The Story
of
EAST DEAN and FRISTON
including Birling Gap and Crowlink

John and Sheila Surtees

with the people of these Downland Villages

Nestling in the Sussex countryside, the villages were isolated from the noise and bustle of town life for a millennium. The special occasions were ceremonies of the Church, the cycles of farming, Fairs, May Day (or Garland Day) and Bonfire Night.

The Village Green was the centre of community life. It was a play area for the children, a meeting place for many events and, of course, it had the only shop and the pub.

People were not wealthy, they had no savings, but they were always helping each other and sharing what they had. Even when in work you just about survived, if you were ill or had an accident there was little in the way of Welfare. Life was also different in the home - always rented. No running water, gas or electricity meant oil lamps and candles and an open fire or range - and earth closets. Pots and pans were mended, little was thrown away. With large families, time off was something no mother knew before 1950. She would say, "There's time for fun when work is done", but it never came.

After 1920 the A259 was made up, and a new estate added bringing in the retired and commuters. For the first time (except for Army service) many of the youngsters left, yet the ambience and community support of a country village has been maintained.

S.B. Publications

Other books by John Surtees
House Physicians' Handbook
Barracks, workhouse and hospital St Mary's Eastbourne
The Princess Alice and other Eastbourne hospitals
St Wilfrid's, the Eastbourne and district hospice
Chaseley a Home from Home
Beachy Head
The Strange Case of Dr Bodkin Adams
Eastbourne a History
Eastbourne's Story
Images of Eastbourne

First published in 2008 by SB Publications
14 Bishopstone Road
Seaford BN25 2UB

© SJ Surtees
Medical Archivist
District General Hospital
Eastbourne BN21 2UD

A catalogue record for this book is available from the British Library.

ISBN 978-1-85770-344-3

Front cover illustration: East Dean and Friston from Went Hill
Back cover: The Three Graces on the Green, Golden Jubilee Fancy Dress, East Dean Shepherd

Designed and Typeset by EH Graphics (01273) 515527

CONTENTS

Acknowledgements

The attribution of this book is made to 'John and Sheila Surtees' for without my wife Sheila's academic historical expertise, her knowledge of the villages and her support the work would not have come to completion. Thanks also go to Peter Armiger, William Armiger, David Arscott, GA Baker, Miggs & Bill Bailey, Mr & Mrs EG Batt, AD Baxter, Jane Beavan, Arthur Bennett, Mollie & Reg Bertin, Fred & Delia Bicks, Alex Bransgrove, Ray Brigden, Jane & George Booth-Clibborn, Kathleen Cater, Oliver Cater, Mrs Kathleen & Diana Banks, Fred & Helen Breach, Jack & Ivy Breach, Sir John & Lady Chatfield, Raymond & Lieselotte Cheal, Mavis Clack, Gordon Clark, Harry Comber, Julia Cowley, Camilla Crump, John Dann, Charlie & Octavia Davies-Gilbert, CJ & L Davies-Gilbert, Phyl Dean, Joyce Donkin, Janet & John Dougan, EM Easy, Vida Elvin, John & Barbara Eve, Frank & Pam Eveleigh, Diana Eyre, Ted & Sara Fears, Ted & Florrie Flint, Jackie and Mike Florey, Tony Francombe, Ken & Marianne Frith, Christine Fuller, Fred & Kathleen Fuller, Mary & Jolyon Fyfield, Ken Gerry, Eileen Goldsmith, ET Goodman, Jean & Roger Gordon, Jonathan Greenway, Doreen & Howard Greenwood, Anthony and Gill Harbottle, Reginald Haffenden, Jill & Adrian Hamilton, John & Berenice Harper, Vida Herbison, Arnold Hills, Peter and Sue Hobbs, Vera Hodsoll, Jimmy Holter, Maureen & Bill Honey, Chris Howden, Elizabeth Howe, Phyllis & Ronald Hughes, Brian and Janet Johnson, Chris Johnson, Peter & Rosemary Johnson, Ann & Wendy Jones, Lionel Jones, Pauline Joslin, Derek Keay, Ian Kerr, Kay & Leslie Ketcher, David Kingsley, PG Langdon, Trevor Larkin, Kathleen Leach, Margaret & Nigel Lees, Jane Leete, LB Manners, Pauline Markquick, Gordon & Hazel Matley, Gerald & Jean Melling, Rosemary Milton, Freddy & Hazel Moureau, Simon & Kate Morgan, Hugh & Annabel Moseley, Frances Muncey, Alan & Joy Mundy, B Murphy, Geoffrey & Ann Nash, Joan Nash, Leslie & Gay (Gladys) Ockenden, Michael Partridge, Charles Peck, LA Pelecanos, Alf Pelling, Noel & Jean Powell, Hilary, Ron & David Pringle, Mr & Mrs Derrick Pyle, Nigel Quiney, Antony Rapson, Chris Ray, JF Riley, Joan & Guy Heath Robinson, Joan Russell, Barbara Scott, Joanna Shawcross, Duncan Smart, Mrs IV Smith, Lawrence & Pat Stevens, John Stevens, Fran Stovold, Jane Stubbs, the Revd Clive Taylor, Grace Taylor, Jesse & Vera Taylor, Nick Taylor, George & Betty Tickle, Peter & Valerie Thomas, Jill Thornton (née Ticehurst), Joan & Ken Thurman, June & Vic Travis, Mary Vickery, Florrie Vine, Jean & Ken Warriner, Roxy Wickens, Vera & Ron Wickes, Irene & Cecily Wicking, Eddie Williams, Iris K Wilson, Lindsay Woods, Phyll Workman, Richard Worsell, Esther Worsfold, Pam Young.

Thanks for photographs are especially due to Peter Armiger, John Dann, Harry C Deal, Kevin Gordon, TM Gordon, Jill Hamilton, Edward Reeves and Esther Worsfold.

Beckett Newspapers, Crowlink Ladies Club, Harry C Deal, Eastbourne Central Library, *Eastbourne Courier,* Eastbourne Local History Society, East Dean & Friston Art Group, East Dean & Friston Local History Group, East Dean Players, East Dean & Friston WI, East Dean with Friston Parish Magazine, East Dean with Friston PCC minutes, East Dean & Friston Gardening Club, East Sussex Record Office, HB News Features, Roy Hudson, Micheldene WI, Royal British Legion East Dean branch, Royal Geographical Society, Salmon postcards, Towner Art Gallery and Local History Museum and University Library Cambridge.

Every effort has been made to include relevant individuals and organisations, it is regretted that at the time of going to press it has not been possible to publish all names. Those involved are asked to accept the author's apologies.

Please Note

Except in spoken or directly quoted words [when p is in brackets] money is in decimals. Similarly time is mainly a 24-hour clock except for spoken or quoted words.

Only one form is used for spellings of place and proper names that have changed over the years, e.g. Hobbs eares (not Hobsares 1542, Hobsehares 1568, Hobbs' arse). See English Place Name Society Vol VII pp 417-20.

Vancouver referenced[1] items have more details against that chapter in Appendix 1, and a square bracket [1] in the text means that more information about the subject will be found in Chapter 1. Abbreviations used are given in Appendix 10.

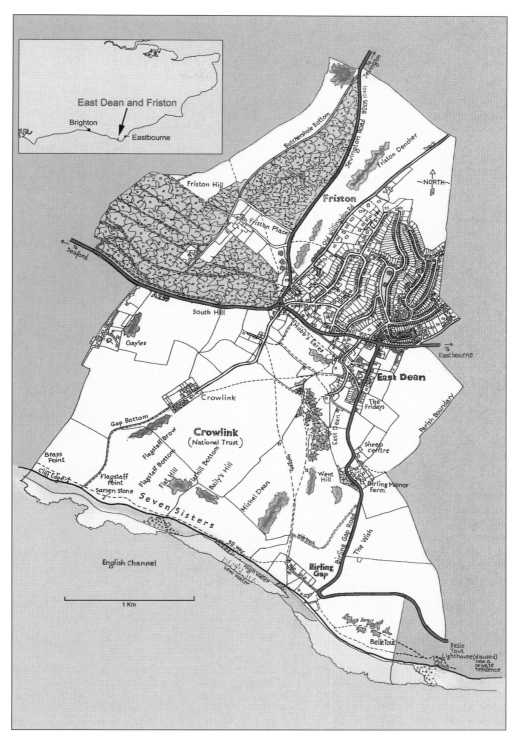

Millennium Map of East Dean and Friston including Crowlink and Birling Gap

General view of the Old Village with above in the background the beginnings of the Downlands Estate c.1929. *The Dipperays* is just left of centre with above *Friston Lodge, Maryfield* and higher up *Middle Brow*. East Dean church is to the lower left edge and Friston church is on the skyline. In the right foreground is *Haligarth,* now replaced as *Little Garth.*

Looking south-east from Crowlink Corner 2002. In the foreground is *Underhill House* (behind the nearby trees) with *Went Acre* to its right. *Birling Farm* and the *Sheep Centre* are in the mid-distance, with Went Hill to the right. The old *Belle Tout* lighthouse is on the sky line

1. Another Merry Millennium and a Golden Jubilee for East Dean and Friston to celebrate

The villages of East Dean and Friston [ED & F] are set in beautiful idyllic countryside, lying in the heart of a quiet valley yet with a cusp of sea in view at Birling Gap. The Seven Sisters and the majestic cliffs of Beachy Head afford a shoulder to protect the villages from gales, and provide exhilarating walks on their doorstep. There is a timeless and tranquil feel about the flint cottages surrounding East Dean's venerable Village Green, with its *Tiger Inn,* and just along the road is the Manor House with historic associations. Both churches could date back to Saxon times, and both villages were recorded in the Domesday book, while Friston's pond was the first to be scheduled as an ancient monument.

A strong community spirit exists which comes to its height when there is the slightest excuse and certainly if a Millennium or a Royal Jubilee is on offer.

Members of the Organising Committee for the East Dean & Friston Millennium Festival were L to R: George Booth-Clibborn, Peter Hobbs chairman, Rita Laws, Sue Hobbs, Frank Eveleigh, Jackie Florey secretary, John Eve, and Frances Mace. Audrey Horlock, Roy Peyton and Alan Starr were also on the committee

To herald the Millennium, Services were held at East Dean Church on 31 December 1999, and at Friston Church the next morning, just as might have happened a thousand years ago, conducted by the 70th priest since 1261. Some 70 ED & F residents saw in the 21st century (as some would say) on New Year's Eve 1999 with a dinner in the Farrer Hall. The celebrations continued in two marquees on the Green, viewing the worldwide television coverage and the soggy fireworks released from the Horsefield, which could not have happened in 1000. Everyone enjoyed themselves and volunteers cleared away the debris.

The organising committee wasn't bothered by the dull, damp and misty opening to another 1000 years of the ED & F story because sensibly they had arranged the main commemoration for the Merry Millennium Month of July.

Meantime, in March, a speed limit of 40mph was introduced on the A259 through the village. In the first week of April, the Players slipped in a long-time favourite, *A Murder has been Arranged* by Emlyn Williams at the Bardolf Hall so that four audiences could enjoy their offering and thank the Davies-Gilbert family for allowing the Players to use such a well-loved venue over many years. Vivyenne Willings directed for the first time.

At the AGM of the Residents' Association [RA] Joe Dempsey agreed to keep a Village Diary to avoid clashing of the myriad of activities generated by the new Village Hall.

An Open Day on Saturday, 6 May, was an opportunity for residents to inspect the new Village Hall. [7] It appeared ideal for a range of meetings, lectures, luncheons, concerts and, of course, coffee mornings. The large hall had room for badminton and short mat bowls, and adorning the walls were local photographs transferred from the old halls.

In a memorable Parish Council [PC] meeting chairman, George Tickle, who had worked so hard to bring the venture to fruition, welcomed councillors to their first meeting in the new Village Hall. George and vice-chairman, Jesse Taylor, were re-elected and a welcome extended to Nicki Terry who had been co-opted on Chris Ray's resignation. The agenda was much as usual - car parking and difficult access due to overgrown verges.

Visiting the new Village Hall on one of the Informal Open Days in May 2000. L-R: Jean Wagstaff, Carole Naylor, Ron Naylor, Eric Mace (near door), Maureen Honey, Frances Mace with (sitting) Michael Sentinella and Ken Gerry promoting the village's Neighbourhood Watch. Vic and June Travis, who worked so hard for the scheme, had retired in 1999

The inception of the Village Hall Luncheon Club by Muriel and Val Wills, on 1 June, was received with acclaim and developed into an essential village feature.

On 16 June the NSPCC held their annual Ploughman's Lunch at Alan and Anne Robson's charming garden and raised £1064. This was a moment to thank Pam Eveleigh and her committee, following the lead taken by Betty Rowson for over 20 years.

Near the end of June the Gardening Club held their annual Garden Party at Anne and Abner's lovely garden also in Warren Lane.

The two Women's Institutes [WI] of the village joined up for a Millennium celebration in the new hall on 24 June when Margaret Clegg and Daphne Dempsey presented a wall clock for the hall, and after supper and entertainments Rene Wicking proposed a warm vote of thanks. Sadly, the ED & F president, May Thorne, recovering after a fall, was unable to attend. No-one could believe it, but the clock was to be pinched shortly afterwards.

The 'Millennium Month' proper opened with a Cocktail Party at *Friston Place* on Friday, 30 June, when 140 guests enjoyed the hospitality of the Shawcross family, and the music of the Clements' Trio playing in the gallery of the Great Hall. It was a marvellous occasion - even the weather co-operated so that guests spread out into the grounds on a balmy evening. Special thanks went to Joy Preen, Sue Walsh, Mike Florey and Hugh Moseley for the arrangements; the proceeds going to the Parochial Church Council [PCC].

The next day was a full one. In the morning, Claire & Ian Hunt opened their attractive Mill Close garden for the funds of St Wilfrid's Hospice, and raised over £1100.

This was followed by the local branch of the Royal British Legion [RBL] chiming in with their annual Village Fête on the Village Green. There was all the fun of the fair - colour, and music, and activities for every interest, with the Eastbourne Scottish Pipe band, the Brownies' Maypole Dancing, a Bouncy Castle, a Punch and Judy, and all the stalls were there from a White Elephant to Face Painting, from Books to Bric-a-brac, and Hoop-la to Coconut Shies. The inner man was catered for too, by Ron, Hilary and David Pringle's hot dogs, and there was so much else; what with Raffles, a Whisky Draw and a Tombola it seemed there was a prize a minute. This great effort brought in some £1700.

The Fête also witnessed the re-launch of East Dean's Neighbourhood Watch scheme thanks to the enthusiasm and hard work of Ken Gerry and his committee of Johnny Johnson, Michael Sentinella and Derek Burton.

This was only one of the RBL's village events in the Millennium year. As usual they put on coffee mornings, Bridge drives, Treasure Hunts with American suppers, Golf competitions, and their Annual Dinner and Dance. Over the years there had been changes, for example, the Old Folks' Outing was no longer on the programme, but essentially what was good for the RBL was good for the village.

The Royal British Legion Fete 2000. **Lt:** John and Elsie Allan, their Whisky Draw stall ready to start with Derek Ockmore. **Rt:** White Elephant stall with Doreen Greenwood and Valerie Thomas

Not forgetting 'Pat's Party', the RBL Christmas Party, which ran from 1979-2003; no, not named after a voluptuous, party-loving Patricia, but after Robert 'Pat' Paterson, a bachelor who started a popular annual Carol Supper. Pat became secretary of the RBL almost as soon as he came to *Barncote,* 19 Deneside, from India in 1964. He was a devoted secretary for 15 years until 1979, and honest - when apologising for a delayed reply he wrote that he had 'completely forgotten all about it'. Was there some connection for his hospitality was unbounded: whatever the time of day the visitor was greeted with a dram!

The Fête was followed on the Sunday by a Garden Party, again at *Friston Place* organised by the PCC on a glorious afternoon, blessed with such warmth and sun that the Wealden Brass Band welcomed the shade of the marquee.

Another fine evening on Monday, 3 July, saw a tremendous blossoming of interest in the story of East Dean and Friston. Esther Worsfold took over 60 people on a two-hour historical tour of the villages, and in the new Village Hall John Surtees spoke to more than 100 on *Memories of East Dean and Friston - the voices of the people of the villages.* This was a part of the Micheldene WI's commemoration of the Millennium, which began with their Annual Supper for Senior Residents.

Midweek, the Crowlink Ladies Club held an Open afternoon, again in the Village Hall, and the Friday Barn Dance was a sell-out, with live band, and a lively caller too, for a swinging evening. Amid all the excitement the new Badminton Club, promoted by Ron Laws and Ken Thurman, was launched.

On Saturday morning, 8 July, in East Dean church, the East Dean Players presented the first part of their Millennium trilogy *These You have Loved.* Devised by David Hunn, this consisted of dramatised stories from the Bible (Jonah and the Whale amongst them), scenes from *Everyman* and *Pilgrim's Progress,* and a selection of favourite hymns.

That evening, as the second part of their Millennium Festival, the Players presented readings and excerpts from some of the most popular English plays.

Kicking off was Ben Travers' *A Cuckoo in the Nest* with regulars David Harmer as Peter and Viv Willings as Gladys. The next was a favourite, Priestley's *When We Are Married,* which had Gordon Matley as Helliwell, Des Thorne as Soffitt, and Marc Symons as Gerald. Other extracts came from *The Winslow Boy* by Terence Rattigan, with Kate Liddiard as Catherine and Christopher Killick as Ronnie; and Goldsmith's *She Stoops to Conquer* in which Val Wills was the landlord. *The Importance of Being Earnest* by Oscar Wilde, with Julie Hunn as Lady Bracknell, Trish Kennard as Gwendolen, Mike Bale as Algernon, Alison King as Cecily, John Moore as Chasuble, and Maire Lucas as Miss Prism, left nothing to be desired, and *Living Together* by Alan Ayckbourn included Marilynne Sharpin as Sarah, and Jane Tullis as Annie. There was also *Private Lives* by Noel Coward, and *Twelfth Night* by the Bard himself, which had Derek Drury in the part of Fabian, and Stella Hutchings playing Olivia. It was a full evening's entertainment, cheese and wine included.

The Village Green venue for the Players' *Pied Piper of Hamelin.* It was perfectly timed, almost as soon as the last tiny tot left the Green, the heavens opened and the village suffered yet another of the promised 'rain and heavy showers' which were regularly delivered throughout the summer

Part three of the Players' trilogy took place on East Dean Green on Sunday afternoon, 9 July. This was a new dramatised version of Robert Browning's verse legend *The Pied Piper of Hamelin,* produced by Stella Hutchings. The cast consisted of most of the Players along with all the parents and children of the village. It really brought the village together, it was carried off so well, and the audience and everyone involved enjoyed themselves immensely.

The next day was the occasion for the RA Get-Together for new residents, and a few not so new ones, to meet up over wine and nibbles.

A busy Greensward on Saturday 15 July for the Millennium Family Picnics. Among those enjoying the evening are Left-Right: Anne Theroux, Michael Kaye, local MP Nigel Waterson and his wife Barbara, Geoffrey Williams, Maureen Honey, George Booth-Clibborn, Joan Thurman and Jane Booth-Clibborn

Thursday, 13 July, was lucky for the Village Hall and the local Tories who held a successful Tea and Cakes Party that day, with all the proceeds going to the hall.

The next evening was a preview of the Art Exhibition, followed on the Saturday and Sunday by a wonderful all-day free entrance Display and Sale of Work by the Village Art group. The standard and diversity of works on show confirmed what talent the village can call upon and the number of red stickers showed how well they were appreciated.

And if your pocket or senses needed refreshing on the Saturday evening what better place than the Greensward to listen to the Glynde & Beddingham Brass band and enjoy a Family Picnic. Hot dogs were on sale and popular, but most folk brought their own grub and drinks and, very wisely, seats and blankets as well, for it was a typical English summer evening - the lovely colours of the sky and the Downs were so enjoyable, so long as you were well wrapped up.

Friday, 21 July 2000, in the new Village Hall, was about 21st Century Woman.
Jean Crask and Marie Mancey helped to organise the display by East Dean & Friston WI of their hobbies, crafts and interests

After a short rest, Tuesday, 18 July, saw the Millennium Festival Golf Tournament and Supper at the Royal Eastbourne Golf Club. Not wonderful weatherwise, but all proceeds to the Village Hall fund.

A group of young-in-heart ex-East Dean school children and relatives outside the new Village Hall on 22 July, Jane Booth-Clibborn (née Nash) in centre front. Grace Taylor, Sandra Goldsmith and Kath Fuller are to the left front and Lois Pelecanos and Miggs Bailey to the right

Andrew Clements and Friends presented *That's Entertainment (Yet Again)* at the hall on Wednesday with a glass of wine thrown in. His Friends came from every line of entertainment from singers (duets included), and pianists, to guitar soloists.

The Social Bridge event, with all standards welcome, was Thursday's offering, but Saturday was a much anticipated evening, the East Dean School Reunion organised by

Jane Booth-Clibborn, and it lived up to its expectations. Over 100 friends and relatives chatted away to fellow pupils, whose time at the school ranged from 1918 to its closure in 1964. Richard Worsell helped to produce a video of the occasion.

At the same time, in complete contrast, another 100 filled Friston Church for a Frank Bridge concert; a programme of music by the Tavec Quartet with works by Haydn and Bridge. There was an introductory talk by Anthony Payne and in the interval the audience were able to view Bridge's refurbished gravestone and favourite seat. Faultlessly organised by Geoffrey Mantle, Sue Walsh and Jean Powell of the PCC, thanks were also due to Margaret and Nigel Lees who lent their garden for handy parking; another memorable evening.

Appropriately on Sunday, 23 July, there was a Millennium Festival Service at Friston Church, again packed to hear the Bishop of Lewes, Dr Wallace Benn. For the rest of the day the Village Hall was filled with visitors entranced by Esther Worsfold's Photographic Memories Exhibition, pictures of the villages and its people throughout the 20th century. There were lots more besides, from architectural details of the oldest cottage in the village to printouts of the comments by the village school's ex-pupils concerning their happiest days, their colleagues and best of all - yes, all the low down about the teachers.

The Jazz and Supper Night with most people in 1920s styles. Left: Louise and John Reynolds with two friends (centre). Right: Frances and Eric Mace

The PCC was again to the fore by arranging four Open Gardens. Local residents who opened their gardens on Tuesday, 25 July were Alan and Vera Tame at Lower Street, Anne and Abner in Warren Lane, Don and Beryl Boucher from The Link, and Bill and Pip Hewitt of The Brow. Those who supported this initiative saw a tremendous range of garden size, slopes, steps, and design, with so many solutions to all the inherent questions, from what plants to which glasshouse. All deserved and received plaudits, not to mention the Eve family's refreshments. As a result of the *Friston Place* Cocktail and Garden parties, the Frank Bridge concert, and the Open Gardens, church treasurer Ian Killick was able to report that £3,465 accrued to church funds.

The Gardening Club's contribution to the Festival followed two days later. Suitably, it was a Ploughman's lunch in the village hall, with tickets from Jackie Florey, Jeanne Maull or Sylvia Shilton. It raised £250 for the Village Hall funds.

Another village favourite, the Bowling Club, held an Open Day on Saturday, 29 July, with demonstrations and assistance to those who might be interested in joining. That night things were hotted up by the Vintage Hot Five Jazz Band at a 1920s Jazz & Supper Night in the new Village Hall. Organised by Sue Hobbs, again all the proceeds went to the new hall.

A hectic month (did anyone make all the events?) finished with a leisurely Festival Cricket Match & Family Picnic on the Recreation Ground. Having said that, Russ Perkins organised a bouncy castle, archery, and train rides to completely exhaust anyone who didn't take up the cricket tuition on offer.

August wasn't much more restful. The Luncheon Club was now fully running, and you had to book your seat for 3 August. The Birling Gap Safety Boat Association held their Open Day on 12 August; the RNLI village flag week collected £754; and the East Dean & Friston Millennium video was on sale, produced by a team which included John and Berry Harper, Camilla Crump, Derek Drury, Esther Worsfold, Martin Grundy, David and Julie Hunn, and you've guessed, all the profits to the Village Hall fund.

The Festival Cricket teams. Front row: Ben Evers, Tim Woodward, David Abrehart, Joe Rees, Paul Feist, Tim Guest, Alan Ray, Chris Francis, and Karl Osborne. Back row: Peter Ainsley, Ian Sands, Matthew Ray, Dave Breach umpire, James Luckhoo, Mark Dunford, Simon Purkiss, P Belverston, Rex Roberts, Phil Marchant, Steve Hopkinson, and B Stevens (umpire). East Dean Cricket Club, included 71-year-old president Peter Ainsley who scored 4, and Tim Guest who made 57, totalled 139. The Media XI reached 135, with Dan Hill (not shown) claiming their last wicket. In the Cuckmere Valley League, however, East Dean could come only second for the third successive year

You may wonder where the Village Annual Flower Show was held? In the new Village Hall, of course, which proved to be a most successful venue, although the occasion was tinged with some nostalgia for the Recreation Field, the Dunwick barn, and *Birling Manor,* which had witnessed so many shows. Peter Johnson, as usual, ran off with the Challenge Shield, the Challenge Cup and the *Garden News* Top Tray Gold Award, but everyone hoped that he would rethink his suggestion that he might not enter in future because of his judging commitments. He did leave the Flower Arrangements Cup for Viv Gardiner, a Foliage Pot Plant Cup to Sheila Surtees, the Challenge Shield for Vegetables to Esther Worsfold, the Rose Bowl for Carole Naylor, and Miss Riddle took the Children's Challenge Cup.

With the autumn the usual courses started up, but now at the new Village Hall. From *Calligraphy,* through *Literary Landscapes,* to *Sussex History,* alongside the *Art Group* and *Keep Fit* - everyone was kept in shape. In contrast to these traditional events the next month saw the inaugural meeting of East Dean's own Computer Club, arranged by Tony Rix.

The event of this remarkable year was the official opening of the new hall on Saturday, 7 October, by Nigel Waterson MP. Everyone who helped was invited, including Cllr Jim Fordham, chairman of Wealden District Council [WDC], Christine Swan of Action in Rural Sussex, and representatives from East Sussex County Council [ESCC] and the Lottery.

George Tickle welcomed the residents of the villages and thanked all those closely associated with the project, including members of successive PCs, the 'Clerk of Works'

Ken Thurman, Frank Eveleigh who did much of the negotiating with the architect and builders, and those who helped to raise awareness such as Frances Mace. He went on to say, "I am sorry better arrangements could not have been made for the weather, but you just can't get the staff for that".

The cost of the hall came to about £500,000, including equipment, which had been raised by community functions, £40,000 from ten charitable trusts, lottery grants reached some £120,000, along with individual donations, loans, and by every resident by means of the PC setting aside £6,000 annually for some years.

Unveiling the plaque at the official opening of the Village Hall on 7 October 2000, with (left) George Tickle, chairman of the hall trustees and of the Parish Council, Maureen Honey and Nigel Waterson MP

Nigel Waterson commented on the speedy completion of the project after years of hard fund-raising work, and also on the village's enthusiasm for the hall - he understood that it was no longer 'the new', but 'our village hall', and already so popular that it was difficult to make a booking. "At this rate it would soon have more visitors than the Millennium Dome!" He paid tribute to the chairman of the project committee, George Tickle, and all those involved. The Revd Hugh Moseley offered a specially composed prayer for the occasion, and Maureen Honey proposed a toast to East Dean & Friston's Village Hall to which the hundred or so residents present heartily responded.

Over the six months since events started in May, the hall had been booked solid. The use of the new hall had exceeded all expectations, providing a sound financial position.

Apart from the regulars, such as the PC, the Art Group, the Flower Show, the Women's Institutes, the RBL, the Church Fellowships, Parents and Toddlers, the RA, the local

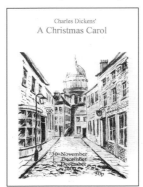

Conservative Association, table tennis and the Gardening Club, there have been many newcomers. These range from a Rubber Bridge Club by Frank Eveleigh, a Local History Group run by Esther Worsfold, to Alan Robson's Short Mat Bowls, with a Line Dancing and a Jive Club also on the cards.

If the Millennium year started with boisterous celebration, the last event of the Millennium year, the Players' presentation of *A Christmas Carol,* touched the heartstrings. Dickens' wonderful story, adapted by producer David Hunn, was ideal for the Players' first production on the new Village Hall stage. The limited space tested the back stage staff, provided a hurdle for the marshalling of the cast of 50, and required the initiative of all, but the show was a resounding success. Yes, all the obstacles were overcome and it was so enjoyed by the audiences - every performance being a sell out. It could be catching.

In between, on 10 September, the Revd Hugh Moseley was instituted and inducted into the United Benefice of East Dean with Friston and Jevington and the same month Peter Thomas started a weekly Church Newsletter, run from 2003 by the Revd Clive Taylor.

Ah, Yes! and at midnight on 31 December 2000 at the end of an eventful year the lease on the Farrer Hall expired and ownership reverted to the National Trust.

The Queen's Golden Jubilee 2002

We don't know how the villages commemorated the Jubilees of King George III, but we know plenty about Queen Victoria's, King George V's Silver, and Queen Elizabeth's Silver Jubilee. [14] So, being vastly experienced, East Dean and Friston went to it for the Golden Jubilee in 2002, with a Jubilee committee well in place before the year started.

East Dean & Friston's 2002 Golden Jubilee committee. L-R: Tony Rix, Alan Tame, Jackie Florey, Mike Florey, Frank Eveleigh, Maureen Honey, Joy Preen, Gillie Willcocks, David Hunn, Julie Ford, John Reader, Maureen Barr, Janine Davies, Rita Laws, John Dann, Ros Brownlee, Fiona Barr, Sue Hobbs (in rear), Margaret Reader, Viv Manchester, Tony Roberts, Frankie Roberts, and Peter Hobbs (chairman). Liz Graves, Frances Mace, Geoff Mantle and Hugh Moseley were busy when the photo was taken

The first golden event of the Jubilee year, however, had been an Accession Service on 6 February 2002 at Friston Church. The packed congregation heard a stirring address by Prebendary Clive Taylor who drew upon reminiscences, mixed with hopes for the future.

Friston Place Great Hall, the ideal venue for a Golden Jubilee
Cocktail Party, seen from the Minstrels' Gallery

They're a loyal lot in the village. Preparations began with some doubts as to whether anyone would want to be involved, but by May the portents were for another great success.

Some of the Millennium exploits were repeated, but with a different slant and a golden theme. One attempted repeat of a Silver Jubilee triumph, the stoolball, had to be cancelled due to atrocious weather on that one day. The big change compared with the millennium was that the eleven events were compressed into nine days in early summer.

On Friday, 31 May, Lord Shawcross invited the village to a Golden Jubilee Cocktail Party in the Great Hall of *Friston Place*. The hospitality of Dr Joanna Shawcross, the attractive floral arrangements by the church flower teams, the 2000 canapés prepared by Joy Preen and her team, and the music of the Clement's Trio, were enjoyed by the 140 present. While the picturesque setting and the warm summer evening ensured a wonderful start to the village's Jubilee celebrations, the proceeds went to Kidscape; 'keeping children safe'.

For the Jubilee Bank Holiday Monday the Greensward was packed with folk who thoroughly enjoyed all on offer including Hilary and Ron's Hot Dog Stall and Terry Wigmore's Mobile Farm Display.
Below: the Fathers and Daughters having trouble with the Mothers and Sons in the Tug-of-War

The next afternoon, 1 June, the Village Green hosted the annual RBL Village Fête, organised under Alan Tame's chairmanship, managed by Derek Ockmore, and opened by Grace Taylor. In remarkably hot sunshine, Punch & Judy, Bouncy Castle, Name the Scarecrow, Surprise Jam Jars and many other attractions vied for custom. The customers were royally entertained by the RBL Cooden Brass Band, and refreshments in the Village Hall were organised by John Eve and family.

That evening a Golden Jubilee Variety Concert came to the Village Hall, with Harmonica and ukulele duos, Eastbourne Academy Dancers, an accordionist, a yodeller, and a Gilbert and Sullivan quartet. Produced by Viv Manchester with input from Audrey Freemantle, Frances Mace and Fiona Barr. Three days beforehand Maureen Honey and willing helpers had decorated the hall in a patriotic theme to form the backcloth for all the functions held there during the week.

A Jubilee Service at East Dean was held on Sunday evening, 2 June. The preacher was the Rural Dean, Canon Gordon Rideout, with the congregation in full voice for the popular hymns. Both churches were beautifully decorated, as part of the weekend Flower Festival. The proceeds went to the Church Fabric Fund.

The highlight of the week was Monday afternoon, 3 June, Jubilee Bank Holiday, when hundreds came to the Jubilee Family Carnival on the Greensward, bring your own picnic, drinks and seats. They enjoyed all the events in tune with the Glynde and Beddingham Brass Band in John Corke's marquee. When the Children's Patriotic Fancy Dress was judged each received a prize thanks to John Reader. The Children's Races, egg and spoon races, sack races, three-legged races, were organised by Julie Ford, Lesley Pyle, Janine Davies, Fiona Barr and Jean White and most of the other mums as well, and the events were cheered on by crowds of relatives until the band brought this part to an end with a rousing *Land of Hope and Glory.* Tug-of-War Mums and Sons versus Dads and Daughters (shown) and a two-hour youngsters' Disco, finishing at 7 o'clock, completed a memorable day.

The Players' *The Way It Was,* produced by David Hunn, on Tuesday evening, 4 June, was such fun that an extra performance was demanded. Memories of the 1950s, with news items, narrated by David and Julie Hunn, alongside songs from shows of the time, mixed well with the popular format of wine and cheese at candlelit tables. Val Wills was everyone's star when he forgot his lines whilst singing Maurice Chevalier's *I Remember It Well.*

Another sell out was on Wednesday, 5 June, for a bring-your-own-grub Barn Dance. Accompanying the scarecrow on the stage was Sean Goddard and music from The Rakes. Organised by Margaret Reader with help from Geoff and Gillie Willcocks and Rita Laws.

A packed East Dean Church on Friday evening, 7 June, greeted *A Garland for the Queen,* a choral and vocal concert beginning and ending with the anthems sung at the Queen's Coronation in Westminster Abbey on 2 June 1953. In between various works, by British composers spanning the 16th to 20th centuries, were sung by the Cantamus Choir, Eastbourne Tudor Singers and soloists. Devised by Sir John Chatfield and

To mark
HM The Queen's Golden Jubilee,
East Dean & Friston Parish presents
A Garland for the Queen
East Dean Parish Church
7th June, 2002 at 7.30 pm
Ticket: £10 including programme & interval drink
All profits to the NSPCC
Please see reverse

organised by Geoff Mantle, Sue Walsh, Joy Preen and Simon Wood, £823 went to the NSPCC.

That evening also had a Disco in the Village Hall for the over-25s, bring-your-own-drink and nibbles. Janine Davies and Maureen Burr and about a hundred young mums, husbands and partners, danced the night away.

Sold out for weeks before, Saturday, 8 June, witnessed a sparkling and romantic climax to the village's celebrations: the Grand Golden Jubilee Dinner Dance. It had everything - village hall, pre-dinner cocktail reception, cash bar and waitress service. Over 90 danced to the popular five-piece Bob Durant band, in 'dress formal, but with a hint of gold'.

All the week tickets were on sale for Rita Laws' Jubilee Prize Draw, with magnums of prizes, this also took place at the Grand Dinner Dance. The behind-the-scenes team included Frank Eveleigh, Frances and Eric Mace, Mike and Jackie Florey, Ken and Joan

Thurman, Margaret Reader, Ros and Ian Brownlee, Sue Hobbs, and Janet Johnson, not forgetting Gwen and Ron Franklin who got the notices out.

As a lasting memento of the Jubilee a commemorative porcelain mug was produced. It had a picture of the Village Green by local artist, Tony Roberts, and his wife Frankie had the task of delivering over 500.

After a short pause for breath, the village activities restarted. On Sunday, 30 June, Jo Shawcross (seen left with daughter Alice) and husband Charles Peck opened the garden of *Pond Cottage, Friston Place,* and raised £1151 for church funds.

The excellent village website was set up in December by webmasters Tony Rix and Henry Branson, but as 2002 closed all the residents agreed that yet again the village's Jubilee Celebrations were just right. They evinced regal pleasure and mirth, while revitalising the Village Community. In Peter Hobbs' words, 'Not many towns or villages could boast such a detailed programme as ours'. None could have enjoyed it so much.

2. Going back, from early times to 1918

East Dean, four miles west of Eastbourne, lies in a dry valley carved by melting Ice Age glaciers that leads to the sea at Birling Gap. On either side are the chalk cliffs of Beachy Head and the Seven Sisters. Just inland from the Seven Sisters is the hamlet of Crowlink, famous for smuggling in the 1700s. The parishes of East Dean and Friston have some 4 km (2.5 miles) of shoreline and a picturesque coast it is too.

The name Dean, or Dene, derives from an Anglo-Saxon word for a Dell or hollow. In the Domesday Book the village is referred to as 'Esdene' or 'Dene'.

Friston is further west at the top of a hill. The name comes from a Saxon 'Fritha' who had his 'tun' or enclosure here, although it goes under 'Bechington' in the Domesday Book. For many years, until 1926, it had the local mill.

Dinosaurs roamed the area 100 million years ago when Beachy Head chalk was being formed under a shallow sea; it took over 15 million years to form the cliffs. No flowering plants existed, the vegetation being mainly conifers and ferns. A million years ago we know the climate was sub-tropical by the finding of elephant and rhinoceros teeth near the centre of Eastbourne. Mankind appeared here much later, but we know man has been walking the Downs for at least 100,000 years, way back in the early (or palaeolithic) Stone Age, and although his stays were transient during the Ice Age of about 90,000-12,000 years ago his flints turn up in the fields. In those days he kept to the hills for the valleys were thick with dark dangerous forests, and he needed to keep a lookout for any enemies.

Stone Age, Bronze Age and Iron Age were a continuum. There is little evidence of Bronze Age (4000-2700 years ago) dwellings, hence the importance of the artefacts near Belle Tout and the Shinewater finds in Eastbourne, but we know they farmed sheep and how they died from the profusion of bowl barrows (tumuli) on the Downs. Pottery dating from the Iron Age (2700 years ago to Roman times) has been found at Crowlink. Ancient terracing (lynchets) can be discerned in Hobbs eares field, and there is an even older trackway, Went Way, (from the verb 'to wend'). Ancient agricultural squares can be seen in the shape of the fields, which have names going back centuries.

Looking over Hobbs eares field, with the shadows running horizontally across delineating the remains of fields, where the ploughing of Iron Age farmers inadvertently raised banks of spoil, or lynchets, at the edges of their small fields

The woodland of the Downs was cleared in the Bronze Age to keep sheep and other livestock; even until the early 1900s life centred around sheep farming.

Canobulinus [Shakespeare's Cymbeline], king of the tribes north of the Thames, had been expanding his kingdom southwards so that the Sussex tribes, who traded with the Romans, were threatened. Claudius, in Rome, was looking for conquests and had a treaty of friendship with the Sussex king Cogidubnus. Eventually, in 43 AD the Romans landed in Kent and defeated the tribes from north of the Thames on the Medway. Crossing the

Thames they captured Colchester, the main town of the time. For his support the Romans left Cogidubnus to rule over SE England.

With many different tribes, there was no concept of 'Britain' except in the eyes of the Romans. Some 2000 years ago they radically changed the ways of the 'Brits'. They imported produce, from oils to rabbits, and introduced goods, such as mosaics and glass utensils - and straight lines. Not only their roads, but for the first time 'British' house walls were straight and smooth. Coins, intaglio rings, law and order also came in, and hot water offered the 'Brits' their first (and until 100 years ago their last) chance of a decent bath.

In Roman times tenant farmers on Beachy Head cultivated the Downs intensively and finds of Roman coins are common. A Roman settlement nearer Birling Manor is possible, for evidence of markets and graves has been discovered there. In the 1930s Harry Sellars found a fine 1st century Roman brooch or fibula in Glebe Field.

The Romans left c.410 as coastal raiding by the Saxons abounded and around 500 the Saxon tribe of Beorls, or Berl, settled here. [5] By 600 the area was part of the Saxon kingdom, which had reverted to paganism until reconverted by St Wilfrid who found the natives jumping from the cliffs to escape a three-year famine, and taught them how to fish.

Over 17,000 Roman coins have been found on Beachy Head over the past century, mostly by farmer Eddie Williams. Examples are L-R: one of Tetricus; a reverse of Gallienus (who was murdered with his wife in 268) and what is probably a Barbarous Radiates, or a counterfeit, possibly why it was buried

The next round of invaders were the Danes, kept at bay for a century by the efforts of Alfred the Great who held court near here in 884, although West Dean is a more likely spot for burning the cakes.

East Dean folk would have seen William of Normandy's fleet in 1066 if he had landed at Normans' Bay, as some believe. When he conquered the Saxon King Harold at Hastings he became King William I of England. He ordered the first recorded parochial history with the Domesday survey (1086) when it is recorded that East Dean, in the land of the Count of Eu, had '1½ hides and 1½ virgates, Walter has 2 ploughs with 3 cottagers value then 10s [i.e. before 1066] now 20s. Wibert has 2 villagers with 2 ploughs. Value is and was 17s'. Friston, in the land of the Count of Mortain, had one hide and 1½ virgates and 1½ ploughs.[1]

Both East Dean and Friston have churches dating from Conquest times. The village retains its beauty, and its woods and Downland are largely preserved. Building has taken place north of the A259, so far within acceptable limits.

East Dean and Friston are now combined, but in the past they were separate, the dividing line started at Baily's Brow to meander above Michel Dene to the flint wall at Crowlink Corner, where the east stone stile brought you to East Dean by Went Hill and the north stone stile lead you to Friston through Hobbs eares field. The boundary skirted *Little Hill* and the gardens of Upper Street to turn sharp left at the twitten and along the hedgerow to turn right across the A259 about *Friston Corner* (3 Mill Close) cutting Windmill Lane just by The Ridgeway. It crossed Warren Lane at No 36 *(Downside)* and went through the old Peak Dean farmyard to the Eastbourne boundary. These wiggles meant that *Linden*

Mead lay in Friston, *Friston Corner* and *The Gables* (8 Windmill Lane) were in East Dean and some houses in 'Peak Dean' were in Friston.

The ecclesiastical and secular boundaries were not identical, e.g. the church boundary with Eastbourne ran through Halfway Cottages, the secular one runs along the back of Cophall Lane. There is no record of the last beating of the bounds, but up to the 1400s boundaries were marked by 'doules', little mounds of earth at each change of direction. They are not mentioned after 1560. The reason why boundaries twist and turn lies in the system of land tenure in feudal times. Each manor was self-supporting and held a mixture of arable land, pasture, meadow and woodland. If one sort was not available the Lord of the Manor held rights in another parish, e.g. *Peak Dean Manor* held grazing land on Pevensey Marshes. The three local houses of *Birling Manor, Peak Dean Manor* and *Friston Place* and their changing importance could be why there is such a discrepancy between the parish and manorial boundaries and why two churches are so close together.

East Dean developed because of the favourable conditions for mixed farming. The Downs were ideal for sheep/corn farming, the rule being one sheep to an acre, while cattle and crops thrived on the scarp and in the valleys. The valley was also strong defensively, and potable water was easily available, so the village prospered.

Sheep were always important and even more so as English wool became sought after on the continent. In 1286/7 it was recorded that 96 sacks of wool, each 364lb [165kg], and 7000 sheep skins left Seaford for the continent. Pigs were popular for they looked after themselves, and in October 1326 it is recorded, 'For carrying 6 hogs from Birling to Pevensey Castle (5 leagues by 2 horses), 3 pence'.

Land was owned by the Lord of the Manor - East Dean had two manors, Birling and Peak Dean. The feudal system meant that each family had to work for the lord as required. Life was hard, hygiene unknown and the death rate high especially in infancy. The local houses of mud and straw on a wooden framework with thatched roofs, clustered round the church and manor - although as in East Dean often at some distance from the latter. Smoke from the central fire wafted through the hovel covering the unpleasant smells, but ensuring that the residents' eyes were permanently red and sore. Animals frequently wandered in and out and the only furniture would be a wooden table with a bench or a few three-legged stools - in style because of the uneven earth floors. You slept on the floor in your day kit.

Living near the coast had some disadvantages even then, for in 1341 the French raided the village, destroying 14 tenements.

Routines had been steady for centuries until the Black Death (probably bubonic plague) appeared in 1348. Sussex lost almost half its population to this pandemic. [Even in the flu outbreak of 1918 the general mortality was not over 2%]. More than one East Dean vicar exchanged livings with the parish priests of badly affected 'Excete', a village near the Cuckmere, which was almost wiped out and after subsequent French raids never recovered.

The shortage of labour afterwards meant that labourers were in demand and the position of the Lord of the Manor was somewhat weakened. Changes were slow in Sussex, but the situation of ordinary folk improved, tenancies increased and land strips were often farmed together or even aggregated into fields. More sheep were put onto the land so fewer farmhands were required.

Gore Farm goes back to at least 1332. [9] The Payne family in 1563 had pasture at 'Hobsares'; and possibly *Payne's Dene,* Crowlink, is called after them.

Around 1570 a family of Hobbs lived in the village and one theory is that the name 'Hobbs' eares' (to ear is to plough) comes from them, but others believe that the poor soil refers to the Devil's backside. Records exist of a Goldsmith in 1547, Foord (1550), Martin (1552), Fowler (1563), Hills (1616) and Fuller (1632), but there is no evidence that they are related to the families of the 1900s. Many names left about 1650 and did not re-appear until the mid-1800s. The 1850s were a difficult time for farming and perhaps there was better chance of work at East Dean, with Mary Ann Gilbert (1776-1845) creating jobs with her philanthropic agricultural works.

A will at Lewes Probate Registry dated 1540 states, 'I Robert ffrench of East Dean … will that Agnes my wyfe has all my lande and my black mare. Witnesses John Parker and Robert Collingham'. The Collinghams lived at Underhill and some of the family were buried in East Dean churchyard. In 1563 Robert Collingham had 'land and tenements at Crowlink and Fryston', and the East Dean parish register has a later entry of houses liable for a Poor Rate, which includes 'Collingham's under the hill'. The family left the village around 1700.

In 1542 John Selwyn, of *Friston Place* [8], held five acres in 'Fryston' in a field called Hobsares with one acre in the upper part of a field called 'Hedacre', between John Gage's land and the 'Kings Way Fryston to Estdene'.

Chimneys came into fashion in the late 1500s and the use of bricks and flints for houses increased. *Little Lane Cottage,* the oldest in the village, started timber-framed, was covered with flint in the early 1600s and had a chimney inserted.

In 1591 the Revd Arthur Pollard was appointed vicar of Friston, and of East Dean the next year, being the first to hold both livings in plurality. His entire ministry of 47 years until his death in 1638 was devoted to the parishes. He was responsible for the erection of East Dean's magnificent pulpit in 1623, and he had a special pew for his family so that he could keep an eye on them.

His son-in-law, the Revd Mark Harry, dispossessed under the Commonwealth for refusing to take the Covenant oath, was restored under Charles II in 1660, only to die the next year. There weren't any hard feelings for William Wallace (1654-1661), the Scottish Puritan intruder (who figured in Calamy's works), because he stayed in the village after his replacement and is buried in the churchyard. There had, however, been complaints about his impenetrable Scottish accent.

On the domestic scene, in 1642 William Punter of Eastdean, described (with tongue in cheek?) as 'husbandman', was 'bound in £1 to keep the peace especially toward his wife'.

The inconclusive Battle of Beachy Head 1690 between the French and a combined Anglo-Dutch fleet, of inferior numbers, was about where the present Royal Sovereign Light Tower is today, so it could have been seen by any locals from Beachy Head. It was variously said to be on 30 June (English) and 10 July (French) - for they were using different calendars

There is mention of a miller at Friston, James Prodger, in 1647, after he and Richard Bannister of Eastdean were found guilty of stealing sheep worth 25p.

The Savoy Conference of 1661 resulted in a revised Book of Common Prayer that came into use in August 1662. Yet twenty years later Transcripts of the East Dean Register state, 'We profess ye want of a Common Prayer book in ye parish church of Eastdean'.

The last sole Vicar of Friston, Dr William Urquhart, died in 1688. His vicarage, opposite the church, continues to be called *The Old Vicarage Cottage.* [8]

Some records of church collections have survived. In 1699 'for assistance to Protestant refugees from France', East Dean's 24p included 2½p from William Griffiths the Vicar, and the two churchwardens, Edward Crunden and William Waymarke each gave 2½p, as did George Gies, while Robert Collingham of *Underhill,* farmer, gave a half-penny. At Friston the Vicar also gave 2½p, but was topped by Sir Edward Selwyn who chipped in 25p towards Friston's total of 38p.

In the Parish Church Registers of 1705, recording the consent of the Bishop to Jonathan Darby, Vicar of Friston and East Dean, also becoming Rector of Litlington, there is added in a later hand, *Take note that ye above Jonathan Darby was the person who formed the cave called Darby's Cave by the Sea Side.* For a time he was also Vicar of Wilmington and it is said he conducted Services in all four churches every Sunday riding to and fro on horseback. Otherwise he probably wasn't all that busy for in 1707 it seems that there were no births, marriages or deaths in Friston.

The coast-hugging sailing ships found Beachy Head a handful. Many wrecks went unrecorded, and the earliest we know of was the *Marie* of Santander[2] in 1368. It was not only the rocky outcrops, which ran under the sea for almost a mile, ready to rip out the bottom of any ship, but the winds about the Head were most capricious and ships could become uncontrollable. Parson Darby was so distressed by the number of shipwrecks and having to bury sailors' bodies washed ashore that he decided to hollow out smugglers' caves and display a light during storms.

This wasn't entirely popular for no doubt the villagers 'devoutly prayed that some well-laden ship may strike their shore' to provide a little extra.[3]

Darby's Cave. **Left** 1797, as sketched by Francis Gross, and **right** a photograph of 1899. The hewn-out steps, likely to have been smugglers' stores, are clearly seen. They lead to the balcony where Darby displayed a light on stormy nights to warn ships of the dangers of Beachy Head. No doubt they were cold, wet watches

In 1870 it was said, 'In the face of the cliff near Belle Tout is an excavation called Darby's Hole which was excavated by the Revd Jonathan Darby, a benevolent though eccentric Vicar of East Dean, as an asylum for shipwrecked mariners. In one instance it afforded refuge to a crew of 12.'[4]

Victorian times saw the cave became quite a tourist spot, and although impassable after a storm in 1917, Bill Armiger said some features could be discerned about 20ft up from the beach into the 1970s. Jonathan Darby's burial in East Dean churchyard is marked by an incised stone.

The findings of a 1724 Bishop's Visitation to East Dean and Friston is in the Chichester Archives. 'Friston church is in good repair, with only a few shingles wanting. The chancel wants to be whitened and the seating mended. East Dean church is in good repair, only some seats want boarding at the bottom. One needs repair. A good Bible and Common Prayer Book in both, but no linen or carpet in either. One silver chalice and three bells in each. The chancel to be repaired by the Dean and Chapter. No dissenter in either parish. Friston vicarage house very mean and out of repair, the fence quite down. East Dean vicarage burnt down in the time of William Griffith, the previous incumbent [1686], and when he died his widow was insolvent. Mrs Judith Medlicott has willed a house at East Dean to the Minister and his successors, which is improved by the present Minister, but not in good repair. In Friston four families. In East Dean 29 families. Friston in the King's book worth £1, East Dean £8. Have a service and sermon once a day alternately. Number of communicants ten. Friston Glebe 30 acres, East Dean Glebe 23.'

The Church Registers also mention a great storm on 8 January 1734, which blew down many barns and trees, and again on Sunday, 24 August the following year, 'a mighty wind did much damage to ye corn standing'.

Intermittent conflict with the French had not ceased. On 21 May 1747 a French privateer captured the *St Paul,* an English sloop, off Cuckmere Haven. In the process the French ship and its prize got into shallow water. A band of men volunteered to go out in boats, and managed to cut the *St Paul* adrift and recapture the vessel and her prize crew of 27 Frenchmen. Two men from East Dean, William Bodle, fisherman, and George Pierce, mason; each received £5 prize money.

On 29 November 1747 the Spanish prize, *Nympha Americana,* came ashore near Birling Gap. It was built of cedar and may explain why some old houses in the village have cedar wood in their structure. Thomas Fletcher is probably the horse rider near the lower edge

Smuggling was rife and well organised: there was the 'Venturer' who financed the operation, while the 'Captain' owned the ship and held the money to buy the cargo and the 'Lander' brought the cargo ashore and moved it inland, involving many locals. As part of the anti-smuggling measures, about 50 Riding Officers covered Kent and Sussex with the help of the militia. Thomas Fletcher, born 1715 in East Dean, became an Exciseman and played his part in guarding the rich cargo of the wrecked *Nympha Americana,* earning the thanks of the Lewes magistrates. One dark night in 1750 while Fletcher was tracking smugglers along the cliffs he was tricked into stumbling over the cliff edge and as he hung on by his fingernails a smuggler stamped on his hands sending him to his death on the beach. He is buried in one of the two box tombs to the east of Friston Church (Appendix 3).

In another village tale, his predecessor, Joseph Simpson, is said to have once allowed himself to be hauled up the cliff with a smuggled package and put the smugglers to flight at the top by letting off his pistols. John Shelley, his successor, lasted until 1789.

The Sussex Weekly Advertiser [SWA] reported on 2 December 1776. 'Early on Tuesday morning last Revenue Officers assisted by Dragoons seized near Friston Mill in this

County, upwards of 17cwt [850kg] of tea and 9 casks of 'Geneva' (gin). The smugglers, returning to rescue the seizure, were fired upon by the soldiers, who killed two of their horses and wounded a man, which obliged them to desist.'

On a lighter note a rash of clandestine marriages at Friston ended in 1754 with the passing of an Act which required the reading of Banns and residence or Licence. It appears that Friston had briefly become a Gretna Green of the south.

Well before the appearance of the RNLI and the Coastguard the people of East Dean were ready to help the shipwrecked. On 28 March 1763 a frigate of 22 guns came ashore at Cuckmere in fog, and the people of East Dean, having heard the guns of distress, upped and saved all the crew, including women and children.

East Dean c.1780. Artist William Lambert, commissioned by Sir William Burrell, was sitting in the garden at the Pendrell family's *Cophall House.* That building has gone and a house was built on its foundations in 1959, but the stables survived as the *Old Barn.* In the centre, is the most striking building *New House,* complete with gazebo, now *The Dipperays,* built c.1769 and apart from bow windows there has been little change. On the left East Dean church is visible near trees with a substantial building to its left. *Underhill* cannot be seen for trees, but was the property of James Dipperay, who also owned the *Tiger,* which he let to William Shoulder. On the right side is the *Old Parsonage,* home of East Dean vicars 1724-1935. In 1780 the parsonage was occupied by the Revd Richard Michell, curate to the Revd Hickes Coppard. *Little Lane Cottage* is hidden, but would have been there and known as *Merrifields.* To the left of *New House* some of the houses in Upper Street can be seen, *Darby Cottages* stand out, and the roof and rear of the *Tiger Inn. New House Farm* has hardly altered, apart from the barn conversion, and South Barn by the Green is now apartments and a tea shop. The cottages on the far side of the Green are much the same. The *Old Bakery* could be hidden by the trees. A corner of *Gore Farm* is just visible on the right, probably occupied by the Fletchers. *Forge Cottage* would be there for we know that alterations were made in 1784. The old road can be seen climbing the hill along the line of the present twitten, the new road came into being with more coach travel. Above on the right is Friston Church with its tall shingled spire of the time. The windmill is not visible for in 1780 it was on the Seaford/Brighton road near today's *Gayles*

Although a Court in 1689 had confirmed the right of the Lord of Birling Manor to wrecks, beachcombers rushed to any wreck to 'liberate' anything worthwhile before the Lord of the Manor or the Admiralty Agent could get there.

The *Lewes Advertiser* of 5 April 1779 states, 'On Thursday 15th Nicholas Friend of Crowlink, farmer, brought before George Fuller Esq., one of his Majesties' Justices of the Peace, being charged upon oath by Capt. Gideon Duncan, late Commander of the *Golden Fleece* an armed victualler wrecked at Birling Gap, for having taken and concealed sundry materials taken at the said wreck.'

The Captain asked that 'the Act of Parliament be read at the two churches of East Dean and Friston on the Sunday after the shipwreck stating that plundering and robbing a wreck is felony without Benefit of Clergy.' Nick Friend was ordered to pay three times the value of the goods appropriated. The *Golden Fleece* was returning from the American War of Independence with convalescing wounded soldiers.

Items rescued by the Customs could be sold by auction at the request of the owners or to defray expenses. In 1787 the *Uffrow Catherine Maria* from Malaya bound to Rotterdam was stranded at Beachy Head. All tastes were catered for - a poster declared that, '600 chests of lemons, 100 barrels of raisins and eleven butts of Malaga wine, with all the anchors, cables and rigging' were to be sold off.

Sailing remained hazardous. There is an entry in the Parish Registers that the *Harlequin* and six other vessels were lost off Seaford on the night of 10 December 1809 and 32 seamen drowned. Shortly afterwards two of the bodies were washed ashore and interred in East Dean's churchyard.

As late as 1843, Captain William Cole, Lloyd's Agent at Newhaven, said that Birling Gap was one of the most dangerous spots on the coast for shipwrecks. This was 15 years after the building of the first of the Belle Tout lighthouses.

East Dean had its share of absentee Vicars. The Revd William Hickes Coppard started as Vicar in 1764, a living he held until 1808, along with the livings of Westfield, St Clement and All Saints, Hastings. Over his 44 years his signature never appeared in the East Dean records, and he only visited once a year to collect his Tithes. His duties were performed by a succession of eight ill-paid curates, one so poor when he died that subscriptions had to be raised to bury him; to this fund the Revd Coppard donated one guinea.

Richard Michell commenced as curate to East Dean and Friston in 1779. He was a scholar who contributed to the *Lewes Advertiser,* wrote a two-volume work, and ran a penny-a-week school - the earliest record of a school at East Dean. He even advertised in the SWA of 6 January 1783. 'Revd Richard Michell, curate of East Dean, now occupying the whole vicarage can accommodate two or three more pupils. Terms 20gns.' When he died in 1790 a county-wide subscription raised £350 for his three children. Medical care in East Dean was almost unknown, although a 1797 doctor's bill exists charging five shillings for lancing an abscess.

The last of the absentee incumbents was the Revd William Miller (1808-17). In order to redeem the Vicarial Tithes he sold three pieces of glebeland [churchland] at East Dean as well as part of the Friston Vicarage cottage and garden.

Part of an hour-long 1779 Sermon by Revd Michell printed for sale

The Revd Christopher Gardner was the deacon and curate in charge until, most unusually, he was appointed Vicar in 1817. It was not his only surprise, for on 5 July 1813 he was standing on the cliff at Beachy Head when he thought the ground was shaking and saw a crack appearing. He instantly stepped over the gap just as a 370-foot [110m] length of cliff, some 84ft in breadth, gave way and fell onto the beach below. The noise of its fall was heard at both Eastbourne and East Dean.

James Dipperay followed his father as tenant farmer at East Dean. Some hinted that he was involved in smuggling: whatever, he bought Birling Manor Farm in 1763, built *The New House,* now *The Dipperays,* and died a rich man in 1791. He left the bulk of his estate to two nephews, but also left an annuity of £20 to his gardener William Worger, three of whose children received £2000 each and the youngest son was bequeathed £1000 and 13 acres in Herstmonceux. The will gives no clue to the services rendered for these rewards. Had the Worgers been involved in Dipperay's smuggling, or were they James' children?

Eastbourne was put on the holiday map by the 1780 visit of the Royal children, during which they visited East Dean. Yes, times were changing. The shepherds didn't miss a trick either. John Dudeney, a Lewes shepherd, is quoted by Beckett in *Spirit of the Downs,* "I have heard them speak of a hundred dozen [1200] wheatears [a migrating bird considered a delicacy] taken in one day in 1799 by a shepherd of East Dean near Beachy Head. He had so many that he could not thread them on the crow quills as usual but took off his round frock and made a sack to pack them in; his wife did the same with her petticoat. This must have been a great flight."

Friston Church by Lambert *c.*1785

East Dean Church of 1882

For some reason, there is a record that the parish supplied a bottle of port to Sam Akehurst of Eastdean on 25 October 1805. There is no record, however, of either the 1801 or 1811 census, but the returns for East Dean under the Defence Act of 1801, which were to report what was available for defence against Napoleon, showed that there were 45 able-bodied 'Home Guards', ten cows, 24 oxen, 22 steers, 3 colts, 1705 sheep, 650 lambs, 9 riding horses, 10 wagons, 14 carts, two carriages, 24 draft horses, and 41 draft oxen. No baker, but 14 private ovens capable of producing 105bhls of bread in 24 hours.

The Revd George Pinnock (Vicar 1841-1880)

We do have East Dean records for the 1821 census, taken on 28 May 1821 by Jas Hodson, Overseer, when East Dean had 297 inhabitants in 30 dwellings.

Census records are available for both East Dean and Friston in 1831, for which the overseers were Messrs Scrase, Hodson and Willard-Ashby. An enumerator was needed to fill in the form because most of the population was illiterate and this census required extra information including the number of houses, how many families in each, the number of males and females, and the males were divided into those below and over 20, and the category of employment was required for males over 20. Names include Foord and Vine. Friston had only eight inhabited houses, with 16 families totalling 50 males and 39 females.

In 1824 Friston Mill blew down. In those days it was situated along the Brighton road at about Gayles' entrance today, and the story goes that a worshipper in the gallery of Friston Church looking west along the Brighton road saw it fall during Sunday Service. [8] It was replaced in 1826 on a new site near, what is now, the entrance to the Downlands Estate hence Windmill Lane.

In 1828 the bell-cot and gallery at the west end of Friston church needed repair, and William Pierce, a local carpenter, took on the job. His bill to the churchwardens was '6 Pounds of led yoused att the Stepell, - 2 shillings; 2 boushells & haff of heare - 15 shillings; for beer - threepence'.

The 'orchestras' of both churches sat in the west galleries. In East Dean there was a fiddle, a bassoon, and a grandfather bass. There had been a flageolet, but one day at practice in the *Tiger* a fat farmer accidentally sat on it and afterwards the instrument failed to play. Today it sounds a fearful combination, but the congregation loved the scrapings and pipings and regarded it as a sad day when 'a box of whistles' (or an American organ) came.

Before 1835 the duty of relieving (assisting) the poor fell on the Overseers of the Poor of each parish, often the churchwardens, who looked after the parish in general including the roads. Most of the parish expenditure went on the poor. East Dean in 1800-01 paid out £403, and for Friston in 1815 it was £191, rising to £308 in 1817. These were huge sums, and the same picture was found over the country. The rapid discharge of so many troops after the French wars, most without any peacetime trade, led to unemployment and penury. A majority of the community in our villages was in receipt of some assistance. The breakdown for the main items in East Dean was: cash £143, flour £128, meat £4, clothes and shoes £73, firewood £12, medicine £7, rent £19.

As Trevelyan put it, 'The payment of rates relieved the big landowners from the need to pay a living wage' and forced the middle class to contribute towards a sum which the large farmers simply redistributed as relief to their own workers. It meant that the term 'pauper' embraced all those who depended upon the labour of their hands. Others believed that the poor brought their condition on themselves by not working hard enough and this faction came to the fore with the introduction of Union Workhouses. These workhouses took most of the responsibility of the poor away from the parish, but only gave relief to those prepared to enter the workhouse where conditions were Spartan - to discourage admission.

The 30 March 1851 census revealed that eight paupers from East Dean and one from Friston were in the Eastbourne workhouse.

Louisa Paris' 1852 watercolour of *Belltout and Burling Gap* looking SW shows Belle Tout, central, and to the right *Hodcombe* cottages and *Cornish Farm* buildings. Her picture of Birling Gap clearly shows the brownish stony cliff of Coomb Deposits at the Gap.

Mary Ann Gilbert did not believe that the unemployed were work-shy. She gave every new employee a card showing the cost of two glasses of gin a day for a year (£4.56, some £500 today), and also what alternatives could be bought with that money. She was an enlightened farmer, who ran an East Dean agricultural school, possibly in *Little Lane Cottage,* and also tried a smallholding system by giving an acre of Downland to locals so that they could grow their own fresh produce. An acre proved to be insufficient to live on, but the tank system she introduced of storing water on the Downs proved most successful. [5] During the 1800s the Davies Gilberts had a bailiff living at Birling or let it out.

In 1848 extensive repairs were again necessary to Friston Church. The main bills were from William Pierce, bricklayer, and James Peerless, carpenter. The main repairs were to the pulpit and desk, painting, new glass and leads, and 2000 tiles at a cost of £90.

There is a record of a Village Shop run by John Hayter in 1836. John Mills ran it from 1837-40, followed by James Float, John Colwell, George Woolgar, and James Float again. It probably started small with a few necessary items sold from a cottage. Shopkeepers from 1850 include Pierce, Fletcher, Markwick, and Dennett. [7]

Cross-channel telegraph cables to Paris via Dieppe and other continental destinations passed through the village to enter the sea at Birling Gap. Near the top of the path up Went Hill you might see amid the vegetation the stumps of two of the poles that carried the wires.

In 1866 the resident telegraph manager, the hi-tec of the day, was Edward William Adamson who lived above the telegraph office on the Green, now *Glebe Cottage*. He was engaged to Grace, daughter of William Osborn, the tenant farmer of *Gore Farm's* 730 acres, who employed 14 men and five boys.

The wooden ribs of a ship wrecked off the Seven Sisters cliffs (near Beachy Head) in the late 1800s and visible over a hundred years later

Figurehead of the *Coonatta* by the *Birling Manor Farm* pond. The barque *Coonatta,* carrying wool from Adelaide, went ashore at Crowlink on 21 February 1876. The statue was originally at *The Dipperays,* house of Lloyd's agent Mr Ashby.
Don't go rushing for a sighting, Sibyl Davies-Gilbert, who couldn't stand it, sold it to an American in the 1970s, allegedly for £17, 000

The Gilbert Institute, *c.*1907. Built by the Davies-Gilbert's in 1884, the original intention was to keep the young men out of the pub and away from the flesh-pot temptations of Eastbourne on a Saturday night. The Birling Gap Hotel was first licensed about that time

An ideal match of the day you might think, but it was not considered 'proper for a young lady to live above the shop'. When he mentioned this to the telegraph company, they fully concurred with the suggestion that their employee's wife deserved better so the company built a substantial flint house on Friston hill, now *Friston Lodge* (was *Hillside*), to which they extended the cables.

The Adamsons had a large family. When Edward died in 1898 his widow moved to Bexhill and a Mr Smith assumed charge of the relay station. After the Post Office took over the submarine telegraph from Cable & Wireless, Eastbourne Waterworks bought *Hillside* for Mr Jack Baxter, the manager of their pumping station at Friston. His twin daughters (one a school teacher) continued to occupy it into the 1960s.

There has been a forge on Friston hill since around 1635. We know that Samuel Gill, the village blacksmith, and his wife Sarah Gill lived at *Forge Cottage* in the 1700s, for a plaque in Forge Cottage, that reads *S & SG 1784,* refers to them. It was known as Gill's Hollow.

The Hills family came to East Dean about 1825 [no relation to the Village Constable Jack Hills who took up his post around 1900]. John William Hills, his wife Flora and daughter Caroline aged two, are mentioned in the 1831 census and JW Hills is in the Register of Voters for East Dean in 1832, along with the Vicar, and the occupiers of *Birling Farm, Gore Farm* and *East Dean House.* One of his 1837 bills to the church for 'gate hooks, screw bolts, repairing padlocks, and lock on porch door' came to 51p and was not paid until March 1841. From 1836 to 1847 he was the Overseer of the Poor for East Dean.

When the *Coonatta* went ashore near Birling Gap in 1876 the cargo of wool was lifted out by a grappling iron made by blacksmith John Hills. Luther Hills remembered the event because his elder brother was paid, unbelievably, a shilling [5p] for carrying a telegram.

Henry Hills came from Lewes in 1872 with the aim of taking over the Forge from his uncle John William Hills. Henry's son, Luther, two when his father started at East Dean, later began an apprenticeship so that when his father met with an accident in 1890 - sparks from the forge fire affecting his eyes - Luther was able to take over, while his father became mine host at *The Swan,* Falmer.

MA Lower described East Dean in 1870 as 'a parish in the hundred of Willingdon, and Rape of Pevensey, four miles west from Eastbourne its nearest railway. Population in 1811 249; 1861 334. Acreage 2431. Birling Manor possesses medieval vestiges, particularly a barn with remnants of a hall of some size. To the east of Birling Gap the cliffs rise with bold undulations to Beachy Head. Between the two points is Belle Tout, site of an ancient entrenchment where stands the Beachy Head lighthouse.' [see Bibliography]

The Diamond Jubilee Day of Queen Victoria on 22 June 1897, was blessed with lovely weather. 'The Church Boys' Brigade band paraded at 11 o'clock and marched to the Church where at 11.30a.m. the *Te Deum* was sung.' They are shown here on the Church Green. Behind is 1-2 Gilbert Cottages

The Cricket Club is first mentioned in 1848, although the club records date from 1880. Of the 15 members paying the 25p subscription that year, the names Fuller, Breach, Hills and Kemp were in the village at the club's restoration in 1947.

By the Local Government Act of 1894 there had to be a parish meeting for every parish, and a parish council for every parish with a population of 300 or more. Those under 300 could only have a parish council if requested and agreed by County Council, or by grouping a parish with another. The 1891 Census found the parish of East Dean with 268 residents, and Friston 92. The parishes of East Dean and Friston took no immediate action.

A meeting in the schoolroom resolved 'to mark the 1897 Diamond Jubilee of Her Most Gracious Majesty, Queen Victoria', by a public dinner, sports, and tea for the inhabitants. Subscriptions were invited to Mr Kwell at the Post Office, Mr Carey, or Mr Drew, the schoolmaster. Sixty subscribers contributed £56.28; ranging from £7 to 2½p, and came from familiar names such as Foord, Fuller, Hills, Russell, and from organisations such as the Stoolball committee - 50p.

After the Diamond Jubilee repast came Maypole dancing and Morris dancing, in the Frontfield (now Horsefield) and then 'A Public Tea for all residents of these two parishes'. One of the daughters of the vicar, the Revd Parrington, was crowned Queen of the May by the Russell twins from Gore Farm

The main event came at 1230h, and was set out in the programme as, 'A DINNER to all residents in East Dean and Friston in Mr Carey's field. Each person must provide himself or herself with a plate, knife and fork and mug or glass'. Mr Carey was the tenant of *New House Farm* and his field is now better known as Horsefield. People were not overfed those days, in photos their arms are thin, and food was a notable social cement, and possibly had somewhat the same taste.

East Dean village from Cophall 1897 by Edward Reeves. In the foreground is East Dean church and on the skyline beyond Hobbs eares field is Friston Church. *New House Farm,* the *Darbies* and *Pendrills* stand out in the centre. *The Dipperays* is near the right margin, with above the white 'Telegraph House', now *Friston Lodge*

At 5.30 in the afternoon a lengthy schedule of sports started including sack racing, a wheelbarrow race, and three-legged races. For women there was racing, but also an extra, a Sunlight Soap Washing Competition with a first prize of a case of plate valued at 75p, and a second prize of three dozen cases of Sunlight soap.

Birling Farm were the winners of the tug-of-war, and Mark Fuller won the prize for throwing the cricket ball. Blacksmith Luther Hills came second in the Hat Trimming competition. The day finished at 2200h with a beacon fire on Friston Hill, sprinkled with brown sugar to start it off, one of a chain throughout the land.

The cost of the dinner and tea was over £30, the band - all the way from Eastbourne - cost £6, prizes £5, the bonfire £6 and Jubilee Mugs for the children £4. A memorial evergreen oak planted on the Green, just where the war memorial now stands, not unexpectedly, died.

About this time HA Colwell was appointed East Dean's rural messenger, that is, the letter carrier or postman. Eastbourne was the postal town for ED & F except for the years 1912-20 when it was Polegate. Colwell managed to hold on to the job until 1906 even though he was often cautioned, or having pay withheld, for being intoxicated on duty.

In 1898 St Mary's Sunday School Annual Treat went to - East Dean. The girls came from Eastbourne on a wagon with a crowd of noisy boys following on foot.

Talking of walking to and from Eastbourne, there is a story from around the turn of the century about the time the host of the *Tiger,* David Fowler, was taken ill and the blacksmith volunteered to call the doctor, which meant a walk to Eastbourne to call Dr Frederick Marsden of Moat Croft Road. It was said that the doctor was 'ever the friend of the needy poor and many a pound of gravy-beef went into his tail coat pocket for some poor patient at East Dean or Willingdon, which he visited once a week on his beautiful black horse'.

The well outside the *Tiger* used until 1896, and re-opened in 1940 along with the Church Green well. A wise move, for the Germans tried to bomb Friston waterworks

Roused by the messenger the doctor, complete with tail coat and black bag, mounted his horse, the blacksmith grasped a stirrup to keep pace and they set off for East Dean. At the *Tiger* the doctor was led upstairs to examine the patient. Shortly, he came down to the bar room crowded with curious folk, "Out you go", he ordered, "our host has an inflamed appendix and needs an immediate operation". The surgeon took out the offending organ on a trestle table cleared of tobacco ash and beer rings. He used carbolic for antisepsis, chloroform for anaesthetic and a candle for light. Mine host recovered and lived until 1922.

Mrs Fredericks, a daughter of the Revd Walter Parrington, who lived in the *Old Parsonage* says, "One of my sisters was born in *Birling Farm* because the Old Parsonage was thought too damp for a mother and new born child. There were six farms nearby, *Gore Farm, Peak Dean, Summerdown* (restored now as a private house) and *New House Farm. Birling Manor* and *Friston Place* were also farms, both had donkey wheel wells for water. Meat could be delivered from Pocock's in Old Town, when a boy would ride out on a pony after school with joints strapped to his legs. In winter he would have to be thawed out."

Bill Armiger said, "Before 1895 the villagers drew their water from various wells. The two main public ones being just outside the *Tiger* and on Church Green, Lower Street." Mrs Fredericks added that the mechanism for raising the well buckets at the *Tiger* was stiff and difficult for the women and water carts were also a source of supply.

Mr Armiger explained, "In 1896 the Eastbourne Water Company laid a main from Friston to Eastbourne, it passed through the village and ran under Horsefield. Pipes from this main were laid to two waterhouses, one by the Village Green, next to *Pendrills,* the other at the entrance to the Gilbert Institute. Each waterhouse had a tap with a drip tank underneath. A blessing because the *Tiger* well-handle was hard work. One of the men's jobs was to carry buckets of water to their homes each evening. In 1934 when we moved into 4 Upper Street there was a tap over the kitchen sink, which was a luxury, but no flush toilet, which was only found in one or two cottages."

Bert Holter, carrying buckets of water with the aid of a yoke

In 1896 Mr Drew, headmaster of the school, calculated that the population of East Dean was 266, and 69 for Friston.

In 1900 Roderick 'Ronnie' Hall began a long and respected association with the villages when appointed Chief Assistant Agent to the Gilbert Estate, working at first from the Estate Office in Borough Lane, Eastbourne. This was also about the time *Gayles* and *Little Friston* were built. [8]

One person who left was the Vicar, the Revd Walter Parrington. Among many works that he started and left in good hands was the *Tiger Inn* Equitable Association. Members paid 20p entrance and 11p a month, the benefit was 62$\frac{1}{2}$p a week for three months if they were off work through illness, 52$\frac{1}{2}$p for the next three months, and 25p for six months. Members' contributions over the year amounted to £49 and £36 was paid out, and there was £444 in the funds.

Church restorer Walter Parrington, the vicar 1881-1900

Arnold Hills said that his grandfather Jack Hills (no relation to the blacksmith) was the village policeman from about 1900 to the end of the 1914-18 war. He lived in the *Police House,* Lower Street [now *Pear Tree Cottage*]. After retirement he moved to Birling Gap Cottages; later he was caretaker at the Gilbert Institute until his death at 87 in 1949.

At the 1901 Census East Dean had 254 and Friston 135 residents. The next year there were nine baptisms in the parishes including a Laura Vine and a James Fuller. The four burials were a baby of ten months, two women, one aged 33 and the other 53, and a 'man unknown found shot on Cop Hall Down'. Rene Wicking said, "The grandparents of my husband Jim came to the village in 1903; and his grandmother was the local 'midwife', yet two of her daughters died in childbirth."

Also in 1903 the Rector of Jevington, the Revd EE Crake, a well-known writer, and the Revd William R Nightingale, the new Vicar of East Dean with Friston, 'at last realised a long cherished desire' and published a monthly Parish Magazine. The *Jevington, East Dean and Friston Church Magazine,* consisting of two pages with an insert, was printed on pale pink paper in London and sold for 'a penny a copy' or a shilling (5p) for twelve months.

In June 1903 the locals noted, 'the District Council have recognised the justness of our representations as to the dangerous condition of the footpath between East Dean and Friston by putting up posts at each end to prevent horses being brought through'. Bill Armiger added, "This footpath or twitten, from 1 Upper Street, only ran halfway up the hill, you walked along the highway after that. Years ago the road ran along this route as Little Lane, when the twitten was the path which now leads to the Bowling Green and now called Little Lane. The land between the 'new' footpath and the present road was fenced off and Friend Fowler used it for his cows, but it was common land and he had to take the fence away."

By August 1904 the parish magazine had become the *East Dean & Friston Church Monthly,* a single quarto sheet bearing a stylised picture of a country church on one side and the other the local church news.

On Monday, 8 August, 12 members of the Mothers' Meeting were entertained at the Vicarage and on 27 August some of the old and infirm were invited to tea. 'It was unfortunate that for different reasons not a few were prevented from coming.'

The ss *International* came ashore at Birling Gap in 1899 and, as she was driven along the beach, she pulled up a telegraph cable, the very one she had helped to lay years before. The ship-breakers for the wreck were so rowdy that they were refused admission to the *Tiger Inn,* whereupon they bought themselves a barrel of beer from the *Star Brewery* at Eastbourne and noisily regaled themselves outside the *Tiger*

On 10 August 1904 a party of 23, men, women and children, left the vicarage for the choir outing. As usual, they walked to Eastbourne station, caught the 10.05h Brighton train (which needed a second engine to get up the Falmer bank), were whirled to the Aquarium in an electric tram, had a splendid luncheon at the *Albemarle Hotel,* saw Brighton from a horse-drawn wagonette, and did 'ample justice' to a first-rate tea. The train brought them back to Eastbourne, whence they walked back to East Dean arriving at eleven at night, although apparently 'some got back a little later'. The total cost of £8 was provided by Mrs Davies-Gilbert, Miss Swift, Mrs Costobadie, Mrs Smith, Mrs Hole, Mrs Brock, Mr JA Maitland, Mr Hargreave, Mr Drew, Mr Dennett and the Vicar.

The Revd Nightingale moved to a richer living in 1904 being succeeded by the Revd Herbert EC Marshall. Sunday Services in 1905 were held at 0800h at East Dean with communion at 1100 alternate weeks East Dean and Friston, at 1500 at East Dean, and 1830 alternating East Dean and Friston. The evening Service at Friston was discontinued in the winter from 1905.

Stoolball, this ancient Sussex game, was re-started in the Vicarage paddock in July 1905 and about a score of ladies turned up, but the enthusiasm came and went.

Mark Fuller, the best batsman of 1905, was vice-captain of the Cricket Club the next year. At this time Friston and Birling Gap had their own teams. Mark had been employed as a labourer on the 'new' lighthouse 1899-1902, going down from the cliff top in the cable car to the work platform near sea level.

At the Annual Sunday School Treat, about 100 sat down to tea provided by Mr Drew, the schoolmaster. Afterwards regular attenders received Bibles, Prayer Books, Hymn

Books and suitable books as prizes. Races were next for the older boys and girls, and for the younger ones hunting for hidden coins caused time to fly. Each child was allowed to pick a suitable toy for free, and after singing the National Anthem they dispersed home with a piece of cake and a bunch of grapes.

For the 1905 Christmas Treat for the Sunday and Day School children, 'Mrs Grace Davies Gilbert, as usual, was kindly enough to give the tea and a garment to every member belonging to the Sunday School'.

In 1906 the vicar said that he was exceedingly grateful to Mrs W Hole, of Birling Manor Farm, for having acted as churchwarden for so long and hoped for her kind support, but the Archdeacon was averse to having women churchwardens where it could be avoided. That year the Revd JW Parrington visited the parish and said what a pleasure it was to come to his old parish for 'my heart is with the South Downs and the people are ever in my prayers'.

Progress was made with an East Dean & Friston band under the leadership of bandmaster Lias and vice-bandmaster Blundy.

Mr Dennett senior, the shopkeeper, died at 80. In the previous week a baby girl of four months and her father had died.

Charles Frederick Russell, tenant farmer of *Gore Farm,* harrowing in the Home Field, now Wayside, 1907

The first Flower Show was held on 24 July 1907 at Birling Gap. It was 'So successful we trust it will be the first of many', with a profit of £6.50. Tents were provided free and put up by the coastguard, Mr Corwin Martin arranged all the exhibits, the schoolchildren had a holiday, Mrs Wycliffe-Taylor, of *Gayles,* offered prizes for the best calico night gowns, Mr Carew Davies Gilbert gave an extra prize of 50p for the person who took the most prizes, and Mrs Grace Davies Gilbert motored over from Eastbourne to present the prizes.

The first parish nurse, Miss Candy, was appointed in June 1909, paid for by a levy of 10p annually from each household. She lived temporarily at the Gilbert Institute. The Nursing committee had been compelled to secure the presence of a professional nurse under the Midwife Act of 1902. 'Now that it is a penal offence for any but a trained nurse to attend maternity cases, the old and familiar system by which any motherly woman could attend is absolutely debarred.'

One hundred magazines were printed each month in 1910, with an average monthly sale of 92 and an adverse balance of £8 over the year.

Over June and July Mark Fuller spent his time as one of those employed in extending and improving the Downs Golf Course.

In November 1910 Major SF Cooke of the British Red Cross Society gave a lecture 'with limelight pictures'.

On Wednesday, 26 March 1911, there was an Evening Concert by the East Dean & Friston Choral Society. Pianoforte solos by Alfred Ticehurst and by Sidney Fillery were interspersed with Miss Carrie Selmes singing *Still I love thee* and Luther Hills' *Long Live the King,* along with a recitation by Miss AB Lintell, and with Messrs L Hills, J Lias and C Harris as a Humorous Trio.

Easter Day communicants totalled 74.

Mr CWA Ticehurst remembers seeing Halley's Comet at Friston, 'with a tail like a peacock' and clearly visible in a night sky unlit by lights from Eastbourne and Brighton.

The Revd Alfred Arthur Evans became the Vicar in October 1908 when Mr Marshall moved to the family living at Occold. He devoted the next 21 years to the welfare of his flock. He introduced church guides, produced many historical pamphlets, and copied and had the Parish Registers re-bound

King George V's Coronation was celebrated on 22 June 1911, with a Festival Service, and a 'General Meat Tea' provided for every resident in the parish, 'it will be necessary for everyone to bring his or her plate, knife, fork and spoon'. The celebrations ended with a bonfire on Friston hill and fireworks set off by Major FJ Maitland. Unfortunately, global warming was late that year and the day was dull and showery throughout and at 1600h, the time appointed for the meal, the rain fell so copiously that the children decamped to the schoolroom. Dancing, however, 'was kept up on the wet grass' of the Horsefield loaned by Mr E Miller for the day. Bill Armiger said that people came from surrounding villages to see the beacon on Beachy Head. "There were games and sports and fairy lights were strung from the Elliott's [now *The Grange*] and the trees round *The Dipperays*".

The profits went towards a new oak door for Friston Church, repair of the organ at East Dean, and a village library that opened later in 1911. Suitably, that year author Edith Nesbit came to live at Crowlink.

William Joslin said, "Before the 1914-18 war our family had holidays at *Hodcombe,* near Belle Tout. My old aunt Grace said that as a child she was expected to walk half a mile to the nearest farm and back again, whatever the weather, to fetch milk for breakfast."

The Parish nurse was now Miss Dyke on a salary of £48 per year. She also received £5 for the rent of her cottage, £2 for a uniform, and another £10 for various essentials such as a hot water bottle, thermometer, lint and bandages. She reminded residents that there was a stretcher and a supply of splints and bandages in the Gilbert Institute for any emergency.

Farm labourers' pay was minimal, a few shillings a week and most would be on parish relief. An Eastdean Rural Workers Union was formed, but the only person to take an official post, Tom French assistant to William Ashby the miller 1876-94, received a note from his employer to 'chuck this nonsense or out ye goes'.

Sussex has always been strong in celebrating Bonfire Night - a great feature of village life, and while the records of the East Dean & Friston Bonfire Society only date from the 1880s, it was going long before. The aims were to commemorate the thwarting of a dangerous plot to destroy the King and government of the day, to put on a public entertainment, and to bring a degree of happiness to the less fortunate by donating profits to a worthy charity or towards presents for local aged.

The Bonfire Boys had a bugle, pipe and drum band and carried flaming torches. First stop would be *Little Friston* where the Bonfire hymn would be sung, the band would play, and they would be given money and a mug of beer. Down to *Friston Place* where Major Maitland and wife would welcome them at the door, same again. Then to *The Gore* and on to *Birling Manor* where Major Harding and family would eagerly await the procession with large mugs of ale and buns, and admire and judge their costumes. Off they went to Birling Gap and back to the allotments where, between Underhill and Lower Street, Charles Harris would give his famous speech by the flaming fire, and effigies of the culprits were committed to the flames to ensure that such a plot would never be tried again. The first verse of the Bonfire Boys' song ran,

> *Please remember the fifth of November*
> *The gunpowder treason and plot.*
> *We see no reason why gunpowder treason*
> *Should ever be forgot.*
> *'T'was Guy Fawkes' foul intent*
> *To blow up King and Parliament.*
> *Three score barrels he'd laid below*
> *To prove Old England's overthrow.*
> *By God's providence, he was catched*
> *With a dark lantern and a lighted match.*
> *Holloa boys, holloa boys. God Save the King,*
> *Holloa boys, holloa boys. Make the bells ring.*

Into the 1940s separate and fiercely competitive bonfires were held at East Dean and at Friston, the latter had theirs in the field opposite Waterworks Cottages.

Bernard Fowler, who started the Eastbourne Aviation Company, rented his first airfield site in 1911, some 50 acres of marshy ground between the gas works and St Anthony's Hill Eastbourne, from Mr CF Russell of East Dean who held the lease from the Duke of Devonshire. A clause was inserted to the effect that 'Should any farm animals be injured or killed by the planes, compensation was to be met by the Eastbourne Aviation Company'.

Mark Fuller noted in his 1911 diary 'after a wettish early spring came a dry, hot summer, and cutting oats started on 24 July, and harvesting finished 12 August.'

In 1912 Mr JA Maitland JP of *Little Friston,* which he had built in 1900 as a dower house [8], gave £5 for the repair of the billiard table in the Gilbert Institute.

On 15 May Lydia Annie was baptised, the daughter of 'Gypsy people of no settled abode'. Another daughter of 'gypsy pedlars' was baptised in November.

The churchwardens at East Dean were Mr CF Russell and Mr E Miller with Mr L Hills as Sexton and Miss E Lias as cleaner. At Friston there was Major FJ Maitland and J Wycliffe-Taylor, with Mr and Mrs WG Morris. Mr EC Drew was organist at both churches. The Vicar noted that the East Dean churchyard needed to be kept in better order. 'We regret to note that several new tracks called 'short cuts' have appeared. We hope all will follow the gravel paths.' Friston church bell was not rung, but struck by a hammer, for it needed re-hanging. The school managers were the Vicar, Carew Davies Gilbert, Major FJ Maitland, J Wycliffe-Taylor, CF Russell and E Miller. The teachers were Mr EC Drew, headmaster, and Mrs EC Drew, with Miss AB Lintell and Miss LE Burch as assistants. [6]

Of the special church collections in 1912, the least (15p) was for the churchyard fund and the most for the Princess Alice Hospital Harvest Festival at £4.12½.

Those days the Downs were not cluttered up with wire fences. A shepherd pitched his fold of wattles in the morning and took his 500 or so sheep over the hills. "If the hunt met at Friston pond the shepherds always moved to South Hill. He could stand there all day and have a clear view of the hunt." By mid-afternoon he had rounded up the sheep and headed for home. Once a year he drove the sheep for a wash in the Cuckmere. Many of the shepherds wore bowler hats for they were waterproof, Bill Armiger said, "The shepherds wore them, such as Dick Fowler, his brother Fred Fowler, Mr W Wooler and Mr Duffy".

Bill Armiger said, "Between haying and harvest the sheep were washed in the Cuckmere at Exceat to clean the wool before shearing. At a bend in the river by the A259 bridge there are several rotting posts which mark the sheep wash set out in a crescent, with a platform running out to the deepest part where the sheep were put in and then ducked at least four times before allowed to scramble ashore.

"A man from each farm would form a six-man shearing team and go round to the farms in turn. Each farm would catch their own sheep and roll up the fleeces. The shearers worked from 0700 to 2000h, and often they had to walk several miles home. As a lad shearing made a change from mangel hoeing." Jesse Taylor adds, "My job was to put a dab on any cut from my lime pot. Latterly the shearing was done at Dunwick Barn, all by hand, of course."

The Russell twins Harold and Arthur, at Gore Farm, 1912. The stables are where the doctors' surgery is today in Downlands Way, with the barn of the Barn Stores behind the white horse

Bill Armiger carries on, "Teams of horses worked a reaper/binder which cut the ripening corn, laid on canvas by the turning sweeps. The cut corn - barley, oats or wheat - was carried to the packer who tied it up in sheaves, and these would be stood up in bunches of six for drying - known as 'shocking' in Sussex. When gathering in the hay the children took a ride on the wagons. As soon as the stacks were finished, the thatcher immediately put wet wheat straw on top making it all neat and straight and fastening it with string and stakes cut from hazel wood to keep the hay safe and dry to provide good fodder.

"Working between the rows of shocks, wagons would bring in the harvest. All summer we children were in the fields loading the corn into wagons. As you moved to another shock you shouted 'Stand hard' to warn the carter loading his wagon. When the last sheaf had been loaded and the last load of corn moved across the deserted field of stubble, with the harvest moon penetrating the evening autumnal mist, we knew that the next Sunday we could sing that all was safely gathered in.

"After the fields had been cleared the land would be ploughed and sown with winter corn as soon as possible. Sometimes this was done by horses, but steam engines were also used, borrowed for the occasion. There would be two traction engines, one at each end of the field, pulling with a thick steel hawser a six-furrow plough back and forth.

"As soon as a threshing machine was started up the whole contraption came alive. The string was cut off the sheaves which were fed into the mouth of the drum, drawn in by the revolving drum and beaten against a concave plate. Part of the corn and chaff fell onto the riddle plate while the straw passed to the shakers and tumbled out of the back. The corn and chaff shaken out of the straw fell through the shakers to the riddles. The short pieces of straw passed out near the back while the corn, chaff and dust fell on to a plate over which a current of air was blown to blow the light chaff out near the straw. The somewhat heavier cobs (or unthreshed ears) fell on a slope and fell out. The heavy corn and dust fall onto a fiddle which allows the dust to fall out but retained the corn that passed to the elevator, which lifted it to a screen. Here the small imperfect grains were separated from the best and passed out by a separate spout. The best grain fell onto more riddles, passed through another air blast from a fan to the dressing box where, brushed and polished, it came cascading down as clean grain into an attached sack. The full sacks would be securely bound and carried up the granary steps high above the ground. One man would carry about 150 of the $2^1/_4$cwt [125kg] sacks a day.

"The mice would run as you lifted up the sheaves, so we wore whirlers on our trousers. Many's the time when I came home a mouse would scuttle across the floor giving my old Mum a fright. Underneath the thresher the chaff had to be cleared. Essential, but a job I hated as it made your eyes smart and lungs choke with the dust. I was glad when I was old enough to work upon the stack.

Gore Farm 1912, the Russell's horses by today's Michel Dene Road. The main road was unmade, and farmers dug flints from their fields and piled them by the farm gate, as here, to be sold to Eastbourne Corporation for laying on the roads

"When threshing out the oat stacks, as the chaff was clean and new, we would empty our beds and fill them up. It was a special treat to nestle down on such a sweet bed which would keep us warm all winter.

"Autumn was a busy time on the farm. Ploughing and drilling in the winter corn, and pulling up the swedes and mangel-wurzels and making them into long clamps covered with straw and earth. The corn stacks were threshed out to obtain oat straw for fodder, bedding down for horses and for the steers and heifers in the farmyards. No animals stayed out in the fields in those days. The oats were for the horses to eat, with crushed oats for the hens. They were crushed at Friston mill until the 1914-18 war. On wet days the mangols were cut up, corn was winnowed, and there was sack mending, with the men sitting on trusses of straw telling tall stories. Of course, twice a day the cattle would be brought in from the meadows to be fed with fresh oat straw and piles of sweet new hay."

In August 1912 the parish magazine took on a new look with cover pictures of the two churches, printed locally by Bennetts on white paper. Mr EC Drew produced the design, and Miss B Thornely furnished the photographs. That year Charles Fears became bailiff of *Weston's Farm* (or *New House Farm*).

Other happenings would be recognised today. Bill Armiger said that there was a Village Fayre in the Horsefield with swings and roundabouts, Ray Kemp understood it was a shadow of what it had been, but agreed it had hoop-la and coconut shies, and the first church guide had appeared in 1911; the printing of 2000 cost £7.15, and over the first two years 1400 were bought by visitors paying £5.22.

They had Flower Shows, too, every now and again. "The first Flower Show I can remember" said Bill, "was in 1913. Staged in the village school, it was supervised by Corwin Martin, head gardener to the Maitlands of *Little Friston.* The show included entries from Jevington and Crowlink, as well as East Dean and Friston."

Would we, however, be able to match Mark Fuller's haul of 43 rabbits for the pot taken at Butcher's Hole on 3 November 1913? We wouldn't be able to accompany the choir to Portsmouth to view the entire British fleet at Spithead for the 1912 Naval Review. Nor could we see 'the Church Lads Brigade's Fife, Drum and Bugle Band' escort the Vicar from the Old Vicarage to the church for the morning Services at East Dean and Friston, and play him back again. Perhaps the reticent Revd AA Evans found this custom just too much, for the Church Boys' Brigade was disbanded prior to 1914. We certainly couldn't join Mark Fuller enjoying his blackbird pie, for in February 1913 he recorded catching eight starlings and two blackbirds - although he was probably after sparrows, of which he trapped six dozen in three days. They were considered a menace by eating the seeds.

What we wouldn't have was women working in the laundry, an enterprise of Mrs Davies Gilbert. The laundry vans came daily to, now, 5 Upper Street.

Surely we wouldn't wish to relive the sanitary arrangements. Grace Taylor said, "When we lived at Foxhole [at Cuckmere Haven] the lavatory was a bucket. It was near the front door, but if we were going there mother wouldn't allow us to go out the front door, no, the proper way was to go out of the back door and walk round. In Crowlink we just had an earth closet and I presume it simply went over the fields. You weren't long on cold days".

Bill Armiger's grandfather, George, came from Norfolk to Foxhole. After his marriage to a Miss Head of Alfriston the couple walked from Alfriston to the reception at Foxhole. He went on to be carter/farm manager and champion ploughman at *West Dean Farm* 1907-11.

A carter was in the stable by 0530h with his hurricane

Mrs French, cleaner at East Dean Church 1913-48, outside *Little Lane Cottage.* The village children knew her for the triangular toffees she made and would save the wrappers to use next time

lamp to feed and groom the horses. "I cannot think of a more pleasing scene than a stable with its soft warm glow and the sweet scent of the horses munching their oats, with twitching tails." A carter groomed with a Currie comb and brush until the horses' coats shone. He hurried home for his breakfast and started work at 0700. He stopped at midday to give the horses their nose bags and to have his bread and cheese and a drink of stone tea. At 1530 he left the field to take the horses home, give them a good rub down and their meal, before he went home for his dinner. About 1800 he would bed the horses down and rack them up with hay.

Peter Armiger's father Bill tells us, "Apart from work, which was often long and backbreaking, what did we do before radio and TV?

"Well, the children played *Gathering Nuts in May, Poor Sally sits Weeping,* rounders and other ball games, *Oranges and Lemons,* skipping, hoops, conkers, *Egg in the Hole* and Maypole dancing. In Lent the boys played marbles within white circles - you had to knock the marbles out.

"After the children went home the village school was a meeting place for discussions, and entertainment, Miss Lintell, one of the teachers, presented concerts with the children, and the Revd AA Evans gave social evenings. The Choral Society, 30 strong, met every Tuesday evening. There were Jumble Sales with clothes given by rich for the poor. The Mummers did plays, Ray Kemp said he could recite his Mummers' part as Little Johnnie Jack in his eighties. There was a billiard table in the Gilbert Institute and whist drives were held there.

"Sixteen adults and as many children were in the combined church choirs, that practised every Thursday evening. Through Lent there would be lantern slides of the Crucifixion, and Lent ended with Stainer's Crucifixion sung with great sincerity by the East Dean choir assisted by Mr Fillery's St Anne's church choir. Choir outings went to Portsmouth, Folkestone and all along the south coast.

"The Mothers' Union was strong and they had their outings. The men would meet at the *Tiger* to play dominoes, and the long room upstairs was used for club and committee meetings, such as the very active Bonfire Society, and a dance once a week. Canadian soldiers came in during the 1914-18 war.

"Sometimes we went to Litlington tea gardens - taken by your father in a horse drawn wagon. Occasionally folk went to a dance at the Devonshire Park when they didn't get home till three in the morning."

Ray Kemp said, "Young men and women danced at the *Tiger,* the *Eight Bells* at Jevington or at Polegate and less often went to the Town Hall or Drill Hall in Eastbourne's Goffs, walking there and back."

East Dean now appeared on the holiday map. 'I travelled down to Eastbourne by train to spend a holiday with friends who had taken a cottage on the Green. At the station we engaged an open horse-drawn Victoria and with our luggage piled high trotted up hill and down. I remember so well that 8-10mph leisurely journey over the Downs. I was so excited I couldn't keep still, and the red cherries on the brim of my straw hat bobbled happily in time with the hoof beats. As we reached *Half Way Cottages* it was as if the whole of the south of England was before me in rolling Downland green, broken by the yellow of gorse.'

'We had quarts of cream, dozens of new laid eggs from *Gore Farm,* crusty loaves from the bakery, honey on the comb, and enormous joints of beef, far too big for any cottage oven. These we left at the Bakehouse on our way to the Gap for our morning bathe, and retrieved them on the way back to be borne in triumph across the Green. Great ribs of rich, juicy meat and piles of crisp roasted potatoes tasted so good and soon disappeared.'

The first shadow of war clouds appeared when the men's Red Cross Society gave a demonstration to a visiting representative of the War Office. After inspecting their work he said he was impressed by their smart and efficient manner.

In October 1913 yet another body of an unknown man cast up by the sea was buried at East Dean; the previous year there had been one at Friston. December saw the death of a more prominent figure, Carew Davies Gilbert, at the age of 61, quite old for the time (the average age of death for men was 47, women much the same). The funeral at a crowded St Mary's Church, Eastbourne, was followed by interment at East Dean. [5]

By 1913 magazine sales had increased to 120 per month but it was the vicar's 'melancholy duty to record a reoccurring deficit'. The magazine adverts were all from Old Town:- Bennett Printing; TH Gander bicycles 34a Church Street; RC Miller 29 High Street; WF Mosley Optician 22 Church Street; AE Fillery watchmaker 'opp. St Mary's church call for repairs'; WH Miller upholsterer 26 Ocklynge Road; H Bradford baker 17 High Street 'German yeast sold' [but not for long] and R Blackmore of 24 Okehurst Road.

The village observed Mothering Sunday, in Lent, when girls in service went home for the day and took a present for their mother. The churches were dressed for Easter by Mrs Russell, Miss Hole, the Misses Baxter; Mrs Wycliffe-Taylor, Miss Scott, Mr & Mrs Freeman and Mr C Martin. Easter offerings were described as 'large at £11.20'.

In 1913 Charles Frederick Russell sold the lease of *Gore Farm* to Mr Davies, a London businessman, who ran it as a hobby. By this time Mr Russell ran *Birling Farm* for the Davies Gilberts and *South Hill* for the Maitlands. His younger sons, Fred and Reg, went into the Army in 1916, and when the twins Harold and Arthur were called up in 1918 Mr Russell moved to Mill Road, Eastbourne. In the 1920s the family bought *Lodge Farm* Ringmer, with cattle-fattening meadows in Pevensey. After selling this they rented *Home Farm* Laughton to 1996.

Bill Armiger says, "Mr Davies had a chocolate factory and he sent down cakes of chocolate dust for his pigs, which we could buy." He adds, "We lads would sit on the steps of Chapman's open char-a-bancs and ride up Friston hill. Mr Dennett, of the Post Office by the Green, would bring telegrams to the school and the boys would deliver them for 2d. If they were important Mr Drew would let us go straight away, if not they would be delivered at lunch time or after school."

The reaper-binder with the usual three horse team at East Dean before the 1914-18 war

The Parish Registers were re-bound by the generosity of Mr JA Maitland of *Little Friston*. Turning the pages it is noticeable how the names vary over the years, Caleb, Jabez, Hepzibah, Lettuce, Mercy and Philadelphia were common in the 1800s, and others were in alliterative alliance with the surname - Parnell Pendrell, Francis Fowler, Dinah Dunstall. Some entries are curiously incomplete 'Old John buried 1634', or 'Goodman Fletcher's child buried and his daughter married'.

Many of the old farming ways continued almost unchanged. Bill Armiger said, "The cowmen would be at work early in the morning. The cows made their way to the cow byre to be milked by hand. Beforehand the cowman had to give them their feed, which he had prepared the day before, oats, cake and pulped mangels mixed with hay chaff. I can still hear the milk splashing in the pail and the soft lowing of the cows and the swishing of their tails, mixing with the jangle of the loose chains around their necks. The cowman took only half the cow's milk for he had to leave enough for the hungry calves, who would be calling out to remind him it was breakfast time. When he'd finished the calves went eagerly to their mums who had been waiting anxiously for them.

"Back at the dairy the cowman would ladle out milk into cans for those who bought it, and any surplus would be sent to the farmer's wife, to churn the cream into butter; the rest was used for cheese. The skimmed milk was sold to the poor at never more than half an old penny a pint. After he finished milking the cowman would have to muck out, bring in new wheat straw, and fill the water troughs.

"The cowman would go through it all again in the late afternoon. In the winter the cows stayed in their stalls all snug and warm and dry. By now the calves had been weaned and would be in a nearby yard.

"The calves, steers and heifers had to be fed in their own yards. The oat straw was cut for forage and the wheat straw for the animals to lay on. The hay had to be cut from the rick and the straw from the stack.

"A special diet had to be prepared for the bullocks being fatted for the Hailsham Fat Stock Show. Week by week they got fatter and fatter until they would puff and blow." They had to walk to Hailsham over two days. And then 4 August 1914 changed the world.

In August 1914 Nurse Dyke, still on £48 a year, went to London, to be replaced temporarily by Nurse Parker and later Nurse Nickels. The outbreak of the 1914-18 war was also reflected in the October issue of the magazine, giving details of the church Services; Matins daily at 0800h with 'prayers for our sailors and soldiers, engaged in the struggle forced upon us, and for our allies'. There was a shortened Evensong daily at 2015, and every Thursday Holy Communion 0730. Besides the Services the church bells were rung every day at noon 'as a call, wherever people might be, to lift up their souls in prayer'.

A Roll of Honour was placed in each church naming those from East Dean and Friston engaged in the armed services.

Early signs of war ahead, Naval Volunteers outside the *Tiger, c.*1912

On 10 September 1914 Private Robert Hall, scarcely 22, of Friston Waterworks Cottages, was wounded in the retreat from Mons, being first shot in the right arm near Parcy village, and soon afterwards hit by a piece of shrapnel in the chest, which knocked him backwards. He recovered at the Royal Victoria Hospital, Netley, but was to be wounded again and gassed twice before his death at the battle of Cambrai in November 1917.

The outbreak of war made it difficult to travel far away so in 1914 the choir had their day-out in Eastbourne. In 1915 it was decided that in the circumstances no choir outing would be held. Instead the choir held a supper at the *Tiger* 'and the evening passed very pleasantly' with speeches and songs. Friend Fowler took over the *Tiger* in 1914 from his father David. [7]

February 1915 saw the children give a three-act play *The Lace Makers* in the schoolroom. Local families were represented by Laura Vine, Florrie Hills, Elsie West, Bertha Wicking, George Armiger, Winnie Ticehurst, and Isobel Dickens.

In September a special Service of Intercession on Wednesdays was introduced as well as the noon bell and the reading of the names of all those in the Armed Forces at Thursday's Holy Communion.

News was received of the deaths of Ernest Miller of the Coldstream Guards at Ypres (missing since November 1914), and William Walker and Alfred Ticehurst both of the 5th Royal Sussex, 'somewhere in Flanders'. James Pengelly, lately coastguard at Birling Gap, was lost on *HMS India* in the North Sea, and Thomas Maynard, King's Royal Rifles, of Friston, was killed in France aged 18. The 'simple but kindly' letter from his unit read, 'From the Field Post Office 4 October 1915. Dear Madam, With deepest regret I have to inform you of the death of your son Rifleman T Maynard who was killed on the 2nd inst. The lad was struck by a piece of shell in the back. Everything was done that human hands could possibly do, but he passed away. I may say he did not suffer. He was a good lad and no one could have done his duty better. I thought you would like to know, as the War Office is generally slow letting one know. Your son had just recovered from a slight flesh wound. You will please accept my deepest sympathy also from all the lads of No 1 section.'

The profits of a 1916 concert went to an Eastbourne Red Cross hospital, and £3.60 was collected for horses and mules wounded in the war. A tragedy nearer home was the February 1916 burial of an infant of Richard and Annie Patching aged 5 months.

In a count by Mr Drew, the schoolmaster, the population of the two villages came to 404 on 1 August 1914. By 1 January 1916 this had dwindled to 284, but rose to 320 in the June. The Gilbert Institute was now not opened in the winter, there being so few men to use it, but Mr Drew and his son Kenneth manipulated the magic lantern for a Good Friday Service.

Mrs Wycliffe-Taylor canvassed for names of women willing to assist on local farms to make up the serious shortage of labour and quite a number volunteered.

By August 1916 the Roll of Honour in the churches had over 50 names. That year the East Dean Marriage Banns' book was filled having been in use since 1828, and *Birling Farm House* had a sale of furniture on 25 September 1916.

The Vicar said he was informed that 'the hygiene regulations which have restricted the keeping of pigs, rabbits and poultry will not obtain for the time of the war, subject to permission from Mr Waghorn, the local Sanitary Inspector'.

The Friston Church roof was repaired over 1917-19 by Messrs Bainbridge and the Gilbert Estate. The East Dean Church guide books showed a profit of £2, 'the Friston one has paid for itself, but the extra cost of a new edition would barely cover the balance'.

On his marriage the village presented table cutlery to Mr Sidney Fillery, the Eastbourne organist who also conducted the East Dean Musical Society.

The Vicar announced that he had offered to leave the parish for some form of National Service, but the Bishop replied that his responsibilities in connection with Military Tribunals, the Rural District Council, and the Board of Guardians, as well as his parochial duties, demand that he should remain. In November he baptised Michael, son of Major Charles and Patience Harding.

For the rest of the war the morning Services were held at Friston and the evening ones at East Dean. Bill Armiger says, "It was also decided to hold the children's Services at three in the afternoon, so that the verger, Mr W Morris in his rich tenor voice, could warn of any Zeppelins lurking around. None came, but there were several scares as our airships from Polegate airfield passed overhead returning from convoy duties in the Channel".

In December 1917 came the Jevington airship disaster. Four airships had to make emergency landings in fog, two on Beachy Head. When the wind rose they were given orders to leave, one made Polegate safely, but the other collided with one moored at Willingdon Hill near Jevington. Both were burnt out and it was only by the bravery of rescuers that two of the crew were saved.

Villagers were now scattered all over the globe. Albert Martin was in Salonika - down with malaria, his brother Tom had been wounded twice. Ernest Hills in Mesopotamia fighting flies as much as the Turks, and William Dann, Richard Patching, and Walter Mantle in Palestine. Frank Ticehurst, after Gallipoli with the Naval Brigade, was scouring the Mediterranean, and Albert Stephens, Charles Hall and Fred Wicking were in India, Walter and Fred Dennett on the NW frontier. As the Revd AA Evans wrote, 'Who would have thought four years ago that so many of our youths tending the sheep and following the plough would be out world-wide grappling with terrible foes. They are out of sight, but never out of our thoughts.'

Bill Armiger said, "During the 1914-18 war I was in the little farming community of *Friston Place*. The Monday before Christmas 1917 my father received his share from the *Tiger* Slate Club. Each member paid sixpence a week and was entitled to ten shillings [50p] a week for six weeks if they were ill, and the surplus was shared out in Christmas week. It was usually about a pound depending on how much had been paid out in sick benefits. Father gave mother his share, and mother, a sister, and I walked to Eastbourne to do our Christmas shopping. At this point in the war everything was becoming scarce and expensive, but we managed to obtain most of what we needed with our pound, including a bottle of Port and a pound of walnuts for Dad, and an orange bottle that was Mum's favourite wine. By this time she was getting anxious because it had started to snow and we had our five-mile walk with our purchases, but we reached home safely much to the relief of Dad who was pleased to see how well we had done.

"Christmas morning came and I awoke to find that Father Christmas had been, my mother had made me some warm clothes and a sugar mouse out of her sugar ration, and my sister had repainted several old toys to look like new. My elder sister, who was in service in Hove, had found a clockwork motor car which gave me great delight for it was the first I had seen; my brother Jim, who was fighting in France, had given my mother some silk cigarette cards, which were a great thrill.

"After breakfast my mother put a fat cockerel and a rabbit in the oven of our iron range and we set off to Friston Church. Inside the church all was bright with holly, a Christmas tree and a manger by the pulpit. Mr Drew was seated at the harmonium, and the old coke stove was smoking as usual, but made it warm for those nearby. As the Vicar was preaching we became aware of a profound silence and that the church windows were no longer chattering from the vibration of the guns on the Western front. We hoped it meant Jim would be safe for another day.

"We hurried home for our lunch to which my father had invited two of the Canadian soldiers who had their Signal Station in one of the requisitioned cottages. After the meal one of the soldiers said, 'Watch this', and he turned a handle and a man appeared on a screen drinking a glass of water - he was actually moving. The soldiers were surprised we had never seen moving pictures before.

"We played party games and sang carols when suddenly Spot, the dog, ran to the door and my brother walked in. He had received a 'Blighty wound'[5] and been sent to the Summerdown convalescent camp at Eastbourne, where he applied for leave and managed to obtain a lift to Friston Mill. He said he almost cried with joy when he saw mother's lamp shining out as he turned the corner, and mother felt that all her wishes had come true."

In May 1918 a Memorial Service was held for Charles Gay, killed in action. There was a house-to-house collection for the Red Cross, as there had been every year since the war began. Gunner JS West wrote home, 'When we went to the St John Ambulance class at East Dean some people laughed, but I found it one of the best things I ever did. When a shell dropped in and wounded several of our chaps, there was only me to bandage them'.

The 1918 accounts of the Rat and Sparrow Club were passed, they showed that several hundred rats and house sparrow eggs had been destroyed, 'useful work done by destroying these enemies of field and garden'.

Bill Armiger said, "In the summer of 1918 the first tractor appeared on the scene to pull the reaper/binder. My father worked the binder, and a man from the Ministry drove the tractor. Everyone was surprised by how many acres they could cut in a day. It was the start of the horse's decline, the tractor did the job much faster - even faster than the land girls."

Bill Armiger recorded, "On 11 November 1918, Luther Hills, on his way to ring the church bells, called at the school to say the war was over. All the children went mad, Miss Baxter kissed and hugged Luther, and Mr Drew shouted, 'Hurrah, no more lessons for today'. We children went off with fife, drum and bugles making a merry din parading round the village until early dusk and rain drove us unwillingly home.

"At the Thanksgiving Service in East Dean Church that evening it was with heart-felt thoughts that all sang the old hymn, *Now thank we all our God*. All the children remembered Martinmas Day, 11 November." One village family learnt the special news that Mr WH French, who had been 'missing' was a prisoner-of-war.

A few aspects of life returned to a semblance of normal. Mr Reginald Fears, having been fined 25p for riding a bicycle without lights, remarked, "What's the use of a bicycle if you've got to walk?" Miss Bertha Wicking, daughter of Mr Thomas Wicking of Gilberts Drive, went away from her wedding on a motor-cycle combination; quite the smart set for those days, capped in December when Mervyn Stanley Stutchbury married Rosamund May Wycliffe-Taylor. The ceremony was in London and the Revd AA Evans assisted.

3. Village Life, 1919-1939

"Up to the 1914-18 war", according to William Joslin, "East Dean was a tiny Domesday village, buried in the depths of the ancient Sussex countryside, completely removed from the unknown and hectic activities of towns and cities."

Others have memories as a country child. 'Playing in the hay, making nests, burying each other amid the sweet smell. Gathering the sheaves of cut corn to build into stooks. The hessian sacks which came filled with fertiliser or corn could be transformed into a hat or a cape, a tent, a hammock, a scarecrow's dress, curtains, leggings, horse blankets, windbreaks, or even a towel *in extremis.* And then there was milking a quiet cow, with the farm cats gathered round hoping for a share, most unhygienic but free from clatter.'

East Dean Smithy on Friston hill around 1920 with blacksmith Luther Hills at the door, wagon wheels and a scythe at his side and an ox yoke above.

Grace Taylor said, "Luther Hills, would, after a few choice words, repair my father's [Dick Fowler] sheep bells. I loved to stand and watch Luther shoe cart-horses, although I didn't like the smell as he put the hot horseshoe on"

Life was hard for the women. "I rose at 3.30, for washing 23 sheets was a day's work. Walked into Eastbourne once a week pushing a pram, not easy and the passengers were bumped around. Often back by 10.30. Bread was baked, the oven fired by bundles of furze collected on the Downs. Rabbits cost $1^{1}/_{2}$p or $2^{1}/_{2}$p depending on size, and herrings were 40 for 5p. The fishmonger came in pony and trap from Eastbourne, but lobster catches at Birling Gap were sold at the *Tiger.*"

Kathleen Banks (née Burgess) said, "My first view of East Dean and Friston (ED & F) stays vividly in my mind. Towards the end of the 1914-18 war, when I was eight-years-old, my best friend invited me to go there in a Hansom cab with her parents. This meant an early start from Seaford. The road was of chalk, narrow, treeless and traffic-free. I remember my surprise on reaching Friston Church and looking down upon East Dean, a lovely little village nestling in the trees, with the sea beyond. After dismounting - to make it easier for the horse - we walked down Friston hill and were thrilled to watch the calves being fed in the yard beside *Gore Farm.*"

Ted Fears said that in the 1920s and 30s East Dean was a farming village, houses were tied to the estate, and travelling carters visited regularly. "Even in the 1940s children could safely play in the roadway."

Into this life came discussions about the peace celebrations. Mr and Mrs Herbert Elliott, of *Grey Walls,* [he was the proprietor of Elliott's Stores, high class grocers of South Street Eastbourne] led the debate. There was great diversity of opinion, although all agreed that boisterous rejoicings would be out of place with the sufferings and great loss of life. In the event, as bonfires and fireworks were not allowed, the residents had to confine themselves to Admiralty flares and rockets under the control of local coastguards on the Horsefield.

The question of whether the Gilbert Institute should be reopened for the winter months as village life got back to normal was answered with a firm 'Yes'. The Vicar even wrote of opening a 'night-club', which was his interpretation of a billiards match and a whist drive between East Dean and Friston - which Friston won. At another whist drive, on 12 December 1919, Dorothy Dickens won first prize and Tom Martin was voted the best-looking man in the room. Over the 1920s the Gilbert Institute went on to house a succession of successful billiards and darts matches, and the in-vogue whist drives.

Any dances were held in the 'Assembly Room' of the *Tiger*. At one Mrs George Wicking won first prize in the Fancy Dress as an Italian lady, her husband won second prize as a flunkey, and Harry Sellars won third prize as a golliwog.

Grey Walls, associated with the Elliott family. [7] Sir John Salmond bought it in the 1930s, after the war the Hudsons took it over. John Kent, allegedly 'the sort that gives entrepreneurs a bad name', converted it into *The Grange,* now a BUPA residential home

The next question was the War Memorial, so a War Memorial Committee was formed on 5 May 1919. Charles F Russell and others suggested that any memorial should take the form of a village cross on either the Green or just outside the church gates. Others, such as Alfred W Yeo, of *Hodcombe,* thought Went Hill would be the best place. The Revd A A Evans favoured the Green, as did Arthur S Haynes, the artist, who recommended that the memorial should consist of a shaft of green sandstone, with a suitable capital, set on a plinth with shallow steps or seats of York paving stone. This went ahead later in the year. [7]

The effects of the war continued, for in April there were another two burials of unknown men washed up by the sea.

At the opening post-war concert of the East Dean Choral Society in 1919 Luther Hills sang *The Powder Monkey,* but the Society's future remained uncertain. Records show that in 1925 Sidney Fillery agreed to conduct the Choral Society for another year, but the last mention was in 1927.

In May 1920, the gun of the U121 submarine that had run ashore near Birling Gap was allotted to the parish by the War Trophies Commission, Harry Sellars, of Friston Old Vicarage, was to convey it to the Green or the Gap. There was, however, no enthusiasm for the venture and the wreck remained on the beach until salvage operations began in 1927.

Cyril Tolley who as a child lived in East Dean, perhaps playing at the Birling Manor golf course, won the English Amateur Golf Championship in 1920 and 1929.

In the summer, as part of the village's rehabilitation, a 'large and handsome' pavilion for the use of the Cricket Club was opened by Mrs Patience Davies Harding. She announced, "So long as a cricket club exists you may be sure the field is at your disposal".

There wasn't much else to do in the village - no *Delphines/Hiker's Rest* or *Grimaldi's* existed in the East Dean of 1920, one tourist complaining, "There's no place for lunch". On Bonfire night, however, a motley host of local Kings, Bishops, and Red Indians sat down to supper at the *Tiger* entertained by the Friston handbell ringers.

The postman's 1920's routine was to walk from Eastbourne, deliver the morning letters, and walk back with outgoing mail in the afternoon. In between he did odd jobs or availed himself of the *Tiger's* hospitality; it was known for him to be found drunk on the roadside. The first public transport plying between Eastbourne and East Dean was a horse-drawn charabanc, but in August 1919 a single-decker bus began a regular (or more likely irregular) service three journeys a day stopping at the Forge.

The Recreation ground in the 1920s with the old 1920-1956 Pavilion. Before power mowers, the grass was kept mown by an ancient Downland method

The Church Services were restored to the pre-war alternate morning and evening times at each church. An illuminated scroll of vellum with the names of those of the parish who had taken part in the war was donated by Herbert Elliott.

Also in 1920, Edward Oliver Hobden, often called EOH, a farm manager at Parkwood Farm, Upper Dicker, bought *Gore Farm* at auction from the Duke of Devonshire. He was joined by his brother Stanley, said to have emigrated to Australia, but returned alleging that the work was too uncongenial there.

EOH had a mixed welcome, for the next year his corn ricks suffered an arson attack and three local boys were summoned for doing £114 of damage.

His daughter, Kathleen Hobden (later Cater) said, "In the early 1920s there was only a dirt road to Seaford. My father's flint carts had a flap opening in the bottom and when a lever was pulled the flints dropped down on the road. The flints from Peak Dean Plat, a bed of flints now the Greensward, were used to make up the road from *Gayles.*"

Arnold Hills confirms, "The flint wagons collected flints from the fields which were dropped by pulling the lever on the wagon. The flints were thrown by hand onto a Foden Steam Lorry that took them up to *Gayles;* you would need a team of horses to get that weight up Friston hill." Mark Fuller mentions in his diary the amount of flints collected from the fields varying from '6yds' one Saturday to '40yds' on the following Monday.

"In the 1920s", said William Joslin, "My father, a busy oil broker in the City of London, would take the family down to East Dean at every opportunity for he loved it dearly. It was a tough journey in an old-fashioned open tourer. Often, *en route* from London, the car could not surmount a hill, when the ladies in their long dresses would be asked to dismount to lighten the load, and my father would scout around until he found some farm workers eager to push the car up the hill in return for the wherewithal to buy some liquid sustenance."

Old plagues continued, for in November 1920 the eldest daughter of the Revd Parrington (ex-East Dean vicar) born in 1882 at *Birling Farm,* died of TB.

The first meeting of what became the Parochial Church Council (PCC) was in 1920. The parish magazine doubled its price to 2d and the circulation increased. The Vicar bemoaned, 'The newspapers are admonishing the clergy to make the pages more lively, spicy and entertaining, but in little country parishes where only one page can be afforded there is no room for local news.' There was a mention of a fierce storm in 1921 when tiles were blown off the roof of Friston church.

East Dean's Church of St Simon and St Jude played a central part in the village in the 1920s

Perhaps the most famous local establishment of the time was the Bee Farm where visitors came to admire beekeeping skills. There is a record of a bee expert coming in 1921 to demonstrate bee-driving, a method of getting honey out of old boxes without the 'barbarous system of sulphuring'. Pauline Joslin said that the bees were reared in a quarry by Mrs Sogno's *Dene Lea* along Downs View Lane and by *Falmer House* according to Cicely Hunnisett. The grave of Arthur Sturges, 'beemaster', is in East Dean churchyard, and the bus stop near where Cophall meets the A259 was called 'Bee Farm' for many years.

The 1921 Armistice Day commemoration consisted of the church bell tolling not for a Service but for a general pause for prayer in the parish. Shortly after the war East Dean formed its own football club that played in a field behind The Gore.

About this time a cyclist riding down Friston hill was killed after crashing into the wall at the end of Upper Street opposite the Forge.

A Jumble Sale in December raised £13.37½, which went towards the churchyards, the parish magazine and the parish library.

The numbers in the Mothers' Provident Club, a thrift club, had fallen off, and by 1922 only eight belonged to the Club, paying between 5p and 25p a month.

The Vicar announced that the bathchair left by Mrs Snape, and never used, was available free for the use of parishioners, and that East Dean & Friston's annual quota to the Chichester Diocesan Fund was £14.

A church Rummage Sale raised £23, the largest amount ever. Mr P Lake of *Pendrills* (although he spelt it *Pendrells*) organised such events in the early 1920s.

Among the newcomers were Charlie Grayson, his wife and three children. After Army service, he set himself up as a baker in two huts where 19a Hillside is today. It was also alleged that when he'd finished baking, he would put a large onion in the warm oven, go down to the *Tiger,* have 'a couple' of pints and a game of dominoes with Harry Corner, and come back to a meal of bread, butter and onion.

The channel telegraph cable wires were removed in October, and the Birling Gap cable hut moved to Holywell. Five remaining coastal wires were left at the Gap.

Capt and Mrs ER Scott, who lived at *Meadow Hill* while *Thatched Cottage* [later *Went House*] was built, came to the village in 1923. [7]

That year Mrs W Hall became cleaner of Friston church and Nurse L Gay, the District Maternity Nurse, visited all the homes soliciting subscriptions to the Friston churchyard extension fund. The Parish Nurse charge was raised to 20p per year per house by 1927.

The Vicar proposed that he would give an occasional address after the Sunday Service on the history of the churches and parishes of East Dean & Friston if parishioners would stay. Apparently these talks were well received and attended.

East Dean village pond, 1925. Edward Hobden's daughter, Kathleen, said, "My bedroom window looked out over the village pond, which was as large as Friston pond with many ducks on it. There was another pond, too, past the shops just by the maisonettes today"

The Revd AA Evans also wrote, 'Our Downland parishes are crowded during the holiday season with two classes of visitors. One of which we are glad to see - those resident in our midst for a week or two and who find real charm in the hills and sea; for the other we have no reason to be grateful. These are the day-trippers, who reach here on Sundays, by char-a-banc, motor-cycle, some in half-nude condition, whose loud hilarity and frolicsome manners are more suited to a showground than to the countryside. They leave behind soiled sandwich papers, newspapers, chocolate bags, cigarette packs, banana skins and bits of broken glass even in the churchyards. We attempt to keep the village clean, but must leave nature to slowly cover up the rubbish.'

That East Dean remained a farming community was reflected by the announcement of Harvest Thanksgiving on 23 September at East Dean church, and at Friston on the 30th, along with the heartfelt plea 'when we hope the harvest will be fully gathered'. The collections and farm produce went to the local hospitals.

At Rogationtide there was the usual out-of-door Service, the congregation meeting at the church door and processing to the village school where a prayer was offered for God's blessing on the seed sown and on the husbandman's labour. For 1925 Canon W Streatfeild, the Rural Dean, gave an address on the Green by the new Village Cross.

In the course of 1923, after selling the Eastbourne Manor House (later the Towner Art Gallery), Grace Davies Gilbert, her daughter Minnie, and the Hardings (Patience Harding was another Davies Gilbert daughter) moved from Eastbourne to *Birling Manor,* and the 1924 Summer Fair took place in its grounds on 22 July, with Lady Dent opening the proceedings. Stalls offered 'fancy and useful items for sale, including vegetables. The sideshows and diversions included a mile-of-pennies, a coconut shy, and buried treasure'. Two concerts were given and teas provided - 'at a price'. The evening saw dancing with 'drinks which cheer, but don't inebriate'. The Fair was in aid of church funds, 'the church needs an efficient heating apparatus and like healthy children it is always hungry'.

The Vicarage or the Birling Manor 'Fetes' of the day were good shows, with military bands playing, dances, the usual variety of sideshows and always sports.

There was some discussion about the right title for the occasion, but the PCC were quite certain, 'Fair is the title by which it is to be known. The word *Fete* often used for such gala days is both un-English and uncouth.'

*Gore Farmhouse c.*1925. Kathleen Hobden (later Cater) said, "The farmhouse was a substantial building with a slate roof, lower walls of brick and flint with daub and wattle above, but no gas or electricity in the early 1920s"

Confirmations were held in June 1924, four years since the previous time. The vicar announced the preparation classes as, 'one for each sex in the village, and also at the Manor Hall, Eastbourne for those girls of East Dean who are employed in the town on domestic service.' Mr RE Fears became Sexton of Friston church.

The next month Captain Besford Sworder of *Cophall* died of his war wounds. He came to Eastbourne with his private nurse after the 1914-18 war. They married and after a search for Utopia bought land at Cophall from Col Elliott and began a smallholding.

Mrs Margaret Sworder was a well-known and endearing character. On her land she reared goats, chickens and bees, and had a stall by the side of the main road, from which she sold goats' milk, honey, eggs, poultry and vegetables. The poultry were a gourmet's dream; free range in the cornfields, they fattened on goats' milk, honey and gleanings - an unbelievable flavour. She hardly ever left the village, but in spite of her isolation, she kept well informed about world events and relied on the radio to satisfy her deep love of Music and the Arts.

To augment her small income, she had a cottage made out of *Old Barn,* to let to holidaymakers. Around 1930 she sold off a plot to a Chichester family, who built the *White House,* although they lived in a caravan and let the house. In the 1930s Miss Chevalier-Rivaille and Miss E Barnard built the next house, *Beauvallon,* and over the 1930s Ron Rowney rented the *Old Barn* until just before the 1939 war when he bought it from Mrs Sworder and built *Bremlings* in the garden.

The Vicar announced that 'for the first time in years new houses have been built and probably many more will be erected. If asked, I would fulfil the ancient and beautiful ceremony of blessing the house'. The Vicar's Easter offering amounted to £44.81, considerably more than ever before.

The Outlook Tea Gardens *c.* 1925. Started during the 1914-18 war and regularly patronised by Canadian servicemen from Seaford, by the 1920s the building was of two huts from Eastbourne's Summerdown Convalescent Camp. Mr DR Cairns said, "*The Outlook* had a tin roof set among buddleias and butterflies."

Charlie Vine and Jack Breach used to empty Mrs Sworder's cesspit. When they had cleared the liquid Charlie would go down to the bottom to shovel the sludge into a bucket for Jack to haul up. Every now and then, as the bucket came up, it hit the side and its contents would drench Charlie below, but his only comment was, "Be careful up there, that went all over me".

The Children's Winter Treat went off with all its old time splendour. 'An entertainer from Eastbourne brought a mannikin and greatly amused the audience with the dialogues which took place between them.'

Not for the first time, in 1925, Mrs E Macandrew of *Little Hill* dispersed sums of money to various needs in the parishes, Lady Purves Stewart of the Old Lighthouse gave a number of books to the parish library, and Mrs Maitland of *Friston Place* donated twelve hot water bottles for use in the parishes. Among the new houses was *Friston Corner,* whose Mrs Marshall gave £5 to the parish magazine fund.

Mark Fuller of The Green died in April aged 88. A countryman through and through he knew where to find adders and even caught them with a forked stick.

In June the Mothers' Union had their day's outing to Battle.

Margaret Sworder and her dog, Squib. She handled animals with expertise and sympathy. Slightly eccentric and something of a recluse, she displayed a complete disregard for the mundane matters of life

John Wycliffe Wycliffe-Taylor died at *Gayles* in the October, aged 66. He was replaced as a school manager by Mr CO Oakleigh-Walker and Mr BF Simpson. Mr and Mrs Oakleigh-Walker lived at *The Dipperays* and Benjamin Simpson was at *Little Friston.*

Charlie Grayson, an ex-serviceman from Lincoln, was becoming the main village baker. He later had a three-wheeled Royal Enfield pop-pop tricycle for deliveries, bought from *Bondolfi's,* the Eastbourne confectioners. His wife Ida ran the Downland Tea Rooms. [9] As a *Tiger* regular, he said that it was a touch of beer which gave his bread its special flavour.

On 31 December 1925 Edward Drew retired as headmaster of the school after 35 years. [6] The Davies Gilbert family built a cottage for him and his wife along Underhill (Went Way), named *Yescombe* after a Sussex place name.

The year 1926 was notable for the collapse of Friston Mill [8]; the restoration of Bardolf Hall [5], and the first measures to stop development on the Downs.

Looking west at East Dean and Friston hill along the Eastbourne road *c.*1920. *Gore farmhouse* is on the right. The road is not made up and, apart from the windmill, there are no buildings above the forge, where the Downlands Estate is today

An Appeal was launched by the Society of Sussex Downsmen, the National Trust and many individuals, including the Revd AA Evans, to buy the land above the Seven Sisters threatened by developers [5]. Eastbourne County Borough was stimulated to formulate the Beachy Head Downs Purchase Bill, to keep access to those Downs free in perpetuity.

As far as East Dean was concerned, by 1929 Eastbourne Corporation had bought *Black Robin, Bullock Down* and *Motcombe farms* (1749 acres for £35,000); 402 acres of *Gore Farm* and 805 acres of *Birling Manor.* [9]

The same view c.1922 showing Charlie Grayson's bakery on the hillside above the forge - comprising two huts from the army camps around Eastbourne auctioned off after the First World War. It had a water supply, but even by 1948 no electricity

East Dean churchwardens in 1926 were Major Charles Henry Harding and Alfred Dennett, and Friston Benjamin Simpson and George Armiger. Roderick 'Ronnie' Hall was organist at both ED & F; Mr RE Fears continued as sexton, and Miss W Hall as cleaner. A concert on Shrove Tuesday for the Parish Nursing Association raised £5.30.

Edward James Pindred and his wife had come to East Dean in 1920. Edith Pindred was a Kemp, the Kemp of Forge Garage was her mother's younger brother, and she was aunt to Ted Fears. In 1925/6 they built on the north side of the A259, the house known as the Corner Stores *(now Long View Cottage and Beech Tree Cottage)* and started a business, taking over the Post Office from Mr Dennett on the Green. The new stores was on the left of the Michel Dene Road entrance today, although then it was just a muddy lane by the side of which was a shed used by Bertie Akehurst, as a mobile butcher's shop. He was noted for his pork sausages, home-killed meat and chops. When delivering he carried the piece of meat over his shoulder on a wooden trough.

In 1926 Hugh Dennis Goodman, known as "Jack" came out of the army and joined his brother Sid's business. Sid Goodman had worked in the Old Forge [Luther Hills shoed the horses just downhill of the Old Forge] after the war and started a haulage business. Reg Fears, who had a bad stutter, delivered coal for Sid Goodman. One day he delivered coal to Arthur Sturges at the Bee Farm, who also stuttered, and when Reg stuttered Mr Sturges took it badly thinking he was mimicking him and told him to clear off. Sid Goodman had to rush in to calm him down and explain about Reg, for Arthur Sturges was a good customer. When Sid sold out to Sydney Stevens about 1932, Jack got a lorry and went hauling anything he could find. The brothers Jack and Sid Goodman were often at odds with each other, but co-operated at church where they were both sidesmen.

Ida Grayson's Downlands Tea Rooms sign on Friston hill, looking east c.1925. Cyclists dismounted and carried their bikes up the slope to her hut. The Vicarage is in the middle distance, as a horse struggles up the unmade road with its load

Jack Goodman suffered terribly from indigestion and got through bottles of Milk of Magnesia, "Gut's Ache" as he called it. He would come into the village shop, ask for Gut's Ache, and swig it straight from the bottle.

The church collections in 1926 amounted to £62, the least of 91p was for the National Lifeboat Institution and the most, £7.20, was to the Princess Alice Hospital, where pre-NHS you had to pay.

The Vicar took a holiday in the south of France from 10 January to 1 March 1927 having received 'an ample cheque to cover all expenses … from a group of friends.' During his absence his duties were undertaken by the Revd JH Cabot of Harvard University.

Contributors to the cost of the Annual Children's Treat at the Bardolf Hall included Major & Mrs Harding, Mrs Mason, Mrs Macandrew, Mrs Binney, Mrs Bugler, Miss Boniface (the vicar's housekeeper), the Misses Baxter (daughters of the Water Co manager), Mrs Hall, Mrs Wycliffe-Taylor, Mrs Oakleigh-Walker, Miss Thelusson, Miss Thompson, Mrs Stutchbury, Lady Purves-Stewart (of Belle Tout) and the Vicar.

The Vicar had suggested the formation of a PC in 1923, but this was not taken up for 15 years and the village Parish Meeting continued to meet just once a year leaving most matters to the Hailsham Rural District Council.

The Annual Parish Meeting on 18 March 1927 discussed clearing litter, making a firm path across the Green, and the provision of wayside seats. For the first time the meeting did not need to consider the appointment of Overseers. For centuries the unpaid, un-honoured and un-thanked Overseers had been the bane, burden and rock of villages, but with the demise of that office they passed beyond the demands of rating authorities and auditors. The meeting also talked about the local Fire Brigade.

The mandatory excursion in the 1920s and 30s was to tea rooms with a view. By now, Annie Sogno ran popular tearooms and a B&B at *Dene Lea,* Downs View Lane. Geoff Nash says his parents would walk from Seaford to the tea gardens

The live spark of the 1920s Bonfire Boys was Harry Sellars, a most outward-going chap. He was potman at the *Tiger* where he lived with landlord Friend Fowler. In the mid-1920s 'a movement had been set on foot' to form a local Fire Brigade under, guess who? Harry Sellars. An old fire-engine was bought, years passed and thankfully it was never used, but it was decided to have a grand practice in the presence of most of the village and the Chief of the Eastbourne Fire Brigade. The hose was attached to a hydrant near the church and run out across the Green and Horsefield to discharge into East Dean pond. Onlookers lined the route in expectation, and at a given signal Harry turned on the hydrant and water gushed forth - in all directions all along the perished hose. The watchers were drenched. The only part short of water was the pond where the merest trickle, accompanied by loud sucking noises, was all that emerged from the nozzle of the hose.

At a meeting convened to decide the purchase of a new hose, someone tactlessly suggested that calling the Eastbourne Fire Brigade might be a more effective line, whereupon the East Dean Brigade resigned *en masse* and Eastbourne has looked after the village ever since. The old fire engine was bought by Charles Davies-Gilbert and put to work, with a new hose, at *Birling Manor.*

Sussex Sheep Bells

Kathleen Banks said, "When my parents acquired a pony and trap, we had many outings to East Dean to see the Hobdens, with picnics on the Village Green and refreshments at

Friend Fowler's *Tiger Inn,* or sometimes at *The Outlook* tea-rooms. My parents would spend a week's holiday travelling to Cross-in-Hand.

"After I got a bicycle we often included East Dean in our itinerary from Seaford. One visit I remember was with a group of six cycling to East Dean to explore Went Hill. We left our bikes at *Underhill Cottages* (now a charming house, converted by Sir John and Lady Chatfield) [7] and, after refreshments under the *'Lemonades Sold Here'* sign, we went up the hill. Imagine our surprise and delight on beholding the magnificent view across the Downs to the sea at Birling Gap.

"I well recall a 1926 outing when a group of us cycled to Friston, left our bikes inside the churchyard and set off to Crowlink to view the ship that had been driven ashore in a violent gale and was now breaking up. [5] Large flocks of sheep were grazing the Downs at this time, and I recall seeing the little hut on wheels where the shepherd lived and slept, with his dog, during the lambing season. The tinkling of the sheep bells, and the song of the larks, plus a myriad of Downland flowers made the climb well worthwhile.

"Another treat was the Bee Farm. This was in the grounds of one of the few buildings in what is now Downs View Lane, a long bungalow, *Dene Lea.* A board on the main road said, *Teas with New Laid Eggs 1/-,* and the owner did keep chickens."

East Dean garage *c.*1931. The Corner Stores *(Long View Cottage)* is on the left and the first flowerings of the Downlands Estate are seen in the background above

Kathleen Banks went on, "My parents bought a motor car in 1926 and promptly drove to Scotland - this was well before the days of Driving Tests - but they got home safely having had a wonderful holiday. My brother Harold first drove when 15 and he bought a Rover when there were only about half-a-dozen cars in Seaford. With one of my brothers or sisters I would sit in the open dicky seat at the back in all weathers. One day we went to Litlington and were late getting back, the car hadn't any proper lights so we had to guide it back to the main road. One day my sister Dot borrowed the car without any idea of how to turn round or reverse, so she embarked on a much longer journey than she thought as she had to take the roads which were curving in the right direction for home.

"The roads were very variable, for example, the one to Birling Gap only went after a fashion to Birling Manor, but after that it was merely a track down to the Gap." Renee Wicking, who first came to the village on holiday in 1932, said "Gilberts Drive was a cart track. We went by way of Beachy Head when we went to the Birling Gap Hotel."

Among the news, a collection for the RNLI reached £5.05 thanks to George Worsell's efforts. There was the burial of Henry Walker from the Guardians' Institution [workhouse] who had been found drowned. Mrs Llewellyn Davies of Birling Gap made a donation to the nursing fund, and an October Baptism was of Ronald, son of Archibald and Winifred Marsh of *Friston Place Cottages*. It was also reported, 'Wind and rain hindered the hay and corn crop; many are feeling sore at heart'.

In 1926 the last Exceat oxen team was bought by Major Harding of *Birling Manor* who had them for show just for a year or two, for the usual routine was to replace a pair out of the team of six every year. [5]

From the 1920s, as the forge business declined, Luther Hills made many pieces for the village including the war memorial railings, and also these models of old Sussex farm vehicles, treasured by the recipients

When Arnold Hills left the village school at the age of eleven in 1928 he had to go to the Cavendish School in Eastbourne. "The East Dean children went where they were sent: Dick Breach and Reg Haffenden also went to Cavendish; Wally, Charlie and Johnnie Vine went to St Saviour's, while Maud Dann and Ethel Gallop went to St Mary's Old Town. We were taken by Sid Goodman in his coal cart, which had a canvas tilt, and we sat on wooden forms. Sometimes we were dirtier when we got to school than when we came home."

Arnold Hills also recalls the *Dene Lea* Tea Rooms in Downs View Lane, the Bee Farm, Summerdown Cottages, and Charlie Grayson, the baker on Friston hill. Charlie Vine helped to deliver his bread. "A third baker delivered to East Dean, Thorpe's from Seaside, he came from Eastbourne with horse and cart and served Jevington, Friston and East Dean. His daughter married Syd Stevens, who ran coaches and took over ferrying the school children to Eastbourne."

Ray Cheal was eleven in the early 1930s when he went to the Cavendish School in Eastbourne. "We went in a char-a-banc of Sydney Coaches. If you were kept in at school the bus didn't wait and you had to walk home. It was a long way, but you didn't think of it." From 1938, when all the older children went to a Seaford school, they caught a bus.

According to Reg Haffenden, "When the main road was made up in the late 1920s a regular bus service of single-deckers started. They were not powerful and, especially if full, had difficulty getting up the hills. It was not unknown for the flywheel to overheat and for sparks and smoke to come out of the back around the transmission and engine. For such occasions the conductor had a shovel to throw road dust onto the engine to cool it down".

The petrol tanks of 1920s Model T Fords were gravity-fed and unless they had full tanks when going up a steep hill, like Friston, they developed an air lock and the car stalled. Edward Hobden installed petrol pumps at *Gore Farm,* hence instead of hauling the car to the top he pulled it down to the bottom of the hill for it to be filled up - the beginnings of the garage at East Dean. Run by Jim Kemp, Edward Hobden's brother-in-law, until it was commandeered by the RAF in 1942. [10]

Work started on salvaging the *Ushla* and the *U121* from Birling Gap beach. The team came from South Wales under Fred Schafer working over 1927-9. [5] A Newhaven firm removed the last salvageable material in 1960, and fragments continue to be found.

Bill Schafer was the crane driver for the salvage operations, who hoped to marry the daughter of a farmer at Gayles. His father, the head of the team, would be lowered down to the beach site by the crane to save walking round to the Gap. Bill had asked his dad for

Dick Fowler, shepherd,
1874-1939

a rise, but without any response, so the next time his father was halfway down on the crane he stopped the descent and demanded his rise. He got it, even though his father chased him round the cliff top when he got back. Edward Hobden had a 6-wheeler Guy lorry to take the scrap to Eastbourne, driven by Bill Dark. 'Part of the scrap was ballast; which consisted of steel nuggets each weighing about 1 cwt [50kg] and one of the workers, name of Pettifer, could lift one of these nuggets in each hand and throw them onto the lorry.'

The Parish Library flourished in 1928 although 'a few people had not been returning borrowed books'. There was also the first suggestion that the Guides and Brownies be extended to East Dean.

Mrs Wycliffe-Taylor endowed a cot in perpetuity at the Princess Alice Hospital for a sick child, in memory of her husband and son. She stipulated that, 'the cot shall be for a child from East Dean & Friston when needed'.

Bill Armiger said with a touch of irony, "In our village we realised that what had been used as a cattle shed and a dump was a charming old house, Jacobean or Caroline, and one of dignity and charm. At one end was a deep fireplace and there were quoin stones of greensand, and a mullioned window with transom and drip stones. It might have been a parsonage house at one time, and in 1928 it was given to the village by Mr Francis Arnatt for use as a Village Hall". The first houses of the Downlands Estate were completed 1927-8. [9]

After the 'new' Village Hall had been adapted, the usage of the schoolrooms and the Gilbert Institute fell away. The Village Hall took over as a cinema, for school dinners, Christmas parties, coffee mornings, jumble sales and such like.

The Vicar noticed that tradesmen's carts were increasing on Sundays, especially butchers and grocers. 'Many will think the Vicar hopelessly old-fashioned but he does not think that the steady secularisation of Sunday should be encouraged. One would think tradesmen would welcome a day of rest.' He also preferred the name Went Way for Underhill Road, and thought 'Twitten a charming Sussex word for a hedge-bordered lane, instead of Little Lane which is undistinguished'.

Those present at the December meeting of the PCC, in the schoolroom, were the Vicar, Mrs Harding, Mrs Gallop, Mrs Fears, Mrs Samways, Miss Boniface, Messrs Simpson, Drew, Lake, Hills, Fears, Dennett, and Bugler.

Mildred Pownall, of Waterworks Cottages, mentions seeing yellow fields of rape in the 1920s, and makes reference to ordinary incidents in East Dean life. 'My birthday presents from Gran were an apple, a banana, a Swiss roll, sweets and a new sixpence. For Christmas we made paper chains from the blue bags that the sugar came in and the red bags that the tea came in. Cut up and flour-pasted they formed our decorations along with holly and ivy, reddening any berries with red ochre, used to colour bricks. Christmas stockings contained sugar pigs/mice, an apple, orange, nuts, a chocolate watch and a game or puzzle.

'Our hair was washed regularly to keep lice at bay. Dad would go through our hair with a fine-toothed comb and if he found anything, out would come the *Derbac* soap and a hair cut. My brothers sometimes looked like convicts.

'A Boot Inspection was held nightly to see how many studs were missing. Dad did all the footwear repairs himself. He bought leather from Woolworths, soaked it in water and nailed it on, inserting metal segs at the scuffing points of the heel and toe. I can see him with the shoe last between his knees knocking in fresh studs.'

Interior of East Dean Church *c.*1931, with oil lamps. A small niche in the north wall of the nave can be discerned on the left, here the 14th century pewter chalice and paten, found in the 1880s, were placed behind a glass cover so that they could be viewed by all

Ronnie Hall's first wife, Florence, died in November 1928. The funeral cortége went from *Maryfield* on Friston hill to the church - when the custom of laying straw along the route to reduce the noise of the carriage wheels as a mark of respect was practised for the last time in the village. Miss Louisa Gay, of 1 The Green, was still the Parish or District Nurse in 1929, "We all called her the Nittie Nurse". She married Ronnie Hall in 1942.

ED & F Women's Institute was formed on 7 February 1929 by the initiative of Mrs Batten, with Mrs Harding as president and Miss Catling vice-president. Their first meeting was held in the Gilbert Institute. In December the WI gave two performances of plays and a concert led by Mrs Bugler and Miss Catling when the sum of £6 was raised for their funds.

"On 18 June 1929", said Grace Taylor, "My father, shepherd Dick Fowler, lent his best crook to the Revd Walter Andrews, acting assistant Bishop of Chichester, who had come for a confirmation but forgotten his pastoral staff. Father made his crooks of willow with a crosier of stainless steel and one he kept at home for sheep sales was lent to the bishop. After his death it was in East Dean church fixed to the Vicar's stall, from where it was stolen in the 1960s, although of no monetary value. Another has replaced it in a glass case."

That June the Vicar sent in his resignation, 'I am nearing my 67th birthday and my weak lungs have betrayed me sometimes. The parishes are growing and need a new Vicar to bring freshness and youth. I have seen many changes. When I came East Dean was a remote village, separated from Eastbourne. A few, and only a few, carts rumbled along its track-way. No houses were built, for ten years no bricklayer was seen except for repairs.

Now the road is a main highway of increasing traffic and noise, new houses, some attractively built, dot the hillsides and the voice of the stranger is heard. I will go to Chichester and help out. I shall be free, I hope, to read more books, grow a little wiser and perhaps do more writing.'

Kathleen Cater (née Hobden) remembers the Revd AA Evans, "He was very prim and proper. He rode a bicycle and wore a black soup-plate hat, and was really knowledgeable about the countryside. One day when I was a little girl, he came to tea at my father's *Gore Farm,* and I told him the story of Sid who was a pupil on the farm. Sid slept rather too soundly in one of the top rooms so there was a bell on a string to the room, which my father would ring whenever it was time for Sid to get out of bed. As he rang it, whatever the day, my father would call out 'Time for church'. The Revd Evans wasn't amused."

Renee Wicking said she met the Revd AA Evans on two occasions. "He was a small man, who wore a flat hat, and was very quiet."

The new Vicar from October 1929 was Canon WF Pearce, known for his flat 'pancake' hat. The choirmaster was now Sidney CG Fillery with Miss King as the deputy organist.

There were about half-a-dozen children in the choir, the boys sat on one side and the girls on the other. The organ still had hand pumps worked by Ernie 'Spud' Murphy. If it was a long sermon he would fall asleep and had to be given a kick by Ronnie Hall the organist. Hubert Foord, who had a good voice, sang in the choir along with Ray Kemp and Bob Seymour.

Crowlink's Rubbish Dump, 1972. With no bin collections before the 1939-45 war the locals had used a hollow or pit for centuries. It was not a throw-away society, pots and pans were repaired, wrappings were reused, no plastic was seen, so the only rubbish was rotten wood, really dirty paper (both burnt), hopelessly broken pots and some glass. This site, filling with old fridges, was covered in the 1970s, but the depression can be made out above the hamlet. East Dean's site was above Cophall

Fred Fuller's father was a farmworker for EO Hobden at *Gore Farm.* "He was a thatcher, did hay tying, straw tying, and shocking (making hay stooks). The pay was sixpence [2½p] a day. He lived at *Peak Dean Manor."*

After leaving school Fred got a halfpenny an hour 'for pulling swedes and mangel-wurzels', then he looked after Mrs Sworder's chickens, and later went milking at *Gore Farm* for 80p a week.

Harry Comber's father said that in those days you had to go into Eastbourne to vote in a general election. It became a day out and everyone went in by horse and cart. "He said that in 1929 he voted for Edward Marjoribanks, the Tory, a member of the Hailsham family, who was elected but shortly afterwards shot himself.

"My uncle, who served in the 1914-18 war, later worked for a farmer at Seven Sisters. He was told to work on Sundays, but said, 'I go to church on Sundays' and when he refused he was forced from his Foxhole cottage and went to Peak Dean."

In March 1930 the PCC held their first meeting in the new Village Hall. The agenda included heating and lighting for the churches, and by September quotes of £36 for East Dean and £122 for Friston Church lighting had been accepted.

A Whist Drive and Dance held in April raised £12 for the Princess Alice Hospital, thanks to the support of Lady Purves-Stewart, of Belle Tout lighthouse, and a Dance at the Bardolf Hall raised £10 for the Nursing Association. Later there was an entertainment to help wipe off the debt on the Village Hall.

On June 12th the new Women's Institute [WI] held a Garden meeting at *The Dipperays.* In November the WI held an open meeting with a guest speaker talking on *The League of Nations,* and their Gala evening the next year filled the Village Hall to capacity, so the WI was flourishing.

An excellent start was also reported to the cricket season, and the team went on to win 14 of its 29 games. As ever, 'The pitch was not all that was desired and will need attention before next season.'

At the Parish Meeting on 15 October 1930 Major CH Harding was in the chair. Others present were ER Scott, RG Hall, WH Lishman, EC Drew, Mrs EH Drew, Mrs M Sworder, Mrs EM Oakleigh-Walker, Mrs PA Lake, F Fowler, L Hills, HD Goodman, I Samways, and B Carter. They discussed diversion of a footpath near Belle Tout, clearing of a drain opposite the Forge on Friston hill, and the Parish Magazine fund's deficit of £3. The disposal of refuse also came up and the decision was that the Parish would dispose of its own rather than add to the rates.

The Village Band: L-R Tony Cheal, Jim Wicking (with big drum), Jessie Eve (at back), Harry Sellars, Walter Eve, and Olive Cheal. Reg Fears, who played a number of instruments including the flute, and George Cheal were also members

During the early 1930s only two or three parish meetings were held a year, which increased to six in 1937/38. The Parish Council [PC] began in April 1938 (with separate East Dean and Friston members) meeting five times a year for its five members, increasing to eleven meetings in 1948, and including sub-committees there were 16 meetings in 1951. From 1931-6 the Clerk was paid £5 a year, then £6, and £8 in 1939, and £20 in 1949, and £50 plus £10 for typing in 1953. In its first year the Clerk dealt with only four letters (excluding notices and cheques), by 1957 the Clerk was dealing with over 300 a year.

The PCC at its March 1931 meeting proposed to level some of the hummocks in East Dean graveyard; and the Southdown Bus Co was allowed to place a bus shelter against the church wall at Friston. Guests at Birling Gap Hotel had suggested that notices of church services be posted in the hotel.

Mrs Binney of Birling Gap donated to Friston Church repair fund, and Mrs Monico supplied a parcel of up-to-date novels for the library.

The Eastbourne Courier of 3 July 1931 reported that the Summer Fair at Birling Manor was opened 'in kind and genial weather' by His Worship the Mayor of Eastbourne, Lt-Col Roland Gwynne. He gave his opening speech from a farm wagon, in which he said he went to church regularly and hoped the proceeds would be large. Total receipts were £164, with expenditure of £47. This would go towards electric light at the churches. The Bowling-for-a-Pig stall was run by Mr B Simpson; Character Reading was by Mr A Bennett; Shooting Mr R Fears; Darts Mr WR Sellars; Teas Miss Mary Harding, Mr WSD Marshall, and Mr E Lawford; Hoop-La Mr RG Hall and Mrs Lake; Coconut Shies H Elliott, RF Wood, and MO Tighe; Pony Rides Mr J Wicking; Aunt Sally stall Miss Marianna Beran and the Hon Patrick Grant; and Hit-the-Nail was by Miss Catling.

Hollington Boys Club, with some village lads, 1933. The Club was started by Cambridge University men in 1893 to keep Camberwell boys off the streets and to feed and clothe them. In 1896 the first camp was held at Birling Gap on the invitation of the Davies Gilberts, and annual camps continued to 1939. They had tents of varying complexity, a marquee for dining and a pot-bellied cooking stove

By 1930, Armistice Day, 11 November, was observed as a Day of Remembrance: with a short Service and a two minutes silence at the Village Cross.

A pertinent record of June 1642 states, 'It is ordered that Thomas Fremlyn of Eastdean, a soldier heretofore imprest out of the country and maymed, shall be allowed a pension of £3 per annum during his life to be paid quarterly.' It is uncertain that it was our East Dean, but this gesture in bygone times by those who were mindful of a soldier's sacrifice was more than many victims received for their 1914-18 wounds, gassing and other incapacities. Some co-ordinated response was necessary and in 1921 the British Legion [BL] had been founded as a national, non-party, non-sectarian organisation. Ex-servicemen's claims were pressed, improvements in the pension achieved, help was given to find a house, and ex-servicemen and women were trained and employed, e.g. in the Poppy factories. Even peacetime life was hard, Arthur Wicking died tragically, aged 41, on 17 October 1931.

Local men and representatives of the Willingdon BL branch to a total of 12, met in Ida Grayson's 'Downland Tea Rooms', on Wednesday, 14 October 1931, to 'accept the charter of the BL and to formally establish a branch of the Legion to be known as the Eastdean *[sic]* branch'. HD 'Jack' Goodman was elected chairman, Wing Comdr JH Wilford treasurer, and Capt ER Scott secretary. Committee members were R Bagg, FC Etteridge, G Wetlesen, FA Cunningham, H Fears, J Dalton and W Penn. Charlie Grayson was later elected vice-chairman, and J Pownall to represent Westdean. Major Harding was president, and RG Hall vice-president. In the 1930s the membership averaged 40, and they little thought that the branch would become one of the largest and most active in the area.

Examples of members were Capt Scott and Frank Bagg. Scott had served in France until invalided out with shellshock in 1917, and came to East Dean in 1923. [7] Apart from the BL treasurer for many years, he supported the Cricket Club, became a representative on the 'Rating Authority' (in the days of the Eastbourne Rural District Council) and continued when the parish was transferred to Hailsham RDC in 1938. In the lounge of his *Thatched Cottage* was inscribed, *'I will build a house with deep thatch To shelter me from the cold; And there shall Sussex songs be sung, And the story of Sussex told'*. Frank Bagg, groom to Miss Prideaux Brune at *Went Acre* and whose wife was her housekeeper, had been gassed in the 1914-18 war and as a result spoke in a soft, husky voice.

On 12 November the committee of the new BL branch counted the first local Poppy Day collections which came to £14.29, plus a church collection of £3. It was resolved to open a bank account. At the December meeting the branch received five pounds worth of Relief Fund vouchers, and they obtained permission to issue 75p worth for three weeks of groceries to Jack Hills of Peak Dean, who was temporarily unemployed following an accident. Decided not to order the *British Legion Journal* - it had to be paid for in advance.

When Mrs Simpson, the local RSPCA secretary, organised a meeting on the Society's work the lantern 'was skilfully manipulated by Mr Killick'.

There were 62 communicants at Christmas, and the parish magazine, which cost 1p in 1932, opened with a letter from the Rt Revd George Bell, Bishop of Chichester. 'The world is suffering from the effects of the war, such as unemployment, due to the economic consequences of the peace, so unexpected by the statesmen. Our thoughts should fix on the Disarmament Conference in February 1932.' The Vicar commented, 'the world in general, and England in particular, are in a distracted condition. Let us hope that the clouds of 1932 will disperse and in 1933 clear skies of peace and prosperity will cheer us.'

'The electric light' was installed in the Village Hall in January 1932 by Mr J Kemp, thanks to a donation from the WI.

The first function by the local British Legion [BL] was a Concert party at the Bardolf Hall on 24 February which showed a profit of £5.07. At their next meeting at 1 The Fridays it was agreed to issue ten shillings [50p] worth of grocery vouchers to Mr C Hartwell of *Friston Place,* and to order copies of the *British Legion Journal.* Later the branch co-opted Mrs Nora Hobden (WI), Miss Gay (District Nurse), Mr Drew (who acted as auditor), Mr Lake (an estate agent); the Revd Pearce was to be chaplain.

Miss Linda Wood and Miss Diana Eyre joined the PCC in March, while Mr Drew retired as churchwarden and was replaced by Mrs Harding.

The population of the villages was now bordering on 500 and over the 1930s it was increased in the summer as the village was popular for Territorials, Boy Scout and Girl Guide Camps. The village was happy to receive such guests, 'they conducted themselves in a very orderly manner and the hope was they would come back'.

A good spell of hot, dry weather helped all round and was ideal for harvesting.

The BL held their AGM at the *Tiger* for the first time, and decided not to send a representative to the Albert Hall Festival on 11 November because of lack of funds. The following year the branch decided against holding an Annual Dinner 'on account of so much unemployment in the district'.

When Arnold Hills left school in 1932 there was no work. "I did odd gardening and went prawning at Birling Gap. We sold the prawns as best we could and lived on them." One of the school governors, Mrs Batten, offered him a job as page boy at the *Hydro Hotel* and he was there for 3$\frac{1}{2}$ years. With the help of Mrs AM Hornsby, one of the directors of the *Hydro,* he went to Gravesend Sea School to train as a seaman. This led to him being a merchant seaman all through the war, and to being torpedoed three times - twice in one day.

During the school holidays the children would ask the Pindreds of Gore Post Office if there were any telegrams to be delivered. 'There weren't many but you were paid 3d to deliver in the village, 6d [2¹/₂p] for Friston and a shilling beyond. Southdown Buses had a box at the back of the Gore garage where parcels off the No. 12 could be collected, Dennett's would order from their wholesaler if they ran out. One day a village lad was found pinching a bunch of bananas from the box.'

Charlie Vine was born in East Dean at the *Darbies*. He never knew his parents and was brought up by his grandparents. He went to the village school, and from the age of eleven, about 1932, went to St Saviour's School in Furness Road. The transport to Eastbourne was, of course, Sid Goodman's coal lorry. The pupils did their craft work in a room below the Library in the Technical Institute. He spoke of the times at the village school when Mrs Grace Davies Gilbert would visit on her birthday, providing a bag of sticky buns, one for each of the pupils. "This was a special treat as things were hard in those days. Often as a boy I would be sent over to Dennett's Stores to get one pennyworth of stale buns or biscuits for the family's dinner.

The Military Muddlers gave another concert raising £8 for the Nursing Association and Cricket Club. Taking part were Misses H Fletcher, and M Dann, Messrs HE and R Fears, R Kemp, I&J Worsell, RG Hall, FJD Long, with accompanist Sidney Fillery. It would seem that the only 'fancy dress' was their old army uniform from 1914-18

"For excitement on a Sunday afternoon", said Charlie, "The village lads would stand at Upper Street opposite the Forge to watch any traffic go by. It was quite an event." Peter Armiger recalls getting his exercise by running up Friston hill after the Foden steam truck that delivered beer to the *Tiger*.

Blacksmith Luther Hills made the wrought-iron coronal lamp fittings that hung in the churches. He was also the Sexton at East Dean church, and Charlie would help him to stoke the boiler with coke, "On a dark winter's night it was eerie". Another job he did to earn a few pennies was flint picking, for which he was paid something like a penny a bucket.

The Vicar wrote of the 1933 influenza epidemic, 'Laid low a few of the parish, with the deaths of Laura 'Lottie' Wakeham servant of the Hardings, Alfred Dann of Peak Dean and Dorothy Gibbs, daughter of Mr & Mrs Hills of the Gilbert Institute.'

The PCC formed a separate finance committee, perhaps because the Waterworks Company had donated £10 towards the funds. Mrs Seymour was now cleaner at Friston. On Charles Oakleigh-Walker's death Percy J Budd of *Green Hedges,* The Ridgeway, replaced him and shortly proposed that the PCC met quarterly rather than 'infrequently'. Mervyn S Stutchbury was appointed school manager in place of Mr Oakleigh-Walker, and Mrs

Rosamond Stutchbury brought Mr John Hunt to give a piano recital at East Dean Church.

The onset of summer meant that the Boxing Club meetings finished for the year, with cricket taking their place. Strangely, the boxing gloves were supplied by Miss Beatrice Prideaux-Brune of *Wentacre*. Mrs Thorpe late of *Flint Cottage* donated jumble to the Summer Fair, held in gloriously fine weather, and £110 was raised.

Armistice Day 1933, on a Saturday, commenced with Holy Communion 0800h, a Memorial Service around the cross 1100h, and a Service at 1930h in East Dean.

The *Military Muddlers* excelled themselves, at a Sing-Song in the Bardolf Hall, and raised £11 for the Nursing Association and the BL. Mr Fillery, the choirmaster, brought St Anne's choir to East Dean on Christmas Eve.

Aerial view of East Dean & Friston, October 1934. The water tower is top central, the old village is in the middle. Compared with now the main differences are the few Estate houses in the loop of The Ridgeway and Warren Lane and the sparseness of Friston Forest, only begun in 1927

Bill Armiger started in 1933 as a full-time gardener with Mr Cory of *Friston Corner,* at £2 a week. "Mr JJ Brown bought the house in 1937 and increased my wage to £2.50, and when Sir Frank Burnand bought it in May 1939 and gave me £2.75 with two weeks' paid holiday I thought I was well off. The average farm wage was £1.50 with only Bank Holidays paid. I contributed to the Gardeners' Royal Benevolent Society for help with illness and to receive a small pension.

"The Society brought gardeners for a week's holiday at the Alexandra Hotel, welcomed by Mr Lloyd Smith, Mr & Mrs Daly and Carol Newall. It was an appreciation for the beauty brought to so many gardens, by humble men mostly with ragged faces."

In 1934 the BL stated that the Village Band had ceased to exist for some years and the only member left, Edward Miller of *Elmlea,* agreed that they take over and repair any instruments. Harold R Fears of *Underhill* was unemployed in April and although now employed he incurred debts that he saw no possibility of clearing, so the BL agreed that a cheque for £2.25 be lodged with Dennett's to his credit.

Miss Ada Absale lived in *Haligarth* (later *Little Garth*), another use for ex-army huts. She always wore a navy blue beret, which in real countrywoman's style she pulled down well over her face.

The East Dean Sidesmen were now Mrs W Gallop, Mr AH Dennett and Mr P Lake, with Messrs P Budd, W Armiger and T Martin at Friston. The PCC put in abeyance the idea of a new Friston organ. It was thought that it would be out of proportion, and if placed in the roof under the tower, the cost would be £1000.

Bill Armiger said, "By 1936 water was laid to most cottages. We were asked to move to *Little Lane Cottage* with no mains water, so we had to go back to carrying buckets from a farm lodge opposite. We had a water closet at the bottom of the garden and you had to carry water there whenever you used it. Mains water was laid on just before the 1939 war."

The Women's Sewing Meeting and the Mothers' Union enjoyed the air of Bognor Regis on 12 June arranged by Mrs Gallop and Mrs Samways. On 22 August the Junior Choir Outing left by 'Sydney' coach to Brighton, where they found no dearth of outlets for their pocket money and visited the Aquarium. The Geranium Day for the Blind raised £3, organised by Mrs Hobden.

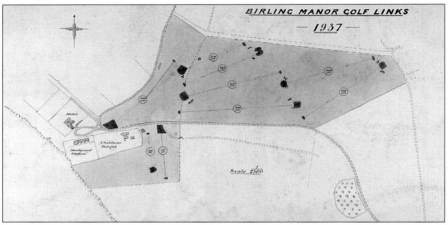

Birling Manor Golf Club opened 1894. A 9-hole 'sporting course', you drove off 125yds towards the cliff edge and then, if lucky, 170yds back, crossed the Beachy Head Road and played back and forth over where the sewage unit is in 2000. Owned by the Davies-Gilberts, it rapidly became popular because, unlike the Royal or Willingdon, it opened on Sundays. To the left are labelled Hotel, Coastguard Station and *Childrens' Delight* [5]

Those receiving relief through the BL United Services Fund were Mrs DK Cheal £1.50 cash over ten weeks, Mr G Wetlesen 35p in kind and 35p in cash over 13 weeks, and Mr GH Cheal £1 cash over four weeks. Wing Cmdr Wilford had retired because of ill-health and the treasurer was now Lt-Col KD Allan, and the secretary Mr J Brace. The committee was Messrs Hyde, Budd, Dann, McNally, Wilson, Dashwood, Bagg, Watson, and Miller.

After leaving school Ray Cheal was an errand boy for Dennett's Stores. "I would leave the shop at 8 in the morning with a full basket, newspapers, milk and the like, and walk to *Friston Place, Gayles* and all places in between, getting back about one o'clock. Sometimes of an evening, four of five of us village lads would walk into Eastbourne to the Hippodrome, spend sixpence [2½p] in the Gods, and walk back, stopping to buy a pennyworth of chips at a shop near the *Tally Ho.*"

An October baptism was of Maisie, daughter of Ivan and Ida Worsell of 7 Coastguard Station, Birling Gap, and a burial was of Muriel Thurlow of *Windover,* The Ridgeway, Friston, one of the new houses.

Armistice Day 1934 fell on a Sunday, so this year as well as the usual Church Services there was a short Service at the Village Cross just before 11 o'clock and at 3 o'clock [1500h] a British Legion Parade at East Dean.

During the year a doctor's surgery (from 6 College Road) started at East Dean.

For the Sunday School Treat, a Christmas Tree and a cinema entertainment was provided by Major Charles Harding of *Birling Manor.*

In early 1935 the Vicar was diagnosed with 'a strained heart muscle which necessitated hospital treatment for a month and then convalescence in Bournemouth'. The Revd AA Evans helped out.

The local branch of the BL held a whist drive which showed a surplus of £11.25. They also stopped relief to Mr G Wetlesen, of *Mill Cottage* because he was now receiving 50p a week from the Public Assistance Committee.

Queen Mary visited the Bardolf Hall in 1935, and Princess Elizabeth, later Queen Elizabeth II, drove along Gilbert's Drive to Birling Gap the next year.

Edward and Edith Pindred (she was Mrs Hobden's sister) celebrated their Silver Wedding in 1937 with a party for the whole village at the Bardolf Hall. They are 4th and 5th from the right in the first row. The girls sitting in front are l-r: Hazel Hobden, Stephanie Fears, Pauline Markquick, Peggie Hyde and Norah Haffenden

Bill Armiger said, "When King George V and Queen Mary stayed at Eastbourne in March 1935 their favourite morning drive was Beachy Head, Birling Gap, East Dean and back to *Compton Place,* Eastbourne. They preferred to go through East Dean rather than continuing along Gilbert's Drive so they passed by the village stores, the Green and the *Tiger Inn.* My wife and I were thrilled as the Royal car passed a few yards from our cottage and when the Royal party saw us His Majesty doffed his hat and Queen Mary gave a regal wave. During their stay the two little princesses waved enthusiastically, and I understand that during their stay they were allowed to play on Birling Gap beach for a few minutes. It was said that they found Birling Gap more private than Eastbourne's beaches". Ray Kemp says that they played with his daughter and other local children.

Bill Armiger added, "It was with deep sorrow that in January 1936, less than a year after his visit, we listened to the radio bulletins informing us that the King's life was drawing to a close. There was no sound between the bulletins, save the ticking of a clock, which stopped with the last bulletin at thirty to midnight."

At the PCC of April 1935, E Miller, replaced P Lake as a sidesman, but the Vicar was absent ill. Tommy Dickens, Dennett's baker, replaced Luther Hills as sexton at Friston on £12 a year.

The BL organised sports and a tea for the children on Silver Jubilee Day, 6 May 1935, to which teenager, Mildred Pownall recorded wearing 'brown shoes and short socks'. The Games included a Fancy Dress Competition when one of the Pownall children went as

Adolf Hitler and won a prize. Other Jubilee Day Games included a Slow Bike Race, and a Flower Pot Race - no, not an early version of Bill & Ben, but walking on two plant pots, holding a string through the drain hole to move one pot as you stood on the other. Every child was given a Jubilee mug and silver medal. The day showed a surplus of two guineas [£2.10], thanks to Mrs Bugler donating a guinea and Miss Prideaux Brune 50p.

Mildred Pownall went on, 'We would go blackberrying on the Downs and come home laden, and with a bunch of wild flowers for Mum. Some blackberries were stewed with boiled rice and some made into jam - a change from the usual economy 7lb jars of *Mixed Fruit*. When one of these became empty whoever's turn it was would bag the jar and get to work to scrape out every tiny particle of jam.

'We moved to a four-bedroom Waterwork's cottage No 2 in 1934. After leaving school I went to help on the farm, where I learnt to bake and spent time in the dairy turning the separator to obtain the cream of the milk. Some of the cream was churned into butter, which was put into 1lb [450g] and ½lb pats, wrapped in greaseproof paper and, with no refrigeration, lowered into a tin bath down the well to keep it cool. Most nights I went home with two pennyworth of skimmed milk for Mum to make rice puddings. Later Mum got me a job as a parlourmaid to the Bensons, a nearby family. The uniform was a dark-grey corded velvet with white collar and cuffs, apron and cap. The summer outfit was Tyrolean style.'

Among village activities were the *Clodhopper's* and *Military Muddler's* concert parties made up of working men and a few women; the WIs had a Country Dancing team, and there was a Rocky Shore Dance Band, with Mr Fleet as bandmaster and Harry Sellars on the drums. The last appearance of the Village Mummers, who included Jim Wicking and Stan Fuller, was as a special request on the occasion of a visit by Mr Leslie Hore-Belisha MP [of Beacon fame] to *Birling Manor* in the early 1930s. Before 1939 the village had a Tug-of-War team led by George Wicking.

Peter Mander wrote, 'I first visited East Dean in the mid-thirties. There were four of us; Boy Scouts who had cycled from London and were camping in the grounds of *Cophall*, a large straggling bungalow owned by Margaret Sworder who grew a variety of vegetables and at the front of the bungalow was a fair-sized lawn.

'One day walking through the fields I came across five or six cows making the most appalling noise, wailing and howling in torment. I made a wide detour. I'd always regarded cows as docile, stupid animals. When I reached the *Tiger* I inquired of the locals, "Why are those cows making all that racket?"

"Cos their calves have been taken from 'em".

"Why have their calves been taken away?"

"Cos they're big enough to eat grass and farmer wants milk from his cows. Don't worry boy dem cows will be right as rain in a couple of days." One learns.'

In those days the *Tiger* was an Old Boys' social club, serving Star Brewery Ales, to the likes of war-hero Bill Dann, Jack Goodman, Harry West, Harry Corner and James Wicking, who would play dominoes there. Friend Fowler, with his waxed moustache and brother-in-law of Luther Hills, was the landlord 1914-48.

Canon Pearce died 7 November 1935. The PCC suggested as successor the Revd William Edward Miller Williams who had done locums during the year. That month the Parish Magazine stopped publication, although a single typed 'pink sheet' eventually appeared, which carried through to 1947.

So the Revd William Williams became Vicar and took his first meeting of the PCC on 14 February 1936 in the Village Hall. He had some good ideas, but pushed them too early. He suggested a Free Will Offering - the matter was deferred, as was his suggestion of forming a Ladies' Guild to do the church flowers, and only reluctantly was it agreed to move the East Dean church safe from the vicarage to vestry. "Not really a country parson, always wore a suit", was one comment.

The Vicar and his wife also weren't prepared to tolerate the cold, damp Vicarage. At the Vestry meeting on 14 April, it was revealed that the Diocesan authorities had already been contacted and agreed that the Vicarage/Rectory was uninhabitable, and that it had been sold to the Gilbert Estate. The proceeds would be enough to build a new house and augment the income, and shortly afterwards, a committee of ladies was formed to deal with the question of flowers and church linen, and after all it was decided to buy a safe for Friston Church instead of storing valuables in the Vicarage or other residences.

The village Bowling Green in 1944. It was constructed over 1936-7. L-R: W Axten, W Sidney Ostler, Bill Armiger, George Wicking, ?Charles Parris, Lt Col TM Gordon, Harold Burgess, ?, ?Percy Budd, Douglass Curtis, Ronnie Hall, ?, Luther Hills

The Bowling Green began with village locals, such as George Wicking, Harry Sellars, Frank and Tom Martin, George Jenner, Corwin Martin and Ray Kemp, deciding about 1935 that they would like a local bowling green. They thought that an area of wild land behind Little Lane Cottage would do. It needed some excavation, but was spare so they approached Major Charles Henry Harding for permission to convert this space, assuring 'the Little Major' that they would do all the work required, and that they had the support of 'Ron' Hall (the Davies-Gilbert agent and church organist, of *Maryfield*), Cecil Dennett (village green shopkeeper), Ted Pindred (shopkeeper and postmaster at *Long View Cottage*) and Friend Fowler (mine host of the *Tiger*). The Major gave his permission willingly.

Over 1936 some 17 of the locals worked on it in various capacities. Fred Fuller said, "It was all voluntary work except for Bill Haffenden, who was unemployed at the time and received 9d an hour. We dug it out, levelled it, and Ken Lemmon and I cut all the original turf for the Bowling Green from the Greensward." Play started in 1937 when Edward Pindred won the singles. In the early years when George Jenner was Secretary of the Bowling Club the membership fee was 15p a year. Stan Fuller won the Singles Cup in 1939 beating Bob Melling (groom and chauffeur to the Hardings) who was one of the doubles winners. Just before the war both Fred and Stan Fuller played bowls, and the brothers also played in the cricket team, Fred being only 15.

Another future long-running campaign started in 1936 when the Parish Meeting that year asked for a 30mph speed limit on Friston hill.

While at school in the 1930s Fred Breach helped Charlie Grayson on his bakery rounds for pocket money. He would take bread and cakes in a bicycle basket to the top of the estate. "Charlie did the outlying ones such as *Hodcombe, Gayles* and the Gap in his trike. After four of us lads had been by bus to an Eastbourne cinema or theatre we would buy one of Charlie's plate-sized jam tarts for about a shilling [5p] and share it out".

Jesse Taylor says he probably only went to Eastbourne about three times a year. More often he went to Alfriston, taking a bus to Exceat and another from there to Alfriston, and catching the last bus back. "On one occasion we reached Exceat to find that we had missed the East Dean connection, but the conductor of the Alfriston bus said, 'Don't worry. When we have emptied at Seaford we will take you from Exceat to East Dean'. Sure enough, the empty bus came back to convey us to East Dean, just paying from Exceat to East Dean, and went back to the Seaford depot when they'd finished. You wouldn't get that service today."

A BL whist drive showed a surplus of £10.97$^{1}/_{2}$, but Pc Hyde complained about remarks made concerning him during the competition.

First-Class GROCERIES AND PROVISIONS.

Chemistry, Hardware AND Greengrocery.

Licensed for the Sale of —— WINES, CIGARETTES AND TOBACCO.

GOOD BACON a Speciality.

DENNETT'S STORES, East Dean.

Phone: East Dean 255
R. HOBDEN,
Family Butcher,
THE DIPPERAYS, EAST DEAN

Prime English Beef, | Finest Chilled Beef AND
Lamb and Pork, | New Zealand Lamb.
Families waited upon Daily

Phone: East Dean 248.
H. GOODMAN,
Coal, Coke & Wood Merchant,
General Carrier, &c.
1 THE FRIDAYS, EAST DEAN.

Hurdles, Poles, Stakes, Pea Sticks, &c.
CARS FOR HIRE.   INQUIRIES INVITED.

Local advertisers just before the 1939-45 war. Dennett's was the village shop on the Green. The Hobden's (they were Edward Hobden's parents), had a butcher's shop in *The Dipperays'* outhouses run by Arthur Raylor. H (Jack) Goodman was a character. A doyen of the British Legion he started the day with a paper round, followed that with a coal round, and then went to look after his pigs at *Underhill*

Pc Harry J Hyde had replaced Pc Etteridge as village constable in 1933 and remained until his retirement in 1948. He was a Cockney and when he took up his appointment he let it be known to all the local poachers that he knew who they were and he didn't expect any trouble from them.

Each policeman's patch was regularly inspected by the County Sergeant, and just before he next called at Pc Hyde's house for the inspection, a row of rabbits appeared in his garden with shot gun cartridges scattered on the ground. After that Harry Hyde took the line that 'if you can't beat 'em join 'em', and the main poachers of the village became Reg Fears, Jack Goodwin and Harry Hyde.

Reg Fears, Sexton at Friston, has a story that in the 1920s the Sextons had to watch over any coffin due for burial the next day. Over one night they got a bit thirsty and opened a bottle of Communion wine, just to wet their whistles, but before they knew they had an empty bottle, so they added a drop or two from each of the other five bottles that were there, topped them all up with water, and no one noticed.

Nothing to do then with Luther Hills replacing Reg Fears as Sexton at East Dean, at 25p a week, plus an extra 25p on weeks when the heating was on.

The BL interviewed an applicant for relief who asked for £2.31 towards arrears of rent, 98p for rates, and an amount for six pairs of boots and shoes. Another member asked for payment of doctor's bill of £1.12$^{1}/_{2}$ and hospital charges of £1.18; the hospital charges were turned down by HQ. Later it was agreed that our RH Fears could have 50p credit at Dennett's stores and £2.50 - to be spent on clothing for his son and a working suit for himself. By now the Secretary was Major AW Farrer (with Capt. Scott as his assistant) although TA Ryde, of *Sparrow's Nest,* became Secretary the next year. Only ten were present at the Legion's AGM. Meetings were again in the Downland Tea Rooms, for which Charlie Grayson was paid 50p a year. The wreath for the war memorial cost 62^1/$_2$p.

The 1937 PCC Vestry meeting in February had 60 present, indubitably to see another of the new Vicar's innovations, 'refreshments were provided by the Revd and Mrs Williams followed by music and dancing'. The Vicar lived in *The Cottage* over 1935-8 waiting for his new Vicarage. Fred Fuller said, "I had the back bedroom in Gilbert's Drive and I would see the headlights of his car coming in late at night; said to be a good bridge player."

On 5 May 1937 Miss Gladys Penford started her kindergarten in Downs View Lane. She had retired early from teaching and built *Woodbury* in 1930, although she helped out at the local school in 1933. Billy Bonnell of *Swallows* was the first pupil and Maureen Burgess of *White Gulls* (2 Warren Close) the second. Many local children attended including Anthony Williams, the Vicar's son, the Soden children from *Middle Brow,* Patricia Vos of *The Dipperays* and the Davies-Gilbert children - Patricia, Sylvia and Jimmy. [9]

The proceeds from the Village Fair held in August were divided between the two churches, where Death Watch beetle had been found. Mr Drewett asked if water could be laid on to East Dean church, but it was decided a rain-water butt might solve the difficulty.

Mrs Elizabeth Bugler was a benefactor to many village activities. 'She was a soft touch for the carol singers' and no doubt an actress manquée, for she ran play readings, plays and fancy dress pageants as here in her garden in 1938. Among those present are Peggie Hyde, Maudie Dann, Roy Fears, and Charlotte Cairns

In January 1938 the BL gave the village children and their mothers a tea party at the Scout Hut [later Farrer Hall] at a cost of £5.77, when each child was given a Union flag. In the February they held a whist drive which made £14.

East Dean Church sidesmen were HB Fletcher and JW Drewett, at Friston PJ Budd and AW Farrer. BF Simpson resigned as churchwarden at Friston, and was replaced by WG Wickenden. The Churches had a Gift Day the last weekend in July. As previously the Vestry meeting was followed by music and dancing, but Miss Mary Parker's reply was to express her concern that the younger generation was not being drawn into the Church.

Mrs French, who had been cleaner at East Dean Church for 25 years was given an honorarium of £4; and was succeeded by Mrs Fuller, at £10 a year. The next year the salary of Friston church's cleaner was raised to £8 per year from £5.

Two of the local notables died that summer, Mr Mervyn Stutchbury of *Gayles,* and Mrs E Macandrew of *Little Hill.* She was succeeded by Mr PS Cradock, who had George Jenner as his gardener and chauffeur for his Rolls-Royce.

The Revd Frederick Ingall Anderson (mentioned in dispatches in 1914-18 war) agreed to become branch chaplain and Capt. HL Wynne, secretary of the BL, now back at the *Tiger* paying mine host Friend Fowler £1 a year for the use of the Club Room. The BL agreed a Christmas present of £1 of groceries and 5cwt of coal to be given to Mrs SA Funnell of Coastguard Cottages, Birling Gap.

Tom Goodman said, "It was in early 1939 that the chap who used to do the newspapers for East Dean broke his leg; my father, Jack, visited him in hospital and said he would keep the business going. When the chap came out of hospital he didn't want to continue and so that's how the Goodmans started in newspapers in a caravan on the garage forecourt".

The other local carrier, Syd Stevens, used three coaches, a Manchester, a Maudesley, and a Bedford, and continued to transport the children to Eastbourne schools, until he lost the contract in 1938. By that time the buses were reliable and the older children attended a Seaford school with a bus pass. 'The buses in those days were so punctual you could set your watch by them.'

Derrick Pyle's farming uncle, Louis Pyle, moved to *Chalk Farm* in 1939, and later had *Chalk Farm* and *Ringwood Farm,* about 1000 acres at peak, with 400 acres under corn (mainly during and just after the war) and two dairy herds, one at *Chalk Farm* and the other at Summerdown Dairy. "The crops were wheat/barley/oats rotated. The oats were fed to horses, the barley went to animal feed, although if of extra good quality it would go for malting. Wheat went for bread; the millers always mixing it with the harder Canadian wheat. Harvesting remained different from today. The corn was cut with binders, sheaves were stood in stooks, then carried to the ricks which were thatched. Most of the threshing was done in winter. During haymaking and harvesting a working day could be 15-16 hours and lunch had to be carried as they were often working far from home."

General view of East Dean village looking west from Cophall in 1930s.
Haligarth is the long cabin in the foreground, *Little Garth* is there now. Above (on the other side of Gilbert's Drive) is *Grey Walls* (now *The Grange*) and isolated way above is *Little Hill.* In the centre are *The Darbies, Pendrills* and Upper Street with Hobbs eares field above

In the early 1920s, before the Downs Purchase, *Birling Farm* was over 1000 acres and had 30 employees. Even just before the 1939-45 war the neighbouring farms were a considerable source of employment. *Birling* employed eight men, *Crowlink* another five, and *Peak Dean Farm* and *Ringwood Farm* about the same. Mr Weston who ran *Peak Dean Farm* also ran *New House Farm* at that time.

Before the 1939-45 war a Wall's Ice Cream tricycle was kept at East Dean and topped up by a van from Eastbourne.

On 1 December 1939 Dick Fowler died of cancer aged 65 and brought a way of life on the local Downs to an end. His shepherding had been the way of centuries, but when the Southdown sheep became uneconomic, mainly because they seldom had twins, his ways were over. [5] Just before the war James Stickland brought the black-faced Suffolks to *Birling Farm* to replace the Southdowns. They were a bigger breed, like a St Bernard dog, and didn't have such a good temperament, but they did have twins.

Dick Fowler used the Sussex dialect. His grandson, Jesse Taylor, remembers, "How you sim then met?" [How you seem then mate?], for "How are you?" and "I'll be down there prencil" for "I'll be there shortly".

Into the 1930s the Downs were free and wild, without fences, gates or stiles, but with many wild flowers such as cowslips, meadowsweet, scabious, and bee orchids. A shepherd looked after a flock of say 4-500 sheep; one in 20 had a bell, folding them in at night.

Grace Taylor said, "In cold weather I can recall my father, Dick Fowler, having icicles on his moustache and bad chilblains on his ears. He came back for dinner every day at noon and finished at five in the afternoon, except at lambing time when he lived in the lambing-hut. This was like a small caravan, kept near the Dunwick Barn when working for Major Harding. He had a lambing yard and went round many times a night with his hurricane lamp. If a lamb died he would skin it and use the skin to cover a twin birth and give the lamb to the mother who often accepted it as her own. Each mother and lamb were kept in separate pens with a bucket of water in each.

"He didn't wear a smock, but had a thick jacket, corduroy trousers (strapped up to keep them out of the mud), supplemented in winter by an overcoat and an enormous umbrella. Usually he had three dogs, two collies, Rock and Quick, and an old English bobtail, always called Bob. Over the day he wandered with the grazing sheep for there were few fences. Each day he pitched a fold for the sheep made up of five-foot length hazel wattles with pointed poles at each end. They would be pitched in fields of rape, mustard, tares, and new growing corn in the spring. This firmed the ground and gave 'goodness' into it. He used an iron bar with a point to make a hole for the wattle poles. If the ground was frozen I have seen him dislocate his fingers when using the bar - he put them back himself."

East Dean Forge and to the right *Forge Cottage* c.1939, where the blacksmith Luther Hills lived, on the A259 Friston hill. Not looking too changed from 1920, but the job had almost gone

Richard and Judith Gorringe recall that shepherd boys used wattle hurdles for sheep folds, changed to wire netting in the 1950s. 'Netting was hard work: the rolls of wire were heavy to carry and to uncoil a roll of frozen wire was hard on the hands. Later electric fences meant that what had taken a morning's work could be done in half-an-hour.'

Many old parish families - the Cairns, Collinghams, Creightons, Hills, Marchants, Paynes, and Willards - have also gone from the village. Fred Breach said the Cairns lived in *The Croft* and the Creightons in *The Cottage* until both families moved to the *Waterworks Cottages* in Old Willingdon Lane. Jack Breach said that the Creightons were a big family and he doesn't know how they managed, especially as before mains drainage *The Cottage* used to be flooded every winter.

William Joslin concludes, "East Dean now seems a very different place, thanks to the 'March of Progress'. Much has been lost, but fond memories are indelible, and I can only look back on those 1920s times as a Golden Age".

Perhaps, but while farming has always been a gamble, in those days when every blade of corn was harvested with scythes and sickles, and every sod of earth broken up by animals guided by man, farming was a dull, backbreaking grind as well. Now the toil has been replaced by innovations which produce much more in less time and at less human cost.

4. The Churches of East Dean and Friston

The churches are not mentioned in Simon Jenkins' *England's Thousand Best Churches,* although both could have Saxon elements, they are listed, and open to the public. East Dean, a delightful example of the evolution of a church, has a pulpit worth seeing and an interesting font. Friston is a tiny, picturesque gem of the Downs, seating barely 100. Simple and unpretentious, it exudes peace and awe, incredible when just over a century ago there were tiles missing on the roof, the door wouldn't close and sheep grazed in the aisles.

St Mary the Virgin, Friston (OS TQ 552982)

In the 1800s and early 1900s the patronal Saint was James the Greater, whose festival was on 25 July. The ancient dedication, however, was to the 'Blessed Virgin Mary', as in the 1505 will of James Peyrs, and this was resumed in 1957.

The Tapsell Gate of Friston Church. The oak frame to carry the electric light over the gate cost £14 in 1946, the lantern was by blacksmith Luther Hills. Damaged by vandals in July 1990 the gate was splendidly restored by local carpenter John Dann with assistance from Bill Bailey

The Church stands on a high tableland of the Downs and looks out on one side to the waters of the Channel, on the other through a cleft of a valley to the Weald of Sussex. The view of the church from across Friston pond, registered as an ancient monument since 1973, is a favourite subject for artists and photographers.

"How old is the church?" is the question asked by visitors. Parts of the nave walls could be around 1060, but as with most old buildings, it has been altered, added to, and in parts refashioned; and many individuals as well as centuries have left their marks on the stones.

Do not miss the Selwyn monuments, which compare to those in any Sussex parish church; the nave roof beams of *c.*1400; or the medieval graffiti in the porch. The Tapsell gate and well-tended churchyard also justify a visit, being the last resting place of composer, Frank Bridge, and an Exciseman killed by smugglers in 1750.

So when you enter you pass through the same wall as the subjects of William the Conqueror. The awe-inspiring oak beams above your head were placed in position over a hundred years before Shakespeare, and even the repaired pulpit might have been there since the days of Queen Anne.

Outside the church the flint house near the pond is *Old Vicarage Cottage,* now considerably extended. The last Vicar of Friston to reside there was Dr William Urquhart, 1674-1688, since when the benefice has been joined with that of East Dean. There couldn't have been much to do in Friston where only four families lived in 1724.

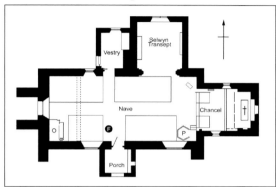

Plan of Friston Church. O - organ; F - font, P - pulpit

Visitors to East Dean and Friston express wonder at the church gates. "This is a curious gate." "I've never seen one like this before, what do you call it?" "A Tapsell? Really, what does it mean?" The answer is that no one knows for sure, it could refer to the part of a wagon where the axle entered the wheel hub, or it could be named after carpenter John Tapsell from Battle, or the Tapsells of Ferring who were bell-founders 1577-1633, or the Tapsells, ironmasters from Wadhurst. You can see similar gates at East and West Dean, Jevington, Kingston, and in West Sussex, Pyecombe and Coombes churches, although the one at Jevington is a modern reconstruction of 1933.

The earliest reference to a Tapsell gate (spelt 'Tapsel') is in the churchwardens' accounts of 1729 for Kingston Church near Lewes. The gates balance on a central pivot and require half the radius of a conventional gate for opening, ideal for keeping livestock out of churchyards. When swivelled open the bearers of a coffin can pass on either side without breaking step, or if the gate was lifted, a hearse could pass over the pivot to draw up to the church porch. The Jevington gate incorporated a stile, removed in the 1990s because it caused extra wear on the central spindle. In the 1990s Sir Peter Tapsell MP heard about the gates from Lord Harris of High Cross and had one made for his home which has a stile.

According to Bill Armiger the main purpose was to enable the pallbearers to rest the coffin while waiting for the Service to begin. Often the body was of a workmate and the bearers may have carried the coffin several miles from an isolated farmstead.

There is a custom to tie the gate during the wedding ceremony and the bridegroom has to lift his bride over, which is said to bring good luck. At other villages the bride must jump over a rope, or climb over a wall, to demonstrate her healthiness and that she was leaving spinsterhood behind. In East Dean and Friston it became a charming and graceful act with the wife leaving for her new life being assisted by her husband over their first obstacle [11].

The earliest memorial in the churchyard is to the right of the path from the gate, a fine example of an early table tombstone, now well sunken, *'Here lyeth interred the body of John George who departed this life the 22nd day of August 1694 aged 80 years'.* Others were destroyed by bullocks allowed to roam in the 1870s. Near the east window of the church lies Frank Bridge. Further down are two Fletcher family table tombstones. The one to the memory of Exciseman Thomas Fletcher records his death on 8 June 1750 aged 34 years; he was pushed over the cliff by smugglers. Four Commonwealth Graves Commission Merchant Navy headstones are to be seen. Until 1955, when all German remains were moved to Cannock, there were also four German graves in the NE corner, airmen killed on the Downs during 1939-45. To the SE lie AA Evans (where the aconites are always the first of Spring), journalist Arthur Beckett, and the Maitlands of *Friston Place.* The nearby seat is in memory of Alice Beckett, who died in 1938 and 'Who Loved the View'.

There are numerous accounts of bodies, found washed ashore at Birling Gap, being buried under a wooden cross carved with *WASHED ASHORE.*

For many years Jack Breach looked after both churchyards on his half day off from his hospital job. Charlie Vine and he used to push the mower up to Friston Church from East Dean. John Eve mowed the grass from 1978 to 2006.

The walls are flint with greensand quoins and windows. On the outside of the church two buttresses sustain the bell-cote tower at the western end. The small bell-cote on the west gable contains one E bell, although the 15th or 16th C oak bell frame would hold three. In 1828 the bell-cote and the gallery at the west end of the church needed repair. William Pierce, a local carpenter, took on the job and his bill for the churchwardens was put down as, '6 Pounds of led yoused att the Stepell, 2 shillings; 2 boushells & haff of heare, 15 shillings; for beer threepence'.

The bell, which has never been tuned, is inscribed *John Palmer made mee, 1651, William Fletcher, warden;* John Palmer cast his bells at Canterbury. At the time of the 2000 Millennium the cast-iron clapper staple had rusted away and the frame was in need of repair. The bell-cote is surmounted by a curious weathervane copied by Luther Hills, the village blacksmith, from the dilapidated one in 1892. Recently re-gilded and like that of East Dean it has no cardinal points.

A weather-worn corbel face at the NW gable has some resemblance to the leopard's face on the heraldic charge borne by the Norman family of de Dene.

A blocked-up doorway and a high lancet window in the nave may be discerned on the south wall, just to the right of the Porch.

Hubert 'Bill' Bailey lifts his bride, Muriel or "Miggs" (née Ticehurst) over the tied up Tapsell gate of East Dean Church in 1954

In 1936 the area of land adjoining Friston churchyard along the road was scheduled as a churchyard extension to prevent development. Neglected mounds in the churchyard were further levelled in 1951-2 and the Garden of Remembrance was created the next year. The Revd Anthony Harbottle (Rector 1981-96) mentioned in 1992 that Nigel and Margaret Lees wished to donate part of the adjoining paddock for use as a churchyard extension; this was finally agreed 2006. See Appendix 4 for details of the graves and Garden of Remembrance.

The **Porch.** It is difficult to assign a date. From the weatherworn appearance of its lower stones, the doorway to the church had been exposed or with only a hood above in its earlier years; however, the Porch is certainly pre-Reformation, for within are many medieval graffiti, protected by a grille since 1938. Of special interest to the right is a mutilated carving of Our Lord on the Cross, done on a piece of hard chalk, roughly and simply, perhaps with the point of a whittle such as the medieval wayfarer carried. Almost every old Sussex church near the coast has graffiti, they represent vows and promises of travellers upon hazardous voyages. The notice board had 'unbreakable' glass fitted in 1990.

In the right hand corner, near the church wall, is the broken half of a holy water stoup. By the door, buried in the left wall, will be seen the fragment of a medieval stone coffin slab, found among the paving of *Friston Place* and restored to the church by Major Francis Maitland. In the porch floor, not quite inside the church, is a 350-year-old stone to *Edward Reading, M of Music.* He was a music tutor to Judith Selwyn about 1650 - well esteemed, but not of sufficient standing to be recorded inside the church. There were several gifted musicians in the Reading family, an Edward died in 1653, but none with any known parish associations; however, the records were not maintained scrupulously about that time. The present oak door was presented in memory of Frank Bridge (1879-1941) by his widow, Ethel, on 18 June 1949. They lived in Old Willingdon Road. [10].

Lambert's sketch of Friston Church *c.*1785, looking N. The tithe barn is to the left. What remained of the spire was removed in the restoration of 1892-7. Described in *Topographical Miscellanies of London,* 1792, as 'a small plain structure of flint and stone, with a low shingled spire; the inside is small but neat with new pews, pulpit and gallery. The chancel is quite separated, and the entry to it is by folding doors over which is a neatly painted altarpiece' of 1774

The **Nave** is the oldest part of the church *c.*1050. Parts belong to a period from the Saxon Edward the Confessor to William the Norman Conqueror. Two interesting vestiges to be seen, which could be Saxon, are the built-up doorway on the south side [on the right as you face the altar] and near it high up, a small slightly splayed window, the one showing outside as a narrow closed-up slit. This window belonged to a time when glass was all but unobtainable and such an aperture needed to be placed, for comfort's sake, well above the heads of the worshippers and even covered with shutters or oiled cloth. The light it admitted to the Nave would be slight, but the Chancel had its lamps and tapers, and in those days the worshippers rarely or never used books; they watched the priest at the altar, listened to the words of the service and joined in its familiar responses. As larger, glazed windows became general, any other pre-Norman openings were removed. Most of the nave windows date from the 1890s.

Oil lamps were converted to electricity in October 1931, when alms boxes were let into the walls. The lighting was extended in 1953 thanks to Charles Meller, and extensive upgrading of the lighting was carried out in 2001. In 1968 the small wall safe was damaged, but the policy is to keep the churches open. Bob Seymour, verger for 30 years always with a smile, carried the communion vessels to and from *Old Vicarage Cottage* before a safe was fitted in 1936. The built-up doorway, the original entry to the Church, gives another clue to the history of the Nave. About a century after the Church was erected, a 3m [10ft] extension at its western end was added, west of the huge beam, which sustained the bell-cote.

This extension had the awkward effect of making the entrance door open into the upper half of the Nave, so it was blocked off and the present one, a perfectly plain Norman, or Romanesque, doorway was inserted.

Francis Grose (1739-91), the antiquary, visited Friston in May 1771 during his fifth tour, where he commented on, 'some fine monuments of Selwins'.

The Nave south wall 1999; **left** a blocked-up high window; a blocked-up doorway with a Selwyn Brass below the arch; the oak door presented by Ethel Bridge, and **right** the font

The earliest of the Selwyn monuments is on the south wall, set in the blocked-up doorway. It is a brass, originally inlaid in Sussex marble, on an oak base. It consists of two figures in the costume of the time of Henry Vlll. Above is a shield with the family arms, three annulets on a band cotticed within a bordure engrailed, and below are the words: *Off yr Charite py for the soulles of Thomas Selwyn & Margery his wyffe -- whiche Thomas decessyd the XXII day of Septrbr A°dm MDXXXIX [1539] & the sayd Margy decessyd the XXVIII day of Octobr A°dm MDXLII [1542] o whos soulles Jhu have mcy.* Margery brought the Friston lands to the Selwyns being the daughter of John Adam who married Alys Potman. [8]

This brass was originally in the Chancel. AC Bouquet in *Church Brasses* says that in 1892 it was re-fixed in the central gangway of the nave and covered with a carpet. When the carpet was replaced in 1959 it was decided to move the brass to a safer position and examination revealed it to be a palimpsest - a brass that had been used for an earlier engraving on the other side. Sheet brass was not made in Britain until about 1600 so it had to be imported and was so expensive that pieces were often used for another customer. The Friston brass was cut from eight pieces. On the reverse side there is a piece with a lion's head; another has a draped arm holding a book; others have one male and one female foot resting on an animal; a lion's head; part of an inscription to Arthur and Katherine Walbe dating from the reign of Henry VII which is of exceptionally high quality and workmanship; two pieces of drapery and a quite unidentifiable piece.

Inscriptions on ledger tombs in the gangway, covered by carpet, are:-

Alice wife of Edward Selwyn of (Bec)hinton, Squir. Shee left this world April 30 AN 1624.
Here lieth the body of John Willard Gent. Who departed this life on the 2nd day of
November 1716 aged 53 years. This is towards the west end:
Also near this place lieth the body of Nicholas Willard late of Crowlink, brother to the
said John Willard who died the ? day of July 1728 aged 62 years.
Here also lieth the body of Jane Willard the wife of said Nicholas Willard who departed this
life May the 17th 1747 aged 81 years.

The Font, near the entrance, is small and shallow and of Puritan parentage *c.*1650, with a plain pedestal. It is of 'winkle stone', otherwise 'Sussex Marble', and fossilised shells will be seen in it. It must have replaced an ancient font.

The view in 1999 from the nave showing chancel and altar with part of the east window. In the nave the lectern is to the left of the chancel opening and the pulpit to the right, above are the 15th century roof beams.
During redecorations in 1959, the tray used for magazines was left empty and the workmen used the vacant spot for their lunch boxes, until a group of Scouts came to look around. The workmen remonstrated when they saw the Scouts consuming their oranges, but their attention was drawn to the notice left on the magazine tray,
Please Take One

Apart from the blocked-up apertures and Selwyn monuments, you have to be impressed by the massive oak beams above. This noble timbering, the panelled ribs, crown posts, tie beams, wall plates, and struts of the Early Perpendicular roof *c.*1400-50, though so old, is in a good state of preservation, apart from beetles. Such well-moulded timbering gives a quiet dignity to the interior of the little Church, a mixture of strength and repose.

The tie beam at the eastern end of the Nave, lying across the Chancel walls, ought to be especially noticed; it is purposely bowed and was made so as to give room in earlier times to the Holy Rood, the carved figure of Our Lord on the Cross. This figure would be attached to the king post which rises from the centre, and until about 1890, so it is said, the large iron staple which had held the Rood was present. The early church just consisted of the Nave, when the east wall terminated in an apsidal altar, now the approach to the Chancel.

Behind the pulpit are the remains of a piscina [to wash vessels]. This may have been for the apsidal altar, but could indicate that, pre-Reformation, a side altar stood against part of the adjoining Chancel walls. The windowsill, just above the broken piscina, has a flattish rise in the stonework, which possibly acted as the support of a long-vanished Rood loft.

Every ancient Church in this district, however small, had a north door in the Nave (now usually blocked-up) as well as a southern entrance. A name for it was 'Devil's door', probably due to ideas about exorcism in the service of baptism. The simple Norman doorway in Friston Church is of the same date as the south one and now opens into the Vestry. This is an 1892 addition, built in flint to harmonise with the rest of the building, and contains the heating boiler. For many years an old coke stove was near the vestry door, it usually smoked and only kept those close by warm. It was replaced by electric heating in the 1930s and in December 1947 the central heating system was converted to gas.

At the western end of the nave the visitor will find a framed account of the many priests who held this small cure of souls, commencing with John War in 1414 (details of earlier vicars have been lost except a Henry in the Assize Rolls of 1347/8), along with some notes of the Parish of Friston and the Great Tithes. Nearby is a plan of Friston Airfield in 1947, and alongside is the 1914-18 Roll of Honour.[1] On the west wall is the Baptism Roll.

There was a gallery at the west end and it is recorded that in 1824 the people in the gallery saw the windmill (then along the Seaford road by today's *Gayles*) blow over. This gallery, taken down in the 1890s, was likely to be used by the minstrels, later there was a harmonium near the front, replaced by a reed organ in 1936.

The present organ is in the south west corner. Built by FH Browne of Brighton, it displays a plaque, *Given in Memory of Ethel Bridge, Frank Butcher, Edward Bailey Page, Dorothy Norman, Woodward Powell, by Sir Frank & Lady Burnand, Guy & Cecily Smart, Lord & Lady Shawcross, Charles & Margaret Meller, Percy & Kathleen Budd, and dedicated by the Bishop of Lewes 25 February 1962.*

On the south wall, near the organ, is a tablet in memory of John Wycliffe Wycliffe-Taylor of *Gayles*.[2]

On 15 February 1953, in the absence of the Bishop with influenza, the Vicar dedicated a window, given by Mrs Rosamond Stutchbury of *Gayles* as a memorial to her husband Mervyn Stanley Stutchbury. A mining engineer, he was churchwarden from 1931 until his death in 1938. Mr Maufe supervised Miss M Forsyth who carried out her design; it represents St James, the pilgrim soul of man.

In 1955 the church was renovated inside under the direction of Bill Pratt of CH Prior.

The visitors' book is kept in the Nave and, taking 1985, reveals names from Australia, Bangladesh, Canada, Egypt, Germany, Holland, Italy, Japan, New Zealand, South Africa, USA, and Zimbabwe. The comments varied from 'peaceful and lovely' to 'married here 40 years ago' and even, 'I am the great-great-great grandchild of Jemima Dunstall christened here 16 January 1820'.

The tiny **Chancel** is in Decorated style *c.*1350, built to replace the apse, as at Newhaven and Exceate, and East Dean's Tower chapel. A low segmental arch gives entrance from the Nave, and on either side of the Chancel are arcaded depressions in the wall which give to the little Sanctuary, when viewed from the Nave, relief and grace.

The Sanctuary and altar of Friston Church. The new east window of 2002 represents an interpretation of The Ascension. On the left Mary, His Mother, kneeling by the reeds and flowers along with an angel, witnesses to the right Christ rising high over Birling Gap

There is no doubt that in medieval times each of the projecting stone slabs on either side of the altar carried a statue, probably a figure of Our Lord on the north and of the Virgin Mary on the south. The recess behind the altar was probably built to carry a stone coffin containing the relics of a Saint. The greensand stone of this arch was evidently brought from the seashore, for there still remain the deep borings of a bivalve mollusc, the 'piddock', and in one the shell still adheres. To the right is an aumbry, a recess for sacred vessels.

The altar, delicately carved by the Revd Walter Parrington and the village carpenter in the 1890s, is of open gothic arches with a vine motive along the top front; exposed, of course, only on Good Friday.

The east window was a small square-headed one of two lights until the restoration of the 1890s. On 8th September 2002 a new stained-glass east window was dedicated. This was in memory of Raphael, the daughter of Jane Patterson who designed it. The lead working was by Alisoun Howie, and installation by Roger Barton with Richard Crook as architect.

The lancet window on the south side is evidently made of material from an earlier window; the jamb stones show marks of axe tooling, the kind of rough tooling on stones before the use of the chisel. Incised on these stones there are two small crosses of the kind sometimes called pilgrim or votive crosses.

The Selwyn alabaster monument on the west wall of the Transept is to Thomas (d. 1613) and Elizabeth Selwyn, and their nine children. The three sons, who died as infants, are shown in swaddling clothes under the table. It displays 38 armorial bearings including. the Adam, Camoys, Covert, Dunk, Dyke, Goring, Gratwicke, Hawtrey, Marshall, Nethersole, Parker, Pelham, Radimylde, and Woodward families.
An inscription translation is to hand in the church

This window holds the earliest stained glass of the village churches and has some merit. It was gifted in 1896 by Cecil, Lord Hawkesbury, a descendant on the Medley female line of the Selwyns of *Friston Place,* in memory of his grandfather the 3rd Earl of Liverpool, and represents St James the Apostle in the garb of a pilgrim with staff, water bottle and scallop shell. Close beside the window is a humble 'Priest's seat' or sedile, and in the corner a piscina or its remains, for the basin has gone.

The Selwyn marble monument on the east wall of the transept.
The monument is mainly a record of Sir Francis Selwyn and his large family, but the left-hand column records the death of his grandson in 1704 when Edward Selwyn's only remaining son and heir, William Thomas, died aged 20, the 'last of the ancient family' and for whose early death and many virtues, 'the very marble (itself) might weep *[flebit marmor ipsum]*'. Much of the paint has been lost over the years and parts are almost illegible, but a record has been kept

Opposite in the north wall is a similar stained-glass window, of the Virgin with child, in memory of John Andrew Maitland (1838-1914) 'from friends EC and WH'. The Maitland family owned *Friston Place* from 1897 until 1938.

The Selwyn **Transept**. According to Stephen Glynn writing in 1857, 'A north transept chapel has been recently added' to the nave. Said to be at Miss Anne Gilbert's instigation.

A purpose could have been as a place for two of the Selwyn Monuments that had stood in the Chancel and must have reduced its space considerably. The Selwyn family laid their dead within the flint walls and the Selwyn memorials, large and handsome examples of their date, have stood in the Transept since at the latest the 1890s.

The splendid, if rather pretentious, one on the west side in alabaster, with quaint effigies in ruff and wimple, is a record of Thomas Selwyn, Elizabeth his wife and children. By the 1900s Thomas had lost his legs, but a new pair has been provided.

On the opposite side of the Transept is a large marble slab surmounted by the family crest, a flaming torch held by lion's paws. This monument is a record of Sir Francis Selwyn, and his large family. He was succeeded by Edward, his fifth son, but the male line died out with the next generation.

The initial page of the Friston Parish Registers, begun by the vicar in 1546 - the last years of Henry VIII's reign.
There are several entries that give sidelights on parochial history.
The writing dates from 1597 when, in compliance with an ordinance of Elizabeth I, registers were made compulsory and any earlier paper sheets had to be transferred to parchment. This copying was done by Arthur Pollard (of Merton College, Oxford) Vicar of both East Dean and Friston. The 'Register Booke' is now kept at the County Record Office in Lewes

The Revd AA Evans supervised a restoration and repainting in 1927. The £50 cost was raised by visitors' contributions, the Gloucester Selwyns, and £18 profits from the sale of church guide books. Painting was by GG Godfrey, masonry by CF Bridgman of Lewes, all under the direction of WH Godfrey of London.

Sunday, 10 July 1960, saw the dedication by the Bishop of Lewes of a new stained-glass window in the Transept. Depicting *The Annunciation* of the Blessed Virgin Mary by a talented local artist, Marguerite Douglas Thompson, it is remarkable for its flowing movement and depth of colour, although some feel it is dark for the simple church. The window was given by Mr and Mrs CH Meller in thanksgiving for mercies received. Charles Meller, churchwarden for many years, made a crib for the church in 1954; although the present one is by Fred Abery.

There is the story of a Friston priest Thomas Wyllis (1482-1508) who had a crib built for the Christmas Eve Service as a surprise for the congregation. After he had secreted it into the church before the Service a young girl entered carrying her baby and fell asleep in the warmth of the church. The priest was impressed by the reverence of the congregation and no one was surprised when the cry of a baby seemed to come from the crib. As a result of the priest's homily that at Christmas one should help the weak and helpless, the child was brought up at *Friston Place.*

Minor damage to the transept ceiling was caused by high-explosive bombs in January 1943 and by flying bombs in June 1944. In 1946 Percy Budd reported to the PCC that a cheque for £30 had been received from the War Damage Commission to defray the cost of damage to Friston church.

A century before, in 1848, more extensive repairs were required. Churchwardens were John Guy (Crowlink), William Scrase *(Friston Place),* and the £90 expenses were agreed by the Revd George Pinnock, George Ashby (Friston Mill) and Richard Scrase *(Gore Farm).* Subscribers were Miss Gilbert £35, Mr Gilbert £5, Lord Liverpool £20, Lord Gage £10, W Smith £2, Child Building Society £17, Mr Scrase 75p and Mr Guy 10p. Main bills were from William Pierce bricklayer and James Peerless carpenter, for repairing the pulpit, new glass, leading, and tiling including 2000 tiles.

The work didn't last too well for on 1 January 1887 the Bishop closed the Church, 'being an ancient edifice and so much out of repair as to be unsuitable for public worship'.

Later that year Dr Edmund Downes of Eastbourne recounted the ugly desolation of Friston Church and its churchyard, covered in weeds and over-growing vegetation.

'Applying the name of God's Acre to such an abomination was a hideous mockery. Inside everything was in a broken and decaying condition with dirt and dust everywhere.

A priest's armchair in oak with elaborate carving on the arm rests and a lifting seat was sent on permanent loan to Michelham Priory in 1966. The age is in doubt

There were gaping holes in the roof and many of the windows were broken, it was apparent that this state of neglect had been allowed to continue for many years.'

Dr Downes decided to start a movement to save the church and create a garden around. Little else was on the top of Friston hill apart from a few farm buildings and the windmill, so when Dr Downes and his friends appealed for funds they were met by the objection that as it had been allowed to decay for so long it would be better to let the process continue. This common-sense view did not prevail.

On 22 August 1891 an application was made for a Faculty to rebuild Friston Church: remove plaster ceilings, reinstate tiles, two new windows in south wall and one in the west, repair walls, provide gutters, refloor and install open seating.

The church was officially reopened on 21 March 1892, but it was over 1891-97 that Parson Parrington turned his vicarious DIY attention to Friston Church. He carefully repaired the windows, doors and roof, built the altar and added the Vestry (paid for by Grace Davies Gilbert) with its entrance through the original *Devil's door,* all at a cost of £862, raised by Dr Downes. One of the vicar's daughters remembers being held up to see the restoration work at Friston church. "The roof was lifted while the beams were repaired and let down again, and the carved wooden altar was replaced by my father and the village carpenter." Victorian 'church improvers' are often castigated, but there would be no Friston Church today without them.

Churchyard regulations from 1997 allowed only biodegradable caskets of cremated remains, with a small plaque on a Memorial Board, and cut flowers only. Gravestones required permission from the incumbent, while only bulbs and annuals in removable containers were permitted on graves.

St Simon and St Jude, East Dean

Another of the charming, unpretentious tiny Downland churches in which Sussex abounds; quite adequate for East Dean's 29 families in 1724.

The church stands near the centre of the village, one gate opens onto Gilbert's Drive and the other, a Tapsell gate [see Friston Church], leads to the Church Green and Lower Street. The Church Green originally was one with the present Village Green and registration was applied for both in 1967. A well on the Church Green was in general use until 1897, when the Water Company put a water tank near the Gilbert Institute opposite. The Green is owned by the Gilbert Estate, but kept mown by the PC. To the left of the churchyard, when facing the Tapsell gate, is the weather-boarded garage/store of *The Grange* residential home. Some believe that this is the old Tithe Barn, others think that a barn at nearby *New House Farm,* an 18th c. listed building, now converted, is more likely to have been the Tithe Barn.

The south side of the church from the Church Green in 1999, showing the Tapsell gate, porch and, to the left, the 1962 extension

The church, of flint with greensand quoins, shows five main building stages. At the 2000 millennium the Tower was almost 950 years old. About 100 years after the Tower the Nave was built followed by the Chancel another 50 years on, with changes of beams and windows over the years. The church was reconstructed over 1882-7 when the roof and the west wall were replaced, and in 1961-2 the nave was extended with a new west wall. There is talk of adding a lavatory suitable for the disabled, a small kitchen and even a meeting room.

The **Churchyard.** Before the 17th c. prelates and people of note were buried within the church in coffins of lead or stone and their names recorded on memorial brasses or stone slabs. Hence the term 'stinking rich' if the coffin wasn't well sealed. Ordinary folk were wrapped in a shroud and laid in mother earth outside, marked by a wooden cross, their names not being recorded until parish registers began about 1550. So there is no record of Robert ffrench who requested to be buried at East Dean in his 1540 will.

The shroud was of fine or coarse linen according to the deceased's pocket, but when wool became the staple wealth of the country, wool was made obligatory.

One acre of land was allotted to every parish church as a burial ground and this sufficed for centuries; the population stayed steady and without coffins the bodies soon decayed. Hence 'God's Acre' was used over and over again, its grass was cropped by sheep and it was used for village activities on Holy Days. As the social structure altered a middle class arose who felt that their names should be perpetuated and coffins and gravestones became general and games were banned.

Gravestones provide much village history over 300 years. On the south wall by the porch is an oval tablet to Lieut Samuel Jacobs, North Hampshires, 50, who died in 1804. Christopher Gardner, Curate and later (most unusually) Vicar, with his wife Jane are by the porch. The Davies-Gilberts are towards the SE corner. Nearby a memorial has been put up to Willie Elijah Tshabani, a Zulu of Natal washed ashore at Birling Gap, one of a volunteer battalion on the *Mendi* which sank in a snowstorm in February 1917, with the loss of 650 troops. On the Tower side is the grave of John Pearce, aged 21, of the coastguard station at Birling Gap who was found dead on the beach having fallen over the cliff while in the execution of his duty, 11th day of July 1831.

Lambert's sketch of East Dean Church in 1780 from the NE, showing the tower with possibly the tithe barn behind.
The outline of the apsidal chapel is discernable on the tower.
Around 1200 Richard de Combe granted the Tithes to the Abbott of Grestein, suppressed in 1414

The most famous stone is of Parson Jonathan Darby, 1705-26, by the Chancel. He was 'the Sailors' Friend' for his efforts to prevent shipwrecks. It is related that in 1961 the Vicar had the words re-incised because he was fed up with visitors knocking at the Vicarage asking for *the* tomb. Other priests, James Leyland and Richard Michell, were buried nearby. Leyland has a striking 18th c. tomb, but Michell lies unmarked (Appendix 3). Among the unknowns were burials in April 1920 of two men washed up at Birling Gap.

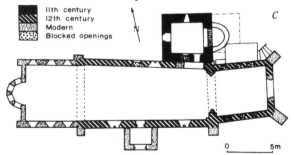

Plan of the church showing the stages of construction with the, not unusual, but marked declination of the added Chancel. The reason for the practice is unknown, some say it is to remind worshippers of Our Lord's head on the Cross, another suggestion is that it is to create a sense of mysticism. Other proposals are that it is an attempt to give a more correct eastern orientation, or that the builders just didn't get it right

In 1923 Major and Mrs Harding (a Davies Gilbert) gave land for a northern extension to the churchyard, and a £200 wall was built to enclose the gift. The PCC decided that no right of burial should be granted to those who did not have a link with the parishes, but the burial of cremation ashes should be allowed. A new oak gate for the Gilbert's Drive entrance was donated in 1960 by Arthur Carter. The Remembrance Garden, started 1963, is to the left of the Tapsell Gate [see Appendix 2].

The **Tower** of *c*.1050 is most impressive and unconventionally on the north side of the church, as at Pevensey. It is a square tower of three stages each slightly receding, and while the windows are not Saxon in style it has some character of a pre-Conquest edifice. The metre thick walls were perhaps built by Edwin the Saxon, who held Dene as a Manor of King Edward the Confessor, when Norman influences were spreading in southern England.

We know the tower was built first as a separate building because it has four external corner stones. As at Jevington, it served as a place of refuge in times of danger as well as a church with its tiny apsidal Chancel. Evidence of this double use inside is an early chancel arch, springing from an impost or slab, on the eastern wall; and outside, notice the high, narrow windows originally unglazed, and exposed in the gravel are the semi-circular foundations of the apse. An excavation in 1979 found human bones underneath which led to suggestions that there was a cemetery and a wooden church here before the tower.

After a 1950 Gift Day when the Revd Norman Lycett sat all day to raise £335.38, the rotten timbers of the tower of East Dean church were restored. Close inspection of the weather vane reveals that it dates from 1801 and has three bullet holes in it from a visit by the King's enemies in 1944. A place of refuge indeed.

Of East Dean's five **Bells,** two are of pre-Reformation date with Latin inscriptions and were cast by Thomas Bullisdon; one was cast in 1640 by Bryan Eldredge, and the two by Mears and Stainbank dating from 1962-3, were donated by Mr & Mrs Fawssett Briggs and Mr & Mrs Harold Down. One of the medieval bells in the tower boasts the inscription *Me Melior Vere Non Est Campana Sub Ere, or Surely no bell beneath the sky, Can send forth better sounds than I.* The 1640 bell bears a more solemn inscription, *St James pray for us.*

A set of bells is a Ring, the sound is a Peal. The assigned note is the Strike Note, accompanied by overtones, the Hum Note, which should be an octave below. A Ring may consist of five bells (such as at East Dean) to 12 (as at St Paul's). With five 120 Changes or variations are possible, with 12 some 480 million that would take 30 years of unceasing ringing. Change ringing, as practised in England, is unknown on the continent where carillons are the rule.

By 1970 the bells could not be pealed as the bell frame needed strengthening, so they were

The Jacobean pulpit, finely carved by local craftsmen, with sounding board or canopy above. Under the overhang is inscribed: *In the yeare that William Hermitage and George Gyles was churchwarddens this pulpet was made anno domno 1623.* The aumbry is seen behind a flower holder, one of those donated by Andrew & Sian Palmer and by the Church Fellowship in memory of Leslie & Gay Ockenden

harnessed for hand ringing (striking the stationary bell with the clapper). At the 2000 Millennium they were given a hand board so that all may be rung by one person, and the cords were replaced in 1999 by churchwarden, Andrew Palmer.

The **Porch** has a Mass dial over the entrance (there was one at Friston until it was pinched some years ago). This was set to give the times of the Services - if the sun was shining. The porch builders appear to have re-used greensand blocks, which had been shaped for another site. In the porch are set out details of the Benefice and a list of its Clergy. This list was first set out by the Revd A A Evans in January 1923.

The congregation worshipped in the **Nave,** with its central gangway. Built by the Normans a century after the Tower, it probably replaced a wooden church. The worshippers stood or knelt, for there were no pews, only a stone shelf round the nave walls on which the old and infirm could rest, hence the expression, 'The weakest to the wall'. On the walls were frescoes of Biblical scenes to instruct the people unable to read or write.

A niche inside the church door, with its trefoil-headed arch, has been there 650 years and was a Holy Water stoup for the congregation to dip their fingers. Along the wall are the Baptismal Rolls, and just to the side of the pulpit is an ambry, or aumbry, a recess for Sacrament vessels, probably to serve the apsidal altar before the Chancel was built; it might have been for another altar on the south wall. A nearby pillar shaft aisle staircase to the Rood has been covered over.

East Dean Church nave with the Norman arches over the door to the Vestry (was the base of the Tower), and the niche recess with grille in the wall between the arches which held the medieval platen and chalice until they were stolen. The Bardolf coffin lid is also to the left of the door; the lectern is to the right

Originally, stone screens would have divided the Nave and Chancel, only to be replaced by carved wooden ones surmounted by the Holy Rood, or figure of Christ on the Cross. With the Reformation all statues were destroyed, the frescoes covered over, the screens removed and the stone altars replaced by wooden altar tables. Bibles were provided, and in 1623 a canon ordered **Pulpits** from which the priest could expound the Scripture, the Lectern being where the Scriptures were read. The Revd Walter Parrington replaced a rotted pulpit panel in 1882, and also found Scriptural wall texts beneath whitewash, which were covered over again.

Near the north front of the nave are two partly filled-in stone arches. The smaller, outer one, is the older, and was an entrance to the tower, the inner was much later and was probably a prop for the wall, now it spans the 18th c. vestry door. The Coat of Arms of George III is kept in the vestry, and it is where the priest and choir robe.

Royal Coats of Arms in churches were introduced in 1563. The East Dean one is a fine example by James Lambert of Lewes, painted on plaster with a massive wooden frame, the colours are clear, it is in excellent condition and foliated letters unusual.

To the right when facing the vestry is a shepherd's crook in a glass case. To the left is a 13th c. Sepulchral cross slab, bearing the arms of the Bardolf family, found under the floor of the Nave; the base is not part of this coffin lid. Further right in the north wall towards the west is a niche, which contained a 1225 pewter paten and chalice. The War Memorial is within the frame of the north doorway.

The windows and roof timbers of the eastern Nave are 15th c. In the 1700s a west gallery was added to provide more accommodation, but a century later population drift rendered such galleries redundant and as the East Dean one was in a poor state it was removed at the 1880s restoration. The west wall was rebuilt in 1882-5, only to be demolished in the 1961-2 extension. So the western end of the church is 20th c. although the Vicar insisted that the new walls were of the same thickness as the existing.

Fonts, the receptacles for baptismal water, were for adult immersion in the early church and set below the floor level; in the Middle Ages, when infant baptism became the rule, they were raised up. The East Dean font bowl dates in part from Norman times. This fragment was found in 1885 (AA Evans says under one of the roof beams, M Drummond-Roberts says in a farmyard) and was married to a block of greensand to make an attractive font. You can observe the joins on the window side. The pedestal is original, but in the 1700s it had been replaced and used as a mounting block outside the village inn, so it was also replaced in 1885. Originally the font was just inside the south door, as at Friston, but at the time of the 1960s extension it was moved to the apse below the west window. The remnants of the 18th c. font pedestal are kept in the tower.

There are records of at least seven chalices, or cups, at the church, and a 1691 chalice has East Dean spelt as two words, so the form is not a recent conceit.

The pewter chalice and paten found in 1882 came into Major Maitland's museum at *Friston Place*. He donated them to the Revd AA Evans on condition that they were in a glass case so that everyone could view them. Kept behind the pulpit at East Dean church until May 1930 when they were placed behind glass and a grille in a wall niche created near the vestry. The chalice was a type A with rounded foot and a shallow bowl. The paten was 11cm across with a depression of over 1cm. Apart from Chichester Cathedral these vessels of 1225 were the oldest in the county. In 1959 the insurance value was raised to £500.

The locals cherished most the shepherd's crook, which Dick Fowler had lent to the Bishop when, in 1929, he came to a confirmation having mislaid his Bishop's crook. Richard Fowler gave it to the church on the death of his father in 1939.

The chalice and paten and shepherd's crook were all stolen on the last of the old style August Bank Holidays, 3 August 1964. Bill Armiger said, "I was the verger at East Dean and discovered the theft of the chalice and paten. The thief had broken the glass and bent the relics to pull them through the protecting bars. He also snapped the crook from its hazel shaft".

Around 1800 the church 'orchestra' of fiddle, bassoon,

The font showing the joins of the original Norman section towards the left. The basketware carving of interlacing circles in the centre, and the pellet and cable mouldings top and bottom have been skilfully carried through

bass and flageolet sat in the west gallery. They sound a fearful combination, but congregations loved the scrapings and pipings and, as recorded by Thomas Hardy and Flora Thompson, regarded it as a sad day when a 'box of whistles, or an American organ' came.

In 1920 the Vicar appealed for funds to buy a 'real organ, a pipe organ', and after six years the new organ was dedicated. Edward C Drew, the schoolmaster and organist for 35 years, clearly thought it was time for him to go for in December 1925 he retired from both posts, to be succeeded as organist in April 1926 by the Gilbert Estates' Agent, Roderick G Hall, always known as 'Ronnie'. Starting on a six-month trial he went on for 34 years, only relinquishing the post in December 1960. "I've never known him not to preside at the organ, Sundays, weekdays, choir practices, never a grumble. All gratuitously". Ronnie said it had been a wonderful experience and added his thanks for the great kindness and support received over the years that it had been his privilege to act as the organist. In 1954 the organ was repaired and re-sited from near the vestry to the SW end of the church.

On Palm Sunday 1960 some 200 packed the church as the Rt Revd Bishop of Lewes dedicated a new loft organ, along with a silver paten (given by her family in memory of Mrs Dorothy Norman) and three new pews, where the old organ had been, given by local residents.[3] The new organ, designed by Denman and built by FH Browne, was the gift of the Vicar and Mrs Burns-Cox in memory of their 21-year-old son Richard Michael, killed in a 1957 car accident while hitch-hiking on a continental holiday. Mrs Burns-Cox was a Robinson of soft drinks fame.

During the 1882 renovations workmen found the remains of a priest on whose chest lay this 13th c. pewter paten and chalice. This was when it was customary to inter priests with church furnishings, silver for a bishop, pewter for a parish priest

The **Chancel** (or Choir), where the clergy and choir sit, and where the priest chanted Mass, is Transitional Norman and was added *c.*1200. The Altar stands in the Sanctuary; the small table is in memory of Horace Rew, 'devoted Lay Reader'.

With its three Richard I lancet windows separated by deep splays and jamb shafts in the east wall and twin windows in both north and south walls the Chancel must have impressed the folk of the village. You can see the remains of lancets at the side of the east window, which replaced them. The side windows were closed up, possibly to strengthen the wall when the east window was put in *c.*1300. This single, wide window was replaced by the present design in the 1880s.

Chancel memorials on the north wall are inscribed *Nicholas Willard 8 February 1762 (aged 61) and wife Sarah 14 July 1761 (57); James Dippery Gent 11 September 1791 (88). On the south wall is one to Carew Davies Gilbert son of John and Anne 1 August 1852 - 1 December 1913.*

Wills are recorded gifting buckram for an altar cloth in 1556, and a font cover in 1686, and on 3 June 1949 a new stained-glass east window, altar, and reredos (or screen) were dedicated by the Bishop of Lewes. The altar and reredos were presented by Elizabeth Cradock of *Little Hill* and Major & Mrs CH Davies-Gilbert.

East Dean nave interior from the chancel in 1943 showing the old west window. The pulpit is to the left, and the original shepherd's crook is on the right

The east window is a representation of Our Saviour as the Good Shepherd with the dove of the Holy Spirit above. In the tracery are the symbols of the four Evangelists, the Agnes Dei and the Instruments of the Passion, on either side the arms of the Diocese are balanced by those of the Davies-Gilbert family. Worked along the bottom margin is: *This window is erected to the Glory of God and in memory of the Snape family 1949.* The story goes that when Churchfield was built in 1947 it supplanted the green field view through the plain east window and hence stained glass was welcomed instead. [11]

On either side of the altar are two handsome oak sanctuary chairs carved with the names of the churchwardens, the vicar, and date 1913. They were presented by Charles Frederick Russell (carved 'FC'), the *Gore Farm* farmer, who was about to give up the lease.

Sometime before 1189 Earl William ('a turbulent man, brave but perfidious, who in his old age quieted his conscience by giving his property to pious uses') gave East Dean to Grestein Abbey, near Honfleur, one of the alien priories suppressed in 1414.

The list in the porch gives the earliest name of a vicar at East Dean as Brother William in 1261, and perhaps the most notable was William Bradbridge, 1542, who became the Dean of Salisbury and Bishop of Exeter.

The East Dean Parish Church Registers begin in 1550 in the reign of Edward VI. In his book *By Weald and Down* the Revd AA Evans gives examples of comments such as those about Agnes and Johan Payne, daughters of Edward Payne, who in 1575 died within a few hours of each other.

In 1705 there is reference to Jonathan Darby 'the sailor's friend'. [2] In 2001 the Revd Hugh Moseley started an annual Sea Sunday Service which finishes with a visit to Darby's slab.

Richard Michell, curate-in-charge 1779-1790, 'an excellent scholar' died in poverty. [2]

A Bishop's Visitation in 1724 had reported, 'East Dean church is in good repair, only some seats want boarding at the bottom. One seat needs repair.' By the 1880s, however, although the church was usable it was not in a good state.

From 1882 the Revd John Walter Parrington (1881-1900) led the restoration with architect Gordon M Hills. He completely rebuilt the west wall of the church, removed the gallery and the chancel arch dates from this time. In 1885 all seats were declared free, and by 1887 East Dean Church had been restored for £1604.

View from the chancel in 1999 of the extension past the organ loft, with the distant font in the apse of the west wall. The tiny west window above the apse was dedicated on St Valentine's Day 1965, by the Revd Burns-Cox. This new Marguerite Thompson stained-glass window shows the Christ Child and Mother and was provided by the children of the parish

Electric lighting was installed by Messrs Beney on 27 September 1931; in 1956 the aged heating was replaced with an automated gas system, and a sound amplifying system was donated in 1965.

In 1962 Bill Pratt (Peter Pratt the actor was his son) made an oak table for the church literature, Joyce MacGowan undertook the supervision of its use.

With an increasing population in the 1950s the nave of East Dean Church needed to be extended, for as Mollie Bertin said, "Unless one was in the church 20 minutes before the 11 o'clock service, it was impossible to get a seat."

The Revd RW Burns-Cox (1956-1964) who, like Horace Rew, could wheedle money out of a stone, started a fund to extend the church to cope with the overcrowding, and raised over £12,000. The Bishop of Lewes dedicated the extension on the morning of Sunday, 25 February 1962, when some 400 people were in, or outside, the church. [11]

In 2000 Peter Mander wrote, 'The workmanship was of a high order and 40 years later where the ancient knapped flints abut the more recent the difference is hardly discernible'.

5. *Birling Manor,* Birling Gap and Crowlink

Birling Manor

While the Downs above the village were occupied by Stone Age, Bronze Age and Iron Age peoples, the Birling Manor valley site was probably first occupied by the Romans who extensively farmed the Downs around the future Eastbourne.

The first Saxons appeared *c.*490, and Birling took its name from an offshoot of the Saxon tribe of Beorls, warlike Saxon sea rovers who harassed the coasts of Sussex and France, before eventually settling down. They were obviously a vigorous crew for there is a Birling near the Medway in Kent and similar names in northern France. The Gap was too good a landing place so the settlement was situated a mile inland to allow warning if other 'sea wolves' tried to pillage the coast.

Countess Goda and locally Edwin the Saxon held the manor of Dene, in the Hundred of Willingdon, from King Edward the Confessor until the Norman Conquest.

After winning the Battle of Hastings, William now the Conqueror granted part of the Pevensey Rape (including East Dean, but not Friston) to the Count of Eu, later it fell to William's half brother, Robert Earl of Mortain, Lord of the Court of Pevensey. The Rights of Presentation were held by Ralph de Dene from the Mortain family, but Mortain's son backed the wrong succession and in 1106 his lands were forfeited to the crown, when *Birling Manor* was held feudatory to the Lords of Pevensey by Hugh de Gurnay. In turn his successor incurred Royal displeasure and the manor went to the Cressek family.

In 1225 the manor was restored to the Gurney family of Norfolk. Three generations on it passed to the sole heiress Juliana, who married William Bardolf *c.*1255. Birling was probably part of her marriage portion, and it is said there was a Juliana Dene locally. In the old medieval manor house, where the hall was the centre of life, William and Juliana as the Lord and Lady dined upon the dais with their retainers below at a long, central table. You can imagine the scene today when you're in the Bardolf Hall.

Davies (Giddy) Gilbert (1767-1839)   Mary Ann Gilbert (1776-1845)

A Charter was granted in 1267 to William Bardolf by Henry III to hold a weekly Tuesday market and an annual Fair on the day before, the day and the day after the feast of St Simon and St Jude, the patron saints of the church. This Fair continued until near the end of the 1800s.

In love, the Bardolf family was adept at marrying heiresses - and was inept by backing the wrong side in war. In 1406 Lord Thomas Bardolf was in revolt against Henry IV, but was killed in battle and his lands forfeited to the crown. The family did manage to regain the lands, but in 1461 they finally lost them, Lord William Bardolf having supported the Lancastrian cause against Yorkist Edward IV.

Grace Katherine Rose, the beautiful daughter of Capt. GKS Massy Dawson, married Carew Davies Gilbert in 1881. They had five daughters, but no sons

Around 1490 the Carew family probably built the flint and thatched early Tudor style manor house on the present site, whereupon the old house became a barn, known into the 1900s as Chapel Barn, now Bardolf Hall, in which there are some medieval remnants.

The Darcy and Carew families swapped properties and intermarried over the 1500s while the land was farmed by a succession of tenants growing flax and running flocks of sheep. However, by 1575 the flint walls of the 'new' manor house were already described as being in poor condition.

A succession of Lords of the Manor of Birling followed, including in 1690, Thomas, Bishop of Down and Connor. Over the years the many tenants included the Ottleys and the Gibbs, until in 1707 the Dipperay family became tenants, and James Dipperay, a son, bought the manor in 1763-4.

The Willard family had lived at Crowlink in the 1600s, moving to Birling Gap in the 1700s, and it was Nicholas Willard who received *Birling Manor Farm* from the 1791 will of his father-in-law, James Dipperay. Nicholas sold it to Charles Gilbert, an attorney of Lewes, in 1807, but continued to live there for a while. Nicholas was related to the Eastbourne Willards, and the Gilberts and Willards were also interrelated.

Charles Gilbert held the Gildredge sub-manor of Eastbourne at the manor house in The Goffs. In 1792 he bought from Stephen Lushington the house in Borough Lane built in 1776 by Stephen's father, the Vicar of Eastbourne, Dr Henry Lushington, and when in 1797 Charles moved there it became the Gilbert sub-manor house.

In 1817 the sub-manor passed to Mary Ann Gilbert who had married a Cornishman, Davies Giddy, in 1808. By Royal assent he took the name and arms of Gilbert to become Davies Gilbert.

Davies (Giddy) Gilbert was the possessor of a large fortune and MP for two rotten boroughs, Helston and later Bodmin, from 1804 until the Reform Bill of 1832. He supported scientists Beddoes and Davy, and introduced an Act permitting the burial of victims of

The Address and Presentation to Grace Massy-Dawson 'from her father's grateful tenantry' on her marriage to Carew Davies Gilbert

the sea in churchyards. His career peak was as a stopgap President of the Royal Society 1827-30. It is said that he only mentioned his wife twice in the course of his diaries. Mary

Ann Gilbert, greatx4-grandmother of Charlie Davies-Gilbert, was a respected agriculturalist who encouraged an interest in the land. She built smallholdings on Michel Dene, measuring out the land herself, but they were too small to eek out a living, and although her system of water storage was a success, wood and coal supplies were precarious. [2]

John, Mary Ann's son, succeeded in 1845. He married Anne, daughter of Robert 1st Baron Carew, and became Lord of the Manor of Bourne by drawing lots with the future 7th Duke of Devonshire. So the Borough Lane building became the Eastbourne Manor House.

Their son, Carew, succeeded at the age of two in 1854, and with his agents (in particular Nicholas Whitley, after whom Whitley Bridge, Eastbourne, is named) was responsible for much development around The Avenue and Seaside in Eastbourne. Prince's Park, formerly the Gilbert Recreation Ground, was given to the Eastbourne Corporation. He also built the East Dean Gilbert Institute in 1884; you can read his initials over the main door.

Roderick 'Ronnie' Hall was appointed an assistant Gilbert Estate Agent in 1900 and Agent from 1921, with Mr Christian his number two. Both were very correct and worked out of the Manor Office, 1 Borough Lane, Eastbourne, where Jimmy Davies-Gilbert describes them sitting on Dickensian-style high stools. Ronnie built *Maryfield,* on Friston hill, where he lived from 1923. Now there is only a retained agent, mainly for valuations.

Guests at the celebrations for the 21st birthday of Charles Gilbert Davies-Gilbert (was Harding) and the opening of the Bardolf Hall, 1926. He was the father of Jimmy Charles Davies-Gilbert and grandfather of Charlie Davies-Gilbert

Carew Davies Gilbert died in December 1913. His body was conveyed for burial at East Dean on a farm cart drawn by two pairs of horses. One of the accompanying farm worker bearers walking alongside in smocks and gloves was Tom Wicking, grandfather of James.

The title fell to Patience, one of Carew's daughters, who had married Charles Henry Harding on 19 April 1904. He saw service in the Boer War and Great War. A story goes that after 1918, when both CH Harding and RG Hall held the rank of major, Ronnie was taken aside by Major Harding and asked to drop the title and call himself Mister.

In 1922 the Davies Gilberts sold the Manor House in Borough Lane to Eastbourne Corporation for £19,000 to house the Towner Art Gallery, and eventually History Museum. The Harding family had visited East Dean and Friston, but only moved into *Birling Manor* from the Manor House with her mother, Grace, and a sister, Minnie Davies Gilbert, in 1923.

Chapel Barn, the original manor house, was restored by Major and Mrs Harding for the 21st birthday party in 1926 of their son Charles Gilbert Harding. One tale has it that an uncle bought a job lot of panelling and decided the old barn would be the best place for it. The Ante Room, or Lady's Bower, does have a beautiful medieval window with trefoil heads and a stone window seat. The barn was renamed Bardolf Hall and the son renamed himself by deed poll Davies-Gilbert with a hyphen.

From the 1920s the Hardings and Davies-Gilberts allowed the Bardolf Hall to be used for village activities such as meetings of the Mothers' Union, charity appeals, the East Dean Players' productions and dances, although it was understood that it was not available during Lent, except for the most deserving and close-to-home charitable causes.

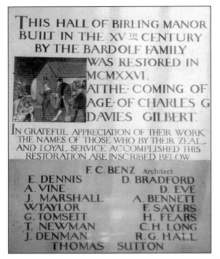

THIS HALL OF BIRLING MANOR
BUILT IN THE XV TH CENTURY
BY THE BARDOLF FAMILY
WAS RESTORED IN
MCMXXVI.
AT THE COMING OF
AGE OF CHARLES G
DAVIES GILBERT.

IN GRATEFUL APPRECIATION OF THEIR WORK
THE NAMES OF THOSE WHO BY THEIR ZEAL
AND LOYAL SERVICE ACCOMPLISHED THIS
RESTORATION ARE INSCRIBED BELOW

F. C. BENZ   Architect

E. DENNIS	D. BRADFORD
A. VINE	D. EVE
J. MARSHALL	A. BENNETT
W. TAYLOR	F. SAYERS
G. TOMSETT	H. FEARS
T. NEWMAN	C. H. LONG
J. DENMAN	R. G. HALL
THOMAS	SUTTON

Plaque at Bardolf Hall to commemorate the the estate employees' help in the restoration

The trefoil headed window in the ante room, or Lady's Bower, of Bardolf Hall

In 1926 Major Harding bought the final team of oxen at Exceat. Oxen were last worked at Exceat Farm by Charlie Pope in 1925. He trained up a Mr Burton of Major Harding's farm when they were sold off to him. [3]

Normally six in a team, the beasts' sharp horns were fitted with a metal cover at the tip to stop them damaging each other, and they wore nose nets to stop them grazing. They worked a 7 to 3 day, and their diet was cheap - hay, straw, swedes in winter, and in summer grass twice a day and for a treat cake. Major Harding's team at Birling Manor were Sussex Reds, not as resilient as Welsh Blacks, and they were not shod as was the custom because the team was not used on the roads.

Beckett in *Adventures of a Quiet Man* writes, 'Major Harding must have took them out of good nature. No replacements were envisaged and as usually two retire each year, it was no surprise when they were pensioned off the next year.'

Bill Armiger said, "Oxen could match any horse team for ploughing, but they were too slow for the reaper/binder. For a heavy load they had the advantage that they did not snatch at the pull. I have seen them shift a threshing machine stuck in a ditch when neither steam engine nor team of horses could move it. They were used extensively over 1914-18 when horses were requisitioned for the military."

Major and Mrs Harding were kindly and would bring a parcel of goodies if any family was on its beam ends, for in those days families experienced extreme poverty. Mrs Grace Davies Gilbert came to the school once a year on her birthday in December, driven by her groom in a pony and trap. She gave all the pupils a new penny and a currant bun. The girls had to curtsey and say "Good Morning Madam", a source of some dissension. [6]

Oxen were very gentle beasts, **above** are Sussex Reds, the last team at Exceat in 1925, although not as hardy as the Welsh Blacks. Oxen worked in pairs, Quick and Nimble, Gold and Gallant, Duke and Diamond, the single syllables to the left. Each knew their name and place and obeyed the voice. Pictured above ploughing at Exceat, with Charles 'Curly' Pope (left) as the oxen driver and Ray Kemp, or a Holter, as oxboy with hazel goad. In the picture **below** Welsh runts are pulling a Sussex wagon

Right inset: a rusty ox shoe, dug up by Roxy Whicker in a Deneside garden in 2000. Actually, half an ox-shoe for, unlike a horseshoe, they consisted of two separate parts

The farm employed about 30 people. "At one time" said Grace Taylor (née Fowler) "the Hardings employed most of the Fowler family." Her father, Dick, was the shepherd, her brother, another Dick, was a carter, her sister-in-law was the cook, and she was a part-time kitchen maid. "I thoroughly enjoyed my time. There was a big Eagle range with two ovens, and I had to keep a kettle of water boiling all the time. We were well fed."

Lady Wilson, Lady Pelly and The Duchess of Hamilton
at Home
Dorchester Hotel, Park Lane, W.1. (Park Lane Entrance)
Tuesday, 16th July,
on the occasion of the forthcoming marriage of their niece
Miss Sibyl Poore
and
Mr Gilbert Davies-Gilbert.
7th Queen's Own Hussars
R.S.V.P
25, St Edmunds Terrace,
Regent's Park,
London, N.W.8.
4.30–7 p.m.

Notice of the impending marriage of Sibyl Poore and Gilbert Davies-Gilbert

In the early years of the 20th century, shepherding was an important occupation. Harry Comber said his grandfather, William West, who always had a full beard, was a shepherd, and Jack Breach's grandfather, David Breach, and his uncle Tom Breach were also shepherds. "They all wore bowler hats because they were shower-proof. They ran the sheep over the Downs, folded them in wattles for the night, and 'lookered them', a Sussex term for checking or counting animals."

BARDOLF'S HALL.
Wednesday, November 27th, 1935.

PROGRAMME.

"Miss Pilkington takes the Plunge."
Characters in order of appearance.

Sally	... Beatrice Wootherspoon
Mary	... Mary Harding
McDougall	... C. Graham Robinson
Miss Pilkington	... Esme Matheson
Colonel Talbot	R. Winslow Patton
SCENE—The Shores of a Loch in Scotland in Summer.	

"The Twelve Pound Look."
Characters in order of appearance.

Harry Sims	... P. Dilberoglue
Emmy Sims	Elizabeth Harding
Tombs	... P. Halstead
Kate	... Diana Black
SCENE—Harry Sims' Study.	

PRODUCER - Esme Matheson

Mary and Elizabeth Harding enjoyed their own amateur theatricals in the 1930s

The Hardings had a few mixed experiences in the 1920s. Having sold their Manor House in Eastbourne to the Eastbourne Borough Council for £19,000, they had an expensive law suit with the tenant of *Birling Farm* before they could move in. Then in 1926-9 came the Downs Purchase when the Hardings lost 805 acres of their farmland, but gained £18,875.

Major Harding continued to donate free milk to deserving families. The Breaches had to collect theirs from *Shepherd's Cot,* where the Davies-Gilbert cowman (yet another Harris) lived, and at the time was a hovel. Other locals collected their milk in cans from *Gore Farm,* where Bill Boarer was the cowman. When the Hardings gave an Easter Egg party for their children the village children were invited along. They were fun occasions with numerous eggs hidden all around.

Miggs Ticehurst said, "Major and Mrs Harding were lovely. She would come to the village shop in her apron with ladders in her stockings like everyone else. She was always with dogs. The Major was a little man, who wore a pork pie hat and often held his hands behind his back. Jimmy was also always nice to us." The donkey wheel well at *Birling Manor* was a source of endless joy to the village children until its dismantlement.

Kathleen Butler's family lived at Windsor and she worked near London but wanted to move out so she applied for jobs on the south coast and on 4 March 1939 she came to the Hardings at *Birling Manor.* "It was a wonderful place and wonderful people. Major and Mrs Harding had seven children: Gilbert (Jimmy is his son), Mary, Michael, Elizabeth (she married John Congreve in 1939), Ann, John and Sue." Shortly afterwards Kathleen was to meet Fred Fuller at a dance in the Bardolf Hall.

Four generations in *Birling Manor* garden, 1945. L-R: Major Harding, grandfather to Jimmy Davies-Gilbert aged 4, and Charles Gilbert Davies-Gilbert his father. Seated, in black, Grace his great-grandmother, and standing, Sibyl, his mother and right, Patience Harding, his grandmother

Kathleen Cater's father, Edward Hobden, farmed *Birling Farm* as a tenant of Major Harding from about 1935, around the time that Fordson tractors were replacing horses locally. Farmer Hobden used the Gilbert land mainly for sheep. Dick Fowler, "a lovely man", ran a flock of Southdown sheep and used the awnings around the Dunwick Barn for lambing. The barn was full of hay and bales of this were used to protect the sheep. As soon as they were fit they were put out in the fields. The Dunwick Barn was also used for sheep shearing. The Revd AA Evans said 'Dunwick' was Saxon for 'Cottage on the Hill', although you wouldn't describe the barn being on much of a hillock.

The Harding's Southdown sheep seldom had twins and became uneconomic to run, so in 1939 just before the war, when Dick Fowler retired, James Stickland, a shepherd from Tring, was brought in with a flock of Suffolks. [3] His sister, Emily, came with him and worked in Gore Farmhouse. "She only had one eye as the result of a bicycle accident as a child. I can still recall her always 'cleaning my brights' [brasses]." Brother and sister lived in *Shepherd's Cot* and later *Underhill.* When Edward and Nora Hobden moved out of Gore Farmhouse at the end of the war, she went to work for the Hardings.

Gerard Melling, groom/chauffeur to Major Harding, had originally been his batman in the 1914-18 war. He was called up in 1939 and as a sergeant in an armoured regiment, won the Military Medal in the western desert, but was killed in Italy in 1945. [10]

Miss Beatrice Prideaux-Brune, who lived at *Went Acre* from the time it was built in the 1920s, was a relative of the Davies-Gilberts. 'Deaf as a post', she was an accomplished horsewoman, who always rode side-saddle. Frank Bagg and his wife, chauffeur/gardener and cook/housekeeper, cared for her for over 22 years, until her death, at 91, in 1950. [7]

The next year, 8 July, Grace Davies Gilbert died age 89, for 38 years widow of Carew.

Ricky Hodgson said, "Major Davies-Gilbert, Mrs Patience Harding and Miss Minnie Davies Gilbert were closely involved in the village activities and you could easily obtain permission to use the Bardolf hall for any function."

In 1952 neither Major Harding nor Mr Hall sought re-election to the Parish Council [PC]. Major Harding had been chairman of the Parish Meeting for 16 years and from the time the PC was instituted in 1938 he was chairman until 1947 when he was succeeded by Mr Hall. Major Harding attended every Parish Meeting and 81 of the 96 meetings of the PC. Ronnie Hall missed only one of the parish meetings and only eight of the meetings of the PC.

Thirty boxes of relief clothing for 1953 East Coast flood victims were sent off, with help from George Jenner, Mrs Houghton, Dorothy Dickens, Fred Saunders and John Eve. Major and Mrs Harding waived their embargo on dances in Lent for one in aid of the National Flood Relief Fund on 7 March, and raised £25.

In the December of 1953 Major Charles Henry Harding (above) died of a heart attack, aged 85, having been in good health up to the previous day. The 'Little Major' went to Uppingham School and after marriage to Patience Davies Gilbert the couple lived in Ireland and Cornwall as well as Eastbourne. He was elected churchwarden at East Dean when he was on active service in 1916 and held the office up to his death. Apart from his long tenure of the chair of Parish Meetings and PC he was president of the local United

Nations Association, the district British Legion [BL], The Players, Cricket Club, and the Bonfire Society. A generous subscriber to village needs, he was deeply concerned about the welfare of East Dean and Friston.

James Gallop (left, with his sack) came to East Dean in 1921 to farm Dunwick and had a smallholding up by the Red Barn possibly a remnant of Mary Ann Gilbert's agricultural efforts (right). He grew potatoes, kept hens and every day about lunch time, in all winds and weathers, aided by two sticks for his rheumatics, he would go there with a sack of corn on his back. "Never saw him come back with any eggs, but his wife sold them." He had a snow-white beard and blue eyes and was ready to talk of country matters. They managed to bring up a family of four. Daughter Ethel married Sid Winter; one son, Alf, was a valet and later gardener for Mrs Batten at Crowlink; Walter was at *The Knoll* renamed *The Gables,* Windmill Lane, where he laid out the garden for Mr Cater and worked on it full time into the 1980s and Ted went into the Army.

The Gilbert Estate Trustees considered the request in 1953 for the Green to be dedicated as a Village Green, but came to no decision. Again no reply came from them when a number of locals protested about the resumption of summer camps at Birling Gap.

In 1958 David Eve died, he worked on the Gilbert Estate for over 50 years, finally in the *Birling Farm* stables. Albert Vine died in 1962 aged 84. He joined the Estate in 1894 tending the Estate gardens in Hartfield Square. When the Corporation took them over, he moved to the Estate building side. In the RA for World War 1 and Home Guard in WW2, on retirement in 1950 he was one of the longest serving members of the Gilbert Estate.

Janet Johnson said, "Jimmy Davies-Gilbert used to go prawning at the Gap with my father Frank Martin when he came down from Herstmonceux, and Charlie, the next generation, would come down here for the cricket."

As a lad Oliver Cater collected flints and mushrooms for pocket money. "It was said that the wagons carrying flints to *Gayles* would pass the tallyman and, if possible, wheel round, have a smoke, give the horses a rest and repass the tallyman with the same load. The best place for mushrooms was on Went Hill and Mrs Harding was always our first port of call, for she paid best (yet didn't take all the best of the crop) and gave us a drink."

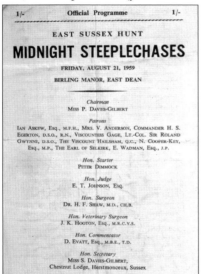

1/- Official Programme 1/-

EAST SUSSEX HUNT

MIDNIGHT STEEPLECHASES

FRIDAY, AUGUST 21, 1959

BIRLING MANOR, EAST DEAN

Chairman
MISS P. DAVIES-GILBERT

Patrons
IAN ASKEW, ESQ., M.F.H., MRS. V. ANDERSON, COMMANDER H. S. EGERTON, D.S.O., R.N., VISCOUNTESS GAGE, LT.-COL. SIR ROLAND GWYNNE, D.S.O., THE VISCOUNT HAILSHAM, Q.C., N. COOPER-KEY, ESQ., M.P., THE EARL OF SELKIRK, E. WADMAN, ESQ., J.P.

Hon. Starter
PETER DIMMOCK

Hon. Judge
E. T. JOHNSON, ESQ.

Hon. Surgeon
DR. H. F. SHAW, M.D., CH.B.

Hon. Veterinary Surgeon
J. K. HOOTON, ESQ., M.R.C.V.S.

Hon. Commentator
D. EVATT, ESQ., M.B.E., T.D.

Hon. Secretary
MISS S. DAVIES-GILBERT,
Chestnut Lodge, Herstmonceux, Sussex

In the 1950s and 60s the younger Davies-Gilberts organised Midnight Steeplechases and Dances at the manor (left). George Worsell rigged up lighting, or car headlights were used to illuminate the fences and some jolly times were had with BBQs until, after one of the horses had to be put down, it was decided that night time racing was too dangerous. [11]

At the 21st birthday of his eldest son on 7 December 1961. Major Davies-Gilbert speaking to tenants, farm workers and members of the East Sussex Hunt of which he was Master, mentioned that other happy occasion when he was 21 and the Bardolf Hall was renovated, and he was pleased to see some had been at both occasions. The new-of-age gave a sincere thank you to his grandmother, Mrs Patience Harding, and to his great aunt, Miss Minnie Davies-Gilbert, before cutting the cake.

In 1965 Miss Minnie, who was becoming frail, resigned as President of the Eastbourne division of the Girl Guides Association, and she died on 20 February 1968 aged 85. [12] Two years later, on 30 November, her sister Mrs Harding died aged 87. Patience Davies Harding's retiring nature did not stop her playing a full part in village life, even when staying at *Went Acre*. She didn't seek the limelight, but had the knack of gracefully saying a few apt and amusing words.

Jimmy Davies-Gilbert remembered, "Grandmother [Patience Harding] used to make the farm's butter and clotted cream. She always insisted that the milk churn for the butter making was not fully cleaned out, she preferred a slightly tart taste."

With her death, son Major Charles Gilbert Davies-Gilbert and his wife Sibyl moved to *Went Acre* while *Birling Manor* was renovated. George Worsell was in charge of the work and the Davies-Gilberts resumed residence when the manor house was ready. George, father of Richard and Julia Worsell, was also the organist for the East Dean Family Service.

Mrs Sibyl Davies-Gilbert was intelligent, had a strong personality (it was not unknown for her to refer to villagers as 'peasants') and participated in many local events. At the

Church Christmas Fair on 6 December 1969 the Bardolf Hall was crowded, despite poor weather, all came to hear her open the Fair, when she expressed the hope that no one would resist the temptation to spend their money. Organised again by Reggie Smith, it raised £487.

When, in 1967, Capt. Norman Davies retired from farming the Davies-Gilbert land after more than 20 years, Major Davies-Gilbert took over, but he was not a fit man and after a few years son, Jimmy, came to East Dean to run the farm.

For most of 1973, on the invitation of Sibyl Davies-Gilbert, Harold Spears and Jack Gryspeerdt of the Eastbourne Local History Society, were sorting D-G papers rescued from the old Manor Office to decide which should go to the Lewes County Record Office.

It was the same year, when the ED & F Bowling Club was exclusively male, that Sibyl Davies-Gilbert pointed out that the Old Town Ladies' Bowling Club welcomed new members. She once again opened the Church's Christmas Fair which raised £600.

Two years later, it was Sibyl Davies-Gilbert who first suggested a Gardening Club for ED & F and at the inaugural AGM held at the Gilbert Institute on 23 March 1976 Sibyl was elected the first president. That summer the 97 members were invited to a coffee morning in the grounds of *Birling Manor*. By the millennium the club had more members than any other local club. [13]

In 1977 despite the tragic death of Charles Gilbert Davies-Gilbert, Jimmy's father, the Davies-Gilbert family gamely went ahead with support for the Queen's Silver Jubilee celebrations which included opening their gardens. [14]

Sibyl Davies-Gilbert also continued her family's support for the Scouts and Guides Association. At the 1978 AGM when Lt Col Grattan Hart presented the prizes, Debbie Fielder, who then ran the Brownies, made an appeal for a Scouts and Cubs' leader, as there were none in

Major Charles Gilbert Davies-Gilbert died tragically on 10 March 1977. It was for his 21st birthday that the Bardolf Hall had been renovated, and also the date when he changed his name from Harding to Davies-Gilbert by deed poll. Here he is leading a local hunt; it was said, "He lived his life for the Horse"

the village. The Association was able to hold a Spring Market at *Went Acre* thanks to Sibyl Davies-Gilbert and raise £114. The next year at the Scouts and Guides Association meeting, Cmdr Peter Winter presented the RBL Shield to Kingfisher patrol, and Sibyl Davies-Gilbert presented a Trophy to Susanna Chapman and Michele Wilson, who had tied. The pack of 14 had won the District Swimming gala.

Again in 1980, when Cmdr Peter Winter presented the RBL shield to Patrol Leader Mary Oliver, Sibyl Davies-Gilbert presented a trophy to Brownie Lucy Jarvis.

When that year Jimmy and Louise Davies-Gilbert heard that the Annual Flower Show had lost £30 in 1979 and could not afford the £120 to hire a marquee, they offered the Dunwick Barn as a site and supplied transport for the chairs. At the Show Wally Eve won both Challenge Shields and Mrs RS Johnson the Webb's Competition. Jack Pearce won the Red Ribbon award for the best exhibit at the show. Elsie Armiger won the Rose Bowl, Dolly Alloway won the Floral Art Award and Susan Greenway was the youngest winner of the Home Produce Cup. Fewer people attended and there was a small loss, but the Davies-Gilbert's involvement and hard work by the committee kept the show afloat.

In August 1981 Sibyl Madeleine Davies-Gilbert died aged 75. She had undertaken a mammoth reconstruction of *Birling Manor,* while supporting her husband, and after his death lived at *Wentacre.* As well as initiating the Gardening Club, and her unswerving support for the Guides and Brownies, she helped the Bowls Club, the Eastbourne Local History Society, and the Friends of the Eastbourne Hospitals.

Until the Downs Purchase of 1926, the Davies-Gilbert family held 1000 acres (300 hectares) with 30 employees, afterwards they had about 300 acres of their own land and leased 600 from the National Trust (NT) on which they ran 3000 sheep and 300 cattle.

Birling Manor from the main drive c.1960 before the refurbishment of the 1970s.

Terry Wigmore, who had worked as a shepherd from his teens, came to care for the animals after Alfred Pelling retired in 1981.

In July 1984 Jimmy Davies-Gilbert reported that rustlers had got away with 36 lambs and 26 ewes from the NT Crowlink Farm.

The Davies-Gilberts came out of livestock farming in 1987, which was not paying; Jimmy also gave up the 600 acres of NT land. His holdings were 250 acres of arable, 30 of wood, 4.5 km of walls, 15 listed buildings, one acre of common and 20 bore holes. "It is wonderful land for modern arable farming." Employing only one person, he rotated wheat, barley and rape, "which is so easy at East Dean. Most of our set-aside land is at Pevensey, the only piece in East Dean is usually the Cophall one which is riddled with rabbits.

"The farm buildings are redundant now. There are stables, a tack room, a slated tractor shed, the old cow shed, and a lovely old restored Sussex Barn. We have permission for light industrial use, but rents are so low in Eastbourne that it is not economical to use them."

When made redundant in 1987, Terry Wigmore and his wife Pamela decided to start the Seven Sisters Sheep Centre at the entrance to *Birling Farm* near the Dunwick barn. "Hordes of people would watch us lamb down the sheep in the front yard. With that interest we thought we should make a go of it". Within four years, at the 1992 Sheep Dairying Association conference, Terry was awarded First Prize for his sheep's milk yoghurt. The Centre became a great success except during the foot-and-mouth outbreak of 2001.

In 1993 Terry and Pam Wigmore put in new facilities to serve light refreshments, and Twiggy, one of the ewes at the Sheep Centre gave birth to quins for the second year running. As he put it, 'What she'd have produced standing still no one knows'. He now had 250 sheep as well as hens, pigs, goats, calves and rabbits. Pam makes cheeses and yoghurt.

There are 49 breeds of sheep including Southdowns. The British Milk sheep have a high lambing ratio: one ewe produced 23 lambs in five lambings. Shearing is not done by gangs, but is staggered, with four sheep a day being shorn from May to September. 'This enables visitors to see the shearing and we will put aside a special colour or quality of wool for home spinners and weavers. Modern sheep farming has its problems, people will leave gates open so the wrong rams get in with different ewes, ramblers scramble over walls cracking the top and give you abuse if you remonstrate. Perhaps with all the restrictions on export and lower production costs elsewhere we could see the demise of British sheep.' [1]

Mrs Louise Davies-Gilbert was a firm supporter of the Flower Show. After a few years at the Dunwick Barn, she and her husband Jimmy were instrumental in rejuvenating the annual show by allowing it to use the Bardolf Hall. She also won many prizes and in 1984 presented the awards.

The Eastbourne and Lewes district branch of the NSPCC held their annual meeting in the Bardolf Hall in October 1990 with cheese and wine and a talk by the Bishop of Lewes, the Rt Revd Peter Ball. Presided over by Lady Monk Bretton, it was chaired by Barbara Chatfield, and Louise Davies-Gilbert was presented with a bouquet for her hospitality.

A glorious afternoon in 1994, with the *Birling Manor* gardens looking their best, witnessed the full recovery of the Village Flower Show. Since 2000 the Show has been held in the new Village Hall.

Noel Powell about to be awarded the Floral Cup by Maureen Honey at the 1994 Flower Show. On the extreme right in front of the Bardolf Hall are Peter Johnson and Kate Boyle. Other winners were Esther Worsfold, foliage pot plant, George Booth-Clibborn and Patrick Coulcher vegetables, Eric Smith's flowering pot plant and Kay Ketcher's flower arrangement

What other recent changes? Well, unfortunately, the returns from grain halved after the Millennium due to intense competition. The income from wheat in 1999 was £120/acre and by 2005 it was only £64, and rapeseed fell from £300 to £100/acre. With tax subsidies ending in 2012, and noting that there are 20,000 visitors a year to the Seven Sisters Sheep Centre, it was decided to develop a business plan for promoting the welfare of the countryside with job opportunities; this involved taking into account animal welfare, for example, continuing to use the local abattoir at Hailsham, where the cattle have always been sent.

On 80 acres of organic, rotated with livestock - Sussex cattle, the sheep increased to 300 (mainly Southdown again) - and with woodland coppicing, the concept is to promote a "Beachy Head' brand of 100% organic products (which retail at up to three times the non-organic - at present). This would be coupled with diversifying into holiday packages (facilities such as gas, electricity, TV and even bore holes and sewers are already laid on) and other leisure pursuits as diverse as tea shops, metal detecting, an RSPB partnership and, an as yet to be constructed, replica Saxon settlement.

Jimmy Davies-Gilbert lives at *Birling Manor* and runs the Gilbert Trust, letting out properties and some arable farming. His son Charlie, who lives in *The Dipperays* with his wife Octavia and young family, started a popular Wednesday Market at the Village Hall in 2003, has promoted the diversification approach and is taking up the reins.

Birling Gap

Landing places were always danger spots, and up to 1342 the parishes even benefited by a remittance of taxation because more than half of their crops had been destroyed by Norman pirates who landed at Cuckmere Haven or Birling Gap, and into the 1800s church records refer to the spot as Birling Gate.

In Good Queen Bess's days every able-bodied man in the parish had to have 'trayninge at shott and avoiding of great expense and waste of powder'. The men were under Yeoman Captain George Gorringe, a name still extant in the district. Horsfield states that the remnants of a gate and portcullis existed at Birling Gap up to 1800, perhaps reminders of the 'We hold yt beste to be ramed uppe' advice of the 1587 Coast Defence Survey just before the Spanish Armada. More peacefully, fishing was reported there in 1697.

Pencil drawing by John Graham of Birling Gap, September 1832. In March 1831 the Coastguard took over the preventive work, lifesaving and other duties from the Coast Blockade. Over time the relative importance of the stations at Beachy Head, Crowlink and Birling Gap fluctuated, but full-time coastguards lasted at Birling Gap until 1951

In 1663 the Court Rolls of Birling reveal that a 'Samson Birthwood had impinged upon his Lord's rights' and that 'John a'Brook hath one hogshead of wine, two small masts, two fathoms of small cable'. A Court case as early as 1689 confirmed the right of the Lord of Birling Manor to wrecks, but while the Gap might lie just on the edge of the sea, it would appear that it was long distant from the laws of the sea or land, and in the 1700s, along with Crowlink, it became a centre for smuggling.

While all were agreed that the Davies-Gilberts were the owners of the foreshore rights, as Jimmy Davies-Gilbert explained, "It sounds grand, but when a Russian vessel unshipped Baltic timber everyone else made off with it and I had nothing, except it was established afterwards that I was entitled to 10%".

The Coastguard service was an anti-smuggling unit, aligned with safety and rescue operations. By 1870 the coastguard cottages at Birling Gap had been completed, with their usual gardens so that the coastguards could grow much of their requirements and reduce the temptation for collusion with the locals.

The Eastbourne lifeboat dates from 1822 and its most remarkable achievement was in 1883 when the *William and Mary,* an oared boat, rescued the crew from the *New Brunswick* which was in distress a mile off Birling Gap. In view of the extreme weather conditions the lifeboat had to be dragged - partly by manpower, partly by horses - from Eastbourne to be launched at Birling Gap. A Naval Club team attempted to re-enact this famous episode in July 1991. The weather was much the same, but this time it was deemed advisable not to launch the lifeboat and it was towed back to Eastbourne - by Land Rover.

By the summer of 1915 Birling Gap presented an unusual appearance of barbed wire and vigilant sentries with the far away accent of Glasgow. In 1916 an Italian freighter the Ushla was stranded near the Gap followed in 1919 by a German U-boat *U121*. [2, 3]

The *Eastfield,* a 2355-ton tramp ship, came ashore 200m east of Belle Tout on 3 December 1909. She looks high and dry, but she was floated off and sailed to Tilbury for repairs

In 1920 the full-time Coastguard service had Chief Officer Lavour in the officer's end cottage, *Leander.* Coastguards who resided in the cottages at Birling Gap included the Breaches, the McNallys, the Wilsons, and the Worsells. Others there over the years included the Norketts, the Hills and the Schafers.

Luther Hills had noted in his 1916 diary that, 'An Italian freighter, the *Ushla,* came ashore at Birling Gap, unladen. Her crew, mainly Chinese, scrambled ashore.' In 1919 the wreck of the *Ushla* was joined near Flagstaff Point beach by the U 121 on the left. The *U 121* was one of two U-boats on tow to Cherbourg as part of German reparations to France, when both broke away during a storm. Kathleen Cater remembers the submarine. "We used to play round it, by then it was only rusted metal." [5]

Jack Breach was born in East Dean and his family lived in one of the coastguard cottages at Birling Gap. "There were two bedrooms upstairs and with eight in the family one was for the boys and one for the girls." His parents slept downstairs. As the children left his parents took in a lodger. After war service he came back to the village and eventually was head porter at the local hospitals. Ivy, his wife, worked for Cmdr Smith for 20 years.

Coastguard work was redefined in 1922 to mainly life saving and rescue, and in 1919 Chief Petty Officer James E Worsell, Richard Worsell's grandfather, came to the station from Fairlight. He had joined the service in 1901 and it is said that he was one of the last to be issued with a standard Admiralty cutlass, and he certainly led a famous rescue in 1925.

At 0440h, on 30 December 1925, the vessel *Contesse de Flandres* ran ashore near Haven Brow. The horse-drawn Life Saving Apparatus [LSA] cart was taken by road to the Cuckmere because of the bad state of the tracks. Having reached the westerly Haven Brow it was found that the vessel was being driven eastwards and the cart had to be taken to Short Bottom, under conditions of a Force 8-10 wind, rain and poor visibility. The ship had now drifted to Limekiln Bottom and the coastguards had another detour to make before they could fire their rocket line. The first man to be rescued from the boat was landed at 1140h and, in all, 27 were brought ashore. Frequent stops had to be made for the exhausted horses; and they finally got back, 14 hours later, at 1823h.

On the **left,** looking east, the *Birling Manor* Golf Clubhouse is extreme left edge, centre is Mrs Binney's timber building, *Children's Delight,* that became *White Horses.* All cleared away by the National Trust in 1987. On the **right** looking towards the Gap is *Children's Delight* and in the distance the Coastguard Cottages and hotel car park

Tommy Taylor was a carter who lived in Peak Dean barn, not unusual then. When the maroon went up to indicate a ship in distress Tommy's horses were used to transport the LSA, but he always insisted on feeding them first. James Wicking's horses were also used.

James Worsell retired in 1932 and was replaced by HT Dashwood. After the full-time coastguards left the station in 1951, the last Senior Officer being WT Maynard, the Auxiliary Coastguard Service [ACS] continued, with Ivan Worsell (1923-61)) in charge, when the pay was 50p per call out for a full member and 25p for an assistant.

Richard Worsell's father, George, married Maud Dann. He was the Gilbert Estate manager and received the Queen's Commendation for his coastguard work over 1925-76. Maud was a stalwart of The Players and an assistant at the school. John Dann's father, Cecil, was in the RN during the war when he married Rose Betteridge of the WRNS. He also received the Queen's Commendation for his coastguard work December 1937 to January 1976. Rose was involved with the Guides, the Church choir and also The Players.

In the 1930s Ivan Worsell was the self-styled professional at the Birling Manor course. Fred Fuller played golf at the course before the 1939-45 war when the artisan fees were 15p a year. He caddied for Sir James Purves-Stewart who owned Belle Tout and who paid him 4p a round and another $2^1/_2$p for carrying his clubs back to Belle Tout and cleaning them. [3]

Many people pay tribute to the beauty of the Downs in those days. Prebendary Colin Kerr loved walking there in the 1920s, and prawning and swimming at Birling Gap. 'Some of the first camps of his Campaigners were at Birling Gap and Hobbs eares from 1926.'

Joyce Donkin said her family regularly came on holiday to East Dean. "We stayed at the *Birling Gap Hotel,* run by charming people, Margarite and Ruth Alder. You climbed out of your room window for a swim and went back the same way. At that time the

Hardings, of *Birling Manor,* had a bathing hut at Birling Gap." Joyce went on to say that during 1939-45 ammunition was stored on the Golf Course. Ronnie Hall did get the golf going again in 1950-51, season tickets £1, green fees 7¹/₂p a day, and Bill Bailey played there with David Brown (who married Kath Taylor), but it only lasted about 18 months to 1953.

William Joslin said, "In the early 1920s the Downlands Estate did not exist, and my father, brother and I wandered all over the Downs, you could walk almost wherever you liked. My father would go down on the shore below Belle Tout before five in the morning, for he was a keen prawner using gin nets, and knew just where to catch the best prawns or even a succulent lobster on a good day".

Miggs Bailey (née Ticehurst) said, "Most Sundays before 1939 our family walked to Birling Gap. We kids weren't allowed in the pub, but lemonade and chips were passed out. Best of all, my father would carry me on his shoulders on the way back".

Mrs AR Llewellyn-Davies (and later Joyce Holden) lived in *Seven Sisters Cottage,* and Dr and Mrs Coit, and a butler, were opposite in *White Horses,* with Adela their daughter. When Mrs Binney had it in the 1930s she had children staying there for holidays in the summer and it was called appropriately *Children's Delight House School.* Hugh StD King-Farlow lived there when the Coits moved up the lane to *The Birlings* where Bobby and George Stein were later. Mary and Michael Mordaunt were at *Seven Sisters;* Dr Broun at *Broadchalke* and Phyll and Trevor Baker at *Trevyllis.* Reg Haffenden's father, William, was gardener at Dr Stanton Coit's house. "He had nine statues in the garden, but they've all been pinched." He agreed the Hardings had a beach hut at the Gap.

Tents above Birling Gap in the 1930s. Before 1939 many Territorial units, Scout patrols and clubs, held their annual camp on the Downs. They used a variety of tents, a marquee for dining or talks, and a pot-bellied stove for cooking. The Hollington Boys' Club camped down nearer the Golf Clubhouse.

Ted Fears said, "Pre-war steps were cut down to the beach at Birling Gap. To protect the chalk, railway sleepers held by metal pegs were laid on each step. In 1940 a Sergeant and a group of Sappers turned up, laid charges, and said to a relative, Bob Fears, if you press that plunger you will remember this day for the rest of your life. When he did the steps were blown up as part of the anti-invasion measures. The concrete plug the Sappers put in was used as a base for steps just after the war." The 'Big Rock' became stranded as the cliff eroded, showing where the cliff edge had been in 1940, and it was used as a diving platform, a source of fun by generations of children, until demolished by the NT in 1994.

Pre-1939 Ivan and George Worsell lived in the coastguard cottages at the Gap. Ivan had a taxi business, meeting people at the station for the hotel and B&Bs, and George worked at the *Birling Gap Hotel,* where Miss GG Knight was the manager. Rene Wicking says, "Very elite it was too, owned by the Misses Ruth and Margarite (Margie) Alder, (after the Fowlers). They lived in Milnthorpe Road, Eastbourne, before moving to *Twitten Cottage* and later *Elm Lea* in Gilbert's Drive. At one time they owned the village shop as well.

In the 1960s an artistic colony developed at *Crangon Cottages,* with Rebecca Betts (Barbara Castle's mother), Jean Cooke (wife of painter John Bratby), and Jean Fawbert.

The Ward Lock guide of 1932 stated, 'the road that leads to … Birling Gap from East Dean has for years been in such a deplorable condition that few motorists think of using it'.

Birling Gap 1911. The wall around the Coastguard Gardens is entire as is the Rocket House along the seaside wall. The central look-out hut and the telegraph hut are well away from the cliff edge with the officer's cottage and the hotel even further back

Aerial view 1925. Extreme right is *Children's Delight.* The Coastguard Cottages are at an angle to the cliff edge with the circular car park and the hotel to the left. The Rocket House is now on the edge of the cliff and was lost by 1928

Birling Gap 1986. The Gap is looking 'slightly' neglected. The hotel is near left, and the Coastguard Cottages are centre. The Coastguard watchtower or look-out is seen on the Downs skyline to the right, it was demolished in 1991

Truly the road to Birling Gap was mud before the war. "The track from East Dean to Birling Gap was very uneven and full of potholes and it took an intrepid motorist to venture down there at all, especially at night. Cars were a rarity, Mrs King-Farlow had one, although such a terrible driver".

During the war the *Birling Gap Hotel* was taken over by the Canadians and the kitchens used to prepare meals for the Canadian troops. The nearby houses were commandeered for NCOs and local troops while the artillery units who came for practice firing ate in huts. [10] Immediately after the war the hotel was run by the Smiths.

Birling Gap beach between the wars when you could walk to the beach down about 25 steps cut into the chalk. Originally cut to convey oil from a barge to Belle Tout lighthouse, they were dug out or refashioned each year by the Gilbert Estate

Jane Beavan (née Ellis) wrote, "The lovely summer of 1947 meant the time for swimming had come round. The first day we went to Birling Gap I was staggered to find there was a cliff and just a rope ladder attached to a frail-looking spike. My uncle, just out of the army, swung nonchalantly down, sometimes with a dog under one arm and a baby under the other. Not surprisingly we had the beach to ourselves, although with its thousands of pebbles it wasn't a beach as I understood the term. You could go shrimping or prawning and in those days the pebbles were entirely free of any oil or tar." Not everyone knows that it is illegal to collect winkles from Birling Gap beach between 15 May and 15 September.

Jimmy Holter said, "Of an evening after the war a couple of us would walk to the Smith's at the *Birling Gap Hotel,* where there was a bowling alley. They also wouldn't recognise that we weren't 18 and we could buy a drink, which we couldn't do in the *Tiger*".

Gerald Melling confirms, "I only went to the *Tiger* twice because your mother had heard about it before you got home. Went to the Birling Gap instead."

The Canadians had put a hard-standing road along part of the way to *Cornish Farm* for their tanks, "But there was an outcry" explained Jane Beavan, "when it was suggested that the Birling Gap road should be upgraded. I thought that the potholes were easily negotiated by bicycle. When the road was finished in 1956 the volume of traffic to the Gap multiplied along with the number of people on the beach". In the course of the work several ancient skeletons, some suggestive of Roman origin, were found near *Birling Farm.*

One day Tom Bridger, the foreman at *Cornish Farm* for 34 years, invited all the farm workers for a drink. When they got to the Gap the hotel was empty of customers and the Smiths were sitting comfortably, Mrs Smith rolling cigarettes for her husband. Tom said, "Business must be better now that buses go along the road?" "That's the trouble", replied Mrs Smith, "Far too many people are coming here wanting drinks."

Cornish was a 1300-acre farm owned by Eastbourne Council. In the 1950s it gave work to six, and over the years Albert Vine, Harold Shaw, Ted Flint (hedger and thatcher), Ned Bailey, Don Ellis, Frank Parsons (mechanic) were there - all good workers. *Cornish* abutted *Bullock Down,* the farm of Percy Williams and son Eddie, where Charlie Hollingdale worked.

Chris Johnson, and son Paul, put in the £32,000 concrete road from the Beachy Head road to *Cornish Farm* in the 1970s. Chris was the manager 1972-89; he restored the shepherd's cot and in 1985 had a trial of organic alongside conventional cultivation.

In the 1950s the ex-Coastguard Cottages at the Gap, including *Leander,* the officer's cottage, were sold for £8,000. They were bought by Mrs Barratt-Terry who lived in *Leander* and let the others as holiday cottages, eventually selling them to the residents.

Jean Gordon says that pre-war her grandparents, Tommy and Emily Dickens, right, walked from the Bakery to Birling Gap every fine Sunday. Here they are, lounging on the beach, in hats and their Sunday best, for no East Deaners had special beach kit in those days. [7]

Post-war each summer Ian and Diana Shearer would walk down to Birling Gap with all their needs for the day packed in a pushchair. "The steps weren't so big in those days or we were younger, at least we were able to get the pushchair down and spend the day there."

The last time the local breeches-buoy was set up was for the 1955 rescue of the *Germania* crew at Cow Gap. In the end it was not used because the lifeboat, with difficulty, took the men off. The breeches-buoy was finally put out to grass in 1982.

On 14 December 1956 the Lifeguard Corps were called out because the duty man saw a flare off Flagstaff Point. Cecil Dann, John Eve, Walter Eve, Teddy Fears, Bert Goldsmith, Ray Kemp, Arthur Pelling, Harry Sellars, Cecil Smith, Rupert Taylor, Charlie Vine, Jim Wicking and George Worsell turned out on a dirty night. Three of them scaled down to the beach to find the flare was a marker dropped by an airplane - but it might not have been.

In a 1960 rescue of a youth who had attempted to climb down Beachy Head to save his tent blown over by the wind, the Police found they couldn't operate their crane at that spot. Cecil A Dann and George E Worsell went down with a lifeline, but they ran out of rope ladder so Richard Worsell and Bert Goldsmith lowered a rope down to them. The Fire Brigade helped by putting up some lights. Cecil came back up first with the youth, not easy because the lad wasn't keen with the rope swinging to and fro in the wind. Meantime, George had to move smartly from underneath the site because of cliff falls. [11]

In 1962 a small vessel, the *Ben Hebden,* came ashore between Belle Tout and Birling Gap. Fourteen members of the Birling Gap LSA turned out along with the Newhaven lifeboat which attempted to tow it off, but the vessel refloated under her own power.

Originally Birling Gap coastguard went as far as Holywell, hence their involvement with the *Germania.* When Garry Russell came in 1973 he took over responsibility for the coast up to and including Belle Tout. Garry said to Cecil Dann, in charge at the Gap since 1962, that the two units should join and Cecil could be his deputy, but Cecil wanted to keep them separate. "The relations between the two units were cool, but there was co-operation - Eddie Williams and Dave Piper would go with the Eastbourne unit whenever there was a rescue on Beachy Head." Now it is usual to call a helicopter if the cliff victim is alive.

In 1966 Ray Kemp retired from the Auxiliary Coastguard Service [ACS] at Birling Gap after 35 years. Out of 140 training drills during his service he attended 138.

Mrs A Llewellyn Davies had willed to the NT the bungalow *Seven Sisters* and a strip of her land running west from the Gap and this assured access for some time to come. She also had a drinking trough for dogs engraved, *For all dogs in memory of Kundry.* At this point the cliff walk had become increasingly narrow due to erosion.

In the course of 1967 the NT acquired 65 acres west of Birling Gap under the Enterprise Neptune project. That November a considerable cliff fall at the Gap forced the East Sussex County Council (ESCC) to close the cliff edge bridle path to Cuckmere in front of the *Birling Gap Hotel* where cliff erosion had been 5m (16ft) over six months. A diversion round the back of the hotel was dedicated the next year.

Coastguard *c.*1975, l-r, front:Trevor Hollingdale, Derek Greenway, Alf Pelling, Malcolm Johnson, Jolyon Fyfield, G Smith; back: George Worsell, Bert Goldsmith, Jim Wicking, Eddie Williams, Ted Fears, Peter Johnson, Cecil Smith, Charlie Vine, Fred Breach, John Dann, Brian Johnson, Richard Worsell and Dick Willis, Sector Officer, Shoreham

On Sunday, 7 December 1971, John Dann was on watch at the coastguard lookout when he spotted a motor boat off Flagstaff Point. The anchor chain had fouled the propeller putting the boat at the mercy of wind and tide. The boat grounded and the men managed to scramble onto the beach although the waves were breaking over them. Cecil Dann went down the cliff carrying a spare lifeline, which he attached in turn to three of the men who were hauled up and taken to hospital.

Since the establishment of the local ACS in 1923 every vacancy had been filled at once from a waiting list. Between 1923 and 1972 the Company rescued 41 persons and in conjunction with other services another 16, not forgetting two dogs.

Richard Worsell adds, "There was a coastguard look-out tower above Birling Gap before 1930. In the war a gun was mounted there and gravel was laid around to warn of night visitors. It was rebuilt after the war. Didn't cost much, the rent was negligible, but it was useful to the coastguard - somewhere for protection in the winter and where you could have a cup of tea during the watches. It was ridiculed by the Downs Wardens, so in 1991 it was demolished for the so-called mobile concept". You can see bases of the posts with 1949 etched in them.

The ex-Coastguard Cottages became *Crangon Cottages,* and by 1972 Mr Louis Beilschmidt, owner of what had been the chief coastguard's cottage, *Leander,* was fighting proposals by Hailsham RDC to demolish it. He used it as a furniture store and said 'it is not unsafe at the moment'. His lease ran out in 1973 when it passed back into the hands of the Gilbert Estate, and *Leander* was knocked down in August 1974.

In an unusual rescue on Saturday 13 December 1973, a four-year-old boy who had toppled into a cesspit at Birling Gap car park was safely recovered.

Cecil Dann was awarded the BEM in 1974 for his long and splendid service with the ACS. His son John explained how the ACS was organised, "There were four sections, each of five men and watchkeepers, so about 25 persons in all. Each man had an armband number and would stick to the same job for years.

"The *Rocket Section* was Bill Bailey 1, Bert Goldsmith 2, Eddie Williams 3, Jimmy Holter 5 and Alf Pelling also did No 2. The rocket line was a light rope fired from the shore to the ship in distress for the ship's crew to haul it in and secure. "The *Whip Section* was George Worsell 6 (leader), Richard Worsell 7, Rupert Taylor 8, Malcolm Johnson 9 and Capt. Ian Shearer 10. The whip (a light endless rope but too heavy for a rocket) was attached by the coastguards to the rocket line, for the ship's crew to pull it in and make it fast with a bowline knot."

Leander, previously the house of the Chief Coastguard at Birling Gap, in 1973, right on the edge of the cliffs. Demolished in 1974

John Dann was in the *Hawser Section,* and from 1976 to 1987 the Section Leader. "I was number 12, Jim Wicking was 11, Charlie Vine 13, Brian Johnson 14 and Ted Fears 15. The heavy hawser was attached and, by the coastguards pulling on the endless line whip, the hawser went out to the ship whose crew made it fast above the whip. A breeches-buoy could then be pulled to and from the ship conveying persons to be rescued. Members of the *Anchor Section* included Cecil Smith 16 (Leader), Peter Johnson 17, Derek Greenway 18, and Fred Breach all part of a happy team, always having a laugh."

Richard Worsell went on, "Then London decided that the numbers were not necessary and we could ditch the armbands. The heavy equipment was taken away, we were told half-truths, few replacements came, but plenty of paperwork appeared".

Birling Gap from the west c.1976. Belle Tout is centre on the skyline, and the Coastguard lookout is to the right. Below from the left is the old Golf Clubhouse, next *Children's Delight* (later *White Horses*) the Birling Gap Hotel and the line of *Crangon Cottages.*
The 'Big Rock' at the water's edge marks the cliff edge in 1940

There was a presentation evening in 1982 at the Farrer Hall to mark the retirement from the ACS of Jim Wicking and Bert Goldsmith after respectively 45 and 27 years' service, both held long service medals. Additional presents were the model replicas made by John Dann - appropriately, a rescue rocket line for Bert, and a rope ladder for Jim, who had been known to carry 80-feet [25m] of rope ladder all by himself.

The appearance of Birling Gap was deteriorating. In 1975 the PC, concerned about their dilapidated state, discovered that 'there were no plans for the future of the hotel and the derelict *White Horses* site, although the hotel proprietor said he would try to tidy up the rear of the hotel.' In 1979 the Sussex Amenity Group nominated it the Black Spot of Sussex. The National Trust [NT] bought Birling Gap in 1982 including the hotel and four of the coastguard cottages, three others being privately owned, and planned to spruce it up and turn it into a haven for walkers and nature lovers.

'We hope to remove some of the buildings, and there will definitely be an information centre, café and hostel for hikers.' The next year, Judith Norris, Agent for the NT, said of Birling Gap, "It is so miserable there the sooner we start a tree planting scheme the better", and Stuart Page, an architect said, "The buildings resemble something from the Wild West. Some control of visitors is necessary".

In the September the PC had talks with NT about the Gap. Peter Winter said that they wanted to co-ordinate local views and those of the Trust. George Booth-Clibborn said, "Many view the NT intentions with alarm. To remove the hotel and cottages, without replacement, and to re-site the car park, showed that the NT was remarkably ill-informed. Much improvement is needed, but the NT line would suit outsiders at the expense of locals who prefer a less drastic approach."

People not infrequently got into difficulties off the Gap. For example, in 1962 Ray Trickett and Jeremy Bird rescued a visitor, but a brave effort 21 years later led on further.

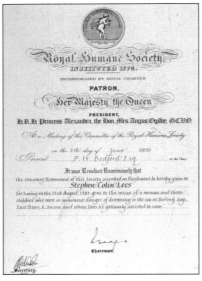

On 15 August 1989 a woman and her 9-year-old son were swept out to sea at the Gap by a freak wave. Her husband plunged in, but got into difficulties. Stephen Lees and Stephen Rummary swam out followed by Geoff Nash with a lifeline. All were rescued, the rescuers receiving Testimonials from the Royal Humane Society

On 19 September 1983 42-year-old Graham Collins fought against strong winds and rough seas to rescue a 50-year-old man drifting out to sea at the Gap. Mr Collins said that it would be a sensible thing for the coastguard to have a small boat there. He later received a Royal Humane Society testimonial, and became the driving force to establish a Birling Gap Safety Boat. A Jumble Sale in May 1984 raised £274, surpassing all expectations, and led to the formation of the Birling Gap Safety Boat Association [BGSBA] that year. The BGSBA became a charity and an Open Day, dedication by the Revd Frank Andrew, raised £840.

One of the first rescues by a loaned Safety Boat, manned by Malcolm Johnson, was of *Guinness*, a springer spaniel that had fallen into the water. Thanks to fund-raising efforts by Florence Whittaker and other ED & F residents over £1500 was raised in 1985 to buy *Florence Whittaker*, an Avon inflatable with a fibreglass hull.

Every year, by means of Fetes or Open Days, the Birling Gap Safety Boat Association raised sums of around £1500 even when, as in 1995, the 'services of the boat were not called upon during the summer'. This generosity enabled them to replace their Safety Boat with a semi-rigid Narwhal to improve efficiency.

On Thursday 25 April 1985 the NT staged a landing of King Neptune at Birling Gap, in the disguise of Paul Milmore, Heritage Coast Officer for ESCC, to christen a new £30,000 staircase for beach access towards which ESCC offered £10,000. Then the problems began. The galvanising wasn't spot on, the design of the handrail had to be altered, the angle of join wasn't right and part of the cliff became unsafe and had to be removed. Access to the beach wasn't restored until June - with the landscaping incomplete.

That was the year the NT claimed that the pub was 'an alien feature', and they would not renew the licence in 1987. *'The Birling Gap Hotel* was about 100 years old, in bad repair, and generally acknowledged to be an eyesore.'

The NT would not commit itself but proposed just to demolish some buildings, provide a 'comfort station with seated accommodation for 70 people' *(sic),* and relocate the car park away from the edge. The PC wrote to the NT saying that they were in favour of a permanent pub licence, and asked Percy Gray, a local architect, to liaise with the tenant of the hotel to produce a viable scheme to put to the NT.

After the lease of *White Horses* was surrendered in 1985, the NT knocked it down. Richard Worsell now spelt it out, "They said they would replace *White Horses* with new toilets, which the place did need, but not at that site. Having knocked it down NT agreed it was not the right spot and placed the toilets just behind the hotel, where the locals had suggested all along".

In January the NT released their architects' report which indicated that the cost of just improving the hotel's appearance would be over £70,000, which the NT was reluctant to finance when the life was unlikely to exceed 15 years. Following this Graham Collins wrote to the NT expressing his willingness to finance the improvements in return for a new lease.

By September 1986 the NT was finding, 'the rehabilitation of Birling Gap difficult to resolve. The NT wants to bring this unique bit of the Sussex Heritage Coast to the point where it reflects credit on the NT'. As Richard Worsell put it, "They've put their site clearance on hold." So the story rumbled on.

That year John Dann produced a postcard series of the village that helped to raise £200 for the Birling Gap Safety Boat Association. Some members had provided safety cover for a film crew beneath Belle Tout lighthouse which resulted in a further donation. The BGSBA received permission to build a new boathouse and their Fete raised £1200 towards it.

The BGSBA organised the 1987 Bonfire celebrations at the Gap. Fireworks cost £150, with £80 for insurance and the total was £282. Income was £61 from raffle, £84 for hot dogs, £90 collections and with about £20 from donations; the profit was £4. [11]

The Birling Gap Safety boat being moved out of its boathouse ready for launching

Life-saving wasn't forgotten. Birling Gap Coastguard won a May 1985 ship-to-shore rescue competition at Brighton. After a 1990 storm the Birling Gap steps were closed as the shingle had been washed away, but the closure lasted well into the year. In 1990 location shots for the film *Robin Hood: Prince of Thieves* were shot at Birling Gap, with members of the Safety Boat on stand-by. Over 1990-91 all the free-range pigs which had been kept along the Birling Gap road for years were removed, the farmer having moved to Norfolk.

April 1990 saw seven people needing assistance when trying to walk round Crowlink with a rising tide. Safety Boat crews who helped included Ann Nash, Geoff Nash, Mick Ranson, Danny Begley and coastguards Derek Greenway and Jimmy Holter.

East Dean's first Collectors' Meet held in the Farrer Hall in 1990 was planned by Rose Dann and raised £107 for the Birling Gap Safety Boat Association.

On Friday, 19 April 1991, Graham, Sandra and John Collins opened the *Oak Room Carvery and Restaurant* at the *Birling Gap Hotel.* The £250,000 extension package could cater for over 300, and all the hotel rooms had been up-dated. It was the venue for a Council for the Protection of Rural England dinner when 85 guests enjoyed an excellent meal. Geoffrey Mantle, one of the speakers said, "Since its formation in 1926 the CPRE had been dedicated to the protection of our fragile inheritance and it was important to continue the work of balancing the pressures on the countryside". Graham Collins added that the NT had proposed to demolish all the buildings, including the hotel, so compromise was needed.

WDC, responsible for the foreshore, proposed in 1991 to replace the lifebelt at the Gap with Balcan safety lifelines and to put up notices warning of the danger of the tides.

Graham Collins, whose family had run the hotel since 1958 was worried about erosion. "In 12 years the hotel will start to go, and an interesting part of the coast will be lost. Boulders could help to reduce the strength of the waves." A spokesman for the NT, presumably not unhappy to see the hotel go anywhere, said, "Let nature take its course". A Birling Gap Action committee was formed to keep the licensed and catering facilities and to improve the appearance.

In 1992 coastguard David Piper died aged 58 while on duty at Newhaven.

The next year three students in danger of being cut off by the tide at Crowlink were hauled to safety by members of the BGSBA. In the November the steps at Birling Gap were closed because of the danger to users, and in January 1994 the steps were dismantled.

No. 1 *Crangon Cottages* was demolished in 1994 having become dangerously close to the edge. London artist, Jean Cooke, who rented the cottage said, "I will just have to find somewhere else to paint". In 2002 the next house, Elizabeth Lazareno's, went.

After a dog was killed in a 1995 cliff fall, part of the cliff was chipped away by a specialist firm to make the beach below safer before the steps were reopened.

Richard Worsell bought 3 *Crangon Cottages* in 2001 for £500, although it might only have five years left, the NT having offered the owners a paltry £1. "I thought I would help to preserve the life of the cottages". He sold it in 2005 to Jean Cooke, who had found her 'somewhere else'. The NT own numbers 5, 6 and 7, which have been re-roofed and decorated, 5 and 6 are leased. Both 5 and 7 have the old coal-fuelled kitchens.

Brian Johnson, whose mother was an Erridge, the Eastbourne fishing family, always wanted to fish. In the 1950s he fished with a rod from the beach, and Geoff Nash would take him out in his boat. The Davies-Gilberts gave permission for a winch and he got a small boat. He went out all the year, fitting it around his work until retirement. He mainly fished for lobsters and crabs, especially May-August, and sold to the Southern Head Fisheries in Eastbourne. His wife Janet said, "He always said, 'Don't worry, we're all right', but it is inevitable that you do." His boat *Sharlisa* was named after their daughters.

Brian explained, "For shellfish there is rock going out ³/₄ mile, from Stones Foot, before it drops from 8 to 12 fathoms. I usually get about 4-6 hours at sea. It's not been an easy place to work a boat. No complaints, you have to watch the weather and I have seen the Seven Sisters in all their moods. The NT has been most helpful - allowing me to move my winch site when new steps were constructed."

On one trip in 2002 when Geoff Nash was helping Brian they caught such a load of sprats that the boat almost overloaded.

Geoff Nash was a coastguard in the 1950s often covering for holidays and Christmas. When he first moved to Seaford he couldn't continue as he wasn't within reach of the maroon. He rejoined in 1968. Maroons have now largely gone with the advent of pagers.

When he came up to retirement Geoff bought *The Boat House* and with his wife, Ann, ran a successful B&B. In 1913 RM Mason had bought four plots, 16, 17, 18, 19, from the Davies Gilberts and built a house on No. 19. You were only allowed to build one house with a coach house and a boathouse, Mr Mason sold plots 17, 18, and 19, and built a boathouse on 16 for weekends. This boathouse was pulled down and a Colt house built to the landward side, where Catherine H Bowyer, Mr Mason's daughter, lived from 1946. She sold it to the Nashes in 1994. Added to and altered this is today's *The Boat House.*

The Gap, the only Sussex beach to gain a premier Tidy Britain award in 1993, was proposed in 1994 as one of the few beaches along this coast without protection under the WDC policy of 'managed retreat'. The Coastal Zone Management Plan's main premise is that erosion of cliffs at Birling Gap should continue unopposed, leading to the eventual loss of all the properties. The considerable local opposition to this approach remained resolute.

Wealden councillors expressed fears that there could be a tragedy if the NT did not speedily replace the Birling Gap steps. Anyone walking along the beach could find themselves trapped and the work would now not be completed for Easter.

Brian Johnson's *Sharlisa* at Birling Gap, the Seven Sisters forming a backcloth.
He would put out some 70 pots for shellfish and worked along all the way from the
lighthouse westwards as far as the River Cuckmere

In 1995 the NT started on the Gap car parks using the Horsefield spoil pile from the East Dean car park construction to remove potholes and resurface with a porous tarmac.

The next year the WDC agreed to a study into addressing the erosion at Birling Gap, but the steps were closed after they were damaged by falls in a January gale. Finally WDC took over the responsibility for the Birling Gap steps from the NT. Posford Duvivier, Engineers, designed an innovative set of steps, free standing and capable of being moved back as the cliff erodes, and officially opened September 1996 by Valerie Chidson, chairman of WDC.

The Birling Gap residents continued the fight for cliff protection and formed an association. NT stated that they care for a living landscape, but in the *Kent & East Sussex NT News* it was admitted that the cliffs between Beachy Head and Cuckmere Haven were one of the last stretches of unprotected coastline. The NT had come down against a revetment because it could only slow down the erosion - it is erosion which keeps the cliffs white and sheer - and may only speed up the process elsewhere. Most locals supported the case for a revetment; it is viable, and the NT has a duty to protect communities.

The Sussex Downs Conservation Board opposed the £450,000 revetment scheme to protect the cliffs at Birling Gap. 'The do-nothing approach clearly means that within 25 years the character of Birling Gap as a hamlet will be lost'. Later, WDC decided to take no action to halt the erosion of the cliffs at the Gap. Residents of the Gap said that the council's policy costs little and does nothing, but the council have the right to demolish any property it considers a danger without compensation. It was noted that the coastguard cottages at Cuckmere are protected even though they are in an Area of Outstanding Natural Beauty.

Storms caused cliff falls and Safety Boat committee member George Booth-Clibborn warned people, "There are dangerous overhangs so keep well away from the edge".

In 1997 over 6,000 signed a petition to save the cliffs at Birling Gap. Jean Fawbert of the cottages, was among those who pleaded for our heritage to be saved. In June three children were swept out to sea on a small 'li-lo' inflatable. They were rescued by the Birling Gap coastguard team, while the Newhaven lifeboat stood by. Graham Collins said that if the inflatable had flipped over they would not have lasted long. "It's a pity these craft are so readily available without parents realising the danger."

That year Birling Gap was again awarded a flag for its clean beaches and George Booth-Clibborn and Matthew Buzza retired from the coastguard. Certificates were presented at the *Birling Gap Hotel,* along with models of rescue equipment made by John Dann. Almost 400 years of coastguard service was represented.

The ED & F PC voted in 1998 to support the plan for a rock revetment at Birling Gap to protect the cliffs from excessive erosion, but there was no movement by the NT.

In the Reader's Digest Good Beach Guide of 1996 Birling Gap was branded as one of the cleanest in the country. The beach was also awarded a Blue Flag in 1999 for water quality presented by Angela Howard to local District Councillor, Brian West. The Gap had won the award every year since the scheme started in 1992.

Cecil Smith and Charlie Vine receiving 35 years' Coastguard Long Service medals with (right) John Dann and (centre) Peter Cross, District Officer at Shoreham. Cecil also has John's model of a 'holdfast', while Charlie has a 'luff' (blocks and ropes) reflecting aspects of their rescue work

On 12 June 2000 John Astbury, on behalf of the Maritime and Coastguard Agency, opened the new Coastguard Station at Birling Gap, built on the site of the old wooden Station office. The Gap will always carry its associations with the Coastguard, there was a full-time coastguard service there from 1831 to 1951, although always Local Supplementary Auxiliaries. Of the local Auxiliary Coastguard Service, John PR Dann and Richard E Worsell (now MBE) joined the Service on the same day, 14 August 1959, and both retired after 40 years' service. In 1981 Long Service medals for Coastguard duties were presented to Hubert Bailey, John Dann, Eric Pelling, and Richard Worsell. Over the years John and Richard, along with Ivan J Worsell, Cecil Dann, John Wicking and Don Ellis have been in charge at Birling Gap. Of the Worsell family, Ivan served from 1923-61, and George 1925-76; of the Danns, Bill served 1936-50, and Cecil (awarded BEM) 1937-1976.

Crowlink

Crowlink has always been regarded as part of the villages, and Crowlink Lane may have been of Roman origin running into Willingdon.

The hamlet, however, became famous for smuggling in the 1700s. It is easy to imagine that a scaleable cliff with an isolated hinterland was ideal for such a trade. So much so that 'Crowlink Geneva', or gin, was well regarded in London.

Crowlink hamlet nestling in a cusp of the Downs c.1960. The road from the right to the sea passes *The Granary, Crowlink House, North Barn* (central) with *Middle Barn* and *Little Barn* further along. On the right skyline are *Payne's Dene* and *Point House*

With changes in taxation and the introduction of the Coastguard Service, smuggling became unprofitable until the recent drug scene. The coastguards were removed from Crowlink Gap Bottom in 1921 - you can just make out the outlines of their cottages looking down from Flagstaff Point, and eroding away with each year. The Chief Coastguard's cottage, which was separate from the others, nearer the cliff edge, was knocked down in 1926, and part of the rubble was used for foundations at *Haligarth* in Gilbert's Drive. Most of what was left of the cottages went in the 1939-45 war.

In April 1911, Edith Nesbit (1858-1924) came to Crowlink. She was the author of *The Treasure Seekers, The Railway Children, The Enchanted Castle* and many other stories, mainly for children. She wrote to her brother, 'an old farmhouse near the sea - very lovely. Part is Tudor and part earlier. It used to be a smugglers' retreat'. She was exhilarated by the salt air, the wide sky and the sense of space, and stayed at Crowlink as often as she could during the next five years.

She wrote, 'The quiet is like a cool kind hand on your forehead'. In 1915 she worked it into one of her novels *The Incredible Honeymoon.* It begins in Jevington and ends with the happy pair installed in Crow's Nest Farm, *alias* Crowlink.

Agriculture was left to rot before and after the 1914-18 war. The Crowlink stockyard also suffered a disastrous fire destroying half a dozen stacks and barns, with no water supply the fire burned for nearly a week and the Crowlink farmer died in tragic fashion.

The land belonged to the Dean and Chapter of Chichester who sold it to a private individual and CT Haywood, an architect of Duke Street, London, became the developer of the Downs above the Seven Sisters. The projected estate had hundreds of plots and an 18-hole golf course. Before they could be saved from development a number of plots had been sold and are represented by houses on the Downs, such as *Crowlink Corner, Point House, Payne's Dene, Greywalls, Glebeland Cottage* and the fields adjacent to *Mary's Mead*.

In *Time* of 18 March 1926 the Revd AA Evans wrote to point out the threat to the South Downs. 'Footpaths across the Downs by the Seven Sisters are being fenced off. This Downland is of value not only to the nature lover, but to all interested in the vestiges of prehistory. Earthworks, barrows, trackways, lynchets and terrace traces of early agriculture are being lost.'

The plaque on the Sarsen stone commemorating the Crowlink purchase and WC Campbell's generosity

Bill Armiger said, "As part of the efforts to raise the money to save Crowlink from the threat of development East Dean and Friston held garden parties and whist drives, and quite a lot of money was raised."

The Mayor of Eastbourne broadcast an Appeal over the 2LO 'wireless' on 24 September 1926, relayed along the seafront, where groups of ladies paraded with collecting boxes.

In October 1926, for one of the many events organised to save the Crowlink valley, Alan Cobham (later Sir) landed his Moth aeroplane on the field opposite Belle Tout and the Horseshoe Plantation. Earlier that year he had flown from England to Australia and back. Coastguards and lifeboatmen formed a guard of honour, and arrangements were made to serve 8000 cups of tea and cakes, the whole of the proceeds going to the fund. A collection reached £300, and Mr Cobham announced that he had been given a cheque for £100 and he proceeded to auction articles donated by Rudyard Kipling and others for the fund.[2]

As soon as Crowlink was in danger of becoming a bungalow colony, the Society of Sussex Downsmen moved to avert the desecration of such a lovely coast rich in historical landmarks. Cuckmere remained owned by the Church Commissioners, Eastbourne Corporation was buying Beachy Head, and the sum required for the part in between was £17,000. Arthur Hornby Lewis of *Chaseley,* Eastbourne, purchased an option on Crowlink for £1700 having only seen it from the Newhaven ferry, and supporters included Lord

Before 1914 you could walk down, after a fashion, to the Crowlink beach

Winterton, Lord Curzon, Lord Leconfield, Eustace Perry, J Ramsey MacDonald, Henry Lawrence, RG Hall, Roland Gwynne, OL Mathias, AER Gilligan, John Galsworthy and, rather belatedly, the Bishop of Chichester.

Not enough money had been raised by the time to exchange contracts so WC Campbell advanced £5,000, providing the largest single contribution, about £7,000 in all.

Crowlink Farmhouse 1925, now *Crowlink House.*
In the 1980s Bernard Hepton, the actor, lived here

North Barn Holiday Fellowship Home in the 1930s.
Almost rebuilt in the 1990s by John Napier the stage director

Crowlink Coastguard Cottages at Gap Bottom between Flagstaff and Brass Points. The site was leased from Viscount Gage in October 1832 for a 'tout and battery', but these cottages were built *c.*1865. One RC family stationed here walked to church in Eastbourne most days. Only mounds of the foundations remain, and the site is part eroded

So on 8 February 1927 the land was conveyed from the London & Manchester Assurance Co., the Eastdean Estates (Eastbourne) Ltd., and Sarah Alice Haywood to WC Campbell. Crocker & Co. did the conveyancing free.

The final cost of the purchase was £16, 717 plus expenses of £1798, and at the end of 1927 the Preservation Fund just covered it with £18,580, about £1m today.

Crowlink farmhouse, cottages and nearby lands were retained by the vendor who wanted another £10,000 for them. CT Haywood acted for the syndicate.

A Sarsen stone was erected at Flagstaff Point by Viscount Gage of Firle to commemorate Campbell's generosity. It came from the Gage estate at *Alciston Court Farm,* and cost £28, George Morley of Brighton charged £10 to move it to the site, and it was in place June 1931. The plaque was by Hadlow's of Brighton in October 1932, the land having been given to the NT by Trustee WC Campbell on 29 September 1931.

Miggs Bailey recalls Crowlink life in the 1920s and 30s. Her parents, Frank and Lilian Ticehurst, lived at Crowlink, with her mother's parents, the Patchings. George Patching was the bailiff and farmer Gorringe would ride over from Exceat to give orders to him. [7]

Will Holter lodged with them and, with her father, broke in the horses. Her father rode with the Ringmer Hunt as First Whip, and helped to teach the Stutchbury children to ride. Her parents would walk down to the beach at Smuggler's Gap to pick limpets, which were used to thicken the soup.

The family went into Eastbourne once a week in a horse and cart, and on the way back called at the *Tally Ho.* Otherwise, they were self-sufficient in most ways. They went blackberrying and collected mushrooms, and her mother used to bake once a week, and once a year would make all their jam and pickles.

Her mother also did B&B in the days when the police regularly inspected Guest Registers. Marjorie Fass stayed on occasions before she lived at Friston, and asked whether a poor young married couple could be put up if she paid for them, and Mrs Ticehurst noted that the entry in the Register was 'Mr & Mrs F Bridge'.

Crowlink also had its share of campers. Alex Bransgrove attended a TA camp at Crowlink in 1932. "We marched from Seaford station carrying 20kg of equipment. It was a tented camp sited between the hamlet and the sea. All the officers brought their horses, and the Officers' Mess had a French chef. The adjutant was Brian Horrocks, later a Lieut-General and knighted. One evening the officers entertained 90 for dinner including Lachlan MacLachlan, the Mayor, and Eastbourne councillors."

Going back to 1900, John and Frida Wycliffe-Taylor were looking for a site to build a house, and bought a curiously-shaped piece of land from the Costobadies on the Jevington Road on the edge of Friston Green. About the same time James A Maitland, 'JAM', of *Friston Place* decided to hand over the estate to his son and build a dower house. [8] He thought that the Wycliffe-Taylor's plot was ideal and offered them in exchange his land on the south side of the A259, (up to Crowlink and the Church Commissioner's land) and, to sweeten the deal, he built a flint drive from the A259 to their new house.

That was how in 1900 JAM came to build *Little Friston* at the top of the hill just opposite the entrance to Old Willingdon Road [8], while the Wycliffe-Taylor's had *Gayles* across the A259 main road. Built of Sussex flint by Sir Edward Maufe, it was notable for the Ionic portico linking the house with the coachhouse.

They were the parents of Rosamund, who took part in the High Diving at the 1924 Olympic Games, when Harold Abrahams and Lord Burghley won gold medals. She practised by diving off the end of Eastbourne pier.

She married Mervyn Stutchbury in 1918 and had four sons and a daughter. The second son, David, born 1923, was a *Mosquito* pilot in the RAF in the 1939-45 war. He recalls that when he came home on leave his mother would meet him at Seaford station driving a petrol-sparing pony and trap, "I quickly felt far away from the high technology of war".

Gayles was used by the RAF early in the war, but after a fire most of the officers and NCOs lived in Friston [8]. The flat area of Ladder's Field was an Advanced Landing Ground for fighters and bombers in distress.[10] Left behind from the war is a Maycrete mess hut visible on the hill looking west from Crowlink; an Oerlikon gun emplacement, two pillboxes on the approach road and some concrete surfacings.

Its flying associations continued after the war, for over 1946-55 it was the home of the Friston Gliding Club. The club had 70 members, with local resident Marshal of the Royal Air Force, Sir John Salmond, as president. The club brought their hangar from Portslade where they had been before the war. Ray Brigden says, "With the thermals off the cliffs, it was eminently suitable for gliders; the only hazard was that the grazing cattle didn't always co-operate while you were landing. On a good day you could sit at 200ft above Beachy Head". Ray Brigden passed one of his glider endurance tests by staying over the airfield for five hours.

The gliders were a Granau Baby, a Kirby cadet, Kirby Tutor, an Olympia and later they had a two-seater, a Slingsby T21B. They were launched by winch, built by the Club as advised

View of the Seven Sisters cliffs from a glider riding the thermals between 1946 and 1955

by SG Stevens, who had been a member before the war.

In 1946 Arthur Pattenden farmed the whole piece, and the Club's payment to him for their first year's use of the land was a tin of chocolate biscuits. The land was part-owned by the Stutchburys, the Church Commissioners, the HRDC and the NT. When the Stutchburys bought part of the ecclesiastical land in 1949 the club was restricted to one runway and moved to Firle in March 1955.

Mary Vickery says that when the WarAg finished in 1952 [8] she and her husband had to move from *Friston Place* and came to *Gayles,* which at the time was "a lovely little self-contained community". Herbert Vickery started a single suckle herd, and "brought the farm up to scratch." Mrs Stutchbury lived in the main house, while the two Gatehouse Cottages had the Vickerys at 1, and Mr and Mrs Roy Marsh at 2. In December 1962 both cottages burnt down and the Vickerys and Marshes lost everything. The Vickerys went back to the flat over the garage, where Mr Funnell, the chauffeur, had been.

After Herbert's death in 1995, a farming friend of the Stutchburys replaced him, but it didn't work out, so Richard Gorringe took over. Now, apart from some Set Aside, it is all grazing, sheep and cattle.

In 1988 Steve Ovett, another Olympic athlete, and his wife Rachel, put *Gayles,* set in 4 acres and with five bedrooms, on the market at £650, 000. They had been there for two years and extensive alterations included an expensively equipped gymnasium on the upper floor.

It is likely that the site of Friston's mills was at the entrance to *Gayles* on the Seaford (A259) road. Rosamund Stutchbury wrote that there were no buildings there before *Gayles* and yet three paths, now hidden by trees, from Friston and West Dean join up at that point. The last mill on that site blew down in 1824. [8]

From Friston pond further along Crowlink Lane is *Glebeland Cottage,* which was owned by a Bruford, one of the jewellers' family. In 1937 Albert Bruford thought that the cement pedestal commemorating the Downs Purchase was inadequate and offered two guineas [£2.10] towards the cost of repair. Prior's of Eastbourne estimated £8 for flint work and completed it in August 1938. Albert thought the result was excellent.

Leonard Stubley and his wife Mabel first came to East Dean when they stayed for weekends at the Holiday Fellowship Home, North Barn, Crowlink in the 1950s, when Charles Sharp was in charge. It was basic accommodation, half the ground floor of the North Barn was the dining room, with trestle tables, the other half was a sitting room, used for dancing, with the chairs moved against the wall. The food was good, but no alcohol was allowed. In the two side sections there were bedrooms on the top floor and showers/lavatories on the lower floor. A Service was held every Sunday. The Stubleys so enjoyed the area that they bought *Glebeland Cottage* from the Brufords in 1958.

'The Holiday Fellowship at Crowlink held an At Home in November 1959 - an opportunity to see this historic building scheduled as an ancient monument, and have tea.'

Middle Templer Alex Kellar lived at *Grey Walls.* During the war he was in the War Office and reached the rank of Brigadier in Intelligence working in both MI5 and MI6, becoming Director of the Political Division MI5. He was a buddy of Lord Shawcross, Lord George-Brown and Lord Healey, but thought strongly (and strangely) that he should have done better than a CMG (wanting a Kindly Call Me God) and died a disappointed man.

The Misses Twigg and Woods (who had a spell at *Crowlink End*) divided *Point House* into two flats, one reached by an outside staircase. Edward and Molly Simmons bought the lot and added a kitchen on the lane end. Since well restored, it has a lovely view.

Payne's Dene, where Graham Mead lived until his death in 2003, was built by Mrs J Batten, who was Mrs Simpson's aunt, and started the East Dean WI in 1929. She was followed by Dr and Mrs Reginald Simpson, he had been Chief Medical Officer at County Hall, London. Their daughter, Jean, was a director of Social Services at Lewes and became involved in the Maria Caldwell abuse case, which she took very much to heart, and died of a massive stroke shortly afterwards in 1978.

Mrs Marie Octavie Haworth-Booth, the French widow of an RN Commander, lived at *The Granary* for many years. This was next door to *Crowlink House* where lived Mr WG Haywood whose family owned most of the hamlet at one time. He did up cottages for letting out and, when indicated, sold a property or two. Mrs Booth had a pile of family silver but wanted that for her niece and after some years of widowhood was finding matters a little tight. A heavy smoker she got to know the Stubleys by asking them to buy cigarettes for her at *The Outlook* on their walks. She mentioned her little difficulty and Leonard Stubley said he would buy *The Granary* for her to purchase an annuity while allowing her to live there. Being a proud lady she asked that their arrangement should not be revealed.

Mr Stubley went to Scotland on business and sold *Glebelands Cottage.* Meanwhile Mr Haywood cultivated the company of Mrs Haworth-Booth allegedly with the aim of buying her house. In 1970 after her death the Stubley's moved into *The Granary.* When Haywood discovered that the Stubley's owned it "he set out to force us out of *The Granary.* He erected new fences encroaching on our land, built a wall obstructing our back gate, would yell abuse at Mabel in the garden and force our car onto the verge if he met us when driving along Crowlink Lane. This was despite two court appearances which found against him awarding damages to the Stubleys, and one Judge told Mr Haywood that if such actions occurred again he would be sent down." Even so the Stubleys were not happy there and it was especially unpleasant for Mrs Stubley who "was subjected to glares all the day long", so they sold *The Granary* and rented 2 *Crowlink Cottages* owned by Dr Joe Chamberlain. As it happens, Mr Haywood and his wife Winifred died shortly afterwards in 1978. A potter, named Perry, was subsequently in *The Granary.* The Stubleys bought 19 The Ridgeway from Martha Barr until Alex Kellar died in 1982 when they moved into *Grey*

Walls. Leonard, who spent most of his last years cruising, only left in 2005 when in his ninetieth year.

Roger and Mary Luscombe (née Spillane) followed Bernard Hepton at *Crowlink House.* She was an Image Consultant, who naturally believed that women should spend 10% of their income on their appearance, and she advised Ian Gow MP when he made the first TV broadcast from the House of Commons. Mark Wigglesworth, Director of the Welsh NO, was in 1 Crowlink Cottages, and the jeweller Cynthia Cousins in No. 2.

Horace and Olive Rew were at *Crowlink End.* Olive Rew, daughter of Sir Frederic and Lady Hallett, died in 1959 at 74. Unfortunately, a housebound invalid for the last decade of her life, but when the hunt came past the Master of Hounds would detach himself, draw rein and doff his hat opposite her cottage window. Horace Rew died at Crowlink after the hamlet had been cut off by the snow. [11]

In the 1962-3 winter it was the constant wind that blew the snowdrifts into the lane and kept it blocked from Boxing Day. "There weren't so many cars then, but the wise ones moved theirs up to the top of Crowlink Lane before the snow blocked it. You couldn't get down Crowlink Lane until Easter 1963." Mary Vickery recalls how eerie it was with no traffic on the A259 and just the snowy tracks of animals.

The Hon. Mildred Leith ("call me Bay") had *Barn Cottage,* Crowlink, from about 1960. Her mother died at her birth. Her brother was Lord Burgh, and the family had property in the Isle of Wight and Aberdeenshire, Algernon Swinburne was related, and in December 1894 he published a poem *To a Baby Kinswoman* dedicated to 'Bay'. She became an accomplished horsewoman and aviatrix.

In 1929 she set up Car and Air departments for Universal Aunts; and she would personally deliver, as ordered, a Gipsy Moth aeroplane to overseas clients. This was when a new Moth two-seater cost £600, and £350 second-hand. After war service, she became Managing Director (1947), and Chairman (1952) of the Universal Aunts Company until 1973. She had retired to Crowlink in 1971. Adrian and Gill Hamilton who took over the cottage (and *Little Barn*) said that they found a flying jacket there.

Farmer Richard Gorringe with his wife Judith and their children were at *Middle Barn* until their flint house along the Jevington Road was ready.

A view of the hamlet of Crowlink in 1950 from the site of the present National Trust car park. It nestles in the Downs with the English Channel in the distance

A Crowlink Road Association meeting in 1969 at the Holiday Fellowship Home had Lt-Col Edward Simmons in the chair, and the Hon. Mildred Leith reporting on the previous year's activities, 'The 3/4-mile lane, a public bridal path in existence prior to 1836, is considered by the ESCC to be in a fit state so they provide no money. The road has been used for years not only by the residents but also the general public and services. The upkeep is supported by residents' subscriptions with some help from the NT and the tenant farmer.'

A number of residents objected to a proposed swimming pool at North Barn and the application was refused. At least in 1981 the Crowlink Road cattle grid was renewed. The following year the 350 acres of Crowlink valley, with a cliff frontage of 1½ miles, were merged with Birling Gap and Seven Sisters by the NT.

In January 1984 Judith Norris, NT Agent, said she would submit plans for permission to move the Crowlink car park into a small hollow the other side of the cattle grid because, 'NT officers thought that the cars could be seen on the skyline and were therefore an eyesore'. The WDC approved the application, but the PC wrote to the NT expressing the hope that the NT would have a change of heart.

After a storm of protest by residents, 'insensitive', 'we can see no reason for removing the car park when money is needed for other projects', the NT decided to defer the car park planning application. Sadly, during 1993, a dozen thefts were reported at this car park.

The NT created another and greater gaff locally after vandals threw the seat at Flagstaff Point over the cliff in 1990. When local residents Mr & Mrs Hoya donated a similar replacement seat, the NT considered that it was, 'not suitable in design or in keeping with the NT open space policy'. Again, there was a massive protest, with the local protesters all staunch NT supporters, until finally, 'The NT agrees to accept the seat donated for Flagstaff Point because of the local feeling even though they prefer benches in rural sites'.

More to the point, the NT stated that grazing and walking on the Downs meant that rare flora were under threat. They were working to control the access for a trial period, and

'this should help to prevent erosion of the steeper slopes at Crowlink'.

Understandably, Sarah Mann was welcomed as the new South Downs Countryside manager for the NT in 1996.

A field archaeology unit (left), under Chris Greatorex, excavated a Bronze Age burial mound just feet from the cliff edge at Brass Point, near Crowlink, in May 1998. It had not been destroyed by treasure hunters, had a flint covering and beneath there was evidence of burials, cremations and pottery, dated between 3500 and 4000 years ago.

In 2000 the PC discussed the retrospective application for planning permission to redevelop *North Barn,* Crowlink, the old Holiday Fellowship Home. Normally they opposed such applications, but the mood was that if refused the site could become derelict.

In brief, to bring the story up to date, John Napier, the famous designer of theatrical sets, such as *Cats,* redesigned *North Barn* in a £1m plus refit, and re-surfaced the ¾-mile Crowlink Lane. In 1995 the NT had agreed to maintain the surface of Crowlink Lane and in 2005 the NT re-surfaced Crowlink Lane from the pond to a cattle grid (renewed) by the Crowlink NT car park where Pay and Display was installed.

Cliff erosion at Flagstaff Point in 2005 alerted the NT to move with alacrity and remove the 1990 seat, but bench seats were provided around the Sarsen stone to comfort tired backs.

6. East Dean and Friston Village School

In the Middle Ages education was almost entirely in the hands of the church, schools being attached to cathedrals and religious houses. In the towns any intelligent child might obtain an education and even graduate, but in rural communities children had little opportunity except that offered by the parish priest.

The priest was required to give instruction, although what rudiments he gave was a variable process. He taught from memory for he had no books; most priests would not possess a Bible. With the Renaissance came printing and the translation of the Bible into English and the new schools founded under Edward VI.

If we go by similar Sussex villages some instruction would have been given in the early 1700s, but the first reference to an East Dean school was in 1779 when the Revd Richard Michell ran a penny-a-week school, and 1789 he advertised in the *Sussex Weekly Advertiser* about his boarding school at East Dean. This enterprise probably finished with him. [2]

In 1814 the parish overseers paid Anne Colwell for 'schooling' at Friston. An agricultural school was started by Mrs Mary Ann Gilbert *c.*1825. The smaller children were taught in *Little Lane Cottage*. [7]

From 1833 the government funded the National Society to provide schools 'for promoting the education of the poor in the principles of the Established Church'.

In 1842 *The Times* reported that East Dean had a school where the master rented four acres of land at forty shillings per acre, besides the rent of his house and cow-lodge. Jesse Piper was probably the schoolmaster, assisted by a 12-year-old boy from Hailsham workhouse. Piper was the village shoemaker, whose shop was in one of the cottages by the Church Green that disappeared long ago. He only opened the shop outside school hours.

We know little about this school, but if it resembled others, the pupils were charged a penny a week for which they were taught reading, writing, accounts, the church catechism, collects and psalmody in the morning, and from two to five o'clock they worked cultivating the schoolmaster's land. In 1848 a Mrs Bradford had a school in her cottage which might be the same one.

In the late 1840s a school house was built on the site of the present Old School House, largely by the generosity of Miss Anne Gilbert of the Davies Gilbert family who in 1851 provided a trust of £500 of 2$^{1}/_{2}$% Consols. The Vicar and the Bishop of Chichester were among the trustees. This Davies Gilbert Trust was the main source of funding until 1896, and the Davies Gilberts took an interest in the school and would inspect it on occasions.

The only surviving reference to the school dates from 1854 when Mrs Bradford's wages were £2 a month, and the sum of three shillings [15p] was spent on books.

Following the Elementary Education Act of 1870 every school was inspected and, after 1872, had to keep a log book, with the school grant and the teacher's pay dependent on the numbers attending and the standards reached. In 1874 the Education Commissioners gave their blessing to East Dean if it could be made more efficient and better desks provided.

The parents had to pay fees of 1/6d [7$^{1}/_{2}$p] a quarter, increased to 2/- [10p] if attendance was irregular. Money prizes from 1/- to 10/- [50p] were, however, available for good attendance. Fees were received in East Dean, but in 1874 there was a complaint from the Vicar, the Revd George Pinnock, about the lack of funds. [2]

We have the school log books from 1875 to 1964 for reference, which show that the years from 1875 to 1890 were marked by a succession of schoolmasters who struggled to impart the 'three Rs' and the catechism into ignorant pupils with uncooperative parents, while striving to overcome the inadequate school house, the deficiency of slates and books, and the long absences of the pupils from illness or being kept away to work on the farms.

The first master was Richard Saunders who, according to the Vicar, 'took up his work on 18 January 1875'. Saunders' first report runs, 'School badly attended during the week on account of the stormy weather and the prevalence of whooping cough'. In February he notes that 'Mr Carew Gilbert, owner of the school, came to inspect it'. That month Saunders' assessment of his pupils was, 'found the children obedient and quick, but very backward'.

The children came from as far away as *Half Way Cottages* and the Crowlink Coastguard Station, and Mr Saunders cited the bad weather as the main reason for not attending, 'but I do not think this is a proper excuse especially from those who live close to the school'.

In June he noted that 'John Weaver and William Pope, both aged seven, left to be shepherd boys, neither can read nor write'. Later that month he complained of children staying away to collect flowers for May Day garlands.

By April 1875 with 65 on the Register, never more than 56 were present. Perhaps understandable when in the December, Mr Saunders records that 'many school window panes were broken, and the roof leaks'. The heating was also inadequate; there is a note, 'no wood, the fire being lit by sticks brought in by the children'. After a heavy snowfall only 22 turned up and the school closed for two days.

On a dull December day with the poor lighting - no gas or electricity, of course - the children would complain of being unable to read by three in the afternoon. To help them and those coming from a distance, Mr Saunders commenced the winter afternoon school at 1.30pm so as to close 30 minutes earlier. Similar measures went on until the 1950s.

From 1876 school attendance was compulsory for under 8-year-olds. That year Mr Saunders wrote, 'the people of East Dean seem to care little about what progress their children make and keep them at home on the least excuse'. On 27 June he 'received a very impertinent message from one of them in answer to my question on irregularity of the children's attendance'.

In the course of that year he commented that 'the village children require double the teaching in every subject compared with the Coastguard and Lighthouse children'. He found it almost impossible to teach Geography, 'few children know anything beyond the village'.

Mr Saunders punished a boy on 15 February 1877 for playing truant, 'being the first case since May 1875'. One day in September only 43 attended with the absentees helping their parents gleaning in the fields after the harvest. Once a farmer's field was empty gleaning was the right of all and sundry and if a family picked up all the corn possible they would have enough to keep them in loaves for months.

Mr Saunders had enough and resigned in July 1878 to be replaced by Robert Bagworth.

In December four children were absent with scarlet fever and others with chilblains, commonly found in cold weather with inadequate heating. On 25 January the next year one of the infant boys died of scarlet fever.

By now the average attendance was 48. The subjects taught included the catechism, grammar, geography, singing (such songs as *My Father My Mother, Oh, I'm a British Boy, 'Tis the voice of the Sluggard*), reading, spelling, and arithmetic - although the HMI [Her Majesty's Inspectors] were unanimous that arithmetic was poorly taught. The pupils learnt five lines a day of Goldsmith's *The Deserted Village;* the rivers that flow into the German Ocean [North Sea]; how to write a letter; needlework (girls only); and they had object lessons on subjects such as Potatoes, Copper, Matches, and Sealing Wax.

All the teaching was in one room, the teacher's wife usually taught needlework, and monitoresses were used to assist the teacher by taking the Infants' class. The first one recorded was Lucy Bradford, the daughter of James and Mary Bradford (he was the farm bailiff at *Birling Farm*) of whom it was said, 'she is by no means the eldest, but is certainly the most intelligent', and she 'succeeded fairly well in keeping order'. Edith Ward is next mentioned as monitoress in February 1879 and when her family left the village that summer she was succeeded by Agnes Barnby (from the lighthouse), with 12-year-old Elizabeth Blaber starting in 1881; her mother Caroline was a servant at the vicarage. Each did from six to eighteen months. They were always girls, not surprising for they mature before boys, and as Mr Saunders wrote in 1877, 'only five boys over seven at the school, for they are put to work as soon as possible'. Boys' jobs were shepherding, dairying, gardening and a few others such as helping in Dennett's shop, the wheelwright's shop or the Forge.

Monitoresses were pupils about a year older than the class they were taking. They taught what the teacher told them, repeating the lesson until every child had read the piece of text or performed the calculation. Nationally, the position was gradually formalised so that at 14 they could go on to become pupil teachers, when they were paid £5-£10 a year. After five years of satisfactory work they could go to a teachers' training school. It was one of the few choices for girls other than domestic service.

The school was inspected twice a year: a Diocesan and a HMI one. The Diocesan exam usually consisted in testing the pupils' knowledge of the Bible, recitations and singing, with a half-day holiday in the afternoon. A typical HMI Report was that of 14 April 1880. 'The children were orderly. General results of examinations fairly satisfactory, arithmetic poor. A deduction of one-tenth of the grant is made for faults of instruction in arithmetic.'

At the beginning of 1881 the school leaving age was raised to ten. On the afternoon of 24 February the children attended the Induction of the new Vicar the Revd J Walter Parrington (the Revd George Pinnock having died in November 1880). Parrington played a much greater part in the running of the school than his predecessor, taking the Upper Standard in Religious Instruction once a week and visiting the school on Tuesdays, Wednesdays and Thursdays and Mrs Parrington visited on Fridays.

The HMI Report in 1882 was that, while there had been some improvement, the full grant should be withheld for the fourth consecutive year of Robert Bagworth's time in post. On 28 November Mr Bagworth recorded, 'the Revd JW Parrington visited and brought me a note to resign charge of the school after the next inspection'. The following March Robert Bagworth duly went and on 2 April 1883 Mr CW Oates took charge of the school.

The new master found 'the children very backward in all subjects, especially arithmetic. The order was bad but improved in the first week.' He records that he punished several children for being careless, and in June he 'had to punish several children for disobedience this week'. The next month the Revd Parrington noted that 'the children do their homework much better than before'.

The school reopened after the summer holiday with a roll call of 71. In the November Mr Oates introduced a fortnightly examination for the children. When one mother 'insulted me saying that she would not allow her children to be punished' he sent all four of her children home. Two weeks later he wrote, 'The mother promised to allow her children to be corrected and kept in when they deserved it, they therefore came back to school'.

In February 1884 the HMI reported Mr Oates had 'brought about a wonderful improvement in the children's work and behaviour. An Excellent Merit Grant is recommended and a trained assistant should be appointed.' Sadly, in May, Mr Oates reported that he was not well and had to be assisted. Over July and August he was too unwell to complete the reports and he died on 13 September of tuberculosis [TB].

Over the summer the school was enlarged, a teacher's house bought and the fees raised.

During and after Mr Oates' illness Richard Saunders and JC Tippers acted as locums until Frederick Whittaker was appointed in December 1884. The next month he examined the whole school to find it in a backward state: 'The children of Standard IV have no idea of Weights and Measures. Children of Standard III are unable to do a problem. The Reading and Spelling throughout the school is bad and several in the Infants are over seven.'

In his report the HMI regretted 'to hear of the death of Mr Oates the excellent master who had been in charge. The attainments of the children have greatly suffered since through the necessary changes of teacher. Mr Whittaker knows the deficiencies and with help should overcome them'. There was a mention that another classroom and a playground would be a boon to the school. The HMI recommended that the Good Merit Grant be continued, 'although the percentage of passes is very low this year. Infants are very backward.'

In May 1885 the Revd Parrington read to the school an Education Department circular *Stone Throwing at Telegraph Wires.* He said, "Much injury is caused by schoolboys who do not think they are doing any harm, and are unaware that they are liable to a flogging."

East Dean School 1883. L to R, back row: Albert and Jesse Carey (of Crowlink Farm). Next row: Mrs Oates (two tiny Oates in front), the two boys to her right have not been identified, the girls in white pinafores are Annie Fuller, Emily Barnby (of Belle Tout lighthouse), Alice Akehurst, Cissie Phillips, Emily and Annie Fowler, Emily Collins, and behind Alice Harris, the two boys in front of Mr Oates are Albert Duly and Walter Fuller. Sitting rows: the first girl in white is May Duly, just behind her is another Barnby, Ada Fowler and the last girl in white Sally Hills. The three boys sitting in front: Ted Hilton, Harry Breach, and Albert Breach

After the holidays Mrs Fowler and Mrs Hills sent the teacher letters expressing their strong objection to homework for their children. Perhaps tongue in cheek, Mr Whittaker 'taught the whole school a new song *A boy's best friend is his mother'*.

On Bonfire Day 1885 the Revd JW Parrington gave an address on *The Burning of Effigies* pointing out how easy it was for poor people to spend money on useless fireworks.

Before antibiotics and vaccines, illnesses played havoc with the children's schooling. Sarah Hills was absent on 22 February 1886 having been taken seriously ill. 'The doctor stated the complaint is typhoid fever.' The next day Mrs Pope informed the Headmaster that 'the doctor had told her to keep Herbert at home because of Consumption' [TB].

Over the year Lottie Walters had an absence of more than three months, Ada Fowler more than four months, and Elizabeth Allery made only 108 attendances out of a possible 435 over the year. There were, however, some children with more than 350 attendances, sufficient for the Revd Parrington to return a proportion of their fees. The HMI was not enamoured of such "Performance Related Pay", in 1889 he wrote, 'Rewards for good attendance cannot be regarded as legitimate expenditure. It is not justifiable to reward the performance of a duty imposed by law. If the rewards are money such payments are returned fees and should not appear on the expenditure side.'

When the school reopened in 1887 Mr Whittaker reported that a boy of eleven, Thomas Wicks, was admitted 'who scarcely knew his letters'.

On 19 May the children had their usual day's holiday after a Service for Ascension Day. A week later they had a half-day holiday because the Village Club was being held in the school, and on 21 June the school was closed for the Queen's Golden Jubilee. Whether it had anything to do with it or not, Fred Blaber was off with a broken arm the following day.

Mrs Parrington visited on 7 December and examined the needlework. She was very satisfied with the work except for 'that of the two eldest girls, Mary Phillips and Annie Barnby, which she thought had been done carelessly'.

In June 1888 Mrs Whittaker, the headmaster's wife who took Needlework, was unwell so 'Mifs [sic] King took the subject' for a week.

The Fisher family left the village on 22 October after refusing to pay the 2½p school fee for their daughter Gertrude. Two days later a portion of the ceiling fell down so the school was closed. It opened the next day because 'there was little fear of any more ceiling falling'. The following afternoon the school was closed while the ceiling was repaired. Ceiling moments were, however, a regular if infrequent, event. On the morning of 18 September 1900 a large piece of plaster fell from the ceiling. Nobody seems to have been hurt. In 1914 Mr Drew knocked down a piece of ceiling to prevent it falling on the children, and 'A large piece of plaster fell from the ceiling of the classroom on 6 July, luckily no children hurt.'

Over 1889 an average of 75 were present. The numbers fluctuated widely, in November Florence, Maude and Nellie Henderson left on their coastguard father's move to Brighton.

William Akehurst drowned in Densher Pond on 4 December. 'He was a very intelligent boy of the V Standard and the sad circumstance has thrown a gloom over the whole parish. The poor boy returning from East Dean had evidently gone on the pond to slide.'

The children were perhaps cheered up when a week later the Revd Parrington visited and accompanied the singing of Christmas Carols on his flute.

The school leaving age was raised to 12 in 1890 and on the first day back, 6 January, 'a number of pupils were punished for coming late'.

The next visitation was influenza. Attendances were poor, and Emily Dann, Rosetta Dann, Louisa Dann, Ada Potter, Mary Lawrence and Charles Potter were absent for two whole weeks in January, John Wooller was absent until the end of February. On 3 February the headmaster 'felt so ill' that after consulting the Revd JW Parrington he closed the school. It didn't reopen until a week later when his first comment is, 'A great number of children at home with influenza'. Mrs Whittaker also had it and the epidemic went on into March. In May the headmaster gave three-month notice to the managers.

The school closed on 31 July for the Harvest holiday and on reopening on 8 September it had a new headmaster, Edward C Drew, Certificated Teacher of the Second Class (Exeter 1884-5), with Mrs Eliza H Drew, also a Certificated Teacher, as his assistant. The next day he wrote, 'I find the children in a very backward state. Apart from reading books and a few slates there are no materials to work with'.

He soon got matters moving for a week later, 'Received slates and other apparatus from the National Society's Depository. Emily Duly agreed to sweep the school room and light fires when required.' And a week later, 'A new time table was being tested'.

He kept order too, 'Owing to a little rain many children made an excuse to stay away the whole day on 25 October, when they returned they were severely reprimanded'.

Two days later Alice Moore, aged nine, was admitted, 'since leaving the school four years ago she has been a patient at the Eastbourne Hospital for a disordered leg. She was unable to tell her letters'.

Near the end of October a stove was placed in position and fires commenced. 'Being

129

the Patronal Festival of St Simon and St Jude a half-day holiday was given to the children.'

Mr Waghorn, the Inspector of Nuisances, having inspected 'the offices', left two canisters of disinfecting powder 'which were very acceptable'. Most understandable when you consider that over 70 children, aged from four to twelve, were using closets at the back of the school yard, without any running water. The next day Mrs Key of *Birling House* saw the work of the children and gave drawing books, pens and pencils to the boys, thimbles to the girls and pennies to the infants. Mr Luther Hills repaired all the desks and cleaned the stove pipe and towards the end of the month the school received 1 ton of coal and 12 chaldrons[1] of coke. A new cord was put to the clock 'which now works better'.

Fred Underhay missed all this activity being off school having crushed his fingers.

On 21 January 1891 a half-day holiday was given to attend a tea provided by Mrs Grace Davies Gilbert. Over the month eleven children from coastguard families left because their parents had been transferred. 'This represented a considerable number in this school'.

On 10 March 'when there was a great gale and snowstorm in the night' only 18 children turned up. The next day children were not able to get to the school and the HMI Inspection was postponed. It must have been some storm for there is a note that 'Amy and Henry Discombe, whose father perished in the gale, left the neighbourhood shortly afterwards'. When the HMI inspection finally took place on 1 April there was a satisfactory report and a grant of £45.12$^1/_2$ was agreed.

In April 'Mrs Grace Davies Gilbert, the Vicar and Mrs Parrington heard the children sing and expressed themselves pleased with their attainments'.

That month Mr Drew set out the level of work. Standard II were taught multiplication up to 100; Standard III long division; IV multiplication of money; and V simple practice.

For two days in May Mrs Drew was 'absent by doctor's advice suffering from a severe cold and relaxed throat'. Many children were absent on 17 June, but this was 'to witness military operations at Eastbourne and to act as bearers at a child's funeral'. Children often acted as bearers for a child's coffin; e.g. on 11 December 1899 'Several boys were absent to carry a small coffin at a funeral. Some were late back through sliding on the ice'.

From the Annual Diocesan inspection: 'The children sing nicely, their written work on the whole good, spelling capable of improvement. They have done much better than last year and under the careful teaching of Mr & Mrs Drew a higher standard will be obtained.'

Rose Gutsell, age 9, admitted was 'unable to name her letters. The father, a labourer at *Friston Place Farm,* has changed residencies many times and neglected her schooling'.

In September Mr Drew reported Clara Armiger for absences, but 'Mr Chapman says that as she lives more than two miles from the school that is a reasonable excuse'.

In December Mr Drew punished Charlie Duly for telling a lie, 'it was not the first time'.

On 21 March 1892 the school was closed because of the re-opening of Friston Church, and confirmations at East Dean Church.

On 25 May two boys were caned for 'visiting a Steam Plough', and three for 'gathering flowers and got late for school'. Mr Drew on 13 October wrote, 'five big boys, William Akern, Arthur Calloway, Henry Calloway, Frank Horton, and Nelson Breach were caned for noisy behaviour in the dinner time'. No doubt examples of the discipline for which the HMI had 'a word of praise' in his Report.

On 25 January 1893 Arithmetic and Dictation was given to Standards I, II, III, IV, V and VI 'instead of Needlework as a punishment for Drawing exceedingly carelessly'.

It seemed to work for the comment after the Drawing Examination in February was, 'the school is again awarded the Excellent Grant. The work is very accurate but might be done much neater'. Mr G Gardner's HMI Report included, 'Children continue in good order and they have passed a creditable examination. Praise is due to Mrs Drew for the condition of the infants' class which is under great disadvantages of accommodation. Grant £57.15'.

Indubitably to general relief, in April a new slab was placed over the cesspool of the school 'offices'.

Outbreaks of severe childhood illnesses continued to interfere with schooling. In May an order was received from Dr F Marsden to exempt the children of Henry Moore of Crowlink on account of a case of diphtheria in the family. The Moores had no sooner been allowed to return to school (their home having been 'thoroughly disinfected'), than the Danns of *Gore Cottage* went down 'through measles', which was so widespread in the village that in mid-June Dr EF Fussell, Medical Officer of Health [MOH] for East Sussex, and Mr Waghorn, visited the school. The next day Dr Marsden reported that one case at the Danns had scarlet fever not measles, whereupon, by order of Dr Fussell the school was closed for three weeks. During this time the schoolroom was thoroughly whitewashed and scrubbed with disinfectants. It did not reopen until July.

Some children with ringworm [a florid fungal infection of the scalp associated with poor hygiene and unsanitary home conditions] were absent for over a year. In 1901 'Jesse Gay returned after one year seven months', and cases occurred into 1906, while measles, impetigo (infected skin), mumps and chickenpox caused school closures into the late 1920s.

When the school did reopen after the 1893 holidays only 61 were present out of 74. Not missing from illness, but again, 'children busy gleaning in the fields.' Only another week on, 'a few of the boys in the Upper Class stayed at home to assist their fathers in preparation to attend Lewes Sheep Fair'.

The Infants were now screened off by a rod and curtain, which Mr Drew greeted, 'This is a great improvement and aids the discipline and working of the whole school.'

'On 4 December Division I commenced studying the Geography of British North America' [or Canada as it is known today].

In the April of 1894 the cesspools of the school closets were emptied by Mr French. Most needed for in December Mr Drew was writing, 'During the dull and damp weather of the last few days the air in this room has become very foul, even though the windows, on a level with the children's heads, have been opened. This state of affairs could have serious effects on the health of teachers and scholars'.

At the end of January 1895 Mr Drew was absent with neuralgia. Not unreasonable for on some days the thermometer registered 27°F [-2C] before the school fire was lit. On the 8th February he reports: 'In order to try and make the room warm before the children arrive the fire has been lighted by myself. When the fire was lit at 8am the temperature was 22°F [-4C], at 10am it had only risen to 32°F'[0C].

Child abuse was not unknown then, if retribution was speedier. 'On 14 February John Jordan was examined by Inspector Akehurst NSPCC, PC Barton and the vicar, Revd Parrington, as his body showed marks of his parents' ill-usage. The lad was taken to Eastbourne.' By 28 February the Magistrates had tried John's parents, found them guilty of cruelty, and sentenced the father to a fortnight's imprisonment.

The next year 'an officer of the NSPCC called at the school to examine Horace Whymark, an imbecile lad of nine, whose father had ill-used him by unduly thrashing him'.

The school re-opened after the harvest holiday. 'Owing to the Eastbourne Regatta only 51 present.' In other words over a third away. On 18 September they had a half-day holiday 'for the cricket match', and the next day a whole day's holiday for the Annual School Treat. When you add that the children were allowed absences for weddings and funerals and Annual Club Days, and a girl would have a month off to nurse an ill mother, (Emily Martin returned after a 15 months' visit to an aunt), and all had a week's holiday for Whitsun, and that Bettie and Ernest Moore of Crowlink (Scarlet Fever) and the Bonifaces of Peak Dean (Chickenpox) had been isolated since July, and in early October some children were kept at home as a consequence of a sale at Friston Farm, you can well understand how some 'pupils' were having difficulty with their three Rs - Reading, Writing and Arithmetic.

On 9 October it was 'a very dull morning, so dark in the room (some decades before oil lamps and candles went) that it is scarcely possible to see the furthest children or for them to see their work. Lesson suspended and singing taken instead.' A similar situation arose on 28 November, 'So dark in the room that at 2.40pm ordinary lessons stopped and singing taken. Dismissed at 3.40pm to enable all to get home before dark.'

In 1896 the school became a Church School conveyed to the Vicar and Bishop of Chichester under the aegis of the Anglican National Society. At the end of March John Best, who had been caned in December for refusing to copy a dictation and 'who evidently is encouraged in his rebellion by his father, refused to write an imposition of 24 words when detained and showed most violent and uncontrollable temper. He was sent home'. Mr Drew won, however, for on the next day, 'John Best being penitent and promising future obedience was admitted after writing his task and giving an ample apology'.

The HMI Report suspended the Infant Class because of the inadequate accommodation, this stimulated the building of a new infants' room in November. The Christmas holidays were extended until 27 January 1897 'because of incomplete building operations'. When the Infants occupied the New Classroom Mr Drew wrote, 'This is simply an inexpressible change for the better'. The dimensions of the classroom were 21$\frac{1}{2}$ x 17ft [6.5 x 5m], height 15ft, planned to accommodate 46 infants.

The weather had its moments those days too. While the children were able to take their recreation out of doors on the morning of 22 February in lovely weather, on 3 March 'a severe gale raged during the morning, only 46 present. The Revd JW Parrington even had to abandon the Ash Wednesday Service'.

From 18 June 1897 the school closed for a week for the Queen's Diamond Jubilee Celebrations.[2] Not that a holiday did George Martin much good for he didn't return from the workhouse infirmary until 5 July after being bitten by a viper during Jubilee Week.

Just before the school closed for four weeks summer holidays, the pupils had their first monthly examination on paper. 'The strangeness of paper compared with slates leaves much to be desired to Standard III.'

Reopened in 1898 'with one new child Rose Glover, age 10, unable to write and say her letters. Dr Marsden asked me to report after a fair trial if the child was unable to learn as stated by her parents'.

On St Valentine's Day Mr Drew wrote, 'I am grieved to report three cases of indecent writing on the walls of the school porch. These are the first while I have been at the school. I have tried by every means to find the cowardly culprit without success.'

On 14 March the Revd Parrington applied to the Lord Bishop of Chichester to take over two unused cottages nearby for use as school buildings or as a residence for teachers.

Mrs Drew gave birth to a son on 16 May; 'her duties were discharged by the late ex-Standard VII girl Eliz. Leaf, and the Sewing was taken by Miss Mitchell'. Understandably, there were a few days over the next year when Mrs Drew failed to attend.

On 10 June the White family left the parish. 'They were the brightest and most intelligent children I have had here and the eldest always played the organ for the musical exercise of both rooms. In their place arrived three Fogartys, the boy rather stupid - in his father's opinion as well - and I find them all the very antithesis of the Whites.'

In October the Revd JW Parrington visited bringing with him as a loan several ancient British stone implements. 'These were placed in the School Museum and formed the object of the afternoon's lesson.' That month 'chintz curtains were placed to the schoolroom windows'; none before, presumably.

In December 1898 Carew Davies Gilbert, now a school Trustee, inspected the school.

Her Majesty's Inspector wrote for 1899, 'A large proportion of the children have been admitted during the year and after allowance for this drawback the Higher Principal Grant appears to be deserved. The infants are properly cared for.'

Mr Drew had one of his rare absences in late April 'In consequence of a severe sore throat I have been unable to give any oral lessons this week.' The next week he was away for three days when 'Mrs Drew took charge'.

In July several children were absent during a visit of the Prince and Princess of Wales to Eastbourne, and when the Agricultural Show was held in the town.

Later that month 'the Danns and Collums, children of Crowlink Coastguard Station, arrived late. Investigation revealed no less than seven partridge chicks in their possession. After conversation with Mr Hole on whose land they were found they were returned to the cover from where they had been taken'.

When the school reopened in 1900 the school leaving age was 13, and 'Charles Hall was caned for upsetting the order of the main room by dancing as I was in the class room'.

On 1 March Mr Drew noted "Ladysmith relieved". On 27 March, as part of the patriotic response to the South African War, Mr Drew wrote 'Recreation extended in Drill to the boys outdoors', and over the following months there were references such as 'Military Drill manual and firing exercises taken from 10.40-11.30 this morning', and 'Drill again taken in the Horsefield, the weather being suitable'.

On 24 May the school closed for Ascension Day, to celebrate the Queen's Birthday and, not least, the relief of Mafeking. Hooray! The next week the school closed one afternoon to celebrate the surrender of Pretoria.

'Mr Kemp altered the inkwells in the desks to prevent the continual wastage of ink.' On the 16 July it was 'very great heat. Master and nearly all the boys worked in shirtsleeves'.

During the five-week Summer holiday half the classroom was refloored, and the premises thoroughly cleaned and scrubbed, and after the holidays the Revd JW Parrington visited and said the prayers for the last time as Vicar.

Dr Stott warned of a more severe line to absenteeism, 'unless the School Managers produced a doctor's certificate, the Attendance Committee would prosecute'.

Many families left the village in the first week of October, including the Blabers, Vines, Whittingtons, and the Vicar. 'In this small place it seems like a gigantic upheaval.' The next week the new Vicar the Revd WR Nightingale visited the school.

In March 1901 John Gay, aged 12, was 8st 2lb [51kg] and 5ft 2½ inches [1.58m] high. William Dann in Standard VIII was the only other boy over 5ft 2½ inches.

In June Mr Drew wrote, '96 children on roll, 40 infants and 56 older children', and, 'the average attendance of the Upper Standards is very low this week. The principal cause being sheep shearing, the absentees being different children each day. This seriously hinders the preparation for the Religious Examination'.

It was 'very warm weather' on 19 July so Mr Waghorn visited the school looking for "Nuisances". Mr Drew added, 'Instead of the usual lesson on Common Things this day I read to the Upper Division an account of the *Capture of the armoured train* and Mr Winston Churchill's escape from Pretoria, from his book *London to Ladysmith via Pretoria*. Most of the children very interested.'

A 1905 letter from Mr Drew to Mr & Mrs Markquick on their marriage, 'permit Mrs Drew and myself to wish you both the best of happiness and health'. He goes on to say they would send 'a small oil stove' for a present

In 1902, the Education Year changed to start on 1 April instead of 1 March. Mr Drew set out the Scheme of Instruction for the year: *Reading.* For Group 1 First Standard 20th century Readers and Royal Science Readers, Second Standard Graphics, Third Standard

Graphics and work at home. For Group 2 Fourth Standard Graphics and work at home. Fifth Standard Lessons in our Laws and work at home. *Writing.* 1 Transcription and Dictation of easy words. 2 Of easy pieces. 3 Of words and paragraphs. 4 Of fairly difficult paragraphs. 5 Composition of simple stories and letters. *Arithmetic,* all Scheme A. *Object Lessons.* As approved Scheme. *Geography.* Group 1 Definitions, England and Europe. Group 2 England, South Africa, India, Canada, maps of England and Africa. *Music.* Group 1 Passages in the open scale semibreve, minim, crochets, rests. Group 2 Passages for tune in C, G and F. *Drill.* Group 1 Turnings and easy drill. Group 2 Military drill. *Drawing.* Group 1 Freehand, with and without ruler. Group 2 Easy common objects, scale drawing. *Needle work.* Cutting out and making small garments. Mending and darning. The subjects for *Object lessons* varied from Mountains to Pigs and Horses; from Latitude and Longitude and the Tower of London to Periwinkles; and from Moths and Butterflies to King John and Magna Carta.

On 2 June 1902 Mr Drew wrote. 'Peace having been declared with the Boer leaders the children had a holiday to commemorate the occasion.'

HMI Report for School 23476 in 1903. 'The teachers have worked well and very creditable progress has been made. Numbers increasing and Mrs Drew needs help in the infants' class. The 'offices' [closets] arrangements are not satisfactory. The staff must be strengthened if a Grant under art. 105 of the Code is claimed next year. The Grant is paid this year under the provisions of art. 92. Edward C Drew Master. Eliz H Drew Mistress. Alice Ticehurst Monitoress. Grants @ 22/- and 17/-. By art. 104 - £10, Fees £40/10/-, Gov £105/7/- total £145/17/-. Average attendance 86.'

On 24 April there were 108 on the books with an average attendance of 55 elder children and 40 infants, and Mr Drew wrote, 'I am in urgent need of extra desks which request has been forwarded to the Education Committee of the County Council.'

The afternoon session on 19 May, 'commenced several minutes late owing to a wheat stack infested with mice being thrashed in adjoining farmyard. Between 1500 and 2000 mice killed. The boys and the master on the invitation of the farmer remained to the finish.'

The usual supply mishaps occurred. 'As needlework materials not received articles had to be procured from Mr Dennett's shop'. 'I received from the Educational Supply Association [ESA] three No. 3 Registers when four No. 2s were ordered. The No. 3s being no use to the school were returned.' On the day the school closed for Whitsuntide, Mr Drew received four ESA No. 2 Registers and as ever - wait for it - a duplicate set.

Trouble continued with the cesspits. In Mr Drew's report of 10 September, 'Owing possibly to the great rainfall there has been much offensive smell from the closets. For the second time this week I have sprayed about 3 gallons of carbolic solution into the cesspits'.

On the building front there was movement - just. In December, Attendance Officer Mr Hargreaves, along with Mr E Haig Brown, CC Inspector of Schools, HM Whitley, the Gilbert Agent, and architect TM Johnson, came to view structural alterations and improvements.

Mr Drew kept his lessons topical with the Russo-Japanese conflict, 'this month's Lessons were on the *War Area Russia and Japan,* and for the Upper Division on *Sailors'*.

The 1904 School Report; 'The migratory character of the children makes the work hard for the teachers who are producing creditable results. Additional help is required and the 'offices' and ventilation need attention.' Mr and Mrs Drew were certainly over-taxed, and the staff was increased by an additional Assistant Mistress, Miss ME Stinton, and the necessary alterations were promised by the County Council, during the summer holidays.

On 14 July the annual Day School Treat took place at *Friston Place* by the kindness of Mr and Mrs FJ Maitland. 'At 2pm 87 children assembled for a short Service and *Friston Place* was reached shortly after 3. The children indulged in all manner of games and races until over 100 children and helpers sat down to tea on tables on the lawns. Afterwards prizes and certificates were distributed by Mrs Maitland and after a brief address by the Vicar three hearty cheers were raised for the Maitlands.'

Back to reality, in September Mr E Haig Brown, the County Inspector, visited to see the progress of the building alterations and found, to his surprise, that nothing had been done.

On 5 October 103 were present, with 107 on the Register. Mr Drew even used the services of his daughter for the Infants. 'Though young she is a good disciplinarian.

The first mention of the Revd HEC Marshall, new Vicar of East Dean, was on 6 February 1905 when he visited the school. It was also the first week 'suitable to take physical drill out of doors'.

An injured seagull was brought to school on 13 February. 'It measured 44 inches [1.1m] from wing tip to tip. An object lesson was given on it, by which time it was dead.'

The alterations to the school finally began on 13 March. 'Conditions are fairly satisfactory except for no cloakroom and lavatory accommodation. The state of the Infants at the school is not only inconvenient but dangerous with scaffold poles and debris.' As a result the managers decided to close the school for seven weeks deducting the Whitsun week, one of the summer weeks and Christmas holidays.

Some pupils of East Dean and Friston School, 1907. L-R back row: Arthur West, J Miller, Maurice Dennett, K Drew, Sid Dennett, G Dennett. Second row: N West, D Hills, B Creighton, F Kemp, M Miller, Lily Kemp, Nellie Miller. Third row (sitting): J Creighton, T West, B Miller, E Kemp, R Hole, Claude Hills (killed in 1918 aged 18), F Hills, Miss Ada Lintell (probably), Jesse Kemp. Front: B Ticehurst, M Creighton, Douglas Kemp, P Creighton, Geoff Drew, Ray Kemp

The school restarted on 8 May, 'although not ready, the room grim and the 'offices' far from complete. The noise of the workmen prevents any real work'. The school was formally reopened on 5 June by the Very Revd Dean of Chichester, 'What with new desks and practically a new building all the children should do Mr and Mrs Drew great credit.' Among those present were Canon Goodwin, Vicar of Eastbourne, Revd HEC Marshall, Messrs CD Gilbert, JA Maitland, and Miss Long. The cost over the year was about £300. Contributions came from JA Maitland (of *Little Friston*), J Wycliffe-Taylor (of *Gayles*), CF Russell (of *Gore Farm)*, the Vicar, the Duke of Devonshire and Eastbourne Waterworks Co.

Miss Stinton left and Miss Ada Lintell (mixed class) and Miss Davis (infants) commenced on 12 July 1905. Miss Lintell lodged with the Hills at the Forge.

The improvements at the school had not come in time for Mrs Drew. Over the past two years she had days off with sore throats, 'lost her voice', neuralgia, swollen face and influenza, all ascribed by her husband to the stress of coping with so many in such cramped surroundings. On 21 February 1906 'her voice has left her', and there were further absences because of 'a slight touch of pleurisy' and once just 'unwell'.

In June 'several children who had been taken to Eastbourne in wagons at the invitation of Mr and Mrs Carew Davies Gilbert to see the fireworks were late to bed and rather sleepy the next day'. When the school reopened after the summer holiday. 'Owing to drought the school rainwater tank ran dry and Mr CF Russell, of *Gore Farm,* kindly sent 300 gallons as a supply for flushing closets and washing.'

Ray Kemp, born 1901, started at the school in 1905. 'The day began with prayers, Mr Drew playing the hymns on a portable organ, then scripture and arithmetic. After a short break, reading, writing and poetry, geography and history were also taken. In the afternoons there were singing classes. The girls did needlework: aprons, pillow cases and articles requiring the mysteries of gussets and gathers to be learnt. As it was a C of E school attendance at church was required on Ash Wednesday and Ascension Day.

'PE meant drill every morning outside. Mr Drew conducted nature walks and organised "wide games" with tracking and ambushes. There were over 100 children so it was crowded and easy to pull the bell, "by accident" - when we all got the cane. For minor misdemeanours boys had to work in Mr Drew's garden or got the cane. At home breaches of good behaviour resulted in the ignominy of being sent to bed.' Ray Kemp said he looked back at his childhood with pleasure.

On 11 October 'William Stevens, a standard V boy of 13 years, was taken with violent pains in head and stomach, but he was well enough to go home'. Some of the other lads were knocking themselves about. Alf Ticehurst returned after a fortnight's absence through a dog bite, and Jesse Gay was absent having fallen on a nail which pierced his hand.

Mr Drew wrote, 'Resumed after Christmas. My best pupils, the Coastguard Mays family, left for Dorset.' During January 1907 the Eastbourne Waterworks Co. laid pipes in the road outside the school, and Mr Drew received a chart of metrication tables and illustrations from Singer Sewing Co.

Mr Drew's troubles weren't over, 'John Scott, imbecile, by his rude conduct is spoiling the school discipline, I have sent word to his father that he must not attend any longer.' At least at Easter the school tanks were connected to the Eastbourne Water Company mains.

The Scripture Report stated, 'with the exception of the Vicar, not one manager has sufficient interest to visit, they deprive both teachers and children of the help and sympathy to which they are entitled'.

When the school restarted in 1908 Mr Drew writes, 'The managers have placed Miss D Miller as Monitoress (she was the daughter of Mr Miller, one of the school managers) and Miss Lintell in the Infants' Room. As they are entirely unacquainted with Infant teaching I have sent Mrs Drew (who had been in the main room) with them to explain the work. A sharp standard VII lad helped me with the lower division.' Miss Lintell stayed for 12 years.

'Sidney Huntley, a most well-behaved and promising Coastguard boy, left on 15 May for Crawley, his father having retired on pension and joined the Post Office service.'

'Six boys (T Martin, E Whittington, Bert Rousell, L Cracknell, W Walker and E Hills) went with the Vicar to play in a cricket match at Birling Gap on 17 June. As this is an organised game I have marked them present, but six children who went to a Primrose Fete at Firle were marked absent.' 'Took the senior boys for drawing out of doors on 26 June, sketched the farmhouses and churches.' On 17 September 'Mr Miller kindly brought a basket of fruit, grapes, figs, and peaches for use in drawing. To obtain the fresh effect a special drawing lesson taken. Curtained off class I & II, to prevent wasted time in minding the business of other classes and to concentrate the student on his own work. With inadequate desk space some boys work at my table'. There were now 124 on the Registers, the most recorded at the school. [See the end of this chapter for the fewest pupils]

'The Revd AA Evans paid his first visit on 9 October, and said a few pleasant words.'

'The boys have started a school football club. By kind permission of Mr EP Gorringe they play at the bottom of Hobbs eares.'

Mrs Grace Davies Gilbert and daughters visited on 10 December 1908 to hear the children sing and recite. 'She was pleased with the illuminated address of birthday wishes from the teachers and class - the work of two upper division lads. Gave the school a half holiday.' She repeated this routine over many years.

School reopened in 1909 with 102 out of 112 present. 'Frank Tutt's mother called in very angry state on 19 January. The boy is very naughty and frequently talking to his neighbours and sulking if reproved. He brought a medical certificate stating he has a weak heart so I am unwilling to give him the whipping he deserves. When I was engaged elsewhere, Mrs Drew called him in front of the class for noise and disturbing the work and good order with the remark, "It will be good for the order of this school when you leave". As I confirmed this opinion his mother has not sent him to school since.'

Sadly, Edith Gay died from meningitis during the Easter holidays; she was buried at East Dean. On 28 June the Infants, children over 13, and any slightly defective children were medically examined. 'The mother of Rose Meads (who has had fits since whooping cough this spring) decided not to have her examined as she might cry.'

In December Mrs Drew accompanied Mrs Wycliffe-Taylor, wife of a manager, to Brighton to purchase Christmas presents for the children. This became a regular feature.

In 1910 'Miss May Dykes now working as Monitoress. Have lost, through removal, four of my brightest children. My best scholar, May Richardson, has to stay away from school suffering from heart trouble and anaemia.' Everyone had a holiday on 21 January when the School was used as a Polling Station for the General Election - and again on 14 December.

While Mr Miller, of *New House Farm,* had engaged a governess for his younger children and withdrawn three of them from the school, Harry Sellars was admitted on 21 March, 'age 6 years, unable to correctly name his letters.'

East Dean and Friston School fancy dress tableau *c.*1910

School Medical examinations held on 18 July. 'Parents kept 20 children away'. Parents continued to deny their children a regular medical examination, although Medicals were introduced only after the Boer War volunteers were found in such poor physical shape.

A new flagstaff presented by Mrs Grace Davies Gilbert was 'in place of the broken one'.

Report of HMI F Freeland in November. 'Upper Division answer questions intelligently. Handwork should be carried through the school, not just the Infants. Several children in Lower Division whose school life is nearing its close need more suitable provision. Geography is spread over too many years; few complete the scheme. Upper Division lessons don't appeal to older and younger children. Work requiring individual effort should be provided for the seniors. Instruction in gardening would be useful and with allotments close to the school a plot should be obtained for a school garden.' Mr Drew's riposte to the 'individual effort' was, 'I have 14 children over 12 years of age in the Seniors. They are backward and dull and my constant attention does more good than self-worked specials.'

On 27 March 1911 'commenced a gardening class on the allotment, twenty allowed to be enrolled, and in April a party of boys transferred two loads of manure from the road to the garden plot.'. Ray Kemp said, 'Three afternoons a week the boys did gardening, each plot was worked by two boys amid some larking about - with retribution'.

The school 'closed for one week from 26 June to mark the Coronation of HM King George V. The children received souvenir mugs and oranges.' Mr Drew noted, 'Received one dozen *Gulliver's Travels* from ESA.'

On 25 October there was a Ploughing Match at Jevington. Six children were excused.

Major FJ Maitland and Mr CE Russell, both school managers, visited on 9 November 1911 and questioned Herbert Knight, 10, who admitted firing ten ricks under a Dutch Barn at *Friston Place Farm* the day before. [8] He was absent from 10 May to 10 July and later played truant for a week, walking on his own to Eastbourne. When he returned on 4 October he had been 'promised a thrashing if any repetition of these freaks'.

On 15 and 22 January 1912 the vicar attended and gave a lesson on *Early Man,* illustrated by Palaeolithic and Neolithic implements and fragments of later clay utensils.

'Elsie Vine was sent home on 31 January as her dirty, malodorous condition, due to an infirmity of the bladder, is offensive to anyone in or entering the classrooms.' She next turned up on 4 December, with the comment, 'Smell not remedied sent home unfit.'

Mr Waghorn visited and left literature regarding the prevention of tuberculosis, and 'During the Easter holiday the whole premises thoroughly saturated with carbolic acid'.

Mr Drew, 'Extended play time on 17 April to watch eclipse of the sun, through smoked glass. Afterwards a lesson on eclipses given to seniors. The following day John Murphy, an old boy, visited on his return from a voyage to Australia.' The next day was 'a lovely spring day, so drill was in the Bakehouse field'. A temperature of 65°F was recorded. 'A strong hot wind from the east, most tiring.'

Around the middle of July Mr Drew records a visit from his nephew. 'Fresh from camp on Salisbury Plain he took several extra lessons on drill with rifles. Boys much delighted. Mr W Goaring, gardening inspector, also visited and very pleased at the work.'

'The Children saw an airship on 7 October.' Miss T Ticehurst appointed Monitoress.

In January 1913, Mr Hart, a professional artist staying at the vicarage, gave the senior boys and girls lessons in colour blending with the new paint boxes supplied. Perhaps equally rewarding Mr Hills attended to a stoppage in the WC flushing and a pipe leak.

The flagpole on the Green belonged to the school to use on Empire Day and other public occasions and on 3 February 1913 the flag was lowered to half mast in honour of Captain Falcon Scott's Antarctic expedition. East Dean needed some warmth for on 14 March Mr Drew wrote, 'Received ½ ton of coal, ½ chaldron of coke and 50 bundles of firewood from Bradford's. I had lent three scuttles of coal for school fires.' 'With Empire Day on a Saturday this year, on 23 May the children marched to the school flagstaff with rifles. They sang several songs, fired a feu-de-joie, and were dismissed after the National Anthem.'

The HMI Report included. 'This school leaves a pleasant impression of good behaviour and steady work. The chief matter needing attention is that the senior class is too unequal in attainments for treatment as a single group. Composition lacks spontaneity. The infants' desks are so long that there is little space for gangways. The main room is very full, the lowest section of the juniors should be placed in the infants' room. A flushing apparatus in the urinal is very desirable in view of the proximity of the buildings.' Mr Drew added, 'I have transferred the Standard I to the Infants Room and rearranged desks'. By 18 June Mr Hills had completed the piping for flushing the boys' urinal as recommended.

The Revd AA Evans 'tested Registers and found them correct, 95 out of 100 being present, the absentees being isolated with measles.' He called the Registers once a month.

Sixteen of the older children were taken on a Nature Ramble on 20 June by the Vicar and Master and given tea by Major Maitland of *Friston Place.* The children were encouraged to bring to school any wild flowers they met to learn their names from Mr Drew or the Vicar. 'By the second week of July there were 104 different specimens of wild flowers on the school window ledge each with a name card.

During the gardening lesson on 21 July the boys were halted and all the children came out to see a team of six black oxen drawing a wagon. It had to draw on one side for a motor car to pass. A week later, 'There was an extended playtime on the morning of 28 July to see the 10th Middlesex Regiment with their band and motor scouts march through the village.'

On 3 October Mr Drew took the older lads in charge of a garden plot to his own garden to observe pruning and propagation of gooseberry bushes.

The Annual Hill Ploughing Competition, Sack Mending and Sheep trimming trials held on 8 October. Nine of the biggest boys excused to attend.

Miss Tamer Ticehurst ended her engagement as Monitoress. Miss Irene Fears took over.

After the death of Carew Davies Gilbert, the school closed at noon on 5 December for teachers and pupils to join the funeral procession and sing two hymns at the graveside. [2]

In 1914 'the Master's Standards IV and V, had 25 children, and 2 in boys' special. The First Mistress' [Mrs Drew] special class of needlework, 12. The Monitoress had Standards II and III, 22. The Second Assistant Mistress had Standard I and the Infants of 26.' That year 'Violet Tremlett aged $13^3/_4$ measured 5ft 8ins, and Alec Cracknell $13^1/_2$ 5ft 6ins.'

During the summer holiday the school was used by a cyclist company of Territorials and later two companies of Boy Scouts.

Miss Lintell's Nursery Rhymes Fancy Dress Show c.1915. Back row l-r: L Osborn, Eric Fears, ?Armiger's cousin, George Armiger, Nellie Gutsell, - Miller, Arthur Freeman, Will Armiger, Margaret Harris, - Dench, ?Will Lias. Front Joan Kemp, Dorothy Dickens, Freda Curwood, ?. Guess the nursery rhymes portrayed - answer at end of chapter

On 24 September the gardening class raised all the potato crop. Four days later, 'The children were taken as far as the Forge on the Seaford-Eastbourne road to see 2000 men of Kitchener's New Army, who had been billeted in Eastbourne, march to camp at Seaford.'

'On 16 October Mrs Patience Harding (née Davies Gilbert) sent 4lb [2kg] of wool to the school, and the special needlework class was given extra time to make it into mittens for the Gloucesters, Major Harding's Regiment.'

On 11 January 1915, 'Two scholars, boys, taken to hospital and operated on for appendicitis.' They didn't return until 1 March.

'Mrs Drew ended her engagement as Assistant Mistress on 31 March 1915 after $24^1/_2$ years. On 6 April Miss L Nellie Baxter, an uncertified Assistant Mistress, commenced in

Mrs Drew's place with Standards II and III, although with Mrs Drew's retirement the Housewifery class was dropped.' Nellie Baxter (later Mrs Straw) was one of the twin daughters of Mr and Mrs Baxter who lived at *Hillside,* now *Friston Lodge* on Friston hill.

On 21 May 'Harold Creighton received two strokes of the cane for playing truant twice. The first time he wandered to Seaford Camp and on both times he slept on the Downs.'

In 1916 Mrs Davies Gilbert replaced Mr Miller, and Mrs Wycliffe-Taylor replaced her husband, as managers of the school. 'Dr Stott visited on 27 January because of the case of meningitis in the Breach family. He isolated the three Dickens' children who lived in the other half of the Bake House. [7] They were declared clear four days later.'

Mr Drew noted a few of the reasons given for absence: 'Mother's leg ulcers are bad and she needs me (W Hall). Father home on leave and we are going to Eastbourne. Mr F is going to the sale tomorrow and wants my help in the work today (H Sellars). Has whitlow and inflamed arm (Violet Fears). Prolonged holiday to strengthen enlarged glands in her neck (Winnie Ticehurst). All reasonable, but hindering their schoolwork progress, and even my son, Geoffrey, had an absence to attend the dentist.'

On 23 May was the first mention of Daylight Saving Summer Time, 'the first day of altered time passed without inconvenience.'

During the summer recess the road in front of the school was tar-sprayed for the second time. 'A great boon as we use it for Drill exercises.'

On 9 October Mr Drew wrote, 'I regret to report that Miss Lintell has been the victim of a brutal assault by an unknown soldier on the highway and is quite unable to attend for many days.' She didn't return until 23 October. Mrs Drew acted as a temporary teacher.

The officers and chaplain of the Western Universities Battalion of the Canadian Expeditionary Force visited on 22 November.

Mr Drew wrote, 'From a private census East Dean population in 1917 was 194 with 19 empty houses, and Friston 90, empty houses 11'.

At the end of May Irene Fears ended her Monitoress duties and Elsie Freeman took her place. 'On 19 June, Sir Douglas Haig's birthday, our flag was hoisted in celebration.'

'Some of the senior girls have been knitting a dozen pair of socks for Mrs Davies Gilbert's Red Cross work. This has been done out of school hours.'

'Six fresh children admitted on 21 July. Very, very backward and probably verminous. Have been working on farms in various parts of Sussex.'

Miss Lintell concluded her engagement on 31 October. In December she was presented with a handsome marble clock for 12 years' faithful work. Miss Webb succeeded her.

The school leaving age was raised to 14 in 1918. On 9 January, 'one hour after fires lit, the temperature was 25F° [-3C]. Pointed this out to the Vicar. At 10am it was 29°F. Desks moved near fires, top coats on and frequent movements, dances and marches.'

Grace Taylor, who started at the school in 1918, when she lived at Crowlink said, "The girls had to wear white pinafores, which I did not like. It was so cold in the classroom, they had a donkey stove which the older boys stoked up with solid fuel and it was all right if you were in the front row, but freezing at the back. The Revd Evans came every Monday morning. The entrance, then at the porch front, had double doors and two of the boys opened them for him. The whole class greeted him with, "Good Morning, Reverend Evans.""

Back to Mr Drew, 'As a result of the Food Control Rationing Order, on 8 March and for the previous two Fridays, five of the older girls have accompanied their parents or sisters to Eastbourne to procure their supply of meat. Parents have no faith in a vegetarian diet.'

Only 42 present on 31 July, 'so many children taken by their parents to Eastbourne to see the Tank Bank. After seeing the Vicar I thought it best to close for half a day.'

On 2 November 'the cash received for the year's needlework (£2.41) and garden produce (£2.76), was sent off to the County Accountant. The receipts were affixed to the school door. Received and distributed leaflets on Prevention of Influenza by MOH'.

The end of the war was celebrated with a spontaneous outburst of rejoicing. [2]

'Small attendance in the week of 22 November through very heavy colds and influenza (myself included). As soon as one batch of children is well enough to return another batch fails. My best scholar, Dorothy Plummer, left. A most intelligent and sensible girl.'

On 19 December the school closed for the Christmas holidays, when Miss AE Webb left. In the evening the school gave an entertainment with actions, dialogue, and recitations.

'Teaching resumed 6 January 1919. The three children of a Canadian soldier have left. Am doing as well as I can with only a Monitoress in the classroom.' Miss Crowley (Miss Webb's replacement) didn't commence duties until 3 March. Elsie Freeman, the Monitoress, finished in May as her parents were leaving the parish, so the Managers re-appointed Mrs Drew as certificated teacher in the infants' room on 18 June, but in July the County Council refused to confirm the appointment so she ceased to act as such.'

Mr Drew found solace in his garden, 'Over half-a-gallon of small potatoes collected.'

East Dean and Friston School, c.1920. L-R Back row: W Armiger, ?, ?, ?, ?, Boy Creighton, ?, Jim Markquick, ?, George Armiger, Harry West. Second: ?, Nellie Grooms, ?, ?, Edith Dickens, Dorothy Dickens, Joan Kemp, Lucy Harris, Maggie Gutsell, Freda Curwood, Miss Baxter, Mr Drew, the two boys in front of them have not been identified. Third (sitting): Irene Markquick, - Crouch, Grace Smith, ?, Edith Armiger, - Crouch, Muriel Gaeson, ?, Emily Wicking, ?, ?, Mabel Smith, ?, Emily Markquick. Front row: fifth along is Cecil Smith

School reopened in September 'including the extra "Peace week". Several fresh coastguard children admitted who had come from Rottingdean, Portsmouth, Wales and Ireland. Miss Irene Fears commenced her duties as supplementary teacher in the classroom'.

'In February 1920 received from EO Lewes garden seeds, seed potatoes and artificial manure. On 5 March received the official book *Syllabus of Physical Training.* I left Miss Baxter in charge while I attended a conference of inspectors and teachers at Hailsham on Physical Exercises and Handwork.'

In May, 'boys of the gardening class angry because jackdaws (the most mischievous of birds) have badly damaged rows of beans', but the report of Mr W Goaring, horticultural adviser, corrected them: 'A 20-rood allotment is worked by 12 boys and three girls. The practical work is good and gardening is a favourite subject on which the subjects take great pains. They are not observant however and attribute peas and beans damage to birds which were really caused by weevils that had escaped their notice altogether. The children are reticent to venture an opinion even on matters with which they are familiar. The headmaster should prepare a syllabus of Gardening Instruction, this should show the garden's use for the study of nature and use the practical interest to give reality to other subjects.'

The 29th of September saw the wedding of Miss Honor Davies Gilbert to Mr Edgar Skinner. She distributed pieces of the wedding cake to the children.

From 25 October 'Miss Baxter was off with scarlet fever. Didn't return until 20 December, but from 3 November Mrs Drew commenced duty in her place. 'On 9 November admitted three children from Chiddingly and as today all were present there were 55 in this room. It is most fortunate that the services of Mrs Drew are available.'

At the Christmas Treat Mrs Patience Harding unveiled a Roll of Honour containing the names of old boys who served their country in the Great War.

On 19 February 1921, Mr Drew 'read aloud to the children the County Council's scheme of scholarships and training courses and I informed the children that if their parents desired further information to call on me'.

Mr EF Davidson, who had replaced Mr C Boutflower as HMI (who, according to Mr Drew, 'it was always a great pleasure to see'), wrote in his report: 'The School is pleasantly managed. Children well-behaved and work steadily. The seniors do creditable work. The main room is over full, while there is space in the classroom. Arithmetic is a weak subject, they show little ability in tackling practical problems. A better supply of books is needed. More advanced work is required for children above standard VI who at present repeat work. More regular physical exercises needed.' Mr Drew added: 'At his suggestion infants are to have frequent breaks of 5-10 minutes during the day.'

A holiday was given on 28 February 1922 for the Royal Wedding of Princess Mary, but in April no needlework, 'owing to senior girls' bad behaviour while lads were gardening'.

The school had its first half-term holiday on 6 November, 'as at Eastbourne and Seaford'; 1922 was also the first year that the children's Medicals, now run by Dr Betenson and Nurse Gay, had almost full attendance.

'Some artificial manure for the school was brought here on 6 December by Mr EO Hobden the new owner of *Gore Farm,* as Mr Dennett was unable to convey it.'

In January 1923, 'Millie Rodway, 10, ran a crochet needle point through her clothes and pierced her chest. Sent with Miss Baxter to my house where Mrs Drew and Mrs H Elliott, a trained nurse, withdrew it. The child remained in comfort at school until 3.45pm, but was absent the following day.'

'As instructed by HMI, on 27 February Miss Fears, the teacher in charge of the Infants, visited Whitley Road School in Eastbourne to see modern methods of infant teaching.'

On opening after Easter, 'only five pupils left from coastguard families owing to alterations ordered by the Admiralty cuts. The lavatory flushing apparatus repaired'.

'Although it is May had two fires going for comfort. It is noticeable that physical discomfort and mental activity are not allies.'

In July lightning struck the chimney of the school house and broke a window. Later that month, 'Mr GB Soddy, Mayor of Eastbourne, visited the school. On 31 July a return visit was paid to the Mayor by the headmaster, six assistants and many of the senior lads.'

Closed for a measles outbreak from 7-21 April 1924, closed for Easter holidays 21-28 April, and closed again by MOH 28 April to 12 May. 'A great deal of arrears to make up.'

Mr Glenister, Vice Chairman ESCC, visited the school on 30 May to inspect the fabric and heating systems. 'Whit Monday, 9 June, was the only holiday because of closures.'

Reopened after summer holiday 'all present with the exception of three children taken to the Wembley Empire Exhibition by their parents'.

Mrs Davies Gilbert visited as usual on 10 December. 'Presented with a bouquet, she had most thoughtfully brought a large tray of buns.' Arnold Hills said "Mrs Grace Davies Gilbert's sticky buns were baked in the village and were most popular and welcome". He also recalls that, "Mr Drew, a little man, was called 'Bantam' by us children."

Whilst the Revd AA Evans was assiduous in testing the Registers about once a month, he forgot to show the HMI report of 1924 to Mr Drew until the next inspection date, 2 February 1925. The Report had stated: 'The work, however, does not reach a high standard. Many of them are not unintelligent but they have not been sufficiently trained to make real effort. Methods of doing this have been discussed with the Headmaster at recent inspections. The science lessons should have afforded the same opportunities but they have been rather general information talks rather than opportunities for observation and experiment. There is no doubt greater progress could be made if the work were more vigorously planned and supervised. Sufficient attention has not been paid to Physical Training and there is a tendency to curtail the lessons in winter time. More time might be devoted to speech training. The infants are pleasantly taught and their teacher has begun to introduce some apparatus for individual work. '

Hence, 'The 24 in the infants' class made perfect attendance in first week of February.'

Some of East Dean and Friston School c.1925. Back row l-r: Bill Burton, Don Harris, Charlie Funnell, Stan Creighton, Charles Pope, ?. Second standing row: Marjorie Ticehurst, Charlie Croft, Ena Fears, Ethel Pope, Edith Wooler, Nellie Akehurst, Emily Wicking, Elizabeth Wells, Edith Wells, Emily Markquick, Irene Markquick. Sitting row: Mary Wicking, Nellie Wells, Elsie Pope, Mr Drew, Miss Baxter, Rose Burton, Eileen Ticehurst, Jessie Akehurst. Front row: Arthur Wooler, Cecil Dann, ?, Maud Dann, Geoffrey Cheal, ?, George Creighton, ?, Eddie Creighton

There was a sense that Mr Drew was tiring. 'In the afternoon of 11 March I sent home Bernard Lemmon and Jesse Mead, two big boys as an example, for continued disobedience and coming late to school through playing "foxhounds" [following the hunt]. This is after previous warnings and punishment.' On 22 March, 'Order and attention of older boys improved. Girls very apt to talk to each other.'

Perhaps Mr Drew felt better after, 'On 12 May, for the first time this year no fires' and 'The valves and stop balls of the teachers' lavatory were repaired by Prior's on 2 July'.

On 7 October 'many boys attended with fathers the farm sale of Mr EP Gorringe of Exceat'; and on 13 October 'six girls at Mr JW Wycliffe-Taylor's funeral, a manager'.

The yearly Diocesan Report ended with: 'The head teacher leaves after a long period of loyal and devoted service in the highest interests of the scholars. His place will not be easily filled, but he leaves with the prayers and gratitude of the church he served so well.'

Severe frost, at 9am on 27 November a temperature of 36°F was registered indoors. Some children with chilblains were excused drill. The last mention of chilblains.

'Miss Irene Fears, ex-East Dean monitoress now Supplementary Assistant Teacher in charge of the Infants, left 30 November to get married. I am trying to proceed with just the help of a senior scholar.' Mr Drew, however, wasn't to be provided with a supply teacher.

The three chimneys were swept on 3 December by Mr Harris of *Underhill Cottages.* 'In December the East Sussex Foxhounds held a Meet on the Village Green.' Afterwards the children were set a composition on the subject.

On 31 December 'I, Edward C Drew, herewith resign the duties of headmaster of this school after 35¼ years of service.'

In February 1926 Miss MG Samuell commenced as Head Teacher with Miss E Bowditch as the Infants' teacher and Miss Baxter in charge of Standards I and III. Arnold Hills said, "Miss Samuell and Miss Bowditch lived together in the school house. Miss Bowditch wore her collar up, she was a typical school ma'm."

On 16 April five girls started at a weekly cookery course in the Seaford Cookery Centre. 'They did not attend on 7 May as it was thought unsafe owing to the General Strike.'

The first mention of Fire Drill was on 17 May.

Empire Day celebrations were held on 21 May this year. Afterwards the school closed for Whitsun. Arnold Hills remembers Empire Day. 'Flew the flag to which the boys had to salute and the girls had to curtsey.' When the school reopened on 31 May the Revd Evans spoke to the children on the British Empire. The school closed in afternoon of 20 July, so the children could be entertained at *Birling Manor* by Mrs Patience Harding.

From 28 July all pupils over 11 went to Eastbourne or other schools outside the village.

On 6 December 'the head teacher attended a conference at the County Hall Lewes'.

From 17 January 1927 Miss Bowditch was away ill, so the Medical Officer closed the school until she returned on 25 January. Mrs French, the cleaner, was also unable to attend until 14 March, but sent a substitute to light the fires.

The February Report of the HMI had a new flavour. 'Did not sign the timetables as I thought too much time given to some subjects. The present head has maintained the pleasant atmosphere. She found the school in a backward condition and has improved the attitude of the children towards arithmetic. Scarcely any of the children can do work beyond standard IV, with little general reading and discussion. In composition creditable work is produced. The infants are being managed with success.'

After the terminal examinations in March, the reports were sent to the pupils' homes - for the first time; and the head teacher attended a conference at Lewes on 31 March on teaching arithmetic, another first.

In April 14 dual desks came from J Bennett of Glasgow, and nine long desks (Mr Drew's favourites - you could cram about four children in each so to hold nearly 40 would present no difficulty) were removed by order of Director of Education. Mrs Davies Gilbert called and gave four prizes for needlework and a packet of sweets for those who did not receive prizes. The first mention of children attending a Dental Clinic was on 6 May.

During the summer holidays, a partition was erected so that there were now two small rooms instead of one large one. 'The three rooms (in all) have each been supplied with Tortoise stoves.'

'On 3 November the organiser of physical education, Mr OR Russell, took the children for games on the Sports Field which had been lent to the school by Major Harding.'

Illnesses continued. First was whooping cough, then 'Five boys were off with impetigo on 18 November, two more cases on 23 November, and on 5 December Miss Baxter was absent having caught impetigo. In December there were three cases of chickenpox.'

Dr Francis Gillett held a routine medical inspection on 3 February 1928, and as a result Dorothy Breach and Nellie West were excluded from school.

Diocesan inspection on 30 March. 'There is a complete change in the school since the visit of two years ago. Head teacher deserves high praise for what has been accomplished.

Discipline excellent. The prayers taken reverently, but could be enriched. The infants are handled quietly and thoughtfully, freer use of the blackboard would be a gain. The middle group is particularly encouraging, the result of teaching on vigorous and interesting lines. The top group has been transformed and the co-operation and activity is most pleasing.'

For the first time, nine children took the Eastbourne Senior Schools examination ['the Scholarship'].

On 30 July Mr Frank Bridge, a professional pianist, played to the upper group during the music lesson. School closed on 2 August. Having attained leaving age, eight are going to Eastbourne schools, one of them to a Central school.

On 23 January 1929 Major Kingham of the National Savings Committee called, and in the week afterwards a National Savings scheme was started at the school.

School closed while staff attended a refresher course at Brighton on 3 May, another first.

From 12 to 29 July the Head Teacher was absent taking a history course at Cambridge. On 18 July the Revd Evans informed Miss Baxter that with the Roll less than 50 her services would not be required after the summer holidays and gave her a testimonial. She obtained an appointment to Portslade Infants' School.

Reopened on 2 September with 49 on Roll. With one exception all children now under 11 years of age. Only two teachers so the classes rearranged with new timetables. The upper group had standards II, III, IV and the other Standard I and the infants.

On 11 November the children were taken to the Village Green for the Silence. Work resumed until 11.45am when school dismissed.' The next week the Dental clinic had an improved attendance of 28 children.

Canon Pearce (Revd Evans' successor) started his regular visits, on this occasion to examine the building fabric as water was coming down the chimney after a storm.

Dr Dunstan visited on 5 March 1930, and Muriel Williams, Flora Fears, David Breach, and Victor Barnard received treatment for defective eyesight.

On 4 July Ivy Etteridge, the village Police Constable's daughter, attended an examination at the Town Hall Eastbourne, on 9 July she went for an oral exam at Bexhill, and on 31 July Ivy had a medical examination at Lewes. As a result Miss Samuell was able to write, 'Six children left for Eastbourne schools - Ivy Etteridge to Eastbourne Girls' High School; Isabelle Fowler to Bedewell Central school; Albert Cairns to Cavendish Senior school; and Reginald Haffenden, John Vine, and Charles Vine to St Saviours'. So Ivy was the first village pupil to 'win a scholarship'.

First mention of a Monthly Test was on 28 January 1931. In June Harry Comber had his tonsils and adenoids out. Later Peter and Joyce Wetlesen, and Bernard Fears had theirs out.

When the school reopened after the summer holidays gas brackets had been fitted in each room. 'Horlicks malted milk served during the morning break on 3 October. The upper group was dismissed at 12.05pm as recreation time has to be extended to 15 minutes.'

The Revd Evans presented Neolithic and Palaeolithic flint implements to the school in March 1933; all found nearby. The next year this collection was transferred to the Eastbourne Natural History Museum, where it was lost in the bombing of 1943.

From 28 August Miss Gladys Penford was assistant teacher until Miss Hayes commenced duty at the mid-term holiday.

The HMI Report: 'The head teacher is most industrious and the pupils' work shows a steady advance. English is well taught, and the arithmetic lesson was well conducted. More than usual interest is shown in the handwork of the school. Lower school work less good.'

Jack (David) Breach went to the village school 1927-33. "The headmistress was Miss Samuell and Miss Bowditch was her assistant. It was a nice little school, and they looked after you; they would dry your clothes if wet, but I found you needed to make up a lot when we went to St Saviour's school in Eastbourne at 11 years of age, taken there in Sydney's [Stevens] coach."

No scholarship successes in 1934, D Breach, C Cairns, B Fears, B Gay, G Hoad and K McNally all went to Meads Senior Church School from 10 September.

Miss MG Samuell resigned at the summer holidays. After a supply teacher from 3 September, Lilian Turk commenced duties on 2 November as head teacher of the school.

Nurse Gay, the local District Nurse, but called by the children 'the Nitty Nurse', carried out a head inspection on 20 March 1935. All 46 present and all clean. Another first.

Eight candidates sat the annual schools examination in March when managers Mrs Harding (morning) and PJ Budd (afternoon) supervised, while Miss L Baxter took charge of the rest of the school.

The school had a holiday on 6 May, the occasion of the Silver Jubilee of HM King George V. 'A very low attendance the next day.'

After the summer holidays, G Dann, E Merry, P Breach, F Fears, R Hyde went to Eastbourne Senior schools; F Breach and H Comber to Eastbourne Central school, and G Parnell Seaford Boys' school. Miss Hayes left and Mrs Vidler commenced duty as an uncertificated teacher. The School Milk scheme started on 14 October.

'School closed 6 November for Duke of Gloucester wedding'. The first record of a lay person checking the Register was on 15 November: 'Tested register and found correct. PJ Budd'. Dr F Gillett and Nurse L Gay, held routine medical inspections on 3 December. This appears to be Nurse Gay's last mention in the school records.

Again school reopened late after the Christmas holiday, 'owing to repairs to roof being unfinished.' The school closed on 28 January 1936 for funeral of King George V. Secular work started the next day at 9.5am to enable children in class I to attend the service of Institution and Induction of Revd WEM Williams.

Mrs JE Batten checked the Registers on 2 March. The next day was the first Open Day with a sale of needlework and handwork. 'Many parents, friends and managers present.'

For their essays on *Kindness to Animals* the RSPCA awarded prizes to Joyce Wetlesen and Muriel Bickers, and certificates to Patrick Fowler, Peggy Hyde and Margaret Pownall.

Coal remained essential and the winter's first delivery, 1 ton, was on 18 September.

The Deputy Director of Education visited on 30 September and brought a Beethoven Baby Portable Radio (model P101) for the school. In November 'the Timetable was adjusted to allow for broadcast talks on the wireless.' The wireless set was returned to Lewes on 24 July the next year.

School opened 7 January 1937, but only 10 out of 41 present, many with whooping cough. On 15 February visited by the Vicar. 'Afternoon session temporarily changed to 1.05pm to 3.20pm, the saving of fuel admits of fires in the third room without the use of which music, PT and handiwork lessons are jeopardised'. Not too popular, so managers and parents met to discuss the times of the afternoon session, 1.15pm to 3.45pm was agreed. There was 100% attendance for the first week after the Easter holiday.

The Head Teacher was at Lewes Music Festival on 21 April. On 11 May the school closed for the Coronation and Whitsun. Reopened on Empire Day when the children had a talk on *Products of the Empire* in the afternoon.

'One scholarship candidate, Reginald Edward Fears, passed sufficiently to take the oral examination at Bexhill, but his mother had died in 1934 and shortly after he had taken the scholarship, the family moved to Ealing. They came back in 1938 to *Long View* with Uncle Jim and Auntie Viv Kemp, when Ted went to Seaford School with Eric Mace.

HMI Report for 1937. 'Classrooms are bright and attractive and the children are trained to be clean and good mannered. Much of the work is praiseworthy notably the infants, the needlework and handiwork. The steady advances however have not been maintained. Arithmetic is accurate but little training in reasoning. English compositions are untidy and the marking is not sufficiently informative. The absence of a playground makes PT difficult. A 360 sq ft enclosed yard adjoining the school is used for the infants, in good weather they use a nearby field, but in winter they use a road with traffic.'

After the summer holiday four were admitted, and 'Lorna Grayson had transferred to Cavendish School, John Fears and Gwen Fears (to St Mary's), Peter Wetlesen, Muriel Bickers, and Greta Vine (St Saviours).'

All the old routines continued. On 23 September the piano was tuned; on 14 October Sanitary Inspector and MOH inspected the premises; 3 November Mr Court held dental clinic at Village Hall when 18 children attended; on 11 November, after the morning session 8.40am to 10.45, this being Armistice Day, the children went to the Green for the Service. Afternoon session 1pm to 3.20pm. Dr Gillett held a routine clinic on 18 November with Nurse Fairs in attendance and she visited for head inspections on 8 December.

On 29 January 1938, the managers loaned a Phillips battery wireless set to the school, and the next day, 'a slight timetable alteration to listen to the reception test by the BBC'.

'Mrs Vidler arrived at 9.45am on 14 February having walked from snowy Eastbourne.'

Mrs Patience Harding (née Davies Gilbert) checked registers and found them correct. She and husband, Major Harding, donated a galvanised wheelbarrow to the school garden.

Recorder made and played at East Dean School by Pauline Markquick

On 14 June Charlotte Cairns heard that she had been successful in obtaining a scholarship place at Eastbourne High School for Girls, but she didn't take it up.

Diocesan Inspection Report by Revd KG Packard: 'The premises are below modern standards, although attractive, well built and in sound condition. The three rooms give ample accommodation for the two classes, and the interchanging is a valuable means of airing the rooms. Two rooms must be rather dark in winter. The most serious deficiency is the lack of a proper playground, it is not desirable that the children should have their PT on the tarmac of a public road. The opening worship is very satisfactory, the children sang well without accompaniment. The teaching was a high standard. A way of dramatising Bible stories would give the infants more expressive work.'

A sample bottle of milk was sent for routine testing to the Public Health laboratory on 21 June. The next day a BBC representative called, 'to test our wireless set and advise with regard to the schools programmes'.

This year the piano tuner said the piano was old and not satisfactory, so in October the old Cramer piano was exchanged for a good second-hand Waldstein. A week later 'temperature 47°F. Fires started'. Miss Dyke, the new Physical Training organiser, watched a PT lesson on 26 October, and was 'pleased to see all the children wearing the PT shoes provided'. She visited the school regularly into the mid-1940s.

On 30 November the Head teacher left at 2pm to visit the new Seaford Senior School on their first Open Day - only two years after East Dean had started their Open Days.

A new manager, Joe Pownall, invigilated at the annual schools examination on 10 March 1939, and on 3 April he checked the Registers and found them correct. He worked for the water company, but as he had eleven children he had educational experience as well.

Miss Turk had attended the Lewes Music Festival for a few years, and once the children's section became non-competitive, she arranged for the school to close so that juniors and both teachers could attend the Festival. The children entered for sight reading, song and hymn competitions, and joined the combined singing at the evening concert.

On 8 June Pauline Markquick heard she had been awarded a special place at Eastbourne High School for Girls. "I went to East Dean School at the age of five, in 1933, was taught by Miss Turk, and Misses Bowditch and Vidler. I was the third pupil to win a scholarship from the School. Ivy Etteridge did in 1930, Charlotte Cairns was the second in 1937, but she forfeited it. My mother had to complete Special Dispensation Papers to allow me to go to the High School (just opened at Eldon Road) instead of Bexhill or Lewes, as East Dean was not in the Eastbourne education area. I received a cigarette card album as a prize."

Pauline continues, "There were 32 in the High School class, only two were scholarship girls the rest were fee-paying, and they did tend to leave you out, for example, to make up foursomes at games. I went there for a year and in July 1940 was evacuated with the school to near Hitchin, but when my parents came to visit me they found at the time there were more raids there than in Eastbourne - as it was near airfields and ammunition dumps - so they brought me back to East Dean. For three months Miss Turk set me special lessons at home until I transferred to Lewes Grammar School which hadn't been evacuated."

The September opening was delayed with the evacuation of children from London to the village. No war, however, stopped the piano being tuned on the 15th.

To cope, Mr PB Coles, HMI, suggested a two-shift system, and that the school should be for the local children, the evacuees to use the village hall. Miss Smith, head teacher of Albion Street London County Council [LCC] School Rotherhithe, and Miss Turk made plans for opening the school and were successful in arranging for the children from any one house to be in the same shift. On 21st the school reopened for local children only.

Miss Dyke, PT organiser, visited the school, the Village Hall, and the Gilbert Institute and considered the arrangements satisfactory. The desks for the LCC children arrived.

On 27th Miss Smith and Miss Turk with senior Albion Street boys arranged the desks while Miss Fraser from the LCC taught the local children. The arrangements were sealed when the next day the local juniors played the LCC school at football, netball and rounders.

The double-shift system was explained to the children, papers setting out the new arrangements were given to all parents and the two-shift system started fully on 2 October. *School I,* consisted of East Dean & Friston scholars, a few Albion Street scholars and some Croydon children evacuated to the village. *School II* was most of the 170 Albion Street scholars billeted around the parish. [10]

School I was in the Village School morning, and Village Hall and Gilbert Institute afternoon. *School II* had the Village Hall and Gilbert Institute morning, and all at the Village School afternoon. Children brought lunches to eat at the Village Hall. The *School* venues alternated weekly.

The various authorities took great care of both sets of children, everyday there were visitors. Mrs Blake Mason, ESCC care organiser, came the day Miss Woods spoke to the children about organising a Wolf Cub pack. Miss Matthews LCC PT organiser visited. 'Dr Bandulska gave a talk to the senior girls', and Miss Dickinson, LCC care committee, visited twice. Nurse Bell did a routine head inspection, the Revd Anderson gave a lantern lecture to all children in the Village Hall on *Capt Scott's Expedition,* and Mr Evans HMI also visited. Mr Henley, the Mayor of Bermondsey, even came to see his flock.

Gas masks were inspected and 'adjusted where necessary'. Two LCC nurses inspected the Rotherhithe children and no doubt adjusted if necessary, and Mr Evans visited again. On 3 November Fire Drill took $1^1/_2$ minutes. Plans were made in case of an air raid, and on the 9th new gas mask boxes were given to those 'whose boxes were in very poor condition'.

The school wasn't closed for half term, but staff arranged to take two days leave in turn. Perhaps understandably the headmistress was absent due to illness from 20th to 30th November. There was a head inspection for LCC children, and Dr Gillett visited as usual. The school closed for Christmas holidays, but continued to be used for evacuees.

The 1940 winter was a cold and snowy one. On 17 January 'heavy snow, only 9 out of 33 present, and Mrs Vidler unable to get to the school'. On 19th Mrs Vidler made it for the afternoon session having walked from Eastbourne, but she was absent for another two days because of snow drifts. There was no water on the premises and the 'offices' were blocked.

The schools were reorganised in March. Local children were separated from evacuees with only one class of Rotherhithe children (juniors) to work at the school. Miss CEL 'Chips' Woods of Crowlink in 1940, started a Wolf Cub pack for the London boys.

John Hills was excluded with scabies on 5 April, and on 8 April 'transparent adhesive paper was attached to all windows as a protection from falling glass in an emergency'.

'Owing to war developments in Holland and Belgium the Whitsun holiday curtailed, and on 15 May gas masks were tested, and older boys shown how to use a stirrup pump.'

On 23 June all the London evacuees left for South Wales. Most locals stayed put, but Alan Saunders who had been awarded a scholarship place at Eastbourne Grammar school, but finally went to Bexhill, was evacuated with them to St Albans.

The Diocesan report stated, 'The experience does not seem to be without profit. Standards maintained and the managers' interest evident. A most encouraging school.'

Mr Miles of the BBC considered that the school wireless set was worn out and not worth repairing; so on 27 August Mr Budd lent the school a radiogram.

Air raids followed. On 4 September an air raid warning sounded in the morning and the children were kept at school until 12.40pm; and the afternoon session delayed from 2 to 4pm. An air raid on the 11th at 3.30pm, kept children at school until the 5pm All Clear siren. On 16th several children arrived at times up to 10am after a very disturbed night. On 2 October children were kept at school until 12.40 waiting for the All Clear. This aerial activity continued into the next year. [10]

Life went on - just. On 27 November Mrs JE Batten gave 'an interesting lantern lecture on *Native tribes of Africa*'. On the night of 9 December, however, three high-explosive and numerous incendiary bombs fell on the parish, without too much damage or hurt.

On 20 January 1941 Dr Gillett visited to discuss a scheme for diphtheria immunisation. In February gas masks were tested and worn for a short time to become accustomed to wearing them. Mrs Blake Masson agreed to visit Mrs Breach at *Friston Place* re the non-attendance of her children, and Mr Percy J Budd, now chief air raid warden, inspected gas masks and arranged to supply ear plugs.

On 27 March Dr Margaret Douglas attended, with Mrs Gillett and Nurse Willis, to give the children their first diphtheria toxoid immunisations, with a second visit on 24 April. Mrs Blake Masson brought along a supply of cod liver oil and malt on 2 May.

Dr Douglas visited on 27 May to Schick Test those inoculated against diphtheria to test immunity; and on 19 June Dr Douglas, Mrs Gillett and a nurse visited to complete inoculations. 'Dr Douglas later gave certificates for the inoculations, the results were good.'

A blackboard was lent to the RAF at Friston Advanced Landing Ground on 2 July, the month a representative from Hailsham left sacks and posters for the school salvage effort.

Among those who left that summer was Jesse Taylor who had been at the school since 1935. "Miss Turk, the headmistress, was tall and slim and very strict, although I can't recall her using a cane, you did as you were told. The standard of teaching was good. After prayers, the first thing we did every morning was to recite our times tables, and on Fridays we had a mental arithmetic test. Mrs Vidler, who took the Infants, was a kindly lady. Unless it was wintry, she cycled in from Pevensey every day with her ginger Pomeranian dog in the basket and it sat by her desk all day, or was looked after by the Institute caretaker. We played on the road outside, but we were not allowed to go outside the confines of the school and certainly not on the Green."

On 15 September PC Sheppard from Bexhill visited to warn the children against picking up objects that might contain explosives.

'Children volunteered splendidly to collect herbs in their own time. Blackberries and rose hips gathered over the autumn were also sent to make syrup rich in vitamin C. Salvage is being collected regularly.' The £3 raised by the sale of herbs and rose hips was donated in February 1942 to the Lord Mayor of London's Air Raid Warden's Distress Fund.

The head teacher talked to the school in September on the care of boots, shoes and gas masks. In October a County Council representative called to enquire about school milk. Mrs Vidler arrived at 10.40am on 11 February 1943 'owing to bombs on the railway line'.

The Revd RL Lycett, vicar and chairman of managers in succession to Revd WEM Williams, visited on 5 May. He gave religious instruction to the Junior class monthly, and checked the Registers quarterly.

It was impossible to hold the usual Open Day because of the restricted space with the six Morrison table air raid shelters delivered in April, so an exhibition of the children's work and a program of singing and dancing took place in the Village Hall.

Teachers and children saw a Ministry of Information film at the Village Hall on 31 January 1944. In May the children heard the special Empire Day BBC program.

Part of the ceiling in the infants' room fell during the night of 19 June - this time due to enemy action by V1s. The school work was hindered by frequent, though short, periods in the air raid shelters. The school even opened on Saturday 15 July for the registration of children for evacuation, but none came to be registered. In spite of all disruptions, Ann Cramphorn gained a scholarship to Eastbourne High School for Girls.

During the holidays the ceiling was repaired, and probably just as welcoming was news on 16 October that extra clothing coupons had been received.

Reopened 9 January 1945 after a fall of snow, only 22 present, More snow on 30th and school closed 30th and 31st owing to lack of coal. Miss Vidler was absent through all this.

Secondary entrance school examination on 2 March Three scholars sat, Miss Baxter invigilating. As a result Kenneth Dark was awarded a place at Eastbourne Grammar School.

The school closed for Victory holidays on 8 and 9 May, which ran into an Ascension Day holiday, followed by Whitsun holiday. School closed again because the teachers attended a refresher course at Lewes in June, and closed all day for the General Election on 5 July; for use as polling station. Closed again for Victory celebrations on 11 July. There were games and sports in the cricket field, followed by entertainment at *Birling Manor.*

With the raids now over, a successful Open Day was held on 31 July. 'Many expressions of appreciation of the exhibited work and of the singing and clear diction of the children.'

When the school reopened in September three infants were admitted, but only 31 on the roll. The Diocesan Report read: 'A nice little school. Quite inadequate under the 1944 Act and difficult to see how it can be adapted. Beautifully tidy, it reflects great credit upon the cleaner [Nelson Breach] who evidently takes pride in his work. I hope that a canteen can be provided, some children come a distance. Head teacher is doing good work, her quiet manner has a refining influence on her charges.'

In February 1946 the children received a gift of chocolates from the Kinsmen's Club of Canada, and on 26 July Maisie Worsell, Esme and Joan Baldock heard that they had gained places at Eastbourne High School for Girls from September.

On 6 November Miss Dyke made her last visit of many to show 'how lack of space could be overcome with Physical Training'.

On 10 December Miss Gregory came to discuss school meals, cook's duties, and food supplies. The next day Miss REM Fish called, first mention of a psychiatric social worker.

The school opened 14 January 1947 when the school leaving age was raised to 15 years (postponed from 1939) there were, however, only 18 present - 14 absent owing to measles and colds. Mrs Vidler didn't arrive until 9.20am. On 28th Mrs Vidler was absent, no buses, and the next day, after heavy snow with an attendance of seven, very little fuel left, with delivery impossible owing to the condition of the roads, and when the severe frost had caused 'unsanitary conditions' the school closed until 3 March.

On 28 April the School Canteen started, 34 out of the 36 children had the Village Hall meal nicely cooked by Mrs Q Brown, promptly served and much appreciated.

Mrs Rock, the new PT organiser, visited in September, and gave a lesson out of doors. School closed on 20 November for wedding of Princess Elizabeth and Philip Mountbatten.

On 19 January 1948 Nurse Summers made head inspections, all clean. The school was instructed to exclude all children who had attended Tommy Eve's birthday party owing to suspected infantile paralysis. Thankfully, on the 24th it was decided that Tommy's illness was not polio and Dr Langford allowed all the children to return to school.

On 4 February Mrs Vidler arrived at 8.55am, but was not well enough to continue and at 9.45 she returned home. Suffering from 'nervous debility' she never returned.

Mr Budd told the head teacher that no supply teacher was available and lessons should be given to class I for half a day and class II for half day. 26 April was a holiday for the Silver Jubilee of the Royal Wedding.

The Wicking children outside the school in 1948, when John the eldest was due to leave for a Seaford school.
From left to right: Raymond (born 1941), David (1943), Cecily (1939), John (1937) and Colin (1940)

The School 'closed on 21 February 1949 on account of the illness of the head mistress'. Miss Turk returned on 7 March, but she was unable to cope after the Easter break and Miss Joan Smith, supply teacher, took over. She clearly believed in cleanliness for in her first week she ordered 22 cleaning tablets, 5 tabs of toilet soap and 1 gallon Jeyes fluid. She left on 27 July 'after a very happy term at East Dean school' and no doubt squeaky clean. Lilian Turk, however, wasn't well enough to return and she retired on 31 July 'after 15 years of interesting work' and went to Sevenoaks. In the October she was presented with a £54 cheque by Sir John Salmond.

G Marsh, R Goodfellow, and M Winter had passed the scholarship examination, and when the school reopened in September Mrs Nellie MV Roberts was the new head teacher with Miss Elizabeth Stein as infant teacher. Mrs Roberts lived in the schoolteacher's cottage [later *Cobblers,* now *Smugglers*] while her husband was with the CMS in West Africa.

John Dann said, "On her first day Mrs Roberts told us how the little black girls had called her 'Ma', so we called her 'Ma Roberts' from then on. When we were unruly she would say that her little black girls could do no wrong, and on occasions she would become faint if we were especially rowdy. The first time we were worried, but after a while we didn't take much notice".

In November Miss Stein visited a modern infants' school in Newhaven for experience. Quite a few 'firsts' came along over the next 12 months. The first mention of the children acting in a Nativity Play for their parents was on 16 December. On 16 January 1950 student teachers from Eastbourne Training College visited, and on 26 January Mr S Bertram gave an entertainment of conjuring to the children. For some reason on Ash Wednesday that year the school 'carried on as usual', apart from a short Service at Prayer Time. Always before and afterwards the school went to a Church Service and had a half-day holiday.

The first ever parents' meeting was held on 15 May. 'About 30 came and asked about modern education and the scholarship exam. They are anxious to form a Parents' Association.'

Miss Stein left to be replaced by Mrs Dilys Baker. She had been a nurse and later trained as a teacher. "My husband, in the RE, was killed in Normandy having gone through Dunkirk and El Alamein." She had a son who worked in the Met. Office. Having remarried in 1951 she became Mrs Blythe and lived in Seaford coming to school on the 0800h bus.

The attendance officer, Mr Fisher, said there was 100% attendance in May. The Diocesan Inspector's Report stated: 'I didn't know that there had been a complete change of staff. I do not propose to make any criticisms. Both are anxious to deal conscientiously with the religious teaching. There will be a great deal of leeway to make up with the infants.'

On 16 June the head teacher accompanied the two candidates to their Eastbourne High School interview, and afterwards both Patricia Wicking and Norma Clark heard they had been awarded scholarships. The school was closed on 30 June to enable teachers to attend a refresher course at Bexhill.

In July PC Page gave a talk on Road Safety, a regular item since the war. John Dann said, "A policeman from Polegate would take us for kerb drill. He would line us up along the side of the road and say, 'Look right, look left, look right again and listen before you cross'. We thought it hilarious and would dash across halfway through his piece because nothing was ever coming to see or hear. We rode our bikes round and round in circles".

The school reopened as a Controlled School on 4 September 1950, taken over by the Local Education Authority (LEA) under the 1944 Education Act. Eight pupils had left, six to Seaford County Modern School, and with five new admissions in the infants, 36 were present. All inspected by Nurse Peck, the District Nurse, on 4 October.

Miss Mayne and Miss Whipp, two students from Seaford College, came to teach needlework in January 1951, while the headmistress took the scholarship children in the small room, alongside Mrs Baker and the infants. That month Mrs Roberts announced to the class that 'Mrs Baker was leaving and was coming back as Mrs Blythe'.

On 22 February at playtime two girls collided and one girl's glasses cut her eyebrow. She went to the Princess Alice Hospital, had three stitches and was back in time for lunch. Mr and Mrs Blythe (Mrs Baker) called and brought a piece of their wedding cake.

After the Whitsun holiday 'William Garish left to go to Australia; the Birling Gap coastguard station had closed and the father transferred. Two boys in hospital after a bicycle accident; John Hearns has a fractured jaw, and Terry Pownall internal injuries'.

The school reopened in September with 38 on the register. Painters were busy, and while the inside was finished, there was no time to get it straight so teachers and children spent the time on the Village Green. The canteen cook had transferred to Lewes, so Mrs Florence Melling began as cook and canteen assistant. She was cook from 1951 to 1964 when the school closed. John Dann said, "Mrs Melling cooked really good dinners. Nobody didn't like the dinners at East Dean School, and they often went back for seconds, which no one ever did at Seaford." Jane Nash added, "The best roast potatoes ever - how did she do it?" One day the Vicar went to the canteen with the children and stayed for the meal.

At a Scripture lesson in church Miss Diana Eyre told stories of children in other lands.

For the first meeting of the new Controlled School's managers, in December 1951, the Head Teacher, Mrs Roberts, emphasised the need for a playground, which was endorsed by the managers. There were strong protests in the village, however, over suggestions that a new school could be between the Rectory and the new Police House.

On 22 January 1952 Mr Ernest Cater, one of the new managers, looked in. Mrs Blythe was absent because the road was blocked by an overturned bus.

'When the children came back from the canteen on 6 February they were full of the news that HM King George VI had died in his sleep.' 'The school kept two minutes silence on 15 February, the day of the funeral, and afterwards sang hymns and the National

Anthem. The children copied a 'piece of loyalty' and the best two by Colin Dark and Jane Nash were sent to the Queen with an expression of love and sympathy. On 25 February a reply was read out: 'The Private Secretary is commanded by the Queen to thank the children of East Dean and Friston for their kind message of sympathy which her Majesty much appreciates.' Mr Cater framed the letter to hang in the classroom.

All the usual school events happened over the next few months. On Ash Wednesday, after milk, the children went to church and the school closed. The head teacher attended a managers' meeting at the Vicarage on 10 March. A week later Hugh Winter ran home on his way to the canteen and didn't return. 'Richard Hearn(s) cut his head on a wall during PT on 15 May. First Aid given and he seemed all right.' The school closed on 27 June to enable the teachers to attend a refresher course at Lewes. The Revd RL Lycett visited the school on 11 July and found 'everything in order', but more cut heads a week later when 'John Dann fell over and cut the top of his head, a nasty gash and sent to hospital'. Innovations were Mrs Maud Worsell starting as clerical assistant to the canteen on 3 March, and on 18 June Mrs Blythe took five boys to Seaford County Modern School to join in the team races.

Mrs Roberts, head mistress of the school, 'regretfully resigned' at the end of August 1952. The Revd Norman Lycett explained that 'since she started the heavy responsibilities of schoolwork have not been easy for her, and not helped by her none too robust health. She will continue to live in East Dean and our good wishes go to her, her husband, and to her two most promising sons'.

She was succeeded by Miss Josephine FP Jenner who lived in Alfriston and came in by car, so she was the first Head not to live in the School House. The managers let the School House tenancy to Geoffrey Dann at £6 per year in quarterly payments.

The managers also announced that 'the new head proposes to form, as soon as possible, a Parent-Teacher Association. Annual subscriptions of 1/6d [7$\frac{1}{2}$p] per family to the Hon. Treasurer, Mrs G Taylor *Underhill Cottages.'*

Sir John Salmond, another new manager, visited on 27 November 1952 and inspected the Registers, and on 18 December there was the now customary attendance of managers, parents and friends to hear the children's carols.

Miss Jenner and Mrs Blythe were good teachers and well-liked, but with their means of transport (Miss Jenner in an ancient Austin 7 and Mrs Blythe on the bus from Seaford) they were increasingly liable to be late or even to fail to get in altogether. On 10 October Mrs Blythe was absent, so Mrs Worsell looked after the Infants. Miss Jenner arrived at 9.20am on 16 December 'having had to walk up the hill because the icy roads were dangerous for traffic, and Mrs Blythe arrived at 10.15am having caught the first bus from Seaford. Mrs Worsell, clerical assistant, had been giving the children choir practice until I arrived.' When Mrs Blythe was absent in October, Mrs Worsell again looked after the Infants.

One result was that Mrs Worsell, who had proved most adept at filling in, took on extra clerical duties from 5 January 1953 in addition to her dinner assistant's work. Whenever Miss Jenner's car had to be repaired, or wouldn't start, or her parents were ill, or Mrs Blythe's bus couldn't make it up the hill, Mrs Worsell opened the school and 'settled the children', which by 1958 had turned to giving them English tests to keep them busy. Before long she was taking a class the whole day if one of the teachers were absent. By 1964 she was officially doing another 10 hours which made her practically full-time.

In February 1953 electricians were busy and the school had electric light at last. It meant that the next month Miss Jenner could show films, on Miss Parker's projector, to the Parent-Teacher Association including one on intelligence tests.

Miss Jenner decided to reintroduce May Queen celebrations, so on 24 April 1953 Class I practised Maypole dancing on the cricket field. The Queen, Jane Booth-Clibborn (née Nash), said, "On the day it rained and my cardboard crown covered in flowers disintegrated, a complete disaster". She went on, "It being Coronation Year we had a tableau with the pupils dressed in the national costumes of all the Commonwealth countries".

In the afternoon of 22 May some parents came to distribute the Coronation Spoons provided by the Parents' Association. On Empire Day (Queen Victoria's birthday, 24 May) the custom survived of the girls curtseying and boys bowing to the flag on the Green.

On 7 September Miss Drew called to renew acquaintance with her father's old school. One dramatic difference from his time was that now only 40 were on the Roll. Mr Drew, however, didn't have to attend regular managers' meetings.

Her subjects kneel to the 1954 May Queen on the cricket field, Saturday 22 May. L-R (of those clearly visible): Jennifer Hopper, Carol Hearns, Anne Stephenson (standing), Faith Taylor (May Queen), Keith Haffenden (Jock O' The Green), Leila Harvey, Jean Richey, Graham Gillam, Jane Nash (who as last year's Queen had just crowned Faith). 'Keith Haffenden, with the infectious smile, made us all feel gay with his high spirits. The boys performed a spirited Tonga dance and the girls a graceful Maori dance. Miss Jenner, who was presented with a box of chocolates, thanked all on the success of their hard work.' Phyllis Hughes wrote, 'nowhere in the country more sweetly and gaily done than in our own village'. Col Gordon took photographs and Miss Parker cine-filmed the Maypole dancing

When a representative from the County Architect came in January 1954 to decide on a place for a new fire extinguisher the head mistress lost no time in pointing out 'another sprinkler', namely, a crack in the roof. On 1 February the toilets were frozen, and the Village Hall canteen was frozen, but 'Mrs Melling borrowed water from a nearby house and managed to cook a meal. Sent the children home after dinner.' On 11 March, when the children were taken for a walk in the afternoon, Keith Haffenden managed to fall from a tree and was badly shaken. 'On return he had a hot cup of tea and was sent home.'

Mr Harris as part of his HMI report stated,. 'About 50% of the children take the school meal daily, this is cooked at the Village Hall. The meal on the day was well cooked and enjoyed by the children under very pleasant conditions.' The dinners were getting known - for on 1 July four international students visited 'the canteen system'.

Venturing further afield, 94 children and adults went to London Zoo on 18 June, thanks to free tickets from Charles Meller and Col JA Burrell. On 30 June, after Miss Parker gave a show of lantern slides concerning the earth, moon and sun, 'all the children were allowed to look at the sun through smoked glass at various stages of the eclipse clearly visible between 1.15 and 2.15pm.' While 'Mrs Goldsmith gave the boys permission to play cricket in the Horsefield providing an adult is with them', Jane Nash and Anne Stevenson were winning scholarships. Jane said, "The scholarship to Eastbourne Girls High School could have been divisive, but I remained on good terms with all my school friends, although envious of them going to school together. Anne Stevenson had moved to Lewes so I went alone."

A succession of visitors came in September: Col TM Gordon gave a series of British wall maps to the school; Miss Callender watched PT; Mr Budd collected milk bottle tops, and Mr Lane, the music organiser, called. On a more serious note in December, after tests by Dr Tony Whitehead of Brighton one pupil was classed as 'Educationally Sub-normal'.

Health and Safety in January 1955, 'Playtime collision between Roy Armiger (age 10) and Clifford Granshaw (6). Clifford bumped the back of his head and afterwards was violently sick, but later he ate a small meal. I don't think he will suffer any ill effects.'

At Easter, school caretaker Nelson Breach wasn't well and had to resign after 18 good years, his place being taken by Geoff and Nora Dann of the school house. A worrying trend for the school numbers started on 25th April when S Pearson left to go to a private school.

Boys of the Village School, 1957, l-r back row: Roger Harvey, Derek Vine. Next row: Graham Gillam, Graham Pyle, John Cheal, Barry Morgan, Dennis Plaice, Edward Vickery, Rudolf Pownall. Next row: Billy Fuller, David Satchell, -Hearns, ?, Graham Haffenden, -Pyle, David Cairns. Front row: Ian Fears, Clive Hearns, ?, Alan Pyle, Tony Richey and Cliff Haffenden

School was closed for the Parliamentary election on 26 May 1955, so the postponed Empire Day ceremony was held in Brigadier and Mrs Hudson's *Grey Walls'* garden on 18 June. The crown and sceptre and green cage were transferred from last year's May Queen and Jock-in-the-Green (Faith Taylor and Keith Haffenden) to this year's holders (Sandra Goldsmith and Colin Dark). Roy Armiger and Michael Evans were heralds, Roger Harvey spoke well as the crier, while Graham Gillam, as St George, conquered an awesome 'five-boy' dragon. After a chorus of bees and butterflies, elves and glow-worms, it was Maypole time. First the infants, followed by the seniors, all cleverly plaited the red, white and blue ribbons. The National Anthem, presentation of flowers to Miss Jenner and Mrs Blyth, and a collection for school books completed the afternoon. The ubiquitous Maypole dancing goes back to pre-Christian times as a fertility rite to assist the growth of crops. Roman youths sang in honour of Flora the goddess of fruits and flowers. In Tudor times much was made of May Day, bunches of may were hung over doorways, although in 1563 Maypoles were referred to as 'stinckyng idols about which people leape and daunce as the heathen did'.

Capt Norman Davies gave a short talk in June on animals which help and hinder the farmer, and in July the school had a coach to Pevensey Castle, by way of the zig-zags and Eastbourne front. The children were thrilled by the dungeon.

At Christmas 'children sang, recited and acted for managers, parents and friends. After refreshments, presents from the Parents' Association were distributed from the tree.'

'Infants' attendance low on 1 February 1956 because of measles and colds. I sent one home as he should be in bed. Lavatory tanks frozen so we had to flush the pans after breaking the ice with hot water. 'The tank is now frozen but the caretaker's wife let us have several buckets of water.' After the Ash Wednesday Service in church at 9.15am the children were sent home as the lavatories were completely frozen, arrangements having been made to provide meals to children whose parents would not be at home. Not until 3 March did a plumber finished repairs and thaw the cisterns.

The May Day revels for the crowning of Valerie Gillam as Queen of the May were postponed because of chickenpox amongst her subjects. On 10 May, Ascension Day, the school remained closed so no Service in the church that year. The deferred May Day celebrations were on the Green in the afternoon of 23 June. The Nursery Rhyme folk present included the Old Woman who lived in a Shoe (Rosemary Cheal), Mother Hubbard (Margaret Ellingsworth) and Humpty Dumpty (Tony Richey).

Sandra Goldsmith heard on 14 June that she was to go to Eastbourne High School,

On 2 July the Revd RL Lycett 'visited the school and found everything in perfect order. Looked at the punishment book and found no punitive offence had been committed'. It was his last visit for he retired in September. 'Dr Collins inspected throats on 10 September, and sent Barry Masters home and excluded Dennis Plaice because of his sister's illness. Miss Nowell called to enquire about a pupil in relation to her father's request for custody.' Miss Jenner reported that 'She was in excellent hands and developing well'.

East Dean School 1958. L-R, standing: Linda Ticehurst, Carol Hearns, ?, Pam Hadrell, Alan Pyle, Ian Fears, Clifford Haffenden, Philip Pyle, Tony Richey, Graham Haffenden (sitting), Dennis Plaice, Edward Vickery, Martin Ketcher. Sitting: Doreen McAvoy, Wendy Haffenden, Miss Jo Jenner, Julia Rust, Janet Stewart. On the ground: Heather White, ?, Jean Richey, Linda Plaice, Leila Harvey, Kathryn Trickett, Christine Maurais

Supervised by their lecturer, students came on 1 October and took a group of children to do local study work around the village.

In May 1957 Jean Dann was crowned May Queen with Barry Maslen Jock o' the Green.

The school gave a half-hour programme of Christmas Carols on the evening of 17 December. The Family Service regulars gathered for a 'get-together' with teas and a film show of *Popeye* and *Mickey Mouse* provided by Miss Parker.

HMI Inspection Report 1958: 'The configuration of this small C of E school presents great handicaps. There is no regular playground and a wide range of ages. The school consists of a long narrow room divided into two teaching spaces by a movable wooden and glass partition and a smaller room. The rooms are neat and orderly. There were 50 on the roll, organised in two classes - juniors taken by the Head and infants taken by an experienced qualified teacher. Many of the children could apply themselves with more determination. The children achieve a competence in figures but fail to obtain an understanding of the processes. Reading given much attention. They enjoy their singing and dancing. The Infants' is friendly and pleasant, they are provided with many opportunities to develop skills. The pupils are friendly and willing and take an interest in local efforts; each day children sweep out the bus shelter and keep the Village Green free of litter. The morning assembly is reverent and the school meal an opportunity to develop social skills.'

Paul Nash (no relation to Jane) won a scholarship to Eastbourne Grammar School.

East Dean School, Infants 1959. L-R back row: ?, Michael Hudson, Christine Pettit (in dark cardigan). Seated row: ?, Duncan Ketcher, Brenda White, Andrew Stewart, Mrs Dilys Blythe, Christine Fears Clive Hearns. Sitting on the ground: Geoffrey Maurais, Chris Hopkins, Ann Winter, Jill Ticehurst, ?Ian Fears, Paul Bennison, and Anne Ransom

'The vicar took prayers on 21 July and announced that the managers had arranged for delivery of a new VHF wireless instead of waiting for the LEA to discuss the matter. It was installed that day.' The school was closed for the Vicarage Fete on 30 July.

Bus times changed in September, 'so Mrs Blythe does not reach school until 9.15am.' Not daunted, the Head arranged to open school at 9.15am 'until the bus timetable is altered. Infants will be dismissed at 3.15 and juniors at 4pm until afternoons darker when juniors' time of dismissal will be advanced'.

On 27 October admitted Christine and Geoffrey Maurais. Roll 44.

In January 1959 admitted Lois Pelecanos, but Sam Barnard left for a private school. 'On 26 February, a student from Chelsea Training College took PT. A slight accident happened when Christine Fears, six, ran out at midday straight into a passing lorry which was fortunately travelling slowly. She was brought into school where we tended her bruises. The mother was fetched and the doctor informed. He said she was suffering from bruises, abrasions and shock.' Christine didn't return to school until 3 March. Normally the children were not allowed to use the front door, coming in through the yard.

'School closed on 12 May to enable juniors to attend Seaford Music Festival.' The school outing this time was to Chessington Zoo on 19 May.

One of the boys came first in the primary event at Seaford's swimming sports. Not all sunshine for him, however, later that year he had to attend the Juvenile Court.

Closed for a teachers' refresher course on 17 July - never in Mr Drew's time! When Miss Jenner returned, 'I received a telephone complaint about bullying and giving and receiving promises by some of the boys. To deal with this today I interviewed two of the parents concerned, the boys and others who had information. I banned the game which led to such roughness, gave a severe lecture on offering and receiving money and telephoned a report to the office. I hope the boys are thoroughly chastened and the business settled.'

In an increasing tendency, two pupils left to go to a private school. Many parents were torn between a happy, local school and a school where there more options such as music and sports. It was a most pleasant, safe school, but as one pupil said, "When I went to

Seaford I couldn't multiply or divide, I'd only been taught to add and subtract." At least there was a first mention of a Speech Therapist when Miss Williams called.

On 2 October children were lent photographic negatives to watch the eclipse of the sun. For previous eclipses in 1912 and 1954 smoked glass had been used. Doubtful if such would be allowed today. The children managed to do quite a bit of damage to themselves, 'Julia Rust had a nasty fall at playtime, banging her head on the asphalt. Afterwards she had a headache and stayed at home in the afternoon.'

When the school reopened in 1960: Miss Jenner wrote 'C Musgrove has left, but two infants admitted.' She went on, 'I attended the Educational Exhibition at Lewes on 9 March, Mrs Blythe took my class.' On 6 May the school was closed for the Royal Wedding. 'I attended a conference at Eastbourne Training College on 9 May.'

A cold damp day didn't diminish the occasion when Carol Hearns was crowned May Queen on the Village Green in 1959, by Lita Curry, the retiring Queen. The Jock O' the Green, Michael West, facing away on the right by the Maypole, had received his sceptre from John Cheal. 'There was a charming performance of Goldilocks by the juniors, climaxed by Maypole dancing' a feature of the festival since Miss Jenner revived it in 1953: all to a wind-up gramophone

The next day Captain Horace Rew came to discuss the Ascension Day Service arrangements on 26th. Up to the closure the children attended a 10am Service followed by - provided they sang the *Te Deum* properly - a half-day's holiday.

For the 1960 May Queen, 'The Heralds Martin Ketcher and Graham Pyle announced Leila Harvey as Queen and David Satchell as Jock o' the Green. When the Queen called for entertainment the whole school performed dances and songs'. The Juniors were taken to the Lifeboat Museum at Eastbourne and the school closed for an afternoon outing to Drusilla's, but Mrs Blythe escaped - absent with tonsillitis. Miss Jenner 'took ten children to Seaford on 13 July for the school swimming sports. Mrs Worsell supervised the rest of the class.'

Matters appeared to continue as pleasantly as ever. On 21 March Mr PJ Budd checked registers, as he had been doing for over 24 years. Miss Hannay called to test the hearing of the six-year-olds on 13 April, no deafness found, and a visual (not auditory) aids official inspected the wireless set and gramophone on 25 July.

Students' Teaching Practice began on 14 November and they had some excitement for Tony Vickers became ill, and his mother was at work at an unknown address in Eastbourne. 'We made him up a bed in the hall where he slept most of the day with three attacks of vomiting and one slight convulsion. After this we sent for a doctor who came quickly and said it was caused by an ear infection. When Mrs Vickers came I took the family home in my car. Mrs Blythe and the students coped with the school.'

More were leaving the school, in November Mary West and Pamela Hadrell left. By the reopening on 9 January 1961 Ian Paterson had moved to Eastbourne, and Christopher Hopkins was off to a private school. There was some compensation for Fred and Susan Upton admitted on 16 February, they had access to a new drinking fountain that had been installed in the Juniors' cloakroom. Fred didn't enjoy the facility too long being transferred to Friday Street School the next year, 'being not suitable for East Dean school'.

Martin Ketcher won a scholarship and left for Lewes Grammar School, despite East Dean school's latest modern fad, for in June 1961 a telephone had been installed.

On 7 June PC Newton warned the children about playing on the wall near the cesspit at The Fridays. Later that month came the first Polio immunisations, a jab not a sugar lump.

For a new departure there was a PTA outing for children to see *Snow White* on Ice at Brighton while the teachers attended a refresher course.

Jill Thornton (née Ticehurst) says, 'On Thursdays in the summer term Miss Jenner took us on the bus to the Devonshire Park Baths for swimming lessons, always followed by a drink of hot chocolate or piping hot chicken soup from a vending machine'. Miss Jenner writes, 'On 27 July the juniors held a Swimming Gala at the baths. In the presence of managers and parents seven children gained 4th class certificates and three reached 3rd class. Of the rest all attempted to swim a length and six succeeded.' The next day was School Prizegiving; some prizes given by Mrs Dreghorn and some won in a painting competition.

'During the 1961 summer break the floors were renewed, but the work was not well done and after discussions with the caretaker and the County Architect's staff along with the head and Vicar the opening was postponed.' The floors were finally repaired at half term.

'A Children's Theatre Company gave a performance in school on 4 April 1962.' The May Celebrations were on the Green and school closed for the County Show in June.

ESCC placed a refrigerator in the Village Hall to provide more variety for the meals.

Mr Karle, psychologist, visited and Sister Thackeray tested Jacqueline Stedeford's sight.

'At the Prizegiving books and tokens and certificates were given for work and swimming. Verses, songs and a lucky dip ended the event. Next term six children will go to Seaford, two are moving, and John Mockler and two others are going to private schools.' Owing to a falling membership it was decided to end the Parent-Teacher Association.

'Mr Doggett and his theatre group came on 13 November. The two plays presented were much appreciated.' Two days afterwards was the first mention of Needlework for a while when Miss Hurst, the organiser, called.

'Could not open school on 7 January 1963 with lavatories frozen and dangerous roof snow. Finally reopened on 17 January as the mains thawed.'

'I took the juniors to Seaford swimming sports on 10 July, where they won first place in the relay race.' 'On the morning of the 12th I took them to the Rural Studies Exhibition at Heathfield where we showed a miniature garden.' They made sure they were back in time for Mrs Melling's midday dinner.

Reopened 12 September, 'Hugh O'Brien will go to a private school. Roll now only 17.' This was fewest number of pupils recorded. On 28 November, 'Notification of the committee's decision to cease to maintain this school was pinned on the school door.' 'Because of the low numbers Mrs Blythe is transferred to supply staff from next term after 14 years of service. While regretting this we realise the necessity.'

On 18 December Mrs Blythe and the head took one child from each class to the Vicarage to present good-bye gifts from the children. The next day was the school party when managers and parents attended to watch playlets and carol singing. Parents provided food and donations for presents. Mrs Blythe had her presentation early in the next year.

In January 1964 five admitted, but roll only 21. Mr Braithwaite, County Education Officer, met in January with managers and parents to discuss closure. On 11 March confirmed that the school was to close at Easter. The following day Mr Lilley came to select books for use at Chyngton, and next day non-teaching staff received notice terminating their employment, the caretaker to continue part-time until all equipment removed.

A managers' meeting to settle final details was held on 16 March, and subsequently 'Mr Doxat Pratt borrowed old school log books to glean material for a talk about the school history.' The managers at the closure were Minnie Davies-Gilbert, Patience Harding, the Revd Richard W Burns-Cox, Maurice Doxat Pratt, Lt-Col Thomas Gordon, Rose Dann, Vida Elvin and Kathleen Burness.

Final day, 25 March 1964. 'Visited by ex-pupils, managers, and the press in the morning. At 3.30pm attended last Service at the church, the Revd Burns-Cox returning for the occasion. There was a large congregation. Afterwards pupils, parents, managers, Mrs Harding and Miss Davies-Gilbert returned to the school for refreshments. Speeches in which reference was made to the history of the school, its value, people who had served it - teachers, managers, caretakers, clerical and kitchen staff, brought the final session to an end. So after 11$^{1}/_{2}$ years with all the memories, happy and sad, I write for the last time. *Closed school* Josephine FP Jenner. Head mistress.'

Final day of the school. L-R, back row: Ann Winter, Elizabeth Graham, Mrs Maud Worsell, Christine Fears, Headmistress Miss Josephine Jenner. Middle row: Peter Markham, Philip Pyle, Stephanie?, Shirley Breach, Lois Pelacanos, Jill Ticehurst, Susan Pownall, ?Wendy Haffenden, Marilyn Prince. Front row: Jenny Pelling, Kevin Winter, Stephanie Pfeifer, Debora Fielder, Thomas Fyfield, Michael Hudson?, Melvyn Breach, David Goodman

As from 13 April all East Dean & Friston children attended Chyngton School or the Seaford Secondary Modern School, a bus picked them up at 0830h from East Dean and Friston to their school and returned to East Dean and Friston at the end of the afternoon.

The final act on 14 May was a presentation to Josephine Jenner, Florence Melling, Geoff and Nora Dann, and Maud Worsell. They thanked the village and in particular Miss Elvin for organising the farewell. They would miss the children, but for the children it was an exciting step forward, and the hope was that they would continue to play their part in the community. Dilys Blythe also thanked the pupils and parents and friends for their gifts. 'The 14 years have been happy treasured ones in a village which has accorded me kindness, warmth and hospitality. Although the closure was probably in the best interests of the children, something precious and irreplaceable was lost.' Particularly sad because, if it was just a case of numbers, by the Millennium there were sufficient children in the village for a 50-pupil school.

Answer to the Nursery rhymes photo of 1915, L-R: Old Mother Hubbard, Humpty Dumpty, Jack and Jill, Old King Cole, Jack Sprat and wife, and Simple Simon and Pieman.

In April 1875 there were 65 pupils on the Register. The greatest number on the Register was 124 in September 1908. The last year with over 90 was 1910, the last year with over 80 was 1922. The least on the Register was 17 in September 1963.

7. The Village Green, the *Tiger Inn* and around

The Green was the heart of any village. Of medieval origins and often at the junction of roads, its main purpose was to secure stock at night against predators - human or animal. It often had a well, and became surrounded by buildings, such as a school, smithy, wheelwright shop or even the church. Use for recreation followed, and maypoles and war memorials became standard features.

The Green and *Tiger Inn*, with well, *c*.1885. No dormers on 2 The Green, but two doors

Most Greens remained unchanged for centuries, and if buildings are found on a Green they were probably gained by squatter's rights and are characterised by a tiny garden.

So East Dean Village Green is typical and when it had to be registered as common land in 1965 it was one of some 1400 village greens; the average size being three acres.

The Green and the *Tiger c*.1895. Roof pitch altered and dormer windows put in from about 1890

Originally it was larger than today, extending to the Church Green by the side of the church, but little documentation exists. In 1811 there was a payment of 12½p for proclaiming an alteration of East Dean Fair, 'held on the Green on the eve, day and morrow of St Simon and St Jude's Day'. The Fair lasted into the late 1800s.

The British Legion [BL] agreed in 1949 that the Union flag be flown from the Village Green flagstaff on 23 April St George's Day, 24 May Empire Day, HM Official Birthday in June, the 15 September Battle of Britain Day, and Remembrance Day in November. Maintenance of the pole was taken over by the Parish Council [PC] in 1966.

In 1971 Hailsham RDC made a Tree Preservation Order for parts of East Dean, and that year Mrs Anne Conduitt and her three daughters took up residence in the old school.

Steve Ovett, the Olympic athlete who lived at *Gayles,* switched on the Village Green Christmas tree lights of 1987, and led the carol singing of the hundred people who attended despite atrocious weather. It was organised by the Friday Club. The Green continues to be used for Fetes and such activities, apart from overflow out of the pub on warm days.

It was the year that the Tiger Tees Golfing Society was formed at the *Tiger.* In 1991 it raised £376 for Eastbourne hospitals, and in 1992 sponsored the Christmas tree lights on the Green, taking over from the Friday Club. Recently the PC organised the lights, although for two years of dissension the tree was sited near the Village Hall.

The Green c.1920, from the hill on the SW where *Little Hill* is today, looking over the *Darbies'* roof, hiding *Pendrills,* towards the *Tiger* on the other side of the Green criss-crossed with paths. To the left is Upper Street with *Little Lane Cottage* behind and towards the centre is *The Dipperays'* roof. To the right is the War Memorial, without railings. The Memorial cost was £127 of which the metal plate absorbed £32. It was designed by Arthur S Haynes who declined any fee

In 1992 Anthony du Gard Pasley reported on landscaping methods to restore and redevelop the Green. He questioned whether the iron railings were suitable, and asked should the flag pole be there? The local RBL replied with the reasons for their presence and why they should remain. The landscaping plan was thrown out.

The Green is surrounded by a pub, shops, houses, and part of *New House Farm.* The letter box was in the wall of the shop which on and off has housed the Post Office. In the 1950s the Post Office announced that any letter to East Dean or Friston posted locally after the 1745h collection and before 0630 would be delivered by the first post that day.

Thieves tried to break into the village Post Office in November 1996. Their efforts were unsuccessful, but as Sam Hodgson mentioned this was the second attempt. It was decided to wall up the post office letter box and erect a pillar post box across the road, which is there today, despite being knocked over by a car in 1999.

Until 1991 vehicles could drive around the Green and pull up outside the *Tiger,* but the battle to unclog the traffic of East Dean's Green had been going on for 17 years, with much argy-bargy about the plans. Maureen Honey, county councillor, said, "Anything has to be better than what we have at the moment", but Pauline Joslin thought that it would only transfer the nuisance.

In 1990 the PC discussed restricting car parking there, but decided that yellow lines would be inconvenient all the year when any advantage would only be in the summer. So the next year a car park was built over part of the Horsefield, with no parking on the Green.

The obvious feature on the Green is the **War Memorial** unveiled and dedicated on Wednesday, 4 August 1920, at a simple but impressive service with the evening light providing an added beauty. Mrs Grace Davies Gilbert and Canon Streatfeild addressed the large gathering. "May this Cross remain, for all who pass by, a solemn remembrance of those who gave their lives for our peace and security." [3]

Remembrance Day Parade, 1950, which included Boer War veterans. L-R: Ivan Worsell, Mrs Sylvia Tompsett, Charles Meller, the Revd L Lycett, Mr WD Curtis (with cross), Col KD Allan, General NG Bannatyne coat on arm, Capt H Lidiard, Bert Foord (two behind ??), Mr R Seymour, Lt Col TM Gordon (back row), George Cheal (standard bearer), MM Harding (with stick), Cecil Dann (sailor), (behind ?), Anthony Tompsett, Major CH Harding (back row), Charlie Vine, (next three ???), Reg Goldsmith (light overcoat), Lt Col EC Simmons (edge of picture). The Church Service was held at varying times over the years, mainly in the afternoon between the wars, but in the morning from 1947

It forms, of course, an essential component of the RBL Remembrance Day parade. Even when, as in 1957, 1969 and 1998, the parade was cancelled because of heavy rain, the wreaths were placed round the War Memorial as soon as the weather permitted.

The war veterans were the leading lights in coaxing blacksmith Luther Hills to make railings to encircle the War Memorial; they couldn't stand people coming from the *Tiger* and spilling their pints over it. Joe Pownall, a 1914-18 war veteran and founder member of the local BL in 1931, never missed the Remembrance Parade at the War Memorial.

In 1950 the PC assumed trusteeship of the War Memorial, and in the July a new tablet was inserted to commemorate the names of those who fell in the Second World War, and a third tablet was inserted later that year to replace the 1914-18 tablet in the same style and adding the name omitted. Remembrance Sunday that year was a lovely day. At the morning Service Sir John Salmond unveiled the 1939-45 tablets of names, and the Archdeacon of Hastings dedicated the memorial. A photographer from *The Times* was present and East Dean appeared in the paper on Monday, 13 November.

As late as 1959 a veteran wore the Boer War medals at the Remembrance Service.

The condition of the War Memorial was giving concern in 1953. The PC agreed in 1957 that the War Memorial railings should be painted, and the flower bed replaced with

York Stone at a cost of £150. The PC said it would oppose any suggestion to demolish it. Two years later it debated whether to add forenames to the War Memorial, but decided against.

There were further repairs in 1964 (when the plinth was paved), 1966 and 1992, and in 1993 the War Memorial and railings were given Grade II status. Sadly, shortly afterwards the PC needed to discuss vandalism by children throwing stones at it.

As in almost every other village in smuggling days it was believed, without too much firm evidence, that there were underground passages linking the cellars of many of these old houses, especially the *Tiger,* the *Darbies* and *The Dipperays.*

The 'Tiger' of the **Tiger Inn** was probably taken from the coat of arms of the Bardolfs or possibly the Norman de Dene family. These depicted a leopard, but as neither animal would have been known to most people at the time it was a reasonable mistake. A tiger serjeant was on the crest of the Medley family, holders of *Friston Place* after 1704.

The first records are in the mid-1600s when the Puritans recorded that the local malthouse was closed. There is, however, a fireback in the bar dated 1622, just how this relates to the age of the inn is a matter of conjecture. Later records of the 1600s state there was a disused malthouse, and Lambert's 1780 drawing of the village shows only a very small building with a large chimney where the *Tiger* is today, so the exact date of the present building is unclear, and like most of the village buildings it just grew.

A public well was outside the *Tiger* until 1896. [2] For many years the mounting block outside was the pedestal of the old font [4] rediscovered in church restorations of 1885, the year a storm damaged the roof of the *Tiger.*

The well outside the *Tiger* c.1895. Tony Markwick is one of the men. Bill Armiger said, "Before 1895 the villagers drew their water from various wells: the main ones being by the entrance to the *Tiger,* and on the Church Green, Lower Street." Another was near the A259 by the old Sorting Office, opposite the Forge, and some private houses had their own - there were three at the Parsonage. The *Tiger* well was renowned for being hard work

David Fowler, who replaced Thomas Anderson as publican, came from the *Dewdrop Inn* Eastbourne in 1881 with wife Mary and family of seven; a son, Friend, was born the next year. It was a hard life, for in those days village inns had to be open 0500h - 2200h. Mary died in 1911. In 1914 Friend Fowler married Alice and took over the *Tiger.* David and a daughter Annie moved to *Pendrills* where he died 1922. Of the other sisters, Lizzie married Luther Hills of the Forge.

When Lizzie died in May 1946 Annie kept home at the Forge for Luther Hills, her brother-in-law, and for her brother Friend after he retired from the pub in 1948. His wife, Alice, had died in January 1945. Friend died in 1951 and Annie died aged 83 in 1959. 'She barely touched 4 foot 9 inch [1.43m] in stature, but she had a heart of gold.'

Bill Armiger said, "Men would met at the *Tiger,* the long room upstairs was used for committee meetings and a dance once a week, Canadian soldiers came in during the 1914-18 war. At one time there was a quoits pitch on the grass outside the *Tiger.*"

Peter Mander wrote, 'Before 1939 the *Tiger* was an Old Boys' Social Club serving Eastbourne Star Brewery ales, but no food. It had dominoes, darts, shoveha'penny and a

Tontine club for Christmas.' The upstairs room was used for functions - from British Legion committees to Church Choir Suppers and Cricket Club Annual Dinners, and at 1920s musical evenings Tommy Dickens, the baker, blacked up and played the bones.

William Joslin wrote, 'In the early 1930s I was taken as a small boy to the *Tiger Inn*. I remember it vividly. The landlord was Friend Fowler, a genial character with a long waxed moustache. Nothing ever seemed to change. He never hurried or got excited, spoke very quietly and used as few words as possible, while being most genial and sympathetic. He was very knowledgeable about every aspect of village life and the inhabitants.

Maypole Dancing on the Green watched by the just-crowned Jubilee May Queen, part of the village's Queen's Silver Jubilee celebrations on 7 June 1977 [14]

'I was allowed to play in the kitchen, and was awed by the vast array of jars of home-made marmalades, jams, pickles, chutneys and fruits - all neatly labelled and stored on long shelves high up near the ceiling, and very exciting to the taste buds when opened.

A Royal British Legion Annual Fete on the Green in 1986 with the Maypole awaiting its dancers, stalls selling household recycles, the hot-dog stand, coconut shys, Find the Treasure, Buy a Ticket - pound a strip and Guess the Weight, and many more ways of extracting money for the good of the RBL charities

'I was not, of course, allowed into the bar - children were never, ever, allowed in bars those days, quite unthinkable. That did not stop me peering excitedly through the cracks in the door. The bar was very small and cosy, and very smoky. Usually there was a great big crackling fire (in the same fireplace as now) surrounded by a small group of villagers, shepherds, fishermen, farm workers and gardeners, all oddly clothed and tied up with string and puffing happily at their pipes. Four or five dogs snoozed gently on the floor, and the latest haul of rabbits was slung up in a corner, sometimes with fish and mushrooms. When the front door opened about every thirty minutes, it creaked on its hinges and all conversation stopped to welcome the newcomer, who was always known to the company. I could hardly understand any of the talk as I was unused to the rich Sussex dialect.

'Outside the *Tiger* I was fascinated by the lively chickens, ducks and sometimes geese that stomped impertinently around the Green, to a background of the vivacious happy yells that emerged from the thriving village school.'

In 1950 the lean-to at the eastern end of the *Tiger* was built over, and since 2006 the main fire at the *Tiger* has been gas-fired.

Pre-1939, the Village Constable, PC Harry Hyde, just happened to be in the *Tiger* when his Sergeant looked in, so he whipped his tankard under his cloak. He wasn't too pleased when the Sergeant expressed a wish to inspect Friston, but trailed along, holding the pint close to his side, until they reached Friston pond when the Sergeant suggested, "You might as well finish that pint before it goes flat".

A happy group of East Dean schoolchildren on the Village Green for crowning of the 1960 May Queen Leila Harvey. They include Janet & John Hearns, Julie & Ray Rust, Denis Plaice, Jean & Tony Richey, Kate Trickett and Ian Fears. Behind to the right is a *New House Farm* Barn

Ted Fears said, "In the war Irish labourers who came to level Friston Landing Ground were billeted in the village, some in Chris Johnson's house, others at *Waverley Post* and others in *Bryn Cottage,* then *Belmont.* They were always fighting, and one day a big fellow had a fork pushed into his face, and as I had just passed my test, I was deputed to drive him to the Princess Alice Hospital. Afterwards he wanted to buy me a drink, but I cried off.

"The next day he saw me as I walked across the Green and called across for me to have a drink on him. I felt I couldn't argue so I entered the *Tiger* where he ordered, 'Two pints'. I was astounded when Friend Fowler pulled the pints, because he knew the age of everyone in the village and normally wouldn't consider serving underage me. In a fresh light I looked at my new-found Irish friend - yes, he was very large, but his face gave the impression as though everyone in Ireland had attempted to walk over it, the once, and I realised Friend knew here was not a man to cross concerning trifling matters of age."

Most evenings Mark Fuller would bring a jug down to the *Tiger,* have half-a-pint and take the full jug back for his wife. At least that was his story. Another regular, old Rachel Patching, wandered across the Green every day in her slippers from wherever she was at the time, *Glebe Cottage* or the *Darbies,* carrying a jug covered with a cloth for a VP wine fill-up, and Albert Ellen, who lived with his wife, Emily, on the Green, would appear at the *Tiger* at nine o'clock with a quart jug, which was filled and he would drink it down. He then had it filled up and would take it home. 'Was a regular, but never said much.'

Ricky Hodgson said, "When we came to the village in 1953 the *Tiger* was a 'spittoon and sawdust' type of pub."

Harry Sellars, the potman at the *Tiger* for some years, was in the cricket club and generally involved around the village, a jolly poacher. Latterly lodged with the Eve family. He was left a considerable legacy, but did not live long to enjoy it.

Overheard in the *Tiger* one night, "How's the old sow to-night then Will?" "Ah, she got so bad we had to kill her to save her life."

Jesse Taylor comments, "Harry Corner, Tom Vine and Mark Fuller taught me to play dominoes, fives and threes, at the *Tiger*. I don't know why, but I was always the one who paid out." Fred Breach confirmed, "The men of the village then were Bill Dann, Harry West, Harry Corner, and James Wicking, who would play dominoes in the *Tiger*".

'Tiger Row', The Green and the *Tiger* looking from Upper Street *c.*1955

Peter Johnson said he started going to the *Tiger* when 'mine hosts' were Albert Edward Langford and his wife. They took over the tenancy in September 1948 from Friend Fowler.

Peter went on, "The regulars used to sing,

> *We are the East Dean boys,*
> *We know our manners*
> *And spend our tanners,*
> *As we drink at the Tiger Inn*
> *Doors and windows open wide*
> *You can hear John Barrett shout*
> *'Put those lights out'*
> *We are the East Dean boys."*

Stan Fuller would sing *The Tinkerman,* the words of which will not be repeated here.

In November 1956 John and Peggy Barrett became mine hosts at the *Tiger,* with its low beams, thick walls and sloping Green. 'When the East Sussex Hunt met on the Green on November 18 it was delightful to see John and Peggy bring out stirrup cups for the joint masters, Major Charles Davies-Gilbert and Captain John Harding, and the hunt.'

Around 1960 the inn had a parrot called *Tiger,* a great mimic, which included imitating the schoolmistress's whistle to bring the children in from play, so well done that Miss Jenner would find them lining up to enter the school before she'd blown.

Infants' teacher, Dilys Blythe said, "When Headmistress Miss Jenner was off having an operation she was replaced by a male supply teacher. At a break while the children were playing on the Green he would sit on the seat keeping an eye on them, but also he would nip down to the *Tiger* and have a pint". Mrs Blythe adds, "In all my 14 or so years at the school and walking across the Green most days, I never went into the pub".

The village raised £250 in 1962 to pay for a Guide Dog for the Blind - and what was the name bestowed on the dog? *Tiger,* of course.

Pauline Joslin recalled, "In the 1962-3 winter when snow cut off the village for weeks, the residents supported each other and gathered regularly in the *Tiger.*" As it happens, in 1963 the *Tiger* did offer 'Bed & Breakfast'.

Grace Taylor said, "Whenever I collected for 'Poppy Day' I would go into the *Tiger* and they would fill up my tin so I had to get another".

Ken Dodd, the comedian, came to Eastbourne for his summer shows and the times he stayed at 1 Upper Street he drank at the *Tiger.*

By the 1980s Jim and Pauline Conroy had taken over as tenants. The *Tiger Inn* remains Gilbert Estate property, and Jimmy Davies-Gilbert ran it for a year or two, but leased it to a brewery and from 1993, managed by Nick Denyer, it did well.

Another view of the Green in the 1880s. Obviously, quite an event to see a photographer. Again, clearly no dormer windows in No.2 the Green

In 1993 the RBL committee decided to meet in the *Tiger* function room instead of the 'cold and draughty' Village Hall. Nick said there would be no charge.

To the left as you come out of the *Tiger* was **New House Farm,** a working farm until 1982. It is one of the houses shown in the 1780 Burrell picture, and was built on the Glebe Field, owned by the Church in the Middle Ages. The old flint barn dates possibly to *c.*1600, but the cowsheds which abutted the Green were built about 1850. Scimpo Weston was the farmer there before 1914, with Charles Fears as farm foreman. After him Len Miller ran *New House Farm* before the Goldsmiths. He had a pony and trap and came round with a churn of milk, which he would ladle out into your container. He went to *Friston Place* to look after the horses. His wife, Nell, collected for the Princess Alice Hospital Box Scheme.

Peter Mander wrote, 'In the thirties we boys explored the village and the surrounding countryside with enthusiasm and pleasure. We watched the cows being milked by hand in the big shed backing onto one side of the village green. To observe this was fascinating.'

Eileen Goldsmith explained, "We came to *New House Farm* in October 1945, and with *Black Robin* and *Half Way* farms our acreage was increased to 1000. *New House Farm* belongs to the Gilbert Estate and derives its name from *The New House* or *The Dipperays,* which was new in the mid-1700s. Nearly all the houses round the Green were originally farmworkers' cottages - carters, stockmen, shepherds, ploughmen, and no doubt some gathered in the *Tiger* of an evening for a drink and a game of dominoes."

Eileen went on, "The cows were kept in what we called the cow-stall [South Barn, now apartments and a shop] alongside The Green. During the air raids it was used to stable Haine's the Eastbourne undertaker's horses. The cows were milked near the house and went to pasture over Gilbert's Drive just by *Sullivans* today.

"In the war the Canadians had Nissan huts near Birling Gap. Mr (Bert) Goldsmith bought the concrete footings (at 25p a sq yd) and used them to cover the farm yard.

"The 500-acre farm grew wheat and barley, with pasture for cows. In the 1940s we took milk in churns to Unigate in Waterworks Road, later a milk lorry collected them, and from about 1970 milk tankers piped the milk direct from the cooler house.

"We had a herd of Ayrshire cows and Sussex beef cattle. Sheep were only at *Half Way Farm*. I kept geese in the yard and chickens in the Horsefield, where the horses retired"

Geoff Nash said, "Bert Foord had been the cowman at the Goldsmith's farm but didn't want to continue when mechanised milking came in and he became a farm labourer again. He was replaced by Bernard Gillam, until he went on the buses, when I took over about 1956. This meant I was up at 0500h to feed and milk the cows, with Mr Goldsmith collecting the milk at 0730. The cows knew their places, and if a young one went in the wrong place the others got most upset. The Goldsmiths treated me well, like a son."

Geoff Nash continued, "I noticed, however, that Ted Flint, who lived in a tied cottage - 1 Cornish Cottages - was only paid £6.80 [£6/16/-] a week although experienced in farmwork, so in 1958 I decided to go into the family building firm. We couldn't afford a house in East Dean so bought one in Seaford."

East Dean Green, 1921, with no railings around the War Memorial.
Pendrills is on the left. The *Tiger* lean-to on the right was raised to roof level in 1950

In 1958 Derrick Pyle went to work for Bert Goldsmith, replacing Geoff Nash. "They had a herd of 18 tuberculin-tested Ayrshires with a daily yield of 50 gallons. The Goldsmith's were keen on their old horses and we used Damsel and Diamond for a year, afterwards we used a tractor for carrying hay and clearing manure.

"I finished at *New House Farm* in 1961 (and milking finished shortly afterwards) and went to *Ridge House* in Windmill Lane as gardener before joining the Post Office."

The Goldsmiths retired from *Black Robin Farm* after 40 years. Eileen Goldsmith said, "We gave up *Black Robin* and *Half Way* around 1980, and the Davies-Gilbert land in 1982, when my husband Bert retired at 70."

The Gorringes succeeded Bert Goldsmith, while Chris Johnson took on some additional acreage at *Cornish Farm*. Bert and Eileen Goldsmith ended their days at *New House Farmhouse,* where daughter Sandra is now.

In 1990 a planning application was made for a conversion of *New House Barns* into nine units and Wealden planning committee agreed a scheme to convert the grade II listed barn next to the Village Green into flats. In 1992, however, the roof of *New House* barn along Lower Street was effectively blown off, and the site remained in a sad and sorry state for over a decade. Starting in 2006 the buildings have been tastefully converted into *Carew Cottages* consisting of seven dwellings and Kim Shearer's teashop the *Hiker's Rest*.

Shops on the Green. The great enemy of wooden buildings was fire. Before fire brigades, once a fire took hold, whether a house or a street, it was only after it had consumed everything that was combustible that it died out. After the Great Fire of London in 1666 Dr Nicholas Bourbon started the first fire insurance company and small medallions were attached to insured properties so the fire brigade knew which owners had paid. Soon insurance companies agreed to attend to all buildings. Sun Insurance is one of the oldest companies, and on *Glebe Cottage,* East Dean, is an excellent example of one of its earliest firemarks with a policy number issued in February 1792. The next door cottage,

towards the shop, was also insured from 1805, but with Kent Insurance. This has a prancing horse, an ensign of Kent from a 5th c. battle. It is a 'fireplate' not a firemark because it was fixed for advertisement rather than to distinguish the property. Now black it would have been a red horse on a white background. The early insurance companies appointed firemen in each village, supplying them with uniform, buckets and axes, but they were not paid. The job was popular, however, for they were exempt from the Press gangs, and grateful owners of property usually rewarded them. The local firemen did not discriminate between the various company's buildings. [3]

Up to 1926 Dennett's Stores was the only shop. The business was established about 1880 by 'Old Dennett' who died in 1907, and continued by Alfred Harry Dennett, known as 'Jack', another with a waxed moustache, and was churchwarden from 1909 to 1931.

Dennett's Stores, with the Post Office, c.1910, behind the wall to the right was their stables

When Fred Breach left school in 1938 he worked at Dennett's Stores. "Cecil Dennett ran the stores after 1935. He was one of the three sons of 'Jack' Dennett, who had dropped dead behind the counter in April 1935, two weeks after his wife Anne died. Cecil went on to cope so well with the rationing of the 1939-45 war. In its early days the shop was only about half the present size but sold china, paraffin, ironmongery, groceries, hams, butter, eggs, bread, garden tools, tin tacks and so on. It was open from eight in the morning to nine at night, and there was a van delivery round at East Dean between five and eight at night. I know because I helped out".

Another who worked part-time in the store was 'Tubby' Harris, 'as thin as a rake' and with a war wound limp. Others confirm, "They sold everything, gumboots, working clothes, candles, and firewood, apart from all the foodstuffs such as cheese, sugar, biscuits and bacon." Dennett's also had the Post Office most of the time.

Kathleen Banks said, "When a teenager in the 1920s my sister and I had lots of contacts around East Dean and we would walk along the paths from West Dean to visit friends, especially the Hobdens at *Gore Farm.* It was not unusual for Mrs Williams of the *Manor*

House, West Dean, to say that she had run out of something and a friend of mine, Kath Williams, and I would often walk through the valley to the nearest shop, Dennett's stores in East Dean.

The village shop was a veritable treasure house, it sold almost everything you could imagine - buckets, brooms, baskets, clothes, all hanging from the ceiling - and a wonderful selection of sweets worthy of the walk there and back. We would think nothing of such a walk, not long for country children of the pre-motor car era."

Dennett's shop, 1943. In front left are Major Harding, Charles Gilbert Davies-Gilbert, bending down, and in between his son Jimmy. Mrs Elizabeth Bugler is to the right and John Eve is behind the counter. "Straight ahead was a little space where the Post Office had been before it went to the Pindred's *Long View Cottage* over the A259 in the 1930s. The PO was surrounded by leather boots and work jackets on hooks. There were ranks of biscuit boxes, while cheese and bacon were cut on request." The shelves look well-stocked for the time, probably many were dummy packets. Miggs Bailey said, "You could get anything from Dennett's stores, except if you dropped a halfpenny. The shop had so many holes in the floorboards that if your coin rolled you never saw it again."

The Dennett's lived to the left of the shop. To the right, there was a narrow passage to the back, and where Grimaldi's is to-day was originally the stable area for Dennett's ponies

A 1944 Dennett's bill for 4qts of ale at 9/6d [47½p] with 4d a bottle deposit

(best known ones were *Topsy* and *Bovril*) and cart, and then came an oil store. Before the war there was an illuminated sign on the wall outside Dennett's; inevitably, it was for Sandeman's, a wine, port and sherry merchant.

Tommy Dickens, who baked their bread, would on occasions deliver it, when he would also take orders for a suit or boots or shoes. The Dennett's ran a school clothing club as well. Apart from sweets the shop sold fruit and vegetables and a packet of six Woodbine cigarettes for six old pence [2½p]. When they had the Post Office Mrs Anne Dennett kept the books in order. On special days the villagers would take hams from Dennett's shop to the Bake House to be cooked within a crust of bread. On any day the shop was the place for catching up on the gossip.

John Eve also worked at Dennett's stores after school until he went into the RAF for his National Service, and he came back to Dennett's. He recalls Bill (WJ) Russell, the drummer in the village band, another who helped out at Dennett's. "At eleven o'clock, no matter how many were waiting to be served, he would drop everything and go and have a cup of tea and a sandwich. Before he retired he'd had his own shop up country, and at one time he was in *Little Lane Cottages."*
Miggs Bailey said, "In the 1930s Dennett's Stores had a lovely smell and Mr Dennett always wore an apron. Cecil, Maurice and Sid were the Dennett's three sons - and Cecil started by driving the van delivering Tommy Dickens' bread."

Dick Patching lived next door to Dennett's. He went to the shop every day with a jug for Tarragona wine. [Tarragona was about 1/10d or 9p a bottle] He would truly be described as a wino these days. His wife Rachel, whom we've met, was knocked over near the Forge where she went to have her radio batteries recharged. Not killed, but never got over it. [9}

The Dennett's shop lease was owned by the Misses Alder, who also had the *Birling Gap Hotel*. In August 1948 Cecil Dennett and wife Edie left for Meads, he to work for Elliott's, the Eastbourne grocers. A Mr Fisher bought the shop installing Mr and Mrs Fred Saunders as managers from September 1948, and it was named GE Godley. In April 1949 Mr Alfred G Weller purchased the shop, and in August 1949 it became Weller's Stores. He had five shops: Eastbourne (Green Street, Seaside), Pevensey and Hailsham. The shop was managed by Maurice Hopkins who married Myra Weller and a daughter, Gail, was born in 1960. When Alfred Weller retired to the Isle of Wight, his daughter, and son-in-law owned the shop and continued to manage it. With Faith Johnson (née Taylor) and Mr W Masson they were a formidable team.

The line of shops c.1955. Weller's Stores meat department is on the right. Going down towards Lower Street is *Delphine's* Tea Rooms with Dennett's old shop (now a deli) where the pavement starts to turn for, now, Went Way

The Wellers had revamped the stables and line of shops, and Arthur Raylor, who lived at *The Cub* and whose shop had closed in the war went to manage their meat section in the right hand side of the present *Grimaldi's;* Fred Breach used to work the mincing machine handle for him on Saturdays when he was making sausages - "lovely they were too".

Arthur had as his main assistant Sydney White, who had a couple of digits missing on one hand - was that the special finger-buffet flavour in the sausages?

When Peter Armiger left school in 1949 his father said, "I've found a job for you, working for Arthur Raylor. He'll pay 22/6d [£1.12$^{1}/_{2}$] a week of which ten shillings [50p] is for your mother, five shillings is savings and seven and sixpence is your pocket money."

He started as the butcher's boy, mainly delivering on his bike to the distant customers such as *Gayles,* Crowlink and Birling Gap, while Arthur and Sydney White did the local deliveries. Mr WF Bunting followed as butcher until retiring through ill-health in the 1970s.

To the left side, now also part of Grimaldi's, a Mrs Haughton opened a little café, *Delphine's,* run for some years by Miss Prince. A 1949 advert mentions '*Delphine's of the Green* for morning coffee, luncheons, and delectable teas'. Jane Booth-Clibborn (née Nash) said, "Memories flood back of buying Eldorado Ice Creams from *Delphine's,* and of the *Tiger* chimney always going on fire with the smoke billowing across the Green".

Ricky Hodgson takes up the tale. "By 1968 the *Delphine* tea-rooms had closed and the site looked derelict. It had a flat above and as I was married by then the family decided to rent the shop and flat for £8 a week from Weller's and open tea-rooms. Priscilla, my mother, had experience in running restaurants.

"The first day over 150 came for the afternoon teas and we were still washing up at six o'clock- no dishwashing machines then. *Delphine's* had been rather rough and ready with lino on the floor and plastic tablecloths and our make-over was much as it is today.

"The name *Grimaldi* had been suggested by a chef, who was going in with us, but pulled out at the last minute. However, the evening before we opened the 'phone went and a voice said, 'Have you got permission to use the name?' It was Mr Sycamore of 38 Warren Lane, well-known on the Estate at the time." He was a businessman, retired after a stroke, who spent his time talking and asking awkward (and unnecessary) questions. Ricky continued, "All settled down and he became a regular customer saying it was good value, which it was, we served morning coffees, lunches at $37^1/_2$p, and afternoon teas for $12^1/_2$p.

"The main difficulty was the kitchen, which was far too small, and used to get incredibly hot. When I worked there I wouldn't dream of going into the restaurant because my shirt would be soaked in sweat.

From left to right: *Glebe Cottage,* the Village Shop, site of Dennett's stable, and *Grimaldi's* restaurant, 2003. Peeping out of the trees above, as ever, is *Little Hill*

"We had some amazing times. I thought it would be a great idea if dishes were served in their own bowls with covers; wonderful, except that once they were covered the waitresses had no idea what was inside and the diners did not always receive the dish they had ordered. Another terribly busy time mother cut herself quite badly and couldn't help blood spurting onto meringues made that afternoon and which could not be replaced in time, so I dumped cream over the blood before serving and they were voted a success.

"After three years we sold out to Countess Diana de Rosso and her brother, although mother continued to help there for another nine years. They took over the butcher's shop next door when Bunting retired, the main advantage being that they were able to double the size of the kitchen."

Priscilla Hodgson left the *Grimaldi* restaurant for personal reasons, hoping to run a Pudding & Pie Service from *Darby Cottage* on The Green.

When the de Rossos retired in 1989 they sold to Keith and Jane Archer. The Countess and her brother went to live in the old school. Diana de Rosso had been an accomplished horsewoman until injured. She had a lovely voice and had developed her talent as a singer and entered the world of opera and the concert platform. She was also said to have performed heroic feats during the war.

Illness forced her to retire from the stage and when she came to East Dean she developed a career in catering with her brother.

Keith Archer, who trained at the Savoy Hotel, has bestowed on Grimaldi's, for a small restaurant, an enviable reputation for fine food and excellent value. Open most days and well worth a visit, but you usually need to book.

After the Wellers retired in 1986 they remained at *Glebe Cottage a*nd Colin, Lorraine and Vicky Heywood ran *The Old Stores,* before John Short bought it in 1987. He lived in Eastbourne, but after a long illness when the shop was open only a few half-days a week, he gave it up in 2005 and the post office was transferred to *The Barn Stores* in Downlands Way. There was a planning application to turn the shop into a dwelling, however, in 2006, following quite a make over, Frith and Little's deli opened.

Houses on The Green. Alongside the *Tiger* are three cottages. *The Cub, The Green & The Cottage,* and they were called Tiger Row. It is not certain when they were built, originally as single storey dwellings with the dormer windows put in around 1900. It is known they were used as billets in the Napoleonic and 1914-18 Wars.

In 1896 the Eastbourne Water Company laid a main from Friston to Eastbourne, which passed through the village. From this supply pipes were laid to two waterhouses, one by the Village Green, behind the central door, above, *Pendrills'* front is to the left. Each waterhouse had a drinking tap, with a drip tank below, used for washing and cleaning water. By 1936 most cottages had a tap over the kitchen sink, but only a few had flush toilets, *Little Lane Cottage* had to wait until 1939 for mains water. The village sign is towards the right, and above the door are East Dean's Best Kept Village plaques

Nearest Upper Street at No 1 The Green are the Breach's, Fred and Helen. Like so many, Fred worked at Dennett's and at Elliott's the Grocers of South Street, Eastbourne and was also a postman. His Dad, Tom, was a shepherd with Eastbourne Corporation. Helen helped the Simpson's at *Payne's Dene* in Crowlink Lane, both retired doctors, and she continued with their daughter Jean. Mrs Rachel Maitland in *Old Vicarage Cottage* was another customer.

District Nurse Gay had 1 The Green until marriage to 'Ronnie' Hall, when her brother lived there. After he died Mr Hall, the Gilbert Estate Agent, offered it to the Breaches and they had been there 43 years in 2000. Both their children, Shirley and Mervyn, went to the school, although Mervyn wasn't old enough to go full-time before it closed.

Capt Davies' foreman, Alfred Pelling, was next door. Alf said, "We lived at 2 The Green with Rube and Grace Taylor as neighbours and my son Christopher played on The Green from a young age. Soon he was playing with the schoolchildren during their breaks and would go back to school with them. When the day came for him to start school, his mother looked round for him and found that he had already gone". No 2 is now leased out.

At No 3, *The Cub,* was Albert Ellen, a big man, gardener at *The Dipperays,* and one of our *Tiger* regulars. He wore an earring, Mrs Cater said, "As a young girl I thought he was a pirate". Arthur Raylor, butcher, whose parents went down in the *Titanic,* lodged with the Ellens. When Rube and Grace Taylor moved there in 1962, she said, "It was wonderful, running water, flush toilets and a bathroom". She stayed until her death in 2005.

Next on the NW side of The Green after the village sign and waterhouse is *Pendrllls* which was built by a man called Pierce *c.*1860, but is named after the Penderell (Pendrell) family who harboured the future King Charles II after the Battle of Worcester. At a house, *Whiteladies* in Hampshire, they fed and disguised him and concealed him from the Roundheads and led him on his way to safety.

A descendant of this family, John Penderell, lived at *Cophall House,* East Dean, had eight children by two local wives, and from 1827 was the beneficiary of the pension of £100 per annum, that was settled in perpetuity on the senior member of the family. The Penderells lived at Cophall from *c.*1750. The pension was still being paid up to 1987 to one branch of the family, and a descendant still owns *Whiteladies.*

Before the First World War the back of *Pendrills* was used as part of the village laundry.

After David Fowler's death in 1922 his daughter, Annie, left *Pendrills* to stay with her sister at the *Horse and Groom,* Polegate. Mr and Mrs Lake lived at *Pendrills* in the 1920s and 30s, he organised the village Rummage Sales.

"After the war," said Miggs Bailey, *"Pendrills,* let by the Hardings, became vacant and my parents moved in. My brother, Leslie, had followed my father into the funeral business, and we were poor but happy. In 1954 I married from *Pendrills* Hubert 'Bill' Bailey at East Dean Church and he carried me over the Tapsell gate. [4] You often had to wait for a house until someone died or left, and then you had to pounce. Captain and Mrs Scott had *Meadow Cottage* at the top of their garden where we lived for a while. When my parents became frail we moved into *Pendrills* to look after them. While my parents were alive all the family came for Christmas and the summer holidays." After her mother Lilian died in June 1958 the Baileys followed on as tenants until 1992. It is now let, and for a while a German doctor, Kirsty, was there and Clerk to the PC, Diane Regan, and daughter lived there for a while.

The *Darbies,* next to *Pendrills,* owned by the Barratt-Terrys from the Gap, was one of the few houses round The Green not owned by the Davies-Gilberts. Pauline Markquick said the school children called the run from the *Darbies* to the wheelwrights shop the 'Alley'.

In the 1930s the *Darbies* were up to five dwellings, called *Pear Tree Cottages,* with three families living there - Dick and Rachel Patching, a Dann and the Vine family - or at least Mrs Vine and an ever-increasing family lived in one cottage and Mr Vine in another.

George Jenner, gardener and chauffeur for Mr PS Cradock at *Little Hill,* was in the *Darbies* from before the war until the late 1950s. George always wore gauntlets and gaiters, when driving the Rolls. He used to play dominoes, threes and fives, in the *Tiger* with Charlie Grayson, Jim Wicking and Tug Wilson (from the Gap), when Stan Fuller would bring in a brace of rabbits for someone else to take home.

The Hodgsons with their two sons came to *Down Dale,* 28 Hillside, in 1953 and after a few years bought the *Darbies* from the Jenners. Mr SL Hodgson was in the leather business, with factories in Eastbourne and Cornwall. His wife, Priscilla, who had been a 16-year-old model for John Logie Baird's first public demonstration of television at Selfridge's in 1926, was a drama teacher 'MRAD advanced'. She gave dancing lessons to the children in East Dean, put on a show in Eastbourne most years, and wrote poetry. Her powers of persuasion were immense and few said 'no' even if it meant appearing in a Greek Chorus or even the back end of a horse in a Greek Chorus.

For example, in 1954 she ran a Christmas Entertainment with sketches and dancing; among the children taking part were Felicity Bishop, Joy Dodds, Valerie Gillam, Leila Harvey, Elizabeth Korn, Leslie Mitchell, Julia Rust, Linda Ticehurst, Kate Trickett,

Rosemary Cheal, Jean Dann, Angela Gillam, Jennifer Hopper, Ann Hudson, Shirley Pownall, Patricia Ticehurst, and Elizabeth Worsell. In 1956 she ran Dancing Classes *Health and Grace* for Women in the Farrer Hall 'only those between 13 and 90 are requested to attend'; by 1958 they had become evening Keep Fit classes with a fee of $7^1/_2$p a class.

She was devoted to drama and her writing, occasionally inadvertently rubbing up the village folk with her efforts. At one of her shows in the Bardolf Hall Ray Trickett, who was a good-looking fellow, sang a duet of *If You Were the Only Girl in the World* and at the time it was considered scandalous that the female vocalist was not his wife. On another occasion Priscilla wrote a piece for the Parish Magazine entitled *Tittle-Tattle Talk* which included a general reference to a 'Mrs White'. There happened, however, to be a Mrs Anne White in the village, whose husband worked at the time for Elliott's Stores in Eastbourne and was a churchwarden, and they were most put out, so Priscilla had to apologise.

Priscilla and son David Lewis Hodgson lived at the *Darbies* until her death at 89 in 2000. David continues there. When they went there it had earth and flagstone floors and massive cellars lined with chalk blocks and once more the story goes, with no real evidence, that in smuggling times there was a tunnel connecting it to the *Tiger.*

Jesse Kemp, the village wheelwright *c.* 1907. The opening in the wall, wide enough for a wagon, is now bricked up, but recognisable today at the Upper Street end of the *Darbies.*
The father of Florrie, Joan, Eddie, Doug and Ray. He, his wife and Florrie died of TB. Eddie left for work and when Joan also died of TB Crowlink neighbour, Mrs Taylor, found that Doug and Ray only had a loaf and a bowl of sugar in the house. She took them, and the dog Spot, into her family

At the other end of the *Darbies,* in Upper Street, was the wheelwright's shop. Jesse Kemp kept the wooden ploughs in order and was also the local undertaker. He had made most of the wagons in the village and if one broke down he would go out to the field where it lay and repair it on the spot. He died young of tuberculosis, but the trade was waning.

The lads of the village used to purloin carts from the wheelwright's shop in Upper Street and let them run down Lower Street. If the village constable caught them they were made to push the cart to Birling Farm and back to Upper Street. Since the Millennium the Gilbert Estate has updated and converted the old wheelwright's shop into a holiday let.

Overlooking The Green from the SW is *Little Hill,* built by Mrs Macandrew over 1923. She had lost a son at Gallipoli and endowed a bed in his name at the Princess Alice Hospital. She was also a generous benefactor to good causes in the village. She certainly didn't want a smelly, noisy motor car polluting her drive so the Rolls was kept in the coach house at the bottom of the drive. Hence, for a trip, she walked down through the narrow gate, after readying the chauffeur. The gateway has since been widened.

Elizabeth 'Betty' Beecroft Cradock came to Cophall in 1934 while she built *Down Dale,* 28 Hillside, completed in 1936. With the death of Mrs Macandrew in the summer of 1938, Miss Cradock's uncle, Percy Cradock, bought *Little Hill,* so Betty sold *Down Dale* and, with Dorothy Dickens, went to care for her uncle, who was a sick man.

On the outbreak of war four evacuees, two sets of sisters, were billeted on *Little Hill*. They had their meals in the kitchen looked after by Dorothy, and after they left in 1940 the house was closed up. It reopened in 1945 but in 1946 Percy Cradock died and Betty inherited *Little Hill*. She flung herself into church life, was a member of the PCC until her death, and along with Major and Mrs Davies-Gilbert gave the altar and reredos to East Dean church in 1949. She was also involved in the Conservative Association, the RSPCA, the WVS and the Civil Defence. Most of all she helped on countless occasions at times of domestic emergencies - sickness, money, burst pipes - she would be there to help.

Dr Bodkin Adams looked after the Dickens family, perhaps on his way to visit Miss Cradock, for as Grace Taylor put it, "Miss Cradock trifled with JBA". The story goes that she would send Dorothy Dickens down to Arthur Raylor, the butcher, to ask for 'two special chops because Dr Adams is coming for lunch.' In January 1958 Miss Cradock died of a pulmonary embolus following an operation at the Esperance Nursing Home aged 52. Hence Dorothy Dickens had to leave *Little Hill* to live with her mother in Upper Street.

*Little Hill c.*1925. It was a 'character residence' set within park-like grounds of 1³/₄ acres [0.5ha], with a wealth of oak beams, an imposing yet elegant oak timbered staircase with carved newel posts and a galleried landing

"Mr and Mrs Colin Pople, another nice family followed in the 1960s, but did not stay long, being replaced by Donald and Julie Green. He had been a POW and had retired from Rhodesia about 1965; also pleasant people. When he died the house was empty for a while until it was taken over by a man who had something to do with a motor cycle business in Pevensey Bay, and was known as 'Sinbad'. In July 1988 the PC had an application for a nuclear fall-out shelter and look-out. Mr Gedge had 'tantrums', and it is alleged he would declaim, 'I'll see all your bodies lying dead when I look out of my shelter'. What can be said is that there are magnificent views from the look-out or belvedere today.

"Poor Mr Gedge thought he was Winston Churchill and would stand on The Green declaiming snatches from Mr Churchill's speeches." Now *Little Hill* is owned by lottery winners, Mark and Nicki Terry, who have been welcomed into the village. In 1997 the coach house was converted into a dwelling for Nicki's parents.

About 1930 Frank Newbold, an artist who had worked for the London Underground, built a chalet of living room, two bedrooms and kitchen, above the village at *Crowlink Corner* on a plot of Mr Haywood's Crowlink development, aborted by the Crowlink purchase for the NT. [5] Mrs Scott advised him on his garden landscaping. Later Bill Bailey added a wing to convert it into the "ballet boys' house". Miggs Bailey has a photo of dancer Brian Shaw, whose partner was Derek Renhchen.

Along the lane that leads to the footpath from Upper Street through Hobbs eares to Friston is the Farrer Hall and to the right the house and gardens of *Linden Mead.*

The Farrer Hall, now in the hands of the National Trust, played an important role in the village - no one who saw the Players production of *1066 and All That* in the Jubilee celebrations in 1977 will forget the part played by the hall. It had been an Army hut in the 1914-18 war, and through the generosity of Major AW Farrer, of *Little Down,* Friston, supported by Percy Budd, Cecil Dann and Anthony Tompsett, converted into a 'double bungalow' Scout Hut as headquarters of the East Dean Scouts. It became an evacuees' classroom in 1939 and went on as an emergency room in the event of heavy casualties.

After the war it was in use as the HQ of the Football Club, but Major Farrer offered the hut to the Parish Council for all in the village to use. The PC took it over on 1 April 1953, and it was renamed 'Farrer Hall'. The official opening on 7 November 1953 was followed by a dance. The conversion work had been voluntary labour by Cecil Dann, Keith Gordon, Stephen Rew, Douglas Richey, Brian Strudwick, Henry Watts, Sydney White, Edward Winter, with Ivan, Richard and George Worsell, supported by Mrs Biddy Kennard, E Cater, Lt-Col TM Gordon, Charles Meller, and Lt-Col ERC Warrens.

The Farrer Hall in 2000. A remnant of Summerdown Camp 1915-20. After its huts were auctioned off, this one was used as the Scout Hut in the inter-war years, and became one of the village halls from 1953 to 2000. Incredibly, it was popular, when you consider that the kitchen arrangements were cramped, or 'compact', and with the low roof it could get hot with a crowd

The villages now had two halls, neither new or ideal. The Farrer Hall was available for meetings, lectures, classes, parties, dances, or social gatherings. It had a piano, but no platform. The Village Hall was used for lectures, meetings, classes, whist drives, concerts or dramatic entertainments; it had a platform but no piano. Both halls had facilities for light refreshments. The rate of hire was - 3/6d, [17^1/$_2$p], not exceeding one hour, 30p two hours 40p three hours, and 7^1/$_2$p an hour beyond, including use of chairs, crockery and glasses. There was a Booking Fee of 12^1/$_2$p, not returnable if cancelled. Items could be hired from either hall, e.g. chairs 7^1/$_2$p a dozen. Caretaker was Mrs Frank Ticehurst, at *Pendrills.* One of the Farrer's last functions was a 1999/2000 Millennium Dinner that was fully booked.

Linden Mead was built around 1930 and was the home of Lt-Col Gordon for many years, he ran a taxi business in his retirement. In the last decade it has been smartened up.

Upper Street. The houses were owned by the Davies-Gilberts and while some families were in the same house for years others moved around depending on family size or change of job. Approaching from near the track to Hobbs eares the first house is No. 5.

This had been the village laundry, a single storey building built around 1900 for the village women to do their laundry and to earn extra by washing for houses such as *Grey Walls* and *The Dipperays.* An upper floor and dormers were added to create a dwelling house. Stan Hobden lived there before and during the 1939-45 war. After the war, when it was called *Roseneath,* Bob Seymour moved there from the *Old Vicarage Cottage* by Friston pond. He was verger at Friston Church for 30 years.

No. 4 also had the dormer windows added, and at one time was probably two cottages. Before the war Herbert Gerard Melling, 'Bob', his wife Florence and children Gerald and Pamela lived there, it was called *Rose Cottage* although it was honeysuckle round the door.

Bob was groom/chauffeur to the Hardings and had been the major's batman. Being in the TA he was called up in 1939 and became a sergeant in the 17/21st Lancers. In North Africa he won the DCM for leading his tank to rescue men trapped in a minefield. In Italy near the end of the war in 1945, he was hit by shell fragments. Strapped to his tank he was rushed to a Medical Post by his devoted crew, but died before it was reached. Florence became the school cook of great renown. [6] Others who at some time were at 4 Upper Street included Ray and Cath Kemp, and Dorothy Dickens and her mother.

From the mid-1930s George and Maud Worsell lived at the *Estate Cottage,* 3 Upper Street, the last of the houses to be built. He was estate manager for the Gilbert Estate, and a coastguard. She played a big part in the school and in the Players.

Fred Fuller said, "When I was eight, in 1928, the Fullers, Mark, Katie, brother Stan and me moved to 2 Upper Street."

Upper Street looking towards the main road *c.*1885. In the left corner is a barn on the site of *Little Hill's* coach house, The *Darbies* are on the right, and above *The Dipperays.* Of the line of cottages on the left of Upper Street, the nearest 5 has not been built, 4 is a single storey with no dormers, there is no 3, and 1 and 2 are to the right of the tree. On the hill behind is *Little Lane Cottage*

Bert Foord, the cowman at *New House Farm,* and his wife Gladys were at 1 Upper Street. A member of the church choir he had a wonderful voice, and he would practise during milking. He milked his cows manually and when mechanical milking came in *c.*1950 he didn't want to know. Peter Armiger said, "They had a grandfather clock in the hallway and as the front door was seldom closed and none of the other houses had a clock, mother would ask me to run to the Foords for the time." Jane Booth-Clibborn (née Nash) adds, "Mrs Foord was the librarian and left books on a chair inside her cottage for me to collect for my mother on my way home from school. Her front door was always open."

This brings us to the ***twitten.*** The safety railings were first erected in 1941 after Peter Armiger, rushing out of the twitten on his way to school, collided with a staff car, sustaining a broken leg. [10] Charles Meller provided the handrail at his own expense in 1954.

Until 1950 the twitten, or footpath, ran only half way up Friston hill finishing where it now meets the road. Concrete tank traps ran across *Mary's Mead* land - and during the war they straddled the road by the bus stop. Jane Booth-Clibborn (née Nash) said, "The schoolboys would play at jumping from one block to another. So for the upper half of the hill you just walked on the A259 or went the long way round through Hobbs eares - although always called Friston Field then. I was only allowed to walk on the main road with my parents, but there was no traffic apart from an occasional bus and you just stood aside when one came. I used to practise my multiplication tables to the rhythm of our steps.

"The excitement was intense when in 1951 the twitten was continued up the side of the main road by a new footpath. Why? Because the tank traps had to be blown up first."

Jane added, "Near the end of the old twitten was a brewing-up point for tramps: we ran past there quickly and quietly. Tramps were quite a feature of life in those days as they trudged from Eastbourne's Institution for Casuals to Brighton's."

Part of Upper Street looking SW *c.*1935, 1-5 on the right. Said to be Jack Goodman's lorry parked there. The wheelwright's shop is along on the left. The *Little Hill* coach house is at the far end of the street, and a chimney of Little Hill is just visible at the left edge

Returning to Upper Street on the left of Little Lane is **Little Lane Cottage,** probably the oldest cottage in the village, ahead the Bowling Club and to the right *Twitten Cottage.*

Frank Ticehurst, who lived at *Cornish Farm* as a boy, married Lily Patching in 1911, and they were at *Crowlink Farm* where her father, George Patching, was bailiff. On the death of George the Ticehursts fell on hard times and Frank worked as groom at the Ringmer Hunt kennels, and at *Gayles.* Subsequently, when in 1923 he managed to obtain a job with Mr Miller at *New House Farm,* the Ticehursts moved from Crowlink to *Little Lane Cottage* and Muriel (Miggles) Bailey (née Ticehurst) was born there in 1926. [5]

Miggs said, "There was no electricity, there were gas mantles downstairs, but candles were needed for light upstairs, and water had to be obtained from a pump in the garden. For the weekly bath the water had to be pumped up, heated in the copper, and poured into the hip bath in front of the fire. As the youngest I had the first bath and the other five children followed. I assume my parents went through the whole process for their bath."

Frank, her father, was badly injured by a kick from a cow and they moved to Eastbourne when he obtained work at Haines the undertakers. During the war their Eastbourne house was bombed and Miss Greenhill lent them *Lye Oak.* [10]

Miggs goes on, "There was always something going on in the village, and if anyone was ill mother would say, "Take this round to Mrs -". Everyone in the village helped each other, doing the other's laundry if they were incapacitated and the Revd Evans' cook would make jellies for him to take to anyone ill.

"I often walked to and from Eastbourne with my brothers singing along as we went. My mother did washing and ironing for Mrs Bugler of *Tatton Corner.* I recall the flatiron, which was heated on the fire, and after use it was rubbed with soap and a cloth. Her brothers carried the clean laundry back in a wicker basket, except for one occasion when they were swinging the basket round and the laundry fell out and had to be rewashed.

"Our front door at *Little Lane Cottage* [sometimes called *Lane End Cottage*] was of oak with inset stones and, to me as a child, it had a massive key. It was so old Major Harding would bring people round to view it. We children were not allowed to use the front door, for the front step was kept white and the red ochre tiles kept highly polished. We didn't have hot water bottles at *Little Lane Cottage,* but we would put a brick in the oven and when warm wrap it in newspapers and place it in the bed.

"Mrs French, who then lived in the other half of *Little Lane Cottage,* made toffee to sell to the children, cleaned East Dean Church for years and for a time the school as well." Mrs French's sweeties made a big impression on the village children and Fred Breach also recalls, "Mrs French of *Rose Cottage,* Little Lane, as her part was called, used to make beautiful treacle toffee, which she cut up into triangular pieces and sold them at about six a penny. Harry West worked for her in her garden."

Little Lane Cottage in 1923, with three front doors and when everyone grew their own veggies. Joints of the original roof collars are of the bare-faced notched-lap variety, which date from the 1200s and could be unique in Sussex

Miggs continues, "It was a wonderful life. All the family sat round the table together, but if too noisy we weren't allowed to talk. If boisterous, father would stop and look up at the pictures overhead which was the signal that children were to be seen and not heard. We certainly weren't allowed to put elbows on the table and if anyone did father would tap them off with the handle of his knife. My mother did like a pleasing comment on her food."

Little Lane Cottage 2003. A single front doorway with greenstone surround, manicured lawn and garden furniture are just the obvious changes of discreet improvement

William James Russell, who died at 85 in 1959, had at times lived at *Little Lane Cottage.* He was in the village 1903 to 1914, and again from 1941 until 1954 (during which time he helped at Dennett's stores) when the Russells left for Ashburnham. The Armigers did a stretch there during part of Bill Russell's time. Another tenant was Mrs R Breach at

2 *Little Lane Cottage.* Maurice Chappell, whose mother was a Holter, and had married Betty Breach, also lived at 1 *Little Lane Cottage* with daughter Faith.

Maureen Honey bought *Little Lane Cottage* in 1998. Entrance had always been from the south via a 'little lane', today's twitten, but main access now was from Little Lane, Upper Street. She commissioned an archaeological survey that confirmed it was the oldest domestic building in the village and apart from the northern aisle the cottage always had upper and lower floors. Initially timber-framed, from the type of joints some of the rafters with soot encrustation date from the 1200s, but were reused for this building. In the early 1600s the external walls were reconstructed in flint, with limited knapping, greensand quoins and a chimney inserted. The north end was rebuilt in the 1700s for an upper storey.

In 1845 the cottage, owned by John Davies-Gilbert along with the adjacent field, was occupied by Jesse Piper, schoolmaster and shoemaker. To the north-east an outhouse is shown on the 1844 tithe map. The main doorway had a greensand surround. By 1874 the cottage had been divided into three dwellings, the windows were reformed, additional doorways and stairways put in, and the roof of the south end was raised to provide an extra upper room. About the same time tiles replaced the thatch. Later the two cottages nearer the main road were amalgamated, and now the building has reverted to single occupation.[1]

Further up Little Lane is the village **Bowling Club.** The first mention of a club was in 1936, and the green was all cut out by voluntary labour ready for play in 1937. [3]

By 1950, when the green was wholly relaid, the club had Ernest Cater as chairman, EG McGlashan captain, Revd Norman Lycett vice-captain, JH Wiles Secretary, Arthur Carter treasurer, Frank Martin groundsman, and Bill Russell appears as a handy hut attendant, serving a total of 29 members. The membership fees were raised that year from 30/- [£1.50] to two guineas [£2.10], with an entrance fee of one guinea.

Members of the Bowling Club have continued to improve the facilities. The green was given another going over in 1954 and needs much attention every year, but with the wonderfully secluded site players can accept the green as it is. The club badge was designed in 1970, whites for matches agreed in 1984, electricity was laid on to the clubhouse in 1985, and a new clubhouse in 2007, envisaged by Roy Webb, meant teas can be served on site - although the subscription is now over £60 a year.

Many village worthies have been long-standing members; Stan Fuller won a cup before the war and again in the 1980s, Ray Kemp, who helped to cut out the Bowling Green, bowled with uncanny accuracy almost up to his death in 1991, and Patrick Coulcher was champion singles player 1999-2005.

The Club's real running story was over the admission of women members. It all started in 1976 when Sibyl Davies-Gilbert decided that women should be admitted and pointed out that The Drive Club in Old Town accepted women members. In 1979 there was a proposal at the AGM of ED & F Bowling Club that ladies should be admitted, but 'there was no support'. In 1981 a further proposal that ladies should be admitted with a member was defeated, but the next year this proposal was carried 27-9. It was not until 1999 that the Bowling Club decided by 21 to 7 that ladies may be admitted to full membership. Ron Wheatley was c that year, David Broughton s (taking over from Alan Mundy), Alan Spencer t, and Alan Robson cap. Joe Dempsey retired from the committee.

The entrance to *Brambledown,* ex-*Darby's Cottage,* which used to be onto Friston hill, is now into Little Lane by the Bowls Club. Tim Hervey, a parish councillor, lives there.

Across Upper Street is ***The Dipperays,*** which apart from the church and manor was the most striking building in the village for many years. Built around 1760 as an L-shape, with wells in the courtyard, later the square was completed, it was *New House* when famously painted in 1780, had a spell as *Little Birling,* and apart from adding bow windows and outbuildings there has been little change. The window tax of 1784 is not the reason for some windows being blocked up, it is merely a decorative conceit - there are chimneys behind. The original gazebo in the picture of 1780 remains in place, as does the porter's lodge which had a view past the outbuildings along the old entrance from the main road.

It was the home of James Dipperay, said to be descended from a Frenchman, De Pres, a religious refugee, who died in 1593. The legends relate that James was a successful smuggler, amassing considerable gains from his illicit trading until he was caught by the Excisemen and, with his accomplices, sent for trial. He turned King's Evidence and having been fundamental in bringing in a sentence of transportation for the rest, he settled to enjoy his fortune. No evidence has been found for the allegations, and Hopkins in *Lure of Sussex* just says that he began life as a smuggler, he gained money, married into a good family - his wife was a Willard - and became a churchwarden in 1729. What is known is that his father, John, was a labourer who became tenant of *Birling Farm*. James built *The Dipperays, as New House,* and owned much property locally - similar to the Gilbert Estate of today.

The Dipperays from Cophall in 2000, when it was leased to the Collins family.
It is now the home of Charlie and Octavia Davies-Gilbert and family. Many of the trees have since been thinned and the central dormer window, as shown in the 1780 painting, replaced

In 1791 James died aged 88; and his name is spelt 'Dippery' in the East Dean Church monument. He left the bulk of his estate to two nephews, and one Nicholas Willard Rowe of Lewes, inherited *The Dipperays,* although he did not live there, dying in 1792. The Gilberts bought Birling Farm from the Willard family in 1807/8, and by 1830 held most of the area.

James Dipperay, a bachelor, left an annuity of £20 to his gardener William Worger, three of whose children received £2,000 each, the youngest son was bequeathed £1000 and 13 acres in Herstmonceux. The will gives no clue to the services rendered for these rewards. Had the Worger's been involved in Dipperay's smuggling, or were they his children?

In the 1870s the house was let to Mr Ashby, the Lloyds of London Agent.

Kathleen Cater said, "From about 1923 to 1933 Mr and Mrs CO Oakleigh-Walker lived there. She was a cousin of Mrs Harding, and they had a daughter Margaret and son Peter." The house name had every variation of spelling imaginable and in 1924 the Oakleigh-Walkers let it be known that they desired the house be known as *The Dipperays.*

Lady Ravensfield opened the Church Summer Fair on 6 July 1927, to gorgeous sunshine in the gardens of the Oakleigh-Walker's at *The Dipperays,* and on the Horsefield. Shortly afterwards, however, a few smatterings of raindrops made themselves felt, but it was warm rain, and the day was a success in the tea tent where some 300 teas were served.

On 12 June 1930 the new Women's Institute held a Garden meeting at *The Dipperays* by invitation of Mrs Oakleigh-Walker.

From 1933-39 Kathleen's grandparents, Robert and Elizabeth Hobden, were at *The Dipperays* and ran a butcher's shop in one of the outhouses, where Arthur Raylor helped.

By 1939 it was in the hands of a lawyer when Mr Philip Vos KC and family were the residents. A Jewish couple, with two children of their own, that summer they entertained groups of Jewish children from Germany. They ranged in age from four to sixteen, and would go swimming at Birling Gap. Some had good English and Ted Fears asked one of them about their parents. "In a concentration camp", was the reply. "What's that?" "Oh it's a sort of prison". "Well I'd always been brought up that criminals went to prison so I had nothing to do with them, and only learnt the truth at the end of the war." The Vos family had gone by 1947. The Collins family later rented it from the Gilbert Estate until they moved out in 2003 when Charlie Davies-Gilbert (son of Jimmy) and his wife, Octavia, moved in. They have done it up, restoring the central dormer window and now live there with their young family. Three of the hay barn and wagon shed outbuildings have been converted into holiday lets of a good standard.

Ricky Hodgson and his partner have been at *Twitten Cottage* from the 1980s, previously the Fergusons had it for a quarter of a century. Miss Catling was there in the 1930s. Originally it was a shepherd's cottage, but greatly enlarged by the Fergusons.

Reflections, near the corner with the main road, was called *Marycroft* with Lt Col WEB Campbell in the 1930s, but John Corke, agent and surveyor, has lived there for many years.

At the end of Upper Street across the A259 was the Forge. [2] Luther Hills, the retired blacksmith, would sit on an ordinary wooden kitchen chair outside his *Forge Cottage.* In those days there was little traffic, and folks didn't have special 'patio' furniture. Luther had sung in the church choir in the time of the Revd George Pinnock.

After Luther moved to a nursing home the architect son of Mrs Phyllis Hughes surveyed and updated *Forge Cottage* over 1961-2. [11] There have been a number of tenants since including for a few years Duncan Smart and family of East Dean's *Strands* hair salon.

Plans in early 1990s to turn Forge garage into a cottage were attractive but access to Friston hill was limited and permission was refused.

Back to the opposite side of the road and up the hill is *Maryfield* built by Ronnie Hall in 1923. He died there in 1969 and the Jones family have lived there since. Micheldene WI gave a standing ovation to Doreen Greenwood and Anne Jones when they reached the finals of the 1973 NFWI Southern Counties Tennis Tournament.

The story of Telegraph House has been related [2], now the white flint building with fine views into Hobbs eares and Gatesfield is named *Friston Lodge,* the home of Michael and Jane Worsley.

Returning to The Green at Weller's *Glebe Cottage* with its firemark and turning left, the upper right hand road is **Went Way.** After the old schoolmaster's house, now *Smugglers' Cottage* (used to be *Cobblers*) comes the de Rosso's old village school [6], with its plaque commemorating the 1939 evacuees. [10] Next is the *Old Bake House.*

Tommy Dickens (1876-1937) married Emily Alice (1880-1965) in 1904 at Burgess Hill and came to East Dean in 1907. At first they lived at *Gore Cottage* until moving to the Bake House, where he baked for Dennett's Stores. He was famed for a speciality, tiny cottage loaf at 1d [$^{1}/_{2}$p] apiece, "They were lovely" according to Grace Taylor.

Tommy, Emily and their five children, shared the house with Mr and Mrs Nelson Breach and their daughter Betty. They each had two bedrooms, a living room and shared the kitchen. Each family had an outside lavatory, and there was a pump in the garden. The house overlooked the allotments running down to Upper Street. In those days, before the New Fridays (1947) and *Cornish Cottages* (1952) the slope down from Underhill (now Went Way) was allotments all the way to the recreation ground. Most of the villagers had two or three plots, and the school children had a double plot.

The five children of the Dickens' marriage were: Isabel, Edith, Dorothy, Thomas, and Florence. All went to East Dean School under Mr Drew, afterwards Thomas, who was a tall lad, went into the Coldstream Guards.

Tommy was the grandfather of Jean Gordon (née Dickens). She said, "A Sunday ritual was for the family to walk to Birling Gap over Went Hill, taking dinner and tea with them.

My grandparents would sit on the beach in their Sunday best, hats as well. We went to a hut that sold everything to buy ice-cream. Other memories include going to Mrs Pindred's at the *Gore* for sweets or up the twitten to Mrs French's [at *Little Lane Cottage*] for homemade sweets and toffee apples. We took old sweet wrappers back to wrap up her sweets." [5]

Tommy Dickens died of a stroke in April 1937 aged 61. He lay in state in the Bake House for all the villagers to pay their respects. The total cost of his funeral was £19/2/- [£19.10, over ten weeks' wages] including 'ruffle and face cloth trimmed with white satin and mauve silk cords'. His wife left the *Bake House* when the Gilbert Estate wanted to sell it and moved to *Rose Cottage* 4 Upper Street with daughter Dorothy about 1954.

The *Old Bake House,* 2000. In the 1930s shared by Rose and Nelson Breach and daughter, with the Dickens family of five children. The bread was baked in the oven on the left side of the house. Tommy Dickens baked for camps such as the Hollington Boys' Club; he would make up a van load, along with Dennett's supplies, to take to Birling Gap

Jesse Taylor said, "I just about recall Tommy Dickens baking at what is now the *Old Bake House.* David Frankland and his wife live there now."

Teachers Miss Mary Hooper and Miss Vida Allison Elvin retired to the *Old Bake House.* They entered into the life of the villages with gusto. Mary started the Art Group, was chair of the East Dean and Friston WI and of the Scout and Guide committee for many years. Vida was on the PC, did a stint as village librarian, her flowers won prizes at exhibitions and she gave talks, often at short notice, on subjects as diverse as *Heraldry* and *Folklore.* Both led the planting of daffodils along Upper and Lower Streets in the 1960s, with everyone contributing bulbs. Even so, they are remembered by some villagers as responsible in 1969 for changing the name from Underhill to Went Way of the road that ran past the school along to *Went Acre.* It is possible that they and others persuaded Maj-General Colin Bullard, who was on the Hailsham RDC, to press for a change. Not, however, popular with the old villagers, James Wicking would fume, "People who have been in the village five minutes overturn things. It'll always be Underhill as far as I'm concerned".

Joan Nash, however, said, "Miss Elvin and Miss Hooper were a charming couple, they were very proud of their old baking oven and were willing to help in anything."

In the early 1920s, when the Davies Gilberts moved from Eastbourne, the Gilbert Estate built *Went Acre* and surfaced the Underhill roadway approach from the Bake House. This old track from East Dean to the shore at the Gap led over the Downs along Went Hill because the valley route to the Gap would be impassable in wet winters. The Estate allowed development of a limited number of 'gentlemen's houses not costing less than £600' on the slope above Underhill and one of the first was built by Capt. Scott and his wife.

Captain and Mrs ER Scott, who built *Meadow Cottage* and *Thatched Cottage,* came to East Dean in 1923. [3] *Meadow Cottage* is reached by the steep footpath, improved over the years, between *Old Bake House* and *Thatched Cottage.* Jane Booth-Clibborn said, "The only person with a car along Underhill just after the war was Mrs Scott." Capt. Scott died in 1954.

Harry Comber recalled, "I cycled to and from work in Eastbourne because I couldn't afford the bus and remember seeing the smoke from Mrs Scott's *Thatched Cottage* as I came home on the evening of 10 July 1958". Mrs Scott returned from shopping to find the house gutted. She had it rebuilt, without the thatch, but with two oak beams that survived the fire and named it *Meadow Hill.* Audrey, a daughter of Captain and Mrs Scott, later Mrs Jenks, moved to Hayling Island, but often revisited the village until her death in 2006.

General Bullard lived there in the 1960s. Now renamed *Went House.*

Next is *Keepings* which was built later between *Thatched Cottage* and *Tatton Corner.* Dr HD Forbes Fraser and his wife Enid lived there for many years in the 1960s and 70s. They had a daughter Elizabeth. He was a canny Bowls Club member, a singles champion 1969 and chairman 1969-73. DF Perrens was a resident in the 1980s.

Mr and Mrs Bugler built the next along, *Tatton Corner,* in 1926 and they also entered fully into the life of the village. He died of a heart attack in 1931, but she continued the work - she was a founder member of the WI, on the PCC, and organized a variety of entertainments from a sing-song in the Village Hall and plays in the school house, to being in charge of the East Dean and Friston contingent for the Battle Abbey Pageant of 1932.

Elizabeth Bugler in her garden, *Tatton Corner,* along Underhill in 1943. Now *Wayside* on Went Way, it looks over to Cophall. She was a friend to all the village, free with encouraging comments, while her house and her garden always had a warm welcome

During the war she ran an open house for servicemen and women, the Carol Singers found a carefully chosen present for each one, and many village children remember her never empty 'magic cupboard'. After the war she gave up *Tatton Corner* (now *Wayside*) with regret, she was always coming back to the village and just before her death she spent the Coronation Festivities here.

In December 1925 Edward Drew retired as headmaster of the village school after 35 years. He and his wife, Elizabeth, also a teacher, retired to *Yescombe,* a Sussex place name, on Went Way built for them by the Gilbert Estate. [6] They died within a few days of each other in February 1940. [10] The Misses ME & PC Bagley (relatives of the Alders) were there in the 1960s, and now *Yescombe Cottage* is occupied by builder Tony Elphick and wife Jill. In 1983 their daughter Pat married Melvin Breach in East Dean Church.

Straight ahead at the end of Went Way, at the approach to Went Hill with its rookery, is *Went Acre* - the name is taken from the piece of land on which it stands. It was built *c.*1923 for Miss Beatrice Prideaux-Brune, a relative of the Davies-Gilberts and a formidable horsewoman, who always rode side-saddle. Her groom and gardener for her last 22 years was Frank Bagg, his wife being her housekeeper. Miss Prideaux-Brune died in 1950 aged 91. The house has since often been used temporarily by the Davies-Gilberts.

On the left at the end of Went Way is **Underhill House** an attractive property that has a long and chequered history.

Underhill was built at the end of the 1500s by yeoman farmers, the Collinghams. James Collingham died in 1550 at East Dean, and John, his son, married Margaret Chambers 1548. In the Parish Register of 1600 the list of donors to the Christmas Penny Loaf includes 'Collingham under the hill'. It was a Tudor house built on the U-shaped plan so popular in Stuart times, with a central courtyard which had a well. Sold to the owners of *Birling Manor* in the early 1700s, James Dipperay lived there while his *New House* [now *The Dipperays*] was being built. It deteriorated from 1800, not uncommon all around the country, and its poor condition worsened with the repeal of the Corn Laws which allowed cheap American wheat into Britain, depressing prices. The 1850s saw the house converted into tenement buildings and it is said that in one of the rooms East Dean's first night school was held. House deeds date from 1873; they describe four 'cottages' leased out and list the four tenants. The flint work had been altered indicating some rebuilding. The farming crises of the 1920s and 30s didn't help, most farm buildings were a pitiful sight. At one time *Underhill* was divided between five tenants with basic accommodation - one of the flats stood in the centre of what had been the courtyard, and the former gardens were strewn with rubbish. An original 1500s oak beam from a fireplace was in the Wilmington Priory Museum, it had a roughly carved Tudor rose on each side.

Underhill Cottages August 1967, tiles off the roof ... October 1968 same south side almost ready

In 1935 five families were there. The Patchings in No.1, replaced by brother and sister James and Emily Stickland. Harold Fears was in No.2, later the Kemp family. Upstairs in 3 were mother and son, Nellie and Harry Comber. Underneath in No. 4 were Bill and Nora Dann, later Rube and Grace Taylor and son Jesse; while in No. 5 were Mrs Pope and son Jesse (he was the road man before Ray Kemp), and when Mrs Pope died, 'Tubby' and Flo Harris and their sons John and Mick. Each family had their own external earth closet (although the one for No. 4, the Taylor's, was across the road - in the mini lay-by) and while there was a well the community obtained their water from a communal tap in the old straw room next to No. 5. Most villagers had spent hard times in *Underhill Cottages.*

The Sticklands worked on *Birling farm,* he as shepherd and she in the house. 'Tubby' Harris was, of course, "as thin as my finger", his wife being about four times his size. He had a leg weakness [foot drop] after injury in the 1914-18 war and devised his own spring that stretched from his leg to the toe of his boot to help his walking.

In 1946 there were four tenants: W Harris paying £13 a year, R Kemp £20/16/-, J Stickland £13, and R Taylor £10/8/-, and these families stayed until 1962, when the Davies-Gilberts decided to sell.

It was advertised for sale by auction in *Country Life* of 3 September 1964, and was bought by Kemping of Croydon in March 1965. Holland's, their solicitors, sought advice as to how fettered they were by covenants to rebuild or build a new house, and when Kemping's decided not to go ahead, solicitor John Chatfield and his wife Barbara bought the main property from them on 2 August 1967. In July 1968 they bought from the Gilbert Estate a small triangle of land across the road, and later the old rubbish dump, which was converted into the main lay-by.

The western wing (near to *Went Acre*) was in poor condition and was removed entirely, but the external walls of the rest were retained. The house had some 17 rooms, and most of the internal walls were gutted down to the chalk-block cellars.

The present central door on the east front had been a window, and both windows on either side had been separate doorways, with small porches. The windows were lengthened except where doorways were constructed. The lintel positions were maintained.

The original wall thickness can be estimated from the interior wall leading from the hallway. It measures 750mm (2ft 6 inches) at the base and 450mm (1ft 6 inch) at the top.

The conversion started July 1967 and was complete in November 1968.

Sir John Chatfield said, "There was a well; at least 30m (100ft) deep, inside the south wing, suggesting it had been in a courtyard and had been built around later. For reasons of safety it was filled with debris during the building work. The site of the new pool and its accessories was where the pig sty had been. Just beyond there is a heap of soot [probably from the chimney sweeping activities of 'Tubby' Harris], it grows a fine crop of polyanthus.

Underhill Cottages east front 1966   East front Underhill House 1970s

"A tree at the bottom of the garden was rotten and I decided to have it down as a bulldozer levelled the site. The man who was cutting the tree down came to me and said 'My chain saw broke and this was the cause; I found it deep in the tree'. He handed me a heavy ball some 30mm in diameter. Could it be a practice round fired by the militia who were billeted in East Dean at the time of Napoleon?" "More recently in April 1982, without prior notice, I was informed that as from 1981 the house was a Grade II Listed building."

All the reactions to this conversion were complimentary. "*Underhill* is fast regaining its original grace. Having watched it become derelict I feared for its existence." Jane Booth-Clibborn (née Nash) said, "I was amazed to see the transformation when I came back to the village." Since 2003 it has been the home of Dr Tom and Ruth Maxwell.

Returning to The Green, **Lower Street** dips down to join Gilbert's Drive and first on the left is a fire exit of *East Dean Grange* and further on the main entrance of this BUPA residential home. A Miss Lorrieman lived in a house called *Glebelands* and built *Glebelands Cottage* for her chauffeur. Bertie Elliott of the Eastbourne grocery stores came to live at *Glebelands* renaming it *Grey Walls*. The Elliotts [3] were there from before the 1914-18 war. Fred Fuller said, "The first private car at East Dean, number HC 5, was owned by the Elliotts, who used *Glebelands Cottage* for their chauffeur too." When the Elliotts left they went to Jevington, where the *Hungry Monk* is now.

Sir John Salmond bought *Grey Walls c.*1930 and lived there with his wife, son Julian and daughter Jean. He was a Marshal of the RAF who had flown in the 1914-18 war, and in the 1939-45 war was involved with attempts to help night fighters locate enemy bombers by means of spotlights - not successful and overtaken by on-board radar detection.

Harry Comber said, "His butler was Fred Weaver, then captain of the village cricket team, and Mrs Weaver was the housekeeper. They had one son Roy". Jesse Taylor said, "I cleaned Sir John's boots and shoes on my way to school; they were well used and cracked. Mrs Stevenson was his housekeeper in my time".

Janet Johnson's mother Rose Martin also worked for Sir John and Lady Salmond at *Grey Walls,* and as a child Janet distinctly remembers that they had a four-poster bed. Florence Dickens started as a maid for the Salmonds, and Jesse Taylor adds, "He was a lovely man. Had a Frazer-Nash car too." [10]

Brigadier John C Hudson and family came in 1953. John Kent, there from 1968, added a swimming pool, sauna and solarium for a high-class retirement home, but only after WDC's 1983 planning refusal was overruled by a Planning Inspector and it opened in 1987. John Kent had his financial difficulties afterwards. Now it is *East Dean Grange*, a BUPA rest home popular with the locals for convalescence after operations, giving carers a break, and for those who would like a little cosseting; it also provides employment for other locals.

On the left, the church side, by the entrance to *The Grange* is a weather-boarded storage and garaging building which could be the old Tithe Barn of East Dean. [4]

Opposite *The Grange* on the slope down from Went Way, with what's left of the village allotments, is a terrace block of three houses, *Cornish Cottages,* built by the local authority in 1952, and all the early occupants, Ned Bailey, Ted Flint, Don Ellis, worked on the authority's farms. Ned died some years ago, but Ted and Florrie Flint celebrated their 65th wedding anniversary in 2003. Don is, of course, now in charge of the Birling Gap Coastguard.

The Lower Street footpath was completed in 1954. On the same side is the **Gilbert Institute,** now subdivided into Caretaker's Cottage, Gilbert Cottage, and Institute Cottage.

Sir John Salmond, Marshal of the RAF, in his 1953 Coronation robes

The Gilbert Institute was built in 1884 by Mrs Harding's father, Carew Davies Gilbert, who gave the building for the use of the village, and his initials are carved over the porch.

The Institute was meant as a working man's club, where they could play billiards and dominoes and be kept out of the pub. A whist drive, with womenfolk, was held weekly, and it was also used for the Mothers' Union and sewing parties for the church. All sorts of activities - meetings, card games and jumble sales didn't, however, stop the young men and women walking to the delights of Eastbourne on a Saturday night. [2] & [3]

On 29 September 1905 members decided to re-cover the billiard table and to obtain new packs of playing cards. 'Besides games there is a choice of newspapers and magazines provided by Mr JA Maitland JP of *Little Friston.'*

In the 1930s Fred Fuller played billiards, darts, dominoes and cards there. "You had to pay a penny a game for billiards, and old Hills, the caretaker, knew the different sound when someone put in a halfpenny, "Who's put in a ha'penny?" he would demand as he opened the door."

Over the 1940s and 50s Miss Gladys Penford took the 'tiny tots' Sunday School, every Sunday at 1500h in the Gilbert Institute. When the PCC secretary was RG Hall, they held their meetings there - all without charge. The East Dean and

Charlie Markwick with the 600th lamb for 1970

Friston branch of the Labour Party was launched there on 27 March 1950 and its swansong, but by 1955 the Institute was back to the old routine of British Legion Jumble Sales (the Charity Shops of the day), and the distribution of free welfare cod liver oil and orange juice every Wednesday afternoon.

In 1958 the Institute was open for teenagers Monday, Thursday and Friday evenings. 'For a small sum they have use of a billiard table, darts and sundry small games, but no bad language and no gambling.'

Fred Harris was the caretaker at the Institute after Hills, he and his wife lived in the left-hand side flat with kitchen downstairs. The Institute had an open coal fire (tended by Fred), superseded by electric heaters, not really warming, but at least they didn't smoke. The billiard table took up so much space that whist drives gravitated to the Farrer or Village halls, until in 1960 Mrs Harding agreed that it could be taken out. The Institute was latterly used by the village library and stored two cases of village-owned books, with the library paying £104 a year for use of the Institute in 1982. The Gallop brothers, Alf and Walter, were only one example of well-read locals, who regularly used the library. [12]

Fred Harris' day job was gardener for the Monicos at *Windy Ridge* on Friston hill, his wife also worked there, 'but there was never a lot of money in gardening'.

Junction of Lower Street and the Birling Gap Road (Gilbert's Drive) *c.*1925. Left is No. 2 & 4, the Police House, (now 1 & 2) Lower Street, next is the Gilbert Institute. The Church Green is central with *The Cottage* (hidden) and No.4 Gilbert Cottages to the right

Charlie Markwick, the shepherd who worked for Capt Davies, lived in *Institute Cottage* with his wife Beryl. This flat was on the right-hand side and also had an up and downstairs.

In 1981 the doctors' surgery moved to the Gilbert Institute, using the kitchen, paying a generous £200 a year rent, despite only $3^1/_2$ hours a week use, with the landlord paying for maintenance. Before long there were complaints about parking, but Mrs D Adams, Health Visitor, started a well-baby clinic in April. The doctors, Chris Savile, Bernard McCullough and John Prosser, were given notice to quit in December 1989 with a new rent of £3,600 and responsibility for repairs of a 100-year-old building. An extension was given, but for a short while there was no village surgery until Dr Richard Adcock opened up in 1991. [9]

The PCC gave up the Gilbert Institute in September 1987. In January 1997 work began to convert the former library, surgery and hall into a one-bedroom flat.

In the Institute grounds, at the left front entrance, there is another Waterhouse where there was a mains water tap for folk before the advent of household running water.

Of the semi-detached cottages next to the Institute, the right-hand one, 4 (now 2) Lower Street, was the Police House before a new one was built on today's Gilbert's Drive. It was where Pc Hyde's only prisoner-of-war was taken in September 1940. [10] Bill and Elsie Armiger lived there for many years. Later called *Pear Tree Cottage,* the name being changed because there was a pear tree, and the name was more attractive to tenants. In the left one, Birling Gap side, 2 (now marked 1) Lower Street, Dick Fowler the shepherd lived, and grandson Jesse Taylor, long time vice-chairman of the PC, was born there.

On the church side of the road are the old Waterworks Cottages: *The Cottage* and *The*

Croft, all that remains of a row of four. The Creightons lived in *The Cottage* into the 1920s. Later *The Cottage* had the Misses Trigg, followed by Lewis Wilson and John Moore, and now Alan and Vera Tame (and Poppy, of course). The Cairns were in *The Croft* until they moved to Old Willingdon Road, one resident was Mrs Brenda Glass.

The **Birling Gap Road** runs along the east side of the village, from the A259 (main Eastbourne-Brighton road) to Birling Gap. Part was concreted by the Canadians during the war, but making it up fully only started after 1955. The stretch from the A259 to Birling Manor is now called Gilbert's Drive; 'East Dean pond was a pond then. It was never the same after the road was made up.' [3], [5] and [11]

On the corner with the A259 (there is a rear entrance from Gilbert's Drive) is the *Old Parsonage,* with the land around (apart from the houses) owned by the Gilbert Estate.

During Parson Darby's incumbency, in 1724 Judith Medlicott, daughter of Sir Edward Selwyn, willed a house to replace a parsonage destroyed by fire *c.*1685, with the condition that a Service of Remembrance be held for the Selwyn family. Since then East Dean with Friston Parish clergy were resident there, the last being Canon WF Pearce 1929-35.

The Old Parsonage on the A259 in 2003

Little was done to the Parsonage over the years, and by 1882 it was not considered suitable for the vicar's wife to have one of her children there. Her husband, the Revd J Walter Parrington, refashioned the Parsonage in 1883, but even after that the Revd AA Evans (1908-1929) was consistently described as having blue hands and a running nose, while the house was said to be dark and damp. These were the days when coal was brought from Eastbourne at 1/11d [9^{1}/$_{2}$p] a cwt [50kg], and a horse and cart was driven once a week to fetch supplies for The Stores and *The iger* for which the driver received 1d. If he brought cods' heads for Miss Boniface, the Vicar's housekeeper, she added a ^{1}/$_{2}$d. "They're not for cats", she would say," I'll make them into fishcakes for our Sunday dinner".

When the Revd WEM Williams came in 1936 he and his wife firmly refused to live in the Parsonage and rented *The Cottage.* The Diocesan authorities agreed that it was uninhabitable and in 1938 the vicar moved into the Burgess-built Rectory [3] just opposite the present Village Hall. All the clergy since have lived there. The locals seem to think Williams a softie, and when compared with their conditions the Parsonage was luxury, "Said to be a good bridge player", was one of the kinder comments about him.

Whether the ex-parsonage was habitable or not the Ticehursts moved in from 6 Old Fridays in 1938, and started a B&B, later run by the Misses Hayes and Greenway. Now a private house, in 1995 with its generous grounds, four paddocks, swimming pool, and carriage house it was for sale at £245,000, but down to £195,000 six months later.

Up the main road from the *Old Parsonage,* on the right, is Cophall Lane only made up in 2004. Ronald Rowney was in *Old Barn,* Miss Y Chevalier-Rivaille at *Beauvallon* (now Trevor Larkin and family), and the Shepherd family at the *White House,* recently enlarged. Mrs Besford Sworder [3] was at the far end of the lane where Pauline Joslin is now.

Returning to Gilbert's Drive, after the war the strip of the former parsonage grounds along Gilbert's Drive was sold off in stages by the Gilbert Estate and four houses built. The plot next to the Parsonage, near the A259 corner, which had been the vicar's orchard, was the last to be sold about 1970. Sidney and Stella Carter had *Birling House* built there by the Southdown Building Co. He was an optician.

Two further plots were sold off in 1959 to build *Paddocks* (now *Medleigh*) and *Maryland*. Arthur and Hilda Carter came from *Wyndways* Deneside to *Paddocks* in April

The Police House from 1952-2001, when it became *Little Beeches*, the cell is to the left

1960 and triggered off a typical East Dean cascade for they had been at *Corner Cottage*, which was taken by Doreen and Howard Greenwood, and when they moved on to 3 Michel Dene Road, Diana and Ian Shearer took *Corner Cottage*. Jolyon and Mary Fyfield's *Maryland*, built by E Powell, was also completed in 1960.

The first house of this group to be built is now *Little Beeches*, the home of Deborah and Dominic Shephard, but in 1952 it was the *Police House* and the present garage was the cell. The story goes that the only time it was used was when the local Bobby locked up a stray dog. The Police Office at the village was closed in 1997 to be replaced by a Community Beat Officer based at Seaford from where the 'rapid response' team could be obtained: 'He would be out on patrol and mainly unobtainable but residents could leave a message, or if urgent dial 999.' The last policeman, Graham Gillam, bought it and sold it on in 2001.

After the gap traversed by the water main to Eastbourne comes the Rectory, now occupied by the Rector, Ian Smale, wife Sue (who is a Reader) and their daughters.

Sullivans, built for the Hawkins family, is followed by *Little Garth* built 1990s and occupied by ex-RN Alan Nash. On this site was a wooden building, *Haligarth*, essentially an old Army hut. Eileen Curryer and Constance Elsie Grose, retired schoolteachers, lived there. Miss Curryer, the PCC secretary from 1954, wrote 'literary masterpiece' minutes. She died in 1963, but Miss Grose went on for another 17 years. After Barbara Nash moved to Downlands Way maisonettes the Nash parents had a decade of happy life there.

Churchfield was built for ex-service families in 1947. Reg and Ruby Haffenden were at No. 1 with children Valerie, Wendy and Graham (who died in a traffic accident at 16); the Bransons, Jane and Henry - he's the local webmaster - live there now. Wally and Jessie Eve were at 2, now the Cowans live there. Cecil and Rose Dann were at 3; and Fred and Kath Fuller at 4 - Fred said, "The rent and rates were 99p a week in 1947". Tom and Edna Goodman were at 5; and at 6 were Charlie and Florrie Vine. John Dann, at 3, and Kath Fuller, at 4, have been there since the opening and Florrie Vine only went into a home in 2005. As Florrie said, "Charlie was overseas so I filled in the form and was given priority by Mr Budd and Mr Meller, who were on the allocation committee. I moved in on 14 May 1947 and my son Derek was born two weeks later". [11]

Elm House, originally *Elm Lea*, was built by Len Miller's father, the farmer at *New House Farm*, before the Goldsmiths. The Alder sisters, Ruth and Margarite, who at one time owned the *Birling Gap Hotel*, had it in the 1940s-60s, and K Wagstaff in the 1980s.

The Old Fridays (1-10) come next, built by CH Prior in 1922. The name comes from Freya a Saxon goddess of good luck and often applied to houses on the edge of a village. Originally half were thatched, but as repairs were needed the thatched roofs were tiled. Details of some of the residents are in Appendix 8.

Returning to the church side of Gilbert's Drive, the Horsefield is where the Village Fair was held. This recent name comes from the Goldsmith's habit of retiring their old horses there, it was previously known as Frontfield or Mr Carey's field. The Glebe, Vicarage field, Churchfield and The Fridays are all surrounded by flint walls built in the early 1800s.

In 1971 the PC first discussed a village car park in the Horsefield to ease parking round The Green. A public inquiry in 1985 upheld the decision to build a car park there, on condition that the Village Green roads were pedestrianised. The Gilbert Estate's appeal against the refusal of planning permission for the Horsefield was withdrawn. WDC earmarked £150,000 in 1989 for a 67-place 1.32 acre Horsefield car park. Geoffrey Mantle said, "It will be a blot on the landscape", and Peter Temple thought that Wealden had looked at the problem in an insensitive way. Eventually, most comments were favourable, although overnight parking became a nuisance for a while.

Celebrating the opening of the Horsefield Car Park on 29 May 1991 by WDC Cllr Bernard Drew, were L-R: Terry Wigmore, Grace Taylor and Florrie Vine in Sussex dress, and sheep from the Seven Sisters Centre. The new car park is in the left distance behind the *Tiger*. The new walls were built with flints from nearby fields

The Village Hall. The halls of the village are mentioned mainly in Chapters 1, 3, and 10-15, the next couple of pages are an account of the years striving for a satisfactory hall.

Most villages have a hall, sometimes attractive, sometimes unpainted and neglected, but all with their own character. Before such halls appeared any village festivities were in a farmer's barn or in the church. With the Industrial Revolution the lot of the rural worker deteriorated and it was inevitable that some of his meagre wages went to the innkeeper. In the latter half of the 1800s philanthropists and the church put up halls where clubs could meet, a magic lantern show could be given, and where children's Christmas parties could be held. Drill Halls were sometimes used for village activities. Many Sussex halls are approached over wet grass, are draughty, have antiquated heating systems, where push-bar emergency doors contrast with rickety chairs, but they are cheerful inside and often have old photographs of the last shepherd, last blacksmith, or last team of oxen.

The 1884 Gilbert Institute was the local clubhouse. After the 1914-18 war there was talk of a new hall, and in 1928 an old building by the main road was gifted as the Village Hall. The feeling was that the best memorial for the 1939-45 war would be a new hall, but as described [11] not financially feasible just after the war, and in 1953 a Scout Hut (Farrer Hall) was donated. In 1965 the Gilbert Estate offered the old school, but again no better and rejected. Although well used and loved, all were too small with inadequate facilities. In a way they each hampered the realization that the only answer was a purpose-designed hall.

The Eastbourne Gazette in November 1978 reported a Village Hall Questionnaire sent to 750 households, with a 35% return, which only had a 22% support for the project. By the mid-1980s, however, the village had come to understand that the Farrer Hall and the 'Old' Village Hall would never be satisfactory, and from 1986 Jean and Max Place and Phyll and Gordon Workman drove around Sussex looking at other halls.

The PC sent out letters on 4 September 1987 asking for representatives on a consultative committee for a proposed new village hall.

A new community hall was discussed by representatives of organisations under the chairmanship of Maurice Hopkins, and highlighted that the Farrer Hall had mounting maintenance costs, and the lease came up for review in 1998, while the village hall was cramped and yet difficult to heat. The Residents' Association AGM had 79 members present for a discussion on a new hall, 53 were in favour, 15 against and 16 undecided.

At a June 1988 Exhibition about a new village hall 151 residents attended to learn the pros and cons. A leaflet was produced suggesting that at a cost of £200,000 it would provide a doctors' surgery, library, plenty of room for functions and leisure time activities, the Players would have stage and lighting permanently in place, and no parking problems. While the Horsefield site was convenient the PC didn't own the land, and whereas the Recreation ground was owned by the PC and the space was available with all services, it was not in the village centre. It was estimated that grants would come to £70,000, the sale of the old hall provide £50,000, with the parish rate increasing by 2p in the pound for 40 years.

On a beautiful 2 July 1999 the building of the New Hall was inaugurated by the oldest resident Grace Taylor who cut the first turf. Front: Nigel Waterson MP, George Tickle, Grace Taylor, Cllr Keith Bridger of WDC and the Revd Clive Taylor, who offered a blessing. Behind, most of the village bereft of their hats and caps in all the excitement

Wealden District Council in 1991 refused planning consent for a new village hall on the Horsefield, because it was in an area of outstanding natural beauty.

In 1993 a new Village Hall committee under Maurice Hopkins, replacing the Community Hall committee, saw sketch plans by Percy Gray and watercolours by Frank Singleton of the proposed building. It agreed that there would be parking problems with the Farrer Hall area and the best site would be the southern overspill area of the new car park.

The year 1994 opened with a mini-exhibition staged at the Village Hall showing the plans for the new hall. The proposal was to submit the plans to WDC and, if accepted, and after a review of costings, the matter would be submitted to a referendum.

That year a planning application for a new village hall was debated at WDC. One Councillor said it seemed strange to apply before the referendum, another questioned the need for a hall as there were two already, others felt that the need was for parking space not a hall, but the view that a new hall was looking to the future was also expressed.

WDC said they would wish the hall to be reduced in size from the 150-seat projected, but the committee agreed that if possible the hall should be large enough to accommodate a badminton court. It was agreed to involve Sir John Chatfield, our County Councillor, and Maureen Honey, District Councillor, to discuss the planning problems. Later the PC heard that planning permission for a new village hall had been obtained.

The next year WDC determined the location of any new village hall as on the left hand side of the access road to the Horsefield car park site in Gilbert's Drive. Percy Gray, the architect, had prepared drawings for a building seating 150 with a stage and provision for a badminton court with building costs of £280,000. Maurice Hopkins, chairman of the Village Hall project, invited organisations to be represented on the Project committee. Because of 'the contentious nature of this subject' the RBL decided to discuss it fully at a meeting.

In 1996 the PC and WDC agreed to the transfer of land on the old Horsefield on a 125-year lease at £250 a year, as a site for a new village hall. Later that year the WDC approved a wide range of uses for the new village hall, overturning its decision in 1995 that indoor sports and sales of goods would not be allowed.

Due to family commitments Maurice Hopkins resigned as chairman of the New Hall Project committee which he had chaired since 1987. He was succeeded by George Tickle.

East Dean's new Village Hall, 2001. *Glebelands Cottage* is just to its left. Gilbert's Drive runs to Birling Farm and on to Birling Gap. Coming off the main road leading to the right is Village Green Lane that leads to the new car park, The Village Green and the *Tiger Inn*

In an October 1996 referendum on a new village hall, if funds available, there was a vote in favour so applications went ahead for Lottery and District Council funding. George Tickle, chairman of the New Village Hall Project committee, said that the hall would probably cost the residents very little. 'The estimated cost was £330,000, the PC had £70,000 already and the parishes should obtain a matching grant from Wealden and we had been invited to apply to the Millennium Commission for up to £165,000. Even if we needed a mortgage of £150,000 it would only cost each elector £7 per year. The existing halls date back over 70 years when the population was 500, they require constant repair, are too small for some village activities, and neither have adequate parking. The population of over 1600 will benefit from the increased use and it will help to protect the village life we cherish.'

The new Village Hall Project committee suffered a set back in 1997 when their Millennium funding bid was rejected due to the intense competition.

In 1997 a Charitable Trust was formed to raise funds from grants to assist with the funding of the new hall. Frances Mace announced the first set of Fund Raising events for the New Village Hall, kicking off with an Exhibition of Paintings, followed the next day by a Sponsored Swim, and continuing with a Coffee Morning and an Antiques Fair, but the RBL branch voted not to share the Fete with the Village Hall Fund on a 50/50 basis. Conversely, president Bridget Rix and members of Micheldene WI agreed that the proceeds from their Spring Fayre would be used for the Village Hall Project Fund.

After some re-jigging by Ken Thurman on advice from ACRE and the PC, the plans for the new village hall went on display in the Village Hall in July 1998, and the next year a Village Lottery was launched in aid of the new village hall funds. George Tickle explained the business plan of the new village hall and the PC agreed its viability.

At the start of 2000 there was an appeal by the East Dean and Friston Village Hall Trust for donations to provide equipment, such as chairs, tables, curtains for the new hall.

Situated south of the A259, off Gilbert's Drive, the hall is close to East Dean Church and The Green. It has two halls, the larger seating 150 and the other up to 60. The big hall has a public address system and a demountable stage. There is a large fully-equipped kitchen with hatches to both halls. An entrance lobby has cloakrooms, there are changing/small committee rooms and a lavatory next to the stage. The garden is landscaped.

The large hall had room for badminton and short mat bowls and table tennis. Over 300 organisations intended to use the hall. The construction was under Tony Sherwin of the Stevens Partnership, based on a design by the East Dean and Friston Parish Council, and the hall was constructed by M&G Contractors and associates.[2]

Just past the entrance to the Village Hall is *Glebelands Cottage,* built for the chauffeur of the big house (now *East Dean Grange*). Miss Mary Rolls Parker and Miss Ethel Bates, retired schoolmistresses, came there in 1932 and Miss Parker nursed Miss Bates bedridden with a tuberculous spine from 1934. [13] Miss Bates treasured a miniature book of Holy Scriptures and after early morning Sunday Service Horace Rew always took breakfast with them. Miss Parker was one of the first in the village to have a cine camera and to record village events. She left her cottage to the parish who gave it to the diocese. Used for visiting clergy, and churchwarden Bob Gardiner, wife Viv and daughter Ann had it until 1999, when the diocese sold it, and has since been upgraded by Mr and Mrs John Stirk.

After the church [4] comes 1-4 Gilbert's Drive. James Gallop was at 1, he famously rescued a villager from a snowdrift near his smallholding by the Red Barn, [5] she worked at Crowlink and would walk over from the village every day. Janet Johnson was born at 2 Gilbert's Drive where her parents Frank and Rose Martin lived. Frank worked for the Gilbert Estate, was greenkeeper for the *Birling Manor* Golf Course and looked after the Birling Gap Camp Site. When his brother Arthur died tragically in 1947 Frank took over tending the bowling green and Janet can recall running through the sprinkler as her father was watering the grass. The Darks lived there for a while, and Arthur Raylor. At 3 was Mrs Wicking, and Mrs AD Conduitt, a relative of the Davies-Gilberts, had 4 in the 1980s.

After Lower Street, going towards the Gap, are the **New Fridays (11-22),** built in 1952 to adverse comments about the 'unrelieved red brick'. The resident families show the same picture as the Old Fridays in that they appear to have played Household Musical Chairs within the village. More details are in Appendix 8.

The Gilbert Estate gave land in the 1960s to build garages and lay-bys and, with the increase in car ownership, in 1997 Wealden DC enlarged the lay-bys.

The War Memorial Recreation Field is some 250m on along Gilbert's Drive. It was bought by the PC from the Gilbert Estate as the village memorial for the 1939-45 war, although the Davies-Gilberts had always allowed sports there. [11] At times when East Dean sported a football team they sometimes played there - always to the horror of the cricketers. There is a pleasant pavilion, sadly routinely vandalised, but regularly restored, a tennis/netball court and a children's playground, recurrently upgraded. Within view of Belle Tout, the Downs around, and the fields coloured by their range of crops or hosting the quietly munching sheep and cattle, it is a wonderful paradise to enjoy playing, or watching, or snoozing on a summer afternoon.

8. *Friston Place,* Waterworks, Forest, Mill and Pond

Friston Place was described by Lord Shawcross (1902-2003) as, 'a typical 13th century 'hall house' in a valley of the Downs near the Seven Sisters cliffs. It is Grade I listed with many attractive features from which one can walk or ride straight on to the Downs'.

AA Evans in 1936 wrote that an early name for the spot was 'Bechington' [Becca's farm or tun] and it is Bechingetone in the Domesday Book in the land of the Count of Mortain. The name Friston (Fryston in 1200) probable comes from Frea's or Fritha's tun.

Friston Place is hidden in a protective fold of the Downs, the red brick entrance with four gables and oak-framed mullion windows concealing a much older timber-framed structure. It was never a manor house, and only ever described as such - probably mistakenly - in one deed of 1579.

It was the medieval smallholding of William Potman, yeoman, and first mentioned in 1428. William's son, John Potman, died childless, and 200 acres of land at Friston, East Dean, Jevington and Folkington went to Alys his sister, wife of John Adam. About 1500 Thomas Selwyn of Selmeston married Margery daughter of John and Alys, bringing him the Potman land at Friston which he made his home and for the next 200 years it remained in Selwyn hands.[1]

Friston Place, NE side, towards the back, from the entrance drive *c.*1910

Thomas and Margery added to the house, and in the tax returns of 1524-5 Thomas Selwyn is one of the largest (but not among the richest) landowners in Sussex.[2] The death of Thomas in 1539, and Margery in 1542, is recorded in a brass erected to their memory in the chancel of Friston church. [4]

A record of 1542 states that their son John Selwyn 'held five acres lying separately in Fryston in a field called Hobsares … part of which lies in a field called Hedacre, between the land of John Gage and the Kings Way Fryston to Estdene'. In 1555 John Selwyn acquired part of the Great Manor of Bourne, and in 1563 Peak Dean was sold to him.

He died in 1594 and was succeeded by a son Thomas Selwyn to whom the arms of the Selwyns were granted in 1611; argent within a bordure engrailed, gules, and band cotticed charged with three amulets sable - in other words on a whitish background there is a diagonal black band with three rings. The same as the arms of the Gloucestershire Selwyns. The crest is a flaming beacon held between the paws of two lions.

Thomas' death in 1613 is recorded in an alabaster monument in Friston Church by his wife Elizabeth, and as his three sons had died young (and depicted in swaddling clothes on the monument) he was followed by his brother Edward who died in 1618. His son, Francis Selwyn, who succeeded him, appears to have been an outstanding member of the family and was knighted. After his death in 1664, a son Sir Edward, an MP for Seaford from 1685, was at Friston Place until his death in 1704, when in spite of seven male children the line ended as his last remaining son, William Thomas, died aged 21 in London without issue. These Selwyns are commemorated on the marble monument in the Transept of Friston Church.

The front entrance, SE, side, of *Friston Place c.*1910

Sir Edward's only surviving daughter, Judith, wife of Richard Medlecott (spelt Juditha Medlicote on the Friston marble) of Burton inherited the estate and sold it to Thomas Medley the same year. He died in 1728, and grandson George Medley was the owner when he leased it in 1785 to the Allfrey family of West Dean. They farmed the land for three generations, George until 1794, son Edwin to 1805 and his son Mortimer to 1828. They were progressive farmers, but allowed the house to become run down, so much so that in 1824 John Bodle, of the Medley estate, writes, 'doubtful if it is worth spending money on repair'. By 1814 it was the property of Charles Jenkinson, later 3rd Earl of Liverpool, who had married a Medley heiress, and in 1869 he sold it to the 7th Duke of Devonshire, who was always ready to buy land.

The 8th Duke, trying to lighten the Devonshire's encumbrances, sold *Friston Place* in 1897/8 to Francis James Maitland, whose father John Andrew Maitland, known as 'JAM', had been the gentleman farmer tenant since *c.*1890. This Duke's policy was shares, not land, so he did not let go of his Water Company shares.

Pelham Maitland ready for a Round-the-World sail, 1932

The Maitlands, JAM (1838-1914) and his wife Margaret (1844-1922), had as kinsman the Earl of Lauderdale. They had a son Francis (1873-1940) and a daughter Ethel (1877-1924). Francis James Maitland was born at Shanghai, China and educated at Winchester. He was a Captain RA 1896-1909, a JP and an Eastbourne District Council member. On 16 July 1902 he married Edith Dorothy daughter of Arthur Mayhewe of *Wyfolds,* Eastbourne, and they had two sons, Pelham, born 1903, and Andrew Fraser, 1906.

Having exchanged land with the Wycliffe-Taylors [5], JAM built *Little Friston c.*1900 as the dower house so that the newly married couple could take over *Friston Place.*

Friston Place Farm in 1890 was of some 1000 acres [approx. 425 hectares] and had five cottages, a wooden granary which had a coach house underneath (in which were two dusty old carriages forlornly waiting for a coachman to drive them as a coach and pair), a wagon lodge, stables, a large pond and two barns. It was a country idyll: swallows took mud from the pond to make their nests in the eaves of the granary, many laburnum trees were scattered around the farm, with some descendants there even now, and after the corn stacks had been built there would be scores of hens scratching around them. An eight-foot high wall, with two oak doors in it, separated the house from the farm.

In 1895, after problems with the quality of Eastbourne water, the Eastbourne Water Company leased much of *Friston Place Farm* and *West Dean Farm* (also about 1000 acres) for water collection, and placed restrictions on what could be farmed, the use of fertiliser and the number of cattle allowed. There were many considerations in these transactions, most are vague, but it is possible that the water company constructed a road to the new waterworks at the back of *Friston Place* to save their coal lorries and workmen having to pass the big house, and at one time the Maitlands did not own *Pond Cottage*. What is certain is the story that the Maitlands had a free supply of 2000 gallons of water a day.

Near the front of *Friston Place c.*1910, from the drive. The main entrance was through the gateway on the left, by the mounting block

In 1905 Henry Curwood took some polo horses from the Channel Isles to the Riviera, where he met Francis Maitland and became his valet. He came to *Friston Place* with him and in 1906 married the governess and Freda, their daughter, was born the next year.

On New Year's Eve 1906 Francis Maitland entertained all his workers to a dinner and smoking concert in the big hall. In 1909 he became an honorary Major in the Sussex Artillery.

The Water Company's restrictions made the farm less profitable and, after arson by a local lad Tom Herbert Knight on 8 November 1911 [6] had destroyed a Dutch barn containing all the winter feed, most of the farm was sold to the Water Company, who leased it to the Forestry Commission in 1927. The land of both farms is now Friston Forest.

Bill Armiger said, "When the Eastbourne Water Company bought most of *Friston Place Farm* in 1912 my father, George, decided to move there as farm manager. One of my first recollections was of the clatter of horses' hooves, sixteen or so, passing our cottage at half five in the morning as the carters brought them from where they had been turned out over the summer nights. In the late afternoon I would eagerly await their return for my father always gave me a ride on one of the horses. I wasn't a popular little boy one day when I realised they had gone past and ran bawling after them only to stampede the horses. On Fridays my father set off to Eastbourne to collect the wages in a trap with a chestnut gelding called Billy and took my mother and me with him. This was a special treat for usually if we went into a town such as Seaford we walked.

"On Saturdays Billy was also used to pull a milk float loaded with sacks of coal, which were sold to the farm hands for a few pence. The farm would buy a truck of coal - enough to last the winter.

Bill Armiger continues, "My mother made one of the rooms into a little shop where she sold mineral water, sweets and chocolate. I remember the chocolate bars of four squares each a farthing. I can still see those bars in their red paper.

Major FJ Maitland

"Before 1914 the *Friston Place* lawns were cut by a mower pulled by a donkey that had leather shoes on its feet to protect the grass, and Major Maitland had a private golf course on the right of the Jevington Road from Friston. Even in those days racehorses from Jevington were training along five-furlongs and the mile.

"The story goes that when the Army was commandeering horses in 1915 Dad hid his champion stallion, *Lion,* in the house to escape their grasp. They requisitioned half the horses including our favourite grey mare. My mother said she would have ridden *her* into the bedroom if she'd known they were coming. Having lost his horses he was given three Land Girls instead. In practice, he replaced the horses by buying a steam plough and used two traction engines at each end of a field with a cable running between. In the summer of 1918 the first tractor put in an appearance to pull the reaper/binder. All were surprised by how many acres could be cut in a day. That was the start of the decline of the farm horse."

Friston Place indoor staff *c.*1925. Left housekeeper, Mrs Morris, third left is valet Henry Curwood, front Mrs West and daughter Nellie, standing are Edith and Freda Curwood

Major Francis Maitland was commissioned into RGA for the 1914-18 war and when his valet was rejected as medically unfit because of varicose veins, he pulled strings for him to become his non-combatant batman.

They both returned to *Friston Place* after the war when the Major appeared a changed man. He and his wife 'went their separate ways', and accompanied by his valet and chauffeur the major lived a racy life of wine, women and song (and not too much of the choral works). He had a suite at the *Grand Hotel,* Brighton in its heyday, had a Mrs Morgan as mistress, went to the races all over the country, and his money went to the bookmakers.

The Maitlands had a place on the Isle of Wight and he often went there of a summer, shutting up the big house. When the Major was at Friston there were high jinks, the guests included Guy Burgess, and actors Tom Walls and Ralph Flynn.

Friston Place outside staff at the front door *c.*1925. Mrs Morris (housekeeper) is seated, Major Maitland is standing just to the left. Top right is Alf West, the head gardener, and next (with folded arms) "Syke" West, an under-gardener

Bill Armiger said, "George, my cousin, and I started work at *Friston Place Farm* when we were 14, in 1921; paid 50p a week. As far as we were concerned the main gain was that we were now allowed to go to the pictures in Eastbourne.

"After the war the shoot was let and both my father and I helped the guns. My father bred ferrets and encouraged us to play with them so that they were really tame. Dad fed the ferrets before use so they hunted for sport and merely made the rabbits bolt. Our dog Spot and the ferrets often walked along together. Spot would catch rabbits by holding them down with his paws, when he tried this with a rat it caught him by the nose and wouldn't let go. When finally it did release him Spot bit him killing him instantly, and Dad was annoyed in case he served the rabbits that way."

Chauffeur, Mrs Morgan and valet at Plymouth Races

In the Victorian walled kitchen garden (to the lower right of the entrance drive) there were laburnum hedges, greenhouses, and arches, with fruit trees (*Beauty of Bath* and *Laxton Superb* apples, plum and walnut trees). There were also asparagus beds, rhubarb, artichokes, peas, onion beds, and five beehives. Flower beds for cutting included pinks, narcissi, and Palma violets for the dressing tables.

In 1936 Alfred West, the head gardener died, and James Markquick, his deputy and Pauline Markquick's father, succeeded. He had married Freda, the Curwood's daughter. The family lived in the middle one of *Friston Place Cottages* where the chauffeur, Mr Attrey and his wife, were in the end cottage next down the lane.

About 1938 the little community at *Friston Place* had Richard Breach who did the carpentry and bricklaying and who lived in one of the brick cottages with gardener, Albert

Breach, his wife and family. Mr and Mrs Rew Marsh and Mr and Mrs Archie Penn lived in *Pond Cottage*. The Penns went to a Waterworks Cottage in Old Willingdon Road and the Marshes (who had lost a son from diphtheria) went to a Water Company cottage by the Pumping Station next to Mr and Mrs Frank Fyfield and their daughter. Jack Watson, the Water Company manager lived at, appropriately, *Aqua Cottage* along the lane to the waterworks.

Friston Place Cottages in the 1930s, where the head gardener, his deputy, and chauffeur lived with their families.
Through the gateway on the left leads to *Pond Cottage*, if you turn right; turning left are other cottages and the Waterworks

Pauline Markwick said, "As gentry Major Maitland had no side and would invite staff to functions and dances at the *Grand Hotel*. On one occasion, when I was a little girl, our family were invited and I asked for a drink of water which was brought in a cup and I said at home we drink water out of a glass. This amused the Major and he demanded that the waiter gave the young lady a glass".

Mrs EVU Young *c.*1935

In 1935 Francis Maitland handed over *Friston Place* to son, Andrew Fraser, who put it on the market in May 1936, as 'one of the finest examples of an old Sussex Tudor house. Exterior in old rose brick, and softly-weathered stone with some oak timbering', along with 50 acres and 'some cottages' all at £20,000. Francis went to a flat in Brunswick Square, Brighton, with Mrs Morgan. Not unexpectedly, he was bankrupt when he died in February 1940.

Mrs EVU Young bought *Friston Place* from the Maitlands in 1938 for £15,000. She decided to do it up which included exchanging the generator for mains electricity, converting the billiard room, that mark of any Edwardian grand house, into the drawing room, with the old drawing room becoming the library. Mrs Young, who thought there were far too many staircases - one having been added with each extension, had the one by the smoking room removed, leaving the one nearby the kitchen.

Mrs Young, born in 1909, was a grand-daughter of Sir Robert Lucas Lucas-Tooth. She had split from Commander Young RN before buying *Friston Place,* although her husband seemed on good terms and once visited her there. She possibly learnt of the sale because she was a friend of Mary Harding, of *Birling Manor,* who became Lady Williams. Mrs Young, an expert photographer, went all over the world for the *National Geographical Magazine.* She was fond of animals, and had a pony, five dogs and a parrot at Friston.

Having arranged the alterations for *Friston Place,* Mrs Young lived in the old head gardener's cottage, next to the Markquicks, with Mrs Fyfield as her charlady.

A cultured, intelligent, well-read woman, who had written travel books and *Pirates of the Caribbean,* she was a 'modern' woman who drove her own car and had no need for a chauffeur. She was also helpful to the children of the estate workers, encouraging them to use the library and to take up stamp collecting to help their geography. Her companion, however, was a Mr Stevenson, who spent half his time trying to get Mrs Young's pet parrot drunk and the rest taking money off her at backgammon - or perhaps the other way round?

Mrs Young received a commission to go on a photographic expedition up the Amazon basin, and off she went in January 1940. When, however, the trip was completed the world had changed somewhat; Germany held most of Europe, and Britain - with Friston at the forefront - was facing the threat of invasion.

So instead of Friston she went to another of her villas *Buccaneer Hill,* at Eleuthera in the Bahamas. She remained there during the war, and where she married Kjeld Helweg-Larson who drank himself to death - not before they had two sons. Her romantic excursions appear disasters, but the boys turned out well.

Friston Place had received about ten evacuees in 1939. [10] They did not live in the main house, but were billeted on the estate cottagers and were moved on when the Germans reached the French coast in 1940. The running of the place was in the hands of a solicitor who visited about once a month.

Soon the Germans were aiming for the waterworks, and high explosive (HE), delayed action (UXB), and incendiary bombs dropped all over the forest; however, on 11 October 1940, an HE hit a barn where the swimming pool is now. Pauline Markquick said, "The greenhouse glass was shattered, our upstairs ceiling came down, a window fell out and there was soot on our best carpet. Mother said, 'I could murder that Hitler if I got hold of him'. One UXB

Richard and Albert Breach, and James Markquick (right) examine the remains of the Friston barn bombed October 1940. Part of the one wall remaining is standing today

was a nuisance at Butchershole, for when it was detonated the rest of the greenhouse glass came out." Another delayed action of the bombs was that when some chickens were killed at Christmas pieces of wire and debris were found inside - to be extracted before roasting.

Pauline Markquick says that between Christmas 1939 and 1942, when *Friston Place* was unoccupied, the staff kept the cobwebs down and opened windows on fine days.

The County War Agricultural Committee, the WarAg, took over *Pond Cottage* for their local base, and in July 1942 the RAF Officers' Mess for the Friston Emergency Landing Ground (FELG) transferred to *Friston Place* from *Gayles*. [10] Not unexpectedly, they immediately converted the Smoking Room into a Bar.

William AF Burdett-Coutts was in charge of the local WarAg. He had been rejected by the navy because of colour-blindness, so with agricultural experience he was drafted into the WarAg. He became a lieutenant in the Home Guard. [10]

Herbert Vickery was the travelling foreman for any land under the WarAg. This extended from growing corn at Butchershole (not Bottom in those days) and The Paddocks, the field between the Jevington Road and Old Willingdon Road (where the Maitlands had a private Golf Course - and the men went shooting rabbits), to land as far away as Saltdean.

Mr & Mrs Curwood, the Maitland's ex-valet, along with the head gardener, now Mr Markquick and family, remained in *Friston Place Cottages,* and grew fruit and vegetables for the Officers' Mess, also supplying the Tanner sisters of the *Outlook Tea Rooms* with cucumbers and strawberries.

Two carthorses were used at *Friston Place* during the war, and later there was a Massey-Ferguson combine harvester. Wheat and flax were the main crops and Pauline Markquick remembers, "The Gallops, on the hill above the house, being bright blue with flax".

Pauline Markquick goes on, "It's a terrible thing to say, but we didn't know there was a war on at *Friston Place*. We kept chickens so there were plenty of eggs and fowl for the table, my father grew vegetables and soft fruits, even walnuts, and kept bees for honey. Before the war the gardeners were not allowed to use manure because it was a water gathering ground, but when it became an Officers' Mess manure was supplied to ensure that there was an adequate diet for the servicemen."

Pauline continues, "My father would present them with grapes set out on dishes with vine leaves and the Mess chef would give us left-overs, 'goodies' as I called them". The young officers at *Friston Place* had lots of parties, which tended to get alcoholic as the evening wore on. There were regular property inspections, all the panelling was boarded up, antler heads put in storage and the RAF was quick to repair any damage. At one party, as a piece of the evening's 'entertainment', booby traps were arranged in the grounds to frighten the guests and one blew up as it was being set and took off a hand of a partymaker.

Mrs Young (now remarried) sold *Friston Place* to Mr and Mrs Miller in 1945, and went to *Brownes* at Robertsbridge, having never lived in the main *Friston Place* house.

Charles Eric Miller and his wife resided at *Friston Place* from September 1948. The Millers came from Coventry and he had been in the coal business, they spent much of 1950 in Switzerland, convalescing, returning in the autumn. *Pond Cottage* wasn't vacated by the WarAg until 1952, when the Vickerys left. After 1952 the Nash's lived at *Pond Cottage*, renting it from the Millers. At that time the back part was only single storey, with two butler's sinks (unused), and two flush lavatories; it was used to store home-made wine.

In 1958 the Millers moved to *Folkington Manor* after selling *Friston Place* to Lord Shawcross, a lawyer. As Hartley Shawcross he had been a Labour MP and President of the Board of Trade, but he was mostly known for his fine showing for the British team at the Nuremberg Trials. At the time Lord and Lady Shawcross had three young children, William, Joanna and Hume. His father, John, also lived on the estate in *Flint Cottage* until his death in 1967.

The House [3] and Grounds

The driveway to *Friston Place* from the Jevington Road is almost ¼ mile [0.5km] in length. It was a surface of flints, but now tarmac. The entrance gate to the house is to the left, on the south side of the drive, just by the mounting block. *Friston Place Cottages* are a little further along the drive on the right. *Pond Cottage* is past the gate in the stone wall and to the right, while to the left are various cottages such as *Flint Cottage*.

The daffodils along the drive to *Friston Place* were planted by Mr Eric Avis; he was the gardener in the 1960s when the greenhouses had lovely carnations. There had been greenhouses in the walled kitchen garden before the Shawcrosses, but in a poor state so two new ones were built on the foundations with the idea of growing for a carnation market.

Lady Shawcross had the greenhouse produce as her interest. Best quality strawberries and carnations went to the market and to the house every day: the second quality went to the staff. After Lady Shawcross's fatal horse-riding accident this project was not pursued further, before long only one was left for vegetables and *Iceberg* roses, and this was knocked down in 2005, only for another greenhouse to appear.

In the gardens there are yew hedges, mature lawns, a kitchen garden, fruit enclosure, an old farmyard, a gazebo, a tennis court and a pool.

Lord Shawcross discouraged villagers from walking over the estate, which had been the custom.

Like all old dwellings many changes have been made over the years, and for *Friston House* many of those mentioned were by Mrs Young over 1938-40, although Lady Shawcross arranged to pull down old garages and war time pillboxes and for the bits to be buried in a pit on the estate.

Outside, the house has brick and flint walls with some greensand stone quoins around the windows and doors. Behind the brick much is flint and timber. On the older north side there is half timbering. The roof is mellowed red tiles.

The front faces SE. The brick entrance façade is of a type after 1650, and probably later here as provincial splayed brickwork is not usually found until after 1683. The dated stones above the front doorway were from elsewhere on the estate.

The original Wealden house of the Potmans was no more than a cottage and stands intact towards the back of the house, the additions tightly surrounding it on three sides. The portion dating to the 1400s is of close upright timbering with jutting sill beams and projecting joints. The oldest part of the house is to one side of the courtyard, but it has a new bay window. The 1950's nursery is now William's study. This early part at ground level was the Drawing Room and Study, which is shown as a little parlour in a 1729 plan.

Open Garden at *Friston Place,* 1965. House is in the distance, and the newish gazebo close up, it was not there in 1930s, although there was a water garden feature near the southern aspect of the well house, removed by Mrs Young

The large Kitchen and fireplace, buttery and hatch are probably next in date, and the lovely open Hall and stone porch have an early 1600s look, although Aslet says the earliest part of the hall is *c.*1500.

The present front door is set out about 3m from the front of the house *c.*1610. You can see latch and hinge supports of the original door, with a sliding wooden bar running into the wall to brace behind the door.

The front door opens to a stone-flagged passage running SE to NW almost the length of the house with many stepped levels. The old Drawing Room is on the right side (north), this became the Library in Mrs Young's time with, beyond, the Smoking Room. Continuing ahead was the Dining Room to the left of which was the Kitchen. There were two staircases - to the right by the Smoking Room and near the Kitchen on the left - Mrs Young removed the right hand one. Above the Smoking Room, the one converted into a bar in 1942, was a room with a king post, said to have been the Chapel. Over the kitchen was a room with carved panels, next was a bathroom and this led to the Fresco Room.

To the left of the entrance is the galleried Great Hall, which led to the billiard room and into the grounds. After the billiard room was converted into a Drawing Room by Mrs Young it was panelled by Lord Shawcross.

This Tudor Great Hall is of goodly proportions at 9m x 6m [30x21ft], and height the full house extent. It survives as one of the best small halls of the date.

It has an over-spanning oak arch, open-raftered moulded beam ceiling with a moulded king post. Upon a wooden framework midway along the front of the gallery a drum has been painted in mellow colours. Two Victorian regimental banners hang from the gallery, which is more recent than the rest of the hall. Lady Shawcross had the 16thc. panelling cleaned, and sold the antler heads, which had hung above the panelling, to a restaurant in London. There was an extra door at the side and a staircase, now gone, under the gallery of the Great Hall. In the Maitland's time it was where the Christmas plays and parties were held, and it also had a chair that could be turned into a table. [1]

The hall windows face east and were put in when the extra porch was added. Of interest are two projections about 1/2m from the floor with a hole, probably fasteners for the door.

Over the front was Major Maitland's bedroom, with his bathroom above the front door. Mrs Maitland's bedroom, which had a four-poster bed, was on the corner partly above the new Billiard Room. The other bedrooms were guest-rooms. In Francis Maitland's front bedroom - he always slept with two dogs in the room - the panelling came from Carisbrook Castle. Towards the southern side of the front a window over the door has an iron projection to hang a wooden shutter.

The little room facing the front was Lord Shawcross' study. The attic just to the right above the main door was made into a miniature museum by Francis Maitland, with glass-topped cases displaying Stone Age and Bronze Age implements and early coins, all found on the estate. Otherwise the top windows were staff bedrooms, along with a few over the dining room. For a fire escape these rooms had canvas on a reel; you placed a loop around your waist and abseiled down.

The courtyard was covered in by the Maitlands, and the staircase is 1930s. Behind the courtyard is now the Dining Room, which was the laundry in the 1600s, with a guardrobe. There was a stairway over the Dining Room, now a bathroom.

There is no regular top floor, but many flights of stairs, said to be over eight in 1936; some of solid oak. They

Lord Shawcross outside the donkey-wheel well house, 1984

were in all likelihood sorely needed for in the 1930s there was only one lavatory on the ground floor. One old staircase is now a lavatory to the right of the entrance.

Looking at the SW side from the garden the upper left room had a bay window removed by Mrs Young, next there is a window on a landing leading to a bathroom and onto the Fresco Room. A flight of stairs led from the landing to the Dining Room and the outside Kitchen door (the back door in Mrs Young's time). The next upper window was a guest room and below was the kitchen that Mrs Young turned into a Servants' Hall, from which there are further stairs down to the boiler room and an old larder. The old Servants' Hall to the left of the Kitchen door was turned into the Kitchen by Mrs Young. The little window at the side was in a loo beside a staircase, and small staggered windows were on the main staircase. The window near the ground was an entrance to the wine cellar - *Friston Place* has three cellars termed Apple, Main and Wine. The top right window was a side window of Mrs Maitland's corner bedroom (as mentioned, partly over the old billiard room).

On the side of the house above William's study is the Chapel Room with a crossing oak beam and king post; this is one of the early 1400s parts. The bedroom over the Chapel has a king post, and the fireplace is 1913.

There is a hatch on the east side of the dining room of mullioned stone with a clock dial let in on one side. The hatch was probably to hand items to people in the courtyard, and

A donkey-wheel well in operation. This was at *Birling Farm,* but similar to *Friston Place*

the dial was to denote the times of meals. The hearth was also on the east side, and the fireplace ran almost the length of wall on the south side. In 1936 it was bricked up. There are two ovens, two spits, cupboards and a long iron shovel for loaves. The left side of the fireplace is worn with knife sharpening. There was a door to the kitchen.

You can enter the kitchen, originally a staff parlour, from the back of the house. The next room (called the Dog's Room) was a staff room. A teeny staircase runs from kitchen to attic with access to rooms upstairs.

Donkey-wheel well house. The wheel reaches to the roof and the inside is worn by donkey's hoofs. There is also an old iron bucket. Pauline Markquick said she worked the donkey wheel in the 1930s; "it creaked awfully. The well was 136 feet deep [40m], but Andrew and his friends went down on one occasion. The water was remarkably clear."

What was a 1950's nanny's room lies on the side overlooking the garden.

Joanna Shawcross' old bedroom, over the kitchen, has panelling said to have come from Carisbrooke Castle. It did have a door into a bathroom now blocked up.

The Maitlands discovered the frescos in the room over the dining room. The chimney there was always going on fire and the plaster must have dried after one fire, whereupon the top layer fell off, disclosing wall paintings with a hunting theme of good quality and unusual in Sussex.

In this 'Fresco Room' there are incised Tudor figures, presumably Selwyns, upon the stone embrasures of one of the windows, and paintings of hunting scenes set in many coloured flowers and greenery. There is one of a likely 17thc. hunter about to skewer a wild boar. The room leads to a bathroom which could have been a hiding place in troubled times.

You may like to know that in the centre of the house there is a secret door that leads to … just a bathroom with a window on a landing!

An abundance of figures, the Fresco Room 1984

As usual with an ancient house there is a tale that a ghost walks. 'It is said' a lady with a baby in a shawl walks in one of the front bathrooms having thrown herself out of the window when it was a bedroom. The Maitlands never saw it, and none of the staff over the years claimed to have seen it although most knew of the fable. Pauline Markquick said, "When the Maitlands or Mrs Young were away and the staff slept in the beds to keep them aired I often lay awake in the hope of seeing the apparition, but was disappointed."

Pond Cottage was sold by Lord Shawcross, but daughter Joanna bought it back and she now lives there with husband Charles Peck, a son and daughter. A granary to the side of *Pond Cottage* had been pulled down by Mrs Young.

Friston Place Garden Party, July 2001. Left is the SW side of the house, in the centre the Donkey-wheel well house roof is seen in front of the trees. Lord Shawcross is third from left

Little Friston.

As mentioned John Wycliffe Wycliffe-Taylor (1859-1925) and his wife, Frida, in 1899 obtained land south of the Brighton road in exchange for a plot of land bordering Friston Green on the Jevington Road that John Andrew Maitland (JAM) wanted for a dower house. [5] They built *Gayles* on their land and JAM built *Little Friston* on his plot.

Little Friston, in the 1930s. It was built *c.*1900 as a dower house for JA Maitland and his wife when he gave *Friston Place* to one of his sons on marriage

JAM died in 1914, and after the death of his widow, Margaret, in July 1922 and daughter Ethel in 1924, *Little Friston* was bought by Benjamin Simpson; there until his death in 1940. It hosted an RAF Sergeants' Mess during the war from 1942. Pauline Markquick recalls her family being invited to a 'do' there in 1945 for a treat of soused herrings and goulash, although her father who had supplied the produce wouldn't eat it.

Francis Arnatt moved there from Downs View Lane in 1946 until 1952 when he left for Guildford. He was the developer of the Downlands Estate [9] and it is said that he moved because, after a slight stroke, he was fed up with residents button-holing him with their problems. The move did him the power of good for he went on for another 15 years.

The next occupier of *Little Friston* didn't want the area on the other side of the road which the Maitlands had used for stabling and a chauffeur's house, so on the far part of the land was built *The Spinney,* where the Powells now are and the assorted buildings converted into a dwelling, *Hillsborough,* where Joyce Donkin, Arnatt's daughter, lived until her death in November 2001, well into her nineties. It was a bit ramshackle, and has since been knocked down by new owners Gerry Armstrong and Julie Ford for a rebuild, although, of course, within the outline of the old. Almost opposite is *Taperlands* where the Hoyers lived.

Returning to *Little Friston,* Bernard and Ellen Lister were the next residents and the most recent occupants were Vincent and Yvonne Argent and their family.

Friston Waterworks

Peter Johnson had played football and cricket for East Dean, but came to live in the village in his early thirties in 1964, and in 1967 joined the Water Company at Friston. He did over 30 years with them until he retired in 1997. He died 10 years later.

"There were eleven on the staff at Friston when I joined. When Friston pumping station became fully automated in 1969, some staff retired, Ray Cheal and Jesse Ticehurst moved to Eastbourne and I was the only one left at Friston. Now, in 2001, there is only one left in the business; Dickie Hearns lives in the *Waterworks Cottages* and works for a sub-contracted company as a meter reader."

The 1896-1934 steam driven, coal-fuelled waterworks on the present site in 1919. Notice the bare, whale-backed Downs around, Friston Forest planting only started in 1927

Friston Waterworks came about because of over-pumping at the Eastbourne Water Company's Bedfordwell to cope with the population increase, resulting in brackish water and even an episode of green water. The company said the water was safe, probably true, but public confidence was low and the Corporation declared that unless an improved supply was obtained they would take over the company. A new pumping station at Holywell was speedily brought into use and Bedfordwell closed, but this meant standpipes for the public. There were protests at the closures and people used the Bourne Stream - even though it had been shown to be contaminated and the Corporation had tried to close the dipping hole. When the first crop of typhoid fever cases appeared, the public mood changed and charges were made that the local authority had not acted promptly enough. Over 80 cases were notified in 1896, some 50 with two deaths from drinking the stream water.

On 6 August 1897 the 8th Duke of Devonshire turned on the new pumping station at Friston. The headings went over a mile and a half into the chalk tapping the aquifers, and producing pure water for many years for all Eastbourne.

The original pumps were steam driven, the engines being brought from the Bedfordwell waterworks to Friston (with the coal coming by lorry from Polegate station). These buildings were completely knocked down and levelled in 1934 when the present pumping station was built. Five new Paxman diesel pumps were installed, three being run each day. Two were long spindle machines each of which could pump 85,000 gallons of water per hour, two submersible pumps capable of 45,000 each, and two booster pumps, 1 & 2, that alternately pumped water to Friston tower. These were taken out in 1962-68 and the Friston station was converted to electricity and automated, now everything is operated from Haywards Heath, with no staff permanently on site.

The Welsh miners who had hand-dug the borehole kipped down on bunks in a shed at Friston. For the staff the first six *Waterworks Cottages* were built around 1896 along the Old Willingdon Road, with an earth bank at the back of their gardens. In the 1920s two more were built near the pumping station and in 1926-7, around the time the tower was constructed, numbers 7 and 8 were built near the original ones, but set a little further back. The money ran out so they weren't as well built as the two near the pumping station, but they did have a bathroom, unlike the first six.

The steam-driven waterworks in 1919 looking north from South Hill. *Friston Place* is in the distance right. With no Friston Forestry Commission trees yet planted a shepherd tending his flocks in ageless fashion would see this new visage of smoking chimney, surrounded by piles of coal

Jane Booth-Clibborn (née Nash) says, "My mother always referred to our house as '7 Old Willingdon Road' and not as '7 *Waterworks Cottages*'. Numbers 7 and 8 were the 'posh' end". The standard rents were 25p a week, with £1 for 7 and 8. In the 1980s the Water Company offered 7 and 8 to the residents for £10,300 each, with a 1% discount for each year of service. There was a *pro rata* offer for the other cottages.

From before the 1939-45 war to the 1960s Jack Watson, the chief engineer of the pumping station, lived in Friston Forest at *Aqua Cottage* [after selling off it became *Five-Farthings* and now *Forest Lodge*]. He was followed by Will Higgitt.

Friston Pumping station well shaft is about 3m in diameter and 44m (142ft) deep. The headings go to Deepdown pumping station, joined with Foredown, which is the highest point where the well shaft is 375 ft straight down.

Mildred Pownall mentions that in the early 1920s, 'There was no pumped water to *Waterworks Cottages*. My father, Joseph, brought drinking water from the waterworks every day in a cart called the Bodge. Next a stand pipe was erected outside the house, but we used it sparingly at first and used rain water for washing. This was replaced by a small tank until the water tower was constructed about 1926-7 when we had running water - especially outside when the tower was overfilled'.

Joseph Pownall from Preston was wounded in France in 1917, convalesced at the Summerdown Camp in Eastbourne, married a Seaford girl, and got work at the Friston Waterworks. As his family enlarged they moved to 2 *Waterworks Cottages* and lived there until his death in 1978. There were eleven children: Mildred, Ronald Joseph, Gordon John, Noreen, Mollie, Tony, Kenneth Harry, Colin George, Shirley, Terry, and Annette. Mildred wrote, 'On some Sundays my job was to take dad's dinner to him at the Waterworks, in a basin with a lid on top and wrapped in a cloth. I had to get it to him hot and I was petrified by the noisy pumping station.'

Work on converting the pumping station to diesel power over 1932-4

There were three eight-hour shifts (6-2, 2-10, 10-6), two of four men and the night shift of one man. Frank Fyfield (no relation to Jolyon) was in charge of one day shift and Fred Nash of the other; Fred had come to *Waterworks Cottages* in 1934. During the day the Friston reservoir was kept topped up, at night the pumps were stopped, but the diesel generator was kept on for lighting.

The water is pumped into Friston reservoir just below *Little Friston*. From there it goes into a 53 cm (21inch) main through the tunnel along Windmill Lane, under Warren Lane, to near the steps by the Old Forge, across the main road to Upper Street (where you can see four manhole covers, two put in recently), across Stan Fuller's old allotment, around the back of the old Postal Sorting building, under the Horsefield, to between the old Police House and The Rectory and on past Wigden's Bottom, near *Cornish Farm*. From here two mains, the 53mm, and one of 35cm, run through a tunnel, which is nearly a mile in length, crossing Black Robin to Warren Hill. The tunnel entrance is near a pond where there is a square fence with a metal door. The smaller pipe serves the Paradise Wood reservoir and the larger one supplies the Meads Hill reservoir, although they are interconnected. Water is pumped up from the Friston well into the Friston reservoir, but is gravity-fed to Meads and Paradise; the valves automatically opening and closing on demand these days.

Ray Cheal said, "Lieselotte and I were married in 1951 and two years later there was a job vacancy on the Water Company staff, with a house. The Company had always been good to its employees, and allowed retired staff and their widows to live on in the company houses. It was like heaven to have a place of our own, and I've been at 3 *Waterworks Cottages* ever since, improving it as we went along."

At the Friston plant he worked on the Paxman diesels pumping the water up to Friston reservoir (with a capacity of 1½ million gallons) feeding into the Meads and Paradise reservoirs (combined capacity 7m gallons).

Richard Worsell said, "Soon after I started in 1964 the water level in the tower was read electrically, but I would note the float and reservoir level on my way in and inform the Friston pumps to act as a check". A booster pump installed in the tower in 1986 improved water pressure. Over the past 10 years the tower has not been well kept and since the booster pump was installed, the tower mainly functions as a mobile aerial mast.

Richard was with the Water Company until he retired in 2000. "I started as Gardener/ Mess Man at Friston Waterworks, following Alf Holter." Alf and his sister Alice came from *New Barn,* West Dean to 4 *Waterworks Cottages,* but they said they missed the peace and quiet and couldn't get accustomed to running water and electric light and 'all these new-fangled gadgets', so they moved back. They both lived into old age, and even when a mains tap was put in at *New Barn* Alice would draw well water for washing.

The newly-completed 23m [75ft] high Friston water tower *c.*1928. It held 55,000 gallons. Before the tower was built there was just a tank on stilts, seen at lower left, mainly just to supply *Waterworks Cottages*. A separate 10cm [4-inch] main ran to the tower, supplying Friston, East Dean and Jevington. Geoff Nash said, "The tower had a needle dial near the top, which could be seen with the aid of binoculars from the pumping station, and when it showed the tower was getting full the pump was switched off. It wasn't unknown for the men to forget, whereupon water gushed out of the overflow and ran down across the road - much to the delight of the children living nearby"

Ever since the Bedfordwell debacle, the company was wary of salt seeping into the headings so one of Richard's first jobs was to check boreholes at Cuckmere. He would move on to the Friston Station in time for 1000h to make the worker's morning tea. "They only had a Kitchener heater, which took about an hour to heat up, so one of the others would put it on at nine o'clock. Later they had an electric kettle."

Richard Worsell continued, "There were lots of happenings to notice on the way those days, wild life and changes in the seasons. On Thursdays I opened up manholes to check they were flowing freely. The sewage disposal was near the headings at Friston and when it overflowed the Company upped the chlorine.

"In the 60s Mr Hazelhurst, of the Water Company's head office, came to install telemetry so that all the data could be read at the Eastbourne offices and thus save on staff, so I went on a day-release course and obtained City and Guilds as an electrician. I was first sent to Ninfield as a fitter/electrician, then Eastbourne as a fitter, and eventually as an electrician at Bexhill, and later covered Eastbourne, Bexhill and Seaford. The company had changed and by the time my retirement came I couldn't wait to get out of it." Ray Cheal was of the same mind, "I walked into Eastbourne during one snowy episode and the old Water Company arranged a camp bed for me and brought me home in a Land Rover. Things altered, however, and by the time my retirement came I couldn't get out quick enough."

On the other hand Peter Johnson said, "Conditions did change over the years, but I enjoyed my time with the Water Company."

Jane Booth-Clibborn (née Nash) recalls, "The steady tread of the men as they came home through the forest from their jobs at the pumping station. Joe Pownall worked down in the well of the engine shed oiling the engines. He had been a miner and never wore socks. The engines were kept in beautiful condition and it was wonderful to see them working, although noisy". Her father was Foreman from 1934 and later Superintendent.

Ray Cheal adds, "In the 1962-3 winter I was on night duty and it was so cold that I bought a fur-lined flying suit to keep warm. I've even cycled through the Friston water tunnel, along the line of Windmill Lane, although you have to keep your head down. There was a time when burglars used it to store stolen property, stacking up furniture there.

"In 1968 the Friston station was converted to electricity and automated. I could control every procedure, from chlorinating to pumping, from the Water Company's Upperton Road main office." Retiring in 1981, he bought the house from the company, "With 28% off the price for my years of service. In 2000, only one of the houses is not privately owned". One was for sale in 1998 for £125,000.

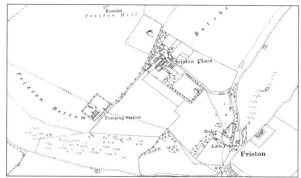

A 1920 map showing the relationship of *Friston Place, Little Friston* and the pumping station.
The six *Waterworks Cottages* (7 & 8 hadn't been built) are just above the name 'Friston'. The water tower-*cum*-mobile phone mast hadn't been built yet, and also no Friston Forest

Over the years Bill Hearns lived at 1 *Waterworks Cottages;* 'Joey' Pownall was at 2 from 1934 to 1978. Archie Penn, who had lived at *Pond Cottage,* was at 3, but moved to 8 in 1953 to be replaced by Ray Cheal, - there until 2007. Alfred Holter lived with his sister at 4 *Waterworks Cottages* followed in 1964 by Harold Maurais, and Terry Pownall was there for many years. Bert Holter (father of Jimmy) was at 5 (Dickie Hearns from the 1960s), Jesse Ticehurst at 6, Fred Nash and wife Lilian were at 7, followed by Charlie Cairns, and later Malcolm Johnson and wife Faith. Richard Worsell is at 8. Rew Marsh lived at *Pond Cottage* in the 1920s until moving to a company cottage by the pumping station. Ted Carter (lived at Jevington), Johnny Grooms, and Joe Cairns were other members of the staff. Joe Cairns, at number 1 for a while, was a big, hearty chap, a driver at the Waterworks, all he wanted out of life was his work, a good laugh and a beer.

Jane Booth-Clibborn (née Nash) recalls, "There was a great sense of a community, everyone was good company. Life was stable, but in line with the times our mothers were not on first name terms, always Mrs Pownall or Mrs Nash.

"There was rivalry between Friston and East Dean. Each had their own bonfire, the Friston one in the field opposite *Waterworks Cottages.* All Friston children went to the East Dean bonfire, but they only came to ours by invitation!

"The children played in 'The Bushes', between the path behind *Hillsborough* and the bridle path further along Old Willingdon Road. There was 'The Park', a tree house, and 'The Pit', a chalk pit. One day in the late 1940s the boys noted tyre marks in 'The Pit' and, as there had been a spate of burglaries, they informed the police who arrested the gang when next they parked their car there."

Friston waterworks now produces 15m gallons a day largely for the western half of

Eastbourne. So when in 1990 one of the tunnels conveying water through East Dean village to the Meads reservoirs was found to be unsafe it had to be speedily opened up for repair.

Friston Forest

Planning started in 1926 as part of Government policy to establish new forests after the 1914-18 war had shown how woodlands and hence the supply of timber had been eroded.

It now consists of 1967 acres (796 ha) of beech, ash, sycamore, red oak and conifers. The forest more or less covers the 2000 acres of *Friston Place Farm* and *West Dean Farm*, which were run jointly by Harry Williams and George Armiger from 1913 for the Water Company until shortly after they were rented to the Forestry Commission in 1927.

The aim of the Commission is timber production (the forest rides are for timber extraction) combined with public access and recreation. In the forest are Neolithic barrows, Bronze Age tracks, remnants from the 1939-45 war, dewpond remains, flint cottages and evidence of past agriculture. Butterflies (speckled wood, comma, peacock), foxes, squirrels, rabbits, other small mammals such as stoats and weasels, owls, sparrowhawks, kestrels, woodpeckers (spotted and green), jays, beetles and snails, abound.

Kathleen Banks said, "When the Forestry Commission took a lease on the *West Dean* and *Friston Place* farms, Mr Harry Williams ploughed up a field to act as a nursery for the saplings. I can remember my father Harold Burgess saying, 'They'll never grow a forest round here', and he lived to be proved wrong. Mind you, as only to be expected on chalk, there are no big oaks there, but the forest does have beech".

Friston Forest in the 1930s from South Hill. *Friston Place* is hidden in the trees, but part of the Waterworks is lower left and just above is a plantation of young trees which, when planted, were no bigger than the average rose bush, so planting a thousand a day was possible

Bill Armiger said, "Some of the first trees were planted by Bob Seymour and myself for 9d [4p] a hundred. We each would plant a thousand a day for 7/6 [37½p] a day. This was piece work, the usual rate was 31/- [£1.55] a week, with no paid holidays except Christmas Day, Good Friday, and Easter Monday.

One thousand a day? You may ask, but as Mrs Katheen Banks explained the young trees were only the size of the average plant from a garden centre, you put your spade in, angled it to make a slit, popped in the roots, heeled it in; 100 an hour - but all for 37½p a day.

"We weren't helped by the many fires caused by the traction engines that pulled the steam coal wagons from Polegate station to the waterworks."

"I left the Army in 1947", said Ray Cheal, "But jobs were difficult for an ex-machine-gunner and there was Direction of Labour, so I started at Friston Forest planting and cutting trees until 1953 when I joined the Waterworks."

Yes, over the years more deciduous have been planted than conifers, but a more dramatic and substantial transformation occurred in October 1987 when the 'hurricane' carved swathes of toppled trees and completely altered the appearance of the top end by the A259. The few trees that survived there continue to stand out over the rest. It took three years to clear fallen timber and many fallen trees have been left (it's expensive to move them out) and 20 years later form features of moss and fungi-strewn vegetation on the exposed rotting roots. In 1993 the planting of more than 50,000 beech trees began in Friston Forest. Broadleaved trees now comprise 55% of the woodland, and when replanting is complete there will be only some 10% of conifers.

The introduction of Pay and Display for car parking by the Forestry Commission in 1998 caused dismay locally because it induced visitors to park on the roadside. Some even used the Downlands Estate roads causing problems of access and damage to verges.

Friston Windmill, said to be one of the prettiest in Sussex, stood about 100m from the main road, just to the north of Windmill Lane, about halfway from there to the Jevington Road.[4, 5, 6] In the 1800s it could be seen out at sea.

The first mention of windmills in England is in the 1200s, 'mill' before then was a watermill. Windmills were once common on the windswept Sussex Downs, and the first mention of a windmill on the Selwyn estate is in a will of 1613, but any Friston windmill of the time was 1km along the Brighton road, about where the drive from *Gayles* meets the A259. Rosamund Stutchbury wrote, 'When my father built *Gayles* in 1900 he said that where the drive meets the main road there had been a windmill. At the time there were no buildings and yet two tracks came from Friston and another, deeply marked, came from West Dean over steep Downland to meet at that spot. One reason for all these old tracks, now masked by trees, to meet up at this point is that it was the site of a mill'. One is shown on a map of 1724 and was probably the one burnt down in 1761, a common fate of wooden windmills, but said to be arson. Its successor was struck by lightning in 1769 and it was the one blown down in 1824. [2, 4] The replacement mill on a new site at Friston Green was re-built with much of the old material, along with a cottage and privy, and started up 11 June 1826; in turn it collapsed on 10 January 1926.

Friston Mill in December 1925 by HS
Swanwick, sketched just before the collapse

The mill just after falling down
on Sunday, 10 January 1926

It was a typical Sussex weatherboarded post mill on a cut-flint round house. The whole working structure was turned into the wind by means of a stout beam with two smaller beams, through which the miller put his head, grasped the beam above and pushed with his shoulders. The four large white sweeps (or sails) would move with the slightest breeze.

Farmers came from miles around to have their wheat or oats made into flour, usually for animal feed. The miller was proud to show off the working of his mill and for special occasions such as Coronations and weddings he would dress it overall.

The miller's stone and wood residence, *Mill Cottage,* was away from the mill towards the Jevington Road. Constructed of flint and brick at ground level and weatherboarded above with tiled roof, the cottage stood entire, of a sort, until 1962. Its top floor bedrooms were at ground level and to reach the sitting room and kitchen you had to go down half-a-dozen steps of millstone fragments, that led to a narrow concrete area onto which the door opened. Presumably built to keep the roof low and not take the wind from the sails.

Friston Mill belonged to *Friston Place* and in 1801 was let to John Ashby. The Ashbys owned it from 1875 and William Ashby ran it until his death in 1894. JA Maitland purchased it for £390 in 1897, largely as an ornament, but installed William George Morris as miller. As Hazel Andrews said, "My grandfather was miller for some 20 years". There was little corn milling after the 1890s, but oats and meal for cattle were ground. Rosamund Stutchbury wrote, 'In 1914 we took corn to Morris at Friston Mill and the flour made excellent brown bread'. Morris was Sexton at Friston Church, and Victor Bryan Morris, on the church Roll of Honour as wounded in the 1914-18 war, was his grandson.

The mill ceased working in 1915 and William took up road mending until he was injured in a road accident at work from which he died in 1922. His widow lived in the cottage until her death nine years later.

Friston Mill reflected in Friston Pond *c.* 1910. Left: is the part-sunken *Mill Cottage* (behind the telegraph post), a gabled coach house and store shed. The entrance to the Downlands Estate would be behind the white signpost directing to Eastbourne. The pond, larger than today, is lapping the Seaford road on the left

It is often stated that the mill was blown down, but although there had been snow showers, it was a calm, cold night and the mill, which hadn't been maintained since 1914, and had no miller from 1922, simply fell to bits. Kathleen Cater recalls being told that Friston windmill had come down in the night. The locals quickly found use for the debris and soon only part of the central post was left - declared a Holy Cross by curious visitors.

A Norwegian, Gary Conrad Wetlesen, his wife, Bertha (née Wicking), and four children lived in *Mill Cottage* in the 1930s. In poor health, he was one of the local barbers. He left for Newhaven where he started a barber's shop just before the war.

During and just after the war Madeline Lillie, wartime postwoman [10], lived in *Mill Cottage,* and for a time one of the mortuaries set up in case of heavy bombing casualties was a garage near the old mill.

Friston Pond and nearby Crowlink Lane

Bill Armiger said, "Before 1914 the pond was much larger than today, and frequently overflowed across the stony road. Later a bank was built on the roadside with a drain. Before the 1921 drought it teemed with tench, we used to catch them and put them in the horse troughs. Many locals dug out the mud and fish to spread it on their gardens. Mr

Morris, the old miller, rescued a few and put them back when the pond refilled. The tench finished after another dry summer in 1926".

The pond is 360 ft [110m] above sea level, fed only by surface water and dried up in 1895, 1911, 1921 and 1945, all dry hot summers. In 1976 measures taken included supplying from a nearby house until officially stopped, whereupon the PC arranged for three separate 1000-gallon loads of stream water from Wannock.

Friston Pond is ancient, some say Roman, and was in the manor of Peak Dean. Used for drinking, watering cattle and horses, it was also a meeting place for the Hunts.

Records show that in 1615 when the pond was cleaned three large stones were discovered, and when in 1634 the pond was cleaned and scoured the stones were taken out and used as a mounting block near the church gate, where they are today.

Legal tangles give more evidence; in 1622 Simon Collyngham was fined 2s for allowing his geese in Friston pond. In 1639 Francis Selwyn and Sir Thomas Gage agreed that Friston pond should be shared although Sir Thomas' farmers should not stake their hogs, horses or cattle on Friston Green. The landowners of *Friston Place,* Crowlink and Birling were responsible in turn for cleaning the pond.

Looking south across Friston Green *c.*1910. Friston Church is on the left, to right of centre *Church Cottages* and the *Old Vicarage Cottage* on the right edge. A cart is in the pond

At the end of the 1800s Friston church, Friston pond, Friston mill, *Church Cottages,* the *Old Vicarage,* and the site of *Little Friston* were on the edge of Friston Green. Now, although it is registered as a Green, it is so intersected with roads, that only a few islands of green remain. A roundabout might be the answer.

At invasion time, 1940, concrete blocks and old cars stretched round the Green, and in 1942 the Canadians drove their lorries into the pond to wash them down.

It was in such an overgrown state that in June 1949 the PC decided to seek the owner. After every effort to trace an owner for the pond had failed the PC decided in September 1950 that it should formally acquire the pond and keep it in good order.

In 1953 the pond was cleared of silt and rubbish, 'which had all but concealed it', although the Ministry of Defence only agreed in December 1955 to fund the removal of concrete blocks around Friston Green and the pond. In 1956 the theft of flowers from Friston pond by the occupants of a car was noted, the number traced to a London resident, and a full apology received.

All the fish died in the 1962-3 frost. At first thought to be due to salt, but none used near the pond because there was such a scarcity that salt was only used on steep hills. The water froze down into the mud so the fish had little chance of survival. 'It was amazing what a number were there, some five inches long. The weathermen said it was 82 years since such a winter; but the Revd Nightingale managed to scratch his name with his skates on the ice in 1903-4 and Ron Pringle had skated on the frozen pond more recently'.

Friston Pond is diminishing and it was decided to remove some of the waterweed. This has to be done in the summer to get all the roots. In the spring of 1982 a floating island was created in the middle. Built of wooden pallets by Ken Warner of *Pondcare,* the hope was that it would be an appealing home for wildfowl. Having sustained generations of toads, frogs and fish, in the December it was found that a terrapin was loose in the pond causing havoc among the fish and frogs. At a PC meeting it was declared that unless something was done nothing terrapin-edible would be left.

The following year the pond was cleared, the first posts erected to stop parking, iron drain pipes put around the pond, and a larger island launched on 17 December. During the work an abandoned nest was found on the island with five eggs, two cracked by the terrapin, which stubbornly resisted capture.

The County Ecologist considered Friston Pond to be one of the best in the county in 1987 and advised minimal trimming of overhanging foliage, regular removal of water plants and topping up with mains in dry spells. The next year the Ecologist doubted that even if cleaned it would attract wildlife and retain water, but both ducks and terrapin had returned.

A more recent picture, looking across the verdant pond towards the church of St Mary the Virgin.
Phyllis Hughes wanted to protect the pond. She found that as it was man-made it could be registered as an Ancient Monument; and this was done in 1974, under section 6 of the Ancient Monuments Act 1931 as 'Dewpond' Friston Sussex B (Monument) 414. It was possibly the first pond in the country to be so designated

The 1990 drought conditions turned the pond into just a few puddles and people used it as a pathway. The danger was that if the puddled clay cracked it wouldn't hold water, although as there is said to be 3m of clay it should not be much of a problem. Maurice Hopkins said, "I am hopeful that the water authority will supply some water which they managed to do last year", they did. The PC decided to remove an old willow and alders nearby to stop their roots extracting water.

The County Ecologist said in 1993 that Friston pond did not need to be repuddled and the low water level was due to evaporation.

Near the island the pond had *Elodea crispa* a good oxygenator, the rare *Hottonia palustris,* the water violet, a protected plant, and round the edge *Tillaea recurva.* The water lilies include *Mrs Richmond,* a large pink, various *Marliaceas,* yellow and small pink flowers; the white ones are *Albatross.* Plants on the edge are iris (yellow flag) and *Typha latifolia* (reedmace, often erroneously called bullrush) and spearwort. Pond life included the great crested newt, and ram's horn snails. Tadpoles hatch out in great numbers in spring, as do dragonfly larvae later. Some rudd and goldfish are seen and mallard ducks are welcome visitors, in 1995 they had nine ducklings, all taken by foxes. Moorhens also winter here.

The PC maintain the pond and arrange for it to be cleaned out regularly by an expert and coppice the surrounding trees at intervals.

Venturing along **Crowlink Lane** the first house on the right is *Old Vicarage Cottage.* This was where the Vicar of Friston lived when the parishes were quite separate. As the last sole Vicar of Friston, Dr William Urquhart, died in 1688 you can see that Friston does not favour frequent changes of house name.

Pauline Markquick said, "We lived in *Old Vicarage Cottage* by the pond in 1929, when it was owned by the Maitlands. First impressions were of a country cottage with American Pillar roses round the door, but the lavatory was a bucket, there was just one tap over a butler's sink, no electricity or gas, you washed in a galvanised bath in front of the fire, and the roof leaked everywhere". Bob Seymour lived there in the 30s and 40s until he moved to 5 Upper Street. Upgraded, it was occupied from the 1950s to 1982 by Mrs Rachel E Maitland, wife of Pelham Maitland. Sold in 1984 for £99,000, it has been repeatedly extended since.

Old Vicarage Cottage, Friston, 1971, in Mrs Maitland's days, when you could just about imagine the likely appearance of the original cottage about the time the last Vicar of Friston died in 1688

A little further along the lane, Fred Fuller said, "Uncle Tom Martin built *Pleasant View* (now much altered as *Meadow Hill*) on the Crowlink Road and his father Corwin Martin, head gardener at *Friston Place* before the 1914-18 war, lived opposite.

"Corwin's family shared *Church Cottages,* then semi-detached, with another member of the Maitland staff until Corwin's death in 1929." It was rented out to various village folk, including the Goodmans from 1940, when they returned to the village after a short sortie to Waldron. It left behind its semi-detached existence when the Misses E and V Lindenberg were there after the war, and they changed the name to *Mary's Mead.* The Lees family followed, Margaret, Nigel, Christopher and Steven, who moved from *Haydon Hill,* attracted by *Mary's Mead's* paddocks for their horses. They have been there since the 1970s and have added to and improved it further.

Jimmy Holter adds, "Before Aunt Rose and Nelson Breach [the Breaches on The Green are no relation] moved to the Bake House [7], they lived at *South Hill Cottage,* which had its own pond, just south of the A259 on the bend of the road about 200m west from Friston Pond. Now all gone."

9. The Downlands Estate

Location, location, location so beloved of Estate Agents, yet for centuries, if not millennia, the villages of East Dean and Friston just weren't in the frame. Yes, they had potable water and they were near the sea, but this was when the sea was a capriciously dangerous place, regularly claiming fishermen to its depths. They also lacked good quality farmland, the thin soil on the Downs only really suitable for sheep, which were far more numerous than mankind, and the rutted, gluey tracks were notoriously impassable for most of the year. There is the no doubt apocryphal tale of the farmer up to his neck in mud being pulled out with some difficulty by a passer-by, only for the farmer to declare, "Right, now we've got to save the horse I was riding." So it was as an average Sussex hamlet that the years slipped by for the isolated tiny community, where everybody knew everyone else, but little outside. The 1914-18 war gave some exposure to the wide world and coupled with advances in transport and communication, some changes were inevitable.

It was, however, the Downlands Estate development that irrevocably altered East Dean and particularly Friston. The first stage was laying out of the ground plan, and although some of the houses were quite small (and intended as weekend or holiday retreats) most were substantial, but tasteful and set in ample breathing space. The garage sizes, however, bring to mind Austin 7s. This phase lasted from 1927 to 1940 when the war put a stop on any new build. The second stage, roughly 1946-65, saw further building along the Old Willingdon Road, The Ridgeway, Warren Lane, the lower side of Hillside, the upper part of Deneside, Michel Dene Road and the start of Peakdean Close, Peakdean Lane, Elven Lane, Summerdown Lane, and Wenthill Close. The third phase was expansion at the edges with the considerable building at The Outlook, Sussex Gardens and Downlands Way. The final phase is essentially infilling, although some projects have been extensive enough.

*Peak Dean Barn and Farm c.*1950. Run down, but used as a residence by a number of families. Peakdean Lane would run just to the right. Evidence of human associations for thousands of years was confirmed by the finding of a La Tene style horse harness at Peak Dean

The Downlands Estate was built on the land of *Gore Farm,* which at one time stretched from *Friston Place* lands along the Old Willingdon Road eastwards to Ringwood, around the Downs Golf Club boundary. It also abutted onto Gilbert Estate land along Horsefield and therefore included *Gore Cottages, Bess Barn, Flint Cottage,* and what became the old Village Hall, now a private residence.

Gore Farm was an ancient feature of East Dean. In a roll of 1332 to pay for the wars of Edward III there is a record of a late contribution by John of the Gore. Gore is an old English word meaning an odd end of land, often a triangular shape that did not lend itself to the furrow-long [furlong] drive of the plough - particularly if oxen were used.

The Payne family were there for centuries. In 1457 Simon Payne held a piece of land *Brambling* (today's Sussex Gardens) from Master Hugh, Lord of Peakdeane,

Tenant farmers included Richard Scrase in the early 1800s, and the Osborns 1850s-1880s. The last was Charles Frederick Russell, who was much involved in the village being chairman of the parish meeting, a school manager and a churchwarden. By 1913 he was also farming *Birling Farm* for his widowed mother, the tenant there, and South Hill for the Maitlands, but after his sons were mobilised, Charles Frederick 'retired' and went to Mill Road, Eastbourne. He later farmed at Ringmer and Laughton up to his death. [2]

Gore Farm had been dairy and arable - wheat and barley with oats for the animals.

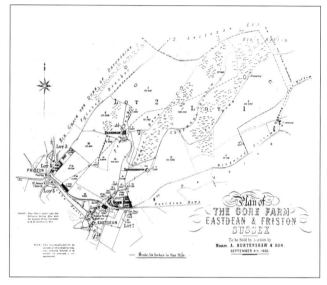

Gore Farm land as it was when sold at auction by the 9th Duke of Devonshire in September 1920.
Edward Oliver Hobden bought mainly Lots 1, 2 and 6. The farm extended from the Old Willingdon Road along the left by Friston Dencher and followed the line of Ringwood Bottom, lower right. Mrs Harding is named as owner of the land on either side of the Eastbourne road, but part had to be given up with the Downs Purchase of 1926-9

After the war the Russell twins managed *Gore Farm* until in 1920 the 9th Duke of Devonshire sold it at auction to Edward Oliver Hobden, known as EOH, an Upper Dicker farm manager who also farmed at Endlewick, where he retired and where he died in 1971. His wife was a Kemp.

Peak Dean Manor was the centre of the area. Near today's 25 Peakdean Lane, by a passing place, was an old flint barn, a well, and a little distance away the ruin of a large farmhouse - *Peak Dean Manor Farm*.

Peak Dean Manor was mentioned in the Domesday book. Owned by the Etchingham family for hundreds of years, a Master Hugh farmed it in the 1400s, and its manor court records go back to 1563, when the Selwyns bought it. Passing to the Lees family in the 1800s they sold to the 7th Duke of Devonshire in 1875 when the house, of no architectural importance, was divided into tenements.

Nigel Quiney said, "*Peak Dean Farm* was in an idyllic position, gentle Downland at the sides with views to the sea and surrounded by a flint wall. Two dwellings with a big barn at right angles. The walls were of flint and wood, for the beams and windows mainly oak was used that over time had turned to a silver grey producing an overall soft, mottled sun-bleached appearance. To the east beyond the flint wall there was a mass of thorny scrub and tangled brambles. It covered quite a few acres and included a few chestnut trees. Little sun penetrated through the thick foliage to the knotted roots and rabbit holes. It was a land of rotting boughs, toadstools, arum lilies, nettles and bindweed. It was called the Shaw, which seems to have been a general term for overgrown shrub land. Local lads used it for *Just William* adventures, making camps and hideaways.

"The house had two storeys, the upper one was merely an attic, used as bedrooms tucked under the eaves. There was no 'electric', gas provided both the lighting and cooking.

"An old crone lived in one of the houses, and the Hopper family rented the end house there during the war. Mr Hopper limped his way to the *Tiger* most evenings, occasionally bringing back a bottle of Guinness or Pale Ale for his wife and mother-in-law.

"Mrs Webb kept a few horses in the barn at *Peak Dean Manor.* She lived with Lawson Wood, an artist. My mother and Mrs Holdway would go riding."

William Haffenden, general labourer, and Sarah his wife, were among those who came to East Dean with the Hobdens. Their son, Reginald, said, "All the buildings opposite *Gore Farm* went with the farm so we lived in 2 *Gore Cottages.* There was no sanitation, no lighting, and for water us lads had to carry buckets from the farm. The lavatory, an earth closet, was at the bottom of the garden. When it was full my father would empty it out into a hole he had dug in the garden. It was not unknown for him to strike the main Friston to Eastbourne water main, which ran down there." When the Downlands Estate started up William Haffenden went to building houses, although he was no relation to Frank Haffenden, a builder with CH Prior who lived on The Green.

East Dean from the unmade Eastbourne road *c.*1922, chalk path to Cophall in foreground. *Gore Farmhouse* centre, to the right the milking parlour and further right the hay barn

Edward 'Ted' Pindred and his wife Edith, another Kemp, also came to East Dean in 1920 and lived in one of the *New Cottages* near Elven Lane. The head cowman, Fred Boarer and son Horace, lived in the other.

Kathleen Cater (née Hobden) said, "Pincher Vine, a carter, and the Breaches, lived at Peak Dean, and Tom Vine lived with the Breaches. Tom had a team of three horses, and Ted Pindred also had a team. The horses belonged to my father, but were looked after by Tom and Ted as their teams. The Lemmons were another agricultural working family who drove a team of horses for the plough".

Fred Fuller's father was Mark, a thatcher - hay tying, straw tying, and shocking (making hay stooks). Pre-1914 the farmworker's pay was $2\frac{1}{2}$p a day. He was another who lived at *Peak Dean Manor* and worked at *Gore Farm.* He had been employed as a labourer on the 'new' lighthouse 1899-1902, going down from the cliff top in the cable car. His wife, Katie, died 1956 and he died four years after her.

Ray Cheal, son of George and Dora, said that at one time in the 1920s the family lived at *Summerdown Cottages.* "You went past *Michel Dene Cottages,* past *New Cottages* and a further field on was Summerdown. No running water, no toilets, to get a bucket of water I had to go to *New Cottages* which is still there, now knocked into one house."

Mr Hobden sold the first plot of land for building in 1922 for £100 an acre.

Bill Armiger said, "The first building on the site of the future Downlands Estate was an old army hut in 1922, bought at auction from the Airship Station at Polegate, and later joined with an Army hut from Eastbourne's Summerdown Camp". [3] Bought by Charlie Grayson, an ex-serviceman baker from Lincoln, he placed them just above the Blacksmith's Forge on Friston hill, where *Downlands* (19a) Hillside is today. In those days there was easy access from the A259. Jimmy Holter said that Charlie carried the Eastbourne hut on his back to East Dean, piece by piece, and re-erected the hut himself on Hillside.

Looking west *c.*1930. The central white buildings on the A259 are (left) *Gore Cottages* and (right) *Long View Cottage*. Above is Charlie Grayson's bakery and the beginnings of the Estate. Just in front of Long View is Edward Hobden's Service Station with petrol pumps

The huts, assembled at an angle, held the bakery, and the family of three children. Florrie Vine said, "Charlie Grayson baked lovely bread which he delivered on his bike". He later had a motorised tricycle for deliveries. "My, that man worked hard." said Tom Goodman, "In the afternoon he would make up the dough, leave it to rise, nip down to *The Tiger* for a couple of pints, or thereabouts, and be back to bake the bread during the evening. First thing next morning he was out delivering, and so it went on. He used coke ovens that produced a lovely crispy bread, not like what you get nowadays". Joan and Ken Thurman say, "Alternate weeks he baked delicious jam tarts at 1/6d [7½p], and shortbreads at 4d". He had no gas or electricity in the 1920s, but they all agree with Florie Vine that, "His Coburgs were something special".

Renee Wicking said, "He went everywhere on his pushbike, all his bread was delivered. Even pushed it to Crowlink. His son John, Raymond Wicking and Ivor Trickett helped him. He was a jolly good baker."

In part of one hut during the summer his wife, Ida, served teas for passers-by, particularly cyclists who used the access from Friston hill. 'Not especially busy, but worthwhile.' In the winter the teashop area was hired out for village functions.

Nigel Quiney adds, "We got wholemeal or crusty white bread from Charlie Grayson's bakery at the top of roughly hewn steps up from the main Eastbourne-Brighton road. He was a dark, swarthy man, often helped by his son, and the bakery was a large wooden shed with a corrugated iron roof. If he had made one of his wonderful Victoria jam sponges, about twelve inches in diameter, we would buy one as well. Everything tasted so good and was so fresh that the lads had to resist nibbling the crusty corners on the way back home, while keeping an eye out for the mouse droppings occasionally found baked in the bread. Some said it was what gave the bread that special flavour, while Charlie would say that it was a touch of beer that did the trick. If that were all."

Shortly after EOH bought *Gore Farm* its viability was threatened when parts of Beachy Head were compulsorily purchased by Eastbourne Corporation in the Downs Purchase Act of 1926/9. *Birling Farm* also lost a substantial acreage. [5] Coupled with the poor state of farming, Edward Hobden became receptive to alternative usage of his land.

East Dean looking north from Went Way *c.*1925. *Went Acre* is the nearest house, the church is just right of centre, *Gore Farmhouse* up left and Summerdown top centre, but no Downlands Estate

In 1925/6 the Pindreds built the house and shop known as the Corner Stores, started a business and Mrs Pindred ran the Post Office after it was transferred from Dennett's shop on The Green. The Pindreds built onto their corner house, a shop, a Post Office and the manual telephone exchange, until by 1939 there were seven bedrooms above. It is now two dwellings - *Long View Cottage* and *Beech Tree Cottage.* The exchange later moved to the single-storey building on the opposite side of the main road. After the Fears family came back from London in 1938 they stayed at *Long View* where Ted's aunt Viv, the wife of Jim Kemp lived, and Ted remarked, "I can recall the large PO batteries on the floor".

Mr Francis Arnatt, always 'Bill', had led an exciting life. Before the Bolshevik Revolution he was the chief representative for Vauxhall vehicles (especially farm needs) in Russia. His daughter, Joyce Donkin (née Arnatt), says that the family lived in St Petersburg from 1908, "I had a Russian nannie, and spoke Russian till I was five". The situation became fraught when the Revolution broke out in 1917 and she went on, "I recall crossing over a frozen river as we escaped after the uprising". Not only did Bill Arnatt bring his family out safely, but he was one of the few businessmen to retrieve the assets of his firm; somehow he brought out all the Vauxhall monies. Naturally, the company was truly appreciative and awarded him a place on the Board.

Joyce adds, "He loved Sussex and from 1920 we came here for holidays and stayed at the *Birling Gap Hotel.* It was just a country lane from East Dean to Birling Gap. My father's intention was to build a house for the family in East Dean, but for the time being they stayed in *Little Garth* on Gilbert's Drive. He knew the architect, Alwyn Underdown, and it was while they were looking over a possible site that my father noticed the corrugated iron roof of Charlie Grayson's bakery on Hillside and other tin roofs of old

Army huts going up after the 1914-18 war. 'What's that?' asked my father and the architect replied, 'Anyone can put up whatever they like. There are no restrictions of any kind'."

In the 1920s lovers of the Downs deplored development, but recognised that with the depressed state of farming some changes were to be anticipated. In many parts of Sussex the landowners sold out to tenant farmers who realised that a good profit could be made by selling on the land for development, for to change land from farm to dwelling use uplifted the value by a hundred fold.

Bryn Cottage, 34 Hillside, in 2000, one of the earliest houses on the Downlands Estate. The house deeds have plans dated 1926. It was called *Belmont* when built in 1927/8

Bill Arnatt wasn't stretched in his new post, and he was no mug. Perhaps inspired by the Thorpness development, he decided to form a company to acquire Downland for an estate so that development would not be haphazard. When Friston mill collapsed in January 1926 [8] the villagers effectively cleared the site in a few weeks, so without further delay Mr Arnatt decided to buy all *Peak Dean Farm* and most of *Gore Farm* and start an estate with restrictive covenants, working closely with farmer, Edward Hobden, the Revd AA Evans and Arthur Beckett, President of the Society of Sussex Downsmen.

This area was sold to the Downland Estate Company, with Arnatt as chairman, in 1927. Each house was to be set in one to three acres of ground with a view of its own; quite achievable for the height of the Downland varied from 45m to over 120m above sea level. He wanted the houses artistically designed in materials to conform with old houses in the village, and he set about buying large quantities of local roofing tiles for this purpose.

Mr Arnatt built a new road, Windmill Lane, ('reserved for more than average houses') across the frontage of the site, effectively camouflaged by a grass bank so that it was not visible from the main road, and brought in electricity and gas. Unemployed men dug the trenches for the pipes and cables. The telephone connections were also underground.

Ray Cheal says the first house on the estate was in 1927, *Friston Field* for Frank Bridge in Old Willingdon Road. Another early completion was *Belmont,* now *Bryn Cottage,* at the bend of Hillside, which then was merely a path off Warren Lane.

Conveyance of the *Belmont* land from Edward Oliver Hobden to Francis and Ethel Marion Arnatt was in October 1927. The transfer of land from East Dean Downlands Ltd [EDDL] of *Gore Farm* to Charles Fears in 1927 (with covenants often meant to maintain standards) and the house was started that year as a B&B. Land Registration followed.

Wayside Cottage (behind the Forge) was given to Prebendary Colin Kerr by his father in 1926, although he came to the village for holidays a few years before. Other houses of the late 1920s soon followed. Included were *Friston Court, Ridge House* (where the Arnatt family lived before the war), *Friston Corner,* all designed by Alwyn Underdown, and *Farthings* along Windmill Lane. In The Ridgeway on the left hand side was *Gillridge;* in The Close, Warrren Lane *Old Style* (now *Haydon Hill*) and *The Cottage,* and Warren Close had *Upmeads* by Oliver Hill.

Next by the early 1930s were *Knoll House* (*The Gables*, 8 Windmill Lane) another typical Underdown house, *Tolmans* (13 Warren Lane), two clusters of houses nearby and *Gainsborough* (38 Warren Lane). Dr Stella Churchill, a lady doctor, owned *High and Over*.

Bill's son John helped him, and he employed Don Harris and Vic Hopper on the estate work. Vic, who was excellent at costing the developments, lived at *Peak Dean Manor* until his death in 1952. CH Prior, a good firm, were the original builders for the estate.

In 1928 Mr Arnatt gave assurances that the amenities of the village would be preserved and invited the president of the Society of Sussex Downsmen to meet Mr Farrier, one of the architects, to examine the plans.

Frank Bridge (1879-1941) with his musician wife Ethel (1881-1960) and their house *Friston Field* c.1930, now a little extended with three front dormers. He was a composer, conductor, string player and teacher of Benjamin Britten, who played tennis with him at the back of the house. Wrote much of his later music here including *Enter Spring,* originally called *On Friston Down.* Both are buried in Friston churchyard

The aim was to complete the Estate with about 550 dwellings and a population of some 1800, compared to East Dean's 400 in 1939. Most of the new residents would be retired from the professions, although some would work from home, and a few commute to Eastbourne or to London.

Bill Arnatt set about a public relations exercise. The unsightly cow yard/rubbish heap opposite *Gore Farm* was turned into a pleasant grass plot surrounded by the old flint wall of the stockyard. *Garden Cottage*-to-be was to the left, and at the back of the Village Hall-to-be were stables, used as stores during the 1939-45 war, and nowadays a bungalow, *Flint Cottage.* In 1920 the 'Village Hall' was two loose boxes for horses. The one nearest the road was also used as a mortuary for tramps who not uncommonly would commit suicide, usually by cutting their throat. To the right is *Bess Barn,* which was a granary converted into an Estate office, with the alterations confined to the interior. Other improvements were to remove corrugated iron roofs on existing buildings. Mr Arnatt also boasted that he had built a flint-walled house for a tenant 'at an actual loss, rather than it be erected by an outside builder of a material which might prove an eyesore'.

In May 1928, Bill Arnatt most generously proffered the ancient building opposite *Gore Farm* for the use of the parish as a Parish Hall. To give permanent tenure it was vested in the vicar and churchwardens. Its history is obscure, but its beautifully tooled quoin stones, mullioned windows and fireplace show it to have been a dwelling place of some repute.

The Estate office moved to the Windmill Lane entrance before the war, where it remained until 1972, The villagers realised that the new hall needed an ante-room for hats and coats, floor coverings, a boiler, sets of crockery and a cupboard, and set about making it workable. By December 1928 one suggestion was that this new Village Hall should be called Arnatt's Hall.

The 'Village Hall', needed about £520 of work. Dances, raffles and such raised £380 so orders for £450 of work were given. The walls were raised, the corrugated iron roof replaced with tiles, a block floor laid, an extra window inserted, a porch built, the walls cleaned and plastered, lighting brackets fixed, the mullioned window re-glazed, the Jacobean fireplace restored, and ventilation, cupboards, chairs and crockery provided.

The feelings engendered were mixed. 'Some people haven't contributed because they don't think the new hall spacious enough for all gatherings, but there is always Bardolf Hall, or even the schoolroom or the Gilbert Institute for larger events, however it is exactly fitted for the greater number of meetings which will occur with the increase in population.'

In 1929 the Downs Purchase by Eastbourne Borough Council was completed. [3] As a result *Gore Farm* lost all its land between Downs View Lane and the Downs Golf Course, 402 acres, but farmer Hobden pocketed £11,580 in compensation.

Celebration for the opening of the 'new' Village Hall in October 1929. Among those identified are Mrs Sarah Funnell, Maurice Haffenden, Cecil Smith, Ben Carter, George Worsell, Mrs Freda Markquick (*Friston Place*), John Grooms chauffeur to Miss Fass, Bob Etteridge the PC's son, Dorothy Stevens, Mrs Lily Ticehurst, Frank Haffenden Prior's foreman and Mrs Ida Grayson. 'Bill' Arnatt performed the opening ceremony and the Revd AA Evans returned to preside over the gathering. Note the oil lamps

Edward Hobden retained the farmhouse and frontage on which he developed a garage and petrol station. He also kept a few hens so many residents will find in their deeds that they are forbidden to sell petrol or eggs. There was no going back, farming in Britain employed one million males as late as 1950, by the end of the century less than 200,000.

In the early 1920s most of the cars were model T Fords that had a petrol tank under the driver's seat (the only one). It was gravity-fed and if they tried to climb a steep incline on a part-empty tank they got an air lock and came to an ignominious halt on the hill - if the brake held. One way round this was to come up Friston hill backwards in reverse and this also gave a lower gear and those in the know, and didn't mind a pain in the neck, also used the technique for Exceat hill and East Dean Road hill. Mr Hobden became fed up with the many others who requested rescue by his tractor to pull the stranded car to the top. Being an astute businessman he installed a petrol pump and if a car became stuck it was towed downhill to the pump for a fill up. And that was the start of the garage. At one time he had five pumps all serviced by different oil companies so that he could sell one company's petrol while paying another whose petrol he had just sold out.

Before long, Jim Kemp, Edward Hobden's brother-in-law, started a garage workshop and EOH became agent for Armstrong-Siddeley cars. The garage closed during the 1939-45 war [10], when Jim branched out and started the Forge Garage on the hill.

Diana Eyre said, "In 1931 cars were few and far between so there was no danger in walking up Friston hill past the *Old Forge*. The only entrance from the main road to our *Hilltop Cottage* [4 Warren Lane] and that part of the estate was up the grassy bank behind what is now *Lye Oak* [1 The Close]". She confirms that, "To enter we had to reverse our Austin Seven in order to engage the lowest gear to get up the slope".

"In this part of the Estate there were only some five other houses such as *Old Style* [now *Haydon Hill,* 4 The Close], *The Cottage* [2 the Close] and *Middle Brow* [2 Warren Lane]. The steep part of Hillside was a cart track which led down to two houses *Belmont* (now *Bryn Cottage*) and *Leinster House* (now *Burford Cottage*)."

Bess Barn (left) a granary, became the Estate Office, converted before the war into two rented flats, the lower one became a doctor's surgery, the top flat, *Grey Cottage,* reached by an outside stairway was rented out in the 1950s to Stan Hobden, Edward's brother. Jack Goodman was in *Bess Barn* in the 1960s and Brian and Janet Johnson in *Grey Cottage*. The building has now (right) reverted to one dwelling as *Bess Barn*

By 1939 the upper side of Hillside was about half built-up, but there were only three houses on the SE side, *Middle Brow* (2 Warren Lane), *Burford Cottage* and *Raycot*.

Before the war the twitten from Upper Street finished where it met the main road below *Lye Oak,* to enter the Estate you went across the road and up the slope to Warren Lane, or walked up the road. To reach Friston church you usually walked up Hobbs eares. [7]

During the war a line of concrete tank traps [dragon's teeth] ran across the road just below the Friston bus stop. Cleared from the road afterwards they continued to obstruct the paths up to Friston until they were 'blown up' in 1951. [7]

Walking up Friston hill changed in the 1950s when three accidents convinced even the most earnest dawdlers that they had to use the paths. Emily Stanley, in service to Prebendary Kerr for many years, was knocked down and seriously injured in February 1952. Rachel Patching and Ronald Townley were others in traffic accidents there.

Fred Fuller said, "In the 1930s all the lads dug for flints in what is now the Greensward. We'd dig there at night with a paraffin lantern and were paid 15p a yard. The flints were piled up in front of the future Gore Garage office ready to be used for repairing roads."

The sewers were incorporated into the East Dean Downlands Ltd in April 1936, the year that an access road (namely, the upper slope of Hillside) was made up by Llewellyn's for a total of £186 including brick gullies and 4½inch of concrete.

Guy Smart, an Eastbourne solicitor, lived at *Belmont* until 1961. His wife was a patient of Dr Bodkin Adams whose Rolls would often be seen parked outside. Next as resident came WT Williams, an engineer who rewired it, put in central heating and renamed it *Bryn Cottage*. He couldn't stand the English weather, or at least the 1962-3 winter, and went back to South Africa in 1964, leaving the central heating fully on.

Joan and Ken Thurman and family came to *Bryn Cottage* in April 1965. Neighbouring houses include 30, *St Mary's Cottage* where for many years Air Vice-Marshall Hugh White and his wife Joy lived. She died in 1999 at Puddletown. At 28 Hillside was Elizabeth Villa, her husband, Helmut, had worked for Mercedes. In the 1970s there was a Finnish woman, Mollie Bjorkstand, a widow with two sons at school, and earlier the Hodgsons lived there with their two sons. Ricky Hodgson said, "The family came to East Dean in 1953, to Hillside when there were no houses on the opposite side of the road. I understood the plots opposite were for sale at £150 to £250".

Upmeads, left, in Warren Close and right *High and Over* in Warren Lane, houses typical of the variety and inventiveness of design shown from the beginning in the Downlands Estate

Opposite *Bryn Cottage* is *Raycot,* built by the Townley's. When Ronald's wife died he had an extension built for his housekeeper. As mentioned, a victim of increased traffic, he was knocked down by a car just above the Forge. He died in 1961. His son, Ray, was in the RAF, and lived there with his wife, Shirley, their daughter and two handicapped sons.

Raycot was rented out for a while and among the tenants were track and tennis stars Chris Chattaway and Shirley Bloomer, there for a year, until it was bought by Mrs Jill Pigott and Richard Wooller's mother, followed by the Hadley-Coates in 1987.

Downland, Daphne Svenson there now, is the site of Charlie Grayson's bakery and his wife's tea-rooms. Ida Grayson would baby-sit for the Thurmans in the 1960s.

Hilltop Cottage in 1932 and 2006. "In the 1930s our garden opened onto Downland, when we mowed our lawn the cows put their heads through the wire fence and ate the cut grass."

Eva Fennell built *Leinster House* [now *Burford Cottage*] - her father was chaplain to the Duke of Leinster. After her, from 1940 to 1959, came retired dentist John Powell and his wife, both keen golfers, followed by Cecil Cornford, a wholesale tobacco merchant. He died in 1973, his widow remarried and, when widowed again, she moved to Majorca. More recently June Pockett was there, the *Grand Hotel* secretary.

Miss Pilley had a caravan near the entrance to what is now Deneside, but was then just a farm gate. The caravan had central wheels and was supported by chocks. Reg Haffenden said that Harry Cleves and Tom Mepham would knock the chocks out late on a Friday night so that when Miss Pilley got up and moved to the other end of the caravan it tipped up.

Miss Gladys Penford retired early from teaching, bought land in Downs View Lane in 1929 and built *Woodbury* the next year. She helped out at East Dean School as an assistant teacher, particularly from August to November 1933 when Miss Crosland left, and before Miss Hayes started. She also ran the Sunday School for many years.

Aerial view of Friston 1934. The white Water Tower - only seven years old - is central, the Jevington Road runs away to the mid-left. The A259 to Brighton snakes to the lower edge, and Willingdon is in the top distance. Notable features are the sparseness of Friston Forest, only begun in 1927, and how few Estate houses are to be seen

Mrs Florence Burgess, of *White Gulls,* [2 Warren Close] who knew her, suggested that she start a private kindergarten at *Woodbury.* Mrs Burgess' daughter, Maureen, enrolled on the opening day, 5 May 1937, and continued until March 1941.

The school ran through the war to 1950. Many local children attended, including Anthony Williams (1937-39), the Davies-Gilberts - Patricia (1941-43), Sylvia (1942-43), Jimmy (1944-45) - and Jane Nash (1948-49). [3]

Miss Gladys Penford, who lived in Downs View Lane, started a kindergarten in 1937 that ran until early 1950

A group of the kindergarten pupils in 1948. Jane Nash (later Booth-Clibborn) is the tall girl at the back

Jane said, "Going to school involved leaving home in Old Willingdon Road, walking along Windmill Lane, Hillside, Deneside, Elven Lane, collecting other children on the way down and taking short cuts through the empty post-war plots. Every Wednesday we had to bring a handkerchief so that we could blow our nose before singing lessons."

Miss Penford wrote children's stories, but from the number of rejection slips it doesn't appear that she had many published. In 1969, the year after she died, George and Jane Booth-Clibborn (née Nash) moved in. "It was most evocative" says Jane, "The pupils' coat hooks were still on the wall in the hall."

East Dean and Friston aerial view 1934. The Ridgeway and Warren Lane form a loop near the left edge. The crossroads (left centre) has *Old Style,* now *Haydon Hill, Penlee* and *Hilltop Cottage.* The straight road (right) is Gilbert's Drive going to *Gore Farmhouse.* Lower Street comes off left on its way to the white *Tiger* Inn on the Green (lower centre)

The *Eastbourne Gazette* of 4 May 1938 stated, 'Aware that the Windmill Lane developments of houses of £1700-£6000 are not within the means of many people, Mr F Arnatt has opened up Deneside for buildings costing less than £1200, but designed by

One of the semi-detached houses on Deneside

Alwyn Underdown. The first ones are near the small triangle reached from Michel Dene Road, a new road opened between the petrol pumps and the post office. They are semi-detached, have old tiles and bricks with modern interiors, brick fireplaces, Oregon pine doors, tiled kitchens, S/S sinks and tiled bathrooms'.[1]

Kathleen Banks said, "When news came that a developer was opening up *Gore Farm* in order to build an estate, my father [A & H Burgess - Harold Burgess was Fred Nash's father-in-law] was keen to buy a plot in Deneside for his retirement home, and he built *Meads,* almost the first house there. This meant that I could spend holidays here with my family.

"There was only wire and posts round the gardens and the children would slip through to pick cowslips. We would take the children to Mrs Pindred at the corner shop to buy sweets, and my son, Ted, liked to go to see Mrs Sworder in Cophall because she always had an interesting animal to see, perhaps a goat, or a rabbit or a chicken. My father eventually went on to build a number of houses before the war including the new Rectory, *Clovers* [26 Deneside], and *White Gulls,* 2 Warren Close, for my brother Percy and family. Later Burgess's built *Sparrows* for Mr Ellis in Downs View Lane." Basil Ellis' daughter is Jane Beavan who now lives in Tasmania.

Before development commenced along Michel Dene Road what is now the *Barn Stores* in the Downlands Way precinct was Big Barn where linseed cake was crushed to feed to the cows, the Hay Barn was on the site of the maisonettes, and Wayside is the site of the dairy parlour. The newsagent's shop [9 Downlands Way] was the bull pen of *Gore Farm* and the other shops were calf pens.

Looking from above Downs View Lane towards *Gore Farm c.*1925.
The nearest dwelling on the right, seen end on, is *Dene Lea* tearooms, with beehives in the garden.
Centre is *Falmer House,* the Pelecano's place, knocked down for Sussex Gardens. In between is where Downs View Close would be built.
In the mid-distance is *Gore Farm* and its outbuildings

Nigel Quiney said, "Children often learnt to drive on the estate and it was not unknown for 14-year-olds to drive on the estate roads, at a time when few families had a car. The real attraction, however, for the lads was East Dean's Sewage Farm, discreetly surrounded by trees. A short track led to an oak gate painted PRIVATE and DANGER, with just beyond three ceramic gullies set in concrete each about the size of a tennis court. In the first a foul-smelling fluid and pieces of toilet paper swirled around, fed from a pipe about 0.5m in diameter with stop-gates and cogs, the second held a soft mud, and the third had a crusted surface."

Interior of the *Dene Lea* Tea Rooms

Although 'the Sewage' was a regular item on the Parish Council [PC] agenda we will move speedily away eastwards, towards another early part of the estate - Downs View Lane. *Falmer House,* knocked down for Sussex Gardens, was the home of the Pelecanos family. Ted Fears said, "Mr Pelecanos, a Greek who dealt in sponges, grandly smoked cigars, had a housekeeper, Rose, and during the war ran a car on producer gas, but its real feature was a car radio - almost unheard of in those days."

Joan Nash said, "My husband and I knew the Pelecanos family of *Falmer House* quite well. Anthony was interested in horse racing and they had property in Nassau. Lyn is now in Eastbourne aged over 102 and her daughter Lois works in the London theatre world."

Another early house along Downs View Lane was *Dene Lea.* Originally associated with bee hives Mrs Sogno turned it into successful tea rooms that you could hardly miss in the 1930s, most of the local postcards had *Dene Lea Tea Rooms* emblazoned upon them, whatever the scene they portrayed, and three signs around the village directed you there.

Before the war many of the residents played tennis on the Estate Tennis Club courts [now Royston Close] between the Ridgeway and the Waterworks Cottages but entered via the twitten from Windmill Lane. Joyce Donkin looked after the junior section.

At the beginning of the war the Arnatts moved from *Ridge House* to Downs View Lane. Just before the war a woman who lived next to Mrs Batten along Crowlink Lane wished to leave for the USA immediately and had offered Mr Arnatt her house fully furnished for £5000, but as he said, 'I couldn't afford it because I was still paying off the interest on my borrowings for the gas and electric works and with the war I couldn't sell plots'.

Apart from the infilling of *Acorns* (Warren Lane entrance) in 1981, The Close, off Warren Lane, had its present quota of houses by 1939, *Lye Oak,* 2, *The Cottage,* 3, and *Old Style* (now *Haydon Hill,* 4) were in place. Between *Lye Oak* and *Deane House* (now *Friston House,* 2 Friston Close) two houses had been built, *Little Down* and *Windy Ridge,* but with access from Friston hill - no trouble in the 1930s, however, with the increasing traffic access and egress can be hazardous today. *Windy Ridge* was built for Emile and Beryl Monico, but Denis and Winifred Arnold lived there for many years into the 1990s.

An inevitable result of the war was that development on the East Dean Downlands Estate stopped, and so the dozen houses scattered round the Greensward remained in isolation, and the four in The Brow were also left to themselves for the duration.

Downlands Estate map of 1939.
Near the left lower edge is the pond and just above *The Outlook* Tearooms, *Little Friston,* the Tennis Club and the line of Waterworks Cottages. About half the plots in The Ridgeway and Warren Lane have been filled. Only the outline of the Greensward is there, but most of Downs View Lane had been built.
Summerdown Lane and Michel Dene Road, however, are empty of houses

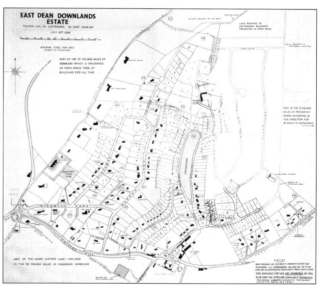

Nigel Quiney said, "Only two houses were at the top end of Deneside by 1940: Major Bell's *Aveland,* number 46 and ours, *Albourne,* Peakdean Lane and with the cessation of building work that's how it stayed right through to 1946. Another early resident of Deneside was Una Ellam who was a member of The Players. She moved away in 1948." The few children around at that time describe playing on building sites with just a few foundations and taking short cuts through building plots.

Aveland was finished in April 1940 for Major Bell, but because of shortages he had to hunt out the timber he required. Said to have the best wood in Friston, it also has undersized hand-made bricks. A housing casualty of the war was a 1939 plan for flatlets surrounding the *Peak Dean farmyard.*

Nigel continues, "Lads would go to the rock pools at Birling Gap to look for sea anemones, shrimps, crabs, cockles, winkles and fronded seaweed. More exciting was the discovery of empty bullet cases, shell cases, and bits of aeroplanes. Just after the war the garden of Belle Tout was popular for an overnight camp, until there were a few cliff falls.

Village lads would climb the trees in the rookery in the lee of Went Hill above the cricket pitch looking for bird's eggs. It was considered right and proper as the farmers classified them as pests.

"Apart from the war there were always tragedies and I recall a couple who lived on the west side of the Greensward gassing themselves because of financial difficulties."

After the war *The Laines* was bought by a Colonel who bred Great Danes, and 'Bill' Arnatt moved to *Little Friston* with his family. [8] They stayed four years, but he had a mild stroke and was 'bothered by enquiries from residents' so he sold the business and his wife took him back to Guildford. The buyer of *Little Friston* was an osteopath who didn't want the stables, gardener's and chauffeur's place, and land on the other side of the Jevington road, so the Arnatt family kept that area and converted the stables and gardener's place into *Hillsborough,* where Joyce Donkin lived for over 30 years.

Upper Deneside looking SW, as it was 1940-45, with just 46 Deneside, *Aveland* (left), and 1 Peakdean Lane (*Albourne*); the nascent Peakdean Lane is running between them. Peakdean Close is a path off the Deneside bend running up the hill. Warren Lane is on the skyline

Jane Beavan (née Ellis) came to East Dean in 1946 from India after the war. 'It was September and my cousins suggested blackberrying. This was a totally new experience for me and I set off in great expectation. We went along Michel Dene Road and up a track to the left that was completely rural and quite beautiful. By the time I left in 1962 it had been completely built over and the lane and blackberries had disappeared.'

Gill Sergeant spent the war in South Africa, for both her first husband and father were prisoners-of-war of the Japanese. Afterwards she met her husband, Ken Imrie, off the boat in Southampton. "He resumed business in the Far East and as my six-year-old son was at school in Eastbourne we rented *Payne's Dene* along Crowlink Lane from the Simpson family. The previous tenant had been a 'British Israelite' who had two male secretaries and Biblical texts were stuck all over the walls. "He said to me, 'It's no use you coming here, the world is coming to an end in July 1946', and this when I was expecting my daughter in the August." All went well however and I had my younger son Tim in 1948."

Alfred Gallop was the gardener at *Payne's Dene* and had been from before the war. "He was very good, but didn't have a high opinion of my efforts in the garden."

"We liked the area and bought a plot of land in The Brow intending to retire there. At that time the only houses were *Poyle Cottage (2), Old Bridle Way (4), Greystone Priors [Grey Friars* 5] and *Furze Close* (11, later the Greenwoods), all built before the war."

On 11 March 1951 her husband was killed when his plane crashed into the Peak at Hong Kong on take off from the notorious Kai Tak airfield.

'Sir John Salmond's daughter was due to move to *Payne's Dene,* but he most kindly said I could stay on for a month or two.' It was difficult to obtain permission for building, and she rented *Blackthorns,* Warren Lane and stayed at *Gore Farm* for a while.

Gore Farm was a big house; when the Pindred's gave up the shop they moved into *The Gore* farmhouse. Mrs Edith Pindred lived more or less in the large back kitchen, and Gill Sergeant rented a sitting room on the ground floor (on the other side of a corridor was another tenanted room), her bedroom was on the first floor and son Tim had a bedroom on the top floor. "I don't recall a Mr Pindred, but he was about. Kathleen Hobden [later Cater] ran a kiosk outside. Mrs Pindred looked after us well and cooked lovely meals. I recall, however, that after we complimented her on her Yorkshire Pudding, we got Yorkshire almost every day for weeks on end."

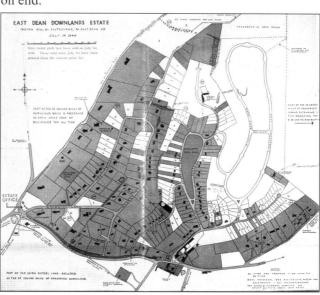

Map of the Downlands Estate July 1946.
A few more houses have been built, especially around Deneside, and in Elven Lane.
Summerdown Lane and Upper Michel Dene Road remain house-free, and *Peak Dean Farm* is intact or at least as much as it had been for the previous 100 years

Eventually she managed to get a permit to build. About that time she got talking with a builder who had a sparklingly clean van labelled *Butler,* and mentioned that she and her husband had rented a house from a 'Butler' in Rangoon. "That would be me", replied the builder and she found he was part of Butler Brooker house builders, who were putting up houses on the estate.

"I didn't have a car then and one day I was on the bus to Eastbourne and I found that the lady sitting beside me had also been to South Africa. I said that I was looking for an architect to build a house and she said her husband was Alwyn Underdown, an architect. He designed a house for me but it was a typical Underdown and not what I wanted, but he understood and suggested his partner who designed *High Gorse.* This would be about 1954 and there were still many restrictions on the height of windows and timber was difficult to obtain. Butler Brooker (who were building *Robin Hill,* and the farm at the end of Old Willingdon Road, at the same time) managed using bricks and tiles obtained from old houses by Alwyn Underdown, and even put in parquet floors, although I do remember radiators were difficult to get.

"Sir Alexander and Lady Grant lived at *Furze Close.* He had been in the RAF and they were very kindly to me. Whenever I came down to see how the house was doing I would stay with them. The Gleggs, Robert and Milly, were having *Robin Hill* built, the land of which extended into The Brow and lived in the Ridgeway while it was being constructed and on occasions I stayed with them when I came down.

"In the 1960s I rented out *High Gorse* in the summer mainly to people from the Glyndebourne theatre: At different times, Elizabeth Söderström, the singer, and a flautist in the orchestra would take the house for the whole season.

"On the other side of the road the Revd Gustav Aronsohn had his house built by his brother who was an architect; the Cooks, a talented and pleasant family, are there now, with the Curzons next door and then Tony and Bridget Rix. Bill & Pip Hewitt at *Poyle Cottage* are other good neighbours. I recall the Baxter's further along too.

Peakdean Lane 1950 looking towards Deneside, mid-left, with 'upper' Hillside on the right and silhouettes of Warren Lane houses

"On my side of The Brow old man McIlvenny built the 'Spanish house' and the other two houses in the 1970s, but later lost money and his son died tragically. His daughter-in-law, Anne, lives in the brick-built Georgian-style one, next to *High Gorse.* Visitors always ask 'What is it?', with guesses varying from a telephone exchange to a smallish factory."

In 1959 Mr and Mrs Walter Broughton built their house in The Brow, where she lived until 1993. Joan Nash adds, "Marjorie Watson was another great gardener there".

The manual telephone exchange equipment was moved from *Long View* to the building (later *Wild Cottage*) on the opposite side of the main road. This became the Postal Sorting Office in 1948 when the present telephone exchange was built in Deneside.

Most of Dene Close and Elven Lane were built in the 1950s, with Elven Close a little later. Peakdean Lane was built in the late 1950s and early 1960s. Most were 3-bedroom bungalows and varied from £7450 (the Hellingly design) to £9250 (Birling 2 design).

In 1952 the estate comprised 260 acres of which 75 had been left as open space. The brochures said it lay amid 35 sq. miles of Downland protected by the NT and Forestry Commission 'for all time'. The plans included footpaths, 'and there is a flourishing Bowls Club, Cricket Club, Football Club, and one of the best Amateur Dramatic Societies in Sussex. Main drainage, water, gas, electricity, telephone are largely underground. To cater for all (almost) needs a Post Office, general store, off-licence, butcher's, baker's and a pub.'

Pauline Joslin said, "From our house at Cophall we watched the new houses gradually creep up the hill, until at night the lights along the Link looked like a train.

Kay Ketcher's family came from Sussex. Both Kay and husband Leslie Ketcher were teachers, Kay having trained at Eastbourne. Les had been a prisoner-of-war in Timor and Japan, and afterwards was an accountant in the city, but they always wanted to move to the country, and they came to East Dean in 1958 with their two boys, Martin and Duncan.

They dealt with Mr Halliwell, Draycott's negotiator, the agents for the EDDL, buying the plot of 7 Peakdean Lane for £540. Given a choice of five designs - two houses and three bungalows; only six of each design were to be built, they selected a house, but Hailsham RDC turned down the application, on the grounds that a house would overlook others nearby, so they chose one of the bungalows. As one of their parents was to live with them, they had it converted to a chalet bungalow with a staircase and two extra rooms.

"When we moved in there were no houses above us on our side of Peakdean Lane and only two on the other side. Up the road, by a passing place, there was a well, and a section of old flintstone wall, and a little distance away the ruin of a large farmhouse Peak Dean *Manor Farm*. When demolition took place Mrs Phyllis Hughes tried to get part of the old barn preserved. There was also the remains of an orchard of apple trees where in the late 1950s our sons, Martin and Duncan, played football. Now all gone."

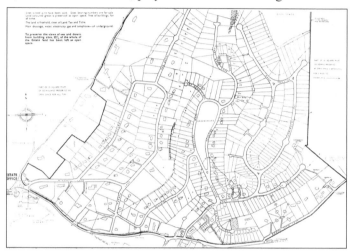

Downlands Estate, 1954. The general lay out is much as it is today, with the projected Closes off Michel Dene Road and The Link joining to Summerdown Lane. *Peak Dean Manor* is extant

At a 1958 meeting of the PC fears had been expressed by residents that building might occur beyond the permitted 365 ft contour, but the chairman reported that both Hailsham and the Downlands Estate had assured him that such fears were groundless.

The development was rapid, and allegations continued that Mr JD Tupper, the Estate Manager for Fairway Homes from 1965, had laid the upper part of Michel Dene Road not to one side of the slope to avoid the houses being too obvious, but on the top of the hill.

If we move down the hill to the front of *Gore farmhouse* we are where Tom Goodman's father, Jack, had a caravan near the garage from which the family sold papers. About 1960 the Goodman's took over the Corner shop at *Long View* when the Tompsetts sold out. The Tompsetts had already given up the Post Office to Weller's after they were asked to deliver a telegram to Belle Tout on their Sunday off.

Reginald Dean, and his wife Phyl, came to East Dean on 8 August 1957 to 20 Wenthill Close. Phyl said, "Many people bought houses because of the Greensward, and there were even adverts in the *Evening News,* showing the Greensward with the caption, *Stop the Car, I Want to Buy a House."*

Library Cottage, so-named by a retired librarian, was about the last house on Michel Dene Road when Mollie and Reg Bertin and family came to ED & F in 1958.

Kathleen Banks said, "After living away for 33 years there was no doubt where we wanted to retire. Although my husband, 'Cabby', was a Lancashire man, he had grown fond of East Dean and in 1966, when he was 60, we came to our house at 28 Elven Lane. Cabby became a member of the Residents' Association [RA] to fight to keep the Greensward as an open space.

"Cabby hadn't been interested in gardening when younger, but with Dig for Victory during the war he took an allotment and continued to garden after the war. Whenever we visited East Dean I always went to the Flower Show in the little hut on the recreation field, but Cabby didn't go until he retired here. Fred Nash said to him that he should join the Flower Show committee and he was one of those who helped to rescue that too."

Howard and Doreen Greenwood both came from Halifax, but their parents had moved out, and in those days without residence the Vicar wouldn't marry them. "So we were married in Friston Church by the Revd Norman Lycett assisted by Horace Rew, who had a lovely voice. Being married on Easter Saturday the only place we could find for the reception was the *Golden Galleon,* at Exceat, which did it well. Frankie Howerd, the comedian, was sitting in the pub garden with his Rolls Royce in the car park below.

Part of Michel Dene Road *c.*1950. The central road leads to Deneside, but no Hillside here yet

"We went to *Corner Cottage* after marriage, buying it from Arthur and Hilda Carter. They had a plot for sale in Deneside, but when we discussed it we didn't think it was just what we wanted so Hilda Carter said out of the blue, 'What about buying this?' So the Carters went to *Spurfold* and we bought *Corner Cottage.* Arthur was a quiet man and Hilda was very good with children and taught elocution into her 80s. She taught our daughter Jill who won a first at the Eastbourne Drama Festival. Arthur died in 1970 and when Hilda died six years later she was all by herself and every door in the house was locked.

"We had checked that there was planning permission for an extension at *Corner Cottage,* but after four years we decided to move to *Ashdown Cottage,* even if it didn't have a garage." After 18 years there the Greenwoods came up to *Furze Close* in The Brow, and were there until Howard's death in May 2001.

Joan Nash came to 31 Michel Dene Road in 1957, when there was only one house above her and one on the opposite side of the road. "I used to complain to Mr Cornford, the Agent for the Estate, about the cows and sheep coming into the garden. There was a gate, about where Michel Close, is now but it was often left open. Mr Cornford would reply, 'You like lamb don't you?' Mr and Mrs P Fairchild, next door at 29 Michel Dene Road, were a charming couple, he had been a headmaster."

"My husband, John (no relation to Jane Nash), commuted to London until about 1970. He was a keep-fit fanatic who did his exercises at Birling Gap, and would sometimes have a dip there in the summer, before catching the 0700h train to London. I can't recall a day he didn't go in, whatever the weather and even when the train was late, until he retired.

"Dorothy Alloway, who also came in 1957 from Walthamstow, was at 8 Peakdean Close. She was so bustling, and still worked at Croydon in the banana business with Albert Palmer, of *St Christopher,* Warren Lane, until both her mother and sister died when she, who had never cooked, had to run the house. Mrs Peggy Fuller was another in Peakdean Close, she ran the WI choir for many years." Joan added, "The Steins lived at *Topthorn,* in Warren Lane, he was much older than Rosalind."

As mentioned, another couple who came to East Dean in 1957 were Reg and Phyl Dean. Phyl said, "The bungalow had been the Wenthill Close show house, Bobby's furnished it, and we were its first residents. Although August, it rained the whole of the first week and I thought if I liked it then, I would always be happy here.

"The A259 seemed a country lane when we came. You could tell where they widened it - you could see the cracks of the joints for years afterwards. When we came here there was a notice at the entrance to Downs View Lane stating, *Lorries not allowed on this road between 6pm and 6am."*

The 16th c. Peak Dean Barn, alongside the start of the newly laid-out Peakdean Lane, that ran through the old farmyard. Photograph taken by Phyllis Hughes in 1961.
A few of the houses in The Brow and Warren Lane can be seen on the skyline

In October 1959 Reg Dean was active in East Dean Scouting and also called a meeting that led to the formation of a Residents' Association [RA]. The problems that engaged the RA included maintenance of the estate, television relay, speed limits, and possible encroachment on land designated as Open Space. Their immediate target was a weekly refuse collection instead of fortnightly and this was achieved in 1965.

The standard 1950s discussions by the PC were all the usual chestnuts, a new Village Hall, speeding on the new estate roads, fouling of footpaths by dogs, the amount of litter at Birling Gap, and whether the double white lines on Friston hill were enforceable at law. In 1959, however, the PC considered a letter from a Friston resident complaining about an unsightly fence erected around a property. He was told that if the Downlands Estate Company had given permission nothing could be done.

A further letter from several residents complained about the rewriting and repainting of two large notice boards at the entrance to the estate. It was pointed out that the boards had been there for many years, but the Clerk said he would ask the Estate manager to alter the wording. The RA secretary had asked whether there were plans to build blocks of flats and shops between Wayside and Michel Dene road; the Clerk said that no plans had been submitted, but there had been rough plans for shops.

At another 1959 PC meeting there was discussion about a planning application for a pub at the entrance to the Downlands Estate. It came to naught, but recurred most decades. A request for a weekly refuse collection was considered, but the PC pointed out that this would increase the rates and most people were able to burn or bury their refuse.

The next year concern was expressed by residents that an increased charge had been proposed for the Estate sewerage, but the PC understood that the Sewerage Works on the new estate had improved recently. By 1960 the future development of the Estate envisaged another 100 houses in the Michel Dene and Summerdown area, but the extension of the Peak Dean area had not yet been requested.

Sewerage developments went on the back burner for in March 1962 the East Dean village sign had been taken down because the oak post was rotted and the PC dithered over whether to re-erect it in view of the £58 cost. Was it a conciliatory measure by Mr LA Pyle of the Estate office who had designed the sign in 1930 and now offered to repair and replace it? Eventually, in 1964, the East Dean sign was re-erected in the same site by the village hall alongside the A259. The sign business was Mr Pyle's swansong for in 1964 Mr Tupper was appointed Estate Manager of Fairway Homes Ltd, responsible for Estate maintenance.

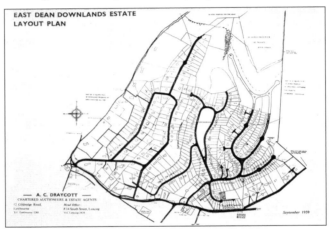

Downlands Estate 1959. The heavy lines show the extent of building along the roads. Yet to be started are The Outlook, Lindon and Royston Closes, the close on Old Willingdon Road, and Sussex Gardens. Developments along Peakdean Lane, Michel Dene Road and Summerdown Lane are only about halfway along

The RA held a special meeting to discuss the demands for increased subscriptions to the Estate maintenance fund. It was agreed to establish a small Legal Aid Fund and refer the matter to their solicitor. Membership now 300.

New postboxes were installed, in Michel Dene Road and Peakdean Lane.

In 1963 the Estate Company submitted plans for building on the Greensward. It was viewed by most residents as a wanton threat to destroy some of the finest sea and Downland views in Sussex, with utter disregard for assurances over the years. The RA launched a protest supported by over 700 residents and others from far afield.

In August 1963 Major-General Colin Bullard, East Dean's representative on the Hailsham RDC, led a campaign to stop building on the 3½ acre [1.5ha] Greensward. Mr LA Pyle, the agent for East Dean Downlands Estate, said the Green was always considered building land and added, "There will be 12 houses there next year." Mr AW Parsons of the RA said the Association was determined to stop it, and Mr JF Marshall said, "The residents are opposed". AS Meanley, Hailsham RDC Surveyor, said the area was intended as an open space and he could see planning refused.

The PC decided to inform the planning authority that it held the strongest views against developing the Greensward, and that the RA also expressed opposition in the strongest terms. 'Since its inception the Downslands Estate has used the fact that it is an inviolate open space as a carrot to prospective buyers, it is now proposing an operation which will seriously detract from the neighbourhood.'

That year the PC also agreed that it was no use trying for a speed limit on Friston hill, but suggested that 'No Overtaking' signs might help. The PC discussed the flooding in Downs View Lane and referred the matter to the Downlands Estate.

Back to the Downlands Estate Sewerage system. The PC said 'it was now working well and when the trees around grew it would be well hidden'. The situation was that while the system had been quite adequate up to 1958 the extra building meant that it was now overloaded, and in the 1970s a moratorium was placed on more building until the Estate sewerage system could be taken over by the water utility. At that time electricity and gas and water were provided by public utilities, and sewerage and roads on the Estate were maintained by the developers.

Summerdown Cottages as they are today, tucked away along Elven Lane, but before the Estate a field away from *New Cottages* across which residents had to trudge to fill their water buckets.
Those were the days

A 1965 Map shows *Gore Farm,* the Link and most of the outline of the estate roads, but no Outlook cul-de-sac, Lindon Close or Royston Close. That year there were 471 houses on the Downlands Estate, with another 48 about to be built. It didn't stop developers coming up with unsuitable schemes. For example, on the last day of March, plans for eight flats in a two-storey block at the Michel Dene Road entrance to the estate were deferred, but in December the Greensward battle was renewed.

An all-out attack was the response to yet another resurrection of Seaside Homes' proposal to develop the Greensward, 700 had protested in 1963 and the matter had rested, now a formal application had been lodged. Lt Col EC Simmons said "An Estate Agent's business is hard and fierce with no holds barred, but this proposal would destroy the amenities in a cynical disregard of the feelings of all the inhabitants".

Major-General Colin Bullard, of *Shepherd's Cot,* co-opted on the PC in place of Fred Bicks, considered it outrageous, 'Even the most apathetic persons pricked up their ears at the danger posed by the application to build on the Greensward.' Hailsham RDC stated that a public enquiry was to be held on 24 November 1966 into its refusal to permit Greensward development. The RDC suggested that if the Estate Company sold the Greensward to the RA, the RDC will ask the Minister for a loan to purchase it from the RA and maintain it as an Open Space. The RDC would pay towards the RA costs, if the parishes agreed to accept part of the sum. This would mean that the cost would fall one-third to the RA, one-third to the General rate and one-third on the parish. The ED & F Parish Council agreed.

Meanwhile in 1966 the PC received the certificate of Registration for Friston Green. Good news, but a cloud on the horizon was obtaining clear demarcation of the path (twitten) between The Brow, Peakdean Lane, and Michel Dene Road. This had seemed to be finally agreed by the Estate Company; however, in July 1967, the PC remained in discussion with the Estate management about this footpath. Sure enough, eventually the Estate owners refused to alter the footpath [13].

The *Evening Argus* of 29 March 1967 had a picture of a Union flag on the Greensward to commemorate the news that a planning application to build there had been rejected by the Minister of Local Government on the advice of his Inspector who upheld the residents' objections. Unfortunately, the Union flag was flying upside down.

Haydon Hill, 4 The Close, Warren Lane, en fete for a 1996 Open Garden. It started as *Old Style*

It was in early 1968 that the Ministerial Inquiry final report set out that it considered the Greensward formed an integral part of the Estate and it would be most unfortunate if it was destroyed by allowing development. But you would be naïve to believe that was that. The PC had understood it would be granted legal title to the Greensward, but the Inquiry stated that the Greensward was registered in Leighton's name, so it was not certain that the PC could be granted ownership. It was thought that the only part of the Greensward to come under PC ownership was the road island, so it was arranged to tidy this part, only to discover some years later that the island was owned by 14 Deneside.

In the middle of the fracas, on 11 December 1967, Francis Arnatt died aged 85. In 1927, having bought the greater part of the *Gore* and *Peak Dean Farms* he created the Downlands Estate. To his energy and vision many owe their Downland homes.

Elsewhere, building continued and sometimes involved a preliminary knocking down. John Dann said, "I went to work one morning and saw they had stripped the roof of *Gore farmhouse* and I thought they were repairing it, and when I came back at the end of the day the house was flattened. Same thing at *Peak Dean Farm,* that old barn was said to be Elizabethan. The Dann's and Fuller's had lived in the farm cottages. My great grandfather was a shepherd at Peak Dean, my grandfather, Bill Dann, worked for Priors the builders. My father, Cecil Dann, was born at *Underhill,* in what is now the garage, and lived with his grandmother at Peak Dean.

The PC in 1968 advised all motorists to take care on the Estate, as the PC couldn't undertake signposting danger spots and the developers refused to take action.

All the houses on the Estate were named, which was popular with the residents, but not with the services because names changed and there were even a few examples of duplication. Numbering had come up in 1963 without any enthusiastic response and the

PC had asked for the matter to be deferred. In 1968 the PC decided that time had come for numbering of houses on the Estate. The next year this went ahead and by the summer the plan for numbering had been agreed.

There were complaints to the PC that new houses at the top of Michel Dene Road were not as varied as the earlier developments built in conformity with the planning policy.

There was another example of lack of cooperation from the Downlands Estate for a well-meant scheme. In 1970 the PC set aside £26 to provide salted grit at nine points on the Estate. They were careful to state that the action was taken without responsibility and the cost should be refunded by the Estate. The PC soon found that £26 was inadequate to cover the salted grit required, and the Estate owners refused to provide reimbursement or to accept responsibility. The PC took advice to the effect that the provision of salted grit on the estate was a matter for private arrangement between the Estate owners and the residents. The point was that if you did nothing and an accident occurred it was an Act of God, whereas if you gritted or salted and a mishap occurred the victim might claim it was thanks to your efforts.

Looking back at Michel Dene Road entrance in the 1967 snow, before Downlands Way, now on the left

The same year the first tenants of the Downlands Way shops moved in, and plans for the re-development of the Service Station were found largely acceptable by the PC, especially that the footpath from the main road to Downlands Way was included. [13]

Goodman's at No. 9 were the first newsagents from 1970 until the family sold to East Dean News in 2003. A butcher's shop has been at 10-11 since 1970, first one was Des Wood, then Jim McNamara, Norman Smith, and from 22 April 1991 Julie & Graham Croucher's Downland Butchers and Jack. The present Doctor's Surgery had been a tea shop and then the *Old Granary,* a restaurant. There were about three proprietors of *The Barn* before Pauline & Keith Hawkins. After Keith's death Liz Moshref rented it for two years from May 1996. "I want to specialise in providing what people want. It is good for the village". She was followed by Michael Neil Toms as *The Barn* licensee, the *Greenhouse*, and later *Bel's Store,* Simon Flux has it now. At 15 Ann Arnold ran *Janda* 1970s-1985, Rita Laws had a fashion shop there for a short time until Terry Spinks' Estate Agent office. He still owns it, but since 1996 it has been St Anne's Veterinary Surgery. The hairdresser at 16 from 1970 was Cheryl's, and after 1982 Duncan Smart (he owned it after 1985). In 2006 it became a Redken Strands and later Strands Unisex hairdresser.

In the Autumn of 1971 Hailsham RDC took over the maintenance of the Estate sewerage plant. Another high point that year saw most of the Estate road repairs completed.

The first whisperings were heard that year about development of *The Outlook,* which had not been functioning as tearooms for a while, and this cul-de-sac development of a dozen bungalows off the Old Willingdon Road went ahead in 1972. Most people agreed it was a pleasant addition. About the same time the Windmill Lane entrance to the estate was completed by three houses appropriately 1, 3, and 5. Good enough houses, but three all of the same style and at the same angle to the road, quite unlike the variety of the rest. Happily, once occupied they have matured with extra garages and porches to add some interest.

The Estate office had been demolished in the course of the building, and in 1973 the PC decided that as it was not possible to determine who owned the estate sales notice board at the entrance to the estate it should be removed.

The RA in 1974 discussed new developments on the estate, the general state of road signs, and impact of main drainage. Two years later the Association noted additional rates demands with the connection of the estate to the main drainage system and the possible take-over of the Estate sewers by the local authority. Eventually, Southern Water agreed to take-over the remainder of the private sewers on the Downland Estate as public sewers from 1 January 1978. Even so, Downlands Estate Ltd had objected to adoption of estate sewers.

When the Estate sewerage site was no longer in use Reg Dean suggested screening by conifers and barbed wire, but people broke them down, "Until the only bits remaining were opposite our house." The result was that for a short while the old refuse site was used as a dumping ground, fires were lit, and often children played there at some risk.

In December 1980 residents of Old Willingdon Road were up in arms over the "disgusting" state of the road. Bill Honey criticised it as "dangerous and disgraceful", Robert Caffyn commented that 'the grass verges had been destroyed by the heavy traffic' and Mr K Sharpin said the road surface was being broken up by the vehicles of developers.

The Outlook Tea Gardens at its peak *c.*1935, run by Miss Tanner and Miss Lowe; Mrs Ada Harvey also helped there. Their advertising jingle ran, 'Sometimes there's ham, And sometimes there's jam, So call at The Outlook for tea'

The Outlook, as it is today, a quiet little Close, with most of the houses not too altered from the concept of an ideal chalet bungalow spot for newly-marrieds or the retired

At least in 1982 the RA succeeded in forcing the Estate Company to do essential maintenance on the Estate roads. It was becoming more and more difficult to obtain any response from the now various companies involved in picking over the scraps of development profits - Downlands Estate, Fairway Homes, the Leighton Group, their common factor was that they had no money to spare on maintenance and they hadn't made any returns and were heading towards liquidation.

By 1983 the state of the roads concerned the RA. Fairway Homes were unable to contribute more than £500 a year when some £10,000 was required. When, following Ron Pringle's assiduous delving at Companies House, the Association learnt that East Dean Downlands Ltd had been liquidated and Fairway Homes Ltd was likely to follow, the view was that the time was right to bring the Estate roads back under local control. Old Willingdon Road and Downs View Lane had now been adopted by the ESCC.

While on about roads, John and Carol Hollick, now of *The Barn Stores,* reminded residents that the adjacent car parks were now their property and asked that residents 'do not park there as more vehicles are parked when the shops are closed than when open'.

The RA reported on the result of their Roads Questionnaire of which 67% of forms were returned. There was support for a flat rate of contribution, with most prepared to pay £25. The committee decided to approach the Estate Company to determine whether they would transfer the Company's assets to a residents' company, 'although no resident can be committed to any change without their approval'.

In 1984, when no roads demands had been sent out, the RA established the East Dean Downlands Roads Ltd, owned by the residents, to take over responsibility from the old Estate Company for restoring and maintaining the seriously deteriorating roads. In general, the move has been most successful; almost every road had attention over the next 20 years and they are clearly a great improvement over their condition in the 1970s. With that matter, we hope settled, it was pointed out that the Estate Water Hydrants needed repainting.

Mrs Lyndell Pelecanos lived at *Falmer House* in Downs View Lane on original Bee Farmland. She was an American who came to Europe for a tour, met Anthony Pelecanos on the boat and married him. He had a business in sponges and bought *Falmer House* before the war. Lois Pelecanos is their daughter. Mrs Pelecanos sold part of the land on which Sussex Gardens is now built and *Falmer House* was knocked down.

Sussex Gardens building started 1982 on the old sewage works. At least the developers agreed to include some maisonette type dwellings as requested. By March 1983 the Sussex Gardens development was nearing completion. Described as a high-quality scheme with architecture in sympathy with the environment, it had 13 different styles within the 34 units which range from flats to three-bedroom houses

Otherwise, problems subsided until 1989, which started off with routine topics, such as: posts first placed on the A259 at the Downs View Lane junction; planning applications for the old Postal Sorting Office on Friston hill were refused, and a house in The Brow had been incorrectly numbered by the resident, when the next big issue blew up - Wheely Bins.

The RA had a meeting with the WDC head of works who explained the introduction of Wheely Bins and, despite the protestations by Maureen Honey, he stated the new system would go ahead. Bins should be placed at the edge of the property to be dealt with by the dustmen, and it would be up to each resident to return bins to their usual location, there would be no compulsion, it was up to each resident. Headlines appeared such as, *Wheely Bins for most of East Dean & Friston in September in spite of appeals that they were inappropriate to the long sloping drives of the village.*

The RA continued to complain about having to wheel out the Wheely Bins and encouraged people to apply for exemption, but the WDC were adamant, stating that most people supported the new method of refuse collection.

Also in 1989 there was discussion about the Local Plan, in particular that while Old Willingdon Road was proposed as 'very low density' housing, the rest was subject to the overall density policy.[15] Speeding on the estate and the difficulties of introducing sleeping policemen as a preventative measure produced mixed opinions.

At least, the next year the WDC proposed to extend the very low density category to Windmill Lane, The Ridgeway, The Brow, Warren Lane and any adjoining closes.

East Dean Downlands (Roads) Ltd stated that in 1990 The Brow and Hillside had been resurfaced. It was recommended that the voluntary contributions per household, if applicable under their deeds, should remain at £40. By 1993, however, the Roads Company decided that all the Estate roads would be in asphalt as the cheaper Fibredeck top did not last.

On 1 August 1991 the PC held a special meeting to consider whether they should take over the responsibility of the estate covenants for the benefit of the community, as requested by the RA. There were concerns that in the event of an applicant having a planning appeal allowed did the PC give consent or seek an injunction to withhold the development bearing in mind that if they failed in court their costs and those of the successful applicant would have to be born by the Council tax. Members wished to comply with the estate covenants, but was it appropriate for the PC? The PC voted 6 against and 5 for, with the chairman Maurice Hopkins abstaining. Hence they decided not to take over the responsibility, which essentially meant that most covenants were non-enforceable.

All the Downlands Way units were occupied when that year Pauline Hawkins opened her new shop of gifts and haberdashery on the site of Tony Spinks' Estate Agency.

The Estate office (just left of centre) by the Windmill Lane entrance to the Downlands Estate from 1938-1972 when it was demolished with the building of The Outlook and three houses on the left side of Windmill Lane. Debris from the old mill and cottage was found in the garden of number 1

Minutes of both the PC and the RA in the early 1990s show an almost constant concern about speeding on the Estate with the potential for accidents, 'despite 20mph notices'. It was also pointed out that with the compactness of the estate even if you shot along at 50mph you would only exit from the estate about a second ahead of someone doing 20mph.

In 1992 the Roads Company completed resurfacing of Summerdown Lane, The Link, Mill Close, Friston Close, The Close and Windmill Lane in dense bitumen and in 1993 the RA arranged for attention to the trees on the Greensward, where a seat was vandalised.

Representations from the RA in 1995 resulted in the bridleway near Downs View Lane being sited further up the hill and advice was given on how to reduce the damage to verges. That year Ken Smith retired as chairman, replaced by Ron Pringle, and Phyll Workman came on the committee. Brent Duxbury of the RA had replaced worn out or damaged road signs around the estate, but from 1998 Wealden District Council were prepared to replace signs as needed, with their blackened supports and dark green background format. By 1998 the PC owned the Downlands Way parking area, resurfaced it and widened the footpath.

The Editor of the *Wessex Review* wrote in the 1930s, 'It would be very difficult, if not impossible, to find a more delightful site for a country home than is provided by the Downlands Estate, East Dean, near Eastbourne. Although it provides absolute perfection as regards peaceful seclusion, with widespread views over untouched land and over a wide expanse of sea, it has all the advantages of town life.'

A resident commented that the bare hillside of 80 years ago had been transformed into a richly wooded spot in which the houses are not intrusive.

Times move on, but the old story holds. The plans look good, the guarantees are given and everything goes well until someone decides that they could make a few extra dollars by applying for infillings, extensions, adding, or even knocking down, often disregarding its impact upon others or whether there is truly an unmet need for such extras, until if you're not careful the 'location' is lost. Obviously, the location in mind is Eastbourne's Sovereign Harbour, but possibly the principle applies to locations in general.

10. War comes to the Villages 1939-45

The air raid siren at the outbreak of war at eleven o'clock on the morning of 3 September 1939 nearly caused Britain's first casualty. People were expecting immediate air raids with poison gas in any future war, so when the siren sounded Jack Goodman leaped out of his lorry in such haste that he caught his toe on the running board and fell headlong. Fortunately, the only damage was to his pride - for the alarm was declared false.

The real action was more prosaic. "I was at Cooden", Kathleen Hobden (later Cater) explained, "When one of the maids at *Gore Farm* rang to say that six evacuees had just been deposited at the farmhouse. Mother and father [Nora and Edward Hobden] were in Scotland, where he went shooting every year, often with Dr Bodkin Adams, so I rushed back to East Dean and what did I find - the Whipp family from Rotherhithe disporting themselves in the family home.

"There was Leslie, age 4, Barney 5, Reg 7, Albert 8, Rita 10 and Doris 12. They came in what they stood up in, without the mother - who had other children, and their docker father was dead. Reg was a bit of a handful at times, but they looked after each other as they always had done and Doris was a mother to them all. They thought it was wonderful to have clean clothes once a week on a Saturday.

Friston Place had ten evacuees at the beginning of the war. They weren't housed in the empty big house (which was being renovated at the time) but billeted around the estate cottages

"Two of their teachers came down with them and commented that their school work improved greatly at East Dean. They stayed with us until in July 1940 things got a bit 'noisy' on the coast when they were moved to South Wales. Doris, Rita, Barney and Leslie paid us a visit after the war."

Fred Fuller said the Foords had three evacuees at 1 Upper Street, and Peter Armiger said that his parents had two, "and Dad dug our own air raid shelter".

One hundred and ninety one London evacuees, 170 from Bermondsey and 21 from Croydon, were billeted over East Dean and Friston at the start of the war; Sussex being designated a 'Safe Area'. Most came from Albion Street School and each host family had two or three, and were paid 10/6d [52$\frac{1}{2}$p] a week for the first and 8/6d for any others.

The evacuation was organised because of this fear of immediate heavy air raids. On the day war broke out Kathleen Banks was wheeling her two-year-old round the village and was passing by *Grey Walls* (now the *Grange*) when Air Vice Marshal Sir John Salmond, who lived there, rushed out yelling, "What are you doing, mother? Go home, London is about to be bombed".

Biddy Kennard said, "On 3 September the Reception committee for the evacuees was waiting at *The Outlook* tearooms from where they heard Mr Chamberlain's broadcast announcing that we were at war with Germany. When the evacuees appeared one of the billeting officers, a retired Army gentleman, lined them up as if on parade and read them a lecture on good behaviour."

The evacuees fitted in remarkably well. In general, their school classes were held in the Village Hall and the Gilbert Institute, while Miss Turk continued to teach the East Dean children at the Village School. [6] After France fell and the evacuees were moved on people who had objected to them saw them off with tears in their eyes.

A store for billeting material was opened up in the cottage behind the Village Hall; it also housed the Billeting Officer and the First Aid Post.

Evacuees playing with the Nash children on Birling Gap beach 1939, the Londoners revelled in the beach. One day a group came to school screaming that they had seen a wild beast which turned out to be an especially mangy fox

A long association with the school was broken in February 1940 when retired headmaster and teacher, Mr & Mrs Drew, died within a few days of each other.

Ray Cheal, in the regular Army, landed in France on 19 September 1939. Coming home on leave March 1940, in uniform, the admiring village children followed him asking, 'How many Germans have you killed, mister?' "I thought of that when I went back, for I am a terrible sailor and there was this fine soldier seasick before the boat had even set sail."

The local branch of the British Legion [BL] bought £26 of National Savings Certificates out of their funds 'to assist the country', they discussed whether to entertain the NCOs and men of the anti-aircraft post near *Birling Manor,* and held their usual Christmas tea party for the village children on 4 January 1940.

After the air-raid warning and all clear of 3 September, and another false alarm the next day at 0750h, the villagers settled into the 'Phoney War', nevertheless they spent those nine months preparing for the worst. Air-raid drills, First Aid lectures and gas tests were well attended, while the food rationing became more severe, and the news from France was not good, culminating in the June 1940 Dunkirk evacuation - stirring stuff, but you don't win wars with evacuations. Ray Cheal was one evacuated from Dunkirk, and when the Germans reached the other side of the Channel, East Dean went from a Safety Zone to the Front Line.

Mrs Banks said "East Dean and Friston were transformed: huge anti-tank blocks of reinforced concrete went up at strategic places including Michel Dene Road [some can be seen today] and Friston pond. There was no access to the beach or Went Hill, and I had to obtain a permit to visit my parents in Meads."

With the German Panzers only 60 miles across the Channel, the school was opened for residents to register their children for evacuation, but nobody turned up. Tom Goodman said, "In 1940 when people were being evacuated Dad said, 'You're not going, we're going to stick together and die together if it comes to that'. So there was no official evacuation from East Dean although a number of children were evacuated by the family making their own arrangements."

East Dean and Friston Home Guard 1940. Fred Milton of *Tolmans*, Warren Lane led in its formation. One hasn't been issued with his uniform and others display their Local Defence Volunteers' armbands. At different times it was B Co'y of the 20th Hailsham battalion and D Co'y of 21st Eastbourne. "They used to drill on Sunday mornings on the main A259 road, of course, there was no traffic at all."

Nigel Quiney says that all access to the seashore was forbidden and not only kept that way by barbed wire and sea defences but the beaches were mined. One effect of being denied access was that he did not learn to swim until after the war. As mentioned in Chapter 9 all building on the Estate ceased during the war.

In the centre, partly overgrown, is one of the few remaining 'Dragon's Teeth' (anti-tank traps) by the Upper Street wall near the A259. In 1940 Jack Breach helped to put up these concrete blocks at Friston and around. "I don't know if they'd have been any good at trapping tanks, but they certainly got in everybody's way"

For the war effort farmer Edward Hobden of *Gore Farm* had to plough up the Seven Sisters from Crowlink to Brass Point to grow wheat.

"The covenants on our house didn't allow you to keep hens or sell petrol" said Kathleen Banks, "but during the war Mr Hobden, the farmer, allowed my father to keep chickens and white Belgian rabbits in a hutch in the farmyard where the shops are now. Mother used to make lovely rabbit pies, with more meat in them than the whole 2oz [60g] a week ration."

East Dean's first real air raid was on 3 July 1940 at 0845. Five high-explosive [HE] bombs dropped on Michel Dene Down, near the Seven Sisters, but only one exploded. Percy Budd, the chief Air Raid Precautions [ARP] warden for the village, wrote, 'Saw

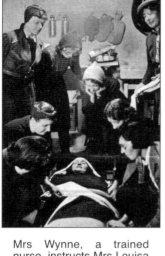

raider pursued by one of our aeroplanes which sent bursts of machine gun fire into it.'

When an air raid threatened, Mr Budd's daughter, Kathleen 'Biddy' Kennard, drove round the new Downlands Estate with her young son blowing blasts on a warning whistle. Tom Goodman was a messenger boy for the ARP, and his brother, Jack, was a messenger boy for the Fire Station, housed in the chauffeur's garage/ house of *Little Hill,* that was converted into a dwelling in 1997.

Derrick Pyle moved to Ringwood Farm in August 1940. As ever there was only an earth closet, and no gas or electricity. Water was from a well, the supply driven by a petrol motor (in a barn) to a tank that gravity-fed a tap, but by the time his parents left in 1957 it had mains water. "Part of Ringwood Cottage was empty and about 1942 was requisitioned for the Canadians who operated a Bofors gun

Mrs Wynne, a trained nurse, instructs Mrs Louisa Roberts in First Aid at the cottage behind the Village Hall, 1941. Mrs C Kemp is the patient and Minnie Davies-Gilbert wears the white cap

on the Downs Golf Club course. They were a most pleasant bunch and, originating from a wheat growing area, were given a week's leave to help out during harvesting. The work was without extra pay but popular as a change. Other extra help came from the Women's Land Army."

Ted Fears started work at Cater's Service Station. His first job was to mix up cement to fill tubes which were to be inserted into the pipes of the garage petrol pumps as a sabotage measure if the Germans came. "I wasn't too keen thinking that if they came I'd be the one blamed, but Jim Kemp, a 2oz of tobacco-a-day man, munched on his pipe and forecast, 'The Germans won't be coming lad'. From the time harvesting came in 1940 I never stopped working till I was 65."

September 1940, local Home Guards watch the Me 109 just to the south of the A259 with East Dean village and early Downlands Estate in the background

Percy Budd lived at *Greenhedges,* 13 The Ridgeway. There is a story that one morning Jack Goodman, a firewatcher, said to him, "A lot of bombs and guns in the night, weren't there". To which Percy replied, "You know, I didn't hear a thing". So it wasn't all activity, but there were upheavals in the village. South Barn along the SE wall of The Green was commandeered for stabling the horses of Haines the undertakers of Eastbourne, while the Village Hall was taken over as a morgue to cope with the expected casualties, but only used for a tramp who committed suicide. Much later it was a YMCA canteen.

On 12 September 1940 Mr Budd went to Hailsham for an issue of babies' gas helmets. He also proclaimed the capital news that the wardens had their own, 'TEA RATION ISSUED of ¹/₂lb tea and ¹/₄lb sugar'.

Tom Goodman says, "I was flint picking at *Gayles* on 30 September when we saw a German plane come down alongside the A259, between Cophall and *Halfway Cottages*. It wasn't shot down, some say it was shooting at us and others say he ran out of petrol". Jesse Taylor says that it circled round before landing, "So it didn't look as though it was shot down. Pc Harry Hyde, East Dean's 'W'at abaht it?' cockney policeman, crammed on his helmet and hitched a lift on a greengrocer's van to reach the spot, but we boys weren't far behind to see Harry march the pilot, wearing a maroon scarf with white spots, down to the village, with hands raised. Harry said that his main job was to protect his prisoner; Mrs Dooley of *Beach Tree Cottage,* who had lost her husband in the 1914-18 war, was yelling 'String 'im up', but the first gesture towards him was a cup of tea from Mrs Hyde".

Ted Fears, a founder member of the Air Training Corps said, "Unlike the expected tall pilot with blue eyes and blonde hair, he was about five foot six with dark frizzy hair". The Me 109 plane can be seen in the Imperial War Museum at Duxford, the only surviving German plane brought down in the Battle of Britain.[1] It probably ran out of coolant.

During the war Pc Hyde was assisted by a War Reserve Special Constable and Specials, including Joe Hayward, Tom and Frank Martin and Harold Fears.

Friston Place was bombed on 11 October, leaving three craters near the house. *Friston Place Cottages* were damaged; a barn was demolished and the glasshouses lost their glass.

The bombed barn at *Friston Place* after a raid on 11 October 1940. The barn was on the site of today's swimming pool, and the present wall alongside (with ventilation holes) is a remaining part of a side wall of the barn [8]

The next day Mr Budd went with Pc Hyde and Harold Fears to *Friston Place* and found four more craters in the grounds. He returned on receipt of a message that there was an unexploded bomb [UXB] at Butchershole. He arranged for the cottages to be evacuated, placed warning notices, and advised the ARP Control at Hailsham. The Control's only concern could be deduced by their phone call the next day asking for the distance of the UXB from Friston Pumping Station.

Pauline Markquick, daughter of the head gardener at *Friston Place,* says, "Some of our chickens were killed and the rest escaped from their pen. My father went round catching and examining them, and if they were severely injured he wrung their necks. We had chicken every day for weeks, and at Christmas when one chicken was carved we found wire inside - a legacy of the bombs."

Friston Place house was empty, with just a few staff left to care for it. Mrs Young, the owner, having gone off on one of her photographic expeditions in January 1940. [8]

Back at East Dean Mr Budd wrote, 'at 1905h on 20 October an aeroplane presumed to have come down in the sea off Crowlink, but no details are available'.

The Armistice Service at 1100h on the 11 November 1940 was attended with special fervour. The BL agreed to send a Christmas parcel to all men of the village serving in HM Forces, each to cost 6/- [30p]. All 26 of them were sent cigarettes, chocolates and a diary.

Bombs dropped around the villages, but East Dean had its own ambulance. In 1940 Major Harding adapted a 1928 Chrysler to pull a horse box which had brackets to take stretchers. In 1941 the village was given a proper Ford ambulance which was to be used for both air-raid and civilian purposes, with Jim Kemp as the driver. The only time it was used was in 1944 when it took Mrs Pownall to Southlands Hospital, Worthing, to have her eleventh child, Shirley.

January 1941 opened with the death of the composer Frank Bridge who lived at *Friston Field* on the Old Willingdon Road. He was a mentor of Benjamin Britten.

Later that month Mr Budd distributed sandbags round the village, and in February he collected five stirrup pumps from Hailsham. The first action of 1941 was on 11 March 1941 when HE bombs were dropped near *Hodcombe*.

German planes regularly attacked ships off the coast or the radar installations on Beachy Head. On 23 May 1942 a strafing Me 109 was shot down near the *Black Robin Farm* barns (seen in the background and there today). The 23-year-old pilot, described by local farmer's wife, Eileen Goldsmith, as "looking hardly 18", escaped uninjured

Poison gas attack was still a worry and when, on 3 April, the Gas Van came to East Dean 197 people had their gas masks tested.

Jack Goodman's family were now chicken farming at *Church Cottage* [now *Mary's Mead*] just by Friston Church. It was owned by Lady Beatty, one of the Maitlands, and comprised two cottages, the other half being for the gardener at *Little Friston*. "One night", says Tom Goodman, "We heard noises and voices in a strange language; Dad said, 'Be quiet, it's the Germans'. It turned out to be French Canadians on a night exercise, who had entered our garden to help themselves to our broad beans."

East Dean had suffered a little from the attention of our allies. Apart from Belle Tout being holed by practising Canadian Army gunners, Friston pond (designated as an emergency supply of water in the event of invasion) was polluted by Canadian drivers who would drive their vehicles in it to wash them.

On 19 April incendiary bombs fell between Birling Gap and Beachy Head; and on the morning of 11 May ten HE bombs fell on Beachy Head.

The Friston Emergency Landing Ground (FELG), created from a pre-war private runway at *Gayles* established by Victor Yates, had been used in training by Hawker Audax planes from Hawkinge and Odiham, and from 1940 for emergency landings. It was upgraded to a forward satellite airfield in May 1941, but that year its use was confined to Lysander reconnaissance aircraft, and fighters in trouble. Even so, on 18 October 1941, a Miles Magister crashed shortly after take off near New Barn, West Dean, killing the two

Canadian officers on board. Jimmy Holter recalls that about May 1942 dummy Hurricanes were scattered about the airfield - without fooling the Germans.

From June, however, real Hurricanes were stationed there and on 9 July German Me 109 fighter bombers hit a Hurricane on the runway and caused slight damage to *Gayles* and to airfield huts, with Canadian casualties at Cuckmere. Later that day two airmen were killed when a Hurricane collided with their vehicle.

The airfield had two runways, the main one for bomber landings ran NW/SE from Haven Brow to near New Barn. A shorter 'fighter' runway ran almost N/S in front of *Gayles*. About this time *Friston Place* became the RAF Officers' Mess, and the grounds and greenhouses were devoted to growing food for their table. [8]

The 'bombed-out' Ticehurst family, back row: Eileen, Marjorie, Ron, Les and Jesse, front: Miggs (centre), with parents Frank and Lilian in the garden at *Lye Oak,* The Close. Miss Greenhill stayed at Mrs Scott's *Thatched Cottage* in Went Way before the war, and decided to have *Lye Oak* built. She declared that she preferred a bombed-out family there than the army who would knock the place about

Belgians, Canadians, Poles, Australians and Americans passed through the airfield - the latter especially thrilled to find the Officers' Mess at *Friston Place* had a musicians' gallery, a painted room, and a donkey-wheel well.

Ted Fears visited the Friston landing ground with the AFC and saw a Boulton-Paul *Defiant* land, piloted by Jack Dunphy, and a pet dog jumped out with the crew.

The emergency landing ground was protected by RAF Regiment gun sites all over the Downs. One was in the trees above the Farrer Hall, another in the chalk pit at the top of Michel Dene Road [now filled in and built over], and there was a searchlight at Crowlink.

The Irish labourers who levelled the landing ground were always fighting and weren't too popular, but the village welcomed the airmen and women. One pilot was billeted with the Ticehursts at the *Old Vicarage,* the wife of another was at *Waterworks Cottages* with the Nashes, and Audrey Scrase (née Smith), one of the first WAAFs at Friston, who came from Biggin Hill airfield to work at *Friston Place* said, "A WAAF was billeted with the Markquicks at *Friston Place Cottages"*.

Among the WAAFs was Ruth Williams, later to marry Seretse Khama, president of Botswana 1966-80.

Typical of the village response, Mrs Elizabeth Bugler of *Tatton Corner* [now *Went House*] organised play readings, East Dean Players' productions, and threw open her home for servicemen and women in the area.

Muriel 'Miggs' Ticehurst said that when they were bombed out of 'Bomb Alley' Eastbourne (where the family had moved for her father's job) Miss Greenhill offered them the use of *Lye Oak* for the duration. "There was no bath in the Bourne Street house and it was wonderful to get into a bath. From *Lye Oak* we saw the barrage balloons being carried along to help protect the ships at D-Day."

Miggs was in the Women's Land Army, working with Mr Miller and Jim Wicking, "who was a lovely, kindly man. If my mother was ill he would always visit with a bunch of flowers, although where he got them I wouldn't like to say."

Kathleen Hobden (later Cater), also in the Land Army, worked on her father's *Gore Farm*. She looked after six sows, and one Large White boar called *Henry*. She did the milk round as well: Birling Gap, Belle Tout, the RAF station at *Gayles* and, of course, the village and the estate. In the summer, Crowlink and the Old Willingdon Road were added. Kathleen also took the bull calves to Hailsham market, "I used the same van for the milk and the calves and had to clean it out between trips. During the war we had synthetic rubber for the tyres and punctures were a problem."

The Williams family continued as the farmers at *Bullock Down Farm*. Their son, Eddie, only gave up in 2000, but continues to live on the farm.

East Dean Fire Service 1940 outside the *Tiger*. On lorry Freddie Breach, Jim Fears. L to R: Maurice Haffenden, Don Hearns, Rupert Taylor, Harry Sellars, Arthur Raylor, George Wicking, Fred Harris, Frank Martin, Bert Breach (mine host Friend Fowler in doorway), Bill Armiger, Harry West, Dick Patching

One day in 1941 Peter Armiger, on his way to school, rushed down the twitten [footpath] into Upper Street and was knocked down by a staff car, so he was the reason why white rails were put up at the bottom of the twitten. He had a broken leg and was in the Princess Alice Hospital. When there were raids most of the patients were moved to the shelters, but he was in plaster and couldn't be moved so a nurse sat with him throughout any raid. "I always thought that was brave of her".

Peter Armiger's father, William, joined the Auxiliary Fire Service [AFS], which became the National Fire Service and he was transferred to Eastbourne and later to Denton Corner. "He would take me there on his bike. The field in front of the road was mined and one day a cow strayed onto it and was blown up."

Miggs' father, Frank Ticehurst, joined as well because he said he liked the uniform. Her brother Ron was on the *Iron Duke* at Scarpa Flow when it was torpedoed, and the two younger brothers were in the Home Guard until they could also go in the Navy. When Arthur Raylor went into the Fire Service his butcher's shop closed and it was used to collect and store paper for the war effort. He was in the Eastbourne Fire Station when it was bombed and although he escaped (it is said by crouching under the billiard table) he was understandably affected by it with six of his colleagues killed.

What with chickens and eggs and cuts of lamb the residents didn't do too badly for rations compared with the big towns. They also adapted to the situation and many took to keeping a pig. Along with others, Frank Bagg, gardener and groom to Miss Prideaux-Brune at *Went Acre,* kept pigs near Underhill during the war and when one was killed he shared the cuts with the Underhill residents.

Pond Cottage at *Friston Place* was now the headquarters for the East Sussex War Agricultural Executive Committee, which directed food production and told farmers exactly what they had to grow and where. William AF Burdett-Coutts, from one branch of the Coutts' banking family, was in charge of the local WarAg; his father being chairman of the national WarAg. The Royal Navy had rejected him because of colour-blindness, but he became a Home Guard lieutenant. The locals have a few tales of him, Ted Fears recalls, "He always looked a tramp, but he was not short of cash. On one occasion he put his hand in his pocket to pay a petrol bill and pulled out half-a-dozen of his pay packets - all unopened".

East Dean Home Guard 1942, now all in smart uniform. L-R Back Row: Mark Fuller, Don Dann, Rue Marsh, Archie Penn, Ronnie Hall, Ted Fears, ? Frank Fyfield. Middle Row: Charlie Goldsmith, ?Tompkins, ?, ?, Albert Vine, Revd Fl Anderson, ?WarAg, Bob Seymour, 'Geoff' Tompsett. Front row: Cpl Cramphorn, Sgt Stan Hobden, Sgt Tom Grooms, 2/Lt William Burdett-Coutts, Lt Stringell, ?Capt., Sgt Bert Foord, Cpl Stan Fuller

Ted also joined the Home Guard. "Charlie Goldsmith and Bert Foord, a most pious man troubled only with his false teeth, were other members. The Home Guard's HQ was in a Deneside semi-detached house, near the present telephone exchange, which wasn't there then. A .22 rifle range ran alongside.

"Lieutenant Stringell in charge of the Home Guard Company was a confectioner in Eastbourne and whenever I was about to go for drill my aunt would say, 'Don't forget to take the money'. This was to pay for the slab cake which the lieutenant would bring over from Eastbourne. I am reminded of such exploits when I see Dad's Army on the TV. The lieutenant was always getting hold of what he called 'goodies', namely special weapons. One day he brought a Spandau machine gun with plenty of ammunition which we fired off in the chalk pit at Peak Dean, and another time an EY gun adapted to fire grenades.

"There were too many sergeants in the Home Guard, Tommy Grooms was one, and Joe Cairns another. Joe had been a Guardsman in the 1914-18 war and came on parade dressed immaculately - razor sharp creases to his trousers and you could read small print reflected in his boots. No one knew why we needed the sergeants; because what the Home Guard was short of were chaps who could 'see'. Typical of them, when they were practising with this adapted EY gun none of the shots hit the target. It came to my turn, last because I was the youngest, and I had noticed that the shots had passed over the target so I reduced the elevation and hit it smack on. Not the thing to do, for I was put in charge of the gun and its tripod, which weighed about three pounds more than the regular rifle.

Charles Gilbert Davies-Gilbert, with son Jimmy just peeping over the wagon side, Minnie D-G with her white pony and Elizabeth Bugler, outside Dennett's Store, 1943. Note the 'East Dean' has been scratched off the British Legion notice board to confound any enemy

"We saw the last of our slab cake after the lieutenant came up with another 'goodie', this time plastic stun-grenades designed for house-to-house fighting. He brought them along one Sunday and a group went off to Litlington to try them out. They were about to throw them when he noticed one lying on the ground, without thinking he kicked it out of the way, it exploded, and he lost three toes."

On the greater scale of things, Exercise Beaver IV in May 1942 involved the Queens Own Rifles of Canada advancing over the Downs from the west to Friston protected by its Home Guard but, perhaps fortunately, the exercise was called off on 13 May.

The RAF from Friston commandeered the Gore Service Station as a Motor Transport Centre, so soon afterwards Jim Kemp, who had run the Service Station, opened the Forge Garage on Friston hill. Ted Fears worked there with Wally Eve. "There weren't too many cars and sharpening cylinder mowers was a standard job."

On both 8 and 9 August 1942 there were raids on Friston airfield. One HE fell on the airfield, with numerous incendiaries there and in Friston forest.

Colin Wicking, aged almost three, had been taught to sing *When You Wish Upon a Star* by the Canadians, so he could sing it by heart. One day in mid-August 1942 hundreds of Canadians came to the Wicking house, put Colin on the wall outside and asked him to sing for them. The next day they had all gone to Dieppe. Mrs Renee Wicking says, "When I went to Dieppe, a few years ago, and saw the memorial with all the names I wondered how many were among those who listened to Colin that day."[2]

Nineteen planes were lost at Dieppe including two from Friston, but most of the pilots were rescued. The airfield saved others by hosting several lame ducks.

Ted Fears added, "There were many Canadian troops in the area during the war and we got on well with them. I'm still in contact with one of the Stewart brothers who were stationed at the Gap. Canadian troops working the Beachy Head and Michel Dene anti-tank ranges were based in and around the *Birling Gap Hotel*. The hotel, along with *Children's Delight* and the Golf House, were the kitchens, the meals being served in nearby Nissen Huts. They always had plenty of food, especially cheese.

"Mr Pelecanos of *Falmer House* [knocked down for Sussex Gardens] kept pigs during the war, and Sid French, (son of Mrs 'toffee' French) who worked for the Pelecanos family, collected pigswill from the Canadians. At the same time Sid would 'liberate' huge amounts of cheese to distribute around the village."

East Dean and Friston's Reading Circle carried on, here they are meeting in Elizabeth Bugler's house, 1943. Those plainly visible are L-R: Major CW Bell, Miss Read, Mrs Cuff, Mrs McDonnell, Mrs J Donkin, Mrs E Bugler, Mr AL Pring, Mrs Wynne and Mr HL Wynne

Peter Armiger says the Canadian troops also had a cookhouse near the Scout Hut by Upper Street [later Farrer Hall], "and they would give us a snack or two".

A succession of Canadian gunnery units came to use the ranges, and could be found firing most days from *Cornish Farm*. A light railway ran from near *Hodcombe* across the road up towards Belle Tout lighthouse. An old car pulled a wire with a mock-up of a tank. There was also a 2-pounder range at Shooter's Bottom which ran E-W between the cliff edge and the road. As a result the Belle Tout ex-lighthouse was hit on 18 occasions (although mainly on one day) from about August 1942 to February 1943. This brought owner Sir James Purves Stewart along to inspect the damage.

Harry Comber, another villager, said the valley below the Red Barn was used for artillery practice during the war, also firing at a moving target near the cliff edge.

Otherwise the Canadians were most helpful. They built a concrete road from *Birling Farm* to *Cornish* because the tanks and self-propelled anti-tank guns churned up the ground excessively, and when on 5 July 1943 a haystack caught fire and the NFS had no water the Cdn 2nd Anti-Tank Regiment, under Captain Ray Manbert, organised a fire-fighting detail.

Through all this turmoil Jane Nash was born in 7 *Waterworks Cottages* during an air raid, with Mrs Alice Holter (who lived at No 5) acting as midwife. The British Legion's children's party in 1942 cost £2.33, and it was decided not to send Christmas parcels to villagers in HM Forces, but to send each 30p instead.

In the spring of 1943 the Revd W Williams moved to a Westcliff-on-Sea parish having exchanged livings with the Revd Norman Lycett.

Mr Budd had noted on 20 January 1943 that enemy planes were seen attacking a convoy off the Seven Sisters, and his next report of activity was for 14 March at 0030 when enemy planes dropped flares and bombs, with the AA [anti-aircraft] guns in action. Two HE bombs fell in fields near *Friston Place,* and windows were broken both there and at *Little Friston.* The greenhouses lost all their glass again, and the transept ceiling at Friston Church was damaged. HE bombs also dropped near Exceat Farm and two UXB were found at Charleston and Jevington.

A marauding FW190 downed into the sea off Cow Gap on 23 January 1943 was probably hit by Bofors guns of the Princess Pat's Canadian Light Infantry.

The RAF station at Friston would collect the village children to give them a Christmas dinner. Peter Armiger explained, "I remember that Father Christmas came in a Hurricane. The men had saved up their sweet rations for we had plenty of sweets and, as there were no toys available, they had crafted toys out of wood; I was given a lovely Spitfire one time. Wish I had it now.

"There were AA guns in Friston forest along the ridge behind *Friston Place.* The gunners used to let us kids turn the handles to elevate or traverse the gun. Once when we were enjoying ourselves a German plane came roaring up the valley and thanks to us the troops weren't able to get in place in time to fire at it."

By now Friston airfield accommodated 1248 RAF and 152 WAAF personnel. The HQ was at *Swallows* (Old Willingdon Road) for a time, with *Little Friston* the Sergeant's Mess, *Friston Court* (No. 2) the WAAF Mess, and *Ridge House* (No. 9), on the other side of Windmill Lane, the medical centre. Fred Bicks, who returned to *Almonds,* 2 Hillside, after the war, was the dental officer, billeted at *Payne's Dene* along Crowlink Lane, until he leased *Gainsborough* in Warren Lane. The RAF used other unoccupied houses for storage.

A number of officers from Eastbourne units were billeted in East Dean, for example, Col Laycock, medical officer for the Commando Training Centre at the *Queensborough Hotel,* was in Michel Dene Road.

Coastal raids by low-flying FW 190 and Me 109 fighter bombers had now reached serious proportions. For example, on 3 April 1943 at 1150h, enemy planes swept ashore at Birling Gap and flew over East Dean and Friston at roof-top height on their way to bomb Eastbourne and then to escape out over the Channel before any warning could be sounded. To combat these tactics a Spitfire squadron was moved to Friston.

On 4 June a group of some 18 FW 190s were seen racing towards Eastbourne by way of Belle Tout. The attack was broken up by the defences with two 190s brought down by Spitfires and another by AA fire, although this was the raid when Eastbourne's Technical Institute was wrecked.

Eastbourne was again raided on Sunday, 6 June 1943; this time the planes came in over the Crumbles. On their way back they cannon-shelled the Beachy Head radar and East Dean and Friston. There were no casualties in the villages, but numerous unexploded shells were found afterwards. Many houses were hit: in Warren Lane - *High and Over* (now 22), *Dormers* (24), *Down Ash* (28), *Blackthorns* (30), *Tolmans* (13), and *Pippins* (15). In The Ridgeway - *Cavans* (1); in Old Willingdon Road - *Upfolds, Friston Field,* and a car was damaged in the drive at *Chalkfield;* and in Windmill Lane - *Friston Court,* and *Ridge House.* In the village - *The Cub* (next to the *Tiger*), and in Downs View Lane - *Algoa* (the Benjamin's house) suffered. It is said that the damage to *Friston Court* was from an exceedingly depressed Bofors gun firing at the low-flying enemy planes.

This was the last serious village raid. In an aerial engagement over East Dean at 2200h on 6 September Elizabeth Bugler's house, *Tatton Corner [Wayside],* had damage to its roof from shell fragments. It was clearly a legitimate target for every weekend she entertained men and women from RAF Friston to tea.

The Quiney family legends include being chased over the Downs by a low-flying Messerschmitt chattering its guns at them. Fortunately no hits were reported.

Derrick Pyle's memories include diving for cover when hay making: "We were working on Butt's Brow, with low cloud and the threshing machine whirling away, when we noticed spurts of soil across the field as low-flying aircraft fired at us."

For part of the war little Mr Philip Vos KC was at *The Dipperays,* with his wife and daughter Patricia and their cook, Jean. Most Sundays a pipe band of the RAF Regiment would play on the lawns and locals could sit there and listen. The musicians were based at the cookhouse, a large marquee put up in the grounds of *Underhill,* along today's Went Way. Many folk remember piper Tommy Hoy.

The Village Hall YMCA canteen was run by local ladies every evening 1944-45 for the Friston RAF/WAAF. Back row L-R: Mrs FW Penrose (later Headland) of *Oak Cottage,* Mrs Lilian Ticehurst, Elizabeth Stein, Mrs Catherine Kemp, Mrs Florence Harris, Margaret Wicking, Mrs Kay Kennard. Centre row: Mrs Delia Bicks and Wendy Kennard. Front row: Mrs Penn, Mrs Eleanor Budd, Nora Vine, Mrs Wilson and Joan McGlashan

In October 1943 Mr Budd reported enemy planes over East Dean and Friston on six occasions, but with slight damage to roof tiles only. That month a Belgian Spitfire squadron, 349, flew its first operational sorties from Friston, and later another Belgian outfit, 350, was deployed.

Amongst the lesser happenings, on 7 November a bomb dropped near *Cornish Farm* and, according to Mr Budd, left a crater 45ft [14m] in diameter and $9^{1}/_{2}$ft [3m] deep. In December there was a fire at *Gayles* and the airfield SHQ was moved to *Treetops.* David Brown, stationed at *Gayles* during the war, was in the parties deputed to search the coast for corpses on the beach. He always said it put him off shellfish.

The November Armistice Day service was held as usual, although now at 1500h, while the Christmas parcel saga ran unabated. Apparently, not all the troops had received their money last year, so it was decided just to send a 'Good Wishes letter' and keep the money for their return. The British Legion children's party, proposed for Friday, 7 January 1944, was held in the school because the Village Hall had been taken over as a YMCA canteen.

Mrs Eileen Goldsmith recounted having to show passes whenever they left the farm, and said troops and tanks were everywhere. She saw Winston Churchill reviewing tanks one day. "In spite of all the activity, crops were sown and harvested in the old-fashioned way and Canadian troops helped with the harvest."

Stricken homecoming bombers continued to make desperate emergency belly-flops at Friston. On 6 September 1943 six B-17 Flying Fortresses landed safely from a raid on

Stuttgart. The record was 68 planes during January 1944; including B-17s and B-24s that often burnt out because the station fire crews just couldn't cope with the numbers of such large aircraft. Mrs Betty Hollingdale, of *Bullock Down Farm,* said they often saw the stricken planes coming in, "And we would yell, 'Make it, you can do it, you're almost there', and often all would be well, but sometimes all we saw was a puff of smoke from behind the airfield trees".

The Luftwaffe also raided the airfield on 21 January 1944, Mr Budd reported, 'the alarm sounded at 2033h and soon after large numbers of raiders passed over. They sent down many HE and flares with incendiary bombs. Saw two planes come down in flames, one at Firle and one Alfriston way. All clear 2220'.

Aircrew and ground crew under a Stirling bomber's wing at Friston airfield in 1944

On 9 February, at 1020h, a Mitchell bomber crashed in flames at Crowlink. It had been hit in Northern France and was losing height, but could not make a landing at Friston because a plane had already crashed on the runway. The Mitchell narrowly missed buildings at Crowlink and came down within yards of *Little Barn Cottage,* bringing down telephone wires. Of the crew of four, one was killed and two injured, one seriously. Dr Alex van Someren, a retired doctor of *Deanbank Lodge,* 6 Warren Lane, was first on the scene.

On 23 February bombs were dropped near Belle Tout, and the next day two delayed-action HEs fell on Went Hill at 2230, and exploded at 2330 and 0020. A plane was seen to fall towards Jevington tracked by the Friston Forest searchlights. The RAF had Bofors guns in the field at *Crowlink Corner* by the stone stile and Grace Taylor said, "One day they celebrated when they thought they had downed a German plane. Afterwards an officer came to *Underhill Cottages* to apologise for his men's language, 'They don't shoot down a plane every day' he explained".

One of the Belgian pilots of 349 squadron came to make his home in East Dean. At 1055 on 29 April 1944 Ft-Sgt (later F/O) 'Freddy' Moureau's Spitfire developed a glycol leak and crashed in Gate Field, Crowlink, after clipping a pylon. He was pulled from the aircraft by Maurice Haffenden, and farmer Stan Hobden, who later said to his daughter, "Hazel, why don't you visit him in the Princess Alice hospital?" She did, they were married at East Dean Church, after the war he became an airline pilot with Sabena, and they retired to the Downlands Estate.

Kathleen Banks reminisces, "In spite of all the raids we spent some happy holidays at East Dean during the war, although I recall the eerie searchlights over Beachy Head. My children remember the picnics, the daily walk for the newspaper from Goodman's caravan in the farmyard, and walking where Elven Lane is now to pick blackberries.

"At that time there was no Peak Dean Lane development and much of Deneside was bare of houses. My son when aged about four would run up the bank of Deneside when sent to Charlie Grayson's hut for bread [now *Downlands*]. His bakery was tiny and rather primitive but smelt lovely. I remember calves and poultry at *Peak Dean Farm,* although it was more of a smallholding. As the children grew older, we would rent Miss Lillie's *Mill Cottage* for the August. This was part of the old mill at Friston sited between the Estate entrance and *The Outlook* tearooms."

Madeline Lillie went from working at the *Birling Gap Hotel* when that was taken over, to *Gorsedown.* Her mother came to live with her to escape the London bombing, and as her contribution to the war effort Madeline took over the work of the postmen from March 1941 and for five years delivered in all weathers. She would push the scarlet bicycle, so loaded as to be quite unrideable, up Friston hill and, regardless of the regulations, she would also carry the baker's loaves down to Crowlink. With only one leave of seven days she basked in the knowledge that she was doing her bit for the community and country like so many women. In 1943 she and her mother moved to *Mill Cottage* near Friston Green. When she gave up the post in March 1946 she helped at Dennett's Stores and went back to her real love, gardening, for many of the Friston houses. An unsung heroine, she died in 1954.

A V1 Flying Bomb, or doodle-bug, coming in over Cuckmere Haven, 1944. The Seven Sisters and Birling Gap are in the distance

In the weeks before D-Day troops on the move slept in sheds and barns. Local people would give them cups of tea and the next morning they would be gone, leaving an empty cup and a thank you note. Having moved up to the Southampton area they would be replaced by another group the next night.

D-Day saw Derrick Pyle working along the Old Willingdon Road with hundreds of Flying Fortresses going over. Just after the Normandy invasion, on 8 June 1944, a Spitfire from Friston airfield crashed in fog near Folkington.

On 13 June Mr Budd recorded the first flying bomb (V1) over East Dean, 'First PAC[3] passed over', and on 16 June he noted the first one to be shot down locally. Over the following days he recorded many such incidents, including one brought down by fighter planes over the Old Willingdon Road which caused slight damage to the Estate Office in Windmill Lane, the school building, and yet again *Friston Place* greenhouses lost all their glass; whilst another 'fly bomb', shot down off Birling Gap, once more brought down part of the ceiling in Friston Church.

Peter Armiger said, "I well remember the night we first saw the doodle-bugs. We spotted these lights in the sky and had no idea what they might be."

"In the 1944 summer" says Kathleen Banks, "we were with my parents in Meads, and whenever their old dog came running into the house Mother said, 'It'll be a doodle-bug', and I recall one falling near the Downs Golf Course."

New squadrons were brought in against these flying bombs, and a Polish squadron flying *Mustangs* had destroyed 50 of them by the end of July. There was quite an international involvement, for Cpl Roy W Gates, from Ontario, was part of 6501 Servicing Echelon attached to 501 squadron during this scary time.

Biddy Kennard wrote, 'I remember strange objects moving down the Channel which turned out to be part of Mulberry harbour. At the time of the doodle-bugs the London anti-aircraft barrage was brought down to intercept them near the coast and the hill by *Half Way Cottages* bristled with guns'.

Diversions to Friston airfield were now mainly due to the weather, so on 8 September 1944 there was a stream landing of 22 C47s.

After October the *Spitfires* moved away and Friston resumed its role as an ELG, but was not busy. A fitter at Friston airfield, 1944-45, RF Walker, says that by that time most of the aircraft were Piper Cubs or Austers. "When a Stirling bomber landed for refuelling our pumps had difficulty reaching the tanks in the high wings and it took us all day to fill it up".

Tom Goodman used to take newspapers to Friston airfield to sell to the airmen. "I recall a few raids there, nearly all were in the early morning, but I always recall one day, towards the end of the war, when I saw a Dakota, a DC 3, come in and Yanks get out, all in dress suits. They were stepping out for an evening in Brighton." Such episodes were confirmed by Frank May, a driver on the ground staff, who stayed at *The Outlook* tearooms, run by Miss Lowe and Miss Tanner during the war,

An Eastbourne Old Town resident recalls a 'Day on the Farm' in 1944. "We started off dressed in a pair of overalls and borrowed heavy boots, pushing a borrowed bicycle up East Dean hill. Arriving at the top all the smoke and dust had gone from our lungs and settled on the soles of my boots.

"Mounting our bikes we coasted down to East Dean and into the field where the farmer and his three sons [the Goldsmiths], two farm workers, a lady helper and two German prisoners of war were busy carting oats to a stack.

"We finished the field of oats at 1100h and went into a field of pea haulms. The 'Old Man' was doubtful whether they were dry enough for stacking so father and sons went into a huddle picking up a handful of peas much as you would feel clothes on a washing line. The Old Man shook his head and off we went to a field of wheat, where we began pulling the stacks over for a final drying.

"For lunch, at noon, we were all bundled into a Ford van driven by the Old Man, who dropped the farm workers at *Half Way Cottages* and took the rest to a large farmhouse where the prisoners retired to an outhouse for their rations. The rest went into the kitchen for a wash and on into the dining room where we met the farmer's wife and two charming daughters, 'Draw up your chair and help yourself to the vegetables' soon made us at home. The father talked about the weather and asked where we came from and we had good conversation until the mother shouted, 'Father's off' and with thanks for the meal we all dashed out back to the wheat field. The Old Man had well-worn stockings over his trousers which were tied below and above the knee and both he and his sons worked like Trojans. At four o'clock the prisoners went and we worked another half an hour when we broke off for tea and sandwiches. Afterwards it was back to the wheat field until, with the glorious sight of the sun going down beyond East Dean, the Old Man called it a day from the top of a stack and it was into the Ford, men, bicycles and dog. What an enjoyable day! I had a bath, a meal, went to bed and Hitler could have sent all his doodle-bugs and I wouldn't have heard them."

At the AGM of the East Dean British Legion most of the discussion was on whether to admit Home Guards as full members, the vote was 21 for and 12 against.

A public meeting on 14 December decided by a large majority that the war memorial should be a Village Hall community centre. The next year the idea of a new Village Hall as a thanksgiving was taking shape, with a tentative cost of £3000. Sir John Salmond, a patron of the British Legion, thought that if the village provided £750 the remainder could come as grants from bodies such as the Rural Communities Association.

Peter Armiger recalls sitting in the Shaw above Friston Field [or Hobbs eares] with Gerald Melling who was crying having just heard that his father had been killed in Italy. So the effects of the war didn't finish in August 1945; in fact the rationing becoming worse, with bread being rationed for the first time so that flour could be sent to the starving countries of Europe. Rationing and other restrictions, such as controlling the amount of timber allowed in building, went on until 1953.

It wasn't a normal life, but for the children it was accepted that you had to scrabble around for clothing coupons and if you'd eaten your sweet ration that was that. It was a time of make do and mend with cold winters not eased by power cuts - at least the tyranny of the Blackout had gone - and a sense of humour helped.

The Parish Council complained in 1948 about the abandoned cars, barbed wire, and tank traps left around Friston pond, and last remnants were only finally cleared in 1956, unless, of course, you include the concrete tank traps on the bank at the side of Michel Dene Road and Upper Street, which saw in the new Millennium underneath the ivy. As late as the Millennium time it was estimated that some 10% of Eastbourne properties had evidence of bomb damage.[4]

After the war Peter Armiger's parents moved to the *Old Police Cottage* in Lower Street. "My bedroom was where the German pilot had been kept in 1940".

In 1951 the War Graves Commission erected headstones for the four merchant navy graves in Friston churchyard and the two at East Dean. The graves of four German airmen at Friston were marked by wooden crosses until in 1955 all German remains were moved to a central German cemetery near Cannock.

Friston airfield was de-requisitioned on 8 April 1946. Biddy Kennard wrote, 'My final memory of the airfield, which always had a slight air of the RAF radio show *Much Binding in the Marsh* was of a notice on the entrance gate reading *Mushrooms for Sale'*.

The RAF abandoned the 'hideous' radar array at Beachy Head in the summer of 1958. It cost £6m to erect, and the hope was that removal would be cheaper.

On Sunday, 22 April 2001, there was a commemoration of Friston Airfield by the Society of St George, who commissioned a plaque, now in Friston Church.

11. Post-War Austerity and Cold Times, 1946-64

The Parochial Church Council [PCC] agreed to have a welcome home to men and women returning after service with HM Forces; notices would be distributed with newspapers by Goodman's the newsagents. The Welcome Home Circle arranged a Social at the Bardolf Hall organised by Rosalind Stein, to which the local British Legion [BL] branch donated £10 to buy cigarettes as prizes. Ronnie Hall, secretary of the PCC for some 20 years, resigned and was replaced by Leslie Stein.

The BL not only agreed to look into the question of having a women's section, but decided that Victory Day, 8 June 1946, should be celebrated with cricket, and 6-a-side football (so long as Lt-Col Thomson had completed the grass cutting with his motor mower), finishing the day with a tea, and a dance in the evening. The branch bought cigarettes as prizes. Friend Fowler was advised of an At Home at the *Tiger* on 11 November, to bring local service personnel together, so that he could reserve some beer.

The Boys' Club, October 1946, in the Scout Hut, later Farrer Hall. Back row left to right: Sid French (ran the Club), Donald Dann, ?, ?, Wally Eve, Mrs Vos, Harry Sellars, Peggy Hyde, Ronnie Hall (organist, Davies-Gilbert Agent), Arthur Farrer, Mr Essex, George Worsell. Next row: Hubert Foord, Mrs E Bugler, Joan Baldock, Marie Worsell (Ivan's daughter), Joan Gates, Maud (Monico's housekeeper), Frances Kemp, Barbara Hall, Brenda Baldock. Front row: Bob Saunders, Tony Schafer (now NZ), Corrie Martin, John Harris, ?, ?, Tony Pownall (worked at the petrol station), Stephanie Fears (married Doug Richey), Bernard Baldock, Barbara Worsell, ?Mrs Gates. In front: Jesse Taylor with guitar, John Eve (the horse), and Kenny Pownall (on the horse)

The vicar's stipend had been £305 per annum [average pay £250], out of which he paid £28 towards dilapidations. In 1945 it was increased to £400 if the laity found half the difference. An appeal was announced to raise the money. The Church accounts on 1 January 1947 showed annual turnover £665, a balance of £132, and a £45 quota to the Diocese.

In May 1947 the Parish Magazine was restarted, supported by advertisers and donations. The parish directory was on the front cover, and it was delivered free to all houses. 'A venture of faith … which we hope will bear fruit in the lives of our people … we rely upon the gratuitous and generous gifts of recipients'. The pre-war printer's blocks of the churches had been lost by war damage, but the pictures were restored in time for the August 1947 issue. The Vicar was the editor with Margaret Gardner and Capt. Horace Rew the secretaries. For the first few issues it carried *Helpful Hints* - 'Burnt pie dishes can be cleaned by rubbing with a damp cloth dipped in salt.'

Pre-NHS the Alexandra Hospital Flag Day was going strong raising £16.39. Poppies, organised by Guy Smart brought in £47. The British Legion's Old Peoples' Outing went ahead in June, the branch standing the cost of the coach and Mr Smart the cost of the tea.

The AGM of The Players was on 27 June 1947, when the constitution was adopted, and Major Harding elected president, with Sidney Ostler chairman, William Bonnell treasurer, secretary Biddy Kennard and committee Mrs Stein, Mrs Blake, Fred Bicks and George Worsell. The hope was to arrange an evening of one-act plays to enter the Sussex Amateur Drama League Festival, which East Dean had won in 1938.

The first ever century for the Cricket Club, 111, was scored by Michael Kennard on 4 August 1947. After a winter of snow the summer was magnificently sunny for the game.

Tom Bishop, East Dean and Friston's [ED & F] oldest resident at 90, was able to take a long walk every day 'as it is important to keep fit'. The father of Mrs Foord, he died at 93.

Work on installation of a new gas central heating system at Friston Church was nearing completion in December 1947.

Over 1947 Churchfield was built and allocated to ex-servicemen. The first residents were Reg and Ruby Haffenden, Wally and Jessie Eve, Cecil and Rose Dann, Fred and Kath Fuller, Tommy and Edna Goodman, Charlie and Florrie Vine. [7]

After RAF war service Reg Haffenden worked on building houses in Deneside and later Warren Lane, until he was given his cards. He next worked for a coal merchant at £5 a week. "It was really hard work." When Charlie Gay left Reg became a part-time postman at £3 a week. As the rent alone was £1 he had to find other work and went gardening at 7^1/$_2$p an hour. "It wasn't easy on those rates and you had to work at a number of gardens."

Florrie Vine moved into Churchfield before Charlie came back from the war when he worked as gardener for Mr and Mrs RT Smith, who lived at *Old Style,* now 4 The Close and for Phyllis Hughes at *Lye Oak,* opposite. Both worked for the Axtens at *Southease,* Florrie for 24 years, and for the last nine years after Mrs Axten died she looked after him. "He had worked for the Bank of England and was a real gentleman." During the season Charlie also went harvesting. Charlie loved his garden, growing mainly vegetables, "You can't eat flowers". It was said of him, "He was honest, straightforward and a good worker, who worked hard all his life. What he could never get over was that he never knew his parents".

Capt. Horace Rew, helped by the Revd AW Anderson and Harry Sellars, got the Cricket Club going after the war. There was nothing left; even the roller had been purloined by the RAF to flatten Friston airfield. It was amazing how many people Capt. Rew knew; thanks to him Ramon Subba Row brought a team to East Dean, and in 1952 Jack Hobbs came as an umpire, so he soon raised 800 donations in half-crowns [12^1/$_2$p]. Unfortunately, Horace was firmly against the tide of Sunday play and league cricket.

Mr and Mrs A Rosen played their part by saving the Cricket Club from a 'financial dilemma', in the autumn of 1947. They gave the treasurer £25 when he was wondering how to pay accounts totalling £4 with only 5p in the kitty.

BL's annual Children's Party was held in January 1948 at the Village Hall, however, their Social on 10 March, 'with an hour's dancing instruction from Mrs Alexander' lost 45p. The BL annual Jumble Sale was in June at the Village Hall. 'The secretary would apply for petrol allocations for members collecting jumble in their cars.'

Mr Turnham held a mini-cinema in the Village Hall every Tuesday at 6 and 8 o'clock, the admission being 1/9d and 1/6d.

June 1948 saw PC Hyde retire after 27 years in the Police, 15 at East Dean. It was said Hyde had two punishments: when a youth strayed he boxed his ears, and erring adults were promptly marched to the *Tiger* where they paid a fine by buying a drink for the constable.

The new Pc was Max Soffner. John Dann says, "The lads respected him. He was very fair, and if he caught you up to something you got a clip on the ear".

The Bowls Club was playing again after the war, and the Downland Tennis Club had been reformed. Their Secretary was Miss G Mullins of 13 Windmill Lane, the subscription for players was a guinea [£1.05] a year, and 130 attended their Bardolf Hall dance

"Our present Flower Show", Bill Armiger explained, "started in 1948 in a marquee lent by Major Harding. Tom Martin came up with the idea as a means of raising funds for the Cricket Club. Tom was a member of a few horticultural societies and had ample knowledge of show procedures. Fred Fuller and I said we would help, with Ronnie Hall as president and Harry Comber as secretary. The show, with 80 entries of Fruit and Vegetables (on trestle tables by the road) with Cricket and Village Sports, was a great success".

Fred Fuller won most of the vegetable classes, although Wally Eve took the best swedes prize. Bill Armiger's dahlias won a prize, and Mrs Wynne's posy was a winner. There were many side-shows; Mr & Mrs Feneley (Wheel of Fortune), Mrs Penrose and Mrs Lane (Rolling the Penny), Miss Cradock (Magic Water), Mrs Tompsett (Treasure Island), Mr & Mrs Rankin (Missing the Board) and Miss Absale (Corinthian Bagatelle).

Cricket Club players and officials *c.*1952. Back row: Bob Irons, Ben Muggeridge, Charlie Goldsmith, Ivan Worsell, Geoff Cornford (capt.), Fred Breach, Eric Bourner, Mrs Ann Goldsmith (scorer, wife of Charlie), Harry Comber, Reg Goldsmith. Middle: Hugh Winter (partly hidden), ?, ?, WJ Benton, RG Hall, H Leakey, Bill Strudwick. Front: Jim Cumming, Bill Trueman, ?, Stan Howes

In the Sports part of the day, apart from the cricket, Tony Pownall won the cycle race with John Eve second, Sheila Pattenden the girls' skipping race, Malcolm Gillam under-5's race, Pamela Meller the girls' race, Barry Wilson the boys' under-7 race, and A Winter won the Throwing the Cricket Ball. First in the Under-10 boys' race was Peter Goldsmith, second Colin Wicking, third Richard Worsell, in the older boys' race Edward Winter, Tom Eve and Jim Holter came in close. Mr J Taylor and Mrs Hobden won the wheelbarrow race.

Jimmy Holter worked for Jim Kemp from 1948-52 at *Forge Garage* on Friston hill. The pay was £1 a week from which 12½p was deducted for National Insurance, "but I was able to live on the wage quite comfortably. There were few new cars in those years and the work was mainly keeping cars on the road, re-spraying old Army khaki-coloured Austin 8s, and tractors were kept going by decoking".

Jeff Tompsett had taken over the Corner Stores and Post Office. The manual telephone exchange building on the main road became the Postal Sorting Office in 1948 when a new exchange was built in Deneside. The sorting office is now *Wild Cottage.*

On 8 October 1949 the BBC broadcast *London calling Europe, Life in a typical English Village.* It had been recorded in the village stores at East Dean on 13 September when Max Robertson interviewed the Vicar, Miss Ada Absale, Luther Hills, Sidney Ostler, Leslie Stein, Fred Fuller, Capt. Rew, Joey Pownall, Christine Hansen and the two postmen, Harry West and Reg Haffenden.

The East Dean Players *The Bitter Bit* was a very good production. Jim Perfect carried the main burden as John Westup, Maud Worsell appeared at ease, Rosalind Stein merited high praise, Delia Bicks was entirely convincing as Kate Hoadley, and Sydney Ostler, Rose Dann and Eileen Goldsmith completed a good cast. It was awarded the Walker cup for the best new play in the Sussex Amateur Drama Festival.

On 6 December 1949 there was a meeting of the War Memorial committee with Sir John Salmond c, Mr C Meller s, Mr S Penning t, and Mrs R Haffenden, Mrs G Wicking, Miss Clements, Mr F Arnatt, Percy Budd, George Cheal and Ronnie Hall. Their last meeting in November 1946 had discussed raising a loan for a Village Hall, the popular choice for a memorial, with negotiations left in the hands of the Parish Council [PC]. With the national economic position, it was patently impracticable to proceed with a loan and the PC suggested that the provision of a recreation ground and renovation of the present memorial should constitute the village memorial to those who died in World War Two.

So a new Village Hall as a war memorial had been abandoned. The decision was deplored, but residents realised that the committee had no choice. 'In particular Sir John Salmond had laboured for the success of this venture and that his efforts have proved fruitless comes as a bitter blow.'

In 1950 the BL branch learnt that West Dean members, although within the East Dean area, 'would on no account desire to belong to the East Dean branch'. Did this brush-off decide the BL to buy a regulation sling and white gauntlets for George Cheal who, founder member of the local BL in 1931, was now s; and an extremely smart standard-bearer (1945-67) including a Hyde Park review by King George VI in 1950. He was a v-c (1952-54), entertainment secretary (1945-50), and awarded the Gold Badge by the National Council.

The ESCC agreed a white line along Friston hill. Ray Kemp, East Dean's lengthman, who would do the white-lining by hand and, 'whose zeal in keeping the area tidy sets an example', reported that he was having difficulty disposing of unburnable rubbish.

In deference to Horace Rew the Cricket Club agreed not to play League cricket in 1951.

The vicar flew back from his South African break by flying boat in May 1950. Horace Rew as acting magazine editor had published the vicar's letters, awash with the sentiments of the time, 'motored to see the grave of Cecil Rhodes, that great statesman, whose name and reputation is known all the world over … and also saw a monument to a small party of Englishmen who in 1893 were surrounded by rebelling Matabeles and all killed'.

June 1950 the ESCC agreed to a light in the telephone kiosk, and to add an arm indicating *Crowlink only No Through Road* to the Friston fingerpost. As nowadays there was a three-tier system of local government; the ESCC, Hailsham RDC and the PC. Sidney Ostler, Clerk to the PC, stated that as all efforts to trace the owner of Friston pond had failed the PC decided that it should be formally acquired, to keep it in good order. Originally in the manor of Peak Dean, it now had concrete anti-tank traps round the brambled Green. The Gilbert Estate agreed that the PC should take over custodianship of the village sign.

An entertainment in the Village Hall in aid of the church fabric fund raised £10. Organised by Mr and Mrs Carter of *Corner Cottage,* East Dean, those taking part included

Heather Davies, Kathleen 'Biddy' Kennard (who sang Roger Quilter's *To Daisies* and Frank Bridge's *O that it were So*), Violet Wimbush (sketches of young lady asking questions about her missing fiancé, and of a crystal gazer giving answers about a missing poodle), Hilda Carter MRST (dramatic recitals) with Doreen Boulter and Cecil Chatfield of EODS (duets & solos accompanied by John Chatfield).

With the cold war Civil Defence (CD) was in people's minds. Norman Davies, now living at *Went Acre,* was the senior warden for the CD area. He held a meeting with 70 present at the Village Hall, and 20 volunteered for wardens' training. The next year 22 residents (12 women) passed their CD training course and received their badges.

The Players presented Gogol's *The Government Inspector* in 1950. L-R: Jimmy Monico, Cecil Dann, Jim Perfect, Delia Bicks, Fred Bicks, Sidney Ostler, Maud Worsell and Richard Dempsey. Edward Bowles, Raymond Kemp, Norman Lycett and Leslie Stein also took parts. 'To handle a cast of 22 on a stage barely 10ft deep and 20 ft long was no mean accomplishment.' Produced by Stephen Brewer, it played to full houses. The production came second to Lindfield in the Sussex Drama League Festival

The Football Club was more successful in 1951, when there were at least three football teams, and at times four i.e. 1st and 2nd elevens, with under-18 and under-15 teams as well. The secret was, no doubt, a playing subscription of only 25p.

The team used to play at the Recreation Ground on a pitch parallel to the road, but in 1950 the Cricket Club complained that they had cut up their square, so football moved to the Horsefield. Gerald Melling said, "We had to level the Horsefield before we could play because it had a raised path diagonally across from Goldsmith's farm to the pond. Other players included Peter Armiger, 'Bill' Bailey, Charlie Goldsmith, Charlie Markwick, and Joey Pownall. John Arnatt was the regular goalkeeper, with Fred Fuller as deputy."

The football club returned to the recreation field, but played at right angles to the road so that their pitch did not overlap the cricket square. Better, but they didn't do well, although some success followed. Finally, they were banned from the cricket ground in 1978, and while a team played in Eastbourne for a year or two, disbandment was not far away. [15]

The magazine was in debt to the extent of £22.72 [£22/14/5d], so a Dollar Gap [DG] Fund was started, DG being the OK phrase of the day, 180 half-crowns would cover it.

The DG was closed with a total of £23. Mrs Bugler and Mrs Snape were among the 120 who contributed. The next week Horace Rew discovered that the gap (in sterling) was £42.72 not £22.72. 'I would gladly pay the £20 if I possessed it - but I don't. I can only hope that some splendid soul will see that our attempt to start 1951 clear of debt is not thwarted by the careless senile decay of -.' The amount was raised in a month.

At the beginning of 1951 the PC decided not to participate in the chain of bonfires for the Festival of Britain, on grounds of cost. Before long, however, it was on everyone's tongue. "Have you been to the South Bank Exhibition", "…the Battersea Fun Fair?" were standard gambits in conversation. People were also pointing out that there was much more to see - the South Kensington Museums, the *Punch* offices, St Paul's Cathedral and many other places were en fete. In the St Paul's exhibition, illustrating British life and religion, there was *The Times'* photograph of the dedication of the new tablets on East Dean's war memorial on Armistice Day 1950. The Ministry of Works, however, had not yet been able to remove Friston's tank defence blocks owing to shortage of funds.

East Dean & Friston Football Team 1949-50. Standing: Fred Saunders (treasurer), Jesse Ticehurst, Les Ticehurst, David Brown (the best player), Jim Bland (goalie), Eric Bourner, ?, Harry Sellars, Derrick Pyle, Reg Goldsmith (secretary). Kneeling: John Eve, Doug Richey, (mascots Ronnie Saunders and Oliver Cater), Geoff Cater and Bernard Gillam. "The colours were green with white sleeves and shorts."

In April, a dance in the Bardolf Hall, featured dancing - old time and modern - to the village band: Ivan and George Worsell, William Russell, Harry Sellars and Sid White. In the interval Geoffrey Bowles, Jimmy Monico, Horace Rew, Anthony Tompsett and Henry Watts gave an amusing interpretation of a scene from *Midsummer Night's Dream.* Members of the band complained that, 'Violin strings which used to cost 7^1/$_2$p now cost 25p'.

Other happenings included the full licensing of the Birling Gap Hotel; motorists asked to park only on *The Dipperays* side of Upper Street; the successful introduction of litter baskets at East Dean and Friston fitted with removable liners by Ray Kemp; Mrs Tait Reid was congratulated on her 103rd birthday and the local BL branch decided that the Exhortation should be said and the Silence observed at the opening of all meetings.

An etching of Friston Mill by HG Brown was hung in the Village Hall, and Mrs Bakewell of Hillside presented two photographs: Friston Mill and a Meet on The Green.

The two parish meetings sat one on either side of the Village Hall and each chairman addressed his own meeting, James Monico for East Dean and Percy Budd for Friston.[1] Out of the Babel emerged the desire for Capt. Rew to act as chairman of a joint meeting and it was decided to submit this opinion to the ESCC. The PC considered the bad state of the footpath between The Ridgeway and the Old Willingdon Road. As part of a national survey of rights of way, in 1951 the footpaths in the parishes had been mapped.

A Christian Missionary Society [CMS] Sale of Work opened by Muriel, Lady Hailsham, raised £76. Also in November 1951 the WI with Mrs Chenevix-Trench in the chair 'heard an interesting talk on *The Uses of the Frying Pan'*; thankfully, a women-only meeting.

Unbelievably, the PC again approached the Southdown bus company about placing a Request Stop *half-way up* Friston hill. Sensibly the bus company stated that it would be dangerous and would throw an unnecessary strain on buses and drivers. The bus company were also not prepared to place bus shelters on both sides of the road.

After Ted Fears moved out of Jimmy Kemp's Forge Garage, Doug Richey took over and married Jimmy's niece. When Jimmy died, Doug managed it for Mrs Kemp (she was a Fears). Keith Haffenden helped him for a while, but when Doug retired it was run by Kevin Reeve as *QCR*. It moved to the original Cater's Garage site in 1996 and later to Eastbourne.

Members of the Angling Club in 1948 included George Worsell, Harry Sellars, Cecil Dann, Wally Eve, A Rosen, and Fred Fuller, subscribing 50p a year. Ray Cheal said, "Geoff Nash, Jim Holter and others would get a fire going and cook sausages from butcher Arthur Raylor and have them on bread from Charlie Grayson's bakery. Incredibly, a coastguard used to walk from the Cuckmere coastguard cottages, along the bottom of the Seven Sisters to Birling Gap, I can see his torch coming along. He'd have a few pints in the pub, walk to East Dean and catch the bus back to the Cuckmere".

Cricket on the Recreation Ground with the old Pavilion, 1952. Fred Breach is bowling, Harry Comber on the left, the wicketkeeper is Eric Bourner and Cecil Dann is to the right of the batsman. After 'an indifferent season' out of the league in 1951 the club voted to rejoin the Cuckmere Valley League, and 47 to 30 voted for Sunday play

January 1952 saw the passing of another link with the past - the dismantling of the Village Smithy. Luther Hills, only able to get about with difficulty, sold the Forge, although he continued to live in the cottage next door, his home for close on 80 years.

That month also saw a piece by Capt. Rew (now the first lay editor) in the Parish Magazine about lazy British workers appear in a Sunday newspaper under the caption of *The Vicar's View*. The Vicar was distressed when he received 'abusive and scandalous' letters, 'although two writers endorsed the view expressed'. Capt Rew 'deeply regretted the annoyance caused to the Vicar owing to the methods of 20th century journalism'. The Vicar said that he normally corrected the proofs, but 'owing to an infirmity [failing eyesight] I asked the editor to be responsible. I did not write the article myself and I dissociate myself from the views which I consider quite out of place in a church magazine.'

Capt Rew had a comment about the magazine losses, 'Some financial experts look upon a parish magazine as a business proposition; if it does not pay it should be discontinued. This is a mistake; the magazine is a vital factor in the work of the Church.'

By now local lad Robert Saunders was serving with the navy in Korea as was John Harris and Anthony Schafer, with Jesse Taylor in Suez.

The PC sent a message of sympathy to the Queen Mother on the death of King George VI and received an acknowledgement within 24 hours. The WI observed a minute's silence in memory of the late King and sang *Abide with Me*. Delia Bicks won the first prize for the best rice pudding. The King's Memorial Fund raised £41.94, 'A wonderful gift from the parish due to the love and esteem for the King and his care for us in a difficult reign.'

The PC reported that a guard rail had been erected at *Gore Cottage;* the water company had cut the hedge at the corner of Lower Street into Gilbert's Drive; and the footpath from The Ridgeway to the Old Willingdon Road had been made up again.

The RSPCA junior section, the 'Animal Defenders', held a party at *Little Hill.*

New House Farm near The Green was an active farm when this picture was taken in 1953 of threshing a corn rick. L-R: Don Gurr, Bert Foord, Mary Maltby, CE Goldsmith and Bert Goldsmith

A public meeting at the *Tiger* heard the British Legion case for doubling the basic disability pension from £2.25 to £4.50 a week. There were 23 present and all agreed with a motion endorsing the policy.

Although the Youth Club had held bonfire parties after the war (the 1946 collection amounted to £1.62) the Bonfire Society was not reformed until February 1952, with Major Harding as p, Harry Sellars c, Harry Comber t, and George Cheal s. 'The aim was to give the public a really good show on November 5th.' It turned out a fine evening, all went well, many were in fancy dress and £10 went to St Dunstan's. Friston's 'do' was at *Friston Place.*

In 1955 a special effort was made to mark the 350th anniversary of Bonfire Night. The bonfire had 'the effigy of the miserable traitor, Guido Fawkes, escorted by no less a person than the Queen of the May for 1955, Sandra Goldsmith, to the music of the Eastbourne Silver band. Some 200 torches led the way for the 600-strong gathering as they moved around the parish. The Fancy Dress was judged at Bardolf Hall by Baroness Elizabeth von Zedlitz and Miss Morvyne Fenwick-Owen, the winners being Faith Breach, Valerie Gillam and Derek Vine, with special prizes to Terry Saward, David and Hugh Winter, and David and Ricky Hodgson. The Hardings made sure no competitor left the hall empty-handed. It was an hour before the crowd reached the bonfire site on the allotments between *Underhill* and 'The Hollow' (Lower Street) by which time the numbers had doubled to 1200. Jane Booth-Clibborn said, "We used to get impatient with Capt. Rew who always gave an oration, consisting mainly of a denunciation of the Pope, before the bonfire was lit - which was what we wanted". The firework display lasted 40 minutes and the dancing in the Farrer Hall went on until midnight. All profits went to Poppy Day and the old folks.

Pauline Joslin said, "From Cophall we could watch the Bonfire Night torchlight procession wending its way from the village. Jimmy Wicking would deliver the Christmas parcels bought from the donations to the elderly folk in the village".

"After Bonfire night", explained Alf Pelling, "We went to the Evening Service on the following Sunday and afterwards to the *Tiger.* I remember Horace Rew walking with us from the Service, 'We've been in one church, now let's go into another', was his comment."

In 1956 the Bonfire Society asked for helpers in a lighted-hearted appeal, saying that torchbearers must be 16-106 and of the sterner sex only; the collectors must be of the gentler sex, discretion forbidding enquiries about age but the qualification was the ability to extract blood from a stone. Joan Nash said, "In the 1950s I acted as a Bonfire Society collector, dressed as a Golliwog, we walked up the main road, with George Cheal in his red tunic, to Friston and then along The Ridgeway, Warren Lane, Hillside, round Deneside, knocking on the doors, and back to Upper Street". The total takings were £25.

Bonfire Society Supper *c.* 1955. Standing: L-R Bill (Hubert) Bailey, Miggs Bailey (née Ticehurst), Charlie Vine, Ethel Winter, Lilian Jessie Ticehurst. Seated: Frank Ticehurst, George Cheal, Arthur Raylor, Harry Comber, Sid Winter

In 1957 Sam Hodgson as Father Christmas, accompanied by Jean Dann the Bonfire Queen, and conveyed on a Sussex trolley, drawn by two horses in charge of Jim Wicking and Frank Ticehurst, distributed 50 parcels of good cheer to the old folk. They had previously delivered to each of the old folk 1cwt of coal, the gift of a Friston resident.

In 1958 the bonfire site was moved to Birling Gap, where it stayed until recently except for one year when it was at Gilbert's Drive between the Vicarage and the Police House.

Rogation Sunday had also been observed in the parishes by a procession through the parish, halting at certain points to invoke the Divine blessing. The Vicar proposed a service in the Vicarage garden with the theme of 'you don't have to be in church to pray'.

The PC were a grouped Council, members were divided between East Dean [7 members for 465 voters] and Friston [4 for 180]. Elected for East Dean were: Jim Kemp, Charles Meller, Sydney Penning, Guy Smart, Lt-Col AC Thomson, Sylvia Tompsett, and Ivan J Worsell; for Friston: Percy Budd, Kathleen Kennard, James Monico, and Lt-Col EC Simmons. East Dean polled 55% and Friston 49%. Helpers distributed 600 copies of a *Reminder to Vote,* however, the polling clerks in the voting station seemed to spend most of the day explaining to East Dean voters that they did not live in Friston and vice versa.

The WI choir, conductor Mrs Chenevix-Trench, did well at the Lewes Music Festival.

From 1952 Derrick Pyle helped his father at Summerdown Dairy. "The milking parlour was around where Chris Johnson's barn along Downs View Lane is now. There were some 70 cows, kept out all the time. The parlour would stand six at a time and one man could milk four at once by machine. The cows knew all about it and would wait patiently in line. One could milk the herd in 1½ hours. The milk went along a stainless steel tube to a cooler and in the 1950s into churns. The cows were put to the bull (no AI) December / January/February and they dried up June/July, with new calves September / October / November when the price for milk was best, but it meant more work bringing in silage. Up to 20 cows were in milk in summer calving December / January."

On 14 July 1952 two burglars were captured thanks to Pc Soffner, although one of them managed to flee across the Downs to Wilmington before he was apprehended.

It was a chilly, wet August in the villages, but nothing like the Lynton and Lynmouth floods. The Lynmouth and Lynton Relief fund benefited by £22 from local collection, and a further £12 was sent after a social evening in the Village Hall.

Horace Rew was appointed East Dean's first Reader in November 1952, the Revd Norman Lycett needing assistance because of his deteriorating eyesight.

That autumn the Players presented *Thunder Rock* by Robert Ardrey. One crit. was, 'A splendid disappointment. May we have a laugh next time?'

Mrs Carter arranged another concert and entertainment on Saturday 13 December 1952 raising £10.50 for the magazine fund. It was a great success, with Bernard Barrand singing *Blow, blow thou Winter Wind, O Mistresss Mine* and *The Fishermen of England* which suited his fine rich voice.

During 1952 a Family Service was started at 1000h. The idea was that it would be over by 1030 so as not to interfere with Sunday activities. That year Constable Soffner and family moved into the new Police House in Gilbert's Drive.

East Dean Garage (Service Station) in the 1950s, 'with *Redex* service', and run by Geoff and Kath Cater. A few houses of the Downlands Estate are on the skyline and *Gore Farmhouse* is peeping in on the right

The Hobdens moved from *Gore Farm* to the *Old Vicarage* at *Endlewick Farm* (near Arlington). EOH had farmed there in tandem with East Dean during the war. He died in 1971; his wife, Norah Ada May (née Kemp), having died seven days before him.

Geoff Cater, a good mechanic, worked in the Gore garage before the war, and returned after five years in the Army. He ran the garage while his wife, Kathleen (née Hobden), started a teashop in the showroom, selling sweets, cigarettes, sugar, tea, anything that people wanted. The workmen on the estate spent the day there if the weather was bad.

The BL branch agreed to buy arrows at a cost of £4.50 for Mr Broadley, a war disabled paraplegic, who had come to live in the village. His only hobby was archery. The BL annual children's party was attended by 74 children and 15 adults.

The RSPCA raised £21 for the annual appeal. Miss D Dickens, Mrs ER Scott, Mrs RC Wimbush, Mr Tompsett, Mr Langford, Mrs Houghton (Café Delphine), Mr Smith (Birling Gap Hotel) and Mrs Soffner all helped.

A Master from Brighton College brought boys over to take rubbings, as agreed, of the Selwyn Brasses. In his letter of thanks he noted the graves of German airmen in the churchyard just by the anti-invasion defences of 1940. 'From its Norman window to its Nazi graves your little church touches the story of England down the centuries.' [10]

Bishop of Chichester, George Bell, visited the parish on 28 April as part of the commemorations for the 700th anniversary of the death of St Richard.

Bernard Barrand, the choirmaster, came from London by road every week without any remuneration. Ronnie Hall played the organ at all choir practices and every Sunday, and he also gave his time gratuitously over many years.

The Coronation committee met, with Capt. Rew as chairman. At first the Football Club wanted to have nothing to do with the committee, but relented. Organisations represented were - *PC* The Vicar, *UNA* Mr WJ Boyce, *Bowls* Ernest Cater, *Bonfire* Harry Comber, *Angling* Cecil Dann, *WI* Mrs Evans, *BL* Lt-Col TM Gordon, *Cricket* E Muggeridge, *The Players* EJ Perfect and *Football* W Saunders, Co-opted were Miss Jenner, Mr Barrand, Percy Budd as t, James Kemp, Mrs Kennard, Charles Meller, JR Monico, SH Penning, EC Simmons, Guy Smart, Mrs A Tompsett, Lt-Col AC Thomson, Ivan Worsell, WS Ostler as s. West Dean joined in, represented by Dr RA Stenhouse. The committee decided on 'a Coronation Fair on Tuesday, 2 June, with a children's party, sports on the cricket ground; tea and a dance in the Bardolf Hall' The committee's appeal for £150 raised £154.

Birling Manor Coronation Maypole, June 1953. Boy second left (in dark top) David Wicking, next but one boy (in dark suit) George Fuller, the smaller of the two boys near the Maypole is Derek Vine, next right Faith Taylor, and girl on right in white Rosemary Cheal

The weather was not promising, but a good day was had by all. The children had souvenir tins of chocolates and Smarties after their tea. The Fair included Hoopla, Skittles, Greasy Pole, Tilting the Bucket, Maypole Dancing, and excerpts from *The Merry Wives of Windsor* by The (Strolling) Players. There was a Fancy Dress Ball in the Bardolf Hall, with the Village Band, until midnight. On the morning of 8 June the over-70s were taken to the Picturedrome to see the film of the coronation, *A Queen is Crowned.*

The Flower Show had 302 entries. Marjorie Westbury, radio actress and opener, presented the shield for most points to Wally Eve, winner for the second year running. Fred Breach was presented with the cricket ball with which he took ten wickets earlier in the season.

The Conservative Fete at Birling Manor in September had good weather (East Dean had only 19$\frac{1}{2}$ inches of rain in 1953). Mr W Axten was chairman of the local branch.

The Choir outing went to the Houses of Parliament and Hampton Court Palace. One rail station had a slot machine which, for a penny, stamped a choice of 18 letters on an aluminium strip. The choir used it so much that it ran out of strips. They returned at 2245h.

At the PC strong opposition was voiced against the decision of the Gilbert Trustees to continue with the Birling Gap camp sites after the painful experience of the noise, litter and discomfort with previous camps.

The Coronation events showed a balance of £90, so four teak seats were bought. One went at each East Dean bus stop, one on The Green and one near the top of Went Hill, the exact spot being where bombs fell during the war and which commanded a most beautiful view of the valley. Before the year was up the bus seats had initials carved into them.

The WI invited 32 old people from London to have tea at the Bardolf Hall on 16 July.

ED & F youngsters were doing well. Peter Goldsmith carried off the boys' science prize at Seaford County Secondary school, Brenda Maslen won the girls' prize, Mary Winter also won a prize and captained the school against the parents at stoolball.

The Vicar introduced a Free-Will Offering scheme, and encouraged seven-year covenants so that the parish benefited from the return of income tax, for the parish's quota had been raised from £37 to £77 a year. There were at least two Services every Sunday at Friston and often three at East Dean and the Children's Service was to resume. By 1954 the Free-Will Offering came to £542.70 including tax recovered from covenants.

Horace Rew announced the yearly results for his Stamp Albums - stamps ('stuck by the child, not the mother') recording attendance at his weekly scripture talks. 'If you are even half-a-minute late no stamp. Richard Worsell was late on a few occasions, but this was because of his paper round.' By neatness Elizabeth Worsell won, but all tried. Horace Rew's typical injunction to the young, 'You will not be at school in Holy Week, I hope that you join me in church on Monday, Tuesday, Wednesday and Maundy Thursday'.

Tilting the Bucket. A country sport to celebrate the 1953 Coronation. Richard Worsell is getting the bucket contents as he tries to escape a dowsing. Jimmy Monico is on the left

Stan Hobden, who was at 5 Upper Street and later *Bess Barn,* worked for his brother Edward of *Gore Farm* until in the 1950s he won £75, 000 - £2m in millennium money - on the football pools. Residents say that Stan pinned all the begging letters on his front door. He bought a house at Lewes and worked for a milking machine firm until he moved back to *Oak Cottage,* 32 Warren Lane, before joining his daughter Hazel at *Lye Oak.*

Arthur Carter and Edward Sidney White were elected churchwardens in place of the Hardings. Mrs Harding had thought fit to relinquish her post after 21 years of service.

A reviewer considered that The Players' choice of *Haul for the Shore* ridiculed Christian morality and asked whether the degradation of the church can be edifying, educative or even funny. The parts were played by Sidney White (as Jeff Burden), George Worsell, Leslie Stein, Delia Bicks (as an amusing village gossip), Leslie Smith, Rose Dann, Frank Shaw, Beryl Barrand, Gillian Norman, and Fred Bicks, who also produced.

Fred Bicks was now chairman of The Players, with Major Harding president. Sadly, Mrs Bugler who was about to be asked to become Vice-President, died in August 1954 age 83. Born in Scotland, trained in London in music and drama she married a bank manager and they retired to East Dean in 1926. [7]

There was a Whitsun collection for the lay reader, Capt. Horace Rew, amounting to £24 'which I appreciate very much'.

Although he was on holiday the Revd Norman Lycett wrote a letter as usual for the magazine. He concluded, 'I was going to write a brief letter. As usual enthusiasm and devotion to East Dean and Friston have swept me away. They say brevity is the soul of wit: so it is: so that I must be lacking in wisdom, and remain a stupid old man, but nevertheless, ever your affectionate friend and Vicar.'

The BL hosted a conference of local branches and County Chairman at the *Tiger* on 29 June. The secretary was authorised to provide at the expense of the branch 36 brown ale, 24 light ale, with 12 brown ale in reserve, all to be sale or return agreed with Mr Langford, also 60 ham sandwiches @ $3^1/_2$p and 60 cheese sandwiches @ $2^1/_2$p. The secretary was to issue 25 tea tickets to be presented to Café Delphine @ $7^1/_2$p each.

Empire Day celebrations 22 May 1954 on the Memorial Recreation Field. Jane Nash, the retiring Queen, crowns Faith Taylor the new May Queen. Among those sitting on the left are Jennifer Hopper, Carol Hearns, Keith Haffenden, and from the right Jean Richey and Leila Harvey

In August 1954 Alfred Dockerill working from *Cornish Farm* was killed in a classic farming accident when his tractor overturned on him down a slope just above Cophall.

October's WI had a demonstration of modern washing machines by a Hoover representative. Mrs Roberts, who gave the vote of thanks, said she was the joyful possessor of one of these machines and could testify to the abolition of 'Blue Monday' with its boiling copper filling the scullery with steam, and the corrugated rubbing board and the dolly-peg used to beat and mix the clothes.

The Bowling Club AGM with Ernest Cater in the chair reported 30 members and six matches during the season. Mr AP Carter was t, Mr J Mawer s, Mr PJ Budd was captain and the committee: Messrs Symons, Axten, McGlashen, Brown and Balfry.

The BL AGM elected Major-General NC Bannatyne as president in succession to Major Harding. For Remembrance Sunday it was decided that hats would only be removed during the Silence and Last Post.

The Players autumn production *Without the Prince* was the 13th since the war and 'best ever'. Leslie Smith (the Stranger), Sydney Ostler (the Rector inspired by Shakespeare) were supported by Delia and Fred Bicks, Joy Blake, Cecil Dann, Barbara Waight, Sydney White and an excellent set built by Percy Budd, Cecil Dann, Frank Shaw and George Worsell.

The Mayoress of Eastbourne, Mrs Pyle, opened the CMS afternoon sale. She was charmingly presented with a bouquet by young Edward Davies-Gilbert.

Ten members of East Dean's Civil Defence team visited Tangmere RAF station for instruction in rescuing persons from crashed aircraft.

An evening of Variety at the Bardolf Hall produced the comment that it was, 'good indeed to see again the Nigger Minstrel troupe of childhood days with its old-time melodies and clean simple fun of a bygone age'.

On 1 January 1955 Ted and Florrie Flint came to 1 *Cornish Cottages,* built in 1952 and tied with the job at *Cornish Farm.* Mrs Flint recalls, "When we moved here I thought it was Buckingham Palace compared from where we came from". The farm foreman, until Chris Johnson came in 1972, was Tom Bridger, and the other men Ned Bailey, Harold Shaw, Albert

Vine and Frank Parsons. Ted worked as a stacker, thatcher, tractor driver and did all the fencing, gates and flint walls for 27 years until he retired at 65 in 1982. The farm was 600 acres, mainly arable with a few fields let for grazing, so his stacks were sold at Hailsham market. Ted, who had a magnificent war record - Dunkirk, El Alamein, Sicily, Normandy and into Germany - was the escort for the East Dean British Legion standard from 1955 to 1999. [7]

The WI had Mrs SH Penning president, committee Miss Absale, Miss Burness, Mrs Cheal, Miss Davies-Gilbert, Mrs E Goldsmith, Miss Hooper, Mrs Roberts and Mrs Wood.

For The Players' *Bonaventure* tickets were from Mrs Worsell, Estate Office, or Mrs Kennard, *Gara,* Warren Lane. Nora Evans, who was hardly off the stage as Sister Mary, enjoyed splendid support from Rose Dann, Maud Worsell, and Delia Bicks.

The PC had three standing committees: the War Memorial, the Footpaths and Open Spaces and the Village Halls. It took over the Village Hall on 1 March 1952 and acquired the Scout Hut on 1 April 1953, renamed Farrer Hall. [7] ESCC extended the white line down Friston hill; the first white lines at road junctions with the A259 were painted in 1953.

Police Sergeant Turnbull of Eastbourne gave the WI a most interesting account of a policewoman's duties and experiences, with amusing examples of some prisoners including one woman who had spent the last seven Christmases in prison. 'There are now over 2000 WPCs and they are of equal status with policemen except in matters of pay - justified in 1955 since there are certain things a policeman does which a policewoman cannot do'.

1954 Flower and Vegetable Show committee, l-r: Fred Fuller, Harry West, Bill Armiger, Tom Martin, Bob Irons, Frank Martin and Harry Comber

PCC electoral roll of 1953 was 374. Messrs Carter, Meller, White and Budd were the churchwardens. The church had a Sanctuary Guild (responsible for the Sanctuary upkeep) and a Needlework Guild that overhauled the linen.

The PC considered appealing against a County decision to delete a bridleway, but withdrew when found it would cost at least £50 to obtain counsel's opinion.

In July Mr and Mrs Ernest Cater of *The Gables* opened their garden for a meeting of the WI. 'The wonderful weather enabled members and visitors to enjoy to the full the lovely gardens'. After a talk on *Sussex History* and tea on the lawn, members looked round the plants and borders and a Bring and Buy stall manned by Mrs Foord and Mrs Taylor.

The Mother's' Union met in Mrs Harding's garden when 'the weather was quite perfect'. After the report there was a presentation to Mrs Harding, who was retiring after 30 years as enrolling member, this was followed by yet another Bring and Buy stall.

As in the previous year the BL paraded at the petrol station and after an inspection marched to the War Memorial for a short service. 'The sight of some 100 veterans of two world wars with medals sparkling ...was indeed a spectacle to stir the heart.' They went on to the *Tiger* for refreshments, but this time reimbursed by the BL Group treasurer.

Priscilla Hodgson presented a charming programme of song and dance at the Bardolf Hall on 25 June 1955. Elizabeth Worsell and Leila Harvey interpreted their parts well, and a 'great sense of humour was discovered in David Hodgson'.

At the WI Doreen Greenwood gave 'delightful demonstrations of icing a cake, methods of decoration and how to make a Swiss roll, a vol-au-vent, puff pastry and meringues'.

The Parent Teacher Association held a Penny Party at the Farrer Hall. For a penny one had to guess the contents of various bags. The PTA gained by some £3. [6]

Mrs Powell, distributor of the Parish Magazine on The Green, Upper Street and Underhill for over 17 years had to give up and immediately; Mrs White agreed to take over.

Players did Moliere's *Tartuffe* '- in English'. There was some criticism of the sets but the acting was praised. The play came second in the Sussex Drama League's competition.

Harvest Festival gifts were sent to the Bell Hostel for Unmarried Mothers in Eastbourne.

The Bowling Club reported that 1955 had good attendances despite the weather. Chairman Mr E Cater presided, Mr AP Carter, treasurer, reported a balance of £32 and Mr PJ Budd, the captain, said that they had won two and lost four matches.

Miss M Hooper, the new WI president, asked that all members wear name badges and the committee of the WI were wearing their badges as told at the January 1956 meeting - perhaps it was of some help with a membership of 103 and an average attendance of 56.

The first real combine harvester, a Massey Ferguson, was seen in 1954 on the Williams' *Bullock Down Farm,* cutting and threshing at a rate of two acres an hour.
Since then combines have become larger, which goes with more expensive, and are more usually hired with the driver at harvest time

Doug Richey, East Dean's licensed radio ham, stressed that he is permitted to broadcast only outside normal broadcasting hours. Hence his activities could not affect local reception - simple electrical appliances, however, frequently affect both radio and TV sets.

The WI had a talk on milk by Mrs Delany of Eastbourne's Simmons and Cowley's Dairy, who said that under a law of 1954 milk pasteurisation was compulsory to eradicate bovine TB infection. 'Eastbourne's milk comes from 97 farms and is tested for infection, water content, age, and quality of butter-fat. Any unsold milk is made into plastic.'

On 10 February 1956 Charlie Grayson's bike skidded on an icy Friston hill and he chipped a bone in his shoulder. It took a couple of months to heal and as a consequence Charlie closed down the Downland Bakery. He had served the community for close on 35 years; in snow, rain or hail he was to be seen pushing his antique bike almost hidden by gigantic loads fore and aft, for rarely was there room for him as well. No one heard of him taking a holiday and his most endearing quality was his invariable cheerfulness.

The PC heard that the Gilbert Trustees were prepared to sell the cricket pitch to the Council and grant an extension for the playing field of 1 acre to the south and ¼ acre behind the pavilion, altogether just over 4 acres, to allow for the road widening and to conform with the recommendations of the National Playing Fields Association. The north-west corner would be reserved for a children's playground.

The ESCC took over all the Birling Gap Road from 1 April 1955, and during 1956 widened it and completed the making up. The County Surveyor promised that as many trees as possible would be preserved and that the footpath would be placed between the trees and the new road. From the A259 to Birling Manor the road would be called Gilbert's Drive.

The Players presented *See how they Run,* such a hit at the Comedy Theatre, London, in 1945 to provide a most enjoyable evening. Produced by Fred Bicks, William Brown gave an outstanding study of the clergy locum, Rose Dann was distinctly good as the vicarage general factotum, Maude Worsell had a difficult part as Miss Skillon, while Charles Parris, the well-intentioned vicar, was amusing.

Bill Brown of *Conifers,* Warren Lane, came to Friston in 1954. Connected with Scouting for over 50 years, he had been awarded the Meritorious Service Medal, and he supported Renee Wicking when she formed a Guides company in 1955. By February 1956 he was roped in to revive the Scouting activities which had been in abeyance since the war. No disciplinarian, yet he always seemed to have the boys under friendly control. In the June Mary Pilkington, of *Down Ash,* Warren Lane, (Brown Owl), with Mary Hooper, and Rose Dann (Tawny Owl) established a pack of Brownies, that included June Fuller, Margaret Ellingsworth, Doreen Flint, Pat Ticehurst, Sandra Breach, Linda Haffenden and Jennifer Hopper. Reg Dean took over from Bill Brown when he had heart trouble, with Pauline Joslin taking over the cubs in 1958.

Remembrance Day 1957, walking to the church from the War Memorial. The Guides in view are girl with flag Sarah Vine, fourth back clearly seen is Jean Dann, behind Margaret Hearns and to her side Sandra Breach. The girl not in uniform is Carol Hearns, one turning face is Sandra Goldsmith, behind her is Elizabeth Worsell. At end of the wall is Renee Wicking, behind her Rose Dann, and alongside Rosalind Stein and Pat Down

The Scout committee entertained a Troop from a hospital for the disabled in Battersea. Mrs Patience Harding and sister Minnie Davies-Gilbert greeted them at *Birling Manor,* Lady Shawcross sent strawberries and cream, and Kath Cater sent sweets. One of the Battersea scouts gave a speech of thanks and they went back with a bouquet of flowers for the Matron of their hospital. Miss Davies-Gilbert kept in touch and they revisited.

The PCC reported that the strip lighting installed in the Choir was not to everybody's taste; a new gate at the Gilbert's Drive entrance had been provided by Mr A Carter; and the damp courses had been restored at Friston. Thanks were made to Mr and Mrs Tom Martin who opened and closed Friston church daily. Diana Eyre and Helen Servaes presented a silver paten to Friston Church in memory of Gertrude Eyre, Diana's aunt, of *Hilltop Cottage* who first came to *Meadow Cottage* 26 years before her death in September 1955. Diana Eyre reported on the visit of the Queen to Ibadan, Nigeria when Diana was with 20,000 schoolchildren who saw the Queen and the Duke of Edinburgh as they drove around.

The Post Office agreed to provide a posting box at Crowlink.

The new District Nurse, Miss Phyllis Thackeray, initially worked from Bakewell Road, Eastbourne, but moved to *Gore Cottage* in 1953. The 'District Nurse' first began in 1859, and recent Polegate and Downland Villages Nursing Association staff comprised Sisters Chesney, Douglas, Foxwell and Furnival at Polegate, Peck at Arlington, Thackeray East Dean, and Spooner Willingdon. Over the previous year they made 16,000 home visits, held 3,000 clinics, 600 ante- and post-natal visits, apart from Mothercraft and maternity classes.

With a good season behind them and the prospect of a new ground and pavilion the Cricket Club were optimistic about 1956, except that over the last few years the membership had dropped from 225 to 133 (including 27 players). Trophies went to Eric Muggeridge, Fred Fuller and Maurice Haffenden. The total receipts for the year were £155 and the balance was £38. CJ Parris was elected t, G Gregory s and committee WJ Benton, Harry Comber, RE Irons, Harry Sellars, AFT Roberts, Ivan Worsell and Fred Breach.

Fred Fuller played cricket for East Dean over many years, bowling fast-medium. In 1956 East Hoathly were skittled out for 11 runs; and Fred took 6 wickets for 0 runs. "We never eased up if they lost a few wickets." He followed his grandfather and father into the Village Cricket Club. In the decade 1947 to 1956 his performances were phenomenal. He started with a hat trick maiden in his first over bowled in the restoration match of June 1947, and the next year took 150 wickets at 3.8. Every year he played he had similar figures - in 1949 399 runs and 108 wickets; in 1953 466 runs and 115 wickets. The culmination of his career was in 1956 when as captain he led East Dean & Friston to their only Cuckmere Valley League championship, his contribution being 129 wickets.

The Guides Christmas Social 1955. L-R standing: Elizabeth Worsell, Barry Maslen, Sandra Goldsmith, ?, Pat Down, ?, June Fuller, Eileen Goldsmith, Doreen Flint (inclined head), Margaret ?, ?, ?, Margaret Hearns, Tony Schafer (behind), Jean Dann, Katherine Avis (folded arms), Valerie Haffenden, ?, ?, Jean Haffenden, Jenny Hopper. Kneeling: Faith Breach, Renee Wicking (the Captain). Front: Curry twins, Carol Hearns, Pat Hearns, Sandra Breach

At this time East Dean had 1st and 2nd elevens and a colt's team. Brian Strudwick and Eddie Winter were in the Colts as well as the 1st team. The Colts played local prep school teams such as *Chelmsford Hall* (on Larkin's Field), *St Andrew's* and *Neville House* (played near Butt's Barn) and were usually well beaten.

Bill Armiger said that his proudest moment was when his two sons, Peter and Roy Armiger, opened for East Dean against *Chelmsford Hall OB*. Eric Bourner was a tremendous hitter and once knocked a six into Gilbert's Drive, hitting a passing bus.

Hello to you All, opened with Priscilla Hodgson's pupils marching up to the stage at the Bardolf Hall. Valerie Gillam's Wood Nymph was especially good, Anstice Cornford sang riding a cycle round the stage, Maureen Vickery did a pretty dance, and after Elizabeth Korn sang *Don't dilly dally,* the mature members, Rose Dann, Ivy North and Gwen Roberts sang and danced to *Singin' in the Rain.* Linda Ticehurst and June Fuller were good, and David and Ricky Hodgson were a great success - all helping the Scouts and Brownies.

Over 40 members of the WI enjoyed a visit to Downland villages and Glynde Place finishing with tea at Boship Farm. At their August meeting they held a Produce Show.

Agreement had been reached between the bus company and ESCC for a regular bus service along the new Birling Gap road in the summer. The bus fare to Eastbourne in 1957 was 6p. The PC decided to take up with Hailsham RDC about cesspool complaints for

The Fridays and also the one serving the *Tiger.* The PC members were also concerned about warning bathers of the danger of unexploded missiles on the Birling Gap beach.

Twelve members of the Mothers' Union went to Windsor for the day, including a steamer trip and a coach tour of Buckinghamshire.

The Flower Show, held in the new pavilion, instead of the loaned Hollington Boys' Club marquee went ahead with some trepidation after the gales of the previous weekend. It turned out a fine afternoon with record entries and crowds. Mr RE Irons won the allotment holders shield and Tom Martin the bronze medal, Wally Eve also won a certificate. Mrs Medhurst won the cookery medal and Mrs R Fowler a certificate in the home produce class. The auction in James Monico's hands raised £21, the best ever. The cricket club now CVL champions after beating Selmeston went on to beat *Chelmsford Hall* OB by 37 runs.

East Dean Cricket Team, September 1956, the only year they won the Cuckmere Valley League. Back row left to right, Fred Breach, Maurice Haffenden, Bill Truman, Stan Fuller, Keith Saunders. Next row, Eddie Winter, Ivan Worsell, Fred Fuller (capt), Eric Bourner (wkt), Reg Goldsmith. In front, Stan Howes and Brian Strudwick

The Players spent a gala afternoon in the lovely garden of Mr Ernest Cater at *The Gables,* and in the evening saw *Savonia,* a comedy by Lesley Storm at the Devonshire Park.

The Revd Norman Lycett retired at the end of September 1956 after 14 years, recently greatly handicapped by deteriorating eyesight. He had been gassed and captured while a Chaplain in the 1914-18 war and his eyesight was permanently affected. He restarted the magazine after the war as a service to the whole village. Village children would say, "He'd put his nose right up to your face and say, 'What's your name boy?' in a loud voice". He had quite a few worries with both his wife and daughter, and it was for their needs that he could be seen at times waiting for the *Tiger* to open.

Close on 100 people filled the Village Hall to present him with a cheque for £257, photographs of the two churches and a mahogany armchair and leather handbag for Mrs Lycett. Two stories were told. Whenever a vicar saw a devoted, keen church worker bearing down on him he would repeat, *To live above with the Saints we love, That will be bliss and glory. But to live below with the saints we know - Well, that's another story,* and the other was about a priest listening to a shepherd describing his work and saying to him, "You know I'm a shepherd too, but my flock numbers 10,000". The shepherd cogitated for a moment before asking, "How do you manage at lambing?"

His replacement in November was East Dean's 65th priest, the Revd RWB Burns-Cox, ordained 1924. He became vicar of Fletching in 1933 where he remained except for two years as Chaplain to the Forces in the war. He was married with three sons.

At a Confirmation service in September the Rt Revd Bishop Karney used the shepherd's crook last used for this purpose in 1929.

The BL branch had a further benevolent credit of £10, with vouchers for traders, rent and travel. Regulations had been tightened and vouchers now needed a medical certificate in cases of sickness. The Smoking Concert held on 20 July had not been a success, but the Jumble Sale and Old People's Outing to Chailey had gone well. Mr W Axten did the accounts. Tickets for the Albert Hall Remembrance Festival went to J Eve and H Goodman. L Miller had been granted a Prince of Wales' pension and Ben Carter had a benevolent payment of £1.45. Any 100% disabled soldier now had a pension of £4.25 per week, almost double what it had been ten years before. Thanks to the efforts of H Goodman and C Vine another 20 members had joined, bringing the membership to 98, for which the branch was awarded the Dacre trophy for the greatest increase in membership.

Young People's Service and Sunday School, 1956. L-R Back (zigzag) row: Jane Nash, Julia Worsell, Richard Worsell, Faith Taylor, Sheila Vine, Shirley Pownall, John Dann, Valerie Haffenden, Elizabeth Worsell. Middle zig-zag row: Margaret Ellingsworth, Barry Maslen, Sandra Goldsmith, Jennifer Hopper, Dennis Plaice, Valerie Gillam, Leila Harvey, Jean Dann, Derek Vine, Pat Hearns, and Faith Breach. Next row: Sandra Breach (no relation to Faith), Linda Ticehurst, Lita Curry, Angela Gillam, Jean Richey, Robin Coles, Julia Rust with June Fuller (nearest edge). Front row: Tony Richey, Wendy Haffenden, Linda Plaice, Graham Haffenden [no relation to] Clifford Haffenden, Ian Fears, ?, Billy Fuller, Christine Fears

The BL gave support to a Fete in aid of the Memorial Playing Field, this meant they manned a *Bowling for the Pig* side show and took part in the tug-of-war.

The PC reported that 'it was not possible to obviate the danger to pedestrians at the main road crossing from the Warren Lane footpath.' In practice, people didn't use it any longer.

The Players autumn production was *But Once a Year,* a Christmas comedy. It was an outstanding success. Linn Tolhurst was in her element, and there was a masterly performance from James Monico.

The Christmas Fair of the East Dean & Friston Scouts and Guides was opened by Her Grace Mary Duchess of Devonshire in the Bardolf Hall. Mrs Gwendiline Pyle won a raffle and the prize was a tea set donated by HRH Princess Margaret of Clarence House, with a card to say so. Mrs Pyle wasn't there as she was giving birth.

At the institution and induction of the Revd RW Burns-Cox some 230 people were crammed into an East Dean church that seated 120. The Service was conducted by the Bishop of Lewes, the Rt Revd Geoffrey Warde (acting for Dr George Bell, Lord Bishop of Chichester), with the Archdeacon of Hastings, the Ven. Canon Guy Mayfield. [4]

William West died at 96 in 1957. A shepherd, he came to East Dean from Hastings in 1892, caring for the flocks of Mr Russell of *Gore Farm* and Mr Gorringe of *Foxhole Farm*. Father of Mrs Markquick, Mrs Comber and Harry West, he never learnt to read or write.

The Summer Fete held in August made £120, it was spent in fencing the new recreation ground. Herbert Down was chairman of the management committee.

The Players production of *Dear Charles* was criticised as, 'an English version of a French play which, while jeering at marriage, lauded prostitution and illegitimacy and was an affront to any decent Englishman.'[2] In reply Fred Bicks wrote, 'drama reflects life but should not preach, and the professional adjudicator gave the play a high mark; there is nothing about prostitution in the play; who are those who have been shocked? The views expressed are not representative of the community'.

The PC, referring to a decision of the original War Memorial committee who, in 1946 found it impractical to enlarge the present Village hall due to building regulations, decided that it could be that the time was now more suitable. Discussion centred on resident apathy, for when a meeting was called to approve a proposal only three ratepayers turned up.

The WI resolved that only residents of East Dean and Friston could be members.

The seat at Flagstaff Brow was thrown over the 150ft cliff, so there was an Appeal for a new one.

The BL had a bugler for the Remembrance Service, previously they had a recording.

The Mothers' Union Christmas party had a skiffle group of Cecil and John Dann, Ray Kemp and Derek Vine complete with straw hats. Some Mothers' Union meetings were to be held in the evenings so that mothers with young children could share in the activities.

Mrs Burns-Cox, who had taken over from Miss Penford, gave a delightful Christmas Party for the Infants' Sunday School.

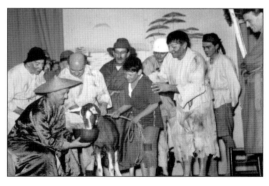

In *The Teahouse of the August Moon* of 1958 James Monico was splendid as Sakini, Leslie Smith showed verve and assurance, Patricia Wicking was to be congratulated, and Fred Bicks was at his best - his phone conversations being absolutely realistic, and his settings a delight. Good support came from Sylvia Tompsett, Leslie Cumberland and Charles Parris. The backroom boys, Jolyon, George and Frank, got a jeep on and off the 10ft stage

When Plough Sunday 1958 was celebrated Mr & Mrs Williams of *Bullock Down Farm* lent the plough and it was prepared by Capt. Norman Davies. The weather was kind and the church was filled despite some regulars being away with influenza. Vicar arranged a visit by patients of Gifford House - a home for severely wounded ex-servicemen.

Thanks to Howard Greenwood and the SE Electricity Board, an electricity 'short' at East Dean church was dealt with promptly so that heating and lighting was available for Sunday worship. 'The nationalised industry provided excellent service.'

Ronnie Hall, the organist, was given a cheque for £50 at the PCC. In April 1926 he had volunteered to play the new organ at East Dean for six months and was to go on for 35 years. He said. "It has been a privilege and a joy".

On 9 March 1958 the milk float was trapped by snow drifts on the top of East Dean hill and Leslie Cumberland, the milkman, walked into East Dean and back to Eastbourne to obtain help. After bulldozers had cleared the way, Charlie Vine, Bill Strudwick, George Worsell, Cecil Dann and Edward Winter willingly expedited the milk delivery.

The daffodils in Friston churchyard were the gift of Mrs May Burgess (of 24 Warren Lane) in autumn 1957. Friston's Book of Remembrance was the gift of Mrs Feneley, the names were printed in by Miss Servaes, the oak bracket was made by Charles Meller and the book itself was made at Sam Hodgson's leather works in Eastbourne.

At the East Sussex Quarter sessions in Lewes one of the light-fingered fraternity was given two years as a guest of Her Majesty for breaking and entering two houses in The Ridgeway. Pc Soffner observed a car in The Ridgeway which he did not recognise and noted the number. Later when thefts were reported, the number Pc Soffner had noted was flashed across the land and a constable was waiting at a London garage when the perpetrator brought in the hired car. Pc Soffner was commended by the Chairman of the Sessions, none other than the Rt Hon. Lord Denning.

Frank Ticehurst with Jim Wicking and the Bonfire Society float. Alf Pelling said, "I got roped into the Bonfire Society, along with Jim and Bert Goldsmith. In 1958 and 59 we entered the Eastbourne Carnival with a horse-drawn float. There was much talk about space travel at the time, so Arthur Raylor had the idea of having rockets on the float and we won second prize"

The Recreation Ground conveyance was formally completed on 30 May 1958. The final cost was £2989, made up of purchase of ground £1037. Transport and re-erection of 'new' second-hand pavilion £829; water supply, lighting, lavatories £752; chairs and fittings £107. Equipment for the cricket ground £142, and children's playground £122. This was met by: donations of £327, Fete £100, loans £600, grants £803, and £1,159 rates contributions over four years. According to Rex Roberts, "The PC are very good and even in 2001 only charge £550 a year to keep it mowed, which works out at under £50 a match, less than many clubs pay. Of course, it used to be mown by sheep."

Pauline Joslin first visited East Dean in 1950 with Peter Joslin. "We walked over to Cophall to meet Mrs Sworder, then to the *Tiger* for a drink on The Green, and onto Birling Gap where I thought it was heaven." She married Peter in 1954, and they came to Cophall four years afterwards. "We rented Cophall from Mrs Sworder in 1958; eventually buying it from her. She was happy to sell for she had no family."

Quite a sick parade in the villages: Mrs Lidiard fell and broke an arm and a leg; two sons of the Parris's were in a road accident, one broke his knee cap, the other a thigh bone. Mrs Rew had a nose bleed and Mrs Sworder had been ill.

Jimmy Monico and Beryl Barrand moved to live in Eastbourne after marriage so he was replaced on the PC by GC Andrews of *Braeside,* 1 The Brow. The Barrands came to East Dean in 1952 and Mr Barrand trained the choir until the family left for Brighton in 1956.

The East Dean Scouts raised nearly £16 in their 'Bob-A-Job' week. Mrs Harding opened Birling Manor garden for The Friends of the Eastbourne Hospitals.

The lay-by for Eastbourne-bound buses was built at the top of Friston hill.

Charles Fears died on his 93rd birthday. Born at Wilmington in 1865, was gardener in service of the Gwynne family, subsequently moved to *Bullock Down Farm,* and in 1912 became bailiff of Weston's farm, or *New House Farm.* Founder member of the Bowling Club, and a member of the Cricket Club, he sang in the church choirs and with his wife, a member of East Dean's PCC when first constituted in 1922. Mrs Fears had died in 1937.

The AGM of the Scouts and Guides showed films of Scouting activities. Mrs M Pilkington, Miss Winter, Mrs Fuller and Mrs R Haffenden resigned from the committee and were replaced by Mrs Nash, Mrs D Plaice, Mrs Vine and Mr Loseby.

George Cheal became caretaker of the halls, and Fred Bicks resigned as chairman of the Players - he had served for five years, Mrs Stein elected for 1958.

In 1957 the Harvest Festivals were on consecutive Sundays at East Dean and Friston churches, but in 1958 the Harvest Festival was at both churches on the same Sunday, one in the morning and the other in the evening..

The Best Kept Village Garden award went to the Vicarage, of course, with Mr Flint's garden second and Mr Jenner's third. The Flower Show was lucky to have a fine day and over 600 paid to see the 266 exhibits. Tom Martin's zinnias were particularly praised, as was Mrs R Fowler's raspberry jam. The most successful exhibitor was Ted Flint, and other winners included Eric Bourner, Mrs Maloney, Wally Eve, and Mrs N Comber. Jimmy Monico had hard work at the auction, but East Dean won the match with Chelmsford Hall OB who reached only 82, their lowest score in the series. Surplus on the day was £14.

Rodney Pettman of Downs View Lane came second in the National Rifle Association's Schools' Day at Bisley.

Other East Dean children proved their ability at the Seaford County School's Speech Day. George Fuller won a certificate, Faith Taylor received the hockey trophy, Rosemary Cheal won a form prize, and Ruth Hopper and Dolores Curry won progress prizes.

At the BL AGM the Revd RM Burns-Cox was now Chaplain. Mr Goodman's health did not permit him to continue as chairman and Lt-Col Simmons agreed to take over. Mrs Soffner complained about a costume she bought at the Jumble Sale. The treasurer reported that they had paid out more than they had received from the only source of income - the Jumble Sale, so it was decided to ask Mr WS Clifford and Cmdr JC Smith to consider raising funds by means of a Village Fete on the Village Green and a Derby Sweep.

When the vicar appealed for a wireless set for an old age pensioner for Christmas, so many were offered that Mr Greenwood was able to give Rachel Patching a beautiful set.

The church was so full for a Remembrance Day Service that people were sitting on the floor of the nave and some had to be turned away. The collection of £23 was a record.

There were now 16 Scouts and Cubs and 25 Guides and Brownies. They had done well and were financially strong, but needed more leaders.

The Angling Club reported a successful season. Mrs Jessie Eve landed a 9lb bass, Geoff Nash a 15lb Conger eel, and Richard Worsell with David Winter fishing from their dingy hooked a few sole, the first flat fish at the Gap for years.

Pc Max Soffner, who claimed a 100% success rate, was thanked by the PC where the chairman described him as fair and honest, and wished him every happiness in retirement after ten years at East Dean. Pc Derek Bashford from Crowborough succeeded him.

Mr & Mrs Ray Kemp offered a photograph of Jesse Kemp, father of Ray, the last wheelwright in the village, for the Farrer Hall to go with the last blacksmith picture.

The WI now had 121 members with an average attendance of 69. President Miss Hooper was succeeded by Miss Burness, with a committee of Mrs Bicks, Mrs Butlin, Miss Butler, Mrs Dietrich, Mrs Fyfield, Mrs Headland, Miss Jenkins, and Mrs Morgan. Miss Creighton and Miss Shipton were welcomed as new members. Before Christmas the WI sent cards to patients at Hellingly Hospital, and gifts for St Mary's Hospital patients.

Among the events in May 1958, Mr Ernest Cater opened *The Gables* garden, in aid of the Friends of the Eastbourne Hospitals; Mrs David Rice spoke to the Mothers' Union on Marriage Guidance; Horace Rew's Church Extension Appeal for A River of Bobs, had 11,000 shillings; Alexander Grant van Someren died aged 76; The Revd and Mrs Lycett had their Golden Wedding; and the Local Fencing Club held a meeting in the Village Hall, however, the burning down of Mrs Scott's *Thatched Cottage* was a big moment of 1958. [7]

Mr and Mrs Shore departed as Verger and cleaner at East Dean to look after a children's home; they had fostered children in East Dean producing wonderful changes. Mr and Mrs Armiger replaced them. Wally Eve appointed East Dean churchyard attendant and Charlie Vine at Friston. Mrs Kathleen Doherty gave Altar linen for Friston church in memory of her brother who died just as he was about to take up residence at *Friston Court.*

In 1959 the Scouts and Guides presented *Show Time.* With Robin Nash, John Cheal, Rudolf Pownall and Oliver Cater as pirates, Leila Harvey as the laughing policeman, the Beachcombers skiffle group, rousing choruses, and George Worsell at the piano it was a good show. There was a good profit too of £21.

The Happy Prisoner, The Players 1959 production was up to their usual standard. Jolyon Fyfield, Frank Shaw, Richard Worsell and John Dann built the set; Fred Bicks painted it, and Delia (in wedding dress) showed her versatility as Violet North. Gwen Roberts (in white) was effective and Ray Trickett (centre back) acquitted himself well. Also in back row (left) Leslie Cumberland, Julia Worsell, and (right) Jack Roberts. Front, Linn Tolhurst, Arthur Perry and Rosalind Stein took the minor parts

Cricket club officers were, Mr Hall p, CJ Parris t, WG Rowland, IJ Worsell c, Cecil Dann s, Fred Breach (Saturday capt.) Rex Roberts (Sunday capt.), committee Mrs Eric Bourner, Maurice Chappell, Bob Harvey, Ronald Hughes and Hugh Winter.

The Guides and Brownies had a Thinking Day on 22 February, the birthday of their founder, and almost their own third birthday and received a pennant. Later in the year the Scouts and Guides celebrated the 50th anniversary of Scouting.

The 1959 Parish Council elections were for an increased number of councillors - five for Friston and nine East Dean. [Appendix 5] W Sidney Ostler decided to retire as Clerk to the PC. In post since 1947, he said lawyer Guy Smart had talked him into it. He had been in the Inland Revenue before the war.

Several members of the WI were missing from the March 1959 meeting owing to flu, and the attendance at the AGM of the local UNA was also not as large as expected.

Mrs Isabel Gibbons died at *Somorlease.* She and her husband were hoteliers and opened Gibby's Tea Rooms in 1933. He died in 1946 but she continued until 1949.

The Players AGM decided that the half guinea [52^1/$_2$p] members were entitled to reserved seats to the value of 6/- [30p] each year. Other members paid 2/6d [12^1/$_2$p] a year.

Another Evening of Music and Drama by Hilda Carter blended serious and humorous items. Scenes from *The School for Scandal, Godstone Nunnery* and *Henry VIII* were on the heavy side, but admirably portrayed. Light-hearted monologues by Heather Davis and Gwen Roberts, duets by Mr Barrand and his daughter Beryl Monico accompanied by Winifred Barrand helped to raise £15 for the Church Appeal Fund.

Fewer entries were received in the WI Produce Show. Mrs Headland won the most points, the outstanding exhibit was Maude Worsell's Fancy Cake. Delia Bicks won the Fruit Cake competition and Doreen Greenwood was awarded a special prize.

The BL ran a successful Jumble Sale, and in the Derby Sweepstake locals won the top prizes: Capt H Rew the first prize of £14, CA Dann the second and RB Mundy the third.

The Fete was fixed for 4 July so as not to clash with the Eastbourne Show on 27 June. A beautiful day and a charming official opening by Miss Vera Mckechnie of BBC Children's TV. There were many stalls and sideshows, but the Archery and Fencing displays were decidedly popular. Another BBC personality, Miss Gladys Young, distributed the prizes, except for the draw when the number drawn was 88 when only 84 tickets had been sold. Even so, the Parish Council benefited by £105 towards playground equipment.

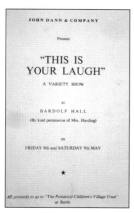

In May (left) John Dann and his company put on *This is Your Laugh* and the large audiences were well satisfied. The song and dance of Pat Wicking, songs of Daisy Place, and Roddy White's impressions brought the house down. A sketch by Fred Bicks and Charles Parris, the 'gay dancing' of Jean Dann, the magic of Alan Hughes, Leslie Cumberland as compére, and the antics of David and Ricky Hodgson made up a side-splitting evening and raised £22 for the Pestalozzi Children's Village Trust. (Right) Lady Terriss-Hicks sent signed copies of her autobiography for sale at the show *1898 and All That* also at the Bardolf Hall in September

The Halls committee of the PC submitted a report on schemes for a new Village Hall, the subject of which had been raised spasmodically since the 1920s. Some 83 residents were present at a meeting in July 1959 to consider the question of a new Village Hall. The PC clerk said there were three ways to provide a new hall:

1. The Parish Council manages the site with a lump sum grant of 30% from the County Council, the remaining 70% by loans payable over 30 years which could be met by hiring charges, any deficiency being a charge on the parish.

2. A Trust Deed is prepared under the Acts with Custodial Trustees who are the legal owners and Managing Trustees who are representatives of the village organisations. Under this scheme 33% of the cost comes from the Ministry of Education and the rest to be raised by the Trustees.

3. A hall combined with a new Village School.

It was estimated that a hall seating 200 would cost £6,000 and costs of £520 a year would necessitate an income of at least £10 a week, which would be impossible without restricting the use of the Village and Farrer halls.

The Scout Camp was at Greatstone-on-Sea, with Bill Brown as Scoutmaster. The troop of R Nash, B Maslen, D Vine, R Pownall, G Gillam and R Harvey had wonderful weather with highlights of sea bathing, visits to Lydd aerodrome and to Dungeness lighthouse.

The BL stated that they would not make any recommendations to the public meeting about a new hall on 22 September. This second public meeting decided that the Trust Deed method would be too expensive, and that a Parish Council-owned hall be adopted at a maximum cost of £6,000, on a central site and that the public be informed that hire charges will increase by two or three times. The subsequent poll showed only 64 votes in favour of a new hall and 308 against, so the PC resolved to take no action.

After only 11 inches of rain from January to September 1959, compared with 25 over the same period in 1958, one old resident, when asked for something from his garden for the Harvest Festival, replied, "I can't help, the long dry spell has washed out my garden". The total for 1959 was a near average 26.5 inches [650mm], two-thirds in the last three months.

Christmas presents distributed in Upper Street by *Damsel* and *Diamond* with Santa Jim Wicking and Les Ticehurst from Bonfire Society to Dorothy Dickens at 4 Upper Street *c*.1959

Mr H 'Jack' Goodman was awarded life membership of the BL branch in recognition of his services, and the BL Old Folk's Outing to Cranbrook on 3 September was a success.

The Players put on *The Prodigious Snob*. It was 'a jolly good show' with James Monico, Sylvia Tompsett, Gwen Roberts and Delia Bicks playing with their accustomed skill, and not one misfit in the cast of 29; they did not, however, reach the final of the Drama Festival.

October 1959 saw the inaugural meeting of the Residents' Association [RA]. [12]

On General Election day 1959, the Brownies had a half-day out at Wannock Tea Gardens. They saw bananas and oranges growing, watched the rabbits and tropical birds, and enjoyed the Model Village which could be set in motion by turning a handle.

A Christmas Fayre was held in the Bardolf Hall to gather money for the Church Extension Appeal. A total of £1,032 was raised, meaning that the Appeal had reached half way to £10,000. On the other hand the Parish Magazine costs rose to over £400 a year.

In the 1960 New Year's honours a knighthood was conferred on Col RF Burnand of *Friston Corner,* 3 Mill Close. He was a Senior Master of the Queen's Bench Division.

The first phase of rebuilding East Dean church began on 4 January 1960 with removal of the old organ. In the meantime a piano was used. The whole work was due to be completed before 10 April. [4]

The Goldsmiths kept their horses in the Horsefield on retirement. Eileen Goldsmith said, "They were *Duke, Diamond* and *Damsel.* Got them from the old farm at Chiddingly. *Duke* had ended his days some years before *Diamond* died in January 1960 leaving only *Damsel,* who was 24 on 29 May, and who died the next year." The Goldsmith's cows in 1960 consisted of 19 Tuberculin-Tested Ayrshires all between 3 and 6 years, with a daily yield of 50 gallons which went to Eastbourne. [7]

Tom Martin who had opened and locked the church door at Friston for many years felt obliged to give up and was replaced by Harry Sellars.

A special Southdown bus was agreed from Seaford to the Eastbourne hospitals, at visiting times on Tuesdays, with a stop at East Dean.

ED & F villages were collecting silver paper and milk tops to provide a guide dog for a blind person. It took 5^1/$_2$ tons to pay for the training, but during 1960 the villages collected over 6cwt [302 kg], which meant £21 to the Guide Dogs for the Blind.

The WI had resorted to two meetings, held in the Village Hall and the Farrer Hall on consecutive days, one presided over by Miss Burness and the other by Mrs Headland. The Village Hall heard a talk on *Guide Dogs* and the other was on *Painting on China.*

At the Bowls Club Mr Budd, captain for seven years, stood down and NH Symons was elected in his place. In appreciation Mr Budd was elected the first president.

In February 1960 The Players presented *As Long As They're Happy,* and every seat was sold. 'The acting of (back row L-R) Leslie Stein, Arthur Perry, Pat Wicking, Jack Roberts and Rose Dann, was of the highest order'. Faith Taylor (next to Rose) and Jo Satchell (front R) had difficult roles, but the bouquets must go to Fred Bicks (centre) who produced the show and played the part of the father to perfection. Heather Anderson, front L, Leslie Cumberland and Joan Nash had the minor roles

The PC decided that old Parish records should be sent to the County Archives at Lewes. Members were informed that Hailsham RDC had given approval for eight flats and garages at the junction of Michel Dene Road and Wenthill Close, but had rejected the request for a hotel at Friston. The charges for the Village halls would remain unchanged. Household Rates were reduced from 8d to 4d in the £.

Cecil Dann presented a picture of his father William Mark Dann, who had recently died, for display in the Farrer Hall. It shows him working an old Sussex plough.

PC Derek Bashford became a Sergeant, meaning that he left East Dean on 14 May after barely 18 months. His replacement was Pc D Newton, an ex-Navy man from Crowborough.

Owing to inclement weather the joint meeting of the two WI sections was held in the Bardolf Hall instead of the gardens of *Birling Manor.* Dr Ronnie Maggs talked on the changing pattern of care for the mentally sick.

In July 1960 the Children's Playground was opened by Mrs Ostler. The total cost was

£3,300, fully paid apart from a small loan which would be paid by 1962. The May Queen, Leila Harvey, presented the opener with a bouquet. The May Queen led the way to the slide followed by a succession of children who returned to the pavilion for soft drinks and lollies.

The Flower Show had a day of brilliant sunshine. Visited by 475 people, the displays were a high standard. Mrs Bourner ran the teas and Jimmy Monico conducted the auction.

Another Midnight Steeplechase was organised in August 1960 by Sylvia Davies-Gilbert of Herstmonceux. The floodlit jumps and fairy lights in the Manor gardens, put up by George Worsell, Cecil Dann and Bert Foord, 'made a gay spectacle'. Of the four races with twelve jumps, Lucy Davies-Gilbert on *Sheila* won the *Teddy Bear Scamper Stakes,* the Hunt race was won by *Golden Sunbeam,* and both The Ladies, and The Midnight Steeplechases were won by *Libkin.* A barbecued ox enabled the dancers to go on to 0330h. [5]

Whist Drives were held every Wednesday throughout the winter. The profits were shared between the Mothers' Union, the WI, BL, Cricket Club, Football Club, Stoolball Club, Parent-Teacher Association and the Scouts.

CMS Day on 1 November had talks on a *New Medical Venture* in Nepal in the morning and *Impressions of Modern Japan* in the afternoon. The various stalls raised £119.

The PC was elected unopposed. A speed limit on Friston hill was again discussed. The County Surveyor stated that while the volume of traffic had increased, conditions had not changed since 1953, and records showed that excessive speed was not the cause of the eleven accidents over the past two years. The PC decided to send all the correspondence on the speed of vehicles through the village to the MP.

Many functions were held for the church extension. Brothers Herbert Down of *Gillridge,* The Ridgeway, and Harold Down, opposite in *Westholme,* opened their gardens. [4]

The PC congratulated Princess Margaret on marriage to Mr Anthony Armstrong-Jones.

The Players offering *The House by the Lake* was 'an excellent production of a poor play. The scene where Mr Howard (Ray Trickett) broke through the window to seize the weapon from Janet (Gwen Roberts) being especially well done'.

With the heavy rainfall of 10 and 11 August the Horsefield pond overflowed and seeped into an adjoining property, the County Surveyor said the only way to stop flooding of Mr King's *Garden Cottage* was to extend the pond.

A dog chased a lamb over the cliff at Bailey's Brow.

Ethel Bridge died aged 79. In 1920s Frank and Ethel Bridge had stayed at *Crowlink Farm* and later at *Old Vicarage Cottage.* They built a weekend cottage *Friston Field,* the first house to be built along Old Willingdon Road. A Nurse Baldock came in 1938 to nurse Frank and when in 1941 her home in Eastbourne was bombed she and her three children were offered a home at *Friston Field.* It is said Miss Vass and Mrs Bridge were like sisters.

At the BL AGM Capt Lidiard addressed members and was greeted with acclamation when he lashed the 'ban the bomb' advocates. "You and I fought in two wars and our comrades died in two wars so that our country may be safe. The BL is determined that there shall be some form of disarmament, but not abandoning friends and casting yourself at the mercy of your enemies". Mrs I Smith of *Foxwold Cottage,* Deneside organised Poppy Day.

East Dean Players presented *The Farmer's Wife* in November. With Fred Bick's usual genius for making the stage appear twice the actual depth, a first-class night's entertainment was provided. Phil Satchell and Delia Bicks gave excellent performances

The Scouts held an Open Night at the Village Hall, when 50 attended. Robin Nash gave an illustrated account of their Normandy Camping holiday (despite the car's clutch packing up they got home safely), and a colour film of the year's happenings was shown.

The Vicar arranged for young members of the villages who are at present away to read a lesson when they happened to be in the village. Alan Hughes studying in London,

William Shawcross at Eton, and Graeme Walker at Marlborough, all took part.

In January 1961 Ivan Worsell, George Worsell, and Cecil Dann were presented with watches by the village for their cliff rescue in September 1960. [5] On 24 March they received the Queen's Commendation for brave conduct from the Minister of Transport.

The football club played 14 matches in the season and won all - their best record. They led the Hailsham League Division II. Greatly helped by coaching from 'Taffy' Jones of Eastbourne United Colin Wicking, captain, and Malcolm Johnson were the leading scorers.

The Register of Electors in 1961 reached exactly 1000 names (787 at East Dean). In 1949 there had been 653 (460 East Dean).

Donors to the Parish Magazine included: 'Mr & Mrs Baird, Mr & Mrs Borer, Mrs HG Brown, Miss Brucesmith, Mrs Butcher, Miss Curryer, Mr & Mrs Doherty, Mr & Mrs Doxat-Pratt, Mrs Edmonstone, Mr & Mrs Fisher, Miss Grose, Mrs Holter, Mr & Mrs Horton, Mrs Jones, Miss Matthews, Mr & Mrs Parrish, Mr & Mrs Peet, Mr & Mrs Pelecanos, Mr & Mrs L Pyle, Mrs Simpson, Mrs Stevenson, Miss Tanner, Mr & Mrs JE Taylor, Miss Umfreville, Mrs van Someren and Mrs Ward'.

The football regulars Jim Cumming, Mike Cumming, Brian Johnson, Malcolm Johnson, Jim Markwick, Brian Strudwick, Colin Wicking, Dave Wicking, Ron Wicking and Hugh Winter, had so enjoyed playing that they decided to form a cricket 'Tiger' club of their own to play non-league cricket on the Horsefield in the summer - minding the cowpats

By 1959 the vicar had decided to enlarge East Dean church. The church seated 120 and on Easter Day there were 162 communicants with a total of 301 for the day. After discussion about inserting a gallery the agreed way ahead was to place the organ in an organ loft providing three extra pews where it had stood, and to extend the church 6m [20ft] westward to give in all an additional 75 seats to bring the total to some 200.

Shortly after Leslie and Kay Ketcher came to East Dean in 1958 fund raising was in progress for this extension. "Beforehand, on festive occasions, you had to be there early if you wanted a seat, and I recall having to sit on the floor of the aisle. We gave a donation, had sales to raise the money and the Hon. Betty Tatum would go to her family business in Stoke and bring back export reject pottery to augment the sales."

Phil Dean said, "The first Sunday we attended East Dean church it was full and so we turned away only to run into the Revd Burns-Cox, who said you must not leave, and put us in the choir stalls." Phil Dean went on, "Everyone, all denominations, was invited to the church to inspect the plans, and forward their suggestions. All the money was raised within the village and the church was never closed during the building work."

The estimated amount needed for the extension was £10,000, so 200,000 shillings was the number required. In April 1959 there was a slide show of holiday photographs at the Farrer Hall in aid of the church extension fund. The hall was filled to capacity, even though the fund-raising campaign had not commenced. In May 1959 Horace Rew started a 'Glad Givers' collection for 100,000 shillings. Maths was not his strong point, but it is assumed he realised that, psychologically, it's best to ask for small amounts and build up. The response was incredible. The Tompsetts at the Corner Stores, the Caters of the Service Station, the Browns at *Conifers,* Warren Lane, the Hopkins of Weller's Stores, Miss Prince of Delphine's Café and the Walkers of *Friston Court* all agreed to act as collectors.

A Jumble Sale by Mrs G Foord and Mrs N Cheal raised £25. Mrs Hilda Carter arranged

An Evening of Music and Drama. Among those assisting her were Heather Davies, Sandra Goldsmith, Barry Maslen, Beryl Monico, Gwen Roberts, Reginald Smith, Leslie Stein, Linn Tolhurst, Sylvia Tompsett and Gwendolen Wynne. After a talk with Horace Rew and the Vicar, Harold and Ethel Brassley said they would meet the cost of the windows in the extension (£1250). They left money to the church to ensure that flowers would be placed on their windows and on their grave, causing a few problems, although anyone living away could send £50 towards upkeep of the churchyard with special attention to a named grave.

In 1960 a Leap Year Market was in aid of the Appeal. Norman Davies, who was giving up driving, donated his 10-year-old Morris Oxford car, with only 18,000 on the clock. Mr Herbert Down gave £500 in shares. In nine months £6,500 had been raised towards the target of £10,500. Sure enough, when the first 100,000 shillings was reached Horace asked for a second 100,000. By Easter 1960 Horace had 128,000 shillings, and in late 1960 the name was changed to 'The Last Lap Appeal' because the work had overrun.

Among the shows for the last 100,000 shillings were a *1920 Roundabout* and films of *The Titfield Thunderbolt* and Charlie Chaplin's *Shoulder Arms.* The Queen supported the Appeal and sent a gift for sale at the 1960 Christmas Fayre which realised £730. Over 21 months the 1000-strong parish raised over £12,000 (about £¹/₂m in millennium money) for the church extension, without reducing the amounts given to other Appeals.

The west wall of 1882/5 was removed and replaced by a perpendicular-type arch across which at gallery level was the new organ loft, the console being just outside the Chancel. The Vicar insisted that the extended walls were of the same thickness as the existing, and that the font was to be moved to the new west end. [4]

Other building work went ahead, *Forge Cottage* was in the process of restoration and remedying structural defects. By 1962 it had taken on a new lease of life. Alan Hughes, with help, renovated the cottage so that it looked a village blacksmith's abode, but inside is a spacious, modern home. Ships' timbers and oars were discovered serving as rafters. In the west wing a blocked-up window was found and this formed the window of a new bedroom to overlook the road and the Downs. The vaulted cellar, of chalk blocks, was remarkably well preserved. The tandem privy, with side-by-side seats, was made into a summerhouse.

Sanitary measures were also needed when a cesspool overflowed across the public footpath on the Village Green to many complaints and calls for a mains drainage system.

At the Vestry and PCC meeting in March Mr Meller agreed to continue as Churchwarden at Friston, but Mr Carter resigned as churchwarden at East Dean, Cmdr RJ Smith succeeded him. Messrs White and Budd continued. There were 75 on the roll. The magazine printing costs rose by £120 and needed an advance of £80 from church funds.

The Players staged the one-act play *In the Draught* at the Bardolf Hall. The play had won them an award at the Eastbourne Festival and the 96 members who attended the evening enjoyed the invitation.

About this time the Goodman's took over the shop on the corner when the Tompsett's sold out with the Post Office returning to Weller's on The Green.

Cricket awards in 1960: batting I Goldsmith, bowling M Wear, and fielding R Armiger.

The WI now had separate meetings both chaired by Miss Burness. In the Farrer Hall Cmdr Smith gave a talk on *The Metropolitan Police* in which he had served for 43 years.

At a WI meeting members of the tapestry class showed their 18 hassock covers for the church in different shades of blue and gold; there were now over 40 kneelers.

The Grayson's daughter Lorna, who married at East Dean in 1945, came back on a visit. She had lived in Canada for the past 15 years.

Phil Satchell produced The Players' *The Sacred Flame* which fully lived up to their reputation. Ray Trickett dominated the first act, well supported by Jo Satchell, and another outstanding performance was given by Meg Horton.

Items discussed by the PC included obstruction by parked vehicles in Upper Street, the question of a site for a new Village Hall (for which a sub-committee was appointed) and there was appreciation of the new bulbs planted on the Lower Street bank. [7] The PC decided to erect a bus shelter at the Gore.

Doug Richey, the village HAM, heard a Polish HAM requesting a drug for a relative with leukaemia. With the cooperation of the Police and the local hospital the drug was flown to Warsaw and Doug received a note of thanks from Poland.

Local Scouts entertained Scouts of the St John's Hospital, Battersea at Birling Manor. They were welcomed by Mrs Harding and Miss Davies-Gilbert with a strawberries and cream tea and home made cakes. A drive around the estate completed a wonderful day out.

For the WI May meeting at the Bardolf Hall the Drama and Music Group gave *Women's Ward*. On left l-r: Beryl Monico (nurse), Joan Nash, Dorothy Snell, Jenny Wynn (other nurse). Right l-r: Ethel Kemp, Rose Dann (nurse bending), Joan Nash, Beryl Monico (nurse bending), Dorothy Snell. Joan Nash says it was fun. "I played a patient with a fractured leg in the play and one of my sons had recently broken his leg but finished with his plaster so I used it in the play." The choir under Mrs Chenevix-Trench sang selections from Brahms *Songs of Love*

The Village Fete was held on Saturday, 5 August, organised by the PC in aid of King George's Jubilee Trust and the War Memorial Fund. The drizzle did not dampen the laughter at Cyril Fletcher's opening remarks. The Players gave an excerpt, the crowds queued to spend their money and the Brownies collected the litter. The most exciting moment was when the pig (of the British Legion's Bowling for a Pig alley) escaped and reached the road before recapture. The pig, from *Tree Tops Farm* Langney, had cost £5.

Derrick Pyle went to *Ridge House* as gardener in 1961. Mrs Phyllis Shaw was the widow of a Captain RN. Her housekeeper was Ruby Hutchison who, it was discovered only many years afterwards, was the mother of three children. In 1973 Derrick started at the Post Office. After a heart attack in 1978 he moved to the Sorting Office in Eastbourne until retirement in 1984. Mrs Pyle worked for Mrs Doxat-Pratt, and Cmdr and Mrs Moss.

The 1961 Flower Show went with a swing although not so well supported, especially in the Home Produce Section. The Cricket Club beat *Chelmsford Hall* OB by 15 runs.

Capt Rew resigned as Warden of the NT Crowlink area, succeeded by Leonard Stubley of *Glebelands Cottage* with Lt-Col CF Sharp of the Holiday Fellowship Home as his assistant. Phyllis Hughes was appointed SAS secretary for the East Dean area.

Davis Relay replaced equipment on The Brow mast to improve television reception.

The Players chose *The Long Echo* as their 1961 autumn production. Much time and patience went into the production. Jo Satchell rose to a most demanding role, and Arthur Perry was congratulated. Meg Horton, Ray Trickett, and Ethel Kemp had a worthy mention.

A new Union flag was purchased for the BL at a cost of £2.70. The successful Jumble Sale raised £22. A talk on the *Murmansk Convoys* by Commodore Bumstead was well received but poorly attended. The Derby Sweep had receipts of £44 after selling 956 tickets.

The PC noted that hot water was being installed in the Old Fridays. Higher wattage bulbs had been fitted in the Farrer Hall after complaints - hall charges slightly increased. Climpson's had maintained the recreation ground in a highly satisfactory state. Members also learnt that only five wardens were left in the local Civil Defence.

Percy & Eleanor Budd had their Diamond Wedding on 5 October. After a Service 'those present repaired to the *Outlook* where refreshments were served'. He said 60 years had passed amazingly quickly, no man could have had a better wife and daughter, Mrs Kennard.

For the first time since the war no Bonfire Society procession or bonfire on the night.

The ESCC agreed to provide No Overtaking signs on Friston hill and a Steep Hill sign. In view of delay by East Dean Downlands Ltd in carrying out measures for improvement of the sewage disposal works, Hailsham RDC deferred planning decisions.

The procession for dedication of East Dean Church extension L-R: Cmdr Reggie Smith, Lord Bishop of Lewes (Rt Revd Lloyd Morell, carrying the 'Fowler' crook), Sid White, Rural Dean (Canon WWS March), Revd RW Burns-Cox, Phyllis Thackeray, M Doxat Pratt and Horace Rew

Mrs E Goldsmith, the new president of ED & F WI, had Mrs Nash as secretary, and a committee of Mesdames Bicks, Doyle, Dunford Smith, Innes, Peet, Rathbone, Ockenden, and Satchell. They agreed to limit the numbers to 125 and to meet in the Village Hall. The inaugural evening meeting of the Micheldene WI had Mrs KE Ketcher as the first president, and members included Mesdames Greenwood, Towers-Minor, Stewart, Smart, Shipton and Joan Nash, who had already organised a whist drive which raised £2.

Kay Ketcher said, "Micheldene WI was started because many of the new residents could not attend afternoon meetings. Working mothers could attend evening meetings and meet new acquaintances. At the inaugural meeting there were about 20 present. The representative of the WI who attended said that there had to be a constitution with officers, and she asked who would volunteer for the posts. Well, naturally, no one rushed forward, so I asked what posts were needed and was told president, secretary, treasurer and so on. At the time I was busy with my teaching and knew I could not spare much time so I said I would do the president and that was how I came to do the first of my three spells of three years as president. The branch fluctuates in strength, has been up to 60 members and occasionally the numbers have dropped right down. It is flourishing now".

That year, 1961, saw the last mail on Christmas Day, and unsealed cards would be 1p.

The East Dean church extension was opened on the morning of Sunday, 25 February 1962 by the Bishop of Lewes. Only half the congregation could be housed in the church, so the Service was broadcast outside. In a truly rural setting the procession crossed from the Gilbert Institute in bright winter sunshine preceded by six local organisations with their banners, W Douglass Curtis, the choir and Lt-Col ER Cabell Warrens. The Friston churchwardens CH Meller and WV Walker were also there.

The Bishop dedicated the extension, the new pews, the six windows gifted by Harold and Ethel Brassley, the font cover in memory of Joseph Lonley and the new porch doors given by William and Audrey Macgowan. [4] The new extension had been designed by John Denman, the diocesan architect.

In the afternoon the new organ at Friston church was dedicated by the Bishop. The church was almost full, although Mr Budd was not able to attend. At a meeting in the Bardolf Hall on Tuesday 27 February 1962 the Vicar read a telegram from the Bishop and thanked everyone who had worked so hard to bring the church extension to fruition, especially mentioning Capt Rew. Major Gilbert Davies-Gilbert thanked the Vicar for his leadership and vision.

The heating, or absence of, in the Farrer Hall was discussed at the PC, as was the suggestion that a tennis court should be included at the recreation ground.

Percy Budd died in March 1962 aged 87. Had been in the Boer and 1914-18 wars, he directed the local ARP in the 1939-45 war and was always ready to help when needed.

After a film show by Mr and Mrs Doherty, the Guide Dog for the Blind collection reached £245 and it was decided to close the scheme on 31 May by which time the £250 will be reached. The dog will be called *Tiger*, the second of that name, the first was named after *HMS Tiger* whose crew also raised the £250. By 31 May £250 had been raised in two and a half years, of which £205 had been raised by jumble sales and donations.

An axe head about 16cm x 50cm [7 x 2 inches] in size and dating from 4000 years ago was found by Mr R Goldsmith on his farm. It was made by Stone Age people from the Mediterranean who colonised this area. The Coombe Hill camp was their work for they probably had a settled social life rather than a nomadic existence.

The Players AGM held in the Farrer Hall with Mrs Harding p, Mr Bicks vp, Mrs Stein c, Mrs Tompsett s and Mr Doherty t, heard that it was not a successful year financially. The committee was asked to devise some scheme to counteract the losses.

Revd Burns-Cox said he would refrain from an Appeal this year but 'if anyone be moved to offer a bell for East Dean church I shall be happy to hear from them. To give a gift that will ring out for hundreds of years is a beautiful gift.' Mr & Mrs Fawssett Briggs and Mr & Mrs Harold Down each promptly donated a new bell for East Dean.

There was no cricket for the 1962 Flower Show, because of the weather, and although only 212 entries, they were of a good standard. Lady Shawcross' *Friston Place Nurseries* provided a grand display of carnations. Miss VL Allsop won a prize in the Home Produce section, in Division 2, most prizes went to Tom H Martin, who was awarded the Blue Ribbon. Best cut flowers went to Bill Armiger and E Flint had the best spike of gladioli.

On 9 September Mr & Mrs Charles Meller were given a presentation after morning Service on leaving East Dean after many years.

A Jumble Sale in October was on the 51st anniversary of the first Village Jumble Sale in 1911, although it was said that similar sales had happened under other guises.

The Players presented *Letter from the General* at the Bardolf hall and it was their entry for the Sussex RCC full length play Festival. The parts were well cast, but special mention was made of Muriel Kidner, a newcomer. Delia Bicks, Jo Satchell, Rosalind Stein, Sylvia Tompsett and Patricia Wicking also gave excellent performances.

John Eve formed an ED & F Youth Club, meeting in the Recreation hut or Village Hall. A Dance at the Farrer Hall in aid of Muscular Dystrophy Research organised by teenager Faith Breach of 2 *Little Lane Cottage* raised £24.

The local BL had now 96 members. Officers the same, but committee strengthened by Major-General Bullard, Mrs Rose Dann, and Mr Charlie Vine.

A Church Missionary Society (CMS) Sale raised £140 thanks to Sybil Parris' efforts.

In a reorganisation of the Scouts and Guides John Cheal became Scout Leader, Pat Down led the Guides and Gwen Pearce, assisted by Rose Dann, the Brownies. Their Christmas Fayre was opened by Her Grace the Dowager Duchess of Devonshire, and assisted by Bill Brown's auction sale, brought in £220.

The Vicar asked that any newcomers should hand their card to him at church so that he may visit them and welcome them to the parish.

Capt Rew gave up the editorship of the magazine and Arthur Carter also felt he must resign. Replaced by Mrs Phyllis Hughes as editor and Fred Doherty as treasurer. The magazine posted 65-70 copies around the country each month.

Mothers' Union had a Christmas party with gifts sent to patients of Hellingly Hospital.

The AGM of the Bowls Club was held in the Town Hall. Mr Axten elected chairman in place of Ernest Cater who was elected President after 12 years as chairman. Trophies to RG Fears for singles and Capt SJ Rodgers and Mr H Dreghorn doubles, and monthly spoons to CH Smart, PQ Smith, HE Down and M Doxat-Pratt. The Budd Cup was won by the Captain's team by one point. The club announced that their membership was full.

Hilda Carter gave her 12th annual afternoon concert, when a cast of ten presented a varying programme of poems, songs and Shakespearean extracts. The proceedings opened with a chorus poem with Gwen Roberts, Jenny Wynne, Sylvia Tompsett and Mary Farren. Shakespearean scenes followed and a recitation of John Masefield's *The Wanderer's Song*. Beryl Monico charmed the audience with her Christopher Robin, and the entertainment drew to a close with votes of thanks and drawing of the raffles. Mr Anderson won the Premium Bond for the second year in succession, and a cake decorated by Mrs Greenwood went to Mrs Dietrich.

The 1962-3 snow. The snow commenced on Boxing Day 1962, the villages were effectively cut off for six weeks, and the remains of some drifts hadn't gone by March.

Diana Eyre said, "The milk float became stuck near *Greenacre,* 13 Warren Lane, even though it had chains on its wheels. I went there from *Hilltop Cottage* for a play reading and took eight pints of milk from the float for myself and others, leaving a note to say what I'd done. The other readers were a little uncertain as to how to react to my action except that I noticed they were all keen to finish early so that they could help themselves to a pint."

For several days no supplies reached the village and Weller's Stores and Kath Cater at the Gore Café coped with the situation. Whenever the road was passable Geoff Cater did a shuttle service to Seaford returning stranded visitors and coming back with bread. Here marooned residents queue for bread at the Cater's Café, that became the Car Sales office and now overbuilt by *Gore Farm Cottages*

Tom Goodman said, "The first day of the 1962-63 snow was terrible. My wife was stranded in Eastbourne in the car, one van was stuck at Alfriston and I couldn't start our other van. Edna finally abandoned her car and came back on Charlie Goldsmith's tractor. The regular bread van became stuck in the snow by the garage [now *Gore Farm Close*], whereupon Pc Debley opened it up and the marooned locals helped themselves."

Ian Shearer says, "I was possibly the last car out of East Dean at the time of the 1962-3 snow. A hire car managed to reach us over the hill, and having collected me, backed to the main road and drove through Jevington to Eastbourne so that I could take the train to catch my ship. We had a bit of digging out to do on the Jevington road - and do you know he only charged five shillings [25p], so I doubled it for a tip".

Diana Shearer recalls that, "There were no milk deliveries, so we had to go to Goldsmith's farm with our bottles and they were filled up as the cows were milked. Nurse Thackeray, the village nurse, was on hand supervising and advising us to boil the milk when we got it home, but I don't know if I did. We also obtained bread from a baker's van, which had been abandoned. You know, we did enjoy the snow". [8]

Joan Nash said, "When the snow was bad, my husband, John, a keep-fit fanatic, went into Eastbourne for the 0700h train every day walking on the tops of hedges, He would bring back a piece of meat or bag of fruit, which he knew we couldn't obtain in the village."

Capt. Norman Davies had to rescue 100 sheep buried in the snow and did not lose one.

Capt. Horace Rew died 29 December 1962, right in the middle of the village's worst snowfall. Nurse Joan Levison, a guest at the Holiday Fellowship Home, laid him out, and Dr Henry Wilson skied over to Crowlink from Eastbourne to certify his death.

Crowlink Lane was impassable to vehicles. John Dann, one of those helping said, "We couldn't get the coffin along the road, so we lashed it to a sledge, pulled it over the Downs and let it down to *Crowlink End*. As we were pulling it back up the hill someone said, 'I bet he's watching us now and thoroughly enjoying it all'. We laughed so much that we almost let the coffin slip off the sledge and run down the hill. Then we pulled it along the top path until two Land Rovers took over." Alf Pelling and Jim Wicking also helped.

Horace was the son of Sir Henry Rew, permanent secretary to the Ministry of Agriculture and Fisheries. He saw army service in the 1914-18 war and became joint-secretary to the Conjoint Board. Horace Rew's 'beautiful readings of the lessons and prayers' were first heard at East Dean in 1935. He was an enormous walker wearing a long cloak, like a monk, who organised walks for youngsters to local spots such as Alfriston. He was interested in sport, especially cricket, restoring the Cricket Club after the war; was editor of the parish magazine 1952-62; the NT representative for the Seven Sisters area; chairman of the Bonfire Society; was a church Reader; took Sunday School,

As the 1962-3 snow was cleared more was blown off the Downs until in places the snow piles were as high as a double-decker bus

and organised church Appeals such as the Free-Will offering and the 100,000 shillings. Many said, "He could get blood out of a stone", but Grace Taylor thought him 'a bit strange'. As John Dann says, "There was no question of volunteering. He would say 'You'll do the carpentry for this event', or 'You'll do the costumes'. If you said, 'I can't stitch', he would reply, 'We'll find a sewing machine for you'." Chairman of the Conservative Association, he was on the PC and when in 1952 he was defeated by one vote in the elections, the council exercised its right to appoint him as their unelected chairman. Very much a man of his time: hard-working, of forthright speech, but his kindness and integrity and an unquestioning absolute faith stood out. Married Olive in 1915 and they had Stephen and Mary. Olive died in 1959, after years of unfortunate invalidism. [5]

The first PC meeting of 1963 was cancelled because of the weather, but in spite of the conditions 47 members attended the WI on 9 January.

East Dean was still in the grip of the cold in February. Not cut off, but the roads flanked by piled-up snow looking more like soot every day and never seeming to melt. If water was coming out of your tap and not somewhere along the way you were lucky, in many cases the mains froze underground. Some folks had to boil snow to make a cup of tea. The owners of one house, away for Christmas, returned to find that the tank above their bedroom had burst, their bed was a solid block of ice and the carpet was frozen to the floor. Cars couldn't get down Crowlink Lane because of the snowdrifts until Easter 1963.

Activities didn't stop. To raise funds for the Freedom from Hunger Campaign Mrs PM Hughes gave an illustrated talk on the history of the two parishes, an anonymous donor and the Eastbourne Waterworks Co paid for a new bus shelter and East Dean Film Club held a Jumble Sale.

Following an exchange between Mr L Gross, the parish clerk, and Mrs PM Hughes, the parish magazine editor after Capt. Rew, the clerk resigned. He refused to have his reports vetted as suggested by the PC. Mrs Hughes had refused to publish his notice of a PC meeting on the need for more housing in the village. The vicar said the he fully supported Mrs Hughes and she was fully within her rights not to publish any matter submitted.

ED&F WI filled the Village Hall to capacity for a film show on coach tours of Britain.

East Dean & Friston Flower, Fruit and Vegetable Show at the Recreation Field, on a lovely day Bank Holiday, 5 August 1963. Prize winners: L-R: Ted Flint, Bill Armiger, Stan Fuller, Maureen Armiger, Peter Johnson, Wally Eve, Mrs V Matthews, Peter Armiger, Jim Markquick, Mary Child, Diana Eyre and Mrs S White.
The entrance fee was 2¹/₂p. No wonder over 500 came

East Dean Players presented *Pools Paradise,* another farce. Many of Philip King's regulars featured the harassed Vicar, unpredictable ex-actress, a Bishop and a militant spinster. Produced by another regular - Fred Bicks. The Vicar thought that it was a really funny play and everyone who saw it felt better for the tonic of laughter.

Planting completed of the box hedge round the Garden of Remembrance at East Dean, donated by Mr RG Hall.

Lt-Col & Mrs EC Simmons opened *Point House* for the Friends of the Hospitals.

Meanwhile Hailsham RDC refused any further council houses saying East Dean already had more than any other village south of the A259 - still awaiting news of garages.

East Dean and Friston WI had talk by Mrs L Stark on her 23 years with the Canadian Pacific ships, including several Princess boats. 'Life at sea cruising was wonderful.'

At The Players' AGM the subscriptions were set at a 37¹/₂p [7/6d] flat rate with no concessions. The subs had not changed since 1946 and financially the Society had been unable to enter the Eastbourne Festival, and their choice of plays was hampered.

Micheldene WI had a large attendance for Vera Maconochie, the famous singer, accompanist Miss Lovering, presenting a selection from Franz Lehar's *The Merry Widow.*

John Eve took over the taxi service when Ivan Worsell left in 1963. "Fred Bicks was going on a long cruise and decided to sell his yellow Vauxhall, so I bought it".

A branch of the Liberal association was formed in East Dean.

In August East Dean & Friston WI went to the new theatre at Chichester to see *St Joan,* while The Players' production *Mornings at Seven* at the Bardolf Hall was most enjoyable. Lorrie Innes, Meg Horton, Maud Worsell and Sylvia Tompsett were well cast. Jo Satchell, Ray Trickett, Arthur Perry and Walter Broughton played their parts well, and Charles Parris gave a finished performance. The set, by Jolyon Fyfield, Anthony Tompsett and George Worsell, was realistic and charming.

Any Christmas Fayre 1963 profits were to help the work on the East Dean church belfry. Although the Vicar was not well enough to attend the stalls did good business. With the raffles and donations £502 was raised.

At *Calanda* the home of Mr & Mrs O'Brien, an audience enjoyed a nativity play performed by the children Jill Greenwood, Penny Shearer, Nicolette and Hugh O'Brien, with a collection for Oxfam. The Youth Club organised a Christmas tree on the Village Green with carol singing on 17 December, and raised money for Christmas gifts to OAPs.

Magazine printing costs rose in 1964 by £6 a month. 'And they will not be ready until the first week in the month instead of the last week of the previous month. The Magazine is a church magazine, but also a local newspaper.' Mrs Carter gave an afternoon of entertainment in the Village Hall and raised £11 for the magazine funds.

There were repeated requests to keep dogs under control, but no mention of fouling.

The Ridgeway home of the Hookers known as *Crossways* was renamed *Lamplands*. In olden times income from fields called Lamplands went to defray the cost of lamps in the church and Taperlands were used to pay for the use of tapers in the church.

ESCC took out a compulsory purchase order for a small parcel of land for the new bus shelter at East Dean. Mr EO Hobden was willing to sell, but there existed a restrictive covenant in favour of Downlands Estate from whom no definite reply was forthcoming.

The Village Hall was filled for the 35th birthday celebrations of ED&F WI, the items were Mrs Chenevix-Trench on *Fifty Years of Motoring;* Mrs Pat Down on *My Experiences in the Mont Carlo Rally* and Mrs Kay Kennard talked on *East Dean in Wartime.*

Cricket Club committee was now EC Bourner capt. and t, Sunday capt. M Wear, v-capt H Winter, M Tatum s, Mrs A Goldsmith match s, members P Armiger, W Hollebon and M Johnson (playing), Mrs EC Bourner, F Adams, HR Hughes (non-playing).

Charles Edward Goldsmith died aged 76. A Son of Sussex his farms were kept in better condition than many a garden.

The Players' 1964 spring play was *Breath of Spring* produced by Phil Satchell. Again it had a skilful set and the frolic of a play had all the cast carrying the fun along in fine style. Sylvia Tompsett looked just right, Maud Worsell was most authentic, Pat Wicking's portrayal had an adorable pertness and Meg Horton's conversations provided perfect little cameos. Linda Stein was in good form and Arthur Perry gave his best performance to date.

PC discussed drainage south of the A259 and decided that cesspools and septic tanks coped with the soil drainage and there was no need to change to mains drainage with a sewage disposal works in the valley leading to the Gap. Occasionally there is an overflow and it must be remedied as the Gilbert Estates have just done on The Green. As a long term project a main drainage disposal of both soil and rainwater would be an improvement but the heavy cost was a factor as long as the Public Health requirements were met.

The new vicar was the Revd Brinley H Howells MBE. A chaplain at Geneva since 1957 and a chaplain to the RAF for nine years, he was married at Eastbourne and wife Molly is a Sussex farmer's daughter. Canon JN Mallinson helped out. He said, "The congregation has renewed my inspiration. I welcome non-Anglicans but encourage them to attend churches of their own denomination in Eastbourne". He introduced a Wednesday morning Holy Communion. Leslie Ketcher conducted the Young People's Service.

The resolutions for the WI National meeting were that more women should be tested for cervical cancer; a different source of water supply than reservoirs should be found; the qualifications for jury service should be modernised, and young persons should be discouraged from smoking and it should be banned in buses and cafés.

Another good year for the football club who won 14 out of 20 matches. Hugh Winter, the captain, played in every match and Dave Wicking scored 25 goals with five hat tricks.

Pc Keith Beard transferred to the village from Uckfield.

The PC considered plans from Mr Pyle as agent for the developers for shops and a flat at the Gore, for which outline planning permission had been in existence since 1956, and had been modified to comply with all planning requirements. The Council agreed that the plans were not objectionable and that the present derelict state should be remedied. Meanwhile, at a public meeting, over 100 residents declared that there was no demand for more shops in East Dean and voted against the erection of shops, saying that they would cause traffic problems and small bungalow accommodation would be more appropriate.

The BL Derby Sweep left £27 for the local funds, and the Annual Jumble Sale organised by Mrs Foord and Mrs Cheal realised £30, again a record. WG Wood of *Shielin, Hillside*, appointed assistant secretary.

Eastbourne Association of Sussex Folk held a programme of events on the Village Green including Maypole dancing, handbell ringing, firing the anvil, and Morris dancing.

The PC stated in reference to plans for a barn at Crowlink that while it was essential to conserve the countryside there could be no objection to the conversion of old farm buildings which had no use provided the original foundation and appearance was maintained.

At The Players AGM Mr Bicks was elected c, Mrs Tompsett s, with Mrs Worsell as deputy, Mr Doherty was t, Mr Broughton continued as front of house committee c. The committee of Mrs Horton, Mr Brown, Mr Satchell and Mr Trickett, with Mr Boden as auditor was re-elected. Total assets £262. The Revd & Mrs Howells elected Honorary members. Meg Horton pointed out that there was a complete lack of young members which made it difficult to cast plays that the Society wished to produce. It was stated that another £10 was needed to complete the basic lighting equipment as advised by Strand Electric.

The Scout Camp was near Midhurst, well away from the Guides' Camp at Dolgellau, North Wales. The Guides spent a night at a Youth Hostel on the way and made expeditions to the Swallow Falls, Conway, Harlech and Caernarvon among others. They had to strike camp during one bout of rain, but the memories were happy ones for Janet Bertin, Angela Pope and Julia Sutherland; numbers few, but enthusiastic.

The 1964 Flower Show brought 550 people to the Memorial Cricket ground to view the cricket and the exhibits. The Challenge Shield was won by Wally Eve and the Challenge Cup by Bill Armiger and excellent prices were obtained at Jim Monico's auction.

East Dean & Friston WI staged a Produce Exhibition at the Farrer Hall with 123 exhibits. The outstanding exhibit for yeast rolls was won by Mr BO Ellis. Prizes went to Miss EM Easy and Mrs DM Dietrich (fruit cake), Mrs RW Down (macaroons), Mrs D Bicks' jam also had top marks and Mrs DE Snell gained highest marks in the flower section. Other prizes were won by Mrs ED Goldsmith and Miss V Elvin.

Farmer Edgar Williams found another horde of Roman coins on Beachy Head which are now in the British Museum. Don't dash to dig there, they are of interest, but of no value.

In October there was a show of holiday photographs in the Village Hall with a collection for the Sussex Campaign.

YJ Lovell built the bus shelter for £550, Southdown Buses gave a donation of £20. The PC could now buy a wreath for the Remembrance Day celebrations as this was now a permitted expenditure, beforehand the wreath had been paid for by the councillors.

Cricket Club only lost out on the CVL championship by losing in the final match to

Glynde, the eventual champions.

No RSPCA collection for 1964, but there were boxes in The Gore Café, The Corner Shop, Weller's Stores and the *Tiger Inn.*

Over the two years 1962-4 the youth of East Dean produced a 20-minute film entitled *The Attempt.* It certainly had soundtrack for the sounds shattered the night air and rocked the Farrer Hall when it was shown and raised £2 for various charities.

No Village Fete in 1964, so an ED&F WI Fete *The House Beautiful* was held in the Manor Grounds raising £190 for WI funds. Mrs Patience Harding, a founder member, was present and Miss Davies-Gilbert. The bottle stall manned by husbands proved profitable.

The Players autumn production by Fred Bicks was *Inquiry at Lisieux.* In the well-chosen cast Delia Bicks and Arthur Perry gave polished performances and there were moving scenes from Mollie Bertin, Gay Ockenden, Jo Satchell and Shirley Pomeroy. All presided over by Charles Parris and ably supported by Bill Brown and Walter Broughton.

The Football Club started the season well. They did lose to a Lewes Prison XI - however, one of the locals said they gained a wealth of knowledge from the prison players!

A strange contraption visible on Crowlink Flat was a cattle oiler, 'as cattle rub against it the insecticide kills the flies which carry New Forest Eye, a disease that can blind cattle'.

The Guides held an Open Evening in aid of the Guides Friendship Fund, to buy equipment for less fortunate Guiders. There were various stalls, a cine film of Guiding and slides of the summer camp. The finale was the enrolment of Katherine Bertin, and two child nurse badges to Angela Pope and Scholastika Zimmer. The evening raised £12.

The villages' last blacksmith, Luther Hills, died in December 1964. Born at Lewes in 1869 he came with his parents to *Forge Cottage* three years later. Left the village school at eleven and went as a carter boy at *Birling Manor* earning 10p a week and later joined his father. He shoed oxen in his younger days. A craftsman, he made the War Memorial railings and the Friston weather vane. When the Smithy work fell away he turned to crafting models of Sussex wheeled ploughs. Was sexton at East Dean church where he dug over 200 graves. Never missed a Service and always took the Collections. He was an essential part of the life of East Dean until moving in 1961 to an Old People's Home in Uckfield. [2] & [3]

East Dean and Friston Parish Churches

There will be a

ROYAL CHRISTMAS FAIRE

in the

BARDOLF HALL, EAST DEAN
(by kind permission of Mrs. P. Harding)
on
WEDNESDAY, 2nd DECEMBER, 1959
FROM 2.30 P.M.
IN AID OF THE CHURCHES APPEAL

UNDER THE PATRONAGE OF

H.M. QUEEN ELIZABETH
THE QUEEN MOTHER
WHOSE GIFT WILL BE ON VIEW

STALLS SIDESHOWS, COMPETITIONS, TEAS, BUFFET ETC: FATHER CHRISTMAS WILL BE THERE!

Nº   23

This Programme makes you a Member of the Churches Christmas Faire

6d. PROGRAMME (Lucky Number) 6d.

The 1964 Christmas Fayre at the Bardolf Hall to raise funds for the church fabric was opened by Lady Gordon, but didn't have quite the regal aura of its 1959 counterpart (above), even so it raised £260. Stall holders were Mr ES White bottles, Mrs T Shaw cakes, Mrs IV Smith children's ware, Mrs Bingley aprons, Miss Curryer hankies, Mrs Hooker with Mrs Kennard presents and Mrs Doherty soaps and scents

12. A Year in the Life of East Dean and Friston, 1965

Wartime rationing ended in 1954, Rock and Roll came in, and before long the nation was told 'it had never had it so good'. The 1960s that saw President Kennedy's assassination and the last of National Service ('the Draft') also welcomed the Beatles and the Permissive Society - bank clerks could now wear shirts of various hues, not just *Persil White*. East Dean and Friston [ED & F], of Hailsham Rural District Council [HRDC], did not lead any of these fashions, but by 1965 the villages showed a pleasant mix of change.

The 1965 Parliamentary Roll listed 1106 names. The year, however, could see Boundary Commission changes - would ED & F stay in the Rural District or be merged with Eastbourne? Major-General Colin Bullard represented the villages on the HRDC.

East Dean occupied 820 acres with a rateable value of £20,000 and a population of 1100; Friston had 1300 acres worth £12,000 and 300 residents. The average yearly parish rainfall was around 30 inches [760mm], mixed with some 1900 hours of sunny periods.

There were 471 houses on the Downlands Estate [10], with another 48 about to be built. HRDC owned 21 cottages in the village, at an average rent of £2 a week, and the Water Company owned 12 at Friston. The Gilbert Estates had 12 cottages, as well as the *Tiger,* The Green, *The Dipperays,* the Institute, the allotments, the *Birling Gap Hotel* and much of the land making up the two remaining farms. During 1965 the Estate sold the empty *Underhill Cottages* to a developer [7], and offered the old school, 'now, alas, unused since last March', [6] to the Parish Council at £4,000 for conversion to a Village Hall. For reasons, such as lack of parking space, this generous offer was greeted with some apathy.

This was a year when the teenagers modelled themselves on Jean Shrimpton or the Beatles, with polo-necked sweaters, long flowing hair, short skirts, black leather boots and transistors. The young families, as ever, were clad in ready-mades, while the more mature women wore cardigans, had curly, grey hair and were invariably accompanied by their dogs, their menfolk had lovat-green jackets, caps and walking sticks. It was also when the Revd Roger Hooker, son of a Friston resident, took his bride to India as missionaries.

Electricity, gas and water were provided by public utilities, while sewerage and roads on the Estate were maintained by the developers. East Dean village did not have mains drainage (until 1977), and the rural atmosphere was also preserved by the absence of street lighting. An Eastbourne pharmacist made three deliveries a week, and sickroom equipment donated by residents could be borrowed as needed from Cmdr Reggie and Mrs Irene (Queenie) Smith, who generously housed it.

The villages, like most round the country, had been entirely farming communities until alternative employment was provided by the Eastbourne Water Company and Forestry Commission. Over the previous 35 years, with the new housing estate, there had been an influx of retired professional and businessmen and their families.

John Norman Davies employed five men farming 964 acres of Davies-Gilbert and National Trust land, on which he ran 600 Kerry Hill ewes (black noses, rest white), 700 lambs, 24 rams (some Dorset Downs, dark faces and legs, to obtain a quicker fattening animal), 90 cows, 81 calves, 74 yearlings and three bulls, mainly Angus/Hereford crosses. He also had 94 acres of fattening marshland at Pevensey, and took over the old *Birling Manor* golf course in 1953.

Captain Davies was hailed as a figure in chalkland farming; being the least staffed, lowest capitalised, quality-meat producer in the county. The BBC featured him in *Farm Fare,* and overseas visitors came to consult. He also encouraged those who wished to enjoy the beauty of the Downs. He retired in 1967. The farm manager was George Markham, with Alf Pelling foreman and Charlie Cumming, Charley Markwick, and Sid Dark.

Alf Pelling said, "He was a pleasant enough boss, but wanted things his way. With the cost of water today it wouldn't be economic to have it in every field - you don't always have cattle there and sheep don't need so much".

Capt. Norman Davies began farming at East Dean and Crowlink in 1945. He and his wife lived in *Little Barn,* and later *Went Acre.* He rode over the farm on his pony every morning. Instead of the sheep being folded at night and the cattle kept round the farmyard, he installed 14 miles of fences and seven water points on the Downs and ranged the animals; now one man could easily oversee 1200 sheep. The locals said it would never work, but it was a success

Gore Farm having been supplanted by the Downlands Estate, *New House Farm* was the only other one within the village. CE Goldsmith and sons leased *Black Robin,* and from 1945, *New House Farm.* Son, Bert Goldsmith, farmed this eastern portion of Davies-Gilbert land until he retired aged 70 in 1980. It employed two men full-time and had 80 acres of wheat, barley and oats, with a TT herd of 20 Ayrshire cows, six calves and 12 Sussex yearlings. The corn was cut by a Massey-Ferguson combine, at 7-ton an hour, and sold to millers McDougalls of Hellingly and Sadlers of Chichester. As Eileen Goldsmith said, "Although some of the romance has gone from farming, so has much of the hard work. Mechanisation produces four tons of corn an acre and TB [tuberculosis]-free milk".

January 1965 was mild, and a wren was seen - a rare bird since being almost wiped out in the severe winter of 1962-3. Rabbits were also seldom seen after the myxomatosis outbreak of 1955. Before 1954 about 2000 rabbits were shot in the parishes each winter, since then only about a dozen were seen until the 1970s when they became plentiful.

Farm work that month consisted of repairing fences and gates and feeding cattle in the yards. Grain, wheat, barley and oats would be taken out of the silos for sale.

On the national field, the death of Sir Winston Churchill on 24 January 1965 was mourned by all. The Revd Brinley Howells preached a memorable sermon at East Dean; 'in our hearts is affection, unbounded admiration for this giant among men, and the deepest gratitude for his inspired leadership in our hour of need'. East Dean and Friston's Memorial Appeal raised £452.

During sunny days in the next month badgers and a hedgehog were seen, ploughing started, and the first lambs were born on 24 February.

March started with two weeks of cold and heavy snowfall with the road to Eastbourne blocked for a day, but soon cleared by snowploughs. The last week was warm and sunny; so much so that some thought it the best of the year.

The local Conservative Association meeting arranged for 4 March had to be postponed because of the snow, and the annual Dinner Dance of the Angling Club was put off from March to April. The Club Secretary, Brian Johnson, had some big catches over the year including a conger eel at 16½lb [7kg], and a bass caught off Beachy Head tipped the scales at 22lb and won the *News of the World* Fishing Rod for the heaviest fish in that class.

On 10 March the Mass Radiography Service visited, and 150 village residents took the opportunity for an X-ray to confirm that they were TB free.

It was time for sowing and lambing. Altogether 1000 lambs were expected over the Downs, with Capt. Davies in the fold along the Birling Gap Road, where he asked folk to keep their dogs under control during the two months of lambing.

In January the last resident Queens' Nursing Sister, Phyllis Thackeray, talked to the local WI on *First Aid*, her advice was to avoid accidents. Here she is outside her home, *Gore Cottage*, in 1965. She was a great help during the 1962-3 big snow-up. Her last home delivery was on Christmas Day 1967 and she retired the next year after 16 years. Died in 1990 leaving £20,000 to the church

The ED & F Women's Institute [WI] Choir under Mrs Chenevix-Trench gained a certificate for a madrigal at the 1965 Lewes Music Festival. The choir had been formed in 1946 with the incentive of taking part in this annual festival. Mrs Chenevix-Trench became the conductor in 1949, inheriting a choir of 20 including Rose Dann and Biddy Kennard. The membership fee was 2d [1p] a week.

The Parish Council [PC], under Chairman Lt Col EC Simmons, decided to plant a willow tree by Friston pond. Sadly, after vandalism, it had to be replaced two years later, and again in 1972. It is now doing too well. PC members noted that the new bus shelter at the Gore was appreciated by all, but especially by 'Knights of the Road' who found it a blessing when tucked up there in an old eiderdown on a cold night.

The Residents' Association [RA], commenting on the excessive speed of vehicles on Friston hill, reported that it had a membership of 400 out of an adults' total of 1150. It was on 16 October 1959 that Reg Dean had called a public meeting to discuss the formation of a RA. At an overflowing Village Hall, 82 voted to form the East Dean with Friston Residents' Association. Jack Roberts c, CF Cook v-c, TA Waller s, and ES White t. The sub. was fixed at 12½p [2/6d] a year per household, and the committee consisted of Miss DE Alloway and Messrs AH Anderson, CF Branch, W Clarke, E Fears and PR Satchell.

Graham Collins, whose family ran the *Birling Gap Hotel,* married Sandra Lloyd at Friston Church, carrying the bride over the Tapsell gate 'which had been suitably secured for the occasion'. The reception was at *The Dipperays.*

The Cricket Club had 80 members at its annual Dinner and Dance when Alan Oakman of Sussex CCC was a speaker. The chairman, Ronald Hughes, reported that Eric Bourner had completed 327 consecutive appearances, and Hugh Winter took 137 wickets in the season, he read a letter from the MCC secretary, SC Griffith, who knew of the Club.

A more sedentary set, the ED & F Literature Group, continued a tradition by meeting for discussions in members' houses. Members of the ED & F WI, however, were visibly affected by Leslie Ketcher's talk on his four years as a Japanese Prisoner-of-War.

On the last day of March plans for eight flats in a two-storey block at the Michel Dene Road entrance to the estate were deferred. On the near national stage two ships, the *Nora* and the *Otto N Miller*, collided off Beachy Head in fog. The resultant seven-mile oil patch was dispersed by the Royal Navy spraying 7000 gallons of Gamlen, hoping to avert any danger to the beaches.

LB Hubbard, Clerk to the Parish Council 1963-68 and 1972-76

The WI national organisation celebrated its Golden Jubilee and at the local April meeting members received commemorative Jubilee goblets. The Queen invited one member from each WI to Buckingham Palace in May; and by ballot Mrs D Anderson represented the villages.

Friston Church had 120 communicants at Easter; with a local Church Electoral Roll of 540.

The cattle were put out to summer quarters, the first cuckoo was heard on 29th April and *Friston Place* opened for a day in aid of the Friends of the Eastbourne Hospitals.

Civil Defence classes and exercises continued in 1965. Norman Davies, who followed Harold Brown as Senior Warden in 1951, resigned in 1964 and Lt Col EC Simmons took over with his wife as deputy. He reported that there was a welfare team of eight to give food and shelter in disasters, whether atomic war or other causes.

The Players' spring contribution in 1965 was *The Happiest Days of Your Life*. Tickets cost from 7$\frac{1}{2}$p (unreserved) to 22$\frac{1}{2}$p. Fred Bicks excelled as the headmaster, and Delia Bicks gave another fine study as the headmistress. Ron Pringle was welcomed, and there were special rounds of applause for David Satchell, Denise Prior and Kate Trickett. It was produced in his usual firm way by Fred Bicks; a busy man that year for he was captain of Willingdon Golf Club.

The East Dean Scout troop held their April camp at *Birling Manor* on the invitation of Mrs Harding. Their trainer for the Starman's course was Mr Pope - from Herstmonceux Observatory, so no surprise when Troop Leader Graham Haffenden and Patrol Leaders Graham Pyle and Martin Ketcher gained their badges. Martin completed all his First Class tests. The Scouts won the coveted Inter-Troop Cross Country run trophy, while the Guides went for a trip on the Dutch canals to see the bulb fields. The seven in the cub pack had Mrs Holmes as Akela. The Scouts and Guides were few in number, but keen and enthusiastic, they even spent an evening clearing up Birling Gap. Their annual meeting was held in the Village Hall in May. Harold Down was t, Reg Dean Group Scoutmaster, Mrs Pat Down Capt. and Miss Gwen Pearce Brown Owl.

Miss Alice Boniface celebrated her 100th birthday in Chichester. She had been the Revd Evans' housekeeper during his time in the parish and went with him to Chichester on his retirement in 1929. She died in 1967.

Over 60 members of the ED & F United Nations' Association attended the 1965 AGM, with Mr CV Nolan in the chair. The Revd Brinley Howells, who had spent several years at Geneva, gave a thought-provoking talk emphasising that while we should support the UN it faced stresses with the inclusion of many newly-independent Afro-Asian countries.

The local UNA, formed by the Revd AW Anderson, had its first meeting in April 1947. By 1952 the branch had a membership of 317 - half the adult population, a proportion exceeding that of any other UK branch, and in 1954 it raised the largest contribution for UNICEF. They met in the Bardolf Hall, Mrs Patience Harding was p, Percy Budd t, WJ Boyce and DJ Headland ms, WS Ostler and CF Parry general secretaries and A Carter auditor. Among many outstanding lectures, in 1960 Lt-Gen. Sir John Glubb gave 'a masterly analysis' of "The Eastern and Western power struggle". The chairmen were the Revd Anderson 1947-9, William Axten 1949-52, Revd George Evans 1952-3, Lt-Col ACU Thomson 1953-8, the Revd Burns-Cox 1958-64 and the Revd Brinley Howells 1965-69.

Local lads fishing at Birling Gap c.1965. The remains of the concrete (the 'Big Rock') used in 1940 to plug the steps can be seen lying in the surf just to the left of the group

The numbers dropped to 200 after the 1956 Suez crisis, and the heady hopes of the post-war days went pear-shaped in 1969 when all the committee resigned. At a special meeting on 21 January only 12 members opposed a motion to close the branch down because of a change of UN policy which they could not accept namely, 'if necessary Britain should use force against Rhodesia'.

At its May 1965 meeting the PC reported that the HRDC had agreed to write to ESCC stressing the dangers to pedestrians on Friston hill, with increasing traffic, and - incredibly - to urge that an underpass be considered.

At the local elections, with separate voting for East Dean and for Friston, H Cunliffe, L Fisher, DC Hodson, Mrs PM Hughes, and Lt-Col EC Simmons (c) were elected unopposed for Friston. East Dean, where only 30% of the 839 electors voted, chose CF Goldsmith, Cmdr RJ Smith (vc), CJ Parris, RN Dean (new), DV Richey, FJ Bicks, BO Ellis, Miss V Elvin and Mrs KE Ketcher (new). Miss KM Burness had decided to retire after seven years.

At their June meeting Micheldene WI decided on a Beetle Drive to raise funds. The month also saw large parties of London schoolchildren staying at the Crowlink Holiday Fellowship Association hostel.

The July weather continued to disappoint and inevitably haymaking was poor. The PC decided to discuss with the Highway Authority what improvements might be possible to the A259 in the interests of safety. HRDC refused planning permission for a derelict barn at Crowlink, but did suggest that the proposed access road to the Gore shops be called

Downlands Way. More rain and gales in August did not deter The Players from an outing to the new Yvonne Arnaud theatre at Guildford on the 14th to see *Say Who You Are.* Previous trips had included the Mermaid and Chichester Theatres.

The weather did change for a glorious August Bank Holiday, held for the first time at the end of the month. A large crowd at the Recreation Ground saw ED & F Cricket Club play the annual all-day match against *Chelmsford Hall* Old Boys, and in the pavilion Commander RJ Smith and his committee organised the highly successful Vegetable Fruit, and Flower Show. For the schedule Broad Beans had been replaced by Cabbages, and Eggs by Apples. The great number of entries received high praise from the judges, and Wally Eve gained the Flower Show Challenge Shield for the third year in succession. This year there was a collection for the National Trust *Enterprise Neptune,* which brought in £6.

East Dean Singers, L-R: Jane Leete, Phyll Workman, Freda Elcock, Audrey Leeder, Georgie Hall, Dorothy Fenton, Elsie Allan, Gloria Saxby, Hazel Matley, Ann Gregg, Doris Tyler, Florrie Vine, ?, and Rose Dann. Peggie Fuller, sitting centre, became the conductor of the Women's Institute choir in 1969 and led it to further activities such as charity concerts. Gradually member numbers from outside the WIs increased and the locals dwindled to five so perhaps the WI Choir could be said to have dissolved itself into the Wannock Singers. As William Byrd put it, 'Since singing is so good a thing, I would all (wo)men would learn to sing'

Any profit went to cover Cricket Club expenses and equipment. The Club was flourishing, although like most organisations the lion's share of the work was done by the faithful few. The club paid £25 a year to the PC for the use of the ground, for which mowing was included, but the preparation of the square was the club's responsibility. Geoff Cornford started bringing in outsiders for the team when he was captain in the early 1950s, and most playing members were now drawn from outside the parish boundaries. The subscriptions were 37½p [7/6d] a year and one shilling [5p] a match for playing members and 12½p for non-playing members - cheap entertainment indeed on a lovely afternoon.

Sylvia Elizabeth Davies-Gilbert was wed to Mr PT Tellwright at East Dean Church.

The Brownie Pack had a drizzly day for their Open Meeting on 10 September, but when Lord and Lady Shawcross held a Garden Party at *Friston Place* in aid of the NSPCC the sun shone and crowds admired the views. RAC members ran the car park and extra police were required. There was standing room only for two bikini parades organised by Bobby & Co beside the swimming pool and compered by journalist and broadcaster

Godfrey Winn. Pony and donkey-cart rides were popular too, the donkey-cart lent by Mrs Voorspuy: Mr J Barker and Mr L Miller sold sweets from a basket carried by another donkey.

The PC decided to hold a referendum to determine whether or not residents wished to acquire the former Village School offered by the Gilbert Estate as a Village Hall. The PC also discussed a modern nuisance, a derelict car that had been left at Friston; the Police arranged its removal at a cost of £2.

The British Legion's [BL] Old People's Outing went to the *Black Rabbit* at Arundel and dropped in at the *Ram Inn* Firle. Suitably lubricated, they had a sing-song from there.

ED & F Art Class were visited by the East Sussex Art Adviser Peter Probyn, who judged the group's holiday paintings and gave a talk on modern painting that occasioned some dissension amongst the group. It was tactfully agreed that painting could not remain static and that experiments were needed. Miss M Hooper and Mrs SJ Snell were the joint secretaries. The indoor Art Show was held in the Village Hall, where new lighting enabled the works to be better displayed. A collection for Oxfam raised £19.

The Art Class, formed four years before with 12 members, had increased so rapidly that it divided into morning and afternoon sections. Members progressed under the encouraging tuition of local resident, Miss Daphne Oliver, a tutor at the Eastbourne School of Art, and Howard Faulkner, a retired head of the school.

In 1965 Kathleen Cater [née Hobden] gave up her café and shop at the East Dean Service Station run by her husband, Jeffrey. Kathleen had lived in East Dean since a child, and as Mrs Phyllis Hughes wrote, 'The following phrases have suddenly gone out of use, "Ask Kathleen, Tell Kathleen, Get it at Kathleen's, Give it to Kathleen, Fetch it from Kathleen's, Leave it with Kathleen, Change it at Kathleen's, Kathleen will know, and Kathleen will have it." She will be missed in many ways'. The next year the Eve family leased the shop and tea rooms while Jeff kept the garage going. John Eve said, "Workmen building the petrol station were customers, and some seemed to be there all the day."

Pigeon fancier, Peter Johnson, of 1 Upper Street entered eight of his 25 pigeons at the Racing Pigeon Show in the Horticultural New Hall, Westminster.

The Church Fellowship started on 6 October 1965 as a monthly social evening, with a Desert Island Discs style programme. In November the talk was on Ancient Musical Instruments and for December Mr Harold Down introduced members of Scott's the Florists, 'who deftly demonstrated ideas for Christmas decorations using *Florapak* and *Oasis,* as well as potatoes and gay ribbons'.

The sisters Minnie Davies Gilbert and Mrs Patience Harding gave strong support to village activities, especially the local Guides and Scouts. In 1965 Minnie resigned as President of the Eastbourne Girl Guides' Association. She died, aged 85, in 1968 [5]

A Bowling Club Social Evening concluded their season when over 60 members and wives gathered at the *Lawns Hotel* followed by a visit to the Congress Theatre.

Most house martins and swallows had departed by October. Starlings formed large, wheeling flocks in the dusk sky, and black-headed gulls followed the plough. A greater spotted woodpecker was visiting bird tables, and rare visitors, a kestrel and a hoopoe, had been seen. The harvest was late, but in spite of difficult conditions cutting was finished on

5 October. 'Typical of our weather' on 7 October the temperature reached 72°F [22C].

The wheat crop was poor, but the barley was fair for malting. Root crops, however, such as kale and swedes were first rate. Sheep from the marshes were moved to their winter quarters on the Downs.

The churches were decorated for the Harvest Thanksgiving, which that year featured corn dollies made by one of the Girl Guides.

The Stoolball Club held its Annual Dinner Dance on 9 October. A mixed team played twice a week, originally on the Village Green.

ED & F WI raised £100 towards the Chichester Cathedral Appeal, and at the Congress Theatre, Eastbourne, Mrs IV Smith and Mrs F Hooker, who were on the Organising Committee, were presented to HRH Princess Margaret and the Earl of Snowdon. To mark the Golden Jubilee of the National WI, a kneeler in the WI design worked by members was placed in East Dean Church. The Jubilee Supper on 23 October was attended by 50 members and friends, with Mary Fyfield leading the country dancing.

The East Sussex Hunt met on the Village Green, 11 December 1965, when cars parked outside the *Tiger*. During the year the road alongside had been renovated

Mrs Patience Harding opened the ED & F WI Fete; their October Jumble Sale raised £18 for funds; Mrs R Stein was elected President for next year, with Mrs Anderson and Mrs Bicks re-elected as s and t respectively, a Coffee Morning raised £8.30. So quite a WI year.

It was a good year for holly berries too which were plentiful for Remembrance Sunday. Each year, at 1050h, a British Legion contingent, about 40 strong, assembled at the War Memorial, flanked by members of the PC, other organisations, Scouts, Guides, Cubs, Brownies, and the public. The Vicar, preceded by the Crossbearer, churchwardens and choir, joins from the church. Wreaths are laid during the hymn *O God Our Help in Ages Past*. At 1102, after the two-minute Silence, a bugler sounds The Last Post, when colours are lowered, followed by avowal of the Remembrance - "They shall not grow old ..." and the Reveille is proclaimed. Prayers are followed by a verse of the hymn *Now Thank We All Our God* and the Blessing; the vicar returns to a full church for a shortened matins, in the same order, and followed by the organisations, all singing *Onward Christian Soldiers*.

The Poppy Day collection amounted to a record £125.97½, over £4 more than 1964, thanks to the organisation by Mrs IV Smith and the efforts of all involved. It was made up of £82 from the sale of poppies, donations of £27, wreaths £10, and proceeds from a whist drive £6. Of the ED & F British Legion members in 1965, some 54 had been in the 1914-18 war, 53 saw service 1920-45, and four after 1945.

November was a month of alternate mild and cold conditions, with snow on the 22nd and a hailstorm on 27th. The atmospheric pressure during the month ranged from 1027mm on the 5th to 964 on 29th. By now Christmas roses and iris unguicularis were showing first blooms, and the tips of spring bulbs peeped through.

That month the Players staged Noel Coward's *Nude with Violin* at the Bardolf Hall. 'An ambitious venture, but carried through by Ray Trickett, with cameos by Bill Brown and Muriel Kidner. Fred Bicks was faultless, and Linda Stein, Arthur Perry, Shirley Pomeroy, Mollie Bertin, Daphne Holmes and Felix Stride-Darnley did extremely well too. David Harmer was to be congratulated on his Fabrice.' The play was entered in the Sussex Full Length Drama Festival at Bognor Regis' Esplanade theatre, but didn't reach the final.

Mrs B Lawrence and Mrs W Harris formed the Crowlink WI on 22 November. It met monthly on Wednesdays at 1430h; yearly subscription 25p.

Gales in December meant extra night watches for the Coastguards, but the Life Saving Corps was not called upon. The LSC comprised 20 men from East Dean, with Cecil Dann the officer-in-charge. They patrolled from Beachy Head to the Cuckmere when summoned day or night by a maroon fired by Mr Dann. They held a monthly practice and stood by with a rocket line for ships aground or people stranded on the rocks. The Look-Out on the cliffs above Birling Gap was manned during gales. On Saturday, 27 November, when there was a Force 9

On 17 December Mrs Clare Chenevix-Trench (left) and Mrs Gay Ockenden (East Dean & Friston WI) (above), Miss K Shipton and Mrs E Horsley (Micheldene WI), planted two ilex trees by the Church Green. Mrs Trench, a WI member for 46 years, served as a transport driver in the 1914-18 war in which her husband was killed, leaving her to bring up their daughter. She drove her split-screen Morris Minor until 1986, dying three years later at 96

NW gale blowing, the maroon was fired at 1700h, after the lighthousemen reported distress signals out to sea. The coastguards searched from Birling Gap to Crowlink and the Newhaven lifeboat stood by, but nothing was found and the men stood down at 2000h.

The ED & F WI meeting heard Vida Elvin talk on *Christmas Customs,* and gift parcels were sent to patients in East Dean ward, St Mary's Hospital, Eastbourne.

At the PC Charles Parris was elected chairman of the Halls committee. Residents mentioned favourably the improvement in traffic flow since the new Friston lay-by, which had been completed to a high standard without disturbing the pond.

December saw an attack on Seaside Homes Ltd plans to develop the Greensward. PC chairman, Lt Col EC Simmons, reminded members that in 1963 the managing agent had said that a plan for houses there would destroy the amenities of the Greensward. [10]

Girls of the East Dean Guide Company, Blue Tit patrol, were runners-up in the Eastbourne Guide Division competition. On 11 December the Guides held a Sale of Christmas gifts made by themselves, they served tea, and gave a vigorous display of Scottish dancing. They went carol singing on 20 December and collected a substantial amount for the Commonwealth Fund for the Blind.

On 12 December the Vicar dedicated a new kissing gate leading from Friston Churchyard to the field above Hobbs eares.[1] Given by Mrs Kennard in memory of her parents, Mr and Mrs Budd, it was made by her son-in-law. Percy Budd, the Head Air Raid Warden for the villages during the war, had been a churchwarden at Friston for some 20 years. The Vicar also opened the CMS annual Sale of Work that made a record £123.

On 14 December 1965 the Youth Club gathered round a Christmas tree erected on the Village Green. A collection, together with the proceeds of a Jumble Sale, was spent on Christmas fare for 36 old people and distributed by Club members. For their Christmas good turn the Scouts sawed up logs for old people.

Over 1965 the Mothers' Union met once a month, with Mrs Molly Howells, wife of the vicar, as chairman. Members had developed a special interest in helping leper children. Mrs Grace Davies Gilbert had started the local Mother's Union in March 1915, although *ad hoc* meetings of mothers had been held at the Vicarage previously. Her daughter, Mrs Patience Harding, continued as the enrolling member until 1954. The local branch closed in 1968, continuing into the next millennium as the Church Women's Fellowship.

Mrs Gladys Foord and Mrs Lilian Jessie Ticehurst had run the Village Library with efficiency and dispatch from its revival in 1951. In 1954 Biddy Kennard produced a card index. After Mrs Ticehurst's death in 1958 Mrs Ethel Winter replaced her. In 1965 there were 164 members and each week about 50 attended. The 700 books were changed three-monthly; 180 going out each week. Every Thursday afternoon Mrs Nora Cheal (Rosemary Johnston's mother) and other villagers gave their time to open up and check books in and out. The library welcomed donations, and in 1961 it received 14 bound volumes of the *Sussex County Magazine,* to form the nucleus of East Dean and Friston's own library.

The library came about after the Coronation celebrations of 1911, when the profits were divided between a new oak door for Friston Church, repair of the organ at East Dean, and a library. The Village Library opened that year and soon had over 500 books - 'a large number are suitable for grown-up people', and each week about 30 books were issued.

By the 1930s it was flourishing under schoolmistresses Miss MG Samuell and Miss E Bowditch. The ESCC took it over as a branch library, and moved it to the Gilbert Institute. When Mrs Foord, who always wore a hat and beads in the library, died in 1971 Mary Fyfield was asked to take over as Librarian, assisted by Joan Robinson, Greta Hoes, Joy White and Dorothy Holt. In the 1980s use diminished - libraries in nearby districts fell from over 100 to 30 in the course of a decade - until on 23 April 1992 the Village Library at the Institute closed. Now there is a fortnightly mobile library in the Village Hall car park.

Back to 1965, the churches were 'beautifully decorated for Christmas and the choir under their organist, John L Bradley, sang sympathetically and lovingly'.

Over 50 children braved wind and rain for the annual Christmas parties in the Village Hall; the seniors' organised by Mrs Joan Towers-Minors and Leslie Ketcher, the infants' by Doreen Greenwood and Molly Howells. Father Christmas and Mary Parker were guests.

During 1965 the Gilbert Estate sold land behind the New Fridays and Underhill Lane [now Went Way] to Hailsham RDC to provide garaging for cars.

The final result of voting on using the old school as the new village hall was: in Favour 216, Against 166, Abstained 724. Despite a Parish Meeting that voted 44 to 20 for the school, the PC decided that the only conclusion was that most voters were not in favour so the Gilbert Estate offer was declined.

13. A Decade of Changes 1966-76

The village suffered a stunning tragedy when Graham Haffenden was killed in a traffic accident on 7 July 1966. Aged 16, he was riding his scooter on the main road going to Seaford, when a lorry in front, with a ladder projecting at the back, slowed down and he ran into the ladder. His parents never got over it and it had a powerful effect on the local Scout troop. The Revd Brinley Howells helped them, especially Martin Ketcher who was a good pal of Graham. The next year the Scouts donated to Seaford County School a canoe made by Graham at the school, but the Troop folded shortly afterwards for lack of numbers.

The village Cub Pack of around 1960 which included Graham Pyle, Graham Gillam, Graham Haffenden, David Satchell, Martin Ketcher, and Dennis Plaice

On 28 July Ray Kemp retired, after 43 years of caring for the verges and footpaths of the parishes. If there was snow in the air he would be out on Friston hill with his spade and grit - and a smile. The PC thanked him for his work. A village lad, his mother ran the laundry, he went to the village school, worked in London for a while, was one of the last to plough with oxen and played a full part in The Players and the Coastguard. Employed by the RDC he painted the first white lines on the local roads - by hand. Raymond Charles Richard Kemp died on 30 July 1991 the day after his 90th birthday leaving his wife Catherine.

East Dean's own constable, Pc Keith Beard, was promoted and moved away. He was "A friend who has always been willing to help while upholding the law".

It was announced that automatic dialling was to be introduced. Beforehand you dialled 9 for a local number and asked 'Florence' to put you through, it wasn't unknown for her to reply, "It's no use trying them, they're out for the day".

The Parish Council [PC] decided to lock the toilets in the Recreation Ground Pavilion when it was not in use. This step was taken with regret, but no other course seemed practicable to avoid wilful destruction and defacing of the toilets.

Environmentally sensitive gardening was coming in. Micheldene WI had the well-known Walter JC Murray speaking on *Wild Life in the Garden.* He said that he planned his garden to attract birds, hedgehogs, grass snakes and even rabbits.

Mrs Agnes Helyar of *Grayscroft,* Michel Dene Road was 100. She lived with her daughter and son-in-law Mr & Mrs FG Cook.

At a ceremony in the Bardolf Hall Queen's Badges were presented to Janet Bertin and Angela Pope, two of the Senior Girl Guides, and Brownie Sarah Towers-Minor was presented with her flying wings.

Gp Capt. HDP Bisley was co-opted onto the PC in place of Mr Fisher, and when Vida Elvin resigned Jolyon Fyfield was co-opted. HRDC stated that it was not sufficient just to state the width of a road for private developments, but the depth and method of construction needed to be specified too. The PC decided that the path from The Brow to Peakdean Lane should be clearly demarcated. After discussions, however, the Estate owners refused to alter the footpath as 'it would be detrimental to their business as site developers', and the PC concluded there was nothing they could do. At least the Ministerial Inquiry of November 1966 into the refusal by HRDC to permit development on the Greensward said that the Greensward formed an integral part of the Estate and rejected the planning application.

The Residents' Association [RA], boosted by its opposition to the Greensward development, had AW Parsons as chairman, JF Marshall vc, W Budd t, Ron W Pringle s, CJ Parris a, and committee Miss Dorothy Alloway, Major-General Colin Bullard, H Dreghorn, Reg N Dean, RW Newland and Cmdr Reggie J Smith.

Among other good news, the Sussex Downs were designated an Area of Outstanding Natural Beauty; naturally East Dean and Friston were included.

A certain Lt-Col Grattan Hart joined the local British Legion branch in January 1967 and went on to be treasurer 1968/9, chairman 1969/70 and president from 1975. As well as playing a full part in most of the activities his was the voice most associated with the Village Fête announcements in the 1980s and 90s.

In the summer of 1967 the PC received the Certificates of Registration for the Village Green, the Church Green in Lower Street, and for Friston Green, although the registration as Common Greens of the Village Green and the Church Green was not completed. In the course of the procedure ESCC found that they owned part of the land between the twitten and the A259 on Friston hill.

General Bullard decided not to stand again for the Hailsham RDC and, as was customary, he nominated his replacement, Cmdr JD Moss.

Hugh Dennis Goodman died aged 72. 'Jack', a founder member of the local British Legion, was chairman from 1931 until 1944, and he came back as chairman in 1957, but gave up due to ill-health. His job was no sinecure and he was in the thick of helping colleagues who suffered hardship in the pre-war depression years.

Micheldene WI heard Mr AE Holter give a talk on *The Sussex Downs Fifty Years Ago,* when teams of oxen were used to till the soil, and a man would carry a 3cwt [150kg] sack on his back for 2d [1p] an hour.

The Cricket Club won the 1966 Tommy Lusted Memorial Knock-Out Competition and Hugh Winter was the Player of the Day.

The new Crowlink WI was going well. In 1966 it welcomed its fortieth member, and its choir gave a concert to the elderly patients at Downside Hospital [now Downside Close]. The next year Mrs V McClelland had a glorious day for a Garden Party at *Beech Cottage* Lindon Close, which added £31 to the funds.

Erik Rosenvinge of Windmill Lane died of a heart attack. He had always worked overseas, not unusual at the time, but with so many servants that neither he nor his wife, Lizzie, had ever boiled an egg, so absolutely every day they went out for lunch at *Crimples,* now *Ridgways* in Meads. Lizzie Rosenvinge died in 1989 at 88.

Farmer John Norman Davies of *The Lodge,* 2 Wenthill Close, retired aged 72 in 1967. He said, "I've bought a dinghy and hope to do some sea fishing. I am not a gardener, but my wife and I are keen walkers and we shall study nature on the Downs." He died in 1979, leaving his house to Grace Taylor.

August Bank Holiday 1967 was blessed with fine weather. East Dean won the cricket match against *Chelmsford Hall* OB 183 to 111, but both teams played attacking cricket. The bowling and batting of Hugh Winter, Mick Weare and Ian Goldsmith was excellent, the fielding was keen, while Eric Bourner gained much applause with his usual display of sixes and fours. The Flower Show was another success with record crowds, the only blot being a swarm of wasps in the tea tent which made life unpleasant for Mrs Bourner and her helpers. With a high standard of entries, Wally Eve won the Tom Martin Challenge Shield, Stan Fuller won the Division 2 Challenge Shield, while Sir Frank Burnand gained a Challenge Cup for his dahlias. As usual the auction was expertly conducted by Jimmy Monico.

The PC agreed that the football club could play on Sunday afternoons. There was agreement in principle that a new doctor's surgery was needed to replace the rented accommodation at *Bess Barn.* No progress was made, however, because the doctors weren't enthusiastic, preferring to see patients at Eastbourne and said they only continued the surgery for those who could not make the journey. The PC also discussed precautions against Foot-and-Mouth disease, and decided to provide a handrail for part of the path in Lower Street past *Cornish Cottages.*

By autumn 1967 the widening of the A259 at East Dean was complete. This allowed for pedestrian refuges in the middle of the road. During the work the East Dean sign was taken down and initially the PC decided not to repair it until - after two petitions and many letters - it agreed that the sign should be restored. There was news of yet another scheme for the A259 road junction at Half Way Cottages.

Snowy A259 at East Dean looking eastwards, December 1967. Cater's Cafe on the left became car showrooms and in the centre is Gore farmhouse, soon to be knocked down

For the first time a Vicar agreed to permit small crosses bearing poppies in the churchyard. Mrs Hilary Pringle raised £127 for her first Poppy collection, when the BL subscription was 17½p [3/6d] and the membership 108. The BL helped Mrs B Simpson of 2 *Pond Cottage, Friston Place* when she could not afford to pay for her husband's funeral: AR Simpson, a gardener, had been a Regular, but died destitute.

A sudden snow storm brought another cold edge to the 1967 winter. Mollie Bertin explained, "The morning was fine yet by noon the snow was thick, and we had to walk back from Old Town. I bought the last pair of Wellingtons at Albert Parade, and any walkers we met looked like Arctic explorers as we tramped over the hill through the blizzard to East Dean. Half way down the East Dean hill we found an abandoned milk lorry so we collected supplies to take to Kathleen Cater's old shop - what became the showroom of the garage."

Mrs Joan Robinson, the PCC secretary, said that on Friday, 8 December 1967, the snow was so deep by noon that the bus became stuck at St Mary's Hospital [Letheren Place today]. "I had to walk back to East Dean, no mean distance. I had my shopping trolley with me and my thoughts were that if I collapse into the snow at least they will see the trolley."

Over the next day the snow went, but following the dislocation to traffic the ESCC stated that a snow fence would be erected on Exceat hill similar to that of Eastbourne Council on the way to *Half Way Cottages*.

The 1968 Cricket Club AGM was poorly attended, but the Club had a successful season. Hugh Winter's average of over 40 was a club record as was his partnership of 156 with Rex Roberts against Selmeston. A special vote of thanks was recorded to Derrick Pyle for repairing the square.

The villages' Milk Tops collection for a Guide Dog raised £150 towards the £250 needed, and Sheila Surtees organised the house-to-house collection for the Friends of the Eastbourne Hospitals.

East Dean Church Choir, September 1968. Back row: Charles Parris, Gerald Mockler, Reginald Smith, the Revd Brinley Howells, Sidney White, Harold Down, Bill Armiger, Douglass Curtis. Mid row: Hubert Foord, Martin Ketcher, Duncan Ketcher, John Bradley choirmaster, Felix Stride-Darnley, Cecil Dann, Leslie Ketcher, Ernest Harman. Front: Judith Stride-Darnley, Doreen Greenwood, Janet Bertin, Jill Greenwood, Stephanie Bailey, Susan Markwick, Florrie Vine, Rose Dann, Elsie Armiger, Kay Ketcher

At the PC elections Friston candidates were returned unopposed and East Dean had the second lowest turnout, 18%, the highest being Berwick at 69%. The PC remained unchanged, Maj-Gen C Bullard, CJ Parris, Cmdr RJ Smith, CJ Goldsmith, J Fyfield, KE Ketcher, DV Richey, G Worsell, RN Dean, Gp Capt HDP Bisley, H Cunliffe, DC Hodgson, PM Hughes, and Lt-Col EC Simmons. The population of East Dean was 1165, and Friston 366. The PC make-up reflected the village's many ex-Service types, hence the story about a village deputation meeting a workman over a building matter. After introductions of General This, Air Vice Marshal That and Commander So-So, the builder riposted with, "Ah, and I'm a general foreman, commanding and marshalling a dozen brickies".

The Women's Church Fellowship members were entertained by a concert given by Isobel Savile's Interlude Singers. Chris and Isobel were to become East Dean residents.

Mary Jessie Rolls Parker died in November 1968. Born 1880, she went to Royal Holloway College and took Oxford Final Honours in Maths and Physics in 1903 and taught maths at a number of schools, including 26 years at St Olave's Grammar School for Girls. She bought *Glebelands Cottage* in 1932 with Miss Bates, who became ill in 1934. Miss Parker resigned her appointment to look after her until Miss Bates died in 1951. She started a Sunday School which developed into the Children's Service, and helped with the Village School lessons at the beginning of the war. She had a three-wheel penny farthing, an early cine camera, was a staunch member of the WI, and drove an open car - cramming on aviator-style helmet and goggles before climbing into her seat. Miss Parker (below) left *Glebelands Cottage* to the PCC to accommodate someone who had served the church. [7]

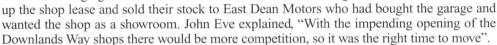

The PCC reported that the Parish Magazine ran at loss of £43 despite a contribution from the church. 'An annual loss is inevitable as each magazine costs more than it brings in.' Mm.

Eight garages and five parking places were eventually constructed at the New Fridays in Spring 1969. The charges were 50p a week for a garage and $12^{1/}2$p (hard standing).

The same year Kathleen and Geoff Cater left for Polegate, having sold the service station to Atlantic Richfield, and David Lambird who had been managing it for them took over the franchise. The Eves gave up the shop lease and sold their stock to East Dean Motors who had bought the garage and wanted the shop as a showroom. John Eve explained, "With the impending opening of the Downlands Way shops there would be more competition, so it was the right time to move".

Another of the villagers, Roderick ['Ronnie'] Glendinning Hall, died aged 90 in March 1969. An assistant to the Gilbert Estate office in Borough Lane from 1900, he married Miss FA West in 1908 and, on appointment as Agent to the Gilbert Estate in 1921, moved to a new house, *Maryfield,* on Friston hill in 1923. His wife died in 1928, and after 14 years a widower he married Nurse L Gay. He served in the 1914-18 war achieving the rank of Major and helped to found the local BL being a Vice-President at his death. He was secretary of the Gilbert Institute Workingmen's Club, secretary to the PCC 1947-60, and church organist 1926-60. Between the wars he played cricket for East Dean, becoming club captain and president. Lately his housekeeper Miss E Dickson cared for him.

An Exhibition of Old East Dean was organised by Phyllis Hughes on 17 May in the Farrer Hall. Apart from Parish Registers, vestry books, rent rolls and manorial accounts, Davies Gilbert archives were displayed showing plans for a railway from Polegate to Birling Gap with a station at East Dean. Ray Kemp was on hand all day to answer questions, and Mrs IV Smith offered to transcribe the old school log.

Most folk agreed with the ESCC proposal to discontinue the caravan and camping site at Cuckmere Haven and create the Seven Sisters Country Park. A not so welcome change, and the first move in the loss of the village bobby, was the introduction of Rural Beat Policing in 1969. This meant that village policemen formed groups *viz* Chiddingly, Selmeston, East Hoathly and East Dean, and could be called to incidents within their group. The Chief Constable gave the spin that this was 'more efficient use of manpower, and that it was not proposed to remove the local officer, but on some days he would be manning the area car'.

The PC discussed yet again bonfires. The conclusion was that anyone has a right to burn garden refuse with due regard to the rights of those who may be affected. It is only a nuisance when in excess - a matter of opinion. The PC did agree the plan for numbering of Estate houses, which they had deferred in 1963. It was timed for 25 March 1970.

The PC had its moments. The cricket pavilion was discussed again because when on August Bank holidays the partitions were removed for the Flower Show the cricket club was unable to use the facilities, and the structure was weakened. To prevent further damage the PC agreed to meet half the cost of a marquee hire for the Flower Show. The Show committee came back saying that they were not prepared to organise the Flower Show if the PC insisted that they had to hire a marquee. The PC decided to form a small committee to look into the matter, which seems to have done the trick, for the Show went ahead and was a great success, thanks to Wally Eve donating the cost of the marquee.

At least the PC and the community were unanimous in one matter, namely that the all-year-round Summer Time trial should continue.

Richard Bradley started Belle Tout excavations above Horseshoe Plantation on 17 August 1968 and continued the following year. The dig proved it to be a site of the Beaker people from about 1750BC, which had gone through many phases. Flint scrapers, arrowheads, axe heads were found and mill stones confirmed that they grew corn. Beaker people from Iberia were named after their pottery of which many fragments were found. They lived in huts within a compound enclosed by a bank and a ditch to keep cattle from straying rather than defensive. There were pits where grain was stored, although almost everything had been destroyed except the pottery. Small fields were discovered confirming that these people were not nomadic, and although no post holes were found clumps of flints suggested that they had been packed around the decayed posts. The Gilbert Estate accommodated all the 'diggers' in the old village school.

Edward Maynard Pinkney, the Church organist, was on pay of £710 per annum and £130 expenses. He was a good player, but was finally asked to leave after over-indulgence in the Christmas festivities. Roy Kibble became choirmaster and organist in June.

At the Bowling Club AGM, the secretary, Dennis Slipper, reported that play had been extended to 24 October, which was a record, the green was in good condition thanks to the attention from Arthur Davidson. The singles winner was president Dr HDF Fraser, doubles winners A Matthews and S Kitching, and monthly spoons were won by A Matthews, GR Mockler, CW Norris, DC Slipper and AW Symington. The treasurer, Charles Parris, captain, Peter Q Smith, and other officers were re-elected. Harold A Down announced that he would be leaving Friston in the near future and he made a donation to the club in appreciation of the friendships he had made and enjoyed on the green.

When the Civil Defence was disbanded ESCC decided to retain some measures to cope with peacetime disasters, and in 1970 an East Dean group was formed of RN Dean, Cmdr RJ Smith, Maj-Gen C Bullard and Lt-Col EC Simmons. They undertook training in First Aid and map reading. Few volunteers came forward, however, and the group devolved into the Emergency Plan for the Village.

About this time Micheldene WI started a Keep Fit class in the Farrer Hall. This was a great success and under Frances Wheeler (later Mace) continued into the 21st century at the new Village Hall.

The PC noted that piped TV had been extended across the main road to the village which was a deviation from the route originally planned. HRDC objected to Friston Green being registered on the grounds that there were rights of way across it. The PC countered that it was impossible to prove whether the rights had been acquired before or after the Green came about and common sense should prevail.

At the AGM of Scouts and Guides in June 1970, the Graham Haffenden Award was presented by the Vicar to the whole Scout Pack. Lt-Col Grattan Hart said that both the Scouts & Guides and the BL aimed at mutual service and help. He presented a trophy to Patrick Burns and a shield to Maria Eve. Harold Down thanked Mary Fyfield, and Gwen Pearce. The new treasurer was Eileen Goldsmith with Fred Fuller secretary, the committee being Miss Eyre, Mrs Dann, Miss Leeder, Mrs Pilkington, Mr Powers, Mr Spink, Mrs Thurman and Mr Thomas. The Guide Jumble Sale, organised by Joan Thurman of *Bryn Cottage* and Diana Shearer, *Corner Cottage,* was its usual success.

A highlight of any East Dean season was Mrs Hilda Carter's *Afternoon of Spoken Word and Song.* 'Her pupils enchanted with a wide variety of items interspersed with songs by Beryl Monico, Nicolette O'Brien, and Letitia Kent, meanwhile Thomas Fyfield gave a spirited rendering of *The Smugglers' Song.* Katherine Bertin, Rachel and Mary Fyfield delighted us, and a light touch was provided by Penny Shearer. We enjoyed Kay Ketcher and Mary Farren's poems, and Phyllis Thackeray's prose, but the outstanding item was Mrs Carter's interpretation of *High Tide on the Coast of Lincolnshire 1571* by Jean Ingelow - no mean feat of memory.' Leslie Ketcher said, "Mr Carter, a retired bank manager, was a churchwarden and treasurer of the parish magazine. The magazine was going through a sticky patch and his wife organised soirées to raise money. She had been a top teacher of elocution whose star pupil had been Flora Robson. These afternoon 'dos' were in the Village Hall and all present were given a plate with a cake and two sandwiches before the readings began. Sometimes this involved dressing up from a theatre box of costumes reeking of moth balls. When invited you felt you'd arrived in East Dean."

In 1970 the Old Village School was restored and converted into a private house. That year Tom Goodman went into his new Downlands Way shop and had to work hard to make a success of it, for the rates were always increasing. "In 1970 £42/year, in 2000 £700/year, and there are extras for business premises."

A British Legion Old Age Pensioners' Outing 1970, arranged by the Vines for the 20th time. L-R: Catherine Kemp, ?, Grace Taylor, Florrie Vine, L Goldsmith, Ethel Winter, ?, Joe Pownall, Wally Eve, Ray Kemp, Bob Seymour, the Revd Brinley Howells, and Jessie Eve. They went to Sheffield Park, calling at the *Ram Inn* Firle, with the usual sing song on the way. The Eve family defrayed the cost of the refreshments

The Players' autumn curtain rose on an *Old Time Music Hall,* at the *Bardolf Empire,* with Fred Bicks in his element as Master of Ceremonies. Led by him the audience joined in the first chorus at 7.30pm and every one afterwards. The jokes were good, and the dances and songs, arranged by Priscilla Hodgson, evoked many memories. The show officially finished with Fred leading the cast in *Auld Lang Syne,* but he went on and on - at 30 minutes to midnight he was calling the cast back for yet another reprise. Fred was The Players, and a fine producer and actor too. It was his life and he was irrepressible - one wag, no doubt edentulous, even suggested he spent more time on the stage than in his dental surgery.

The steps at Birling Gap were removed because of encroachment by the sea. Surely inevitably, in November walkers were stranded at Birling Gap, so the PC asked ESCC to erect warning notices at Eastbourne and Cuckmere.

Patience Davies Harding (a Gilbert) died aged 87. Her retiring nature did not stop her playing a full part in village life, even when as dowager at *Went Acre.* She didn't seek the limelight, but had the knack of gracefully saying a few apt and amusing words.

During a busy year the local BL organised the usual Jumble Sale, a Derby Sweep, the Old Age Pensioners' Outing, and a Dinner/Theatre occasion. From 1971 the old folk's arrangements were by Mrs Dann, and called the Senior Citizens' Outing.

A new venture for the East Dean BL to provide working capital was their first attempt at a coffee morning on 16 May. Organised by Mrs Hart, it was a success and raised £44. The BL also started a Car Treasure Hunt on 22 July, suggested and organised by Howard and Doreen Greenwood with help from Mr and Mrs Money. Finally, a Fête was held on 12 September at the Recreation Ground on the suggestion of Lt-Col Grattan Hart, 'to be a forerunner of a bigger show in 1971, the Jubilee Year of the BL'. In spite of bad weather the takings were £120, thanks to the Eve family donating half the cost of the marquee.

The branch decided not to add Friston to its name of East Dean, but to increase the subscription. Capt Lidiard left for Eastbourne, remaining a Vice-President, others who left included Brig JC Hudson. Maj-Gen Bullard was p, Lt-Col EC Simmons and Capt RS Lidiard vp, Grattan Hart c, Comd JD Moss vc, RC Paterson s, and committee RE Dann, Mrs D Greenwood, CAR Dann, CW Vine, and D Richey, who was also the standard bearer. P Quinton-Smith became treasurer. Poppy Week brought in £151, again organised by Hilary Pringle. Recipients of welfare vouchers were Mrs Goodman, Mrs Melling, Mrs Ransome, Mrs Martin, Mrs Fowler, Mrs Seymour, and Mr Cheal had his usual bottle of sherry.

Unigate introduced a delivery charge for their bottles of milk in November 1970.

The shaft in the cliff face exposed in 1971 by erosion between Belle Tout and Birling Gap (shown by David Galer right) was examined by experts from SAS. A metre in diameter and some 45m in length, although partly filled, it had notches in the sides suggesting footholds. No certainty about age or use, most likely a well shaft but could be associated with ritual ceremonies: thought to date from 1700BC, later than the Beaker people.

The winner of the ED&F WI slogan for the 1971 anti-litter competition was Delia Bicks' *The Country Looks Fitter Without Your Litter.*

The PC discussed the provision of a small roadside car park by Friston Forest on the Jevington road, as at times 20 or more cars were parked along this road.

The British Legion [BL] became the Royal British Legion [RBL] on 29 May 1971. That year the local branch organized the Village Fete and celebrated its 40th anniversary with a slap-up dinner by Edouard Frederic at £1 per head plus tip of 2/- [10p].

The ESCC plan was issued in which the A259 was to be a 24 ft carriageway as a scenic route, whereas the A27 would be made a fast dual-carriageway to Brighton.

Micheldene WI had a talk on the development of the Arlington Reservoir since its commencement in 1968.

Pc John Debley felt that the procedure for contacting Hailsham was unsatisfactory. "With four burglaries in 1971 and numerous thefts in the village, far more than in previous years, don't hesitate to ring my number, 3111, if you see or hear any suspicious happenings. Watch out for strangers, record any suspicious car numbers and secure your property. In an emergency dial 999 and ask for police."

Both the Vicar and his wife, Molly, had become part of the village, and he had been the Bowling Club Singles champion. Kindliness was the assessment of his main quality. The esteem in which he was held was shown by his Retirement Testimonial fund, which reached £1160. He said, "I wanted a fireside chair for my wife and I to use in turns. Now that I have enough for 22 chairs you have set me a problem".

In 1972 Leslie Cumberland ceased being the East Dean milkman after 26 years. He delivered every day, took a warm interest in his customers, and was an active member of The Players. He and wife Barbara said goodbye and thanked folk for their kindnesses.

The Revd Harry Parsons was instituted and inducted as parish priest on 29 April 1972. He and wife Ethel had a son John and an adopted daughter Pat Nickson.

The grant for enlarging the entrance lobby and kitchen of the Farrer Hall and adding new cloakrooms only came through in July. So the start had to be put back from May to October, causing great inconvenience with bookings.

Chess facilities had been available to residents since 1969, with no subscriptions or officials, games being arranged by ATF Roberts of Elven Lane.

The Church Fellowship held another of their *Any Questions?* This time the panel was

Gay Ockenden, Rosalind Stein, the Revd Gustav Aronsohn and Gordon Vellenoweth, the Vicar as Chairman. Formidable questions were answered with aplomb until the panel were stumped by, *Whom would you consider the most lonely, a bowls widow or a WI widower?*

Phyllis Hughes considered protecting Friston Pond by scheduling it as being of historical interest. As it was man-made it could be registered as an Ancient Monument; possibly the first pond to be so designated when registered in 1973.

With a damp morning turning into a bright afternoon, the highlights of the 1972 RBL Fête were an exciting tug-of-war won by Vines Cross, and the Eastbourne Model Flying Club's demonstration. The show made £231, but a youth fell through a tent canopy, broke his arm; and caused damage to the tent.

Over 100 came to the Bardolf Hall for the Revd Brinley Howells' retirement presentation on 1 November 1971. L-R Gustav Aronsohn, Harold Down, Joan Heath-Robinson, the Revd Brinley Howells, Douglass Curtis, Cmdr Reggie Smith (speaking), Major Davies-Gilbert, Molly Howells, Sibyl Davies-Gilbert, Sidney White, and Brig Gerald Mockler

Fred Fuller of 4 Churchfield won first prize in the HRDC Garden Competition, with Wally Eve of 2 Churchfield awarded a certificate.

The PC purchased a new Union flag to replace the one stolen from the flag pole during the period of mourning for the Duke of Windsor. Other matters mentioned were clearance of the excessive growth around Friston Pond; Upper Street to be included in the area regularly swept by the RDC, and under new procedures all PCs would receive notifications of planning applications in the parish. The members agreed to consult the Residents' Association and the District Council representative before any applications were put to the relevant committee or brought up to a PC meeting. News was received that *The Outlook* was to be retained in the name for the new development on the Old Willingdon Road. [9]

A record 103 sat down to the Bowling Club annual dinner at the Lansdowne Hotel. Major & Mrs Davies-Gilbert and the Revd Harry Parsons and his wife were present. The captain, Percy Smith, followed an excellent meal with a witty speech and Enid Fraser presented the trophies. Cmdr Reggie Smith proposed the toast and Mrs Skinner responded. Secretary Arthur Davidson had a presentation in appreciation for all the work he put in, and the Revd Gustav Aronsohn thanked Bill Symington and Cecil Holliss for the arrangements.

As previously mentioned [5] shortly after the dinner Mrs Sibyl Davies-Gilbert initiated thoughts of mixed play by pointing out that the Old Town Ladies' Bowling Club welcomed new members.

Two applications for bungalows went to the PC, they had no objection in principle to them, but thought the developments premature until main drainage had been installed.

The PC noted that pedestrians were having difficulty using the footpath through the Arco garage on the A259 which had not been demarcated, and also that the Southdown Bus Company had withdrawn the 197 bus during the winter.

Cmdr Reggie Smith gave a talk to the Church Fellowship on *Leaves from my Diary,* an account of his experiences as a high-ranking Police Officer during the London Blitz. 'His observations brought a whiff of nostalgia to the many in his large audience who had lived through the events described'.

Returning to 1972 the local shops and services included East Dean Motors automobile engineers and MOT approved testing station; Kemp Bros Forge Garage on the hill; in the new Downlands Way were ET Goodman newsagent at 9, L Wood & Sons family butchers 10-11, Miller's hardware garden supplies and haberdashery 15, and Yvonne's hairdressing 16. Alongside the Village Green were CH Prior builders (based at 19 Hyde Road), *The Tiger* with hosts John & Peggy Barrett, Weller's general stores and post office, and WF Bunting family butcher. Around the village were John Eve private car hire, JPR Dann carpentry, AJ King builder and plumber at *Garden Cottage,* and FW Schafer plumber and decorator *Crangon Cottages,* Birling Gap. Although now living in Hailsham, Jimmy Holter, electrical installations, was the choice of many residents.

Presentation in May 1972 to Poppy Day collectors entitled to Certificates of Appreciation. L-R Florrie Vine, Phyl Dean, Lt-Col Grattan Hart, Hilary Pringle, (Poppy Day organiser), Sybil Parris, Brigadier GR Mockler, and Gwen Wynne. Mrs MY Neale, Mrs FW Schafer, Lady Shawcross and Mrs Molly Simmons, also eligible, were unable to be present

The PC heard in 1973 that vandal drivers had used the recreation ground as a racetrack and as a result the grass was in a bad state. Windows had also been smashed in the pavilion. The police found the culprits, but had not taken them to court because the parents paid for the damage. A resident offered to supply and fit a new sink unit in the Farrer Hall.

Harry West, village postman, retired on 28 February 1973. His residents subscribed £70 to recognise the occasion, and he had been awarded the Imperial Service Medal in 1968 to commemorate 41 years' service. Born in Friston, he was carter's boy, blacksmith's apprentice, vehicle mechanic and gardener. When he became postman he was single-handed, his deliveries were to less than 100 people and a letter cost 1d [$^{1}/_{2}$p]. At retirement he went to 800 houses, had three other postmen part-time, and letters cost the equivalent of 10d. During the 1939-45 war he served with the RAF in Africa, Sicily, Italy and Yugoslavia, and returned to a wage of £4.25 a week. He always rose at 0600h worked till 1000 and again from 1445 to 1845. Towards the end of his life lived at *The Dipperays* with his cats.[1] He died in 1992 aged 84.

"Harry West [shown right] was a lovely man," said Gill Sergeant. "When I was at *Payne's Dene* he came with a postcard that I had posted locally. He handed it to me with the words, 'We try our best but we do like an address'. I had forgotten to put any address on the card, but he had recognised my hand-written message."

After ten years Joyce Macgowan retired from distributing the magazine to the deliverers, and Beverley Winter took over.

East Dean's new sewerage scheme was deferred by HRDC having to prune projects following a pegging of the rates.

Crowlink Ladies WI held a coffee morning in aid of Alexandra Rose Day in place of the door-to-door collection. The £33 proceeds went towards patients' comforts at Hellingly Hospital. In July *Birling Manor* opened for the Friends of the Eastbourne Hospitals.

The Budd Cup of the Bowling Club was won by Percy Smith's captain's team, who received the Cup donated by her father from Kathleen 'Biddy' Kennard.

The Cricket Club presented a silver salver to Eric Bourner, a player for 17 years, on his 600th match for the club, 14 July 1973. His wife was given a cut glass vase for her support. And East Dean won the match against Alfriston, Eric scoring 35.

The PC discussed one-way traffic in East Dean village, and noted that the local doctors' surgery was open only two days a week. 'Plant-a-Tree in 1973' ideas seemed to be in the air except that the PC were all at sea about planting trees on the recreation ground.

In December 1973 Micheldene WI was due to hear a talk on Astrology but the speaker forgot to turn up. At least that year farmer Edgar Williams turned up another horde of Roman coins on *Bullock Down Farm.* They were in a Henmoor bronze bucket, only the second found in Britain, now in the British Museum, and far more valuable than the coins.

There was exceptional traffic congestion around the village on Boxing Day. This followed the blocking of the streets when hunt followers' vehicles obstructed roads, driveways and spoiled Greens. The Police admitted they were caught napping by the crowds, and it would not happen again. The Gilbert Estate, however, considered that the workmen at *Greywalls,* who parked on the Church Green, were responsible for the damage.

Phyllis Thackeray mentioned that thanks to help from coffee mornings the Retired District Nursing Sisters' Association had built the Joan Nightingale House in Haywards Heath, a wardened accommodation of 24 self-contained flatlets for retired nurses.

The annual Church Christmas Fair opened by Sibyl Davies-Gilbert, raised £600.

Over 1973 and 1974 the village converted to 'natural gas', but it didn't help with the miners' strike and the three-day week. At the beginning of 1974 Church Services were held solely in East Dean Church because of the national emergency, and other meetings were cancelled. Joan Nash welcomed Crowlink WI members and thanked those who brought an oil heater and candles to the meeting. Their talk was on the probation service, when they learnt that in 1939 there were 11,000 in prison compared with 37,000 in 1972. Micheldene WI met in the Gilbert Institute (instead of the unheated Farrer Hall) and took turns to sit by the coal fire provided by Joyce Bailey and Fred Harris, while hearing about the Samaritans.

East Dean and Friston's Parish Council [PC], the 'grass roots of local government', met on the first Tuesday every month except August. Most of the work was undertaken by the committees: Finance and General Purposes, Rights of Way, Recreation Ground, and Halls.

PCs are able to incur expenditure which is in the interests of the area to the equivalent of a 2p rate. This is fairly large, but the right is used sparingly because it has to be paid for by the residents. Often the power of persuasion to other bodies is more effective, examples are Friston pond declared an Ancient Monument [8], the ownership of Friston Green, and the kerbing of the Village Green along Upper Street - it doesn't always work, the speed limit on Friston hill is one example. The PC also requests the provision of car parks, such as the one in Horsefield, the re-instatement after laying of cables or sewers, and has the right to be consulted about planning applications. It decides to enter Best Kept Village competitions, helps to organise celebrations such as the Queen's Jubilees, and preserves local amenities - East Dean village is designated a Conservation Area.

Election meeting, 1974. L-R Dolly Alloway, Jane Gow, Frank Lloyd, Ian Gow, 'Cabby' Banks and Phyllis Gundle. Mr Gow replaced Sir Charles Taylor, MP since 1935

In addition, the PC manages the Recreation Ground, Sports' Pavilion and Children's Playground, the War Memorial and flagstaff, the bus shelters, the Rights of Way and Friston Pond. In 1974 the PC was also concerned about the persistently poor TV reception in the village, which was without priority for relay TV. Finally, the PC gave assistance towards the cost of mowing the Greensward.

Wealden District Council [WDC], an amalgamation of Hailsham Rural District Council [HRDC] with Uckfield RDC, came into being on 1 April 1974. It would be responsible for housing development and planning, footpaths and bridleways, transportation, refuse collection and environmental health.

The annual RBL Treasure Hunt, organised by Ron and Hilary Pringle, had almost 50 participants in 12 cars followed by an excellent supper at the *Bull Inn,* Newick, with a profit of £2. This was the last one using cars, for after a barbecue in 1975 it was decided to have Walking Treasure Hunts and save fuel.

The PCC had several photographs of previous vicars framed and placed in East Dean Church vestry. The sum of £321 was collected for Christian Aid, but repair and treatment of a defective beam at Friston Church came to nearly £3000.

A Gift Day for church funds was held on 28 September instead of a Christmas Fair. Although the Revd Harry Parsons was not well enough to attend, £1140 was raised. During the Vicar's illness the Revd Gustav Aronsohn helped out - which included writing a two-page letter for the October Parish Magazine, and a three-page one the next month.

The Post Office Telegraphs closed Upper Street and the twitten to lay cables from *Half Way Cottages* to Cuckmere. The PC had to request the PO to refill the trench.

The first ravages of Dutch Elm disease were noticed and worsened in 1975, with the loss of ancient trees near *Went Acre.*

The Gilbert Institute was renovated by the Gilbert Estate (repairs and rewiring) and by volunteers (re-painting). It was agreed that the Institute would be the responsibility of the PCC, although remaining the property of the Gilbert Estate.

Joan Macpherson, the CMS Missionary link, had resigned from the CMS in 1973 and the following year the parish received its first letter from Pat Nickson, as her home parish, on her way to Bangladesh after three years in Afghanistan.

The 13th Annual Art Exhibition had 90 paintings on view and no less than ten were sold and £18 sent to RNLI. Since the classes started in 1960 the tutors were Daphne Oliver for four years, Howard Faulkner eight years, and now Leonard Breach.

East Dean & Friston Play Group's Jumble Sale raised £41. This enabled them to refurbish the equipment (for the previous five years they had used second-hand toys and small chairs bought by the parish for the evacuees during the last war), and to open two mornings a week for about a dozen children from $2^{1}/_{2}$ to 5 years.

Leslie Kerr filled the PC vacancy left by the resignation of Peter Quinton Smith. The informal question time before the main meeting attracted a few more questioners. Permission was received for a new bus shelter at Friston.

Carols were sung in East Dean Church on 16 December, Roy Kibble directing the church choir and the WI choir conducted by Peggy Fuller contributed in superb style. The selection of poems was beautifully spoken by Meg Horton.

In the course of 1974 the Seven Sisters Country Park opened. Country Parks are not National Parks; they are smaller, freely open to the public and intended for recreation. The Park has examples of chalk grassland established by the grazing of rabbits and sheep over centuries, where the grass is kept short, but not overgrazed, so small plants are allowed to grow, and it also contains shingle and mudflats. A warden lived at Foxhole, and there was a nature trail which started at Exceat.

The Children's Christmas Parties in the Village Hall on 1 and 2 January 1975 were funded as usual by Mr Hunnisett of Windmill Lane. For the 8-14 year-olds the Christmas tree was bedecked by Thomas Fyfield and David Taylor, and they had games, tea and a present from the tree. The under-eights, the next day, had a visit from Father Christmas after games and tea. Santa, through his local agent Leslie Ketcher, appealed for a new costume.

The PC agreed a precept of £3270 and confirmed that there was no change in electoral arrangements, just one district councillor for East Dean, Friston and West Dean.

For the first time the RBL Jumble Sale on 11 April was split between the Village Hall and the Farrer Hall, which had the better quality clothes, to avoid slightly worn clothes being sold off for a song. The event made £120.

There was a Confirmation Service at East Dean Church, the first since 1968. The Sidesmen, J Pearce, FJ Abery, AR Chick, and SW Bourner were re-elected.

The PC said there was a need for a car park to relieve the congestion around The Green, and noted that the cost of maintenance for the Recreation Ground was rising. Maureen Honey asked about the provision of a tennis court for East Dean and Friston. The PC decided to show interest in taking charge of a path by the bollards in Downlands Way, and if after 12 years no owner had come forth the Council could take steps to claim ownership.

The youths of East Dean, having met informally for some months, formed themselves into an official Youth Club.

In July three gardens in Friston were opened for the Friends of the Eastbourne Hospitals, Mrs HA Down's *Westholme* in The Ridgeway, Mrs GM Chapman at 2 Royston Close, and Mr SA Steel 3 Royston Close. Mrs V McClelland and Mrs M Piggott opened their gardens in The Ridgeway for WI funds and raised £92.

At the 19th annual meeting of the East Dean & Friston Scouts and Guides Supporters'

Association with Mrs H Down in the chair, Cmdr Don Moss presented the RBL shield to Suzanne Morecambe, and the president Mrs Sibyl Davies-Gilbert presented the Tawny trophy to Susan Greenway. Pat Down had been chosen to meet Princess Benedikte of Denmark at the triennial World Guides Conference held at the University of Sussex.

The Players' autumn production in 1975, *Lloyd George Knew my Father,* provoked more laughter than for years, but was not well supported. Fred Bicks and Nora Evans, the eccentric general and his wife, kept the play bubbling, and were well supported by Peter Lilley and the rest of the cast - all to the theme tune of *Onward Christian Soldiers.*

Toni Bagshaw, first in every ED & F WI competition all year, at short notice spoke to Micheldene WI on *Reading for Adults.* Mrs R Ginns gave the vote of thanks.

The Players' *Lloyd George Knew My Father.* L-R: Ken Penfold, Fred Bicks, Catherine Clunies-Ross, Delia Bicks, Cedric Best, Michael Knight, with Nora Evans at the piano and John Shortall extreme right

The RBL complained that the colour of the War Pensions Order Book had changed from Red to Buff so that it looked as though a War Pensioner was collecting a Social Security benefit, and members considered this an insult. Cmdr Don Moss retired as president and was replaced by Lt-Col Grattan Hart. Road stewards had been introduced to cope with delivering RBL items, and in view of the expense the practice of sending Christmas Cards would be discontinued. Ian Gow MP was the guest speaker at the annual dinner.

In early 1976 the level of Friston Green was raised, partly to restore land disturbed by recent works and also to deter parking.

The Revd Harry Parsons resigned as parish priest because of heart trouble. Mr Sibson of the PCC reported that the Gilbert Institute was used on 67 occasions July to December; that the parish was required to pay £651 towards bringing the Vicar's stipend up to £2400; and that Mrs Knopp (who had replaced Mary Child) had resigned as organist at the Family Service. Elsie Armiger, who had cleaned East Dean Church for 18 years, also retired.

Mr J Woodhams, of Bruford's, outlining the history of jewellery to Micheldene WI, said that British silver was the best. Afterwards members welcomed the chance to attend a Cytology Clinic, while some members volunteered to run in the Litlington Pancake race.

The Young Wives' Group had a successful year. Their first AGM, led by Nancy Chapman, was followed by a talk *First Aid in the Home.*

Sibyl Davies-Gilbert suggested a Gardening Club, and this was taken up at a well-attended meeting on 27 January 1976 in the Gilbert Institute. The Gardening Club was formed on 25 March with Mrs Sibyl Davies-Gilbert as president, AT Johnson c, JM Chapman t, and Eric G Harris of Peakdean Lane s. An annual sub of 75p and monthly meetings were agreed, and the question of obtaining fertilisers at bulk prices was raised.

The first meeting was a talk on *Spring Gardening* by Plumpton Agricultural College staff, and in June Mr and Mrs Chapman opened their garden at Royston Close. [5]

The PC felt that the general shabby state of Birling Gap was a matter of concern. [5]

Mrs Gertrude Urquhart Thomson, who had lived in Friston from 1932 to 1960, died age 95. She left a legacy to the church.

Jack Pearce, DH Mew, T Abell and Douglas Horsman of the RBL cleaned the Bardolf Hall from roof to floor boards, for which Mrs Sibyl Davies-Gilbert expressed her thanks. It meant that the Derby Sweep and supper could be held at the Bardolf, when 71 attended, catered for by Peggy Bonham, Doreen Greenwood, Grace Taylor and Florrie Vine in expert fashion.

A RBL Barbecue Supper was held in the Pringle's Mill Close garden in perfect weather. There was a raffle, mini golf, as always the

One of Priscilla Hodgson's Dancing Classes at Eastbourne's Central Library Theatre when, with Rose Dann, East Dean children achieved high standards

swimming pool, and £41 was raised for the Poppy Day Appeal. The RBL Fête on 31 July was also well supported, and with Doug Richey kept busy running the coconut shy, and thanks to £60 from the White Elephant stall, £380 was raised, £151 up from 1975.

Micheldene WI enjoyed *Twelfth Night* at the Chichester Festival Theatre in spite of the terrific heat wave, and on 30 August the Flower Show went ahead in the hope that some flowers and vegetables would survive the dry weather. In the event gladioli, peas, lettuce and potatoes were scarce, but roses, tomatoes and runner beans were in abundance. Some 135 entries in the Home Produce section, meant a record number of entries, 442, easily beating the previous best of 414. Peter Johnson was the outstanding exhibitor, though three generations of the Armiger family chipped in, along with Wally Eve, Fred and Stan Fuller. Mrs Kath Fuller won the prize for roses, Mrs V Matthews took the *Amateur Gardening* Red Ribbon for the best exhibit, and Clive Mattock the new Children's Challenge Cup.

By September 1976 the kitchen and cloakrooms had been redecorated at the Village Hall, and with the imminent advent of main drainage the PC had given approval to provide full sanitary facilities at the Farrer Hall. A contribution to the Gilbert Estate to continue the kerbing round the Village Green was agreed.

The Bardolf Hall was filled with 150 parishioners in September 1976 to present a cheque of £1152 to Harry Parsons on his retirement. It marked the end of 41 years since his ordination; 12 in Nigeria, a curacy at Worthing, 21 at Polegate and 4½ at East Dean with Friston. He said the village possessed two of the loveliest churches in the country.

The Players announced no autumn play because the Bardolf Hall was unavailable. It was decided not to repeat the 1975 experiment of playing in the Wannock Hall.

Kay Kennard retired as editor of the Parish Magazine and was succeeded by Sheila Surtees from November 1976.

The annual NSPCC autumn coffee morning at *Tolmans,* Warren Lane, organised by Betty Rowson, raised £89. In anticipation of the usual seasonal festivities, Doreen Greenwood gave a demonstration on the art of icing a cake to the Young Wives' Group Christmas meeting.

14. Another Silver Jubilee Year

The year 1977 was notable for the celebrations staged by the village to honour the Queen's Silver Jubilee. The Parish Council [PC] decided to take the lead with a steering committee and, rather exceptionally, to contribute £100 expenses.

The planning, preparation, fulfilment, and the satisfaction and congratulations on the wholehearted success of the occasion occupied most of the days of the year.

Silver Jubilee Committee at Bill and Maureen Honey's *Appledown* 1977.
L-to-R Douglas Horsman, Hilary Pringle, Margaret Lees, Sheila Surtees, Peter Winter, Lily Donovan, Eileen Goldsmith, Maureen Honey, Dennis Slipper, Jane Booth-Clibborn, Gordon Vellenoweth, and Ronald Pringle

There were other, more routine, events over the year. The Diocesan Pastoral Board decided that the benefice (not the parish) of Jevington be united to East Dean with Friston, and on 3 February the Revd Raymond Lewis, Vicar of Jevington, was licensed as Priest-in-Charge of East Dean with Friston and Rector of Jevington. Appropriately for a former gardener, the new Vicar was a down-to-earth fellow, who got on with everyone, except for one point - his wife was a manager at Marks & Spencer. For some folk vicars' wives acted as another pair of arms and legs for their husband and a working one was unthinkable.

Over 80 members attended the Gardening Club's [GC] inaugural dinner at the Lansdowne Hotel. Toni Bagshaw proposed the toasts, with chairman, AT Johnson, and the Revd Gustav Aronsohn replying. In March the club held their first AGM reporting the expeditious order of 4½ tons of bulk fertiliser at a trade price of £350. The proposed talk had first-night nerves when a faulty projector defied strenuous efforts to get it to work.

Perhaps they should have contacted the East Dean and Friston Community Care Group, now four years old, who had prepared an Information Leaflet detailing the assistance available in any emergency.

At the annual PCC meeting Cmdr Reggie Smith and Leslie Ockenden were elected Vicar's wardens for East Dean and Friston respectively, and Bill Symington and Brig. Gerald Mockler as people's wardens. Secretary, Alison Vellenoweth, reported that East

Dean Church Green would be kerbed with granite setts; that £1732 of work was required on the churches, and concluded by paying tribute to Charles Parris, the treasurer, for his lucid accounts. The PCC re-elected Harold Down, Phyllis Hughes, Quinton Smith and Gordon Vellenoweth, while Hilary Pringle and John Chapman replaced Biddy Kennard and Fred Doherty. New sidesmen were Thomas Fyfield and ATF Roberts (East Dean), and Robert Sibson, Henry 'Bill' Willey, Ian Coombs and Ronald Carpenter at Friston. Cyril Griffin, magazine treasurer, presented the accounts. Diana Eyre expressed appreciation to him, Biddy Kennard, Sheila Surtees (Editor), Lilian Butler, Beverley Winter and the deliverers.

The Vicar congratulated the editor on the new set-up of the magazine and its prompt delivery. He went on to thank the Revd Gustav Aronsohn, the Revd B Tanner and Dr Max Warren, and the lay readers Douglass Curtis, Leslie Ketcher and Geoffrey Coombs.

One sad day in the year was 10 March when the village heard of the tragic death at 71 of Major Charles Gilbert Davies-Gilbert (born Harding). A Master of the East Sussex Hunt, horses were his life [5].

The PC was unchanged except that Sid Worsfold was co-opted in place of LW Kerr, otherwise it was a case of the PC giving the Village Sign a face-lift, while the RBL arranged a Flag Day for the Silver Jubilee, which raised £177. The Gardening Club [GC] got into the act by organising a Jubilee Competition for the Best Kept Front Garden, and before long all the village clubs and organisations had decided to enter the Carnival Procession and vie with each other for the prizes on offer.

The Three Saints with Ron Pringle, Leslie Ketcher, Fred Bicks, and Charles Parris, a scene from the East Dean Players' *1066 and All That*

The villages learnt that the RNLI collection organised by Betty Rowson and EM Timms realised a record £98, and Lt-Col Grattan Hart stated that the Wealden Planning Committee meetings were now open to the public.

While this preliminary work for the Jubilee was in progress, the long-overdue main drainage was being installed in the village. Jolyon Fyfield had been involved in the design of the scheme now taken over by Southern Water. The work in East Dean village finished on 1 June, just in time for the Jubilee celebrations, although the Parish Council refrained from entering the Best Kept Village competition because of the 'mess' caused by the upheaval. Some trees along Gilbert's Drive had to be cut down, but the ESCC arranged for suitable replacement plantings.

The Players had been out of action since *The Dream House* in May 1976 because, so it was said, the Bardolf Hall was in use for storage, but they decided to contribute to the community's Jubilee Festival and use the Farrer Hall.

So on Thursday, 2 June, East Dean's Silver Jubilee kicked off with The Players' role. Over three evenings, with a Saturday matinée, The Players presented the frolic *1066 and All That,* a triumph of dedicated effort over difficult conditions. The Box Office of Fred and Delia Bicks reported capacity audiences, but how producer Ron Pringle managed to convey the essence of this prank in the Farrer Hall by well-judged cuts, playing in curtains and other theatrical devices, only he knew.

It went with great zest, there was excellent teamwork and most effective musical numbers. No space was available for a back-stage, but the back-stage staff of Hilary Pringle, Jo Satchell, Michael Chapman and Jolyon Fyfield, did a tremendous job. Amid a profusion of scenes and props, two stood out: Fred Bick's judge, and Rose Dann and Charles Parris as a Puritan Maid and a Cavalier.

The cast of The Players' *1066 and All That* outside the Farrer Hall: Sitting front l-r: Jo Satchell, Mike Knight, Delia Bicks, Gay Ockenden and Rose Dann. Standing l-r: Val Wills, Jo Perry, Leslie Ketcher, Jayne Leete, John Shortall, Ron Pringle, Arthur Perry, Sylvia Tompsett, Charles Parris and Fred Bicks

On the morning of Sunday, 5 June, there was a Family Service at East Dean, taken as usual by Leslie Ketcher, and later a Jubilee Thanksgiving Service, with latecomers having to sit in the porch. Both churches were florally decorated in regal style. On Sunday afternoon many residents went on from viewing the church treasures on display to Tea in the Vicarage Garden hosted by the Revd Raymond and Mrs Kathleen Lewis.

Holiday Monday, 6 June, was the big Jubilee day. In the morning *Birling Manor* gardens were open through the kindness of the Davies-Gilbert family and proved a great attraction, and kept the Young Wives' Group busy providing coffee.

Showers and cold winds did nothing to hinder the Carnival Procession as it assembled at the Greensward, Deneside, just after one o'clock. Over 150 entrants appeared in Fancy Dress classes for clubs, groups, and for walking individuals, 14-years and over, and under 14-years. There were also classes for decorated floats and vehicles, and fancy dress equestrian groups and individuals, all coordinated by Margaret Lees, Kay Ketcher, Dennis Pitcher and Mrs H Wagstaff.

The Church Fellowship organised a walking group, and the Gardening Club was represented by a decorated barrow and gardening attendants arranged by Marjorie Watson of Warren Lane.

The Royal British Legion Fete opened at the Recreation Ground with the arrival of the procession, and when everyone was assembled the prizes were presented to the winners.

Fete events included the Seaford Silver Band, children's races, country games, and the presentation to winners of the Best Kept Front Garden competition. There were also stalls, side shows, refreshments and a clairvoyant.

Faced by the wintry conditions the large crowd made a beeline for the marquee stalls, the tea pavilion and the fortune-teller's caravan. Most of the stalls sold out early, with the tombola closing up within the hour. The gross takings were over £500 as against £390 the previous year.

The Jubilee cricket on the Recreation Ground, Sunday 5 June, with East Dean & Friston Cricket Club playing WG Gracefully CC of Isfield

The Monday evening Jubilee Dance at the Recreation Ground marquee, arranged by Jane Booth-Clibborn and Dennis Slipper, with a wine and cheese buffet, was enjoyed by over 90 locals.

Tuesday, 7 June, saw the WIs put on an all-day Crafts Exhibition in the Farrer Hall. At noon, the time the May Queen was crowned, patches of blue sky appeared to ensure that at least the Maypole Dancing would be graced by the sun. [7] 'Happy Village Tea Parties' on The Green and in the Village Hall were among other well-attended events, with Peter Johnson doing well in the Tug-of-War.

The Judges for the Jubilee Carnival Procession on the Greensward, 6 June, included Joan Thurman and Ronald Hughes (seen here), and John Surtees

The Village Silver Jubilee was a joyous and memorable occasion. Despite some worries in the January about how it would go, and the weather breaking up after three settled weeks, the celebrations were an outstanding success, thanks to splendid efforts by the organisers, to those who took part so wholeheartedly, and to encouragement from the whole community .

Maureen Honey thanked all who had helped to make the Silver Jubilee celebrations such a success, and the village paused for breath.

The RBL held their now usual split Jumble Sale, using the Farrer Hall for the better quality clothes, with the main sale in the Village Hall.

The float, *Britannia Rules,* with front L-R Peter Connew, John Oliver, Barrie Hearns, Hilary Worsell, Nina Booth-Clibborn and Maureen Worsell, with Rosemary Johnson as *Britannia,* all awaiting the judges' decisions

Floral Jubilee float with front L-R: Susan Greenway, Alison Miller, Sarah Ginns, ? Polyanna Stirling, Susanna Chapman and Lucy Honey. Lynn Johnson is partly obscured extreme right

Leading the procession out of Michel Dene Road across the A259 to the Recreation Ground is the Church Fellowship walking group, Christianity comes to East Dean in 683, with Evelyn & Ron Carpenter, Gay Ockenden, Mary, Rachel & Thomas Fyfield, Ray Trickett, Charles Parris, Bill Symington and Les Ketcher. In the background is Cater's old shop, in 1977 the East Dean Motoring Centre showroom

With the judging complete, the Jubilee Carnival Procession crossed the A259 to move from the Greensward to the Recreation Ground for the Fete. The village policeman, Pc John Debley, halted the traffic in royal style

In a further attempt to return to normal activities, the PC agreed the principle of a car park and public conveniences on the Horsefield, although the need was questioned by many councillors saying that it was only required when the *Tiger* was open. As the Gilbert Estate, the landowner, was not prepared to enter negotiations it would be some time before detailed plans were prepared. When the PC learnt that the Gilbert Estate owned the Church Green; permission was sought to mow it.

The Jubilee Gymkhana in the Ten-Acre field on Monday, 6 June, was much enjoyed by all of the young riders in their carnival costumes - except possibly for one participant

The magazine printed a letter from Link missionaries Roger and Pat Hooker, and their children Richard and Mary. Pat's father, Canon Max Warren, had died in the July.

The Flower & Vegetable Show was held in the Recreation Field on 29 August. The entries showed good support, though the attendance was slightly down. As usual, Peter Johnson won most of the shields and medals, with Elsie Armiger, Kath Fuller, Evelyn Carpenter, Mrs FM Williams, Kathleen Banks, Dolly Alloway and Fred Fuller getting among the prizes. Mary Oliver and Stephen Debley were the main winners in the children's section and they received Jubilee Crowns.

The Carnival Procession and the Fete were followed in the evening of 6 June by the Jubilee Dance in the Recreation Ground marquee. Some folk nipped out to watch the Beachy Head beacon, returning to the dancing which went on well after midnight

The Chess Circle, arranged by Guy Heath Robinson, restarted in the autumn, and the Harvest Supper in the Farrer Hall was as popular as ever; the meal prepared by Alison Vellenoweth receiving rave comments.

After a public meeting on 20 September a Youth Club committee was formed to look into the activities that could be made available in the village. The club was to meet in the pavilion every Friday for table tennis, darts, stamp collecting, needlework and cookery, washed down with soft drinks and crisps.

More than 20 helpers planted 2000 daffodil bulbs around Friston pond on Saturday, 29 October. Guides Susan Greenway, Julie Pownall, Susan and Caroline Chapman had previously cleared the ground. Whether it was the dense shade or the damp ground, the plants failed to flourish apart from those near *Mary's Mead*.

Bill Honey chauffeurs the Jubilee May Queen, Jackie Cuming, to The Green. The May Queen's procession was greeted by the singing of *Hurray, Hurray, it's Jubilee Day*, heralding the Maypole dances, and the crowning of the May Queen

The 1977 annual Art Exhibition of the East Dean & Friston Art Class was held on the same day, and raised £23 for charity.

East Dean & Friston WI held a morning market with preserves, cakes, vegetables and other home produce for sale, while Micheldene WI had a talk on the Seven Sisters Country Park by John Gascoigne, Head Ranger.

Silver Jubilee Maypole Dancing on the Village Green, Tuesday 7 June, commemorating the crowning of the May Queen. Left to right in front, Helen Dann, Andrea Evans, and Lucy Honey - with injured right arm in a sling

At the AGM of the Residents' Association [RA] a presentation was made to John Marshall in recognition of his many services. Chairman for eight years, he had held many offices, and led the opposition to the development of the Greensward.

Mollie Bertin relinquished her work as parish organiser for Christian Aid, but a WRVS 'Meals on Wheels' service continued, run by Olive Newsome and a band of helpers. They were paid 8p a mile for fetching meals from the Hyde Road WRVS kitchen and delivering them to the housebound in the village and about.

Mrs P Roberts, of *Child's Cottage*, 42 Warren Lane, saved the local Brownies from closure after 21 years by succeeding Eva Oliver and Jane Booth-Clibborn. Local secretary, Mrs Hilda Thomas of *Brabourne*, 24 Hillside, said, "The Guides also need help, Renee Wicking is retiring, 22 years after she had started as 'Leffie', Mrs Pat Down is leaving for Wannock, and young Guider Scholastika Zimmer has left the village'.

The Tuesday afternoon Stoolball matches on the Recreation Ground involved East Dean versus Friston, and adults v. children, ensuring hilarious entertainment. L-R Barbara Nash, David Wheeler, Jane Booth-Clibborn (batting), John and Jill Jarvis - and the best teams won, of course

The Estate sewers were adopted on 21 October and the Estate Sewage Works [now Sussex Gardens] were not used from that date. Southern Water agreed to take over the remainder of the private sewers on the Downland Estate as public sewers from 1 January 1978. The cesspits of the village houses, such as those in the front gardens along Gilbert's Drive, could now be filled with garden rubbish.

Tributes were paid to Lt-Col Tommy Gordon, of *Linden Mead*, a sidesman, and a school manager until it closed. He lent his garden every year for the Guides and Brownies Patrol Competition, and helped to build a happy neighbourhood.

Jubilee Barbecue. L-R: Robert Mattock, Charlie Wibley and Ron Pringle. The sight of the roasting of a whole lamb throughout Tuesday afternoon led to crowds queuing up for the feast at the evening Country Dancing that concluded the Jubilee Celebrations

So village routines went on. Two gardens, those of Stanley and Iris Wilson of *Toriba*, 6 Windmill Lane and Sidney Steel of 3 Royston Close were opened for the Friends of the Eastbourne Hospitals; Wings Week raised £85; the RBL Poppy Appeal £289, a record; Carol Singing raised £15 for NSPCC and the Indian Cyclone Disaster - and the library rent for the use of the Gilbert Institute increased from £25 to £45 a year, but the Jubilee permeated people's thoughts.

The village name was perpetuated, too, for when the Help the Aged flats in Granville Road were completed one was named *East Dean and Friston* as a 'thank you' for the generous help of local people.

At their July meeting the East Dean and Friston WI decided that they had enjoyed the Jubilee celebrations so much that they gave three cheers for Jubilees.

Jubilee Brownies outside the Farrer Hall. L-R back row: Jane Booth-Clibborn (Tawny Owl), Sarah Nash (Pack Leader), Eva Oliver (Brown Owl); middle row: Emma Davies-Gilbert, Alison Miller, Catherine Booth-Clibborn, Lynn Johnson, front: Susanna Chapman, Susan Dann, Rachael Booth-Clibborn, Caroline Worsell, Donna Hearns and Carolyn Hicken

Jubilee Girl Guides L-R back row: Rachel Fyfield, Pat Down (captain), Renee Wicking ('Leffie'), Julie Johnson, Sarah Nash; in the middle Helen Dann and Susan Greenway; front Caroline Chapman, Catherine Booth-Clibborn, Julie Pownall, Andrea Evans, Mary Oliver

Members of this WI formally commemorated the Jubilee by making curtains for the Farrer Hall, presented by president Alison Vellenoweth to Phyllis Hughes, chairman of the PC. For their contribution PC members decided on a Jubilee seat to be erected at the Michel Dene Road and Summerdown Lane junction.

Bill Symington retired as captain of the Bowls Club, after ten years in office, but not before the club placed a Jubilee teak seat at the end of the green.

The Young Wives' Group held an evening of Jubilee Memories in the Farrer Hall, and at the same hall on 10 December photographs of the Jubilee events, many by Alan Oliver, were displayed and drew big crowds.

The interest continued into March 1979 when the Church Women's Fellowship saw a film made by John Chapman of the East Dean and Friston Jubilee celebrations.

Joan Nash concluded, "The Silver Jubilee celebrations went off so well. I'll never forget the children with their banners in the procession. The Crowlink WI presented the £100 oak seat at the top of Deneside in commemoration".

The success of the Jubilee events found the committee some £200 in pocket, of which £40 was donated to the Prince of Wales' Jubilee fund, £25 towards the daffodils around Friston pond, and the rest was held for good village causes.

The 1977-78 Parish Council. Left-Right, Back: Robin Miller, Dorothy Bowles, Maureen Honey, Dennis Slipper, Jean Simpson, Maurice Hopkins, AR (Tony) Bish (clerk), John HW Chapman, Jane Booth-Clibborn. Front: Jolyon Fyfield, Gordon Vellenoweth (v-c), Phyllis Hughes (in the chair), Peter Winter and 'Bill' Willey

It had been a truly happy occasion and by bringing together many of the residents emphasised the community spirit that existed in the villages.

Typical of the village spirit was Dad's Army, or Operation Ivy, at Friston Church. Gerald Mockler, Hugh White, John Granville White, Fred Abery, Ronald Carpenter, 'Tim' Rowson, Bob Sibson, Harold Joyce, John Eastham, Sidney Steel, 'Bill' Willey and Leslie Ockenden tidied the graveyard and tended the plants.

As part of the Silver Jubilee every village youngster had received a Jubilee crown, with Doreen Greenwood exhibiting her calligraphic skills for the presentation scrolls. More good news was to receive a satisfactory report on the year's work at Chyngton School, which was attended by 44 children from East Dean and Friston. So the villages' future looked bright.

Wealden DC shelved the proposal for a car park at East Dean, but the PC continued to look ahead. At its December meeting the members agreed that East Dean did not have a hall worthy of the community, but the doubters asked - would it ever be possible to sell the present hall to pay for a new one?

15. From 1978 to the present Century

The Parish Council [PC] received a petition from 25 householders against a proposed ramblers' footpath at the back of The Link. Betty Leatherdale was worried about security, and when Mrs Simcox said it would devalue her property the proposal was dropped.

New members requested for the Flower Show committee. The show had survived the 1976 drought, but marquee hire of £140 instead of using the pavilion meant it ran at a loss.

On 21 February the Revd Raymond Lewis was inducted as Rector of the united parishes of East Dean with Friston and Jevington. The Reception was held in the Farrer Hall. He was one of the few Rectoral incumbents of all the Vicars of East Dean going back to 1261. An additional Remembrance Board was put up at Friston, cost defrayed by Sheila Surtees.

In March 1978 the people of Friston & East Dean unanimously voted to become one PC. This would save having two elections and precepts, however, the annual parish meetings remained separate and met respectively at 1930 and 1915h. Lt Col Grattan Hart elected chairman of Wealden District Council [WDC] for a second year. He represented East Dean.

East Dean & Friston WI committee 1978-9, Hobbs eares field in the background.
L-R: Betty Harms, Gay Ockenden, Elsie Nicholson, Marjorie Jones (stick), Jayne Leete (tall), Dorothy Griffin (handbag), Lily Corbett (at back), Alice Steele (handbag at side), Eileen Goldsmith (back), Ivy Tomkins, Delia Bicks (back) and Toni Bagshaw

In September the Sussex Sheep Dog championships were held at *Birling Manor;* Leslie Ockenden continued his WEA talks on Sussex in the Gilbert Institute.

Swallows in Old Willingdon Road - one of the loveliest gardens in the villages - opened for Friends of Eastbourne Hospitals. Eric Harris, the Gardening Club's [GC] secretary, reported that the November talk had been disappointing - 'so the less said the better'.

The Church Fellowship January 1979 meeting was cancelled owing to the freezing weather and others reported Arctic conditions; at least a new boiler paid for by Pat Down was installed at Friston Church. Micheldene WI's party was called off, and the PC meeting was shorter than usual. Magazine donors, however, were up at 37 for the month.

The next month Micheldene WI had Cecil Baker talking on the RNLI, while Crowlink WI went on a pub crawl, in imagination of course, when they had a talk on *Inn Signs*.

The centenary of the birth of Frank Bridge, composer and tutor of Benjamin Britten, was celebrated by a weekend of music at Friston Church in June 1979. He had lived at *Friston Field* until his death in 1941. The organising committee was chaired by the Revd Raymond Lewis, with Rob Jones as the artistic director, Charles Parris, treasurer, and members Leslie Ockenden, Rene Jones, Sheila Surtees and Gordon Vellenoweth. The event, which was most successful, was backed by SE Arts and the Frank Bridge Trust. Leading musicians who performed included Christopher Bunting, Yonty Solomon,

Christopher Herrick and David Johnston. Peter Pirie gave an introductory talk on Bridge and his music, while Anthony Payne acted as chairman. Local resident Daphne Oliver contributed memorabilia. There was a Commemorative Service on the Sunday.

Charges for the Farrer Hall increased to £1.50 a session and the Village Hall to £1.25.

The PC paid £392 a year for mowing the Recreation Ground. Norah Cheal gave up as halls' caretaker after 20 years and Janet Johnson took over. The PC launched a blistering attack on the ESCC for failing to make Friston hill safer. Sid Worsfold said the hill was so hazardous that few used it. Phyllis Hughes added, "The ESCC are only interested in traffic flows, it is immaterial to them how many people are knocked down".

On the Saturday morning of the Frank Bridge Centenary Weekend there was a display of Morris Dancing, Maypole Dancing (right) and Priscilla Hodgson's dance production *Youth Takes a Bow,* all on the Village Green. Helen Chapman is the dancer mid-right, Christine Hughes and Rob Ginns are in the standing onlookers on the right. Pauline Joslin also organised a party in her garden to celebrate the event

The Royal British Legion [RBL] Village Fete was a great success. In the children's races East Dean beat Friston avenging their defeat in the Silver Jubilee stoolball.

Gifts from the church's Harvest Festival were sent to *Staveley Court* Old Peoples' Home now that Downside Hospital had closed. Florrie Vine gave up looking after East Dean Church and was succeeded by Rose Dann. Mr AW Symington donated a Hoover to the church in memory of his wife! The church insurance premium was £375, an 8% increase.

Youth Club members painting the Pavilion, 1979. L-R: Matthew Honey, Nick Honey, Kevin Elphick (in window), Paul Johnson (sitting), Julie Johnson (in window), Peter Nash (dark top/trousers), Susan Chapman and Sarah Nash. The Youth Club, restarted by Maureen Honey, met in the Pavilion on Friday nights, membership was now 60 with 47 crammed in one Friday. They celebrated Bonfire Night, but instead of each person bringing a few small fireworks the club solicited donations to have a better show, so they walked to Birling Gap with torches, ate 300 sausages, rolls and onions and had a great firework display

Anthony Burns-Cox, sub-organist at Llandaff Cathedral, gave an organ recital at East Dean Church on 5 September at the time of the funeral of Earl Mountbatten which had so moved the country and the concert provided comfort on such a sad day.

John Stanley organised the RBL Jumble Sale. The RBL had arranged for local residents Jane Sutherland and Jonathan Greenway to attend an Outward Bound School course at Ullswater. The Senior Citizen's Outing was cancelled, but instead they had a Senior Citizen's tea party. The 1979 Poppy Collection, organised by Hilary Pringle, raised £371.

The owner of *Marycroft [Reflections]* agreed to cut back hedges to improve uphill visibility for traffic at Upper Street and a second *Slow* sign was put on Friston hill. The East

Dean foootball club had refused to alter their pitch to avoid damaging the cricket square, and as there were now no East Dean players in the team the lease to the club was terminated; they were asked to remove equipment and to stop using the name East Dean.

Membership of ED & F WI was restricted to 105 to be able to fit in the Village Hall.

A letter to RBL Secretary D Poynton presented him with a neat problem to which he replied, *'Thank you for your letter returning a request for a subscription and pointing out that you have paid for this year. I can confirm that you are not in arrears with the RBL, but am returning the subscription demand to you because it is from the Downs Golf Club.'*

Golden Jubilee of ED & F WI 6 April 1979, Bardolf Hall. Present: Mrs Stamper County c and Lady Castle-Stewart, with p Alice Steele v-p Mrs M Jones, s Ivy Tomkins, t DW Griffin; Elizabeth Alston, Toni Bagshaw, Jean Barnett, E Butler, Evelyn Carpenter, Mary Child, B Claus-Harris, Lily Corbett, V Crocher, C Dickinson, K Donoghue, Nora Evans, Eileen Goldsmith, Dorothy Hall, Betty Harris, Jean Hart, Betty Knight, MD Lines, S Muspratt, C Mockler, M Neale, Elsie Nicholson, Gay Ockenden, Olive Reynolds, Ann Scully, Diana Shearer, M Slater, Hilda Spence, VK Stutchbury, Edith Tait, I Tomkins, Alison Vellenoweth, BW Walton and LM Watson. Front facing: Elsie Armiger, Renee Wicking, Grace Taylor, Delia Bicks, Jayne Leete, with front Catherine Kemp

The Friston-Wannock road designated a C road to allow a weight restriction. A direction sign was erected at Friston bus stop directing visitors to the telephone box in East Dean.

Final event of the ED & F WI Golden Jubilee Year was a Wine & Cheese Party at the Towner Art Gallery on 17 October. Nearly 100 members and friends were present.

The Players' production was *Night Must Fall* with tickets at 50p each; followed that year by a minor disaster when The Players forgot to order wine for their Yuletide Party.

Plough Sunday, held on 13 January in 1980, commemorated a time when little ploughing was done in the autumn, and represented the start of the cycle which ended in harvest. Other Church matters included raising minimum stipends for clergy to £4,615, and the Diocesan quota was set at £2,700. Two brass candlesticks stolen from East Dean Church were recovered by the Police, but brass vases taken from Friston were not returned.

Micheldene WI had a talk by Gerry Armstrong on umpiring the exciting 1975 Wimbledon final of Arthur Ashe and Jimmy Connors. He and his family became residents.

The Guides appealed for a leader. Although 14 were in the company and they won the Camp Fire Singing Cup in the Eastbourne Music Festival in 1979, with Pat Down's retirement the only senior was Rachel Fyfield who at 18 couldn't accept responsibility.

New committee of Young Wives was Jean Connew, Rosemary Greenway, Kathleen Lewis, Gill Marlow, Angela Myerscough, Cheryl Veitch, Carol Voake and Janet Whittome.

The East Dean Players presented *Without the Prince* directed by Joy Bryant and Jane Leete, with a wonderful set by Jolyon Fyfield, Frank Leonard and Bunny Banfield.

Long-widowed Margery Alice Wilford was 100; her neighbours, Fred and Diddy Abery at 11 The Ridgeway, had given her unstinted care over the years.

Phyllis M Hughes retired from the PC in May 1980. She first came to East Dean in the 1920s. She was on the PCC, edited the Parish Magazine for ten years, was elected to the PC in 1960s and chairman from 1971. The local Hon. Secretary of the SAS, she wrote a short guide to East Dean and Friston and her broad knowledge of the history of local matters was legendary. A WI member, she instituted collection of bottle tops for a Guide Dog, and devoted much time to the restoration of Michelham Priory. She died in the December.

Alexandra Rose Day collection for Hellingly Hospital raised £84; Joan Jackson's coffee morning at Downs View Close raised £73 for leukaemia research, the Lifeboat Appeal raised £173 - £20 over the previous year - and £155 was raised for Battle of Britain week.

RBL Village Fete was held on the Recreation Ground. There had been doubts about hiring a marquee, which was becoming increasingly expensive, but heavy rain made it essential. Polegate Majorettes marched with precision and Mrs Hodgson's Group danced delightfully within the confines of the tent and £288 was raised.

Pc John Debley was given a presentation when he left in September after 13 years.

The Players presented Nada Bouch's *Lord Arthur Savile's Crime.* Michael Knight as Lord Arthur Savile and Delia Bicks as Lady Merton could not fail. Fred Bicks as the incompetent anarchist had just the right mix of zest and inefficiency. Ron Pringle was the faithful Butler who had his feet on the ground more than the others, but not by much.

The village celebrated the 1981 marriage of Prince Charles and Lady Diana in some style - it was also the best weather of the summer. Here many of the villagers enjoy a street party. The ED & F WI held a memorable commemorative luncheon, and one new house, *Acorns* in Warren Lane, had a plaque built into the wall to record the event

A Hunger Lunch held in Farrer Hall to show concern for underfed people in the world. The final performance of Priscilla Hodgson's *Encore* in Eastbourne's Library Theatre had Rose Dann singing, and controlling the children at the same time, with Gladys Leonard at the piano. Ricky Hodgson repeated *We're a Couple of Swells,* this time with son Sam.

The usual children's Christmas parties were at the Farrer Hall on 2 and 3 January 1981. Kathleen Lewis, John and Vicky Mockler organised the games, Mr & Mrs P Hunnisett of Windmill Lane, provided the presents, the Young Wives ran the party for 28 younger children while Sheila Surtees, Rosemary Greenway and Leslie Ketcher supported.

It was a great shock for the village when on 9 February 1981 the Rector, Raymond Lewis, died of a stroke age 59.

Sick Room equipment for borrowing was now with Mrs Shaw and Mrs Stutchbury at *Meads,* 10 Deneside. In 1994 Don Preen assumed the custodianship, but the items were deteriorating and from 1997 Sick Room equipment was provided by the Practice Nurse.

The Guides and Brownies raised £565 at an auction held in March, helpers included Mr & Mrs B Knopp, Mr & Mrs CR Watson, Mr & Mrs S Hall, Mr & Mrs Barnes, Mr &

Mrs Goldsmith, Lord Hardinge, Mr AW Symington, Mr & Mrs W Tracy, Mrs BM Rowson, Miss V Hilber, Mrs Baldwin and Lord Kingsdale.

Comdr Smith presided and 74 parishioners were present at the Annual Vestry and Church Meetings on 30 March; Mrs K Ketcher said the Electoral Roll had 210 members. Elected to the PCC were Ron Carpenter, HP Steele, Mrs EI Jones and Mrs RA Baker. The next month Roy Kibble presented a musical evening for the Church Fellowship.

Maureen Honey was re-elected PC c, Cmdr Winter v-c. John Chatfield as Hon. Solicitor and Rupert Taylor as Custodian of the Union flag. Jolyon Fyfield re-appointed as Planning Applications Officer and Christine Hughes as Governor of Chyngton School (attended by 50 East Dean children). Esther Worsfold and Michael Chapman were co-opted. After Douglas Horsman had explained that the RA paid the mowing cost of £365 a year with some help from WDC, the PC agreed to help toward the upkeep of the Greensward.

Prizes were presented in an Anti-Litter Competition to ten children, with Susanna Chapman and Lucy Jarvis winning their age groups. Meanwhile Miggs Bailey, John Robinson and Pc Ray Hill completed a 26-mile sponsored walk raising £300 for the disabled, and Micheldene WI gave their annual supper to 16 senior citizens from East Dean.

Bowling Club match Over 70s v. Over 80s in 1981. On the left the 70s l-r: Charles Parris, Jack Pearce, Bert Steele, CW (Rags) Norris, AA Goode, John MR Chapman, Denis Slipper, Mark Lester, Guy Heath Robinson, George Tomkins. To the right the 80s l-r: Sam Kitching, Bert Steele, Leon Ceulemans, Reg Smith, Ray Kemp, [Len Knott, under 50, substitute on the day] Percy Smith, Leslie Ockenden and Gerald Mockler

The film *Fire Gems* conceived by Priscilla and David Hodgson of *Darby Cottage,* had the children of the village develop a story about smugglers and Excisemen. Pc Ray Hill played a policeman, Ray Kemp a fisherman, and the coastguard staged a mock rescue with nail-biting climax amid local scenery at its best. Continuity and camera were in the hands of Susan and Helen Dann, Julie Johnson, Chris Connew and Robert Mattock. Leading players included Cindy Wheatley, Caroline and Hilary Worsell, Carolyn Hicken, Lucy Honey, Rachael, Catherine and Nina Booth-Clibborn, Becky Wigmore, Malcolm Johnson, Sam Hodgson, James Hughes and Sylvia Tompsett. It took two weeks to film, two months to edit and it was shown on two afternoons in the Farrer Hall in January 1982.

The July 1981 RBL "Carnival" Village Fete on the recreation ground, celebrated 50 years of the local branch. Opened by comic Ken Goodwin, and pianist Walter Landauer, the Maypole, Morris dancing, coastguard display, children's display, and fun stalls made £2435 despite dismal weather. Des Walder said that local organisations including the RBL bought equipment for the disabled at the Churchill Rehab. Centre out of the proceeds.

East Dean and Friston had entered the Best Kept Village competition partly in memory of Phyllis Hughes who longed for the village to win, but also to make everyone more litter conscious. The judges had to see that the village was a caring community looking after its open spaces, verges, bus shelters, and overall appearance of private properties.

The news that they were runners-up in the East Sussex Best Kept Large Village group was greeted with delight by the residents and a determination to do better. Elsie Armiger said, "I am very fond of the village, it's so friendly", and Bill Armiger added that he was proud of the village history. Maria Launder also said, "I am very proud of our village". Priscilla Hodgson, "It's like a fairy-tale village" and David Hodgson agreed, "I think it is a beautiful place to live, with a good community spirit". Jonathan Greenway said, "I prefer living here to anywhere". George Worsell thought that there was nowhere as good as East Dean, and Margaret Smith summed up with, "I am very happy living in the village".

ED & F Chess Circle restarted for the autumn, while ED & F Art Group held the 20th Annual Exhibition of their work in September, the first year without a County grant. Eighty-two pictures shown and 21 sold, raising £40 for Talking Newspapers.

East Dean & Friston Flower Show, 1981 prizewinners. L-R: Peter Armiger, Louise Davies-Gilbert, Peter Johnson, Elwyn Jenkins and in front Andrew Johnson who won the *Creature from Outer Space* exhibit.
The unlimited parking at the Dunwick Barn was popular with exhibitors and visitors alike. Other winners were Mrs C Parkinson (Rose Bowl), Mrs J Nash (Home Produce Cup) and Mrs E Armiger (flowers)

Cecil Smith, caretaker of the Pavilion and Recreation Ground since 1972, retired due to illness; Clifford Haffenden of The Fridays appointed in his place.

The Revd Anthony Harbottle was instituted as vicar in November 1981. Since 1968 he was chaplain to the Queen and Royal family at Windsor. At Easter, during his Ministry, he received the present of a whopping Easter Egg from HRH the Queen Mum. Gill Harbottle was welcomed to the December meeting of Church Women's Fellowship [CWF].

The Young Wives went to the Downlands Way hairdresser for pate and wine and to watch the most fascinating feats with comb, hairdryer, dyeing, 'scrunching', a 'hat creation', tinting with a comb-in spray gun, and a free cut and blow dry by 'Nigel'.

The GC AGM in January 1982 AGM was cancelled because of snow, but Meals on Wheels battled through ice, blizzard and fog to collect and deliver the hot meals.

John Dann, assisted by Trevor Hollingdale, gave an account of the Auxiliary Coastguard to the Church Fellowship in February. In May Dr Mark Lester talked to 80 of the Church Fellowship at the Farrer Hall on Eastbourne's new St Wilfrid's Hospice, and raised £122.

Nina Booth-Clibborn, Tracey Barnett, David Chapman, Helen Chapman, Elaine Clarke, Peter Connew, Sarah Dann, Daniel Ginns, Barrie Hearns, Sam Hodgson, Debra Holloway, James Hughes, Lucy Jarvis, Richard Jarvis, David Pringle, Caroline Worsell, Hayley Wheatley and Janine Worsfold all passed the cycling proficiency test.

The RBL enjoyed a Cheese and Wine supper, Elsie Allan interpreted 'cheese' as an appetising three-course meal. Jack Pearce organised the wine, and Don Mew the draw.

Mr SJ Hollick, co-proprietor of *The Barn,* co-opted on the PC. When a vacancy arises on the PC an election is held if requested by ten or more electors, otherwise filled by co-option.

The Gardening Club held their Garden Party at May Cambridge's *Beckon,* Old Willingdon Road, when 145 members raised £248 for the funds.

In Maritime England Year a Cuckmere Valley Smugglers' Festival was held on 19 June 1982. In the morning there was a display of coastguard apparatus at Birling Gap by John

Dann and Richard Worsell; another of photos and artefacts by Christine Hughes in the Farrer Hall; demonstrations by the Sea Cadets; Jane Booth-Clibborn directing Maypole dancing by village children; sailors jigs were danced by the Wendy Beale school of dancing, with music by the Eastbourne Folk Club and the Old Town Band. The highlight of the afternoon was an ambush of smugglers by Preventive Officers on Went Hill with Margaret Lees in charge of proceedings, followed by a mock trial directed by Fred Bicks and The Players. That evening in the Farrer Hall there was a showing of Priscilla and David Hodgson's film *Fire Gems.* Over a day of enjoyment £46 was raised for the RNLI.

The Maritime England Smugglers' Festival 1982. **Left:** back row l-r, Esther Worsfold, ?, Jane Booth-Clibborn, Christine Hughes; middle row Susan Ryder, Janine Worsfold, Sarah Wigmore; front row ?, Kirsty Hughes, Nina Booth-Clibborn, Jo Graves, ?, Hilary Worsell. **Right:** Nigel Lees, as Jonathan Darby, with Margaret, Steven and Chris Lees outside Weller's Stores

The PC agreed to object to East Dean being included in the Lewes Constituency. Yet despite over 1000 (out of a 1400 electorate) signing a petition against being linked to Lewes, the Boundary Commission transferred East Dean and Friston to Lewes.

Betty Rowson's NSPCC Ploughman's Lunch at *Tolmans,* 13 Warren Lane, made £188.

The *Sussex Express* of 11 June 1982 reported that Paratrooper Mark Lambird was among the troops at Goose Green, the famous British victory in the Falklands campaign. His parents, Mr and Mrs David Lambird, lived in East Dean. Mark, later a resident of Friston himself, returned safely to open the RBL Annual Fete at the Recreation Ground on 24 July. The profits from the Fete would go to the South Atlantic Fund.

On 30 August the Flower and Vegetable Show at Dunwick Barn had 430 entries; Peter Johnson was pre-eminent in the awards, his skill and knowledge earning him nine cups.

Some 100 folk attended a presentation by Charles Parris of £316 to Dr Basil Barkworth on his retirement in September 1982, Mrs Beryl Barkworth was presented with a bouquet.

In 1982 fears were expressed about several of the bridleways. Margaret Lees considered that Bridleway 6, was unsuitable for horses. Peter Winter warned that horses were using the narrow path along the A259 between the villages when only the lower half was classified as a bridleway. The NT would not contemplate upgrading the footpath in Hobbs eares field, but finally in 1984 agreed if it ran from the Farrer Hall to Crowlink Lane.

Throughout the eighties Mrs Pat Burnett gave WEA talks at the Gilbert Institute on Art - Baroque and Dutch Art; Renaissance Art; the Rococo style of Watteau and Tiepolo; the more realistic Chardin and Hogarth, and the neoclassicism of David and the Romantico-expressiveness of Goya. As Miss WG Joyce of Micheldene Road, the organiser put it, "There will be slides, much lively talk and a visit to a London gallery".

ED&F WI held a craft exhibition on Motherhood to celebrate the birth of the new Prince William - and there was a new Village Sign by the Village Hall.

The Revd Anthony Harbottle was appointed Hon. Chaplain to the RBL Sussex County; Hilary Pringle and Florrie Vine attended the Albert Hall Remembrance Service; Chris Ray and Reg Mathieson were appointed to the committee and the Poppy Appeal raised £542. John Granville-White died of cancer; a most cheerful, good-humoured and helpful man.

The Players 1982 autumn show was *When We Are Married*. Produced by Lewis Wilson this was a sparkling production and played to capacity houses. The Farrer Hall was also filled for the visit of the Toy Man to the Wives Group.

PC members, including recently elected Mr RE Ginns, were introduced to Pc Graham Gillam the new village policeman.

At 0620h on 6 January 1983, Maurice Hopkins, East Dean's sub-postmaster was beaten up by thugs who snatched a mailbag, and left him needing hospital treatment for severe cuts and bruises. He had collected a sack from the sorting office on the A259 and was walking back to the sub-post office in Upper Street. On Thursdays the bag carried extra money for pensions and the robbers got away with a haul of more than £10,000.

Maurice Norrell who had looked after East Dean's footpaths for eight years retired in March 1983, the PC presented him with a pair of binoculars in appreciation of his work. The PC heard that of 50 Upper VI village pupils at *Seaford Head* 30 had gone to university. Members also noted that the Southdown 12 bus was now 712 and that the *Tiger, Grimaldi* restaurant, and Weller's Stores agreed to contribute to the mowing costs of The Green.

In April 1982 an *All Our Yesterdays* exhibition in the Farrer Hall, was organised by Christine and Christopher Hughes and Esther Worsfold (l-r above). Mrs PM Hughes, had collected most of the items, she had also sent material to the Lewes Record Office. The oldest relic on show was a Stone Age axe, along with a piece of timber from the *Nympha Americana* wrecked in 1747 and a collection of sheep bells. £52 was raised for the Boys' Club

The Women's Church Fellowship had a talk by the Rector on *Butterflies*. He said that there were 69 species and some of the migratory types flew at over 15,000 feet. The Wives' Group had a more 'feet-on-the-ground' talk on electric cooking and most were convinced that a microwave was an essential kitchen item. ED & F WI discussed the threatened move of ENT surgery from Eastbourne to Hastings to which the public had responded in protest. Micheldene WI had a hilarious talk by a driving instructor: about learners who confided their ailments, tried to start the car with their house keys, and caught their necklaces in the steering wheel; Crowlink's talk was on the *Mary Rose;* sunk 1545, raised October 1982.

Lewis Wilson directed The Players' spring 1983 production, the *Chalk Garden*. Full of dark secrets it had excellent dialogue and was consistently well acted by Celia Monico, Joy Bryant, Michael Knight, Nada Bouch and Rona Hurter.

The Farrer Hall strained to accommodate the 90 who were at the GC AGM in April.

Sisters Thelma Shaw and Verrall Stutchbury left for Devon. Frank Shaw had been secretary of the Bowls Club and Thelma of The Players. Verrall had been an Olympic diver in her younger days. After Frank died in 1972 they moved from *Greenacre* to Deneside.

The PC with Maureen Honey c, Cmdr Peter Winter v-c had new members Lois Hurter and Mr E Pelling with John Chatfield continuing as Hon. Solicitor.

The Wives' Group had a good turn out for a talk by Mr Meldrum from the National Trust and found great hilarity in their May visit to the Devonshire Park Theatre to see *Old Tyme Music Hall* with Clive Dunn and Leonard Sachs.

RBL Annual Village Fete had all the usual stalls and competitions around the Recreation Ground, but although it was a fine day and £500 was raised, the numbers were down.

Peter Armiger won the Red Ribbon Award at the Flower Show and Peter Johnson the Banksian Medal. Other winners were Diana Banks, Mrs KA Banks, Susan Dann, Louise Davies-Gilbert, John Eve, Jolyon Fyfield, Mary Fyfield, Mrs M Gillam, Eileen Goldsmith, Doreen Greenwood, SC Hall, Lois Hurter, Elwyn Jenkins, Kay Ketcher, Elsie Lawrence, Carol Morgan, Jack Pearce, Elisabeth Villa, Mrs S Wheatley, Mrs HG White, Mrs DJ Willard and Mrs M Worsell.

Mrs B Parker, 33 The Ridgeway, was the new Meals on Wheels Organiser. Roy Kibble retired as organist and choirmaster after 14 years, replaced by Edward Maynard Pinkney.

In November 1983 an elephant was filmed on the Village Green as part of a TV series *Talking Animals,* designed for children.
Quite independently, the next month the East Dean & Friston WI sent a donation to Hazel Court School for disabled children

The CMS October Sale had Cakes (Mrs Ketcher), Preserves (Miss Eyre and Mrs Sibson), Christmas Gifts (Miss Thackeray and Miss L Hurter) Young People (Mrs Fenton and Mrs Down), and refreshments by Mrs Goldsmith. The Friends of the Eastbourne Hospitals' collection that month organised by Derek Underwood raised £182, a record.

The Players Autumn show was a comedy thriller *Tabitha* directed by Ron Pringle. With an unlikely plot the comedy was essential. Rose Dann, Dorothy Fenton, and Margaret McIntosh kept the audience laughing, strongly supported by Michael Knight, Liz Overs, Doug Beeston, Delia Bicks, Des Throne, Gordon Matley and Nora Evans as prompt.

Crowlink WI held an emotional 1983 AGM when, with several founder members present ready to celebrate 18 years, Crowlink WI was formally suspended because members felt in need of a new direction. The ladies of Crowlink wished to meet old friends and hear good speakers and join in outings, but not under the WI umbrella.

Christmas parcels from ED & F WI were delivered to All Saints' Hospital by Mrs Vellenoweth and Mrs Dickinson, donations also sent to the RNLI and St Wilfrid's Hospice.

The Youth Club collected £16 Carol Singing over a wet and windy night when many failed to open their doors. In December Maureen Honey retired from the Youth Club committee and was presented with a silver tray at the Club's New Year Disco.

The new Crowlink Ladies Club was formed in January 1984, to meet of an afternoon on the first Wednesday of the month. Joan Nash was c, Jean Place s, Dorothy Alloway t, Pam Rich v-c and programmes Phyllis Gundle. By February they had 29 members and four guests for a talk on *A Trip down the Nile.* Kathleen Boulton thanked the speaker.

Muriel and Irene Kidner left The Brow after 22 years and moved into Eastbourne. They used their tennis court at every opportunity and during the Wimbledon fortnight they kept open house. Irene, who at one time held a pilot's licence, played tennis until well over 75.

The GC had a good attendance for their AGM. All the officers were re-elected. Mr AT Johnson p, Mr B Jackson c, Miss K Boulton t, and committee Mr Nicholson and J Pearce.

All four churchwardens, Mr Steele, Mr Rowson, Cmdr Winter and Miss Eyre were also re-elected. The east window at East Dean had been repaired at a cost of £1300, but the Diocesan quota was now £6204.

When Tony Elphick's wife, Jill, had a road traffic accident, village Pc Graham Gillam reassuringly took charge of the situation. [7]

A cycling proficiency course was held before Easter and all the children passed the test. In May Maureen Honey presented the certificates to Michelle Benge, Katherine Gallway, Joanne Graves, Austin Haffenden, Andrew Holloway, Andrew Johnson, Carol Morgan, Claire Nottage, Mark Nottage, John Oliver, Mark Stuart, Amanda Tyrrell, Leon Tyrrell, Sarah Wigmore and Andrew Worsfold.

The Players production was *The Noble Spaniard,* a farce by Somerset Maugham directed by Des Thorne. Mildred English and Douglas Beeston gave sound performances if a little overplayed. Jane Brittain struck the right note and Deborah Monico showed promise. Michael Knight had panache and Ron Pringle, Delia Bicks and Basil Puffer were polished.

In 1984 a Birling Gap Safety Boat Association was formed after concern by residents at several near fatal incidents at the popular beach the previous year. [5]

The PC supported the Crime Alert Scheme and encouraged residents to ask Pc David Smith, the Crime Prevention Officer for advice.

Fred Bicks was killed in a car accident near *Half Way Cottages* on 8 June 1984 aged 75. His friendly presence and encouragement would be missed. The Players was his life from when he was dental officer to the RAF at Friston. Fred and Delia decided to move to East Dean and he established a practice along the coast and helped to re-form The Players which had started just before the war. He never spared himself whether acting or producing. [13]

The RBL Village Fete was on the Recreation Ground with the Newhaven ATC band; CR Davis showed TV from Moscow and Joe Corrigan, Brighton's goalkeeper, fielded a barrage of shots from youngsters. The prize for Tossing the Wellie was won by Pc Gillam (men) and Jill Jarvis (ladies), Andrew Pringle won the Darts. The net proceeds were £550.

Just on 700, almost a record, at the 1984 East Dean and Friston Flower Show in the Bardolf Hall, thanks to the Davies-Gilberts. Vegetable and Flower entries were a little down, but Home Produce and the Children's section (which earned many appreciative comments) were up. As usual Peter Johnson won the Floral Challenge Cup, Dorothy Alloway won a RHS certificate for flower arrangement and Elsie Armiger a challenge bowl for roses. Ted Flint scored a double, the best exhibit in show went to Mrs LG Pearce, and Nina Booth-Clibborn won awards in the children's section. Prizewinners included George Booth-Clibborn, Mrs E Carpenter, Mrs D Griffin, Mr ED Jenkins, Geoffrey Mantle, Irene Mantle, Mr A Mortimer, Geoff Nash, Mrs GJ Nash, Jack Pearce, Chris Ray, Mr & Mrs R Stott, Sheila Surtees and Marjorie Watson. Louise Davies-Gilbert presented the prizes.

The RBL September Jumble Sale raised £165 from the Farrer Hall (quality clothing) and £105 from the Village Hall (general) substantially more than before - despite rain.

A sponsored ride for St Wilfrid's Hospice, organised by Mrs Margaret Lees, raised the worthwhile sum of £307 especially so for it was another wet Saturday morning.

The WDC agreed a TV relay station near The Link to improve reception.

In October 1984 a Neighbourhood Watch scheme was introduced at East Dean and Friston with Ron Bayes as the co-ordinator.

The Players presented *Wait until Dark* directed by Michael Knight. A mystery thriller with the emphasis on mystery as some members of the audience were little wiser about the plot at the end, but all said it was good entertainment. The cast handled the drama well, Jane Brittain, Roland Boorman and Basil Puffer giving good individual performances.

At the RBL AGM Certificates of Appreciation were presented to Douglas Richey who had acted as standard bearer for 20 years and Alfred Pelling who replaced him after assisting him and being a branch member for 27 years.

Disaster struck Tuesday, 13 November 1984, on Willingdon Hill when a light aircraft, carrying journalists to France, crashed killing all nine on board. Malcolm Johnson of Old Willingdon Road said, "We saw a light dropping out of the sky and heard a great thump".

Church Choir June 1985. L-R: Edward Pinkney, Mandy, Trudy Gillam, Molly Mathieson, Revd Anthony Harbottle, Charles Parris, Daniel Peter Connew - grandson of Rose Dann, Rose Dann, Florrie Vine

The Guides, Brownies and the Boys' Club held a Christmas Show over two days at the Farrer Hall and played to packed houses helped by Peggy Fuller and Priscilla Hodgson. The children and the family audiences thoroughly enjoyed themselves.

In January 1985 thick snowfalls in East Dean and Friston provided sledge runs for the children. Friston hill was closed for a short time on Tuesday, 8 January, by a sudden blizzard, The PC, Micheldene WI, and Wives' Group meetings were postponed.

The PC was to pursue the idea of a multi-purpose play area in the village's recreation ground at a cost of £6,000, towards which they had a donation of £1,000. The size of a tennis court, the hard area site would be marked out for netball, volleyball and tennis.

Since the introduction of Neighbourhood Watch the previous year there had been a slight fall in incidents. One success was the arrest of two characters after a report by a suspicious resident that led to the solving of eight break-ins in the area.

WDC proposed to cut the number of constituent parishes, with a reorganisation of the parish boundaries; East Dean, Friston and Jevington would be combined as East Dean.

Alan Ferguson, the first Eastbourne Downs Ranger started in 1985.

In May 1985 work went ahead to stop vehicles parking on the grass verge along the Friston Forest/Jevington road by banking the verges.

The Players' offering was *See How They Run,* a hilarious farce directed by Lewis

Wilson. Grace and pace was injected into such tiny space with well-timed actions that cascades of laughter bubbled round the hall. The interval had a real buzz and even the coffee (prepared perfectly as ever by Hilary Pringle) was rushed for the second half. All the ingredients for farce were there: plenty of bedrooms (suitably, for East Dean, off stage), as soon as two doors closed another three opened, ecclesiastics, misalliances, mistaken identities, mislaid trousers and the magnificent Sylvia Aston and Gordon Matley.

Tree warden, Esther Worsfold, attended a Woodland Forum to learn that East Sussex, with 17% woodland, was the second most wooded county in England. Many trees in the parish already have preservation orders, although Dutch Elm disease had reappeared.

A large family house along Windmill Lane with 'views and 4 rec, 6 beds, 3 baths, gas ch 2 gges' was for sale at £87,500 in 1982. Four years later it was £165,000 and another nearby was up for an incredible £300,000. One of the *Waterworks Cottages* reached £52,500.

ED & F WI entertained 30 elderly and disabled members of the Red Cross Jubilee Club.

The East Dean RBL Fete of 1985 raised £650. There were a great number of stalls, a painting competition, the Newhaven ATC band, and a flag and baton display. All organised by Chris Ray, Lt Col Grattan Hart, Ian Shearer and other committee members.

The Gardening Club had good weather for Head Ranger John Gascoigne to conduct them around the Seven Sisters Country Park. John was due to retire shortly.

The ED & F Flower and Vegetable Show had a new trophy in 1985 - the James Mason Shield for the best rose, donated by Countess de Rossi in memory of her brother-in-law a lover of roses - won by Mrs A Mortimer. Chairman Desmond Lloyd-Davies said, 'The day has gone well'. As usual Peter Johnson had seven special awards and Ted Flint had three. In the children's section Nina Booth-Clibborn and Victoria Nash were prominent.

The winning Bowls Club Davies-Gilbert triple was Ray Kemp, George Crask and Ron Wheatley. After a most depressing season plans were made for next year's 50th anniversary. Bowls Club officers were JMR Chapman c, RW Wheatley capt, MG Place v-c, DAE Hayhurst s, LB Manners ms, JF Riley t, CJW Griffin a.

ED & F again came second in the Best Kept Village competition in the Large Village section. Howard Greenwood, a local councillor, congratulated all concerned.

The Youth Club started again under Frances Wheeler. There was snooker, table tennis, disco, and other activities weather permitting.

The last of the Gardening Club's summer evening meetings was a quiz. The team of Mrs M Gray, Mrs V Whitehead and Mr A Vine won by a few points against Friston represented by Mrs R Jones, Mrs S Lindsay and Mrs S Surtees, with Alan Mundy as Question Master.

The RBL Jumble Sales raised only £119. The Remembrance Parade of 40 ex-servicemen and women directed by Lt Col Grattan Hart was held in bright sunshine. Charlie Vine was the standard bearer and Philip Goldsmith sounded the Last Post.

The Players' production was *Our Town*. The 28 players were brilliantly directed by Michael Knight. Brian Ayres fitted well into the narrator role and memorable performances came from Debbie Green and Gerald Hawley, but all contributed. Two Players, Sylvia Aston and Gerald Hawley, were voted *Eastbourne Herald's* best amateur actress and actor.

Tim Rowson resigned as churchwarden, continuing as sidesman; Colin Fenton replaced him. Mr Parris presented the accounts estimating a deficit of £600 and Margaret Jenkins reported on the Family Social Work. Molly Mathieson and Mary Fyfield suggested that evensong be forwarded to 1600h November to March and this was carried.

Joan Hicken retired as Brownie-Guider after six years. Liz Graves took over, assisted by Carolyn Hicken.

ED & F Wives' Group had a talk in April on *Unusual Salads,* afterwards they devoured them knowing that they not only tasted good but, most important, were non-fattening.

The Bowls Club Golden Jubilee Lunch for 130 was at the Congress Restaurant in May. Among those mentioned were Percy Budd, Ernest Cater, Arthur Carter, Arthur Davidson, Sam Exley, Dr Henry Fraser, Albert Goode, Rags Norris, Frank Shaw and Norman Symons. The annual bowls fixture between the under 75s and over 75s was won by the oldies.

The Players' Spring offering in 1986 was *An Inspector Calls*. Arthur Morris produced an atmosphere of suspense, Gordon Matley was splendid and seldom off stage, and Gerald Hawley showed his talent. Nada Bouch, Ron Pringle and Angela Crockett were convincing.

The RBL Fete transferred from the Recreation Ground to the Village Green in 1986. The hot and sunny Green was thronged like a Brueghel picture, with Maypole dancing, gymnastics and BMX bike displays. The hot dogs' stall sold out in the first hour. The move was clearly the right decision, the profit being £1080 compared with £585 in 1985.

East Dean & Friston won the Best Kept Village competition again. Mrs Honey said, "We are extremely proud. I am now looking forward to the car park to solve our parking problems". Prizes included £50 from Giro, £30 from Men of the Trees, a 56lb bag of bulbs from Eastbourne Mutual Building Society, a wrought iron challenge trophy and the plaque.

ED & F WI had talk on *Magistrate* - 85% of their cases were motoring offences.

The Flower Show entries in 1986 at the Bardolf Hall were down in Flowers but up in Pot Plants. Winners included Peter Johnson, Doreen Greenwood, Lucy Pearce, Marjorie Watson, H Rich, Joyce Donkin, Maureen Gray, M Jenkins, J Nash, E Parkinson, Jack Pearce, Noel Powell, B Riddle, Sheila Surtees, Esther Worsfold and Emma Cowan.

Gardening Club Annual Dinner, 1987, L-R: Gordon & Gloria Saxby, Betty Knight, Elsie & Harold Nicholson

The Neighbourhood Watch team was invited to a Garden Party at the Police House by the village bobby and his family.

Bowls Club had decent weather at last. In the singles Ron Wheatley beat Cyril Griffin, and in doubles Walter Gregory and Albert Slater beat Max Place and Richard Leach.

Carol Evans gave up as leader of the Boys' Club to be replaced by Judith Conlin.

The GC Open Gardens were Mr & Mrs Parker, Mr & Mrs Veitch and Mrs Marjorie Watson. The Club team of Kay Ketcher, A Vine and Noel Powell won the quiz match with Cuckmere Valley Horticultural Society. Jean Powell presided with her usual efficiency.

The Players presented *Sailor Beware*. Directed by Lewis Wilson there was applause for a jolly good romp. Vivienne Singer tackled a wide range of emotions, Daphne Dempsey made her first appearance at East Dean and Gordon Matley proved as reliable as ever.

John Ridley was now RBL secretary. Reg Mathieson replaced Chris Ray. Richard Leach was replaced by Cyril Cloke as v-c. Poppy Day, with donations included, raised £1307.

A Christmas tree was erected on The Green in 1986 for the first time in years. Maureen Honey attended the lighting-up ceremony in a horse and carriage and over 200 were there carol singing, in spite of the rain, all for St Wilfrid's Hospice.

Snow in January 1987 saw meetings cancelled. The new owners of *Barn Stores,* Norma and Kevin Griffiths, toured the village during the snow siege announcing a New Year sale.

Maurice Hopkins, retired sub-postmaster, elected Chairman of the PC. Lt Col Grattan Hart retired from the WDC after 15 years as councillor for East Dean, Friston and West Dean (chairman 1978-80), succeeded by Maureen Honey. John Allan, Howard Greenwood, Malcolm Johnson, Margaret Lees and Esther Worsfold returned unopposed for the PC.

Cycling Proficiency Tests were held on the hard play area. The cyclists were trained by Liz Graves, Pam Wigmore and Cheryl Veitch, the bikes were checked by Pc Gillam and the testing was by County Road Safety Officers.

The GC had a fine day for their Open Gardens, by Mr & Mrs Hirchfield, Mrs A Mann and the Misses Lawrence and Boulton, as The Players did for their coffee morning at *Greenacre*. The RBL Annual Fete raised £1,132 on a warm day in a reluctant summer. Now truly the Village Fete, congratulations were due to the Fete committee, Reg Mathieson, Chris Ray, Ian Shearer, Ray Trickett, Jim Thompson and John Allan.

The Players' *Gaslight* was another winner, with a mention of Ron Pringle's lighting assisted by Jolyon Fyfield. Gordon Matley, Michael Knight and Vivyenne Willings gave good performances, and Ken Penfold, Beverley Byrne, Rose and John Dann did well.

In May 1987 the ESCC made an order banning parking along the sides of The Green and Department of Transport extinguished the right to use vehicles there, [7] while the PC turned down a twinning request for a town in France because it wasn't rural enough.

With the sudden death of Ron Bayes, Vic Travis took over the post as co-ordinator of the East Dean & Friston Neighbourhood Watch scheme.

This tree on East Dean Church Green was blown down and hit the churchyard wall in the 'Hurricane' of 16-17 October 1987.
Most houses lost tiles or fences and many were left without telephone, gas and electricity. Friston Forest around South Hill was quite altered, but it was apparent that the older trees suffered the worst effects.

The PC wrote to BT saying that they wished to retain their old-style red telephone box and received the reply, 'Fine, if you pay for the upkeep of £200 a year'.

The Flower Show had a warm sunny day, although the numbers were down a little the exhibits were of high quality. The class to commemorate the 40th anniversary produced some delightful arrangements. Winners included Peter Johnson, Phyll Workman, Mrs S Wheatley and in the children's classes Emma Cowan, Emma Oliver and David Evans. Lt Col Grattan Hart DL presented the prizes and Gordon Matley conducted the auction.

The Players' production was *Dry Rot*. Starting with the Post Horn Gallop it was ably directed by Michael Knight who also played one of the lovers with Beverley Byrne. The Terrible Trio were Ken Penfold, Des Thorne and Gordon Matley. Sylvia Willings, Sam Hodgson, Margaret McIntosh, Brian Johnson and Sylvia Gregory were convincing.

The Great Storm over the 16-17 October 1987 night left few houses unscathed. It wasn't unusual that morning to find a fallen tree blocking the drive. One house had a chimney stack fall into a bedroom, fortunately without harm to the residents. Another lost all services for weeks when a falling tree pulled them up, the owners had to move to an Eastbourne hotel. Bill Bailey made emergency repairs to Friston Church and Jack Webb also worked on the roof curing the damp in the Selwyn chapel. A tree blocked the path between Michel Dene Road and Peakdean Lane for weeks before being cleared. The Red Barn needed to be re-roofed and a seat at Friston bus stop was so damaged that it had to be replaced (Mrs Kennard donated one in memory of her parents) and the Village Sign needed renovation.

At the AGM of the RBL branch a letter of sympathy was sent to the Enniskillen branch of the RBL to express the horror at the tragic loss of life and injury at their Remembrance Day Service outrage and a donation of £50 was sent to their welfare fund.

Derek Hicken, Frances Wheeler and George Booth-Clibborn resigned from the Youth Club committee after many years, replaced by Diana Hirchfield and Liz Graves. The club's programme included video, swimming, bowling, ice skating, dances, table tennis, and snooker.

Peggy Fuller's East Dean Singers packed the Farrer Hall for a *Carols for All* Concert and raised £148 for St Wilfrid's Hospice.

In January 1988 Crowlink Ladies Club celebrated their fourth birthday with lunch at the *Horse & Groom* before Delia Bicks' talk on *Memories of East Dean* at the Farrer Hall.

Guides and Brownies' changes included Mrs P Elkington taking over as Guider Leader from Mrs Chris Byrne. Sally Shepherd assumed leadership of the Under-5s Club.

The RA had 79 members at its AGM, Brent Duxbury now t. Cabby Banks (after 18 years) and Douglas Horsman (13 years) did not seek re-election.

The East Dean Players Junior Section produced the *Wizard of Oz*.

In May 1988 The Players performed *Night Must Fall* produced by Lewis Wilson. Michael Knight, as Dan, and Nada Bouch, as Mrs Bramson, gave outstanding performances, well supported by L-R Margaret McIntosh, Ken Penfold, (after Nada and Michael) Vivyenne Willings, Des Thorne, Tiffany Conlin, and Daphne Dempsey

There was a change of use for Dunwick Barn to a Seven Sisters Sheep Centre. [5]

For the RBL Fete the Maypole dancing was organised by Jane Booth-Clibborn, and the Black and White Minstrels by Priscilla Hodgson.

East Dean won Best Kept Village in 1986, was runner-up in the Two Counties Championship to Stedham in 1987, but in 1988 came top village in all Sussex for a prize of £80 and trees and bulbs, sponsored by Girobank and Eastbourne Mutual Building Society.

Peter Hewitt co-opted onto the PC. Items of concern were rubbish tipping; and a recent accident at Downs View Lane. The PC requested warning signs, but the ESCC provided only 'edge of carriageway' markings. Members noted that the NT was to buy *Gayles Farm*.

The 1988 Flower Show at the Bardolf Hall had 540 items to a high standard with favourable comments on the Home Produce exhibits. Noel Powell won the Banksian medal, Peter Johnson had eight awards, and Louise Davies-Gilbert generously provided the cakes and teas.

The Bowls Club season left much to be desired weatherwise with matches cancelled and washed out. In 1988 John MR Chapman was Bowls Club c, RW Wheatley capt., PG Dyer v-c (replaced Max Place) PH Buist s (replaced Doug Hayhurst), JF Riley t, LB Manners ms, and RA Miller, FR Livock, J Bebbington and JJ Dempsey.

A sponsored walk for the Sussex Historic Churches visited 11 churches while walking 11 miles from Friston to All Souls, Eastbourne, raising £312; the Bardolf Hall was packed for the Church Fellowship Harvest Supper.

A Table Tennis Club was formed by Cliff Hirchfield and Cecil Holloway, and a Village Preservation Society was started. Aims included preserving the 1940 tank traps in the village and to return East Dean pond to its former glory, sadly, not achieved.

The Players' production *The Happiest Days of Your Life* was of the highest degree. Nina Booth-Clibborn and Sam Hodgson were both in top form. Brian Johnson had done his homework and Gordon Matley and Rose Dann brought the house down. Ray Trickett and Mildred English were convincing. Michael Knight was at home in one of the more exacting parts ably diverted by Lucy Johnson. Arthur Morris' Headmaster, Sylvia Gregory's Principal, Daphne Dempsey's Miss Gossage and Edward Rigby's Rainbow went well and nobody had to be kept in after school. Jean Stanley, Vivyenne Willings and Georgie Hall dealt with the props and costumes. The peals of laughter confirmed that Des Thorne had given his happy troupe and audiences one of the happiest days of their lives.

Jack and Lucy Pearce went to the RBL Festival of Remembrance at the Albert Hall. Capt Shearer reported that assistance had been given to several members in need and in one case, after negotiations, the rent had been reduced from £32 per week to 89p. Certificates of Appreciation went to Elsie Allan and Douglas Horsman.

Brenda Parker gave up as the local organizer when Meals on Wheels was taken over by ESCC Social Services from the WRVS.

The RA - membership now 700 - observed that a mobile home had been placed in the garden of a property in East Dean without planning permission, but learnt neither touring caravans nor mobile homes required planning approval unless used as a separate dwelling.

Sarah Day reported that the Parent & Toddler group was going well. Visits to Drusillas and Treasure Island and the Christmas party (despite chickenpox) had been a success.

A waste paper scheme started in the village in 1988; residents tied up bundles and left them out every other Friday. It was a great success.

Michael Knight produced *The Railway Children* for the Junior Players in April.

The Church Women's Fellowship had a talk on *Lifeline,* an emergency call system run by the Eastbourne Borough Council; East Dean was included in the area covered.

Members of the Parish Council learnt that the WDC had decided to send all planning applications to the local PC, and discovered that postmen in rural areas were obliged to accept cash for stamps and to post letters. The telephone kiosk watch had proved a success, the boxes were cleaner and had not been out of action over six weeks.

A new boiler and timer were working well at Friston Church where wire guards had been fitted on some of the windows. Sidney Bunting elected to the PCC, Cyril Griffin resigned as magazine treasurer after 12 years and Peter Bonham was now treasurer of CMS. Sybil Parris organised the flowers at East Dean for many years.

Players presented an old favourite *Blithe Spirit.* Arthur Morris creditably produced the show with Nada Bouch as Madame Arcarti and Sylvia Aston as Elvira. Michael Knight, Lisa Aston, Joy Bryant, Ken Penfold and Vivyenne Willings were convincing.

Church Women's Fellowship had a talk by Hazel Andrews on her childhood memories of Friston windmill, her grandfather, WG Norris, being the miller for many years. [8]

The Forestry Commission agreed to open three more paths in the forest once timber harvesting had been completed.

The bunting hired for the RBL Fete involved a high insurance premium, but under the direction of Bill & Miggs Bailey and Florrie Vine enough material for pennants was provided by the villagers to avoid hiring. The 1989 Fete went well with the spanking new pennants fluttering in the light breeze. £1200 was raised, although there were some snide comments as to the original use of some of the material gaily adorning The Green.

The GC had a heat wave for their Summer Open Gardens by Peter and Peggy Bonham and Dr Bill and Pip Hewitt. The gardens looked wonderful even with a hose-pipe ban. The Flower Show in 1989 also had a good standard despite the dry conditions.

For the Best Kept Village competition 71 villages entered. As winners last year East Dean entered the Two Counties' section for the seven best villages in 1988, and set a record by winning two years running. Among village events, Mr & Mrs W McClelland of Lindon Close celebrated their Diamond Wedding; Chris Ray became chairman of the ED & F Art Group, while Jean Powell won and Doreen Greenwood came third in the East Sussex WI golf competition held at the Royal Eastbourne.

The RA discussed WDC's Local Plan noting that while the Old Willingdon Road was proposed as 'very low density' of housing, the rest was subject to the overall density policy. After Alan Mundy and Maurice Hopkins represented the RA at the South Wealden Local Plan Inquiry, Windmill Lane, The Ridgeway, The Brow and Warren Lane were included.

Church Fellowship had a talk by Leslie Ockenden on a subject close to his heart, *The Three Churches of East Dean, Friston and Jevington.*

The Players' autumn presentation was *Too Soon for Daisies.* An unchanged set and plodding script didn't help, but Gordon Workman gave a competent first appearance, with Daphne Dempsey, Mildred English and Vivyenne Willings in the other main parts. Ken Penfold, Tiffany Conlin, Desmond Thorne and Brian Johnson completed the cast.

The annual NSPCC coffee morning raised £802. A cook book of *40 Quick Traybakes* available from Jean Powell or Ruth Smith contributed another £295.

The Bowls Club reported on its best season. Despite increasing membership, rises in rent and water charges meant that subscriptions had to go up to £35.

Micheldene WI had Sylvia Wheatley p, Nora Scott v-p, Georgie Hall s, Margaret Jenkins t. Among their members were Margaret Coulcher, Judith Hemsley, Jill Jarvis, Bobby Stein, Eva Oliver, Phyllis Gundle and Maureen Gray.

Fred Breach retired from the Post Office after 24 years, 'Sorry I didn't go there before'.

A severe storm on Burns Night January 1990 uprooted many trees, including those wobbly after 1987. An old hawthorn tree in Friston Churchyard was removed after damage.

The PC budget expenditure was £36,600 which included £6,000 set aside for a community hall fund, and a one-off reserve fund of £8,900, which was raised by adding £25 a head to the Poll Tax because most residents gained through the new Poll Tax. The PC heard that TVS had donated £500 for the Children's Play Area equipment. A planning permission request for a house on land at *Long View,* Michel Dene Road was refused.

A Branch Surgery had been part of East Dean for 56 years, but conditions in the Gilbert Institute were not satisfactory by present standards. The doctors believed it best to attend College Road surgery or request a visit. On the other hand the Family Practitioner Council insisted that there must be a surgery in East Dean. [7] A survey by the Family Health Services showed that the village was split on whether a local surgery was necessary.

Another Diamond Jubilee marriage, this time of Leslie and Gay Ockenden. At the Church Fellowship AGM, with 47 present. Leslie retired after seven years as chairman - succeeded by Mary Fyfield. Guy Robinson also retired from the committee.

The row, that had been simmering since 1984, between the Eastbourne Borough Council, Strutt & Parker the land agents, and farmer Chris Johnson, over the 1074-acre *Cornish Farm,* took another turn when the agents decided to give up overseeing the farm, amid stories that the Council were planning to change the way the farmland was run.

On 1 April 1990 the Parish Council became known as East Dean and Friston PC. For the first time there was no need for separate meetings at an Annual Parish Meeting and the boundary between East Dean and Friston would be deleted in 1991.

The 1990 hot summer engendered fears of a 'puma' stalking East Dean. Miggs Bailey and John Dann said they saw it and local farmers, who had lost stock, threatened to shoot it - there was also an epidemic of litter bags appearing next to the bus shelters on the A259.

The GC had a talk on *Garden Design,* but most interest and cheers resulted when the slides disappeared into the bowels of the projector until rescued by Noel Powell.

The Players' *A Letter from the General* had Rose Dann and Nada Bouch with a group of nuns in the Far East when Stella Hutchings made her first appearance for The Players. Michael Knight, Des Throne, Gordon Matley and Daphne Dempsey were convincing.

Mrs Elsie Allan again organised the RBL annual jumble sale raising £192, the RBL Walking Treasure Hunt was a resounding success devised by Peggy and Peter Bonham and hosted by Doreen and Howard Greenwood. The Branch Golf Competition at the Downs Club was won by Mrs Pat Ockmore, beating her husband into second place.

Bill and Pip Hewitt's garden was one of the Open Gardens of the Gardening Club in June 1990, a beautiful setting for gentle instruction, relaxed conversation and welcome refreshment. Bill was also the Club President.
Members were saddened when they learnt of the death of the long-standing Secretary Eric Harris

Gloria Saxby, as VCO reported to both the ED & F WI and Micheldene WI on the resolutions for the National Conference. Crowlink Ladies celebrated Gwen Strickland's 90th birthday with a special cake and roses from Dolly Alloway and Magda Huntley.

Walter Gallop died aged 80 in July. He was a villager who laid out *The Gables* garden and was the full-time gardener there until his retirement. Tributes were also paid to the murdered Ian Gow, the villages' MP from 1974 until boundary changes in 1982.

The RBL Village Fete with Pipe band, stalls, entertainments and refreshments, raised £1458; the Birling Gap Safety Boat Association Fete £1300; and the RNLI collection £422.

The GC visited the Eastbourne Butterfly Centre; their summer Open Gardens were *The Spinney,* hosted by Noel and Jean Powell, and Joyce Donkin's *Hillsborough* next door.

On 15 August, an East Dean resident, Mrs Rosetta Holderness, had a lucky escape when her car went out of control as she was reversing out of her Hillside garage. It shot across Hillside through a fence, down a lawn and flower beds to finish against a corner of 11 Deneside. Miraculously, apart from shock, the driver escaped with minor injuries.[1]

Despite the drought the quality of entries was good for the 1990 Village Flower Show. Peter Johnson won the Top Tray award and the Red Ribbon Award for the best exhibit in show. Diana de Rosso won the Raymond Lewis Challenge Cup, George Booth-Clibborn the Challenge Trophy, Noel Powell the best floral exhibit, Elsie Lawrence the Cup for Home Produce, John Eve won the novelty section, Peter Armiger the RHS floral certificate, Kay Ketcher the flower arranging, and Emma Cowan the RHS outstanding exhibit certificate. Steve Morgan, 14, won the Challenge shield for most points in the vegetable classes.

The PC again discussed a suggestion that a petition be presented to the MP, Highway Authority and Chief Constable for a speed limit in the village. After four accidents in the village, 'Slow' and 'No Overtaking' signs were required. The new equipment in Children's Play Area proving popular, but vandalism continued at the Recreation Ground.

The RA discussed the possible development of the Horsefield, and the designation of the Greensward as a Conservation Area. .

Micheldene WI had a talk by Mary Seiffert on the *Chaseley Home,* and Crowlink Ladies on the *St John Ambulance Service* which started in 1887 and now had 60,000 members.

In September a full coach took members of the GC to *Great Comp* in Kent. For The Players' outing 31 members and patrons went to the Devonshire Park Theatre to see *Rebecca* followed by dinner at the Devonshire Club.

Bowls Club results were: Singles winner Joe Dempsey, Pairs Bert Slater and Ron Wheatley. The Veterans winner was Roy Leeder with John Riley runner up.

Eight members of the choir visited Tangmere Air Force Museum on their way to Chichester for lunch and finished the day with evensong at Chichester Cathedral.

Esther Worsfold, with John Dann and Richard Worsell, organised an exhibition of old photographs of the village and raised more than £130 for St Wilfrid's Hospice.

The national WI 75th Anniversary Tea party was shared by East Dean & Friston and Micheldene WIs at the Bardolf Hall and declared a great success.

In October the Farrer Hall was redecorated in accordance with the lease. Used for many meetings, one by the CMS raised £525, and the ED & F Conservatives also met there.

A new Chess Season started at *The Spinney* by courtesy of Jean and Noel Powell.

Stan Fuller died in 1991. Cheerful and friendly, a real countryman who knew every badger sett. Born 1915, son of Mark and Katie, he planted trees in Friston Forest, drove tractors for the WarAg, was a gardener and Pest Control Officer

The Eastbourne and Lewes district branch of the NSPCC held their annual meeting in the Bardolf Hall in October with cheese and wine and a talk by the Bishop of Lewes the Rt Revd Peter Ball. Presided over by Lady Monk Bretton, it was chaired by Barbara Chatfield and Louise Davies-Gilbert's hospitality was recognised with a bouquet.

The Players presented an evening of Victoriana, with Ken Penfold as chairman. It was a wonderful innovation of sketches, songs, readings and recitations. Becky Ring of the Juniors was assured and Terry Hutchings proved a great asset with his fine voice. The new logo was on show in memory of Fred Bicks.

The RBL Dinner dance was at the Glastonbury Hotel. Ernie Pearce was now chairman in place of Bruce Money who was elected a v-p. Lewis Cornford, t, mentioned that they had donated £200 towards the children's playground. Elsie Allan, ms, reported that computerisation of the records, after some difficulties, was now on an even keel. Poppy Appeal raised £1104, plus a branch donation of £950.

ED & F Parish Council now run by 14 councillors, meeting monthly with four standing committees: the Rights of Way - looked after the Greens, paths, bus shelters and litter bins; Halls - did halls and car parks; Recreation Ground - pavilion and children's Play Area; Finance & General Purposes was comprised of c of the standing committees and v-c and one other, dealt with planning - studying applications to build. Each met four times a year. They also acted as representatives to various county councils.

Repairs to a landslide on the Friston to Wannock road at Filching involved closing the road in 1990. It meant that the Meals-on-Wheels team had to drive to Polegate via Eastbourne to pick up the meals, and one recipient lived just to the Jevington side of the roadworks. The cost of the repairs meant that the setts promised for Lower Street would not be installed until the summer. There was another landslide on this C40 road following heavy rains in the autumn of 2000.

Despite the cold, many villagers came to The Green for the Christmas Tree lights switch on by Graham Collins. The winter snow guards, along the A259 since 1987, were blown down in Christmas storms and re-erected in 1991 by Eastbourne Borough Council.

East Sussex CC agreed to new village signs for East Dean with the added wording 'Please drive slowly through the village'. Half the £390 cost would be borne by the PC.

There was great excitement on 16 January 1991 when a police helicopter complete with heat-seeker scoured the village for a burglar who had broken into two properties.

At the Gardening Club AGM Kath Boulton was elected President.

East Dean wasn't cut off in a February snowfall, but vehicles were abandoned on the A259 hill. Farmers Chris Johnson and Eddie Williams helped to keep the roads passable. Hobbs eares slopes were full of tobogganing children. The Preservation Society, ED & F WI, GC, and Church Fellowship meetings suffered a snow 'white-out'. Eastbourne Borough Council announced plans to open up the Downland. Fences will be less conspicuous and parking controlled by mounding and ditching. There will be new car parks near the Beachy Head hotel. Local residents were to be exempt from charges, but this was rescinded.

Not much crop spraying now, but behind *Cornish Farm* is a 1½ mile level stretch of Down, Longdown, used by the crop-spraying planes. Jim Pearce was the usual pilot.

The PC expressed concern over accidents on the A259 at the village entrance. Mrs Molly Mathieson, the parish clerk, said that it was a dangerous road. ESCC proposed 'No Entry' signs for some of the roads at the Friston Green C40/A259 junction. The PC, however, requested that traffic should be allowed to go straight across from Crowlink Lane because it was impossible for farm vehicles with trailers to make the otherwise sharp turn from the A259 into Jevington Road.

Steve and Jean White of Downs View Lane were told they had to knock down their garage after a Planning Inspector made a mistake and quashed his blessing for the plans. The plans had been opposed by the PC and WDC, but the story rumbled on.

RBL distributed from branch funds: to Poppy Appeal £950, service committee £350, *Chaseley* £150, Dunkirk Veterans £50, Royal Star & Garter Home £50 and *Gifford House* £50, Birling Gap Safety Boat £30 and Parish Magazine £15.

Pc Graham Gillam, as local policeman, pointed out that for emergencies residents should dial 999, for non-emergencies Hailsham Police Station and for local advice or information continue to ring him at the Police House.

By March 1991 it was agreed that the Savile medical practice would move out, but continue until Dr Richard Adcock opened his new surgery in the old Granary restaurant. [9]

Bus shelters at East Dean again vandalised. The wooden one had been overturned three times and the seat and glass in the brick one broken the day after being repaired. During 1990 the Council spent over £600 on repairs following vandalism - £280 at the pavilion, £174 bus shelters and £180 on the children's play area.

The PC decided to enter the Best Kept Village competition again. Last year they hoped to set a record by being the overall winner for three years running, however, the judges noted weeds around the War Memorial, brambles at the rear of the Village Hall, rubbish at the rear of the pavilion and vandalised seats. The judges did say that the churchyards were worthy of the highest praise. The Southdown Bus Co said that it no longer had funds for the maintenance of the bus shelters on the south side of the A259; the PC owned the two shelters on the north side so would now have to take over all four - completed in 1992.

Crowlink Ladies had a demonstration of the new Japanese finger food - Sushi.

Geoffrey Coombs 'retired' as Reader - he had been at Friston since October 1971. There are no ranks of Reader, and you remain one for life, but can be inactive.

Graham Croucher, and wife Julie, came as the village butcher. The Tiger Tees Golf Society based at the *Tiger Inn* raised £376 for Eastbourne hospital's paediatric unit.

The PC elections had 27 candidates for 14 seats. Howard Greenwood topped the poll with Esther Worsfold, Jolyon Fyfield, John Dann, Ronald Wickes, Kate Boyle, Jesse Taylor,

Peter Hewitt, Maurice Hopkins, Margaret Lees, Derek William Tonkinson, Paul Steele, Duncan Smart and Patricia Laws. Maureen Honey was unopposed for the WDC.

The new village car park, built in three months at the Horsefield site, received a certificate of commendation and favourable comments. [7] Residents were shocked to hear of Chris Johnson's suspension as manager of *Cornish Farm*. He was later reinstated.

In April the Gardening Club's Open Gardens of Mr & Mrs Bexon and Mr & Mrs Thompson showed how sloping ground could be worked to produce attractive gardens.

The RA officers were re-elected *en bloc* with Ken Smith as c, Brent Duxbury t, Jack Bebbington v-c, and Rona Hurter as s. They discussed enforcing Estate covenants. [9]

Molly Mathieson took over as secretary of the PCC from Pam Rich.

Many local gardeners at Ellen Lindsay's Garden Party in The Ridgeway 1991 as Marie Adams buys sticks of rhubarb

The annual parish meeting saw the Village Hall packed to hear about the surgery arrangements, with Dr Adcock's partner Dr John Mason taking three surgeries a week.

Jonathan Greenway returned safely from the 1991 Gulf Crisis.

The May meeting of the Church Women's Fellowship heard Jenny Lush describe how the Friends of the Eastbourne Hospitals started in 1948 and affiliated to the League of Friends in 1953. They had since raised £1,300,000 to help patients and staff.

Four saplings at the Friston Forest entrance were replaced. The Forestry Commission installed barriers at the forest entrances to stop joyriders spoiling the rides. To replace 1987 losses at Hobbs eares NT volunteers planted ash, field maple, bird cherry and spindle trees along the edge.

New granite sets had been placed in Lower Street, and East Dean Downlands Roads Ltd spent £19,000 on road maintenance in 1990, bringing the total since 1984 to over £100,000.

The Farrer Hall was packed for an RA social. The summer's Open Gardens were Vera and Ron Wickes at 38 Warren Lane, and Hazel and Gordon Matley at 13 Windmill Lane.

In June the RBL celebrated their 60th anniversary and welcomed Mr and Mrs Davies-Gilbert and Mr and Mrs Goodman. James Davies-Gilbert's grandfather had been the first branch president and Tom Goodman's father the first chairman. Commemorative medallions were presented to Hilary Pringle and Elsie Allan. At the RBL Fete the heavens opened and the rain just tumbled down. A severely curtailed programme raised £433.

For the 1991 Flower Show, however, the setting at Birling Manor and the weather were superb. Show winners included Ted Flint, Peter Johnson, Peter Armiger, Diana de Rosso, Mrs A Green, Howard Greenwood, Esther Worsfold, George Booth-Clibborn, S Morgan, John Eve, Kathleen Banks and Rebecca Cowan. Mrs Gill Harbottle presented the prizes and Ron Pringle auctioned the exhibits for sale.

Raymond CR Kemp died on 30 July the day after his 90th birthday. A true villager. [13]

Dr Adcock's new surgery in Downlands Way was opened by Maurice Hopkins, PC chairman, on 9 September. Due to have surgeries on Monday and Friday mornings and all day Wednesday, within a few days the surgery closed because the demand had been underestimated. Dr Adcock and his partner Dr Mason considered that they would be stretched too thinly for both Alfriston and East Dean until they took on an extra partner. From 13 September they provided a service three mornings a week.

The village won £100 as second prize in the ESCC competition to find the tidiest village. Maurice Hopkins was kept busy for, as the PC chairman, he received the award.

The Under Fives' Group restarted in September, as did a Music Movement and Play Group. So did the Youth Club, held in the Pavilion on Friday evenings, with snooker, table tennis, darts, disco and outdoor activities - light and weather permitting.

Brigadier Gerald Mockler DSO died 1 October aged 93. Saw service in both World Wars, retired 1953. Was churchwarden for 16 years, a Bowls Club and a RBL member. The PC remembered Fred Nash as well, who had been a founder member of the PC.

In October Esther Worsfold, with John Dann and Richard Worsell, organised an exhibition of old village pictures and raised £130 for St Wilfrid's Hospice. Esther also organised a Photographic Memories event and produced £125 for the hospice. The Hospice Fair at the Bardolf Hall was opened by Rt Hon Dr David Owen MP and raised £1300.

The Cottage, Lower Street, is the near half and *The Croft* forms the far half of these delightful ex-Waterworks Company dwellings.
The garden of *The Cottage* was featured in the TVS series *That's Gardening,* and was opened for St Wilfrid's Hospice on 26 June 1991 by the then owners Lewis Wilson and John Moore. Vera and Alan Tame are there now with *Poppy*

The bonfire prepared for the 1991 Bonfire Night celebrations near the Gap was set on fire by vandals. Safety Boat Association members managed to build another one in time. The next year saw another successful Youth Club Bonfire Night thanks to Bonfire King Geoff Nash's torches, and despite wintry conditions.

By custom, the 1993 celebrations began on The Green with the distribution of 300 hand-made torches. The procession made its way along Gilbert's Drive to the bonfire at Birling Gap where they were eagerly joined by another 200. After the fireworks Graham's renowned East Dean sausages were barbecued and served by members of the Youth Club.

George Booth-Clibborn's team organised great Bonfire Nights in the late 1990s and as Alf Pelling says, "The Society was going strong until one year Lewes had some flooding, their Bonfire Show was curtailed and half of Sussex seemed to come to East Dean. We managed, but when it was over we breathed a sigh of relief and realised that if it happened again and we hadn't enough insurance we would be in trouble." The insurance increased to £400 so the Bonfire Society had to give up, until in 2005 the PC took over the arrangements and led by Roger Notman-Watt had great success with a bonfire on the Recreation Field.

The Players' production was *Bonaventure.* 'Joy Bryant gave a sensitive performance and Vivyenne Willings, Nada Bouch, Brian Johnson, Stella Hutchins, and newcomer Fiona Sayers played their parts well. Apart from occasional dry spells a convincing performance.'

Anthony Burns-Cox gave a delightful organ recital at East Dean Church thanks to Charlie Vine repairing the pedals at the last minute. On 19 November the bells of East Dean and Friston churches rang in celebration of Terry Waite's release from capture in Syria.

The Gardening Club talk was on *Lutyens and Jekyll* and the Church Fellowship enjoyed a trip to the Gardner Art Centre, Brighton, on 3 January 1992 for *Wind in the Willows.*

Daphne Oliver died, 81. A companion of Marjorie Fass, she came to know Frank Bridge, Benjamin Britten and Peter Pears. An artist with Graham Sutherland and Henry Moore, she became a lecturer at the Eastbourne College of Art. Lived at Old Willingdon Road and latterly Crowlink. In the ATS during the war and later did VSO work in Nigeria.

The squeeze gate in the Horsefield was renewed with a donation by a resident.

At the Annual Church meeting Diana Eyre retired as churchwarden and from the PCC. Secretary Marie Adams said the Electoral Roll was 202, Reg Mathieson reported that expenditure overran income by £1300. Sinclair Smith's CMS report showed a shortfall of £40. Jean Powell spoke on the Family Social Work. The Rector thanked Leslie Ketcher for the Family Service, Roy Kibble and the choir, and mentioned that Nigel and Margaret Lees wished to donate part of the paddock adjoining Friston graveyard for use as an extension.

The Open Gardens of Mr and Mrs Greenwood and Jill Sergeant had poor weather.

In May 1992 The Players presented the farce *There Goes the Bride* ably produced by Joy Bryant. Desmond Thorne was masterly and Gordon Matley's suitable vagueness produced a laugh a minute, all well supported by Timothy Westerby and Ken Penfold. Alison Roberts made her first appearance for The Players; everyone hoped to see her again.

Flower & Vegetable Show Bardolf Hall, 1992. Entries down a little, but winners included Peter Johnson, Noel Powell, Jane Booth-Clibborn, Esther Worsfold, 'Cabby' Banks, Patrick Coulcher, Kay Ketcher, Donald Preen, Rebecca Cowan, Peter Armiger and Catherine Booth-Clibborn

In 1992 the Jevington gas main was converted to a ring main extended from Eastbourne.

Lt Col Grattan Hart was presented with a certificate of RBL Life membership, and there were RBL branch awards to Charlie Vine, Ernie Pearce and Lewis Cornford. The RBL Golf Competition was won by John Allan, but his hole-in-one at the 8th cost him a fortune in drinks, 43 had to sit down to the supper in the evening. The rain came down for the second successive year on the RBL Fete, but throngs also came and £1,139 was raised.

The GC Garden Party at Dr & Mrs Hewitt's garden was well attended. It showed no sign of having had 500 people two days earlier for the Friends of the Eastbourne Hospitals. Hilary and Ron Pringle threw an evening Barbecue in their Friston garden on 25 July.

Over 100 patients now registered at the local Surgery, receiving all the usual services.

Canadian ex-servicemen attended the ceremony when a commemorative plaque was unveiled in the Village Hall in memory of those who died in the Dieppe raid of 1942.

New speed limit signs in place 40mph along Gilbert's Drive and 30mph in Upper Street.

East Dean Players did the farce *Post Horn Gallop* in October. It featured Lord and Lady Elrood (Ken Penfold, Vivyenne Willings) opening their stately home, while their daughter (Alison Roberts), a scoutmaster (Gordon Matley), two visitors, and a couple of ex-cons added confusion, not helped by Lord Elrood taking pot shots at everyone. The production was notable for a convincing performance by Stella Hutchings and the first appearance by Maire Lucas at East Dean. All seats were booked and many had to be turned away.

The East Dean and Friston Conservative Association held a Silent Auction at the Farrer Hall, Mr Rathbone MP and his wife attended. One occasion he did not make a speech?

Alice Warren was asking for more volunteers to cover the Meals-on-Wheels service.

East Dean Village sign refurbished. White lines were painted at Michel Dene Road junctions; some residents thought it meant a loss of the rural character. More worrying were the burglaries reported by Pc Gillam and the time taken for police response to calls.

Charlie Vine decided to stand down as standard bearer for the RBL, replaced by John Dann. Elsie Allan gave up as membership secretary and Vic Travis took over.

The Farrer Hall pictures were reframed and an additional picture of Dick Fowler was given by grandson Jesse Taylor. Jolyon Fyfield made a cupboard for the Village Library.

The 1992 Poppy Appeal brought in £1 per head of population, compared with Wealden's 49p. There was a vote of thanks for Ken Penfold's literary efforts publicising the RBL. His Parish Magazine Derby Draw report: 'The evening ended with the nail-biting drama of the draw, performed with punctilious puissance by that Titan of the Turf, Derek (from the horse's mouth) Ockmore and won by Joan Walters' prize quadrupled.'

In December 1992 the *Barn Stores* introduced a reverse credit scheme. After two successful years the recession meant that times were so bad for village stores that Keith and Pauline Hawkins faced voluntary liquidation, the bank would only allow them £500 "and you can't get enough stock for that", so they introduced a scheme whereby the customers paid a lump sum in advance. Over 30 customers stumped up £3300 in sums varying from £20 to £1000. "People have been marvellous", said Keith, who had come to East Dean in 1989, after taking redundancy from Woolworth's in 1981 and running a pub in Wales. Mrs Stella Hutchings, a customer, said, "It is an essential part of village life to have a store". By March 1993 over 100 families had joined the Barn Stores scheme and Keith had attended a seminar at St James' Palace to tell his story to the Prince of Wales. Having said all that, a quarter of Sussex villages now had no permanent shop.

Crowlink Ladies Club, presided over by Joan Nash, was told that greetings cards started in 1843 with 500 and in 1990 some 210 million Christmas cards were sent.

On a miserable wet evening many braved the weather to watch the Tiger Tees Golfing Society switch on the lights of the Christmas tree on the Village Green, but the community singing which followed was in the comfort of the *Tiger Inn.*

In January 1993 the local garage reopened, after being closed for a year, as the East Dean Service Station. Brothers Ray and Gary McDonald took over the Total garage.

Leonard Pearman, wildlife artist now living at Friston, gave a talk to the Art Group.

The PC stressed that permission was needed for any building or tree work within the village conservation area and discussed the question of putting the telegraph lines at The Green underground. Des Thorne took over as Emergency Co-ordinator for the village.

An alert East Dean man noted the number of a van which he thought was suspicious, reported it to the police and when stopped in Eastbourne stolen goods were recovered. Vic Travis, Neighbourhood Watch co-ordinator, declared it an outstanding success.

Mollie Bertin gave a talk to the Church Women's Fellowship on *Malta, the George Cross Island,* while Sinclair Smith told of his experiences there during the war. Later John Surtees gave a talk on *Old Eastbourne and its hospitals* to the Fellowship.

Mountain bikes were now more frequent on the Downs and in Friston Forest; although most riders were considerate, some stray from the bridleways and are a danger to walkers.

The East Dean & Friston Playgroup raised £70 to buy toys for the children's ward of Eastbourne hospital, where they were presented by Beverly Hayter and Sara Rumble.

East Dean's Guides had closed some years ago, but Emma Cowan joined the Jevington group and received the Baden Powell award. Liz Graves, Brown Owl, the Brownie Guider who had been involved with the pack for nine years retired in the summer.

The thriller, *House Guest,* was The Players' contribution for Spring 1993. A film star couple, Maire Lucas and David Harmer, discover that their son has been kidnapped - and one is a suspect. Bob Gardiner, as one of the villains, lent light relief to the suspense.

Maurice Hopkins and Stuart Gammon stood down from the RA committee after many years of valuable service.They were replaced by Jolyon Fyfield and Peter Hobbs.

The Milk Race cyclists raced through the village on 1 June 1993.

The new Family Communion Service at East Dean was well supported in May, but would be shorter next time. At a PCC meeting Reg Mathieson reported a healthy balance thanks to the Gift Day. Peter Hewitt was re-appointed auditor.

The GC's Annual Dinner was at the Hydro Hotel. Their Spring Open Gardens were at Ellen Lindsay's in The Ridgeway and Dennis and Rowena Minns' in Warren Lane.

In June 1993 Graham Croucher, East Dean's village butcher, scooped the top prize at a Meat Federation contest for his home-made pork and leek sausages.

For the first time in three years the weather was kind to the Village Fete. The Green looked attractive; teas were served in the Farrer Hall and stronger fare in the *Tiger*.

A 1993 view of a distinctive house in Warren Lane with the site furnishing wonderfully extensive views but with the usual sloping garden which is tackled in a different manner by every gardener

Frances Wheeler (later Mace) ran her Keep-Fit classes as usual in the Farrer Hall. The Youth Club started again after its activities were allowed to come under the PC's insurance and the RBL Walking Treasure Hunt, devised by Pat and Derek Ockmore and Pauline and Derek Hawkins, was won by Elsie and John Allan.

In June the Gardening Club heard a talk on Organic Gardening. Noel and Jean Powell held an Open Garden for the Diocesan Family Social Work and had glorious weather, but the ED & F WI Ploughman's Lunch had to be held inside due to the moods of the weather.

The Bowling Club managed to win their match against Seaford halting a long losing run.

On 24 August there was the opportunity for residents to have their annual electric blanket check at the car park behind the Total garage. Of the 161 blankets tested, 91 failed the tests, but of these 19 were put right by changing plugs or fuses, and most of the others failed because they did not have a cut-out. Only seven were unsound.

A letter from Rob Jones appeared in the Parish Magazine explaining its finances. 'The magazine was worthwhile, of benefit to the community and a cohesive element. Although 35 people were involved in the editing, administration and distribution the costs were nil. Printing costs for 900 copies each month were £2000 a year. To meet this £1000 came from advertising, the charges kept low because most were local services, the remainder came from donations; in 1985 some 450 residents made donations, but in 1992 only 200.'

A class for the best garlic was introduced to the 1993 Flower Show, otherwise much the same. Over 600 entries with Peter Johnson winning 25 firsts. What prizes he didn't win were scooped up by brother Brian and son Andrew, although John Eve did win the Banksian medal and Maureen Gray won two cups. All presented by Sir John Chatfield.

Graham Gillam, village bobby since 1981, said, "I always wanted to cover the village patch, which in 1993 was extended to cover Jevington, West Dean, Litlington, Wilmington, Folkington and Alfriston, about 28 square miles and 3200 people. You're a part of the community and you cover every range of police work, from escaped sheep on the roads to the Old Willingdon Road plane crash of 1984." His biggest problem was car thefts, with visitors parking to go for a walk on the South Downs and giving thieves the perfect opportunity to break into the car and steal whatever they could find. He believed that talking to schools and youth clubs was one way of reducing crime.

After being the winners in 1989 (for the second year) and runners-up in 1992, in 1993 ED & F again won the East Sussex Best Kept village, large village section, with Battle and Ringmer runners up. The award was a cheque and a wrought-iron sign to be displayed for a year. The village also won the prize for the least litter. Esther Worsfold said, "It's a friendly village and there's so much going on. You can be involved or keep away as you feel".

A party from the village found a 1993 visit to Buckingham Palace well worthwhile and felt privileged to see the beauty, magnificence and splendour. Organised by Mr Pattenden, the return journey was rounded off with a call at the *Anchor Inn* at Hartfield.

Bill Honey, one of the village's best known residents, died after a heart attack at 54. Educated at Eastbourne Grammar school, he was founder and senior partner of chartered accountants Honey Barrett and held directorships in many sectors. He had great boyish charm, an abundance of energy, and a creative and enterprising mind. He was married to Maureen and they had three children.

In October Jane Tullis organised a coffee morning in support of the Macmillan Cancer Relief fund. Despite a continuous downpour, but with the support of the Mayor and Mayoress of Eastbourne, the sum of £300 was raised.

The Church Fellowship heard a talk on the Samaritans and learnt that the Eastbourne branch dealt with 40 telephone calls a day.

The Players in autumn 1993 did *Ladies in Retirement* with Joy Bryant, Vivyenne Willings and Daphne Dempsey. Maire Lucas, John King and Alison King (née Roberts) and Molly Mathieson, in her first appearance, maintained the momentum. Produced by Lewis Wilson, it had a splendid set. Delia Bicks, the prompt, must have thought back 40 years when The Players last produced the play and she took one of the leading roles.

At the ED & F Conservatives' Cheese and Wine evening George Stein gave a talk on his experiences as a POW in Colditz, £205 was raised.

Esther Worsfold arranged another exhibition of old postcards and photographs at the Farrer Hall in October. The RNLI benefited by £177 as a result.

The annual luncheon of the Bowling Club was a happy scene and well supported by over 100 members and guests. The club captain and his wife, Ron and Sylvia Wheatley, conducted the raffle. The Club noted that many members played indoor bowls in the winter.

Mrs Jean Warriner, the ED & F WI treasurer, was the only member to enter the Wellhurst Golf Tournament but came back with the Silver Award. Mrs Dorothy Cullis, on the Village Hall committee, explained the details of the new hall plans to the WI.

The Remembrance Service was now under the direction of Lt-Col Grattan Hart, with the standard bearer John Dann, escorted by Charlie Vine and Ted Flint. Trumpeter Philip Goldsmith called for the lowering of the standard and The Green was enveloped in a quiet calm as those present remembered the fallen. The Revd Anthony Harbottle conducted the service with Cyril Cloke reading the lesson. Col BM Hubbard resigned as chairman of RBL because of other commitments; Treasurer Ron Pringle announced a healthy profit of £1867, of which £1495 was donated to good causes. Ken Frith succeeded Cyril Cloke as Secretary.

Jim Davis won three bowling spoons over the year when play went on until 15 October. Walter Gregory at 94, made an honorary Life Member - worthwhile with a £60 sub.

Village happenings included - Rob Jones relinquished the treasurership of the magazine; succeeded by Lois Hurter; Crowlink Ladies Club held their Birthday Lunch at Grimaldi's and the members said how fortunate the village was to have such a good restaurant; smoke alarms were fitted in all the village halls; Colin Parker, Chartered

Surveyors, purchased the Old Sorting Office for their practice; on Palm Sunday Leslie Ketcher took his last Family Service after 30 years; Mr Pain the Greensward contract grass cutter retired and was succeeded by Mr Pocock; mathematician Marie Adams worked out a game pattern for the Bowling Club to ensure the best way to schedule games for the Davies-Gilbert trophy. A new dialling code came in 16 April, now 01323, with either 999 or 112 for emergencies.

Dedication of a new RBL standard Sunday, 24 April 1994 at East Dean church, borne by John Dann. Afterwards there was a Reception in the Village Hall, thanks to Joan Cloke, and Messrs Vine, Allan, Harwood and Frith. Cyril Cloke had recently been awarded the County Certificate of Appreciation in recognition of his contribution to branch and Legion affairs.

The GC's Spring Open Gardens had over 70 attending. New chairman Patrick Coulcher and members enjoyed the visit to Exbury's azaleas organised by secretary Jeanne Maull.

Under a Local Government Review Eastbourne proposed to expand by taking in six neighbouring parishes, including ED & F, but the parishes were united in their opposition.

Lord Shawcross opened his garden for the Friends of the Eastbourne Hospitals in May.

Dolly Alloway not only celebrated a 92nd birthday, and a move to Eastbourne, but took over the Crowlink Ladies Club chair when Joan Nash was indisposed.

The Players presented a farce *Love's a Luxury*. Brilliantly produced by Desmond Thorne, with Gordon Matley hilarious as Mr Mole, the play went at a cracking pace. John and Alison King were a delight and David Harmer and Vivyenne Willings were perfection. Marc Symons, Stella Hutchings and debutante Debbie Williams were exciting.

The Cricket Club entertained a full Sussex team for David Smith's testimonial, the weather was superb and Sussex made 281 including 23 sixes, with Bill Athey and Franklyn Stephenson prominent. East Dean was dismissed for 122 with two sixes. It was over 60 years since Sussex played on the East Dean ground.

RBL Village Fete on 9 July had the Sussex Army Cadet band, Maypole Dancing and a festive array of stalls. It raised over £1300, part sponsored by Davis (CR Tubes) Ltd.

The Interlude Singers presented a concert in East Dean church in June and raised £220.

The ESCC again turned down PC request for reduced speed limits through the village citing unfulfilled criteria. Vandals smashed up a seat by the twitten near Friston church.

On 7 July Pc Graham Gillam organised a meeting on personal protection. The Village Hall was filled to hear Trish Pybus, Seaford Crime Prevention Officer, give practical hints. Inspector Graham Alexander blamed drugs and greed for most crime and dismissed poverty as a cause. To make the best use of the situation he explained the graded response system.

One of the houses in Warren Lane in 1995 with lovely gardens and magnificent views to the Downs and sea

East Dean & Friston WI had a talk by a farmer's wife on PYO, with anecdotes about pickers who came complete with cream and sugar for a picnic and thus had no strawberries to buy. Patrick Coulcher gave a talk to the Crowlink Ladies Club on *Nature Studies*.

In August the *Barn Stores,* that had pioneered a credit system for village stores, had to close down. Keith Hawkins blamed changing shopping habits as younger people in the village tended to shop where they worked. [9]

The 1994 Village Flower Show at Birling Manor had wonderful weather. Many visitors spent the time just sitting in the beautiful surroundings enjoying the teas provided by Mr and Mrs Davies-Gilbert, with all the cakes baked by Louise Davies-Gilbert. Peter Johnson won the Red Ribbon award, but Alan Nash had a good show and in the children's section Philip Riddle had the most points, with Sophie Hallett a close runner-up, and 7-year-old Cassandra Day won the under-11 trophy. [5]

New RA committee: Ken Smith c, Ron Pringle vc, Michael Hobbs s, Peter Hobbs t, Tim Cullis, Brent Duxbury, Jolyon Fyfield, Louise Gaffney, Kenneth Lucas and John Surtees.

The GC raised over £500 at their Garden party at Ellen Lindsay's; and The Players had over 100 supporters for their coffee morning at Hazel and Gordon Matley's *Greenacre*.

Concerns were expressed that following the property market fall the Church Commissioners needed to reduce costs. Rumours that when the Rector retired the replacement would be a part-time priest from Eastbourne, and that Jevington be split off to join with Polegate, so alarmed the PCC that they decided to organise a petition of protest.

The PC agreed to display Jolyon Fyfield's community street map in the car park, not to install dog poop bins because of cost and noted new steps at the Gap not in place until July.

The cricket club had one of their biggest wins, by 223 runs over Ridgewood. Ten village residents played in the cricket team this season. Peter Buckland was the leading player, but a local, Steve Hopkins, hit 118 in one innings, the highest score of the season. The Club's 1994 Annual Dinner was held at *The Tiger*.

An East Dean Church Concert by the Renaissance Singers directed by Reg Bertin and joined by tenor John Terry sang music by Handel, Mendelssohn, and Quilter, raising £130.

Some village activities: a full Village Hall at the Church Fellowship meeting heard Jean and Noel Powell recount their adventures on the Trans-Siberian railway. The Fellowship's next talk was about the Internet and the following one had the Revd Ray Morrison speak on his work as a hospital chaplain. East Dean Players performed *Dangerous Corner* for JB Priestley's centenary year. The sports news included the East Dean and Friston Brownies coming first in an Eastbourne swimming gala, while Ron Wheatley won the Bowls Club singles and Cyril Dickinson and Eddie Hemmings the pairs.

Esther Worsfold, as tree warden, reported that there were 22,000 mature English elm trees in the area, the largest collection in the country.

At the Art group AGM Chris Ray reported that a goodly number of paintings had been sold at the annual exhibition. Evelyn Ray would not be able to act as tutor in 1995, but the services of Fleur Gray had been secured.

The RA expressed concern that the development for seven houses on the petrol station site would be too cramped. Finally in April WDC planners granted permission for only six new houses subject to 21 conditions, but nothing happened as a result.

The PC meeting commenced as usual with prayer. Representatives had met the NT to discuss remedial work to *Crangon Cottages;* handrails installed on two footpaths from The Brow to Peakdean Lane and from Warren Lane to Peakdean Close. Many familiar faces decided to stand down: Kate Boyle, Rita Laws, John Dann, Duncan Smart, Howard Greenwood and Maurice Hopkins who, elected in 1976, had been chairman for the past eight years - and only missed one meeting in that time. Vice-chair Esther Worsfold presented him with a decanter with thanks and best wishes.

Richard Gorringe asked that dog owners be extra careful at lambing time, and noted that 'recently five sheep had been killed by dogs in fields adjacent to the Old Willingdon Road'. Pc Graham Gillam said 57 had been killed in the year. One dog had been shot as a result.

Dennis Minns succeeded Ron Wheatley as Bowling Club captain, a hard act to follow.

Maureen Honey retired after eight years as Wealden councillor, Brian West was elected in her place. PC members were Esther Worsfold c, Jesse Taylor v-c, Liz Charlwood, Sarah

Day, Jolyon Fyfield, Peter Hewitt, Jill Jarvis, Margaret Lees, Kenneth Lucas, Joanna Shawcross, Kenneth Thurman, Derek Tonkinson, Ronald Wickes, and Phyll Workman.

The new representatives for St Wilfrid's Hospice were Jenny George and Maureen Burr, replacing Phyllis and Gordon Workman who had retired after eight years of fundraising.

The Gardening Club made a donation of £25 to the District General Hospital in memory of Marjorie Watson, a great gardener. The Royal British Legion asked all those who hadn't won anything on the new Lottery to indulge in a dabble in their Derby Draw on 27 May.

The Players had full houses for each of the four performances of *We Did meet Again,* a commemoration of VE and VJ days in revue form produced by Des Thorne and Sandra Goldsmith, with Gill Bebbington as accompanist. In a beflagged and wartime postered Bardolf Hall Ken Penfold set the scene punctuated by extracts of Winston Churchill's speeches, and the talents of members of The Players. Memories were awakened of Robb Wilton ('The Day War Broke Out') Flanagan and Allen ('Underneath the Arches'), Gert and Daisy, while the Dad's Army sketch had all the hilarity and lovable absurdity of the original. Interspersed were quiet spells of readings about the experiences of POWs, and stories of the Russian convoys. A chorus of *A Lovely day Tomorrow* and the All Clear followed by resounding applause brought the show to a close.

After more vandalism of bus shelters and notice boards and graffiti on the pavilion, Ron Franklin agreed to repair the bus shelters. Mr and Mrs S Carter gave up tending the garden of the Village Hall which they had looked after for seven years.

Events of the Gardening Club, the village Club with the most members. Left: Annual Dinner Dance 1995 Ken and Maire Lucas, and guests. Right: Jackie and Mike Florey at the same 'do'.

The RBL Village Fete on 15 July had many attractions including the Eastbourne Pipe Band, Maypole dancing, Bouncy Castle, Face painting and many stalls. Blessed with unimpeded sunshine, typical of the summer, £1500 was raised.

East Dean garage was in the hands of Receivers; the hope was it would remain a garage.

A chiropodist commenced private practice at the Surgery in Downlands Way.

Vast numbers of visitors at the 1995 Flower Show celebrating 50 years since World War Two with wartime recipes in the Home Produce section where entries were up; homage to wartime rationing. By popular request flowers in arrangements would no longer have to be grown by the exhibitor. Mrs JE Tidmarsh won the Wartime Barn Cake Cup, Mrs C Hallett Eggless Cake prize and Dr David Faro Wartime Potato Scones. Otherwise Peter Johnson, son Nicky, brother Brian, Peter Armiger, and Fred Fuller were well in evidence. Viv Gardiner won the outstanding flower arrangement section, Rebecca Cowan the children's section. Lewis Wilson presented the trophies and Ron Pringle ably auctioned the produce.

Ian Shearer and Carole Naylor's RNLI house-to-house collection amounted to £582.

The Residents' Association held a coffee morning on Saturday 9 September to welcome all residents, and in particular newcomers. Representatives of other groups were present from the Bowling Club to the Parent & Toddler group.

The Cricket Club retained the Bourner trophy, (given by Eric and Dolly Bourner) beating Eastbourne Downs in the final, and won the Playfair Shield beating The Boards, the winners for the past three years. However, the Club did not have a successful CVL season.

In policing changes, Eastbourne and Lewes Divisions amalgamated and East Dean became part of the Seaford sector, with Pc Graham Gillam changing to a Community Beat Officer instead of Rural Beat officer. Seaford Police station, like most Police Stations in Sussex, would only be open during the working week.

At their September meeting Micheldene WI had John Surtees talking on *Dr John Bodkin Adams,* followed by a competition for An Unusual Teaspoon. Dr Surtees joined in by showing an X-ray of a teaspoon that had been swallowed. 'Take one teaspoonful a day'.

A mobile phone company requested six more antennae on the water tower at Friston, and the PC thought it best to have them there than on separate masts.

At the Bowling Club Ron Wheatley won the singles and Patrick Coulcher and Alan Spencer the doubles. Only one game had been affected by rain all summer. The Annual Lunch was at the Congress restaurant when Rowena Minns presented the trophies.

By 1995 the East Dean surgery was fully computerised, both surgeries directly connected so that all records could be accessed, and soon to have hospital connection.

East Dean Players' autumn 1995 production was *Man Alive* at the Bardolf Hall. 'A lively comedy which sent us all home with smiles on our faces. The actors playing shop dummies retained their poses in a remarkable way'.

The RBL commemorated VE and VJ Days with a branch dinner (May), the Treasure Hunt (June) and the Fete (July). No annual dinner dance because of lack of support.

Gardening Club held their usual December meeting with mince pies, a 'competition' of photographs depicting flowers, and as ever Vic Travis' slides of meetings over the year.

East Dean Grange, [7] part of the Court Cavendish Group, made its residents feel at home with cuisine to match its elegant dining room, and with three lounges, a music room, and an evening lounge to relax afterwards. There was also a heated indoor swimming pool, and the extensive grounds offered scope for putting, gardening and croquet.

From 1996 the parish magazine changed to A5 size following a take-over of the printers.

The CWF heard Prebendary Clive Taylor, a retired Chaplain to the Metropolitan Police, speak about the Police Service. He was to become a Freeman of the City of London.

PC matters included the village precept increased by 3%; a study of road signs found over 40 on a $1\frac{1}{2}$ mile stretch of the A259, which was thought excessive, however, ESCC agreed to install another *Reduce Speed* sign on the A259 approach to East Dean from Eastbourne; emphasis that cycling is not permitted along the various footpath Rights of Way; only allowed on Bridleways. The Service Station started serving petrol again in April and the new proprietor agreed to the creation of a dedicated footpath. The PC decided to enter the Best Kept Village competition in the Small Village (less than 3000 residents) section despite an increase in the entry fee. Alan Mundy retired as honorary legal adviser to the PC; he had given good advice over the Car Park and pedestrianisation of The Green.

A branch of the Liberal Democrats was reformed for East Dean with Tony Hoadley c, John Edrich s and Kate Boyle t. Kate was also president of the ED & F WI.

In March 1996 the GC arranged a day trip to France, mainly for rehydration. That month Mr & Mrs Cook and Mr & Mrs Powell opened their gardens for the Spring Open Gardens. Any success was in spite of rather than because of the weather which was bitterly cold. At least the clear nights meant that the Hale-Bopp Comet was seen well at East Dean.

Over 1996 the Surgery opened weekday mornings, and practice nurse Karen Surtees held a nurse clinic on Thursdays. Jackie Florey and Cheryl Veitch were the receptionists.

The Players' production *They came to a City* at the Bardolf Hall was superb. The set was by John Dann and Jolyon Fyfield and the improved lighting by Ron Pringle. Stella Hutchings, John King and Debbie Williams were brilliant, Ken Penfold, Vivyenne Willings and Fran Cook superb. Gordon Matley gave a fine characterisation of Cudworth, while Giselle Salisbury and David Harmer provided moving performances.

Esther Worsfold was elected c of PC with Jesse Taylor v-c. Margaret Lees was c of the Rights of Way committee, Ken Thurman of the Recreation Ground and Jolyon Fyfield of the Halls. The PC rejected the option of a National Park and supported continuing with a properly funded Conservation Board.

Rupert Taylor died aged 87. Known as 'Rube', he worked in East Dean as a gardener and married Grace 65 years ago. During the war he was in the AFS and later a postman.

The RBL Derby Draw and Supper held on the Glorious First of June was a great success; raising £162. David and Christine Faro's Save the Children Fayre raised £475.

In July 1996 the bins for recycling paper and tins finally appeared at Downlands Way.

The annual Village Fete in July raised over £2,000 for the RBL funds. A rousing performance by the Eastbourne Scottish Pipe Band got the proceedings away, with a variety of other attractions. Stall holders included Doreen Greenwood and Peggy Bonham at the *White Elephant;* Mrs Warren, Miss Shaw, Mrs Wood and Mrs Shearer *Cakes;* Mr Dickinson and Ian Shearer *Tombola,* Mrs Gray *Produce*, Des Thorne and Mr Wood *Books and Records,* Mrs Ockmore and Mrs Stein *Raffle,* Mrs Dann *Buttons and Bows,* June Travis *Toiletries,* Mrs Cloke and Mrs Harwood *Garden Tools* and Mr Ockmore *Whisky Raffle.*

Gardening Club activities 1996. **Left:** At Barbara and Brian Cook's *High Covert* Open Garden, June, L-R: ?, Mollie Miliffe, Jean Crask, Maud Singleton and Doreen Robinson and **Right** a happy party off to holiday in the Ardennes

The Bowls Club did well in matches, but unfortunately Dennis Minns was unable to devote the time required to the captaincy so Brian Smith agreed to be acting captain.

St Wilfrid's Hospice house-to-house collection raised £371, despite a wet week.

The Gardening Club's Summer Open Gardens were those of Soei and Jennifer Liauw in The Brow and Donald and Joy Preen in The Close.

In August 1996 the Revd Anthony Harbottle, the Rector of East Dean with Friston and Jevington, retired. Over 200 attended his retirement party, hosted by Rosalind Hodge of the PCC. He said, "The parishioners have been wonderful and I shall miss the work." For the interregnum Prebendary Clive Taylor would be heavily involved along with the churchwardens and Rural Dean.

Fine weather ensured that over 500 came from all around for the 49th annual Flower Show. Peter and Nick Johnson, Fred Fuller, John Eve and Peter Armiger had a good show. Other prizewinners included Esther Worsfold, Alan Nash, and Viv Gardiner. There was close competition in the children's section with Simon Shepherd and Rebecca Cowan doing well, but the outstanding exhibit was by Cassandra Day.

Chris Ray arranged the RBL Golf tournament at the Royal Eastbourne following on from John Allan organiser for many years. Dennis Minns won the trophy.

Hilary Pringle gave a lunch party for her Poppy Appeal collectors in appreciation of their dedication. Lt-Col Grattan Hart presented service badges and certificates.

The number of patients at the village surgery increased and an extra surgery was started by Dr Joanna Shawcross on Fridays; Jackie and Heather were now the Receptionists.

Cmdr Peter Winter, a v-p of the RBL, died in August. As observer of a Fleet Air Arm

Fairey Swordfish he played a vital part in the 1941 Battle of Cape Matapan. His torpedo disabled the Italian cruiser *Pola,* slowing the Italian vessels enabling the British capital ships to come within range. Later shot down by Vichy French and captured, but exchanged to finish the war in the Far East. Afterwards he came to be on good terms with those who had shot him down. Locally he was on the PCC, the Deanery Synod and was Churchwarden for East Dean and Friston; v-c of the PC for years, in 1984 p of the NT Seven Sisters Centre, chairman of the RBL East Dean branch 1979-82; an ex-president of Eastbourne Combined Ex-Services Association. He left a wife, Beverley, a son and two daughters.

The 1996 Harvest Supper was a great success, as was David Hunn's talk on his work as a Fleet Street journalist, his last assignment being the Olympic Games at Atlanta.

Colin Bexon's autumnal bulk purchases of peat and compost for the Gardening Club had been such a winner that members were considering a similar service in the spring.

Micheldene WI celebrated their 35th anniversary with an account of the local WI by Mary Fyfield who was founder member. The cake was made by Joy Mundy and Claire Hunt and the refreshments were served by Nancy Chapman, Sue Hobbs and Bobby Stein.

Bert Goldsmith's flowers along The Green entrance by the car park were much enjoyed.

The Players' offering was *Table Manners* by Alan Ayckbourn. Directed by Joy Bryant it played to full houses, and proved an excellent opportunity for the cast to show their skills. Perfect timing was essential, and Marc Symons and John King were without blemish, also requiring mention were David Harmer, Tricia Kennard, Alison King and Debbie Williams.

After a nasty accident at the A259/Upper Street junction a car was written off and the owners badly shocked but otherwise unhurt. About that time hounds of the East Sussex and Romney Marsh Hunt were hit by a bus when they chased a fox onto a busy road at Friston.

An application to build two houses in Twitten Yard, Upper Street was rejected.

The Revd Simon Morgan was licensed Priest-in-charge on 8 December. He came with his wife Kate and young daughter Flavia. Parishioners had decorated the Rectory for them.

The Revd Peter Williams reported that five RBL Christmas grocery tokens, each £45, had been given out that year, and stressed the need of confidentiality for the recipients. The Services committee was C Cloke c, G Wood v-c, P Williams s and R Mathieson. The branch had 200 members. Officers were Lt Col Grattan Hart p, C Cloke c, Capt I Shearer v-c, V Travis ms, R Pringle t, K Frith s, R Mathieson, B Money and C Ray were v-ps, Poppy Appeal Organiser Hilary Pringle (raised £1132), Press Officer Marianne Frith (who took over after the death of Ken Penfold), Standard Bearer John Dann, Ian Killick a. Certificates of appreciation went to Alice Warren, Doreen Greenwood, Peggy Bonham, and John Allan. Cyril Cloke was presented with the National Council Gold Badge award.

Gwen and Ron Franklin took over the job of Parish Magazine distributor to the deliverers, while Ken Warriner became the Parish Emergency Co-ordinator. Bridget Rix took the chair for her first presidential meeting of the Micheldene WI.

Mrs ML Eldrett co-opted to fill the PC vacancy left by Dr Shawcross. The discussion was about the lack of rubbish clearance due to icy roads, it was felt that this is bound to be experienced in a country village. David George became the Honorary Solicitor to the PC.

Further changes were notified in the policing of the village. The Police Office at the village was closed and the Community Beat Officer would be based at Seaford where the 'rapid response team' would be situated. 'He could be out on patrol and mainly unobtainable' but residents could leave a message or if urgent dial 999.

Brian Adams, Andrew Palmer, Jean Powell and Sheila Surtees were licensed to administer the chalice at Holy Communion.

The formation of a Village Strollers Group was announced.

In April, May and July 1997 three village couples celebrated their Diamond Weddings,

Bert and Eileen Goldsmith, Douglas and Phyllis Pitcher and Tim and Margaret Rowson.

Tom Cullis was on parade at Windsor Castle following the award of the Silver Acorn, one of scouting's top decorations in recognition of seven decades of service.

Vivienne Butler won the RBL Walking Treasure Hunt, set by Jackie and Mike Florey.

A letter from Pat Nickson, the missionary link in Nairobi, recounted the invasion of Zaire by Kabila and the overthrow of Mobuto, 'but nothing will change, except the name'.

The PC decided not to support the Ramblers who wanted a definitive footpath to Crowlink. John Clarke took over the responsibilities of Tree Warden.

Magazine donors in June were Mrs Ashforth, Mrs Barlow, Dr & Mrs Bramley, Mr & Mrs P Buist, Mrs P Butterfield, Mr & Mrs Charlesworth, Mr & Mrs P Coulcher, Mr J Davies, Mr & Mrs D Drury, Mrs G Hoes, Mr & Mrs M Horlock, Mrs M Moody, Mrs S Smith, Mr & Mrs L Stubley, Mr & Mrs V Travis, Mrs M Watson and the Gardening Club.

The RBL Village Fete on 12 July 1997 had a perfect summer's day. Bargain hunters, investors in the competitions and raffle lovers invaded The Green and enjoyed the entertainment by the Eastbourne Rapper Sword and Clog dancers and Maypole Dancing by the East Dean Brownies. Chairman Cyril Cloke was delighted with the £2,300 raised.

Left: the trophy table for the Golden Jubilee (since the war) of the East Dean and Friston Flower and Vegetable Show 1997. Fred Fuller is half hidden behind the Parish priest, the Revd Anthony Harbottle who, with Peter Armiger, helped distribute the prizes. Committee members, Esther Worsfold and George Booth-Clibborn, ensure all receive the correct prize. **Right:** Show prizewinners l-r: Alan Nash, Charlie Goldsmith, Fred Fuller, Peter Armiger, John Eve, Peter Johnson, Philip Riddle, George Booth-Clibborn and Christine Nash. Other big winners were Christine Faro and John Chapman. The craft trophy went to Maureen Gray, Mary Fyfield the home produce Rosebowl, Anne Robson the home produce Challenge Cup, Pauline Joslin took the cup in the novelty section and Ann Gardiner the RHS certificate for flower arrangement. In the children's section Simon and Jack ensured that the Shepherd family were in front with Philip Riddle runner-up

East Dean & Friston battled it out with 28 other villages to win the title of Best Kept Village in the East Sussex, small village section. Esther Worsfold said, "This is a pretty village and everyone works hard to keep it tidy". The PC continued to press the ESCC to introduce a speed limit on the A 259 through the village.

The Gardening Club's Open Gardens by Mr and Mrs Brent Duxbury and next door Mr & Mrs Fred King were a spectacular success. Despite dreadful weather Ian and Claire Hunt raised £727 for St Wilfrid's Hospice when they opened their garden for the first time.

Alan Mundy and helpers raised over £600 in house-to-house collections for Friends of the Eastbourne Hospitals, despite no Saturday collection because of Princess Diana's death.

The Bowling Club Budd Cup was won by Ron Wheatley's Vice-Captain's team. Patrick Coulcher won the Bowls Club singles; Jack Bebbington and Alan Mundy the pairs.

In October 1997 Richard Worsell and his daughters went to Buckingham Palace to receive his MBE from Princess Royal. Currently in charge at Birling Gap, after succeeding John Wicking, he had served HM Coastguard for over 38 years. [5]

A capacity audience at the Farrer Hall heard Norman Baker MP speak on *The*

Environment to the local Liberal Democrats.

The Players production for their 50th anniversary after the war was *The Bells are Ringing,* a celebration of all the good things in life. Gordon Matley was Master of Ceremonies for the occasion and 50 persons were involved in the production. The vigour and enthusiasm of those involved augured well for the next 50 years.

After another fatality on the A259 the ESCC finally agreed to institute a study on that section of the road. The PC noted that the police accident map showed 156 accidents along the East Dean and Friston section of the A259, with two fatalities near Friston Pond.

Remembrance Sunday was accompanied by such gale force winds and torrential rain that the salute to fallen comrades was held in the church. Good support was reported for the restored two minute silence on 11 November. Hilary Pringle and helpers raised £1,540 for Poppy Day. RBL Committee meetings were now held in the Function Room of the *Tiger.*

The Cricket Club gained promotion back to Division I of the CVL as joint winners.

South Saxons, Warren Lane, 1995. **Left:** looking at the house from the garden. **Right;** Looking from the house over the garden viewing from Belle Tout to the Downs Golf Club

A Confirmation Service was held at East Dean on 16 December 1997 and was an opportunity to welcome Bishop Wallace Benn to the parish.

At the GC AGM Kathleen Boulton relinquished the post of president and was succeeded by Margaret Enser. Shortly afterwards Elsie Lawrence and Kathleen moved to Eastbourne.

In early 1998 Crowlink Ladies Club heard from Gloria Saxby of her years in the newspaper world in particular dealing with the Hatches, Matches and Dispatches column.

Village news included the opening of the new porous surface for ball games at the Recreation Ground; Carol Starr organising a non-profit making community coffee morning every Thursday in the Village hall for 40p. The Best Kept Village competition was replaced by a Village of the Year based on what each village does for their community.

The Players' *Home at Seven* was produced by Joy Bryant in the Bardolf Hall. Maire Lucas displayed a range of emotions and David Harmer was convincing as her amnesic husband. Des Thorne and Gordon Matley were splendid foils, and Vivyenne Willings played her part faultlessly. The newcomers Derek Drury and Nikki Terry were convincing.

An interim report on the A259 by ESCC recommended measures such as anti-skid surfacing and a possible 40mph speed limit on a limited section, and another redesign of the junction at *Half Way Cottages.*

The PCC reported that Andrew Palmer and David Broughton were churchwardens at East Dean, and Sidney Bunting had retired at Friston. The average Sunday attendance at East Dean was 61 and 22 at Friston, total communicants at Easter were 116, and 161 at Christmas. Ian Killick, t, said that, excluding bequests, there was a deficit of £3,500. Lois Hurter declared a satisfactory balance for the magazine and thanked editor, Sheila Surtees, Gwen Franklin and her distributors. Jean Powell spoke on the Child Protection Policy. Sheila Surtees retired after 25 years on the PCC and Tim Rowson after 18 years as sidesman at Friston.

Cedric Grimshaw and Geoffrey Mantle were elected Friston churchwardens.

The PC set the 1998 precept at £25,180, to include resurfacing of the shops' forecourt. The Mobile Library was now at *The Grange* for 1 1/2 hours on alternate Thursdays.

Esther Worsfold re-elected PC c and Jesse Taylor v-c. The introduction of Pay and Display by the Forestry Commission caused dismay because it encouraged visitors to park on the roadside, a potential obstruction on such a narrow road.

The Duplicate Bridge Club met once a month in the Farrer Hall. Convenor J Thompson thanked all those supporting the Bridge Drive which raised £420 for the new Village Hall.

A Sunday Club was started for 2-10 year olds at 0915h in the Farrer Hall on Sundays. As a contrast, both Joyce Donkin and Maud Singleton, were now 90.

Another fatality on the A259 sadly emphasised the importance of road improvements.

Country Matters was David Hunn's 1998 anthology of readings from Shakespeare to Sheridan by members of The Players and held in the grounds of *Friston Place* by permission of Mr and Mrs William Shawcross. It was a remarkable performance notable not only for the high standards of the production, but for the high temperatures of the day.

Joy and Donald Preen at the Gardening Club Annual Dinner 1998

Hilary and Ron Pringle won the RBL Annual Treasure Hunt, but Alan and Doris Rome offered to arrange next year's event.

June was a wet month causing cancellations for Bowling Club and Cricket Club matches. The Bowls folk at least had their popular Club Supper in the Farrer Hall. In July 24 members entered the Davies-Gilbert Trophy competition, won by Peter Davies, Bill Attwood and Geoff Wood.

ED & F WI had a talk by Liz Gregory on *Ink in my Veins* covering her career in Fleet Street, which included a spell working with Osbert Lancaster, the cartoonist.

Crowlink Ladies Club had Prebendary Clive Taylor talking on *It Shouldn't Happen to a Vicar*. East Dean Players' Summer Coffee Morning had delightful weather at Ron and Hilary Pringle's garden, Ron and Hilary also hosted the Conservative Association August Barbecue. ED & F WI enjoyed a splendid tea-party in Jean and Ken Warriner's beautiful garden under a blazing sun, whereas Micheldene WI were not able to assemble at Ann Merchant's garden owing to the inclement English weather, so met in the Farrer Hall.

The 1998 Flower Show had good weather but some decline in entries. The judges commented on the high standard despite the indifferent growing year. Peter Johnson and Fred Fuller were the main winners, but others included Betty Rowson, John Eve and Hazel Matley. Clive Taylor presented the prizes and Gordon Matley conducted the auction.

A Flower Festival and a Gift Day for the church were held in September. Ian Killick announced that £6,570 was raised towards the Fabric Fund. John and Barbara Eve and their daughters Brenda and Maria worked especially hard to provide refreshments for those who visited Alan and Vera Tame's *The Cottage* next to East Dean church.

Gifts to Families in Need at Christmas were collected by Jean Powell and Mary Fyfield.

The PC had the recreation ground resurfaced, installed basketball posts and completed the refurbishment of the tennis courts. Hire of the tennis court was £2.

The Cricket Club, in line for three competitions in mid-August, lost the Trophy Final, were beaten by CVL champions Firle and again by Firle who took the Challenge Cup.

The Players' 1998 production was *Fish Out of Water*. A tale of the English abroad with Maire Lucas tremendous as Agatha the life and soul of every party and from whom all are trying to escape. Gordon Matley relished organising the search for Stella Hutching's Fiona, controlled by an uplifted eyebrow from his wife played by Daphne Dempsey, while Mick Bale as Len discovered Mikki McNeill's attractions. Thanks to Derek Drury, Gordon Saunders, Des Thorne, Jenny Waldron and Vivyenne Willings there wasn't a weak link in this believable production of an unlikely story that played to packed houses.

At the RBL AGM Certificates of Appreciation were awarded to Marianne and Ken Frith and the appointment of Alan Tame as chairman was confirmed. Carol Starr and Jackie Florey organised Pat's Party with help from Nick of the *Tiger*.

Another Christmas in a Box for Balkan's children was organised by Mollie Bertin.

The RBL Remembrance Sunday parade was again cancelled because of heavy rain. The wreaths were placed round the War Memorial when the weather permitted.

ED & F WI had a talk from their vice-president, Margaret Clegg, who talked about her days as an air hostess with BOAC in the 1950s. Maire and Ken Lucas' Christmas 1998 Party for the Conservative Association was thoroughly enjoyed by the members.

David Broughton and Andrew Palmer resigned as churchwardens and Brian Adams and Peter Hewitt agreed to act until the annual meeting.

Successful Carol Services were held at both East Dean and Friston churches with over 120 attending. It was the first time in recent memory at Friston.

The 1999 Gardening Club AGM elected Sylvia Shilton c, Jackie Florey as assistant s, Colin Bexon took over Christine Faro's role as ms and Margaret Enser and Jeanne Maull were joined by Kay Bondi, John Purdy and Vera Tame on the committee.

The Duplicate Bridge Club continued, now organised by Frank Eveleigh.

The trees on the Greensward were pruned in a combined effort by the PC and RA.

In March 1999 there was a Pie and Wine Lunch which raised the magnificent sum of £357 for Chichester Diocesan Family Social Work. It has continued each year since.

Ted Flint was awarded a certificate for his extraordinary service as escort to the standard, a duty that he had performed since 1955.

East Dean, Friston and Jevington choir members took part in a Festival Service at Chichester cathedral, described by choirmaster Roy Kibble as a never-to-be-forgotten day.

The 1999 RBL Annual Village Fete was held on a hot, dry, sunny day and people flocked there in large numbers. Alan Tame was able to announce record takings of over £2000

ED & F WI celebrated their 70th birthday, presided over by May Thorne. Dorothy Stevenson produced a Scrap Book of WI events covered in an appliqué design by Beryl Boucher. Georgie Hall, Jean Warriner, Barbara Laird, Rosemary Gillett and Sylvia Wheatley were involved in the entertainment.

Betty Rowson as usual arranged for the Easter lilies donated in memory of a loved one to be blessed at Friston Church. Anne de Graf was now cleaner at Friston Church. Marjorie James gave a seat on the Village Green in memory of her husband Jimmy.

The Annual Easter walk on the South Downs way raised £425 for Family Social Work.

The Bowling Club was taken over by a team from the BBC to film the life of member Walter Gregory 100 on 19 June. He was one of eight UK citizens born in 1899 who are the subject of a TV programme to be screened later in the year.

George Tickle was elected PC c and Jesse Taylor v-c. Ken Lucas, Liz Charlwood and Margaret Lees were sub-committee c, Peter Hobbs and Camilla Crump were representatives, Ken Thurman continued as the Village Hall co-ordinator, David George the honorary Legal Adviser, and Maurice Hopkins as the custodian of the Council's flag.

The Players' spring production was *That's Life* in the Bardolf Hall. This was a compilation of excerpts from Congreve's *The Way of the World* to Pinter's *Last to Go.*

The PC again reminded residents that if their property adjoins a public path it is their responsibility to cut back any overhang, ESCC were empowered to cut back the offending growth and reclaim the cost from the property owner. It was agreed that the Cricket Club could modify the storeroom at the Pavilion to provide a score board. News that charges were to be introduced at the Seven Sisters car park was received with dismay. Concern was also shown at the low water level of Friston Pond.

The Gardening Club's Garden Party in July was at Jean and Ken Warriner's garden, after an Open Garden event at Sylvia and Maurice Shilton's home the previous month. The NSPCC Ploughman's Lunch in Anne and Alan Robson's garden, raised £1,112.

Graham Gillam announced that he had been forced to give up front line policing in the village after 18 years due to ill-health. The new Community Beat Officer would be WPC Teresa Hide, working out of Seaford. While on Police matters, local resident Robin Harlowe was appointed to serve on the Eastbourne Lay Visitors' Panel.

In August the Revd Simon Morgan left for a teaching post to be succeeded by the Revd Hugh Moseley from Ringmer, whose wife Annabelle was a teacher at Ringmer school.

The day was just right for the 1999 ED & F Flower Show and the venue at Birling Manor was perfect. It was especially encouraging to see so many entries in the children's classes. John Eve, Peter Johnson, Betty Rowson and Brian Johnson were the main winners, with Di Banks taking the cup for Home Produce, Sheila Surtees the bowl for Roses, and Jack Shepherd and Hannah Riddle romping home in the children's section.

At the ED & F WI May Thorne made a presentation to Phyl Dean on her 90th birthday, and they had a talk on Capability Brown's *Sheffield Park*. Crowlink Ladies Club was regaled with nostalgic memories of life in the village during the war by Eileen Goldsmith.

A Flower Festival and Gift Day at the churches raised £4,592 towards the Fabric Fund. As ever Vera and Alan Tame and the Eve family hosted the refreshments.

Peter Wallis, County Councillor, agreed to see if the 40mph speed limit could be implemented as soon as possible. ESCC stated that they will no longer repair the wooden finger signposts, but replace them with metal ones. The PC thought that these old posts were a part of the village and that the parish should take over their maintenance; ESCC agreed.

The Players honoured the centenary of Noel Coward's birth with *Blithe Spirit*. The ideal vehicle for sparkling performances from Maire Lucas and Trisha Kennard as the leading ladies, while Daphne Dempsey, David Harmer, Debbie Williams, Christine Walbrin and Derek Drury were sterling supporters. Joy Bryant's production was as impeccable as ever.

Alan Tame was c of RBL, with Cyril Cloke as v-c, and committee of Mrs E Allan, Mrs A Warren, J Harrison, G Clapp, M Florey, A Johnstone-Smith, J Dann, D Ockmore, D Thorne, Revd P Williams and Capt I Shearer. Revd Hugh Mosley was Chaplain. Still had a walking treasure hunt, Derby dinner, bridge evenings, Fete, annual dinner, and golf competition. The Poppy Appeal, organised for 32 years by Hilary Pringle, raised £1,815.

The Bowling Club decided that ladies be admitted to full membership of the club. [7]

The villages lost two long-standing residents at the end of 1999. Diana Eyre died aged 84. She came to East Dean in 1931, when cows grazed around the garden fence of *Hilltop*

Cottage and many of the village roads were dirt tracks. She was a nurse and school matron, but her main work was in the missionary field, spending ten years in Nigeria. She was only the second woman to be a churchwarden at Friston. Delia Bicks came to East Dean during the war. Both Delia and husband Fred were talented actors; they formed today's The Players and worked hard to build it up. A staunch member of ED & F WI and president 1980-1, but after Fred's untimely death in 1984, she devoted her time to The Players.

The Village Millennium Map went on sale at £5.50. Ron Franklin's drawing of the parish was surrounded by watercolours by Barbara Burwell, Camilla Crump, Joy Mundy, Chris and Evelyn Ray, and Anne Williams, all part of WDC's "Mapping the Millennium".

Jolyon Fyfield, Sheila Surtees, Ron and Vera Wickes, in 2001, were part of a dedicated band of church members, now under the direction of Betty Rowson, who kept the churchyards tidy, cleared ivy, and hoed the flower beds

Looking to the future, Francis Mace's New Village Hall Fund events continued, with £6,243 raised over the year, as construction of the new hall was almost complete. [1]

At the PCC David and Shirley Gazzard, Margaret Norris, and Simon Wood were elected sidespersons. Rona Hurter was succeeded by Sylvia Sweatman as CWF treasurer.

The local Conservative Association had a Lunch Party that day at the home of Bobbie Stein, with Sir Geoffrey Johnson Smith being the guest speaker.

Fred Fuller died in August 2000. Born and bred in East Dean, Fred followed his grandfather and father into the village Cricket Club. In the decade 1947 to 1956 his performances were phenomenal. [11] In 2000 ED & F Cricket Club finished runners-up in the CVL for the third successive year. Captain Bruce Elkington retired after injury.

Alan Tame was co-opted as Parish Councillor following the resignation of Ken Lucas. John Harper succeeded Ken Warriner as the village Emergency Plan Co-ordinator.

That autumn two well-respected residents resigned from posts after 40 years; Doreen Greenwood from the CMS committee and Florrie Vine from the East Dean church choir.

What was new in 2001 included the first Sea Sunday Service in July and new green waste bins - by that was meant new ordinary grey wheelie bins for green waste.

So the village routines rolled on, as anyone who has soldiered through this last chapter will be well aware. They were interrupted only by the occasional jubilee or coronation or even less often millennium. [1, 14] Even the rare spat which gave enjoyment to the onlookers mostly subsided without trace.

It was truly said, and especially since the new Village Hall, that you could be busy all day and all through the year without leaving the village especially if you had eclectic interests and immense stamina.

If you wish to learn more about the local story, or know more about local events, or the host of clubs and groups at hand, or to discover how long it took to obtain a speed limit through the village, or the village hall saga, or the village's part in beating Hitler, or tales of farming before the tractor; thanks to everyone who freely chatted about their story and memories, it's all here.

Selected Bibliography

Book of British Villages. London: AA, 1980.
Briggs J. *A Woman of Passion.* London: Penguin, 1987.
Becket A. *Spirit of the Downs,* 1909.
Budgen W. *Old Eastbourne.* London: Sherlock, 1912.
Domesday Book Sussex ed Morris J. Chichester: Phillimore, 1976.
East Dean Village Walk. Micheldene WI. Eastbourne: Sumfield & Day 1978.
East Sussex, within living memory. ED&FWI. Newbury: Countryside, 1995.
Evans AA. *On Foot in Sussex.* London: Methuen 1933.
Evans AA. *A Saunterer in Sussex.* London: Methuen, 1935.
Evans AA. *By Weald and Down.* London: Methuen, 1939.
Gilbert R. *Shipwrecks, Cuckmere Haven to Langney Point.* Eastbourne ELHS 1988.
Hannah IC. *The Sussex Coast.* London: Fisher Unwin, 1912.
Kerr J. *A Midnight Vision* 2002.
Marchant R. *Hastings Past.* Chichester: Phillimore, 1997.
Herbert-Hunting K. *Universal Aunts.* London: Constable, 1986.
Hughes PM. *The Seven Sisters, a guide to East Dean and Friston.* Eastbourne: Sussex Ptrs, 1962.
Jenkins S. *England's Thousand Best Churches.* London: Penguin, 1999.
Longstaff-Tyrrell P. *Operation Cuckmere Haven.* Polegate: Gote House, 1997.
Lower MA. *A History of Sussex.* London: John Russell Smith, 1870.
Lucas EV. *Highways & Byways in Sussex.* London: Macmillan, 1924.
Mee A. *The King's England, Sussex.* p170, 256.
Moore K. *Queen Victoria is Very Ill.* London: WH Allen, 1988.
Porter V. *The Southdown Sheep.* Chichester 1991.
Pownall M. *One of Eleven.* Eastbourne, 1983.
Robinson M. *The Quiet Valley.* London: Turnastone 1994.
Shawcross H. *Life Sentence.* London: Constable, 1995.
Surtees J. *Beachy Head.* Seaford: SB, 1997.
Surtees J. *Eastbourne a History:* Chichester: Phillimore 2002.
Surtees J. *Eastbourne's Story.* Seaford: SB 2005.
Surtees J. *Images of England - Eastbourne:* Stroud: Tempus 2005.
Surtees J. *The Strange Case of Dr Bodkin Adams.* Seaford: SB 2000.
Swinfen W & Arscott D. *Hidden Sussex.* BBC Radio Sussex, 1984.
Thomas P, *AA Evans.* ED & F LHG, 2004.
Eastbourne and district Guide Book. Ward Lock 1931.
Wales A. *A Sussex Garland.* Godfrey Cave 1976.
Waugh M. *Smuggling in Kent and Sussex 1700-1840.* Newbury: Countryside Books 1985.
Weiner M. *British Culture and the Decline of the Industrial Spirit 1850-1980.* CUP.
Wills B. Downland Treasure. London: Methuen, 1929.

References

Action Stations 9, 115-8.
Aeroplane July 2000 IPS London; 38-46.
Argus The (Brighton) 21/8/1997 et al.
Aslet C. *Friston Place.* Country Life 19/6/86; 1748-52.
Bedwin O. *Excavations at Belle Tout, Eastbourne.* 1981 Bull. Inst. Archaeology London; 18: 27-8.
Bertin, M *Memories of Friston Airfield* ED & F PCC 2001.
Birling Deserted villages GP Burleigh SAC v 111 p45 v 114 p61.
Bradley R. *Excavation of a Beaker settlement at Belle Tout.* 1970 Proceedings of the Prehistoric Society; 36: 312-79.
Bradley R. *A chalk-cut shaft at Belle Tout.* 1974 SAC; 112: 156.
Budd PJ. *ARP Warden's Diary for East Dean & Friston* 1939-44.
Burton P. *Downs Country* May/June 1998; 22:44-6.
Coats of Arms in East Dean and Friston churches SAC pt IV (Fane Lombarde) vol 70 p134.
Country Life 13/20 April 1972, front cover.
Cuckmere News May 1987 13-14.
Daily Mail. 4/10/1988.
Doff, E. *Celebrating a Royal Occasion in East Dean.* 1981 The Sussex Genealogist and Local Historian; 3 (1): 4-11.

Drewett P. *Section through Iron Age promontory fort at Belle Tout.* 1975 SAC; 113: 184-6.
Drewett P. *Excavation of a Bronze Age Round Barrow, Cornish Farm.* 1992 SAC; 130: 235-8.
Eastbourne Herald 8/1/1983, et al.
Eastbourne Gazette 28/2/1973, 12/10/88, 1/12/1993 et al.
East Dean with Friston Parish Magazine 1903-2002.
East Dean & Friston WI, Scrap Book for 1965.
East Sussex Record Office various.
Entries *Friston Parish Register* (transcribed AA Evans).
Evans AA. *On Field Names.* Sussex County Herald 1/1/1922.
Evans AA. *Parson Darby's Cave.* Daily Chronicle 15/8/1919.
Evans AA. *Prehistoric Man in the Crowlink Valley.* The Spectator 23/10/1926.
Evans AA. *Selwyns of Sussex.* Sussex County Herald 27/1/1923.
Evening Argus 29/3/1967 et al.
Farmer & Stockbreeder 31/8/1965 p 63.
Friston Church SAC N&Q v 2 p 223 (plan), brass C Davidson Houston V 77 p192, Selwyn monument N&Q v 2 p14.
Giddy D. *Account of the opening of a Barrow at Berling.* 1814 Archaeologica; 17: 338-9.
Gilbert Richard. *Eastbourne Gazette* 23/1/1963.
Ginns S. *East Dean a short history of a Sussex village.* 1992 SS BA Brighton Polytechnic.
Harwood J & Eccles J. *Experience Sussex.* Autumn 1998 18.
Herbison V. *John Boyle - Author with a Difference,* Sussex County Weekly 1989; 215: 21-3.
Herbison V. *Ray Kemp One of the Last Ox Boys.* Sussex County Weekly 1987; 123: 21-23.
Hughes PM. Scrap Book for 1958-63.
Kerr I. *A Topical study of East Dean Life and History from Early Times until 1800.* 1966.
Illustrated 31/7/1943 p19.
Lay Subsidy Rolls 1524-5. (Sussex Record Society vol 56.)
Martin D, Martin B. *Archaeological Survey of Little Lane Cottage.* 1998, University College London.
Quiney N. *Coming Attractions, East Dean Memories.* Memoirs nd.
Russell M. *Archaeological investigation Belle Tout.* 1996 Bournemouth University Interim Report.
Sargent G ed Arthur D. *A Sussex Life.* Barrie & Jenkins 1989 London.
Stevens L. *A chalk cut shaft at Belle Tout.* 1979 SAC;117: 260.
Stevens L. *Windmill sites* SAC NQ vol 126 p93.
SAC xi, 330-1. [Friston clergy]
SAC xiv, 126. [human remains urns]
SAC xiv, 263. [Birling]
SAC xvi, 207. [Churches and bells]
SAC xvii, 148. [a Dutch shipwreck (Darby)]
SAC xxxviii, 41.
Sussex County Magazine 1934, VIII; 703.
Sussex County Magazine 1936 X; 5: 294-301.
Sussex County Magazine XXIV; 497-500. [Tapsell gates]
Sussex County Weekly 18/4/1987. [Downs]
Sussex Express 12/3/1971, 11/6/1982, 10/12/1993 5/5/2000 et al.
Sussex Life Vol 4; 10: 42. [Gates]
Tatler and Bystander 13/5/59.
The Times 8/11/1958.
Thomas P. *AA Evans* ELHG 2004.
Wardell R *Sussex in the Old Days.* East Sussex County Age Concern 1987.
Windmill collapse SAC NQ (1926) vol 1 p24,
Worsfold E. *A Short History of East Dean and Friston Parish Council 1894-1994.*
Worsfold E. *Friston Place,* 2003.
Worsfold E. *Friston Pond.*
Worsfold E. *Scrap Books 1972-99.*

Appendix 1 Notes and References on the Text

2. Going Back, from early times to 1918
1. *Domesday Book Sussex* ed Morris J. Phillimore Chichester 1976. A hide was a measurement of the land required to feed a family, it varied in size, about 100 acres. A virgate was roughly a third of a hide. An acre was the amount of land that could be ploughed on a long day.
2. Surtees J. *Beachy Head* 2ed. Seaford SB 1999. p 45.
3. *Ibid* p 36.
4. SAC xiv; 136, and xvii 148.
5. A 'Blighty wound' was an injury sufficiently serious (but ideally not too serious) to require evacuation home to Britain.

4. Churches
1. *Friston Roll of Honour* 1914-18; Trooper James Cairns 2nd Life Guards, Trooper Charles Cairns 2nd Life Guards (wounded), Gunner Henry Curwood Royal Garrison Artillery, Private Bertram Crunden Royal Sussex Regiment, Gunner Edward Freeman RGA, Private Richard Fowler 8th East Surrey (wounded), Private Frederick Funnell labour Battalion, Stoker Sydney Fuller RA CB 22, Private Frederick Gay 3rd Sussex Regiment (killed), Private Charles Gay 147 N Hants Labour Battalion, Private George Gutsell 2nd Norfolks, L/C Robert Hall 2nd Royal Sussex (killed), Shoeing Smith Charles Hall RFA 221 Brigade, Seaman Thomas January *HMS Victorious,* Major FJ Maitland RGA, Private Albert Martin 2nd East Surrey (wounded), Private Frank Martin 3rd Royal Sussex, Rifleman Thomas Martin 4 KRR (wounded), Rifleman Alexander Maynard 3rd Rifle Brigade (killed), Private Victor Bryan Morris 3rd City of London Fusiliers (wounded), Seaman Robert Seakel *HMS Victorious,* Seaman Frank Ticehurst HMS Europa, Private Charles Frederick Thorpe Duke of Connaught's Light Infantry, Seaman William Cranlett *HMS Victorious,* Lieutenant Thomas Wycliffe Taylor MC RHA. (wounded).
2. *Friston Wycliffe tablet;* In loving memory of John Wycliffe Wycliffe-Taylor of Gayles Born Easter Day 1859 Died October 9 1925 & Frida his wife Died May 13 1968 aged 98 also their son Tom Wycliffe Wycliffe-Taylor MC Lieutenant RHA Died March 3 1926 aged 27 & their daughter Rosamond Stutchbury of Gayles Died October 25 1980 aged 84. Gayles is a farm just along the Seaford road.
3. *East Dean dedicated pews were:* (north side) Harold & Florence Burgess; MJ & WV Walker; Charles Edward & Annie Augusta Goldsmith; Reginald John & Irene Victoria Smith; (south side) Richard William B & Una Marion Burns-Cox; JMF & IDF; Ruby Winifred Down in memory of her mother Emily Rebecca Parsons 12/8/1960 aged 100; Horace Hayter Rew in memory of wife Olive.

5. Birling Manor, Birling Gap and Crowlink
1. Downs Country 1998; 2: 44-6.
2. Coverley's *History of the Society of Sussex Downsmen* p57.

6. The Village School
1. A chaldron was a measure of 36 bushels of coal.

7. The Village Green and around
1. *Little Lane Cottage* also has the remains of greensand quoins at three corners, and at the back an early window and vent hole, possibly from the oven. The chimney had four flues; the two from the upper floor have been blocked up.
2. Village Hall M&G associates were: Alincourt Roofing Ltd Henfield, Bonners Music Eastbourne, Norvett Electrical Alfriston, Westgate Joinery Ringmer, Caterers Choice St Leonards-on-Sea, Elphick Plastering Milton Road Eastbourne, Jackson Plumbing and Heating Hove, Tudor Roof Tile Co Lydd Kent, Security Doors and Windows Tunbridge Wells, Hailsham Roadway Windmill Hill, Stevens Partnership Battle, Ian White Associates consulting engineers Upperton House Eastbourne.

8. Friston Place
1. SAC II, 10. XI, 83. XIII, 101. XIV, 122. XV, 211. XVIII 27, 40.
2. Lay Subsidy Rolls of 1524-5 Sussex Record Society vol 56.
3. Lower's *History of Sussex* vol I, 193, and in SAC LX 41. 37, 108. 68, 79-83. 70, 145. XIV, 218. 38, 163. XVI, 292.
4. Gilbert, R. *Eastbourne Gazette* 23/1/1963.
5. Hemming, P. *Windmills in Sussex.* CW Daniel London 1936.
6. Stevens L, *Some Windmill sites in Friston and Eastbourne.* SAC 1982; 120: 93-138.

9. Downlands Estate
1. In 1938 the average house price was about £500, and 3-bedroom houses could be found at £350 with £10 deposit.

10. Wartime
1. The Bf 109E shot down 30/9/1940 was piloted by Horst Perez. Serial number 1190, and built in Leipzig in 1939. It had shot down 2 Dutch, 1 Belgian, and 2 British planes over France. In the Battle of Britain it was flown by the Jagdgeschwader 26 Squadron based near Boulogne. It failed to rendezvous with a group of German bombers and probably crash-landed due to a coolant leak. Not thought pilot was shooting as he circled, but engine was backfiring due to the leak. Pilot just had cuts to his hands and the plane was undamaged apart from dented radiators and bent propeller blades. Sent to Canada January 1941 to raise funds for the war effort and after touring Halifax and Quebec went to over 50 American cities, where visitors, on payment, could scrawl their signatures in it. Spent next 25 years in Canadian Defence College and scrapyards, brought back to Britain in 1961 and in store until bought by Duxford Museum in 1998 as the only German plane brought down in the Battle of Britain to survive.
2. Of the 4963 Canadians who embarked on the Dieppe raid, 900 died, 1800 became prisoners-of-war, and among those who returned only 300 were uninjured.
3. PAC was the term used for Pilotless AirCraft, or more prosaically flying bomb/doodlebug/V1.
4. *Eastbourne Herald* 21/7/00.

11. Austerity 1946-64
1. After 1894 each parish had to have Parish Meetings that consisted of all the electors, but where their number is about or over 300 it is superseded by a Parish Council elected triennially. In 1948 the Parish Meetings of East Dean and Friston were merged. The Annual Parish Meeting has no administrative powers, but it holds the consent of the Council to incur expenditure beyond the product of a standard rate, unless the Minister has

already given sanction, and to the adoption of certain Acts such as Public Lighting and Burial Grounds, and to any liability the Council would incur involving a loan. The business is the election of a Clerk and any voting is by a show of hands, with two or more electors constituting a quorum, but any elector may demand a poll, the cost to be borne by the Parish. The PC can use a parish meeting to sound the feeling of the residents where there is a question of finance.

2. Other plays that were suggested as more suitable in 1957 included *Mrs Gorringe's Necklace, Outward Bound, Flare Path, Laburnum Grove, Mr Pim Passes By, The Circle, Our Flat* and *Caste*.

12. A Year in the Life of East Dean and Friston 1965
1. This kissing gate was removed in 2007 when the churchyard was extended.

13. A Decade of Changes.
1. *Eastbourne Gazette* 28/2/1973.

15. Up to Date
1. *Eastbourne Herald* 18/8/90.

Appendix 2 Church Memorial Gardens plaque details
East Dean Church *Memorial Garden Plaques (* has a close relation on a plaque)*

Oscar Francis Schnitzer 18/5/1963, Estelle Eileen Curryer 28/12/63, Basil Lancelot Pearson 27/9/64, Gerald Charles Marvyn Brown 15/8/64, Charles Henry Smart 20/7/65, Charles Wilmot Turner 13/11/65, Rev John Joseph Tatum* 4/3/66, Florence Hilda Tilbrook 12/4/66, Elsie Muriel Chubb 10/5/66, Gladys Emily Clifford 30/3/67, Margarite V Alder* 3/7/66, Joseph Coleman Flynn 20/5/67, Albert Victor Roach 7/8/67, Violet Lucy Allsop 7/2/68, Richard Burdon Fear 18/4/68, Ethel E Armstrong 11/5/68, Russell H Tilbrook 25/5/68, Robert PE Williams 20/6/68, Constance E Curryer 1/7/68, Lettice Bertha Smith 3/9/68, ?Richard Alfred Fowler 2/12/69, Ruth Alder* 11/1/69, Mabel Blanche Taylor 14/1/69, Charles Arthur Grayson* 28/3/69 (71), Hettie Eugenie Humpston 4/4/69, Arthur Frederick Farren 9/12/69, Deborah Fiona Payton* 4/12/68-22/12/69, Nora Ada May Hobden 27/12/69, Mary Adelaide Fletcher 7/4/70, Phyllis Bayes Joyce 17/6/70, Sydney George Sims 22/1/71, Violet Jeanne Clements 8/5/71, Emily Edith Stickland 12/5/71, John Cotter Baker 13/10/71, Sidney Smith 15/11/71, Hilda Taylor Jefferson 21/6/72, Maurice Leslie Haffenden 2/8/72, Arthur Scott Horsley 7/10/72, Ethel May Winter 27/6/73, Florence Charlotte Spink 27/7/73, Alfred Edward Quincey* 23/9/73, Sydney William Henley 5/10/73, William Slatter Clifford 17/10/73, Harold Frderick Fabb 22/10/73, Mary Ella Read 24/2/74, Irene Victoria Smith 26/4/74, Percy Hails Raimes 31/8/73, Jessie Kathleen Eve 23/12/73, Jessica Waterhouse 30/6/74, John Janatt Blythe 30/7/74, Dorothy Jessie Edgar 9/10/74, Dorothy Eleanor Henley 3/3/75, Gordon Adams 21/3/75, Reginald Noel Dean 26/3/75, William George Fox 29/3/75, Leslie Harold Barnett 28/4/775, Peter Lucian Fowler 5/5/75, Leonard Edgar Brown 22/6/75, Hilda Victoria Fowler 18/5/75, Herbert Arthur Harman 29/7/75, Lilian Constance Roach 12/12/75, Cecil AR Dann* 13/1/76, Meliora Ellen Bagley 4/2/76, Gladys Ellen Brown 30/3/76, Dorothy Mary Harrison 26/4/76, William Slack Spink 28/11/76, Emily Quincey* 19/12/76, Ruth May Hunter 23/12/76, Revd Harry Parsons 2/1/77, Charles John Smith 5/1/77, Thomas Milford Gordon 4/2/77, Betty Foster 25/3/77, Rosetta Ida Grayson* 31/7/77, Sophia Mary Anslow 29/9/77, Jean Davis 18/11/77, Edith Kathleen Baker 24/1/78, Charles Herbert Fears 2/3/78, Wendy Christine Holt 28/7/78, Sidney Winter 12/7/78, Muriel Edith Gorski 22/6/78, Flora Edith Emily Goode 14/9/78, Mary Fielder Hooper 25/10/78, Beatrice Lilian Glass 20/11/78, Olive Margaret Harrison 3/1/79, Emma May Kerriage* 24/1/79, Charles William Snazell 9/2/79, George Edward Robell 11/2/79, Ernest W Harman* 20/4/79, Elsie F Harman* 25/4/79, Irene May Symington 17/5/79, Albert James Matthews 30/5/79, Gordon Vellenoweth* 21/6/79, Frances May Dreghorn* 6/12/79, Elsie Bertha Grose 2/1/80, William Hugh Stockley Curryer 13/3/80, Margaret Innerdale* 27/6/80, Arthur George Stocks 26/7/80, Lydia Bodle 29/7/80, Horace George Lambird* 12/3/08-11/8/80, Albert Kerriage* 8/11/80, Hamilton Innerdale* 9/6/81, Edward J Bailey 5/8/81, Sidney W Powell 30/9/81, Reginald John Smith 8/11/81, Herbert Cyril Spink* 27/11/81, Winifred Alice Spink* 3/12/81, Walter David Eve 26/12/81, Ellen Florence Brown 2/1/82, Winifred Mary Ward 15/.3/82, Ethel Brook 24/3/82, George Elms Worsell 1/5/82, Jean Glenn Hart 4/5/82, Alexsander Gorski 12/7/82, Alan William Symonds 5/8/82, William Leonard Tracey 16/9/82, Vida Allison Elvin 20/12/82, James Richard Monico 4/7/83, May Irene Stephenson 4/12/82, Kathleen Iris Dorothy Collins 5/12/83, Charles Ernest Barker 16/5/84, Stanley Herbert Armstrong 28/5/84, Frederick John Bicks 8/6/84, John Fortune Lawrence 13/8/84, Winifred May Manners 14/8/84, Beryl Doreen Joyce 8/9/84, Reginald Edward Ticehurst 23/10/84, Maya Dorothy Carteret 6/1/85, Constance Mary Lansley 12/1/85, Henry John Hamilton 1/3/85, William Isaac Brook 18/5/85, Sarah Louise Tatum 29/3/85, AA Goode 4/5/85, Emily Mary Ann Hamilton 4/7/85, John Leslie Williams 16/10/85, Alison Vellenoweth* 13/12/85, Cynthia Margaret Jesson 1/9/86, Marion Sanford 6/2/87, Jean P Atkinson 27/5/87, Beryl Elizabeth Pelling 8/7/87, Herbert Dreghorn* 27/3/88, Mary Evelyn Maude Worsell* 13/5/88, Alice Elizabeth Turner 16/5/88, Aubrey William Symington 21/5/88, Margaret Helen Church 29/5/88, Sidney Acason 28/8/88, George William Blick 30/8/88, Freda Ellen Haffenden 1/10/88, Harold Percy Joyce 11/11/88, William Lawrence Porter 18/7/89, Lilian Elizabeth Butler 18/9/89, Florence May Melling 6/11/89, William FS Bedward 7/1/90, May Howard 14/4/90, Douglas Victor Richey 20/5/90, Thomas Loos Cooper 25/6/90, Edward Sydney CH White 4/7/90, Ethel Lucy Parsons 3/10/90, Phyllis Anne Thackeray 8/11/90, Kathleen Mary Ridley 7/12/90, Peter John Joslin 1/3/91, Rose Elizabeth Dann* 1/3/91, Winifred Hannah Acason 16/3/91, Anne White 22/3/91, Peter James Adams 24/3/91, Ritan Viktoria Morgan 24/3/91, Stanley William Fuller 30/4/91, Gladys Amelia Sims 12/7/91, Michael Mahoney 23/7/91, Ray Kemp* 30/7/91, Doris Ethel Smart 13/9/91, David John Piper 5/12/33-20/5/92, Dora Yeo 22/5/92, Carla Valeria Schnitzer* 25/6/92, George Crask 31/8/92, Emily Margaret Porter 29/10/92, Beryl Kathleen Monico 27/12/92, W Thomas-Ellam 2/7/1897-11/1/93, May Ethel Manning 17/1/93, Betty Tatum* 15/3/93, William Arthur Stevens 5/4/93, John Ridley 13/7/93, Robert John Nella 28/8/93, Julie A Slaven 19/5/52-19/9/93, Evelyn Mary James 30/9/93, Trevor James 20/10/93, Constance Mary Dickinson* 13/12/93, Catherine Kemp* 18/12/93, Alfred Charles Gallop 26/2/94, Ethel May Timms 22/10/07-3/4/94, Goolam Mahmad Hassen 28/4/94, Alice Mildred Griggs 30/6/94, Alice Doris Curryer 5/8/94, John Eric Jarvis 24/8/94, John HJ Boyle 7/9/94, Michaelene Marie Benwell-Lejeune 28/3/93, Harold William Gillham* 27/11/95, Hamish Paul Towers-Minors 16/2/96, Maurice Stevenson 3/5/13-16/3/96, Cecil Hollis* 10/4/96, Joseph Foulds-Holt 12/5/96, Rupert Taylor 13/5/96, Olive Anne Stevens 7/11/17-30/5/96, Reinette Eve Martin 27/8/55-6/7/96, Kenneth John Penfold 8/5/26-26/7/96, Janet Mary Buckley (née Benson) 27/11/19-17/4/97, Christine Patricia Maxie Vellenoweth 10/8/43-19/4/97, Gladys EM Abbott 1/8/03-24/6/97, Albert John Gosnold 13/9/13-15/12/97, Kathleen Quilter Gristwood 7/11/08-2/5/98, Charles Spencer Gay 9/5/20-25/7/98, Herbert Charles Siggers* 23/12/00-11/8/98, Dudley Francis Morgan 11/1/23-22/10/98, Kathleen Francis 16/2/12-3/11/98, Evelyn Hollis* 11/12/98, Roger Charles Batchelor 29/5/55-16/12/98, Marjorie M Burn 13/8/24-17/1/99, John L Mawer 17/5/26-16/2/99, Muriel Elsie Gillham* 6/9/14-2/4/99, Sidney Owen James 1912-8/5/99, Gladys Doreen Yeo 1923-1/6/99, Cyril James Dickinson* 6/11/99, Douglas L Atkinson 13/12/99, Dora Ellen Cooper 14/8/15-6/1/2000, Elwyn Daniel Jenkins 22/4/15-12/2/00, Hugh John Gutteridge 20/11/15-19/2/00, Leslie Frederick Burdett Morgan 15/2/05-19/2/00, Walter Henry Gregory 19/6/1899-

12/5/2000, Phyllis Mabel Dean 10/9/09-9/7/00, Christine Gloria Gillam 12/11/48-17/7/00, Keith Hawkins 6/8/27-18/7/00, Frederick Corwin Fuller 9/1/21-12/8/00, Edna Jessie Siggers* 22/7/03-11/10/00, Edwin Henry Sampson 25/7/16-31/12/00, John Harold Joyce 1/8/39-26/2/01, Christine M Payton* 10/6/01, Ivy Alice Barker 18/2/11-21/6/01, Brenda Loretta Hassen 18/5/49-17/7/01, Arthur C Baker 23/9/19-5/2/01, Alice Emma Windsor 11/2/14-9/10/01, Lillie Burnage 1917-2001, Gladys Primrose Rees 19/4/23-27/2/02, Marjorie Stocks 22/2/11-9/3/02, Frederick Ernest Manning 13/6/20-28/3/02, Gratten H Hart 21/7/15-31/5/02, Betty Walter 13/8/05-13/12/02, Josie T Oakes 2/1/45-15/8/2003, Norah Geraldine Wicht 1921-2004, Alice Mary Mann 1907-2004, Rhylda May Symons 20/5/16-6/4/05, Annalie Vickers 11/12/73-23/7/05, Joan Curryer 31/10/21-25/10/05, Saru Carreck 19/10/34-6/11/05, Ronald Burrage 1922-2005, Anthony GW Rees 4/8/25-22/12/06, Eric Lewinton 1910-2007, Peter S Whaley 10/1/19-28/4/07, Louisa Ethel Lambird 7/2/09-29/4/07, Brian Thomas Batchelor 11/5/58-6/5/07

Friston Church *Memorial Garden Plaques*

Will Smith Harris 7/4/1954, Leila Marion Pease 18/4/54, Charles Bass Kirby 23/4/54?25/11/54, Joseph Henry Barber 1/12/54, John William Burrell 18/12/54, Mabel Catherine Barber 30/1/55, Fanny Elizabeth Easy 3/5/55, Mary Isobel Cochrane 26/5/55, Nellie Boden 6/6/55, John Hamilton 30/7/55, Gertrude Eyre 21/9/55, Helen Servaes 23/10/55, Braham Solomon Rosen 23/11/55, Augustus Scott Williams 10/1/56, William Joseph Boyce 26/10/56, Maurice Frank Martin 12/11/57, Arthur Henry Crook 19/1/57, William John Feneley* 13/8/57, Grace Clarke 25/11/57, William Joseph Benton 23/4/58, John Andrew Douglas Thompson 27/5/58, Edith Jane Kirby 6/7/58, Michael Timothy Malone-Barrett 3/8/58, Edward Bailey Page 23/9/58, Cecil Thomas Jeffrey McDowell 19/1/59, John Woodward Powell 29/3/59, Alexander van Someren 25/4/59*, Sidney Harrison 25/7/59, Samuel Arthur Terrey 16/8/59, Dorothy Edith Norman 30/8/59, Ethel Doble 24/10/59, John Cyril Dalton 26/10/59, Lilian Power Jenkins 1/12/59, Joseph Ashforth "Dick" Longley* 10/12/59, Olive Margaret Rew* 15/12/59, Christina Laird Newbound 28/2/60, Joan Erica May Pownall 29/3/60 age 29, Amy Winifred Thompson 29/7/60, Elsie Toms 31/7/60, John Anthony Forinton 4/9/60, Robert Ironside Lindfield 9/1/61, Norah Gibb Terry 16/1/61, Robert Everett Warrier 20/2/61, Leonard Rathbone 6/3/61, Ronald Stanley Townley 23/6/61, Alice Elizabeth Mundy 29/10/61, Harold Burgess 12/1/62, Margaret Sworder 20/1/62, Percy James Budd 30/3/62, John Forest Smith 8/4/62, Walter Sidney Ostler 2/5/62, John Edward Taylor 29/10/62, Mabel Anne Powell 28/11/62, Florence Mary Ostler 10/12/62, Horace Hayter Rew* 31/12/62, Charles John Cairns 24/1/63, Eleanor Kathleen Budd 1/2/63, Florence Burgess 22/2/63, Gordon Edward Fincham 23/3/63, John Raymond Simeons 26/9/63, Marjorie Symons 26/10/63, Reginald Hugh Simpson 1891-2/5/64, Ernest Cater 3/6/64, Col RH Elliott 1896-31//7/64, Margaret Crook 4/12/64, Donald Temple Roberts (MT Crosby) 30/4/03-8/1/65, Leonard Arthur Newbound (70) 6/5/65, WV Walker 13/6/65, ?Anne G Barber , Charles Frederick Oldfield 8/9/65/14/9/65, Mabel Clissold Mawer 25/12/65, Tonie Servaes 11/4/66, Margaret Meller 21/7/66, Albert John Swan* 2/12/66, Ethel Marion Arnatt 9/4/67, William I Forinton 11/4/67, Stuart Leslie Litchfield 13/4/67, Claude Herbert Grundy* 31/5/67, Guy Ross Smart 2/7/67, Erik Rosenvinge* 18/7/67, Kathleen Doherty* 20/9/67, Mary Sheahan 29/9/67, Francis Arnatt aged 85 11/12/67, Arthur Philip Glenny 30/12/67, Michael Xernosites 18/1/68, William Henry Brown 1/9/68, Grace Louisa Cairns 23/4/69, Cicely Winifred Smart 21/11/69, David IJ Edwards 28/11/69, John Arthur 6/12/69, Winifred Mary Huggons* 16/12/69, John Rodgers 3/3/70, Arthur Clarence Stevens 14/4/70, Edith Sarah Penny 2/6/70, William G Johnson 12/8/70, Neil Charles Bannatyne 22/8/70, Margaret Joan Walker 30/3/71, C Ian Adam 20/6/71, John Matthews 28/7/71, Catherine A Roberts 27/1/72, James William Mawer 7/2/72, Charles Harry Meller 29/2/72, Beatrice Pearce 6/3/72, Isabel PM Symons 20/5/72, Hilda T Jefferson 21/6/72, Doris Rathbone 25/7/72, Frederick Charles Rapson 16/9/72, Reginald James Hooker 21/12/72, Mary L Van Someren* 28/2/73, John A Cowie 16/2/73, Ethel Edna Baldock 21/8/73, Joyce Rayner Simpson 26/8/73, Francis Gertrude Pownall 24/10/73, Betty Kendall King 12/11/73, Alan Vodden Rapson 10/1/74, Frances Dunbar McDowell 10/5/74, Douglas Dunn Rowson 11/6/74, Alice Greenwood 1/7/74, Frederick William McPherson 9/5/75, Alice Oldfield 14/7/75, Marjory Hamilton 21/7/75, Dorothy Marguerite Cullen 13/8./75, Harold Toms 13/8/75, Minnie Elizabeth Greeves 3/10/75, Leslie Williamson 17/10/75, Graham Lycett Lycett 7/11/75, Gladys Evelyn Maufe 20/2/76, Honor Meakin 21/2/76, Albert Edward Leslie Tate 13/9/76, Harold Hans Ballin 7/12/76, Fred Doherty* 15/2/77, Norman Holding Symons 28/3/77, Hilda Jane Rogers 19/4/77, Kathleen Forinton 30/4/77, Katherine Miller 30/6/77, R Clifford Cambridge 14/7/77, Harold Ashford Down 13/11/77, Joseph Pownall 12/1/78, Mollie Evelyn Glegg* 6/4/78, Arthur Francis Huggons* 10/5/78, Dorothy Scott Williams* 18/5/78, May Adele West 22/5/78, Frederick Charles Henry Comley 7/6/78, Olive Lucy Bullock 28/8/78, Jean Rayner Simpson 11/10/78, Hilda Wolfenden 7/11/78, Reginald Stanley West 4/12/78, Christine Elsie Nora Simeons 11/2/79, Jack N Dupont 10/12/19-17/3/79. John Donald Moss 19/1/80, Alfred John King 2/4/80, Theodora Bannatyne 2/5/80, Margery Alice Wilford 24/6/80, Sheila Muriel Rodgers 17/7/80, Barry NB Justice 6/8/80, F Constance M (Toney) Boden 1981, Charles F Sharp 10/3/82, Grace Helena Johnson 20/3/82, Ann Rapson 23/7/82, Rose Roberts Martin 3/8/82, John Herbert Granville-White* 1/12/82, William Harry Barker 23/1/83, Timothy Sheahan* 31/1/83, Stanley Wilson 21/3/83, Emily (Diddy) Abery 6/8/83, Hugh Granville-White* 23/9/83, Rosa Lillian Swan* 5/12/83, Adeline Phelps 1/3/84 (aged 103), William Taylor 20/3/84, Rachel Maitland 7/5/84, Geoffrey Arnell Burgess 2/6/84, Ernest A Long 28/10/84, Robert Carcroft Paterson 25/1/85, George Arthur Davidson 8/3/85, Jessie Kate Ada Taylor 12/4/85, Stuart Rapson 27/5/85, Linn Violet Tolhurst 10/9/85, Anne-Louise Thornhill 11/10/84-5/12/85. Elsie Taylor 14/1/86, Douglas Meredith 3/2/86, Harry Cunliffe 6/3/86, Mary Veronica Child 16/5/86, Gustav Aronsohn 19/6/86, Kathleen Dorothy Barbara Grundy* 4/10/86, Maurice John Norrell 23/5/87, Kathleen Rose Kennard 6/3/87, James Frederick Sutherland 13/3/87, Joan Lovekin Mcpherson 23/5/87, John Edward Robertson 3/6/87, Ethel Florence Osborne 30/4/88, Lizzie Rosenvinge* 7/6/88, James Stanley Lindsay 17/8/88, Muriel Rosen 10/11/88, Elsie Brown 12/11/88, Edgar Alfred Young 4/2/89, Mollie Louise Ballin 4/4/89, Robert Sibson 27/5/89, Florence E Sibson 2/8/89, Clare Cecily Chenevix Trench 16/1/90, Daisy Harrison 16/1/90, Marion Winson 8/1/90, Leonard Martin Bertin 26/1/90, Winifred Gertrude Cambridge 13/2/90, Bessie May Cox 28/7/90, James William Baggett 8/12/90, Cedric Albert Styer 17/12/90, Mary Yolande Coulcher 25/2/91, Rita Elsie Marian Cowie 22/5/91, Frederick W Nash 29/6/91, Jack Zoethout* 19/8/91, Hartwig R Schnuppe 11/3/1939-19/9/91 Rechlin, Gerald Ringrose Mockler 1/10/91, Robert Francis Pillans Glegg* 16/1/92, Barbara L Benson (née Milton) 29/2/92, Rene Jones 30/6/92, Charles John Cairns 19/8/92, Leslie Curtis Ockenden* 24/2/93, Doris Evelyn Robertson 11/4/93, Roland Summers 28/4/93, Myra Kathleen Lilian Baggett 5/9/93, Gladys Ada Ockenden* 2/4/94, Lilian Sharp 11/6/94, Stella Myra Illsley* 23/6/24-7/7/94. Molly Evelyn Mathieson 26/8/94, Mary Taylor Burgess 6/5/94, Marguerite D Thompson 14/11/10-11/12/94, Herbert William Vickery* 25/2/95, Jean Zoethout* 9/7/95, Dorothy Winifred Cunliffe 4/8/95, Ray Knott 28/1/96, Lilian Annie Nash 14/10/04-6/8/96, Ellen Lindsay 27/7/12-22/10/96, Mavis Harris 16/2/20-13/3/97, Laura Irene Feneley* 14/1/97, Noel Dennis Hegarty 18/5/98, Vera Simpson 1907-98, Patricia Moya Hardy 18/5/42-19/12/98, Lieselotte Cheal/Diem 19/12/25-27/6/99, Priscilla Elsie Hodgson 13/11/10-9/3/00, Betty Beatrice Mullinger* 13/7/16-24/5/00,. Mary Tate 1913-2000, Jean A Davidson 1903-2000, Robert Roy Mullinger* 1914-2001. Ernest Illsley* 17/1/22-15/1/01. Patricia Stanley* 24/8/01. Mary Elizabeth Vickery* 1/10/01. Lionel Napier Bramley 2/3/08-19/10/01. Arthur Layton (Tim) Rowson 9/6/12-23/10/01. Donna Evans/Hearns 22/2/69-1/11/01. Joyce Donkin (née Arnatt) 15/11/01. Harold Winson 10/12/01. Lloyd Gregory* 6/7/14 18/6/02. Maxwell Henderson 15/9/19-14/7/02. Billy Marchbank b & d 26/9/02. Marion Gregory* 10/4/20-9/12/02. Mary Penn Longley* 1903-2002. John Henry Stanley* 15/3/03. Virginia Royds 1915-2003. Pauline Olive Aronsohn 8/1/1912-13/10/03. Mildred Anne Mortimer 1916-2003, Brian Alan Newman 20/5/38-12/1/04. Frances Marion Clements 25/12/1912-3/4//04. Anna Summers 1919-2004. Evelyn Vera Russell 20/12/27-20/7/04. David F Sharp 6/12/04. Gertrude Platt Matthews 28/10/1903-4/5/2005, Ruby Louise Gibson 5/8/12-12/7/05, Pat Granville-White* 1928-2005, Jamie Alex Cox 23/3/06, Audrey Nelson Jenks née Scott 1919-2006, Vera Doreen Wickes 5/10/1930-10/3/2006, Deidre Ann Barfoot 6/11/46-7/9/06, David Mortimer 1916-2006, Alexander James

Weeks 1921-2007, Brian Evans 1940-2007, Elizabeth Kathleen Kingdon 1924-2007, Ivy Henderson 12/10/17-27/7/07, Kathleen Arnell Banks 9/4/09-26/9/07, Christopher Blom 23/4/54-14/12/07, Joyce Evelyn Meredith 15/4/26-4/1/08

Appendix 3 Churchyard Gravestone details and approximate site
Friston Church

Near gate to the right of path on entering from Crowlink Lane
Mantle, Irene 1909-1999. Box tomb, so sunk more like a slab. George, John 22 August 1694 aged 80.

To left of path from gate. Stevens, Mary Ann Lucy wife of Urban Stevens 2/7/1900. Clifton, John Thomas who died through an accident at Friston Place 27/6/1902 aged 38. Armiger, George 1/10/1930 age 67, & Amy E 4/3/45. Seymour, Robert J 8/9/75 age 75 Verger 30 years, Grace Harriet 18/1/76 age 78. Macgowan, William Stuart 12/2/1898-7/5/1974 foundation member of RCGP. Armiger, William A 22/8/1982 age 75 Verger, Elsie 16/1/94 age 84.

Further along on right side of path near wall by tree. Box tomb. Armitage, M John of East Dean 29/1/1911.

On right side of path nearer porch. Lieut Daniel Leary RN who died at Crowlink Gap 24/8/1839 aged 49 years and six months, also Mary his wife who died ?28/11/1848 in the 52 year of her age. Powers, David de V 1917-1971, Odile Fernade de V Powers 1886-1976 widow of Powers Rev CS 1877-1951. Hobden, Anne 20?28/12/1982 age 86, Clarence Stanley Hobden 16/1/1986 age 87. Carpenter, Evelyn 20/3/88 age 79, and Ronald 14/1/99 age 92.

Opposite porch on right side of path. Box tomb. Rason, Anna Maria of Crowlink 16 July 1806 this tomb affectionately inscribed by her husband. Mary Nash Boore 17/7/1807 who was buried by Henry Rason of Crowlink 23 July.

On left side of path leaving porch. Anscombe, James 13/6/1930 age 65, Amy 17/12/1963 age 91. Slab Indecipherable.

Left side of church by porch. Hamblin, Edith Winifred 22/6/1988 age 82. Skellett, Geoffrey Miles 5/10/1918-22/1/1988, Nora 4/9/1915-26/3/1998. Willey, Henry Riggall 1908-87, Nina Dorothy Willey 1912-2005, Doxat-Pratt, Maurice 1895-1970 lay reader, Marjorie 1893-1987, son Peter Maurice 1927-1990. Alice Ann daughter of Charles and Eliza Tuppen 6/3/1893 aged 22, also Louisa daughter of Charles and Eliza 15/4/1893 aged 36. Holter, Albert Edward 8/9/1973 age 82, Alice Louise 8/6/1970 age 70.

Along southern wall right of path line. Winter, P 1917-1996. Morris, WC 8/3/1922 (68) Jane Morris 14/5/1931 (81), Wootten, Ted stillbirth 4/52006, Reynolds, Edward James 1911-28/4/1992, Olive Hilda Reynolds 1911-17/6/2001. Goodwin, Lucretia Annie Hillside East Dean 14/10/1902 (33), Frances Louie Goodwin daughter 11/12/1908 (17). Lilian Winifred daughter of L and LAG 18/2/1919 (21). Carey, Edgar 23/7/1900, Frederick George Carey 1910-98, Thomas of Crowlink farm 8/1/1894 & Harriett Carey Crowlink Farm 5/5/1891(58).

Maitland memorials near SE corner. FJM Francis James Maitland Major RGA 20/7/1873-16/2/1940. EM Ethel 5/7/1877-14/8/1924 daughter of JAM & MNM. AFM Andrew Fraser 16/2/1906-5/11/1986 second son of FJM. MNM Margaret Nicol 30/7/1844-14/71922. JAM John Andrew of Friston Place 19/7/1838-17/12/1914 father of FJM.

In SE corner past Maitland memorials. Evans, Alfred Arthur Priest 1908-29 16//4/1946 [often has the first aconites in spring]. Beckett, Alice 10/1/1938, Arthur William 8/5/43 age 71. Harvey, Leonard William 10/3/1931, Ada 28/3/1931. Cubitt Smith, Basil Joseph her son 21/1/1951 died at sea. Cubitt Smith, Geoffrey William grandson 26/11/1951 died in New York. Elphick David 5/11/1928 age 67 Mary Ann 27/3/1940 age 81.

Seat. In memory of AB *Who loved the view* 10/1/1938 [Alice wife of Arthur Beckett. It is said that Frank Bridge liked sitting on the seat]

Behind east window of church first row starting near path. Little, Mervyn 28/3/30-21/4/90. Bridge, Frank musician 1879-1941, and Ethel 1881-1960, Oliver, Daphne (1910-1992). Fass, Marjorie (1886-1968). Wycliffe Taylor, John Wycliffe of Gayles 9/10/1925 age 66, and Frida 13/5/1968 age 98. Wyndham, Laura 1937-1983. Kellar, Florence Maud 1877-1960, and James Dodds Ballantyne Kellar 1874-1965, and son Alexander James Kellar CMG OBE 1905-1982. Williams, Peter priest 1922-2005, Wheeler, Bellisa Barne 1/9/1934 age 79, and Marion Catherine wife of Eric Streatfeild 17/11/1882-8/2/1961. Meredith, Ada Henrietta of Windover 8/1/1974. Greenwood, Reg & Alice July 1974. Hooker, Florence Mary 22/12/1974. Hearns, Williams A 1908-1977, Annie Hearns 1912-1978. Haywood, Winifred 17/10/1905-9/7/1978.

Next row from church towards memorial garden. Slab Wilson, Thomas Henry 1904—1999, Margaret Valerie Wilson 14/3/08. Box tomb Fletcher, Wm 10/4/1748. Binney, Katherine 8/3/1933. Honey, William Andrew 1938-1993. Box tomb To the memory of Fletcher, Thomas late of this parish (but formerly of the town and port of Seaford) who died June ye 8th 1750 aged 34 years. Allen, William 3/6/1933, wife Elizabeth Ann 30/7/1943. Attenborough, Elizabeth Annie 29/8/1964, husband Eric George 12/9/1972. Barnes, Ada Jane 21/9/1964 (85). Godsal, Charles William Lloyd 1907-65. Thomson, Alan Chichester Urquhart 26/10/1881-22/12/1965, Eva 11/11/1889-2/5/1976. Essex, Oliver George Victor 3/4/1897-25/12/1965, wife Vera Alice Mary 5/7/1903-30/12/65. Kerr, Colin Causton 1890-1966, wife Beryl KM 1908-1999. Cornford, Cecil David 7/7/1973 (63).

Next row, third between memorial garden and church starts with wooden cross. Washed Ashore (said to be a woman washed up on Birling Gap beach in 1930s). Bassett, William Selby 29/11/1920. Clark, Herbert George 14/6/1966 age 65. Axten, Adelaide Daisy 17/12/1966 age 75, William Axten 8/2/1976 age 89. Davey, Audrey 3/4/1967. St Johnston, Dr Charles Hector 27/3/1901-31/10/1967, Marie Helene 20/3/1907-9/1/1977. Williams, Sydney 15/5/1904-4/1/1968, Ethel May 4/7/1988. Piggott, Joseph 1885-1968, Muriel Clara Piggott 19/1/1991. Howkins, Drina 1886-1969. Evans, George 1880-1969, Nora Annie Evans 1905-1991. Anderson, Rex 1903-1970, wife Mollie Anderson. Moss Violet Alice 5/12/1971. Hahn, Tom 1/11/1909-29/3/1972, Ann Hahn 11/3/1915-3/101993. Smith, Anna Stuart 4/9/1973 age 63. Hannaford, William Henry 4/7/1973 age 83, Eileen 4/9/1989. Chick Catherine Patricia 30/8/1973 age 73.

Middle row between memorial garden and church. McDonnell, Edward Thomas 18/8/1932. Greenwood, Howard 17/5/2001. Thorpe, Charles FE 21/10/1932 age 59, May Thorpe 24/5/1937. Funnell, Frederick John 19/3/1934, wife Sarah 6/1/1954. Thurlow, Muriel Doris Clara youngest daughter of Robert Youngman and Clara Thurlow 13/6/1895-16/10/1934, Thurlow, Gertrude Maria sister of above 3/5/1963 *slightly out of line.* also Thurlow, Cecilia Anne sister of above 14/7/1878-14/4/1969. Norwood, Samuel Burton 16/5/1941, Amy Rachel 13/10/1958. Matthew, Margaret S Sutton 19/5/1854-1/10/1941. Wilford, James Henry 27/10/1941, Mary Louisa Wilford. Milton, Frederick Joseph 6/11/1950 age 71, Ada Beatrice 16/12/1942 age 57. Tompsett, Arthur Stanley 27/10/1945 age 76, Edith Florence 7/6/1953 age 76. Couser, Elizabeth Adelaide 13/9/46. Middlemiss, Donald P 14/8/1947, Celia Elizabeth 31/7/1972. Blake, Dorothy Joyce 7/2/1956. Lycett, Harcourt Montegue Straton 24/4/1877-12/5/1944, Ethel 23/1/1954. Simpson, Benjamin Ferdinand died Little Friston 2/2/1940 age 80.

Second row from memorial garden between garden and church. Three MN graves. A Sailor of the Second World War Merchant Navy 18/4/1941, 19/10/1941. 8/7/1942. Dennett, Dorothy K 1892-1/9/1943 at Trimley Suffolk, & Frederick LS Dennett 1893-1972. Fourth MN A Sailor of the Second World War 4/9/44. Fawcus, Gladys Constance 1/7/1949. Sturgis, Lilian Taylor 16/5/1957. Penn, Edith Maud 14/2/1961. Archibald Victor Penn 19/7/1962, Hilda Winifred 19/6/1982.

Alongside Memorial garden, starting from south. Bell, Cecil Walker 7/2/47 age 78, Frances Ethel 18/4/1872-10/4/1962, with plaque Holme, Bryan (1913-1990) and Elfrida (née Bell 1907-1999). Lister, Bernard Stanhope 1889-1966, Ellen Edith 1889-1979. Lister, Barry 1921-1942. Forth, Vincent Gerard 7/7/1952. Gibbs, George William 1878-1951, Henrietta Tinsley Gibbs 1873-1969. Royds, William Massey 16/61951, Doris Mary 7/5/1974 (91). Lillie, Sarah Alice 26/10/?1968. Farrer, Ethel Florence 3/1959. Langton, March Herbert Innes 18/3/1952 (52). Cowie, John and

Rita 1973 and 1991. King, Catherine 1863-1954. Scott, Edward Rupert 7/12/1954, and his wife. Bowness, Walter Leslie 6/7/1955. Crees, Percival Nelson 22/12/1957 (59). Mudler, Zoe Marie 5/7/1959 (85) widow of Felix 27/6/1957 (ashes in GofR Woking). Butcher, Francis Tom 21/1/1889-21/7/1960. Lycett, Norman Lycett Vicar 1943-56 1870-1962, Ruth Edith 1877-1968. Burnand, Richard Frank 1887-1969, Lea Felicity 1894-1985. Carter, Arthur Partridge 5/2/1970 and Hilda 23/12/76. Haworth-Booth, Marie Octavie 26/8/1970.
NE side between church and road starting near church. Tompsett, Sylvia Margaret Grace 31/5/1982, husband Anthony 6/10/1985. Haviland-Nye, Jessie 1901-1979, John Haviland-Nye 1898-1985. Miller, Helena 23/12/1981, Eric Miller 28/3/1988. Laszlo, Bona 28/4/20 (Budapest)-20/3/1984 (Friston). Hughman, Trevor Montague 1909-1984.
Next row. Simmons, Molly of Point House 1899-1984, Edward Simmons 1899-1997. Gooderidge, Enid 1905-1985. Glen, Eileen 2/2/1988. Bradbury, Marie 1/3/1990. Stow, Eric St John 1903-1992, Gladys Irene Stow 1905-1997. Shaw, Brian (dancer & teacher) 28/6/1928-2/4/1992. Humphreys, Rose Annie 3/7/1906-22/6/1992. Knopp, Margery Doris 4/12/1910-23/7/1992, Benjamin Bowyer Knopp 2/9/1908-14/12/1993. Bonham, Peter John 9/9/1992.
Next row. Richards, William Randolph 1930-1993. Smith, William Sinclair 16/10/1918-25/5/1993. King, James William Henry 18/10/1921-1/9/1993. McAdam, Joan Violet 26/6/1926-21/11/1993. Mathias, née Hart Belinda GCT 17/10/1906-13/8/1994.
Next row. Purkiss, Beryl Mary 18/5/1995. Arnold, Denis Edward 19/6/1909-5/6/1996, Winifred Ethel Arnold 1908-2005. Climpson, Jack Douglas 1918-1996.
By tree Granville-White, John Herbert 1/12/1982. Palmer, Geoffrey George 11/1/1997 aged 73, Violet Florence Palmer aged 82
Next row. Patterson, Raphael 1977-5/9/1997 (unmarked), Mead, Jack of Payne's Dene 1917-1998 and Graham Mead 18/6/2003. Long, Irene Ellen 1909-1999. May, Frank Herbert 25/5/1914-27/11/1999. Hadley-Coates, Marie December 1999.
Near tree. Joyce, Harold a gentle man 6/11/1904-11/11/1988.
Next row. Staite, Jean Christine 1/8/1930-10/10/2000. Wagstaff, Edward Fletcher (Ted) 15/7/1911-19/4/2001 and Jean Margaret Wagstaff 22/10/1917-3/6/2003. Francis, Harold William 1928-2001. Tilton, Lylie Amelia 1906-2001 and Harold Tilton 1905-2002. George, Christopher 18/9/1982-22/10/2000.
Next row. Johnson, Barbara 19/6/1941-13/11/2001. Fyfield, Mary Isabel 17/7/1925-3/1/2002. Hillman, Gilford Bernard Derek, Patricia Hillman 2006 aged 73. Thornton, Charles Henry 1927-2004.
George Henry Booth-Clibborn 27/7/36-24/4/07, Derek John Noel Pipe 13/12/46-13/5/07
Next row nearer pond. Dorothy Edith George 10/11/07 aged 83

On road side of church near tree (by bus stop). Russell, Sarah Ince 20/10/1904 (45). Elphick, Eunice Sarah 26/12/1897 (73) and her husband David 29/11/1904 (79). Dunstall, Robert 7/3/1888 and widow Maria 24/4/1891 (76), also grandson Harry Walter Dunstall who died at ? British Columbia 13/2/1889 (26). *Indecipherable child's tomb ?* January.

Next row. Thomas, Hilda (née Hugh) 30/7/09-16/5/06. Mockler, Catherine (née Cardale) 1914-2004.

East Dean Church Gravestone details and approximate site
From Gilberts Drive gate, the arch is in memory of AP Carter, churchwarden 1953-60.
To the left (south) of path. Row nearest wall. Akehurst, James 20/2/1922, wife Sarah Ann 1/8/1922. Davies, Harry Llewellyn 1/5/1923.
Next row. Waring, Thomas Richard Gainsborough 8/1/1935, wife Marie Eveline 6/8/1945. Dennett, Anne 4/4/1935, Alfred Harry Dennett 18/4/1935. Drew, Elizabeth Hodges 6/2/1940, Edward Charles Drew 9/2/1940, and his sister Annie EM Drew 11/5/1957. Cheal, Dora Kate 14/4/1941. Indecipherable. HBF 1941. Davies-Gilbert, Grace Katherine Rose 8/7/1951 wife of Carew Davies-Gilbert 1/12/1913. Butler-Kearney, Hester Davies 11/4/1972. Harding, John Holroyd 14/9/1920-30/4/96. Conduitt, Anne Dorothea 7/4/1915-12/5/1994. Harding, Michael Massy 28/9/1917-25/2/1979. Davies-Gilbert, Minnie 20/2/1968. Harding, Charles Henry 19/12/1953. Davies-Gilbert, Charles Gilbert 1905-1977. Harding, Patience Davies 30/11/1970. Davies-Gilbert, Sibyl Madeleine 1906-1981.
Third row. Hall, Florence Ada 12/11/1928, Roderick Glendinning Hall 14/3/1969. War Grave Kinley, WL Seaman RNPS JX 174488 HMS Ocean Sunlight 13/6/1940 (19). Dann, Cecil 1920-1976, wife Rose Dann 1922-1991. Vine, Florence 26/12/1953, Albert Luther Vine 1/4/1962. Dark, Charles Murrice 13/1/1934, wife Minnie 15/4/1949. Fletcher, Herbert Bristowe 21/4/1868-21/3/1941, wife Gladys 19/4/1887-26/11/1958. Worsell, Eric Elms 10/11/1924 age 39/12. Hudleston, Robert William Sept 1918. Dennett, James Bernard of Birmingham age 21 drowned at Portsmouth 5/9/1909 recovered at Birling Gap 5/10/1909.
Fourth row. Martin, Corwin 22/1/1929. Snape, Ellen Anne 14/1/1913. Long, Henry William Alner 20/5/1926. Higgs, Florence Alice of Purley and the old lighthouse 5/11/1916. New, Anthony George died at Belle Tout 7/8/1911. Corbyn, Archie died at Birling Gap Coastguard Station 5/6/1903 age 169/12. 9555 Private Willie Elijah Tshabana SA Native Labour Corps 21/2/1917.
Fifth row. Martin, Ruth wife of Corwin Martin 27/12/1902. Emmett, Robert Skinner of Romsey 4/5/1900.
Next row. Slab Darby, Jonathan Parson 'He was the Sailors' Friend'. ?Worger, Will ?29/12/1781, also Will Worger 11/2/?1789/99 age 76. Worger, Elizabeth 14/6/1794 age 30. Wallace, George 10/11/1873 age 50. Anderson, Charles Alfred Thomas only son of Thomas Anderson 25/1/1879 age 49/12.
[?In memory of Ann wife of Will Worger also of Worger, Will 11/2/?1789.]
By yew tree. Hughes, Elizabeth 12/3/1848. Pearce, Mary Ann departed this life at Beachy Head lighthouse ?12/5/1834 age 27/12. Marsh,John, also of Ann Marsh 24/5/1820 aged 17.
Near porch. The son of William & Elizabeth Bodle 22/9/1747 age 9 years, Elizabeth Bodle 4/12/1738 age 3, William 17/3/1778 age 70. Box. Gardner, Jane wife of Christopher, Vicar, 16 May 1810 aged 34 years, Christopher Gardner 26/8/1846 aged 68. West, Mary Marten daughter of John & Elizabeth West 28/5/1799. West, John 16/4/1827.
Oval plaque on wall of church near porch. Near this spot are deposited the remains of Lieut Samuel Jacobs late Paymaster of the North Hampshire Regiment 22 October 1804 aged 50. In front are two slabs SJ which mark his grave.
From Gilbert's Drive gate. To the right (north) of path, row nearest wall. Against wall. Edmondston, David Laurence 11/1/1937 age 22, Henry Saxby 28/9/1941 age 63, Alice Edmondston 28/2/69 age 88, Bridget Ann Edmondston 28/11/1989 age 63, Alice Coffin Edmondston 6/1/1927 age 6. Akehurst, James 2/11/1884, wife Catherine 27/2/1886. Bradford, James 18/1/1886, wife Mary Ann 28/3/1895. Lias, Samuel Hutchill 30/1/1906, wife Martha 9/2/1911. Hole, Mary Hannah 5/8/1907
Second row. Akehurst, Charlotte Sarah 23/1/1915 (73), husband Thomas Robert 12/1/1927 (84). Crouch, Mary Jane 27/3/1919, husband John Alfred 23/12/1922. Lockey, Mary 29/10/1911, husband David Fowler 9/3/1922. Gay, Edith May 17/4/1909, also of Charles William Gay killed in action at Gandiempre France 21/4/1918 aged 26 interred at Gandiempre Military cemetery.
Third row. Harris, Florence 16/7/1936, and daughters Baker, Agnes Lucy May 22/1/1982, Hatley, Phyllis Sarah May 1/10/1987. Gay, John

30/7/1926, wife Louisa 7/11/1942. Thiselton-Dyer, Mary Ada 12/5/1912. Cracknell, Emily Jane 9/3/1910, also Leonard Cracknell 1897-1974, wife Mary 1895-1981. Cracknell, Alice 18/2/1907.

Fourth row. Pearce, William Fletcher 7/11/1935 (66) Vicar of East Dean, Minnie Florence 24/4/1956 (85). West, Alfred 12/6/1938 (46). West, Caroline 28/1/1928 (68), William West 4/2/1957 (90). Cox, Edith Elizabeth 7/7/1921. Norman, Lily Jane 5/12/1918, Charles Frederick Thomas Norman only son of above 8/12/1918 age 16/12. Albright, Christopher John 20/10/1983. Boyle, Jane 7/8/1983. War Grave A Sailor of the Second World War MN 9/9/1941. Just to east A Sailor of the Second World War MN 25/5/1943. In loving memory of Reggie.

Fifth Row. Breach, Laurence N 29/6/1931 age 16. Butterfield, Robert Cecil 1908-1987. Breach, Elizabeth 23/1/1917, husband David 21/10/1920. Huggett, Emily 23/12/1910. Hall, Martin Beauchamp 1914-1984. Powley, Richard 27/4/1899-29/1/1984 and wife Winifred 4/6/1901-14/4/1978. Burn, Winifred Isabel 1911-1982 and John Burn 1909-1987. Donovan, Lily Elizabeth Martha 13/12/1981.

Sixth row. Brassley, Harold Joseph 3/2/1971 (78), wife Ethel 28/11/1988 (97). Gregson, Marion Edith 11/6/1915, Dorothy Caroline Gregson died at Bournemouth 28/8/1960. Rowney, Gloria 30/10/1986, Ronald Rowney 2/1/2000. Caffyn, Margaret 21/1/1939, also her friend Purver, Helen of Haligarth East Dean 25/4/1950. Bates, Ethel 24/1/1951, also her friend Parker, Mary Jessie Rolls aged 89 20/11/1968. Street, Hugh 30/12/1977. Whitcher, Nigel 7/7/1978. Robinson, William 1906-1980. Lidiard, Herbert Seppings 1894-1981, wife Beatrice Dorothy 1899-1983. Miliffe, John Patrick 30/4/1981 and Mary Frances Miliffe 26/8/09-20/11/02. SAS Dennett 17/11/1981. War Grave F/Lt LE Thompson Air bomber RAF 5/10/1943 age 34.

Seventh row. French, Charles 10/10/1907 (81). French, Ann 21/10/1900. French, Ruth Clara 9/4/1879 (11). Hussey, William Henry 17/7/1833, also George Hussey 19/3/1834. Small slab GH 1834. Wooller, Freda 28/121876. Roberts, Nellie Mabel Violet 1896-1976. Fraser, Enid Marcia 1902-1976, Henry Douglas Forbes Fraser 1897-1982. Cheal, George Henry 4/6/1975, wife Norah Florence Mary 22/4/1996. Clarke, William Harvey 7/5/1974. Pelecanos, Anthony Pantelis 20/3/1974. Wilde, Peter George 30/9/1961.

Eighth row. Cosham, Elizabeth 3/3/1802. Adamson, Edward William 9/3/1898. Osborn, Martha 9/6/1885 daughter of William and Mary. Osborn, John Verrall of Gore Farm 1875 youngest son of William Souter Osborn 5/4/1885 and Mary Osborn 19/8/1885. Ashby, George Thomas 3/4/1876 miller at Friston. Ashby, George 12/2/1872, wife Elizabeth Ashby 18/6/1878. Ashby, Annie 24/10/1868 711/12 only child of William Peter Ashby 22/10/1894 and Elizabeth Frances Ashby 22/1/1891. Scrase, Richard 4/8/1854. Young, Sidney Arthur 2/4/1974, and Sophie 28/12/1984. Ellis, Basil Owen 10/3/74, and wife Anne died 4/12/1986 in Hobart Tasmania. Gill, Gladys Ivy May 2/10/1973, and husband Arthur William Gill 18/8/1985. Elliott, Norman Walter 5/6/1972. Stow, Ivor Acton 20/1/1972, and wife Ada Beatrice Stow 12/6/1999. Rivaille, Yvonne Chevalier 9/5/1966. Saville, Helen Irene 10/8/1957.

Ninth row. Curtis, Violet Eugenie Helen (Ena) 22/3/1976, husband William Douglass Curtis 30/3/1983. Foord, Gladys Louisa Lettice 10/2/1971, and husband Hubert Stanley Foord 12/7/1973. South, William Arthur 13/7/1973. Haffenden, Graham Alan 30/6/1966 aged 16, also Ruby May Haffenden 1922-1993 and Reginald Owen Haffenden 1918-2000. Hagger, Elizabeth Gertude 19/6/1966. Taylor, Thomas H 1882-1965. Norris, Mary 22/4/1958, and husband Ellis Cecil Harold Booth Norris 13/1/1960. Cradock, Elizabeth Beecroft (Betty) 30/1/1958 of Little Hill. Tablet on wall Harris, Walter Samuel, and Florence Anna. Eileen, Joyce, John & Michael.

Tenth row. Lewis, Raymond Rector 9/2/1981 age 59. Ashby, John, 15/8/1839, also Jane daughter of John & Elizabeth 15/4/1853. Ashby, Elizabeth 21/11/1830, also Mary Ann 23/11/1830 daughter of George & Elizabeth. Ashby, Maria 1/9/1850 daughter of George & Elizabeth. Ashby, Richard 31/10/1854. Leyland, M James Vicar of this parish 37 years 31/12/1764 died universally lamented a worthy Divine. Breach, Alfred Thomas 12/12/1994. Hayward, Harold Frank 25/11/1970, also wife Emily Florence 12/11/1995. Goldsmith, Charles Edward of Black Robin farm 7/3/1964, also wife Annie Augusta Goldsmith 17/10/1975. Steeles, Beatrice Elizabeth 17/112/1957. Dockerill, Alfred Charles 30/3/1954 died as a result of an accident on the Downs. Wilson, Alfred Joseph Charles 8/3/1967, and Amy Emily Wilson 25/4/1952. Breach, Annie B 14/2/1945, and husband Harry L Breach 4/4/1963. Lanchbery, James John 27/4/1946, also wife Grace Eliza 14/2/1943.

Row going north from chancel. Constable, Thomas 20/12/1796. Pearce, John of the coastguard station at Birling Gap who was found dead on the beach at the foot of a precipice near the said station in this parish on the morning of the 11th day of July 1831 and supposed to have fallen over the cliff while in the execution of his night duty, he was aged 21 years, son of Hugh Pearce a chief officer in the coastguard at Hope Cove port of Dartmouth, Devon. Michell, Mercy wife of Richard Michell curate of this parish 16/11/1786. Miller, John 24/9/1840, wife Frances 29/6/1840. Hollobone, Dorothy 'Dorrie' 1916-1995. Gessner, Charles Ernest 13/10/1970, wife May Eveline 18/3/1986. Wall, Sidney Archibald 30/9/1957, wife Florence Ellen 19/6/1997. Comber, Edwin 29/9/1933 (39), wife Nellie Comber 7/4/1989 (93).

Next row. Pendrill, Mary 6/2/1830, wife of John Pendrill, also of Parnell second daughter of John & Mary Pendrill who died in London 16/2/1838, also of Martha third daughter 13/6/1848. Vine, Charles Wilfred 'Charlie' 9/3/1998. Vine, Doris Edna 1/2/1996 wife of Walter Sidney Vine. Haffenden, Irene May 11/1/1993, & Albert WJ Haffenden 13/6/1997. Hore, CWC 10/1/1970, wife Dorothy 2/9/1979. Ticehurst, Thomas 19/10/1958, wife Kate 5/3/1965. Vodden, 'Ninny' Mary Ann 17/12/1957, beloved & admired nanny of Burns-Lindon Cockcroft & Lycett families for 80 years. Markquick, James 24/1/1942, wife Emily 31/7/1978 (97). Dickens, Thomas 26/4/1937, wife Emily Alice 21/2/1965. Tablets on wall. Vine, Walter S (Wally) 1918-1974. Vine, Thomas E 1860-1944. Vine, Edith M 1872-1953. Grayson, Charles Arthur 18/5/1897-28/3/1969, wife Rosetta Ida 24/11/1900-31/7/1977.

Next row. Winchester, Susan 15/9/1864. Baker, Eliza 11/4/1873. Harris, Florence Grace 15/9/1969. Ticehurst, Lilian Jessie 8/6/1958, husband Frank Bazil 1/5/1963, & Sarah Ticehurst 18/12/2000. Wiles, Mary Edith 28/10/1954. Hill, William Harry 13/7/1952, wife Daisy 1899-1994. Kemp, Roland Alfred 18/2/1949, wife Mary Anne 25/10/1962. Fears, Rosa 20/10/1937, husband Charles 19/5/1958 (93). Kemp, Alfred James 7/2/1936, wife Belinda 31/11/1948. Tablets on wall. Pindred, Edward James 6/2/1962, wife Edith Belinda 8/12/1968. Kemp, James Clifford 13/2/1957.

Next row, north of tower. Breach, Thomas 10/5/1869, wife Lucy 20/5/1889. Hore, Olivia Rose 2/6/1969, Wicking, William George (verger 14 years) 22/1/1955, Susan Wicking 14/8/1969. Carlisle-Bamlet, Major David 23/9/1946 (25), his mother Isabella MG Carlisle-Bamlet 12/7/1978. Johnston, the Revd Francis Boyd died Eastbourne 1934.

Next row, Gap from church by tree. Sellars, 'Harry' Harold NC 11/10/1968. Breach, Emily Phyllis Louisa 30/1/1954, also Richard James Breach 20/12/1957. Harris, John May Milner 19/5/1950. Hirst, Mabel Clarissa 23/2/1947. Carter, Benjamin & Elizabeth at rest. Horwood, William Henry resting. Fennell, James Patrick Physician & Surgeon (born Dublin 1851 died East Dean 1934).

Next row. Gap from church to indecipherable slab. Burns-Cox, Richard 8/7/1957, Richard William Burns-Cox Vicar of this parish 4/12/1979, Una Marion Burns-Cox 6/2/1991. Begley, Simon 1965-1988. Grimmer, Walter died at Beachy Head lighthouse 28/4/1874 age 11/12. Briggs, Harold Fawsett 14/7/1968, wife Monica Pare 7/4/1979. Hills, Ann Elizabeth 29/6/1948, husband John Hills 27/2/1949. War grave, 1259114 AC2 Cheal, GL RAF 15/11/1945, age 23. Wicking, Emily 13/1/1945, husband Thomas Wicking 19/1/1946. Sturges, Arthur Manning beemaster 3/1/1934 he loved all God's fair world. Wall.

Indecipherable box between rows, which waver.

Next row. Green, Scott Roger 6/9/2000. Oliver, Alan 1927-2001. Goldsmith, Bert & Eileen. Carmichael, Yvonne 8/7/2002 & sister Angela Folkes 6/9/2002. Roberts. Guilyn Leonard 27/3/03 aged 83, Peter Thomas 19/12/36-27/4/04, Valerie Kay Thomas 8/6/44-12/7/06, Anthony Frank Field 2/7/34-17/6/05, Cissy Ivy Pearce 11/2/1905-23/7/2005. gap. Breach, David Thomas 24/12/1967 and Annie Elizabeth Breach 4/1/1968. Trigg, Edith

Mary 11/11/1960 also sister Lilian Ruth Trigg 3/7/1962. Winn, Amy Bertha 12/4/1950. Hills, Elizabeth Ann 9/5/1946 also husband Luther Hills 14/12/1964. Fowler, Alice 25/1/1945 also husband Friend Fowler 6/1/1951. Haffenden, Frank & Fanny At Rest. Baxter, William 5/6/1932 also wife Frances 17/7/1951. Wall.

Next row nearer road Christopher Paul Lambird 2/6/67-24/5/07, Peter Johnson 26/10/06 aged 69, Brian Arthur Johnson 19/5/34-28/10/06.

Next row. Young, Amy Ellen 18/4/1996 also husband Donald Mackenzie Young 1/11/1997. Charlesworth, Frances Mabel 3/10/1996. Whitcher, Kenneth 1929-1996. Ashcroft, William 1912-1997. Goldsmith, William Edward 1912-1998 Farmer of these fields. Wood, Geoffrey 1918-1998. Collingham, Lucy 29/8/1829. Bonnett, Trevor Francis 2/2/1999 (Capt Queens Royal Regt 39-45 schoolmaster Chelmsford Hall). Wooden cross Hemmings, Edgar James 3/11/19-23/4/00. Collin, Charles Peter Verrall 1913-2000. Thompson, James Hayward 4/6/2000. tree Robinson, Guy Heath 1906-2000 burial 4/7/2000. Burningham, Jack Handley burial 2/8/2000. Besant, Norah 27/6/1949 & Morris, Harold Watkin 6/2/1950. Lake, Percy Robert 15/12/1948 also wife Anna Maria 4/6/1956. Bugler, Alfred 19/2/1931 and wife Elizabeth 22/8/1954.

Next row. Blake, Cecil Stephen 7/1/1996. Jack Pearce 1911-1994 & Lucy Grace (wife) 1913-1998. Dowell, Joan 19/12/1994 & sister Jessie Margaret Dowell 23/9/1998. Eyre, Edward Charles 1915-1994. Roadnight, Eileen Marjorie Ella 30/4/1994 & husband Dennis Harry 16/10/1994. Walker, Peter Michael 16/11/1993. Kent, John 1924-1993. Parris, Charles James 29/6/1993 & Sybil Parris 25/8/2001. Gill, Jane 19/1/1804 & husband James 21/4/1825. Gill, Samuel 23/7/1785 & wife 28/5/1812. Evans, William Fred Richard 15/6/1993. Smith, Percy Quilter 1895-1993 & wife Doris Ivy 1897-1998, remembering their son Ted died Canada 1997. Comber, Julya Helen 11/11/1992. Bushby, Agnes Naisbit 29/11/1966. Burnett, Alexander Edwin 9/5/1959. Smith, John Dunford 30/10/1959 & Alice Kathleen Smith 12/10/1976. Milton, Stanley William 20/9/1952 also wife Mabel Edith Milton 16/8/1974. Lishman, William Hutton 27/10/1935 also wife Elizabeth Ann Lishman 30/6/1962.

Next row. Griffin, Dorothy 30/10/1992 & husband Cyril Griffin 20/12/1993. West, Harry Feb 1908-July 1992. Beeston, Peggy 27/10/1991. Pindred, Jessie 1/7/1991. Singleton, Edric K 1906-1991 also wife Alice Maud 1908-1999. Parsons, Revd Douglas 1905-1991 & wife Mary Catherine 1909-1996. Lloyd, Henry Frank 11/11/1990. Sherwood, Ellen 15/7/1990. Badcock, John Desmond 30/4/1990. Tune, Thomas William 7/3/1990. Norris, Harry Clifford 7/9/1989 & wife Elsie Gertrude 'Nib' 1/1/1997. Spencer, Dorothy Joyce 1920-1988 & daughter Martin, Reinette Eve 1955-1996. McCarthy, John Henry 1922-1987. Richardson, James 8/2/1987. Hollingdale, Charlie 4/8/1986 Shepherd of these Downs. Piper, Percy Frank 1918-1986. Martin, John Aston 18/2/1965 Medical Missionary & wife Marjorie 31/12/1989. Rumble, Elizabeth E 30/12/1964 & Edward W Rumble 1/3/1984 & son Kenneth aged 6. Miller, Nellie 15/12/1964 also husband Leonard Miller 28/4/1967. Farren, Dorothy 30/4/1964. Absale, Ada Marian 20/1/1962. Spencer, May Blossom 20/12/1960. Brune, Beatrice Prideaux July 1950. Oakleigh-Walker, Charles 31/3/1932.

Next row. Peirce, James 29/5/1818 also wife Elizabeth 19/5/1827. Peirce, Walter child of W & F Peirce aged 28/12, Harman, Mary Ann wife of Sargent Harman 7/7/1825.

Next row (along wall starting from Garden of Remembrance). Peirce, John Gosden 11/2/1865 also Elizabeth Peirce 12/2/1866. Ann Peirce 11/2/1850 also William Peirce 26/6/1881. Harriott, Mercy 13/2/1847. Peirce, Caroline 27/9/1860-30/9/1860 also of two infant daughters 7/11/1862-9/11/1862 daughters of Henry and Martha Peirce. Elizabeth daughter of John & Elizabeth Peirce 6/10/1845 in 15th year of her age, also of James Peirce son of the above 5/2/1846 aged 22. Twin sons of Henry & Martha Peirce who died in their infancy 13/11/1866. Pierce, Alexander 11/3/1797 also wife Mary 21/6/1821. Oliver, Ethel Winifred May 28/5/1976 husband George 25/11/1985. French, Thomas 21/12/1849. Bowyer, Sq/Ldr Frederick Hugh 1898-1982. Mason, Reginald Maxwell 21/12/1939 also Knight, Catherine Mary 9/3/1976 and Renwick, Evelyn Betty 14/1/2000.

Appendix 4 Chairmen Parish Council

East Dean
1924-28 Alfred A Evans
1928-47 Charles H Harding
East Dean with Friston, (from 1990 **East Dean and Friston**)
1947-49 Roderick J Hall
1949-54 Horace H Rew
1955-63 Edward RC Warrens
1963-68 Edward C Simmons
1968-91 Colin Bullard
1971-80 Phyllis M Hughes
1980-87 Maureen Honey
1987-95 Maurice Hopkins
1995-99 Esther Worsfold
1999-2003 George Tickle
2003-07 Peter Hobbs
2007-08 Spencer Wilcox
2008 Peter Hobbs
2008 J Taylor

Chairmen Parish Meetings

East Dean
1895-1906 J Walter Parrington
1907-09 Charles F Russell
1914-28 Alfred A Evans
1928-46 Charles H Harding
1947-49 Roderick G Hall
1950-54 James Monico
1955-58 Guy Smart
1959-62 Edward S White
1963-64 Reginald J Smith
Friston
1894-99 J Walter Parrington
1900 Francis J Maitland
1901 WR Nightingale
1902-04 Francis J Maitland
1905-23 John W Wycliffe-Taylor
1924-25 GO Howship
1926-38 Benjamin F Simpson
1938-39 J Brace
1940-41 WW Bonnell
1943 PercyJ Budd
1945-46 AL Pring
1947-61 PercyJ Budd
1962 KE Ward
1963 Harry Cunliffe
1964 Edward C Simmons

Appendix 5 Parish Council changes and membership 1940s and 50s

In 1947 the PC members had been Major Charles Harding c, Ronnie G Hall, the Revd Norman Lycett and George Cheal, the meetings lasted less than 15 minutes. In March 1948 Friston was grouped with East Dean and the combined Council was RG Hall c, the Vicar, GR Smart, G Cheal, C Dennett, S Penning, for East Dean and for Friston Mrs Goodman, PJ Budd, FW Nash, and H Rew. The first triennial election under the new Act in May 1949 had Budd, Hall, Harding, J Kemp, CH Meller, JR Monico, S Penning, HH Rew (c), Lt-Col EC Simmons, Mrs Sylvia Tompsett and Ivan Worsell. In 1952 Lt-Col AC Thomson was elected in place of Ronnie Hall and Mrs Kennard replaced Horace Rew, who was co-opted as chairman despite not being elected. In 1953 Mrs Tompsett resigned, replaced by Lt-Col EC Warrens. In 1954 Major Harding died. In 1955 Miss V Elvin replaced Mr Penning, Col Warrens became c with Col Thomson v-c. On Mr Kemp's death in 1957 Geoff Cornford was co-opted. In 1959 as Mrs Hughes was nominated in place of Lt-Col Thomson who did not seek re-election, for Friston the sitting members - George Cyril Andrews, Percy James Budd, Phyllis Margaret Hughes, Kathleen Rose Kennard and Edward Clare Simmons were duly declared elected. For East Dean the field was 14 candidates, of whom Frederick John Bicks; Kathleen Mary Burness; Basil Owen Ellis; Vida Allison Elvin; Charles Frederick Goldsmith; Charles James Parris; Reginald John Smith; Edward Robert Cabell Warrens and Ivan James Worsell were elected. Harry Comber, Cecil Alfred Richard Dann, Reginald Noel Dean, Douglas Victor Richey and Edward Sidney Charles Hammond White failed to obtain sufficient votes. In 1952 55% of the electorate voted; in 1959 36%.

Appendix 6 Parish Clerks   and   Village Policemen

Parish Clerks	Village Policemen
1924-36 HJ Woodhams	-1900 Pc Barton
1936-41 W Pickard	1900-18 John Hills
1941-43 JD Drewett	1918-33 FC Etteridge
1943-45 Kathleen Underhay	1933-48 Harry J Hyde
1945-47 CW Bell	
1947-59 W Sidney Ostler [salary £45 a year]	1948-58 Max Soffner
1959-60 RG Fear	1958-60 Derek Bashford
1960-62 James H Parrish	
1962-63 LL Gross	1960-64 Douglas Newton
1963-68 LB Hubbard	
1968-72 W Gordon Vellenoweth	1964-66 Keith Beard
1972-76 LB Hubbard	
1976-80 Anthony R Bish	1966-80 John Debley
1980-86 Pauline Crompton	
1986-94 Molly Mathieson	1980-82 Ray Hill
1994-96 Douglas Smith	
1996-2003 Andrew Clements	1982-99 Graham Gillam
2004- Diane Regan	

Appendix 7 East Dean & Friston Players productions (usually in the Bardolf or Village Hall)

1938 Pageants (some in *Tatton Corner* garden) and plays. Won Sussex Amateur Drama League Festival
1943 Too Many Wives (Village Hall)
1944 George and Margaret [in the NAAFI at *Gayles* Friston airfield]
1946-8 Cradle Song, Great Day, Dark Tide, Eleventh Hour, Nightwatch
1949 The Biter Bit
1950 The Government Inspector, Nov.
1951 Miss Mabel; Chiltern Hundreds
1952 Playlets (Dukes and Fairies, There's no problem, The Bishop's Candlesticks); Thunder Rock
1953 Ladies in Retirement; The Merry Wives of Windsor [Coronation production]; The Happy Family
1954 Haul for the Shore; Without the Prince
1955 Bonaventure; Tartuffe [in English. Came 2nd in the Sussex Drama League competition]
1956 See How They Run; But Once a Year
1957 Dear Charles

1958 Distinguished Gathering; Teahouse of the August Moon
1959 The Happy Prisoner; The Prodigious Snob
1960 As Long as They're Happy; The House by the Lake, The Farmer's Wife
1961 In the Draught [won award at the Eastbourne Festival]; The Sacred Flame; The Long Echo
1962 Elephants to Ride Upon; A Letter from the General
1963 Pools Paradise; Mornings at Seven
1964 Breath of Spring; Inquiry at Lisieux,
1965 Happiest Days of Your life; Nude with Violin. [entered Sussex Drama Festival , but no award]
1966 The Nightingale; Roar Like a Dove
1967 The Happy Marriage; Rashamon
1968 No spring production; The Reluctant Peer
1969 Lord Arthur Savile's Crime; It Won't be Long Now
1970 A Man about the House; Old Tyme Music Hall The Bardolf Empire
1971 When we are Married
1972 Waters of the Moon; Haul for the Shore
1973 A Hundred Years On; Where there's a Will
1974 No spring production; Yellow Sands
1975 Spring production at Wannock; Lloyd George Knew My Father, Nov.
1976 The Dream House, No autumn production, Bardolf Hall not available
1977 1066 And All That [the Royal Silver Jubilee production at the Farrer Hall]
1978 Midsummer Mink; Review mainly written by Fred Bicks [at the Bardolf Hall]
1979 Night Must Fall
1980 Without the Prince; Lord Arthur Savile's Crime (repeat)
1981 The Winslow Boy; They Came to a City
1982 No spring play[insufficient actors], When we are Married (repeat)
1983 The Chalk Garden; Tabitha
1984 The Noble Spaniard; Wait until Dark
1985 See How They Run; Our Town
1986 An Inspector Calls; Sailor Beware
1987 Gaslight; Dry Rot
1988 Wizard of Oz [Junior Players] Night Must Fall (repeat); Happiest Days of Your Life (repeat)
1989 The Railway Children [Junior Players] Blithe Spirit; Too Soon for Daisies
1990 A Letter from the General (repeat); Victoriana
1991 Nightwatch; Bonaventure (repeat)
1992 There Goes the Bride; Post Horn Gallop
1993 House Guest; Ladies in retirement (repeat)
1994 Spring Fever; Love's a Luxury; Dangerous Corner
1995 We Did Meet Again; Man Alive
1996 They Came to a City (repeat); Table Manners
1997 Breath of Spring; The Bells are Ringing
1998 Home at Seven; Country Matters; Fish out of Water
1999 It Must be Spring; That's Life; Blithe Spirit (repeat)
2000 A Murder has been Arranged; Christmas Carol
2001 Moving; Cinderella
2002 Confusions; Respecting your Piers
2003 Laburnum Grove; Our Town (repeat)
2004 Pack of Lies; Round and Round the Garden
2005 Separate Tables; You're Only Young Twice
2006 Cat's Cradle; There goes the Bride (repeat)
2007 Black Chiffon; The Crying Dame-The Play Reading- Easy Stages 60th Anniversary playlets

Appendix 8.
Some Residents of The Old Fridays (see Chapter 7)
In August 1926 'Jack Albert son of Hugh Denis and Rose Lilian Goodman of 1 The Fridays was baptised', and the Goodmans stayed until 1937, subsequently William Haffenden was there. In 2 were the Danns, Bill and Mabel, from *Underhill*. Bill had been in the Middle East with the Royal Sussex Regiment in the 1914-18 war and had earned a commendation, but he was affected by his experiences, had a short fuse with his children, and became a habitué of the *Tiger*. One of their daughters was Maud Worsell. The Fyfields were there for a couple of years from 1957. At 3 was Roy Fears a train driver; the Wickings were there 1940-60. James 'Tiny' Markquick and wife Emily were in 4; 'Tiny', a tall, straggly fellow, helped to dig the water tunnel from Friston to Eastbourne in 1896, and was also on the building of the Beachy Head lighthouse 1899-1902; a daughter married Bill Haffenden; John and Barbara Eve took over. Ben Carter was at 5, a widower, he liked to show off his Boer War bounty of five gold sovereigns pocketed in a

leather case, two being awarded for each year of service; and when Ted and Sarah Fears moved in from 14 The Fridays in 1960 they found gas lamps over the mantelpiece; Ted Fears' grandfather, Charles Fears, was the bailiff and Ted's father led a strike against him on one occasion; the grandfather would say that he hoped 'Ted wasn't going the way of his father'.

The Gallop family was in 6 at one time and the Ticehursts were there until they moved to the *Old Parsonage* in 1938, when they were replaced by Harold Fears, barman at the Beachy Head Hotel, and later Syd and Ethel Winter (née Gallop), she helped in the library. They had sons, Edward, twins Hugh and David, and Kevin, and daughters Mary and Ann. The Winter boys were great cricketers, and at one time the mischievous lads of the village, and if it wasn't them it was the Wicking boys. Jack and Ivy Breach were in 6 at the Millennium. At 7 was William West who at 90 in 1940 cycled to and from *Friston Place* to Dig for Victory; he died at 94 so shepherding didn't do him harm. His grandson, Harry Comber, took over in 1954; his father, Edwin, a Canadian soldier who came here in the 1914-18 war, died of pneumonia in 1933, but his mother Nellie lived to be 93. Arthur Samways, who had been a coastguard at Birling Gap, was at 8. Numbers 9 and 10 belonged to the Gilbert Estate. George Cheal, father of Ray, Geoff and Tony, moved to 9 after his wife died of MS and married Nora Vine (only daughter of Albert Vine) and had a son and daughter Rosemary. At 10 in the 1930s and 40s was David Eve, followed by Bert and Gladys Foord when they moved from Upper Street. Now houses the Wigmores of the Seven Sisters Sheep Centre.

Some Residents of the New Fridays (see Chapter 7)
Among the residents at 11 was Maurice Haffenden and later DJ 'Pip' Piper. 12 had William Ransome. At different times 13 had Jack and Ivy Breach, and JA Goodman. Jim and Rene Wicking were in 14 from 1960 after the Fears. 15 had Derrick Pyle, who moved to Eastbourne, then Mrs Cheal, and now the Revd Chris and Elizabeth Hadfield. At 16 from 1952 were the Coles with EA Pelling at one time. Mrs H Hopper from *Peak Dean Farm* was in 17 after her husband died in 1952, followed by Peter and Rosemary Johnson (née Cheal) Peter worked for the local Water Company for over 30 years. He put on marvellous displays at the Flower Show and a tremendous show of houselights at Christmas. FJ Saunders was in 18 during the 1950s and was followed by Chris Plaice and Mrs D Plaice. Tom Goodman was in 19 for a while, as was FW 'Bill' Schafer, and JA Rust. Mrs Florence Melling was in 20. Bob Harvey was in 21 followed from 1970 by Brian and Janet Johnson (née Martin) the year Brian also started work for the Water Company, fitting in his fishing. Doug Richey was in 22. Locals moved around depending on how many children they had and whether they learnt about any changes in time, assisted by the paternalism of the Hardings.

Appendix 9
Village Directories, officeholders of village clubs and organisations **1965**

Art Group: M Hooper, SJ Snell
Bible reading Fellowship: Mrs BO Ellis (*Sparrows* Downs View Lane)
Bowling Club: Frank H Shaw (*Greenacre* Windmill Lane)
British Legion: Mr WE Green (*Badgers Way*)
Church Treasurer and Free Will Offering: Charles J Parris (*Green Leas* Deneside)
Churchwardens: East Dean: RJ Smith, ES White. Friston Harold A Down (*Westholme* The Ridgeway), VW Walker (*Friston Court* Windmill Lane)
Civil Defence: Lt-Col Edward C Simmons (*Point House* Crowlink) Miss KM Burness (*Senlac* Elven Lane)
CMS: Mrs Sybil Parris
Coastguards: Cecil A Dann (3 Churchfield)
Conservative Association: Mrs M Shearman (*Little Dean* Warren Lane)
Cricket Club: Ian Goldsmith (2 *Black Robin Bungalow*)
Crowlink WI: Mrs Lyn Pelecanos
Diocesan Council: W Douglass Curtis (*Chalvington* Deneside), Harold A Down, Basil O Ellis.
Editor Parish Magazine: Mrs Phyllis M Hughes (*Lye Oak* The Close). Deliverers: Mrs Bingley, Mrs Curtis, Mrs Dietrich, Miss Doble, Frederick Doherty (*South Cottage* Warren Close), Mrs Patricia Down, Mrs E Fraser, Mrs A Green, Mrs Greeves, Mrs MacGowan, Mr E Matthews, Mrs C Mockler, Miss G Pearce, Mrs FW Schafer, Mrs D Shearer (*Corner Cottage*), Miss ES White, Mrs IV Smith, Mr Young
Football Club: Mr Malcolm Johnson (*The Cub*)
Hall Bookings: George Cheal (7 The Fridays)
Liberal Association: Mrs D Anderson
Mothers' Union: Mrs Molly Howells
Parish Council (before elections): Lt Col EC Simmons (c), Cmdr RJ Smith (v), FJ Bicks (*Almonds* Hillside), Miss KM Burness, H Cunliffe (*Summerhill* Warren Lane), BO Ellis, Miss VA Elvin (*Old Bake House*), L Fisher, CF Goldsmith, DC Hodgson, Mrs PM Hughes, CJ Parris, Douglas V Richey, ES White (*Linton Lea*)
PCC: Mr M Doxat-Pratt, Mrs PM Hughes, Mr CJ Parris, Mr C Dann, Mr F Doherty, Mrs PW Down, Miss VA Elvin, Miss Diana Eyre (*Hilltop Cottage* Hillside), Lt Col Thomas M Gordon (*Linden Mead*), Mrs Doreen Greenwood, Miss EB Grose, Mr Roderick G Hall (*Maryfield* Friston hill), Mr Harman, Mrs F Hooker, Miss M Hooper, Mr Leslie E Ketcher (*Grey Gulls,* Peak Dean Lane, Brig GR Mockler (*Pippens* Warren Lane), Mr LC Ockenden (*Stamford House*

Warren Lane), Mrs EM Pilkington, Mr D Powers, Mr ATF Roberts, Mrs IV Smith, Mr PQ Smith, Mr LH Stein, Mrs N Parry (*Weald Cottage*)

Police: Keith Beard, Police House (3111)

Queens Nursing Sister: Phyllis Thackeray (*Gore Cottage*)

Residents' Association: JF Marshall (*Bramble Down* Deneside)

RSPCA: Mrs PM Hughes

Ruri-Decanal Court HS Elton, Cmdr RJ Smith, Mrs White.

SA Missionary Society: Miss Holmes (*Dene Lea*)

Scouts: Mr RN Dean (20 Wenthill Close). *Guides:* Mrs PW Down. *Brown Owl:* Gwen Pearce (*Brackla* Mill Close)

Sextons: East Dean William Armiger (*Old Police Cottage* 1 Lower Street) and
            Friston Robert Seymour (*Roseneath* Upper Street)

Surgery: Drs C Savile, L Snowball, B Barkworth

The Players: Mrs Sylvia Tompsett (*Beech Tree Cottage* Friston Hill)

UNA: Mr CF Parry (*Weald Cottage* Michel Dene Rd)

WI: Mrs D Anderson (*Moray* Deneside), Mrs E Horsley (*Lea Croft* Peak Dean Close)

WVS: Mrs A Green (*Badgers Way*)

Youth Club/Stoolball: Miss Mary Winter (6 The Fridays)

Village Directory around the Millennium and Jubilee.

Art group: R Bailey, S Drury

Auxiliary Coastguard Service officer in charge: Don Ellis

Badminton Club: Rita Laws

Birling Gap Safety Boat Association secretaries: L Raven, C Lamberth

Bowling Club secretaries: David Broughton, Peter Glaser, George Chadwick

Church: Rector the Revd Hugh Moseley, Priest-in-charge later Rector the Revd Ian Smale

Churchwardens: Mollie Bertin, David Gazzard, Peter Jeffery, Dennis Minns, Andrew Palmer, Jean Powell, Paul Summers, Peter Thomas, Jenny Waldron

Church Electoral Roll Officer: Vera Tame

Church/Benefice Fellowship: Maureen Broughton, J Walker

Church Sunday Club: Christine Jeffery

Church Treasurers: Ian Killick, Tim Crees

Church Tuesday Club: Tim Archer

Church Women's Fellowship: M Howes, Evelyn Taylor

Computer and Camera Club secretary: Tony Rix

Conservative Association chairman: Joan Russell, Jackie Florey, George Tickle

Crowlink Ladies president: Joan Nash, secretary: Vera Tame

Deanery Synod members: M Bertin, M Fyfield, M Lloyd, A Mudd, J Powell, P Summers, V Tame

Duplicate Bridge Club chairman: Frank Eveleigh

East Dean & Friston Cricket Club: president Peter Ainsley, chairman Russell Perkins, Saturday captain Bruce Elkington, Sunday captain Alan Ray, secretary Simon Purkiss, treasurer Bryan Buckland, fixtures' secretary Rex Roberts, David Windsor

East Dean & Friston Local History Group chairmen Peter Thomas, Graham Hodgson, secretary: Esther Worsfold

East Dean & Friston Women's Institute president: Margaret Clegg, secretary: Dorothy Stevenson, M Jenkins

East Dean Liberal Democrats: David Hunn, John Harper

East Dean Players secretaries: Cheryl Veitch, Derek Drury

Emergency Plan coordinators: John Harper, Derek Drury, J Hine

Flower, Vegetable and Fruit Show: Julia Langford, J Willcocks, D Banks, J Eve, K Holmes, J Nash, B Watts, E Worsfold

Gardening Club secretaries: Jean Maull, R Frost, Ron Naylor, membership secretary: Dr M Norris

GP Surgery: Dr R Adcock, Dr J Shawcross. Practice Nurse Karen Surtees

Keep Fit Class: Frances Mace

Line Dancing: D Picknell

Micheldene WI presidents: Daphne Dempsey, Eva Oliver, secretaries: Jenny Duxbury, Cheryl Veitch

Neighbourhood Watch chief coordinator: Ken Gerry, secretary: LJ Goldsmith

National Trust local warden: Sarah Mann

National Trust Seven Sisters Centre secretaries: JW Peskett, MGR Marshall

NSPCC secretaries: Pam Eveleigh, Betty Tickle

Organists (East Dean): Isabel Savile (choirmaster), Gill Bebbington, Chris Hadfield, Gerald Sweatman, Jonathan Watt

Organist (Friston): Roy Kibble

Parent & Toddler Group chairwomen: A Rabuszko, L Woodford

Parish Child Protection Policy Representative: Sue Walsh, J Summers, John Newman.

Parish Council Clerks: Andrew G Clements, Diane Regan

Parish Council included: B Alstin, M Bartlett, George Booth-Clibborn, E Charlwood, Camilla Crump, Charlie Davies-Gilbert, M Delaney, Bruce Elkington, J Fox, Ken Gerry, C Gray, T Hervey, Peter Hobbs c, Margaret Lees, Ken Lucas, Frances Mace, Roger Notman-Watt, Charles Peck, C Preece, D Short, G Simcox, Alan Tame, Jesse Taylor v-c and c, Nicky Terry, Ken Thurman, George Tickle c, Derek Tonkinson, Maggie Whitmore, S Wilcox c, David Windsor, Esther Worsfold

Parish Magazine: Editor: Sheila Surtees, Treasurers: Lois Hurter, Dr John Chapman, John Newman. Distributor: Gwen Franklin, Deliverers included: M Adams, B Argyle, J Booth-Clibborn, D Burge, V Butler, N Chapman, A Clements, D Dempsey, S Drury, E Flint, R Franklin, M Frith, J Fyfield, M Fyfield, R Greenway, J Gregory, J Harrison, D Harwood, R Hayes, T Hervey, C Hicken, J Hicken, L Hurter, M Jenkins, K Jones, P Joslin, M Knight, P Lamdin, R Laws, L Manners, P Marshall, G Matley, M Norris, A Palmer, J Patterson, N Powell, C Preece, B Rix, R Robinson, R Shaw, C Starr, J Summers, S M Surtees, V Tame, J Taylor, M Thorne, J Thurman, D Wadsley, R Walters, R & V Wickes, B Winter, P Workman

Parish Readers: Leslie Ketcher, Tony Rogers, Sue Smale

Parochial Church Council: secretaries: Marie Adams, Mrs B Warner, Dr M Norris, Margaret Reader. Members included:Kate Boyle, Tim Crees, David Gazzard, Roy Kibble, Ian Killick, Geoffrey Mantle, John Newman, Joy Preen, N Robinson, Sue Smale, Jocelyn Stubley, Vera Tame, Mrs H Taylor, Sue Walsh, David Windsor, Simon Wood and ex-officio the Rector, Chuchwardens and Readers

Police: PCs Andy Prescott, Dennis Donovan, Ben Stevens, Liz Keenan

Residents' Association presidents: Peter Hobbs, Louise Gaffney; treasurer: Brent Duxbury; secretaries: Jackie Florey, Molly Eldrett, Ron Pringle; committee members: Camilla Crump, Ron Franklin, Jolyon Fyfield, Ken Gerry, Ken Lucas, Alan Starr, Dorothy Stevenson, John Surtees, Beverley Thompson, Val Wills, Phyll Workman

Royal British Legion East Dean branch president Peter Hobbs, chairman Ron Naylor, v-c John Dann, secretary: Ken Frith, C Lewis, treasurer Ron Pringle, membership secretary: Marianne Frith

Scouts & Guides Brownie Guider: M Seabrook, local association secretary: J Hicken

Short Mat Bowls Club: Alan Robson

Table Tennis Club secretary: Ken Thurman

Tiger Tees Golfing Society secretary: N Waldron

Verger East Dean: Jolyon Fyfield

Village Diary: Joe Dempsey

Village Hall Manager S Everest

Village Hall & Pavilion bookings secretary: Janet Johnson

Wealden District Council: Brian West, Charles Peck

Appendix 10. Abbreviations used

ACRE - Action for Communities in Rural England; ACS - Auxiliary Coastguard Service; AGM - Annual General Meeting; ATC - Air Training Corps; BL - British Legion; CMS - Church Missionary Society; CVL - Cuckmere Valley League: CWF - Church Women's Fellowship; ED&F - East Dean and Friston; ELHS - Eastbourne Local History Society; ESCC - East Sussex County Council; ELG - Emergency Landing Ground; ESRO - County Record (Archive) Office; GC - Gardening Club; HE - High Explosive; HMI - His/Her Majesty's Inspector of Schools: HRDC - Hailsham Rural District Council; LSA - Life Saving Apparatus; MOH - Medical Officer of Health; NSPCC - National Society for the Prevention of Cruelty to Children; NT - National Trust; PC - East Dean & Friston Parish Council, and Pc - Police Constable; PCC - East Dean with Friston Parochial Parish Council; RA - Residents' Association; RNLI - Royal National Lifeboat Institution; RBL - Royal British Legion; SAC(S) - Sussex Archaeological Collections (Society); UNA - United Nations Association; UXB - Unexploded Bomb; WDC - Wealden District Council; WI - Women's Institute. For committees/teams:- p - president, v-p - vice, c - chairman, v-c vice; capt. - captain; s - secretary, t - treasurer, ms - membership secretary; a - auditor.

INDEX
In **bold** if pictured

Exercise, lads 64
Exley, S 350
Eyre, D 63, 152, 228, 279, 296, 298, 317, 328, 346-7, 360, 374
Eyre, G 279
Fair (Fayre) 39, 50, 71, 288
Fairchild, Mr & Mrs P 238
Fairway Homes 237, 240
Falmer House **232,** 245
Families in Need 372
Families, old village 73, 184, 386-7
Family Service 329, 362
Family Social Work 362, 373
Fancy Dress Show 16, 67
Farming 20, 72-3, 102, 169, 289
Farm workers 72, 169
Faro, C 368, 370, 373
Faro, D 366, 368
Farren, M 296, 318
Farrer, AW 70-1, 178, **264**
Farrer Hall 7-8, 14, 71, 113, **178,** 277 193-4, 264, 271, 285, 294-5, 301, 317, 319, 321, 326, 328, 330, 337-9, 341-5, 347, 351, 356, 358, 362-3, 370, 372
Farthings 225
Fass, M 120, 290
Fatalities on A259 road 371-2
Faulkner, H 308, 324
Fawbert, J 106, 116
Fayre (see Fair or Village)
Fears, B 146
Fears, Charles 39, 168, 225, 285
Fears, Christine **157, 160, 282**
Fears, E (Ted) 46, 106, 109-11, 146, 166, 183-4, 224, 250, 253, **255,** 257, 270, 304
Fears, Ena **143**
Fears, Eric **139**
Fears, F 145-6
Fears, G 147
Fears H 62, 64-65, 187
Fears, Ian **155-7, 282**
Fears, Irene 139, 144.
Fears, Jim **254**

Fears, John 147,
Fears, Reg 45, 51, 53
Fears, 'Bob' 64, 106
Fears, Roy **71**
Fears, S **67, 264**
Feist, P **13**
Feneley, Mr & Mrs WJ 266
Feneley, LI 284
Fennell, E 229
Fenton, C 349
Fenton, D 307, 346
Fenwick-Owen, M 271
Ferguson, A 348
Ferrets 201
Ferrier, Mr 226
Festival of Britain 268-9
Festival of Remembrance 353
Fete (see also Fair and Village Fete) 9, 16, 51, 274, 282-3, 285, 287, 293, 301, 318-319, 320
Feudal System 20
Fibula, Roman 19
Fielder, D 100
Figurehead 28
Fillery, SCG 35, 40, 47, 60, 64
Film show 153, 156, 301
Fingerpost 267
Fire Brigade, local 55
Fire, drill, 144. 148
Fire fighting 257
Fire Gems 342, 344
Firemark, 170
Fireplate 170
Firewatcher 250
Fireworks 7, 128, 136, 339, 359
Fish, big catches 304
Fisher, G 129
Fisher, L 306, 313
Fish, frozen 217
Fishing 103, 114
Five Farthings 210
Flagstaff 137
Flagstaff Point 124
Flagstaff Point seat 124, 283
Fletcher, C 293
Fletcher, Miss H 64
Fletcher, HB 71
Fletcher, T 23

Flint Cottage 220, 226
Flint, D 279-**80**
Flint, E 389
Flint, F 189, 276
Flint picking 64, 99
Flint, Ted 108, 169, 189, 276-7, 285, 295, 298, 347, 349, 358, 363, 373
Flints **38,** 48, 145, 228
Flint walls 192
Firing the anvil 300
Florey, J **7,** 12, 15, 17, **366-**67, 370, 373, 388-9
Florey, M 8, 15, 17, **366,** 370, 374
Flower Festival 16, 372, 374
Flower Pot Race 68
Flower (& Vegetable) Show 13, 34, 39, 100, **102,** 238, 266, 274, 277, 281, 285, 290, 293, 295, **298,** 300, 314, 316, 326, 333, 338, 344, 346-7, 349-52, 354-5, 358, **360,** 362, 364, 366, 368, 370, 372, 374
Flux, S 243
Flying boat 267
Flying bomb **261-**2
Flying Fortresses 259
Flynn, R 201
Fold 36, 96
Foord, H 60, 169, 179, 247, **255, 264, 271,** 290, 315
Foord, G 179, 247, 277, 292, 300, 311
Foot & Mouth 101, 314
Football 49, 137, 178, 196, 209, 236-7, 268, 300-1, 314, 340
Footpaths, parish 269, 338
Footpath (see twitten)
Ford, J 17
Fordham, J 13
Fords, model T 58, 227
Fordson tractors 97
Forestry Commission 199, 214-5, 302, 353, 358
Forest Lodge 210
Forge 29, 46, 184, 270, 301
Forge Cottage 292

Markwick (née Curwood), F **227**

Markwick, J 291

Markwick, S **315**

Marlow, G 340

Maroons 114

Marriages, candestine 23

Marsden, Dr F 31, 131-2

Marsh, G 151

Marsh, A & W 57

Marsh, R 202, 213, **255**

Marshall, Revd HEC 33, 35, 135

Marshall, JF 240, 313, 334

Marshall, Mrs 52

Marshall, P 389

Marshall, WSD 62

Martin, A 44, 196

Martin, C 34, 39, 40, 69, 219, 262, 264

Martin, F 69, 182, 196, 251, 254, **277**

Martin, PT 44, 66-7, 69, 136, 219, 251, 266, **277,** 279, 281, 285, 289, 295

Martin, R 188, 196

Marycroft 184, 339

Maryfield 93, 184

Maryland 192

Mary Rose 345

Mary's Mead 118, 179, 219, 334

Maslen, Barry 156, 280, **282,** 288, 292

Maslen, Brenda 275

Mason, Dr J 358

Mason, RM 115

Massey-Ferguson combine 278, 303

Masters, B 156

Mathieson, M 348-9, 357-8, 363, 385

Mathieson, R 345, 350-1, 360, 362, 369

Matley, G 10, 346, 349-51, 355, 358, 360, 364-5, 368, 371-2, 389

Matley, H 307, 358, 365, 372

Matthews, V 298

Mattock, R **335**

Mattock, C 326

Mattock, R 342

Maufe, Sir E 120

Maull, J 12, 364, 373

Maurais, C 157

Maurais, G 157

Maurais, H 213

Mawer, J 276

Maxwell, T&R 188

May, F 262

Mayfield, Canon G 282

Maynard, WT 105

Maynard, Thomas 43

Mayor of E'bourne 363

Maypole 8, 30, 153-5, 158, 274, 300, 330, **334, 339,** 342, 344, 352, 370

May Queen 153-6, 158, 161, **165,** 290, 330, 334

Me 109 **250, 252**-3, 258

Mead, G 122

Meadow Cottage 175, 185, 279

Meadow Hill 185, 219

Meads 248, 262

Meads 341

Meads, R 137

Meals on Wheels 334, 346, 353, 356, 361

Meanley, AS 240

Medhurst, Mrs 281

Medlecott, J 191, 198

Medleigh 192

Medley, G 198

Medley, T 198

Meller, CH 82, 154, 178- 179, 192, 267, 272, 274, 277, 284, 292, 295

Meller, CH & M 295

Meller, P 266

Melling, F 152, 154, 160, 178-9, 319

Melling, Gerald 108, 178, 263, 268

Melling, Gerard 97, 178-179

Melling, P 178

Melling, R 69

Memorial Garden names 379-81

Men of the Trees 350

Mepham, T 229

Merry, E 146

Mess, Officers 204

Mess, Sgt's 208

Mew, DH 326

Mice 38, 134

Michell, Revd R 24-25, 90, 125

Michel Dene Cottages 223

Michel Dene Road 231, 237-8

Micheldene WI 8-9, 184, 195, 294, 298, 306, 312-13, 317, 319, 322, 325-6, 330, 334, 337-8, 340, 342, 354-8, 367-9, 372

Microwave 345

Middle Brow 228

Midnight Steeplechase **99,** 290

Midwife Act, (1902) 34

Miliffe, M **368**

Military Medal 97

Military Muddlers **64,** 68

Milk charge 319

Milk float trapped 283, 296, 314

Milk, free 96

Milk Race 362

Milking 169, 179, 272, 278

Millennium 7-14

Millennium map 375

Mill (see Friston mill)

Mill Cottage 215-6, 246, 261

Miller, A 331, **336**

Miller, B **135**

Miller, CE 204

Miller, D 136.

Miller, Edward 35-6, 65-67, 137

Miller, Ernest 43

Miller, J **135**

Miller, L 136-7, 140, 168, 180, 192, 282, 308

Miller, M **135**

Miller, Nell 16,

Miller, Nellie **135**

Miller RA 352

Miller, Robin **337**

Miller, Revd W 25

Stirk, J 196

Stirling bomber 260, 262

Stirling, P 331

Stirrup pump 252

Stone Age 18, 345

Stoolball 15, 33, 275, 309, **335**

Storms 23, **351,** 354

Stott, Mr & Mrs R 347

Strand electric 300

Strands hair salon 184

Straw for funeral 59

Streatfeild, Canon W 50, 163

Street map displayed 365

Street Party 341

Strickland, G 355

Stride-Darnley, F 310, 315

Stride-Darnley, J **315**

Stringell, Lt **255**

Strip lighting 279

Strollers Group 369

Strudwick, B 178, 280-**1**, 291

Strudwick, W **266**

Stuart, M 347

Stubley, J 389

Stubley, L 122-3, 293, 370

Stubley, M 122, 370

Student teachers 151

Sturges, AM 49, 54

Stutchburys 120-1

Stutchbury, D 120-1

Stutchbury, MS 45, 64, 71

Stutchbury, R 54, 65, 80, 215

Stutchbury, VK **340**-341, 346

Subba Row, R 265

Sub-Post Office 345

Suffolk sheep 72, 97

Sullivans 191

Summerdown camp 44, 52

Summerdown Cottages 223-**4, 241**

Summerdown dairy 72, 272

Summer Fair 50, 62, 65, 183

Summers, J 388

Summers, P 388

Summertime 140, 317

Sunday best 185

Sunday Club 372

Sunday play, cricket 270

Sunday School 189, 230, 282-3, 315

Sunday School treat 31, 33, 67

Sunday work 60

Sunlight soap comp. 30

Sunshine 302

Surgery 190, 354, 357-8, 360, 367-8

Surtees, K 367, 388

Surtees, J 9, 330, 361, 365, 367, 389

Surtees SM 13, 315, 326-**7**-8, 338, 341, 347, 349-50, 369, 371, 374-**5**, 389

Sushi demonstration 357

Sussex Amenity Gp 111

Sussex Downsmen 53, 225-6

Sussex Downs Conservation Board 115

Sussex Express 344

Sussex Folk Ass. 300

Sussex Gardens **245**

Sussex sheep dog chp 338

Sussex trolley 272

Sutherland, J 300, 339

Svensen, D 229

SWAdvertiser 23, 25

Swallows 258, 308, 338

Swan, C 13

Sweatman, G 388

Sweatman, S 375

Swedes 38, 266

Swimming gala 100

Swimming pool 124, 203

Sworder, B 51, 191

Sworder, M 51-**52,** 61, 68, 231, 284

Sycamore, Mr 173

Sydney Stevens' coach 145

Symington, AW 317, 320, 327, **332,** 337, 339, 342

Symons, M 10, 364, 369

Symons, NH 276, 289, 350

Table Tennis Club 353

Tait, E **340**

Talks 185

Tallyman trick 99

Tame, A 12, 15-16, 191, 359, 372-5, 389

Tame, V 12, 191, 359, 372-4, 388-9

Tank traps 179, 180, 228, 249, 263, 267

Tanner sisters 204, 244

Tanner, Miss 262

Tanner, Revd B 328

Taperlands 209

Tapsell gate **75, 84,** 304

Tarragona wine 172

Tar spraying 140

Tatum, M 299

Tatton Corner **186,** 258

Taylor, Revd C 14-15, **194,** 367-8, 372

Taylor, Sir C 323

Taylor, D 324

Taylor, E 388

Taylor, F **154,** 155, **274, 276, 282,** 285

Taylor, G 11, 16, 46, 59, 72, 96, 140, 153, 168, 175, 184, 187, 193, **194,** 277, 297, **318,** 326, **340,** 367

Taylor, H 389

Taylor, K 106

Taylor, J 8, 37, 70, 72, 149, 167, 185, 187-8, 190, 251, **264,** 266, 270, 357, 361, 365, 368, 372-3, 385, 389

Taylor, R 109, 111, 175, 187, **254,** 342, 368

Taylor, T 105

Taxi service 106, 298

TB, see tuberculosis

Tea pavilion 330

Teenagers, 190, 302

Telegrams 29, 41, 64, 237

Telegraph hut 107

Telegraph manager 28-29

Telegraph poles 28

Telephone exchange 224, 236, 267

Telephones 267, 340, 351, 353, 357

Tellwright, PT 307

Temple, P 193

Tenant farmers 19, 25, 27, 34, 92

Tennis Club 232, 266

Tennis courts 232, 295, 324, 372